MW00512620

Handbook of Research on Critical Thinking and Teacher Education Pedagogy

Sandra P.A. Robinson
The University of the West Indies – Cave Hill Campus, Barbados

Verna Knight
The University of the West Indies – Cave Hill Campus, Barbados

A volume in the Advances in Higher Education
and Professional Development (AHEPD) Book
Series

Published in the United States of America by
IGI Global
Information Science Reference (an imprint of IGI Global)
701 E. Chocolate Avenue
Hershey PA, USA 17033
Tel: 717-533-8845
Fax: 717-533-8661
E-mail: cust@igi-global.com
Web site: http://www.igi-global.com

Copyright © 2019 by IGI Global. All rights reserved. No part of this publication may be reproduced, stored or distributed in any form or by any means, electronic or mechanical, including photocopying, without written permission from the publisher. Product or company names used in this set are for identification purposes only. Inclusion of the names of the products or companies does not indicate a claim of ownership by IGI Global of the trademark or registered trademark.

Library of Congress Cataloging-in-Publication Data

Names: Robinson, Sandra P.A., 1966- editor. | Knight, Verna, 1983- editor.
Title: Handbook of research on critical thinking and teacher education
  pedagogy / Sandra P.A. Robinson and Verna Knight, editors.
Description: Hershey PA : Information Science Reference, [2019] | Includes
  bibliographic references.
Identifiers: LCCN 2018036352| ISBN 9781522578291 (hardcover) | ISBN
  9781522578307 (ebk.)
Subjects: LCSH: Teachers--Training of. | Critical thinking. | Critical
  pedagogy.
Classification: LCC LB1707 .T3995 2019 | DDC 370.71/1--dc23 LC record available at https://lccn.loc.gov/2018036352

This book is published in the IGI Global book series Advances in Higher Education and Professional Development (AHEPD) (ISSN: 2327-6983; eISSN: 2327-6991)

British Cataloguing in Publication Data
A Cataloguing in Publication record for this book is available from the British Library.

All work contributed to this book is new, previously-unpublished material. The views expressed in this book are those of the authors, but not necessarily of the publisher.

For electronic access to this publication, please contact: eresources@igi-global.com.

Advances in Higher Education and Professional Development (AHEPD) Book Series

Jared Keengwe
University of North Dakota, USA

ISSN:2327-6983
EISSN:2327-6991

MISSION

As world economies continue to shift and change in response to global financial situations, job markets have begun to demand a more highly-skilled workforce. In many industries a college degree is the minimum requirement and further educational development is expected to advance. With these current trends in mind, the **Advances in Higher Education & Professional Development (AHEPD) Book Series** provides an outlet for researchers and academics to publish their research in these areas and to distribute these works to practitioners and other researchers.

AHEPD encompasses all research dealing with higher education pedagogy, development, and curriculum design, as well as all areas of professional development, regardless of focus.

COVERAGE

- Adult Education
- Assessment in Higher Education
- Career Training
- Continuing Professional Development
- Governance in Higher Education
- Higher Education Policy
- Pedagogy of Teaching Higher Education
- Vocational Education
- Coaching and Mentoring

IGI Global is currently accepting manuscripts for publication within this series. To submit a proposal for a volume in this series, please contact our Acquisition Editors at Acquisitions@igi-global.com or visit: http://www.igi-global.com/publish/.

The Advances in Higher Education and Professional Development (AHEPD) Book Series (ISSN 2327-6983) is published by IGI Global, 701 E. Chocolate Avenue, Hershey, PA 17033-1240, USA, www.igi-global.com. This series is composed of titles available for purchase individually; each title is edited to be contextually exclusive from any other title within the series. For pricing and ordering information please visit http://www.igi-global.com/book-series/advances-higher-education-professional-development/73681. Postmaster: Send all address changes to above address. Copyright © 2019 IGI Global. All rights, including translation in other languages reserved by the publisher. No part of this series may be reproduced or used in any form or by any means – graphics, electronic, or mechanical, including photocopying, recording, taping, or information and retrieval systems – without written permission from the publisher, except for non commercial, educational use, including classroom teaching purposes. The views expressed in this series are those of the authors, but not necessarily of IGI Global.

Titles in this Series

For a list of additional titles in this series, please visit: www.igi-global.com/book-series

Higher Education and the Evolution of Management, Applied Sciences, and Engineering Curricula
Carolina F. Machado (University of Minho, Portugal) and J. Paulo Davim (University of Aveiro, Portugal)
Engineering Science Reference • copyright 2019 • 258pp • H/C (ISBN: 9781522572596) • US $185.00 (our price)

Handbook of Research on Critical Thinking Strategies in Pre-Service Learning Environments
Gina J. Mariano (Troy University, USA) and Fred J. Figliano (Troy University, USA)
Information Science Reference • copyright 2019 • 657pp • H/C (ISBN: 9781522578239) • US $265.00 (our price)

Fostering Multiple Levels of Engagement in Higher Education Environments
Kelley Walters (Northcentral University, USA) and Patricia Henry (Northcentral University, USA)
Information Science Reference • copyright 2019 • 316pp • H/C (ISBN: 9781522574705) • US $185.00 (our price)

Study Abroad Opportunities for Community College Students and Strategies for Global Learning
Gregory F. Malveaux (Montgomery College, USA) and Rosalind Latiner Raby (California State University Northridge, USA)
Information Science Reference • copyright 2019 • 324pp • H/C (ISBN: 9781522562528) • US $195.00 (our price)

Identifying, Describing, and Developing Teachers Who Are Gifted and Talented
Meta L. Van Sickle (College of Charleston, USA) Julie D. Swanson (College of Charleston, USA) Judith A. Bazler (Monmouth University, USA) and Kathryn L. Lubniewski (Monmouth University, USA)
Information Science Reference • copyright 2019 • 302pp • H/C (ISBN: 9781522558798) • US $195.00 (our price)

Challenges and Opportunities for Women in Higher Education Leadership
Heidi L. Schnackenberg (State University of New York at Plattsburgh, USA) and Denise A. Simard (State University of New York at Plattsburgh, USA)
Information Science Reference • copyright 2019 • 353pp • H/C (ISBN: 9781522570561) • US $195.00 (our price)

Examining Student Retention and Engagement Strategies at Historically Black Colleges and Universities
Samuel L. Hinton (Independent Researcher, USA) and Antwon D. Woods (Belhaven University, USA)
Information Science Reference • copyright 2019 • 250pp • H/C (ISBN: 9781522570219) • US $175.00 (our price)

Exploring the Technological, Societal, and Institutional Dimensions of College Student Activism
Michael T. Miller (University of Arkansas, USA) and David V. Tolliver (University of Arkansas, USA)
Information Science Reference • copyright 2019 • 303pp • H/C (ISBN: 9781522572749) • US $185.00 (our price)

701 East Chocolate Avenue, Hershey, PA 17033, USA
Tel: 717-533-8845 x100 • Fax: 717-533-8661
E-Mail: cust@igi-global.com • www.igi-global.com

List of Contributors

Table of Contents

Section 1
Conceptualizing Critical Thinking in Teacher Education Contexts

Section 2
Interrogating Teachers' Critical Thinking Pedagogy Across Multidisciplinary Contexts

Detailed Table of Contents

Section 1
Conceptualizing Critical Thinking in Teacher Education Contexts

Teachers are an indispensable part of the debate on the development of critical thinking skills. Much research has centered on examining teachers' critical thinking skills, and on empowering teachers for more effective delivery of critical thinking in instruction. This chapter examines one of the key forces impacting the global context for critical thinking, teachers and teacher education today: an international mandate for critical thinking as a vital 21st century skill for the effective preparation of citizens and workers for life and work in today's society. The chapter begins with an exploration of the meaning and conceptualization of critical thinking. It then deliberates on how the international mandate for schools and teachers engenders a context for critical thinking in teacher education and considers the need for increased pedagogical support for educators. As a final point, the chapter points to some implications for classroom practitioners and teacher educators of delivering on the demands for critical and reflective workers in 21st century society.

This chapter focuses on exploring the role of pre-service teacher (PST) narratives in a research-based model of initial teacher education (ITE) for secondary English teachers across three semesters of a two-year graduate entry, Master of Teaching (Secondary) degree at the University of Sydney, Australia. The model is underpinned by the belief that the development of the teacher's professional identity is an antecedent and generator of their ways of knowing and teacher quality. Initially, the chapter frames the model of ITE through a discussion of the relevant research literature in the field of pre-service teacher development. It then delineates the features of the model at the University of Sydney and provides a close analysis of the sequential narratives of a pre-service English teacher over the course of the first semester of study in the ITE program. Finally, the chapter reflects on the affordances of narratives in shaping PSTs' ways of knowing and professional identity.

Chapter 3

Talia Randa Esnard, The University of the West Indies – St. Augustine Campus, Trinidad and Tobago
Linda Lila Mohammed, University of Trinidad and Tobago, Trinidad and Tobago

Freire contended that teachers' knowledge sets are incomplete without the critical engagement and dialogic exchange with students. Such non-hierarchical and collaborative arrangements are perceived to be at the crux of transformative praxis. As a way of testing the possibilities around this pedagogical alternative, this project encouraged teachers to creatively explore critical pedagogical approaches (CPA) in the classroom and the extent to which this enhanced the engagement of students, and, ultimately, their ability to critically apply their understanding of existing knowledge frames to the formation and presentation of new forms of knowledge. Written observations and self-reflections point to the salience of systemic constraints that were rooted in the structural and cultural facets of the school system, and the effect of these both on teachers' adoption of a bimodal model of instruction, and, on their partial success in this endeavor. Implications for theory and practices are herein discussed.

Chapter 4

Kimberly S. Reinhardt, Texas A&M University – Corpus Christi, USA

This chapter seeks to illustrate how one field-based professor used her instructional coaching knowledge and applied it in a field-based course to develop reflection and ultimately encourage teacher candidates to challenge themselves and take risks in their clinical placements. It reveals how approaches to teacher candidate coaching differ from traditional instructional coaching, which is focused on student outcomes, and how this coaching encourages teacher candidates to push themselves and think deeply about their emerging practice. Through an analysis of five coaching sessions, the use of effective coaching strategies that foster growth for the candidate were examined. The analysis of coaching as critical pedagogy is important to understand not only how the characteristics of dialogical conversations shape teacher candidates' goal choices, but also to situate the place of skilled feedback in the context of learning to teach.

Chapter 5

Kerri Pilling Burchill, Southern Illinois Healthcare, USA
David Anderson, Eastern Michigan University, USA

The contemporary demands of the education environment today require that teachers refine their reflective thinking skills and shift towards the deeper critical thinking skills inherent in reflexive thinking. Reflexivity is a deeper level of critical thinking that assumes a degree of metacognition and "knowing-in-action." Metacognition is a critical tool in helping individuals become more aware of their deeply seeded biases and tacit assumptions about the way the world works. Through a phenomenological analysis of four individual case studies, this study found that student feedback was a key catalyst for building reflexivity skills. Specifically, the study details the key ways by which feedback prompted novice teachers to metacognitively think through their knowing-in-action and ultimately improve their teaching practice. The research details important implications in three areas: 1) practice, 2) theory, and 3) future research.

Chapter 6

This chapter introduces the concept of infusing critical thinking and reflection as part of professional development for teachers, as well as provides recommendations for schools to promote critical thinking and reflection as part of teachers' daily practice. Constructs, such as problem posing and dialogue, are introduced to provide examples of promising practices to consider implementing as a means to enhance critical thinking and reflection amongst teachers when participating in professional development. Additionally, professional learning communities and self-directed professional development are introduced as spaces for teachers to practice these constructs to transform their praxis. Providing opportunities for critical thinking and reflection is one of many steps schools and districts must take, to bring about the positive change required for future success of the education system.

Chapter 7

This chapter provides a method for meeting the educational demands of the 21st century. The Content through Action method (CTA) provides a process to plan integrated instructional units for connecting various subject matter areas. Based on the researcher's experience in designing interdisciplinary units, the chapter includes the CTA process of building a unit and the research-based rationale behind each step of the process. The literature review includes discussion of the Four Cs, the 21st-century classroom, the motivation of learners, and the teacher's role. The theoretical framework is built on the foundation provided by constructivism, heutagogy, design thinking, the theory of change, and the growth mindset. After teaching other methods such as problem-based and design-based learning, the author asserts that the CTA method of instructional planning promotes the development of thinking skills compatible with the needs of the 21st-century learner.

Section 2
Interrogating Teachers' Critical Thinking Pedagogy Across Multidisciplinary Contexts

Thanks to the polarized nature of politics in the world today, students need to learn how to think critically about social issues. Argumentation can be both a type of critical thinking and a tool with which to teach students to think critically about social issues. This chapter lays out a framework for teaching students how to develop critical thinking about real world issues through the use of dialogic argumentation. The impact of dialogic argumentative activities in the classroom are discussed, particularly as they relate to the development of metacognition and theory of mind, as well as how they help students develop an "inner-locutor" that allows them to evaluate both their position and opposing positions. Finally, a model for how these elements contribute to students' value-loaded critical thinking about social issues is outlined.

Wardell Anthony Powell, Framingham State University, USA
Danielle Fuchs, Wellesley High School, USA

This study investigated the implementation of a socioscientific issue curricular unit that was designed to enhance evidence-based reasoning among middle school students. Forty-three middle school students (11-12 years old; 20 males, 23 females) from a summer enrichment program operated by a non-profit organization in the northeastern United States participated in this study. The duration of this curricular unit took place over five consecutive 1-hour period blocks. The researchers utilized qualitative procedures to analyze students' abilities to engage in evidence-based reasoning and the impact it might have on students' argumentation quality on whether the air we breathe makes us sick. Comparison of the findings from pre-test and post-test indicate that students were able to use evidence-based reasoning to enhance their argumentation quality. The results from this investigation suggest that perhaps the use of socioscientific issues as a critical pedagogical tool does enhance students' abilities to engage in evidence-based reasoning.

David Florius Samuel, Providence Secondary School, Barbados

From as far back as the 1980s, many researchers have cited the importance of critical thinking in the citizens of modern societies. Given this importance, the merits of including critical thinking as a major objective at various levels of the education system and in different subject areas of the school curriculum have been extensively argued. This chapter focuses on science and technology curricula and rationalizes the need for changes both in the development as well as the implementation of the curriculum to facilitate the promotion of critical thinking skills in students. There is also an extensive discussion of particular instructional approaches and strategies needed to facilitate this.

Lizette A. Burks, University of Kansas, USA
Douglas Huffman, University of Kansas, USA

The new science and engineering practice of developing and using models is needed to achieve the vision of three-dimensional teaching and learning and should be an important new component of teacher preparation programs. This chapter examined critical thinking and preservice teachers' preconceptions about critical thinking and the practice of developing and using models. The results of the study indicated that when preservice teachers initially described how this practice might look in the classroom, only two of the six categories outlined in A Science Framework for K-12 Science Education for this practice were described by most participants. Of those two categories described by most participants, the majority were at a novice level. These results emphasize the necessity for elementary teacher education to provide opportunities for preservice teachers to better understand the practice of developing and using models, and how critical thinking can help teachers use models.

    Md. Anwarul Azim Majumder, The University of the West Indies – Cave Hill Campus, Barbados

    Bidyadhar Sa, The University of the West Indies – St. Augustine Campus, Trinidad and Tobago

    Fahad Abdullah Alateeq, Al Imam Mohammad Ibn Saud Islamic University (IMSIU), Saudi Arabia

    Sayeeda Rahman, American University of Integrative Sciences, Barbados

In recent years, there has been more emphasis on developing higher order thinking (e.g., critical thinking and clinical reasoning) processes to tackle the recent trends and challenges in medical education. Critical thinking and clinical reasoning are considered to be the cornerstones for teaching and training tomorrow's doctors. Lack of training of critical thinking and clinical reasoning in medical curricula causes medical students and physicians to use cognitive biases in problem solving which ultimately leads to diagnostic errors later in their professional practice. Moreover, there is no consensus on the most effective teaching model to teach the critical thinking and clinical reasoning skills and even the skill is not effectively tested in medical schools. This chapter will focus on concepts, contemporary theories, implications, issues and challenges, characteristics, various steps, teaching models and strategies, measuring and intervention tools, and assessment modalities of critical thinking and clinical reasoning in medical education settings.

    Kelli Thomas, University of Kansas, USA

    Douglas Huffman, University of Kansas, USA

    Mari Caballero, Emporia State University, USA

The purpose of this chapter was to investigate pre-service teachers' noticing of children's critical thinking and views towards eliciting and using students' critical thinking in mathematics teaching. A mixed method study was used to provide a range of perspectives on pre-service teachers' views towards mathematics. The results indicated that the pre-service teachers initially held beliefs that mathematics teaching and learning consist of transferring information and students absorbing and memorizing information. The pre-service teachers based their instructional responses on experiences they had as students in elementary mathematics classrooms. The pre-service teachers described what they had observed about teaching mathematics as the ideal without regard for how the teaching behaviors they observed might influence children's critical thinking about mathematics. After completing a mathematics methods course, the pre-service teachers held beliefs more consistent with a reform-oriented classroom and demonstrated growth in their ability to notice children's mathematics thinking.

Section 3
Situating Critical Thinking in Instructional and Informational Contexts

Chapter 14

Teaching critical thinking skills to students has become a central focus the language arts classroom. It is therefore important to examine what critical thinking may look like for the language arts teacher: How do language arts teachers come to know and understand? How do language arts teachers engage in critical thinking in order to enhance their pedagogical practices? This chapter examines the ways in which teachers' involvement in developing their critical thinking skills can aid them in establishing their knowledge and understandings. The chapter explores findings from a study that involved teachers in Grades 2 and 4 in the development of a framework for reading instruction in the primary grades. These findings make a case for encouraging teachers to engage in critical thinking in professional learning communities that foster professional development and collaboration in an active and reflective process.

Chapter 15

This chapter presents a completely structured training (CST) for the Angoff standard-setting method. The CST was developed to address the challenges teachers face in making the required probability judgments about student performance. It includes a comprehensive curriculum and instruction, practice, and feedback to guide participants on task performance. Overall, the approach is useful for developing critical-thinking skills among teachers in the context of assessing and evaluating educational achievement. This chapter also describes and illustrates how to use the training to facilitate professional development for K–12 teachers through programming. Guidelines, lessons and recommendations for implementation and study of CST are also provided.

Chapter 16

The aim of the chapter is to provide both theoretical and practical ideas about critical thinking development within English language teaching contexts. Encouraging language learners to be critical thinkers is important in teaching English as a foreign language. However, achieving the goal remains a challenge. Using various strategies together seem to be effective when properly implemented. Therefore this chapter outlines these strategies which include communicative language tasks, using authentic meaningful texts, using critical literacy, being aware of whole-brain learning, adopting a reflective teaching, enabling students to become autonomous, using explicit instruction, teacher questioning, using active and cooperative learning strategies, using literature in English classes, using creative drama, and adopting self-assessment. Teachers can enable learners to have critical thinking skills and more efficient English lessons by combining these strategies in a new way or by designing critical thinking activities in the classroom.

Chapter 17
Shaneise J. Holder, The University of the West Indies – Cave Hill Campus, Barbados
Kahdia L. Jordan, The University of the West Indies – Cave Hill Campus, Barbados

This chapter focuses on the importance of planning for critical thinking in language arts instruction based on the Caribbean classroom. It seeks to identify traits of critical thinking, outline suggestions for planning for the inclusion of critical thinking, and highlight methods for incorporating critical thinking into language arts and provide solutions and recommendations. The chapter ends with suggestions for future research directions and summarizes the importance and many benefits associated with critical thinking in language arts.

Chapter 18
Hannah Mills Mechler, Grays Harbor College, USA

This chapter will outline the roles of teachers within early childhood learning environments and how they may promote children's critical thinking skills. Further discussions about how children's cognitive development may be fostered is also addressed. Theoretical frameworks are integrated as well to further decipher and understand how children's critical thinking skills may be promoted within early childhood learning environments. In addition, several curriculum models in early childhood education that are focused on the Montessori, Reggio Emilia, Tools of the Mind, High Scope, and Waldorf approaches are presented and applied to how they may enhance children's critical thinking skills as well as their overall development.

Chapter 19
Katrina Woolsey Jordan, Northwestern State University, USA
Michelle Fazio-Brunson, Northwestern State University, USA
Shawn Marise Butler, St. Vincent and the Grenadines Community College, Saint Vincent and the Grenadines

Critical thinking is not a new concept in the world of education. However, teaching it to university students in teacher education programs can be difficult. Teaching these skills to students in grade school, especially in the early childhood classroom, comes with its own set of challenges. This chapter outlines strategies for teaching critical thinking skills in interesting and innovative ways, both at the university and early childhood level. Of particular interest is the project approach. During the three phases of this approach, children act as young investigators and apply critical thinking skills in their daily work. Future trends in both teacher education and the education of young children are also identified.

Chapter 20

This chapter acknowledges the widespread recognition of the importance of instruction in the area of information literacy and shows how information literacy and critical thinking, another vital skill demanded in more and more fields of endeavor, can be integrated as institutions seek to prepare their students to be able to function effectively in today's knowledge-based environment. Some attention is given to Information Literacy frameworks which aim to guide the development of information literacy and enhance delivery and assessment in this field. It recognizes the importance of information specialists and faculty in higher education institutions to be able to work together to establish and develop Information Literacy programs that will equip students with the relevant skills to be considered information literate. It also touches briefly on pedagogical approaches that may be taken in the delivery of Information Literacy instruction and emphasizes the importance of assessment as a means of enhancing the ultimate value of the process to students who participate.

Foreword

There appears to be a general gravitation towards what many describe as a post-truth era in our 21st century. The word "post-truth", defined as "relating to or denoting circumstances in which objective facts are less influential in shaping public opinion than appeals to emotion and personal belief", was designated as Oxford Dictionary's 2016 Word of the Year (English Oxford Living Dictionaries, 2016). "Post-truth", also associated with the notion of "fake news" or the "post-factual" (Alvermann, 2017), was recently followed by the 2018 Word of the Year, "toxic," a word meaning "poisonous" which first appeared in English in the mid-seventeenth century from the medieval Latin *toxicus*, meaning 'poisoned' or 'imbued with poison" (English Oxford Living Dictionaries, 2018). According to the English Oxford Living Dictionaries, the Oxford Word of the Year is "a word or expression that is judged to reflect the ethos, mood, or preoccupations of the passing year, and have lasting potential as a term of cultural significance."

Considering that these two words – "post-truth" and "toxic"– have both characterized our society in such rapid succession within the past three years, one wonders: What happens to teachers and classrooms when we live in an era where these words seem to have come to reflect the very ethos of our society? What are the majority of teachers in our society to do when their primary goal is to address curriculum in classrooms where learning is often disconnected from the daily discourse of the real world occurring through "social media texts", which continue to function as "the largest source of public opinion" (Alvermann, 2017; Deng, Sinha & Zhao, 2016)? And, if thinking is such a central part of the process of learning, what happens if teachers who scaffold students' thinking in classrooms do not or cannot help learners bridge gaps between the emotions and personal beliefs that tug at the heart of their students on one hand and the decreasing attractiveness of objective fact that beckons to them on the other?

Donna Alvermann, in discussing the ramification of the post-factual for students in this era, points to the need for using critical inquiry as a key part of literacy teaching. Alvermann (2017) describes critical inquiry as "instruction aimed at disrupting myths and distortions in social media texts by accounting for the intersection of politically infused cultural practices (e.g., online networking) with the social and economic realities that regulate flows of information on the internet" (p. 3). Alvermann's proposition for using critical inquiry, which is very much aligned with the notion of "critical literacy" (Luke, 2000), seeks in many ways, to extend notions of critical thinking such as that proposed by Deanna Kuhn.

Kuhn (1999) proposed this developmental model of critical thinking drawing from the idea that three forms of meta-knowing – "knowing about one's own and others' knowing" (Kuhn, 1999, p. 17) – are central to critical thinking. In the model, Kuhn argued that these three forms of meta-knowing are meta-cognitive, meta-strategic, and epistemological (Kuhn, 1999). Emphasizing the requirement of critical literacy which focuses on elements of higher order comprehension and of social power across texts (Luke, 2000), this notion of critical thinking proposed by Kuhn (1999) functions as a basis for critical inquiry (Alvermann, 2017). Critical thinking through critical inquiry asks us to think beyond the limitations of subject matter when working towards training teachers and teaching students to engage in meta-knowing, to consider more closely the ways in which social media functions as a developmental context for enacting critical meta-knowing, and to create opportunities where teachers and students have control over their meta-knowing beyond the predefined curriculum that is limited to classrooms. In doing so, the field comes to see meta-knowing, and therefore critical thinking, as an exercise that relies largely on social media texts such as Wikimedia for engaging in processes such as editing (McDowell, 2017). Practices such as this that foster critical inquiry, Alvermann (2017) notes, are more likely to facilitate students' learning of information literacy skills which foster critical thinking than their writing of assignments that tend to rely on traditional printed texts (p. 8). Through such practices that foster critical thinking, it becomes possible to address long-standing debates regarding whether critical thinking can be taught or not by illustrating how the use and engagement with contemporary and popular social media texts that constitute popular culture, form the basis through which both teachers and students engage in meta-knowing.

Particularly, for teachers who assume the responsibility to develop critical thinking skills in students, Trevor Stewart agrees that critical thinking is a "literate practice that must be developed and nurtured" (Stewart, 2019, p. 212). Stewart (2019) points to what many have referred to as the "two-worlds pitfall" (Feiman-Nemser & Buchman, 1985), which he describes as the "contradictions between standardized instructional practices often modeled by cooperating teachers" in classrooms and the "student-centered theories that [teachers] have studied in their literacy classrooms" that require teachers to engage in the "critical thought" needed to address "challenges they encounter as they prepare students for success in and beyond the classroom" (Stewart, 2019, p. 212). Without first developing critical-thinking skills themselves, Stewart (2019) argues: How will teachers be able to enact instruction in "student-centered frameworks"? It is such frameworks that will allow teachers to draw from social media texts as a contextual basis for engendering critical thinking in their students in what some regard as a "post-truth" era.

The *Handbook of Research on Critical Thinking and Teacher Pedagogy* emerges at a timely and relevant moment, responding to the need for concrete mechanisms that demonstrate how teachers can work to develop critical thinking within and beyond content areas as well as through reflection and coaching to develop pedagogies that support students in the classroom. For instance, by acknowledging the international mandate for critical thinking as a vital 21st century skill that effectively prepares citizens and workers for life and work in today's society, the *Handbook* highlights the global imperative for helping teachers to use critical thinking in ways that impact the global context. It also emphasizes reflexivity as an avenue through which teachers adopt a deeper level of critical thinking – reflexivity – which allows them to have more control over their meta-knowing by drawing from their metacognition and "knowing-in-action". In this way, they are better able to facilitate critical inquiry through student-centered teaching in their practice.

This volume also gives attention to the application of the skills of critical thinking to real world situations beyond the classroom. It shows further how dialogic argumentation activities draw from metacognition and theory of mind to support the development of an "inner-locutor" that allows students to evaluate both their position and opposing positions, a critical thinking skill for addressing the divide between public opinion and objective fact, what many regard as a "post-factual" era.

While we await another Word of the Year that describes the ethos for our current generation, our thoughts must be focused on the ways in which we will develop teachers who themselves can engage in critical literacy through critical inquiry that is premised on critical thinking. Through this Handbook, we see a commitment to helping teachers know how they know, to improving teachers' knowledge about their knowing, and to providing educators with strategies that facilitate this meta-knowing. In turn, teachers can foster critical thinking in their students in ways that allow us to reclaim objectivity as a function of its metacognitive constructs even while acknowledging the place of personal opinion in public discourse through critical thinking in this era.

Patriann Smith
Texas Tech University, USA

Patriann Smith *is an Assistant Professor of Language, Diversity, and Literacy Studies in the Department of Curriculum and Instruction at Texas Tech University. Patriann Smith's work emerges at the intersection of language, literacy, and multicultural teacher education. Her publications include "Accomplishing the Goals of Multicultural Teacher Education: How about Transdisciplinarity?" published by Curriculum and Teaching Dialogue, "Understanding Afro-Caribbean Educators' Experiences with Englishes across Caribbean and U.S. Contexts and Classrooms: Recursivity, (Re)positionality, Bidirectionality" and "Learning to Know, Be, Do, and Live Together With, in the Cross-Cultural Experiences of Immigrant Teacher Educators" published by Teaching and Teacher Education.*

REFERENCES

Alvermann, D. E. (2017). Social media texts and critical inquiry in a post-factual era. *Journal of Adolescent & Adult Literacy*, *61*(3), 335–338.

Deng, S., Sinha, A. P., & Zhao, H. (2016). Adapting sentiment lexicons to domain- specific social media texts. *Decision Support Systems*, *94*, 65–76.

English Oxford Living Dictionaries. (2016). *Word of the Year 2016*. Retrieved from https://www.oxford-dictionaries.com/press/news/2016/12/11/WOTY-16

English Oxford Living Dictionaries. (2018). *Word of the Year 2018*. Retrieved from https://en.oxforddictionaries.com/word-of-the-year/word-of-the-year-2018

Feiman-Nemser, S., & Buchmann, M. (1985). Pitfalls of experience in teacher preparation. *Teachers College Record*, *87*(1), 53–65.

Kuhn, D. (1999). A developmental model of critical thinking. *Educational Researcher*, *28*(2), 16–46.

Luke, A. (2000). Critical literacy in Australia: A matter of context and standpoint. *Journal of Adolescent & Adult Literacy*, *43*(5), 448–461.

McDowell, Z. F. (2017). *Student learning outcomes with Wikipedia-based assignments (Fall 2016 research report)*. Amherst, MA: University of Massachusetts.

Stewart, T. (2019). Supporting teacher candidates' development of critical thinking skills through dialogue and reflection. In G. J. Mariano & F. G. Figliano (Eds.), *Handbook of research on critical thinking strategies in pre-service learning environments* (pp. 211–234). Hershey, PA: IGI Global.

Preface

The demands of the 21ˢᵗ century require critical thinkers. These demands also require a tangible pedagogical and curricular mind shift for schools and educators in order to create and enable literate citizens. In a global society where the problem-solving skills of citizens are becoming increasingly important for effective decision making, educators and curriculum specialists need to 're-imagine' curricula that recognize, through classroom practice and professional development, the need to structure teacher education and development in ways that facilitate teachers in their role of preparing students for the knowledge economy as well as providing opportunities for students to reflect and create. Teacher education in the global context is evolving and needs to evolve to respond to the needs not just of today's learners but also to the challenges today's learners face and will encounter within and without the classroom as they prepare for emerging 21ˢᵗ century jobs. Teachers' exposure to the how of critical thinking in their classroom practice advances their own problem-solving and critical thinking skills and those of the students they teach. Teaching for critical thinking in teacher education and its wider currency for teaching and learning on all levels ranging from K-12 to college and university is therefore central across the curriculum.

Critical thinking in each discipline is a complex set of cognitive skills and dispositions, some of which are shared and many of which are specific to the discipline (Gardner, 2011; Bensley, 1998). Critical thinking is also evidenced by the process that every human being uses to solve problems, make decisions, generate new ideas, and be creative. But it also means different things to different people. It is complex and complicated at best. Yet, it describes the process of taking responsibility for one's own thinking, it explains decision-making through the analysis of information, and it facilitates and documents the evaluation and assessment of learning. More importantly, critical thinking directly impacts student learning and growth. This potential to influence student outcomes and growth has implications for teacher education programmes and teacher education pedagogy (Halpern, 2014).

The importance of preparing teachers on a strong base of knowledge in critical thinking skills is increasingly important in contemporary society. Standards for learning, with heavy emphasis on thinking skills, are now higher as citizens and workers need greater knowledge and problem-solving skills to survive and succeed. Critical thinking is increasingly important to the success of both individuals and nations, and growing evidence demonstrates that teachers' abilities are crucial contributors to students' learning. Every thought or action of the teacher influences students. And they are now expected to prepare all students for higher order thinking and other 21ˢᵗ century critical thinking skills. To meet these expectations, teachers need a new kind of preparation.

While the new kind of preparation and pedagogy involves raising standards, it means more than learning content. It requires the use of critical content and pedagogy as a tool to understand key concepts and principles and teaching beyond the facts, to facilitate deeper thinking. Facilitating learners' successful functioning requires teachers to draw upon beliefs, knowledge, experiences and pedagogical practice.

This volume contains 20 chapters. The purpose of the book is to add to the knowledge and pedagogical base of critical thinking in teacher education with regard to what instructional practices best enable critical thinking in this fundamentally important field. It provides necessary insight into our understanding of critical thinking as an overarching goal of instruction in teacher education across all disciplines. Questions guiding the chapters, and the subsequent, overall narrative/discourse of the book include:

1. What counts as evidence of critical thinking in teacher education?
2. What instructional practices best enable the habit of thinking critically when teaching in teacher education?
3. How are instructional practices in critical thinking best applied in classroom instruction and professional development for teachers?

The authors in this volume situate their discussions about critical thinking within the context of teacher pedagogy, focusing on detailed and situated descriptions of theory, curriculum, practice and reflection. Their discourse is strengthened by the diversity of contexts which shape their perspectives and reflections on the subject: Australia, Barbados, England, St Vincent and the Grenadines, Saudi Arabia, Trinidad and Tobago, Turkey, and the United States.

The chapters are presented in three sections, representing three major themes covered in the volume. Part One focuses on critical thinking and teacher pedagogy. This section, 'Conceptualizing Critical Thinking in Teacher Education Contexts', ponders and reflects on teaching critical thinking with teachers in mind. It considers the thinking classroom in teacher education, teachers' ways of knowing, using critical thinking to structure teachers' knowledge and understanding, curriculum and instruction for teacher thinking and planning for thinking. The context of teacher education and development is interrogated, through discourse about pre-service teacher education courses, and how talk and reflection (Beltman, et. al, 2015; Beauchamp & Thomas, 2011; Zweirs & Crawford, 2011) help to build critical thinking skills, in a way that is important for not only teacher development, but ultimately teacher student achievement and development as well. In Part Two, 'Interrogating Teachers' Critical Thinking Pedagogy across Multidisciplinary Contexts', authors share research and experiences about teaching critical thinking across the disciplines. Critical thinking is a phenomenon of worldwide importance and it is a desired outcome across education disciplines and levels. Development of critical thinking is considered a primary responsibility of educators. And, while educators, at the different levels and within the disciplines, find it challenging, at times, to foster learners' understanding of their critical thinking development (McTigue & Wiggins, 2013; Darling-Hammond, 2006), there is much value in observing how multidisciplinary educators perceive and practice critical thinking within their different and varied educational domains. Part Three 'Situating Critical Thinking in Instructional and Informational Contexts', positions and centres the discourse on critical thinking as instructional and informational. The perspectives within this section, exemplifies what transpires when students, supported and guided by teachers are able to think critically. Within this paradigm of learning – 'Critical Thinking in Language Arts and Early Childhood Education' – both students and teachers are thinking deeply about what they are learning in order to apply that knowledge creatively and effectively as they seek to infuse critical thinking development into their discipline (McTigue & Wiggins, 2013; Boyd, & Markarian; 2011;. McBride, 1991).

The introductory chapter by Verna Knight and co-author, Sandra Robinson, examines one of the key forces inherently impacting the global context for critical thinking, teachers and teacher education today: an international mandate for critical thinking as a vital skill for the effective preparation of citizens and workers for life and work in today's society. This mandate, the authors argue, has resulted in increasing demands on teacher training institutions to produce critical and reflective teaching practitioners. It has motivated increased teacher ownership of their own professional development and subsequent efforts to access a deeper understanding and skillful application of critical thinking in their classrooms in all disciplines. It advocates for providing increased support to educators in the quest to empower classroom practitioners and teacher educators to best deliver on the demands for critical and reflective workers in 21st century society.

In keeping with the emphasis on reflection, the chapter by Jacqueline Manuel and Janet Dutton focuses on exploring the role of preservice teacher narratives in a research-based model of Initial Teacher Education (ITE) for secondary English teachers. The model, underpinned by the belief that the development of teachers' professional identity is an antecedent and generator of teachers' ways of knowing and teacher quality, frames ITE through a discussion of the relevant research literature in the field of preservice teacher development. It then delineates the features of the model at the University of Sydney and provides a close analysis of the sequential narratives of a preservice English teacher over the course of the first semester of study in the ITE program. Finally, the chapter reflects on the affordances of narratives in shaping preservice teachers' ways of knowing and professional identity.

Talia Esnard and Linda Mohammed extend the focus on conceptualizing and reflecting on critical thinking by contending that teachers' knowledge sets are incomplete without critical engagement and dialogic exchange with students. They share research which examined the possibilities around pedagogical alternatives that encouraged teachers to creatively explore critical pedagogical approaches (CPA) in the classroom. Their observations and self-reflections point to the salience of systemic constraints that were rooted in the structural and cultural facets of the school system, and the effect of these both on teachers' adoption of a bimodal model of instruction and on their partial success in this endeavor. Implications for theory and practice are also discussed.

Kimberly S. Reinhard's chapter illustrates how one field-based professor used her instructional coaching knowledge and applied it in a field-based course to develop reflection and ultimately encourage teacher candidates to challenge themselves and take risks in their clinical placements. It reveals how approaches to teacher candidate coaching differ from traditional instructional coaching which is focused on student outcomes, and how this coaching encourages teacher candidates to push themselves and think deeply about their emerging practice. It also situates the place of skilled feedback in the context of learning to teach.

Kerri Burchill and David Anderson, explore reflexivity as a deeper level of critical thinking that assumes a degree of metacognition and "knowing-in-action" (Schon, 1983, p. 50). Through a phenomenological analysis of four individual case studies, their study found that student feedback was a key catalyst for building reflexivity skills. Specifically, the chapter details the key ways by which feedback prompted novice teachers to metacognitively think through their knowing-in-action and ultimately improve their teaching practice.

The concept of infusing critical thinking and reflection as part of professional development for teachers is addressed by Sandra Guzman Foster and Stephen Fleenor. They consider how providing opportunities for critical thinking and reflection is one of many steps schools and districts must take in order to bring about the positive change required for future success of the education system. By capturing the 'tugs and pulls' associated with families' need to provide their children with the best opportunities in a racialized society, this study raises a critical awareness about the contested uses of languages across home and school spaces and the advocates for interlocutors in leveraging language use.

In the final chapter of this section, Harpreet Kaur Dhir provides a method for meeting the educational demands of the 21st century. The Content Through Action method (CTA) is a process for planning integrated instructional units for connecting various subject areas. Based on the researcher's experience in designing interdisciplinary units, the chapter includes the CTA process of building a unit and the research-based rationale behind each step of the process. After teaching other methods such as problem-based and design-based learnings, the author asserts that the CTA method of instruction promotes the development of thinking skills compatible with the needs of the 21st century learner.

Section Two of the text begins with a chapter by N. Leigh Boyd who observes that because of the polarized nature of politics in the world today, students need to learn how to think critically about social issues. Argumentation, she notes, can be both a type of critical thinking and a tool with which to teach students to think critically about social issues. The chapter lays out a framework for teaching students how to develop critical thinking about real world issues through the use of dialogic argumentation. The impact of dialogic argumentative activities in the classroom is also discussed, particularly as they relate to the development of metacognition and theory of mind. In a somewhat similar vein, Wardell Anthony Powell and Danielle Fuchs outline a study which investigated the implementation of a curricular unit based on a socioscientific issue and designed to enhance evidence-based reasoning among middle school students. The researchers utilized qualitative procedures to analyze students' ability to engage in evidence-based reasoning and the impact it might have on the quality of their argumentation. The results from the investigation suggest that the use of socio-scientific issues as a critical pedagogical tool may enhance students' ability to engage in evidence-based reasoning.

David Florius Samuel's focus on science and technology curricula rationalizes the need for changes both in the development and the implementation of the curriculum to facilitate the promotion of critical thinking skills in students. The chapter also provides an extensive discussion of particular instructional approaches and strategies needed to facilitate this. Lizette A. Burks and Douglas Huffman examine critical thinking and preservice teachers' preconceptions about the practice of developing and using models including discourse patterns. They note that the results of a study which highlighted preservice teachers' unfamiliarity with the elements of the NRC's "A Science Framework for K-12 Science Education" (NRC, 2012). This fact, they believe, emphasizes the necessity for elementary teacher education to provide opportunities for preservice teachers to better understand the practice of developing and using models, and how critical thinking can help teachers use models.

The emphasis on developing higher order thinking processes in response to the recent trends and challenges in medical education is addressed by co-authors Md. Anwarul Azim Majumder, Bidyadhar Sa Fahad Abdullah Alateeq, Al Imam Mohammad Ibn Saud and Sayeeda Rahman. They note that critical thinking and clinical reasoning are considered to be the cornerstones for teaching and training tomorrow's doctors. They argue, however, that there is no consensus on the most effective model for teaching the critical thinking and clinical reasoning skills in medical schools. The chapter also highlights concepts, contemporary theories, teaching models and strategies as well as assessment modalities of critical thinking and clinical reasoning in medical education settings.

Kelli Thomas, Douglas Huffman and Mari Caballero discuss a study which investigated pre-service teachers' observation of children's critical thinking as well as views towards eliciting and using students' critical thinking in mathematics teaching. The mixed method study revealed a dated attitude to mathematics teaching on the part of the preservice teachers, an attitude which changed after their exposure to a mathematics methods course.

Section Three, 'Situating Critical Thinking in Instructional and Informational Contexts, begins with Karen Thomas' chapter in which she examines the ways in which teachers' involvement in developing their critical thinking skills can aid them in establishing and centering their knowledge and understandings within the instructional context. She further explores findings from a study that involved teachers in Grades 2 and 4 in the development of a framework for reading instruction in the primary grades. The findings make a case for encouraging teachers to engage in critical thinking in and as professional learning communities that foster professional development and collaboration.

Ifeoma Chika Iyioke presents a Completely Structured Training (CST) for the Angoff standard-setting method which was developed as a tool to facilitate teachers' assessment of student performance, while developing their own critical thinking skills. The chapter describes and illustrates how to use the training to facilitate professional development for K–12 teachers through programming and provides guidelines, lessons, and recommendations for implementation and study of the CST.

Şenol OrakcıF, Mehmet Durnali and Osman Aktan provide both theoretical and practical ideas about critical thinking development within English language teaching contexts. The chapter outlines how encouraging language learners to be critical thinkers is important in English as a foreign language teaching. Shanese Holder and Kahdia Jordan reflect on characteristics of critical thinking skills and their importance and highlight ways in which educators can plan lessons effectively to foster these skills in the classroom, specifically during Language Arts instruction.

The next two chapters concentrate on the Early Childhood Education classroom. Hannah Mills Mechler outlines the roles of teachers within early childhood learning environment and instructional contexts and how they may promote children's critical thinking skills. The chapter situates the instructional context by providing theoretical and curriculum perspectives about a variety of approaches to learning in early childhood and considers how they may enhance children's critical thinking skills as well as their overall development. Katrina Woolsey Jordan, Michelle Fazio-Brunson, and Shawn Marise Butler outline strategies for teaching critical thinking skills in interesting and innovative ways, both at the university and Early Childhood levels. Of particular interest is the Project Approach in which children act as young investigators and apply critical thinking skills in their daily work. Trends in both teacher education and the education of young children are also identified.

In the final chapter of this section, Ann Marie Joanne White makes the case for critical thinking as indispensable to research and by extension how we engage with information. She highlights the value to librarians, and information seekers (teachers and students) who use active-learning in the classroom to interact with one-shot sessions of information literacy. She notes that although critical thinking and information literacy concepts are known to be beneficial to graduates, it is a challenge to embed them into a university curriculum.

In summary, the foregoing serves as a platform for interrogating and advancing the discourse on critical thinking and its implications for emerging 21st paradigms in teacher education and pedagogy. There is no one overarching perspective among the authors; rather, diverse perspectives are presented as the authors interpret and synthesize their knowledge base regarding critical thinking and teacher pedagogy at this time. Within the collection of perspectives and voices, the reader will find contradictions and redundancies. This is as it should be. The contradictions are points of departure for further discourse; they also offer a convergence of ideas that creates a more balanced perspective. The redundancies are also useful in that they serve as a means of emphasizing some of the most important aspects of the broad subject of this text. These contradictions and redundancies also provide sources of inquiry to provoke and invite further investigations and reflections among advocates of critical thinking and teacher pedagogy. In some instances, the voices can seem incoherent. Yet, the incoherence stimulates a discussion that is knowledgeable, experienced and passionate.

As editors, we do not impose a shape on these chapters, except to categorise them within thematic contexts. Rather, what is encouraged is a conversation about complicated and unresolved issues which speak to the complexity of critical thinking and teacher pedagogy. This is an important nuance of the exchange of ideas. It invites readers to construct their own understanding based on their own purposes, experiences and needs. And, in the end, we expect that the reaction to this volume will advance the important dialogue about the dialectical relationship between critical thinking and teacher pedagogy.

Sandra P.A. Robinson
The University of the West Indies – Cave Hill Campus, Barbados

Verna Knight
The University of the West Indies – Cave Hill Campus, Barbados

REFERENCES

Beauchamp, C., & Thomas, L. (2011). New teachers' identity shifts at the boundary of teacher education and initial practice. *International Journal of Educational Research, 50*(1), 6–13. doi:10.1016/j.ijer.2011.04.003

Beltman, S., Glass, C., Dinham, J., Chalk, B., & Nguyen, B. H. N. (2015). Drawing identity: Beginning pre-service teachers' professional identities. *Issues in Educational Research, 25*(3), 225–245.

Bensley, D. A. (1998). *Critical thinking in psychology: A unified skills approach.* Belmont, CA: Academic Press.

Boyd, M. P., & Markarian, W. C. (2011). Dialogic teaching: Talk in service of a dialogic stance. *Language and Education, 25*(6), 515–534. doi:10.1080/09500782.2011.597861

Darling-Hammond, L. (2006). Constructing 21st-Century Teacher Education. *Journal of Teacher Education, 57*(3), 300–314. doi:10.1177/0022487105285962

Gardner, H. (2011). *Frames of Mind: The Theory of Multiple Intelligences.* New York: Basic Books.

Halpern, D. F. (2014). *An Introduction to Critical Thinking* (5th ed.). New York: Psychology Press.

McBride, R. E. (1991). Critical thinking: An overview with implications for physical education. *Journal of Teaching in Physical Education, 11*(2), 112–125. doi:10.1123/jtpe.11.2.112

McTigue, J., & Wiggins, G. (2013). *Essential Questions: Opening doors to student understanding.* Alexandria, VA: ASCD.

National Research Council. (2011). *A Framework for K-12 Science Education: Practices, Crosscutting Concepts, and Core Ideas.* Committee on a Conceptual Framework for New K-12 Science Education Standards. Board on Science Education, Division of Behavioral and Social Sciences and Education. Washington, DC: The National Academies Press.

Schon, D. (1983). *The reflective practitioner: How professionals think in action.* New York, NY: Basic Books, Inc., Publishers.

Zweirs, J., & Crawford, M. (2011). *Academic Conversations: Classroom Talk that fosters critical Thinking and Content Understandings.* Maine: Stenhouse Publisher.

Acknowledgment

We are deeply appreciative of the efforts of all those who contributed to the publication of these chapters, through submissions, reviews of manuscripts, and by providing support and encouragement through this process.

Special thanks to all the contributing authors who worked tirelessly to revise manuscripts so they could be included in our final selection. We are extremely grateful for their dedication, hard work, and professionalism.

Thanks to the IGI Global team for their guidance and consideration at various crucial stages of the process and for helping us to get through the phases required for publication. These include Marianne Caesar, Jan Travers, Josephine Dadeboe, Sharlene Oong and Mark Brehm who were all supportive in every way.

We are very thankful for the time taken by Patriann Smith to write the foreword.

We are especially grateful for the input of the Editorial Advisory Board; their contribution advanced the work. This volume also benefited greatly from the insightful, instructive and thoughtful comments of Victor Simpson.

Lastly, we are thankful for the friends and the members of our families who journeyed with us, especially, Shawn, Saraiah, Ethan, Vilna, Julia, Andrea, Karen and Colin; their support, encouragement, patience and acts of grace throughout the process of this publication, mattered.

Section 1
Conceptualizing Critical Thinking in Teacher Education Contexts

Chapter 1
An Introduction:
Establishing a Context for Critical Thinking in Teacher Education

Verna Knight
The University of the West Indies – Cave Hill Campus, Barbados

Sandra P.A. Robinson
The University of the West Indies – Cave Hill Campus, Barbados

ABSTRACT

Teachers are an indispensable part of the debate on the development of critical thinking skills. Much research has centered on examining teachers' critical thinking skills, and on empowering teachers for more effective delivery of critical thinking in instruction (Perkins, 2014; Gardener, 2011; Duron et al, 2006; Abrami et al, 2008, Choy & Cheah, 2009). This chapter examines one of the key forces impacting the global context for critical thinking, teachers and teacher education today: an international mandate for critical thinking as a vital 21st century skill for the effective preparation of citizens and workers for life and work in today's society. The chapter begins with an exploration of the meaning and conceptualization of critical thinking. It then deliberates on how the international mandate for schools and teachers engenders a context for critical thinking in teacher education and considers the need for increased pedagogical support for educators. As a final point, the chapter points to some implications for classroom practitioners and teacher educators of delivering on the demands for critical and reflective workers in 21st century society.

INTRODUCTION

Education would be much more effective if its purpose was to ensure that by the time they leave school every boy and girl should know how much they do not know, and be imbued with a lifelong desire to know it. William Haley, British Editor.

What is the current situation in which teachers find themselves which necessitates that the teaching of critical thinking be a significant part of teacher education and teachers' professional development agenda?

DOI: 10.4018/978-1-5225-7829-1.ch001

Copyright © 2019, IGI Global. Copying or distributing in print or electronic forms without written permission of IGI Global is prohibited.

Why has critical thinking become so important as an educational goal? Why must teachers and teacher educators be concerned about the state of critical thinking in classrooms today? These are a few of the many questions which can only be answered by delving into an interrogation of the educational context and inherent factors informing the conceptualization and delivery of critical thinking as a skill required of teachers, and teacher education institutions today. Consequently, the complexity of the decisions teachers face require different kinds of knowledge and judgement that they will bring to the contexts in which they work. To meet the education expectations of these 21st century contexts, teachers must be aware of the many situations in which students' learning and thinking can unfold. Making these judgements requires a type of instructional leadership that keeps what is best for the learner at the centre of the decision-making process.

Teaching for thinking is central to education. And, critical thinking has long been an important skill for those who learn and those who teach. This ability to draw together knowledge from many different disciplines enables one to make good judgments about what to believe or what to do; it is an essential characteristic of critical thinking skills. However, translating critical thinking into tangible teaching goals continues to be a pedagogical challenge in teacher education classrooms. The result is a discrepancy between what is valued and what is pursued (Tsui, 2001). In order to ensure teachers' facility to apply critical thinking skills to tasks and the ultimate role of teaching, it is necessary that their education and development provide them not only with practical ways to improve their abilities in this area of scholarship but also to explore and understand how the students they will teach perceive, conceptualize and value critical thinking.

This chapter examines one of the key forces impacting the global context for critical thinking, teachers and teacher education today: an international mandate for critical thinking as a vital 21st century skill for the effective preparation of citizens and workers for life and work in today's society. This mandate has resulted in increasing demands on teacher training institutions to produce critical and reflective teaching practitioners; and has motivated increased teacher ownership of their own professional development and subsequent efforts to access a deeper understanding and skillful application of critical thinking in their classrooms and across disciplines. The chapter begins with a discussion of the meaning and conceptualization of critical thinking. It then moves on to examine the international mandate for schools and teachers, and ends with a discussion of the need for providing increased support to educators in the quest to empower classroom practitioners and teacher educators to best deliver on the demands for critical and reflective workers in 21st century society.

In the last two decades, increasing emphasis on the importance of teaching critical thinking skills and findings from research into critical thinking as an essential component of academic and instructional engagement have triggered changes in strategies and activities which inform instructional practice (Brookfield, 2011; Tang 2009, Paul and Elder, 2006; Erickson; 2007; Browne and Freeman 2000). These changes have collectively provoked a shift towards greater efficacy in instructional techniques and procedures which both engender critical thinking skills and effect a "level of intellectual sophistication required for higher education" such as teacher education (Lauer, 2005; Tremblay and Downey 2004; Guest 2000). As a consequence, as student teachers in training, teachers are deemed to be critical thinkers if they are able to analyze, synthesize and evaluate concepts (Guest, 2000, Gokhale, 1995). In fact, "[for teacher educators], developing and shaping [teachers'] critical thinking skills is an important goal" (Chenault and Dulcos-Orsello, 2008; Vesely & Sherlock, 2005, Siegal (1988) cited in Tsui (2001).

Engendering critical thinking as a pedagogical tool in teacher education has also been central to curriculum policy for decades (Fullan & Hargreaves, 2016; Cole & Ji Zhou, 2014, Fullan, 1994; Hargreaves, 1990). Additionally, this emphasis on thinking reflected in current approaches in education can be traced back to the philosopher John Dewey, who wrote on the centrality of reflective thinking in the educational process (Dewey, 1933). Dewey argued for a nurturing of the scientific attitude of mind as a central focus of educators who teach children (Dewey, 1933). Developing students' critical thinking continues to be a fundamental aim of the educational process, and the wider currency for instruction in this regard especially in teacher education classrooms cannot be overlooked.

Early research work on the concept of critical thinking in the 1900s can also be credited to other philosophers and educators such as Jerome Bruner (1956), Jean Piaget (1959), Lev Vygotsky (1978) and others. Since then, studies into the conceptualization and practice of critical thinking have increased alongside growing demands that schools improve their capacity to effectively teach and nurture the development of critical thinking skills in students through classroom activities (Beyer, 1987; Cotton 1991; Cuypers and Haji, 2006; Abrami et al, 2008). Through some of these studies, a broadening narrative of critical thinking juxtaposed to literacy also surfaces. The narrative situates literacy within critical thinking as moving beyond a limited focus on reading, writing, and arithmetic, to incorporate an emphasis on higher order thinking skills, in order for students to truly be adequately prepared for the rapidly changing society of today (Campbell, 2015; Cox, 2018; Leu and Kinzer, 2000; Leu, Kinzer, Coiro, and Cammack, 2004; Paul and Binker, 1990). Consequently, critical thinking is now recognized as one of the most essential 21st century skills required for success in life and work (Donovan, Green & Mason, 2014; Faulkner & Latham, 2016; Partnership for 21st Century Skills, 2008).

CRITICAL THINKING BY DEFINITION

Thinking in itself is a process natural to the human mind. Consistent excellence in intellectual thought, however, is a process which must be cultivated (Choy & Cheah, 2009; Elder & Paul, 2010; Lai, 2011). Basic thinking patterns left unchecked have been characterised as being potentially biased, distorted, partial, uninformed, and prejudiced (Foundation for Critical Thinking, 2015; Kahneman, 2011). The average person, when faced with a puzzling phenomenon, is said to generally accept the first explanation that makes intuitive sense, or to rely on personal experience, rather than rightfully engaging in scientific study or careful scrutiny of alternative possibilities (Halpern, 1998). The ability to think critically is said to offer individuals the ability to better judge, question, reflect, and apply knowledge and information in novel and creative ways. But what exactly is critical thinking?

Consensus on a generally acceptable definition which captures fully the complexity of the construct referred to as critical thinking has been difficult to formulate over the years (Facione, 1990; Lai, 2011). The American Psychological Association (APA), in an attempt to resolve the issue of an encompassing definition, commissioned a panel of experts in 1990 and produced one of the most commonly used definitions of critical thinking. In its Delphi Report, the general consensus was a definition of critical thinking as judging in a reflective way what to do or what to believe. Additionally, critical thinking has also been narrowed down to comprising two main dimensions: cognitive skills and dispositions (APA, 1990).

CONCEPTUALIZING CRITICAL THINKING

The conceptualization of critical thinking and its development often incorporates four main aspects: Critical thinking skills and dispositions; cultures of thinking; stages of critical thinking development; and Bloom's cognitive taxonomy. A visual of theoretical framework for the conceptualization of critical thinking in this chapter is presented in Figure 1.

Critical Thinking Skills and Dispositions

The first aspect is based on the research on critical thinking skills and dispositions (APA, 1990; Facione, Facione, & Giancarlo, 2000). The term 'skill' generally refers to something a person can do. Skills are usually developed within the range of a person's abilities. A 'disposition', on the other hand, generally refers to a habitual inclination or a tendency to do something given certain conditions. An understanding of a person's disposition allows one to better predict, more or less, how the person is most likely to act or react in variety of circumstances. People may or may not be disposed to use some of their skills.

Critical thinkers are therefore said to possess cognitive skills such as interpretation, analysis, evaluation, inference, explanation and self-regulation (Facione, Facione, & Giancarlo, 2000; Dilley, Kaufman, Kennedy, and Plucker, 2015; Riddell, 2007). However, according to the APA report, the ideal critical thinker must also possess critical thinking dispositions such as being habitually inquisitive, well-informed, trustful of reason, open-minded, flexible, fair-minded, cognizant of personal biases, prudent in making judgments, willing to reconsider, clear about issues, orderly in complex matters, diligent in seeking relevant information, reasonable in the selection of criteria, focused in inquiry, and persistent in seeking results (APA, 1990; Ennis, 2011). The most common thought patterns, or "thinking dispositions," are based on characteristics like motivation, attitude and emotion.

Figure 1. Theoretical model for the conceptualization of critical thinking

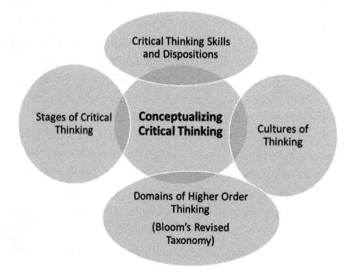

Cultures of Thinking

Another recent addition to the conceptualization of the development of critical thinking has been the theory of Cultures of Thinking developed through Project Zero at the Harvard University Graduate School of Education (Ritchart & Perkins, 2005; 2008; Barahal, 2008). Cultures of thinking are essentially places where an individual (or group's) thinking is valued, visible, and actively promoted as part of the regular, day-to-day experience. Ritchart (2015) specifically emphasized the need for teachers to pay close attention to cultural forces present in every group learning situation which act as shapers of the group's cultural dynamic. These eight cultural forces are identified as: language, time, environment, opportunities, routines, modeling, interactions, and expectations. Efforts to cultivate thinking in their classrooms should involve teachers' use of a variety of appropriate strategies and methods, making time for thinking, developing and using a language which supports thinking, making the classroom environment rich with the documents that stimulate students' thinking processes, and making their own thinking visible to students.

Ritchart and Perkins (2008) also identified six basic principles which should undergird the school's approach to nurturing critical thinking skills in students. These are listed below:

1. Learning is a consequence of thinking;
2. The development of thinking is a social endeavor;
3. Good thinking is not only a matter of skills, but also a matter of dispositions;
4. Fostering thinking requires making thinking visible;
5. Classroom culture sets the tone for learning and shapes what is learned; and
6. Schools must be cultures of thinking for teachers

These principles all necessitate a direct focus on the teacher and the teaching and learning process in any attempt to strengthen the development of critical thinking skills in students at the school level.

Stages of Critical Thinking

Another useful theory for understanding the development of critical thinking is found in the Stages of Critical Thinking, developed by educational psychologists Richard Paul and Linda Elder (2001; 2010). Paul and Elder (2010) asserts that people are not born critical thinkers, but rather progress through five identified universal stages of critical thinking development: the unreflective thinking stage, the challenged thinking stage, the beginning thinking stage, the practicing thinking stage, and the advanced thinking stage. See Table 1 for a brief summary of the characteristics of thinkers at each of the stages of critical thinking.

Four basic assumptions which underlie this theory are that:

1. There are predictable stages in the process of developing into a critical thinker;
2. Passage from one stage to another is dependent on individual commitment to develop as thinkers;
3. Effective instruction in critical thinking is essential to significant student gains in critical thinking; and
4. Regression is possible along the development stages.

Table 1. Stages of critical thinking and characteristics of thinkers

Stages of Critical Thinking	Characteristics of Individuals
Unreflective Thinkers	is largely unaware of the importance of critical thinking and does not consistently practice critical thinking.
Challenged Thinkers	is aware of the importance of critical thinking and their own lack of critical thinking skills.
Beginning Thinkers	has committed to making critical thinking a part of their life, and has begun to self-monitor and observe their own thinking practices and habits.
Practicing Thinkers	understands the types of changes they must make to their original patterns of thinking, and are committed to actively practicing critical thinking.
The Advanced Thinker	has established excellent critical thinking habits, and are beginning to reap the benefits of applying these habits in their lives.
The Accomplished Thinker	regularly, effectively, and insightfully critique their own thinking and improve it. They effectively and insightfully articulate the strengths and weaknesses inherent in their thinking.

Source: Elder & Elder (2010)

The stage theory establishes development in thinking as being a gradual process through which critical thinking skills can be learnt and limitations surpassed over time with practice. This framework provides a benchmark for gauging the status quo as it relates to what is the extent of one's critical thinking skills. This developmental perception of thinking and the framework it presents for assessing one's limitations in thinking serve as invaluable tools for guiding the development of critical thinking interventions in the classroom. Awareness of the levels of intellectual development through which people progress as they improve their thinking can be invaluable to teachers or critical thinking instructors if they are to achieve significant gains in the intellectual quality of their students (Paul & Elder, 2001).

Benjamin Bloom's Hierarchical Taxonomy

Another theoretical contribution was the conceptualization of critical thinking found in the work of Benjamin Bloom. This work has largely impacted the field of education since published in 1956. Bloom's hierarchical taxonomy differentiates clearly between lower and higher order thinking skills. The three highest levels of thinking in Bloom's taxonomy are critical thinking behaviors or actions; specifically analyzing, evaluating, and creating (Anderson & Krathwohl, 2001). Bloom's taxonomy establishes that among the six hierarchical levels of cognitive reasoning, the first three levels (remembering, understanding, and applying) are indicative only of basic thinking skills (lower order thinking). Critical thinking requires students to move beyond lower order thinking which is characterized by mere recall, demonstration of understanding, and applying the acquired knowledge or skill in new situations to solve problems. Higher order thinking (analyzing, evaluating and creating) according to Bloom's cognitive taxonomy, requires student learning to go much deeper. Students must be able to interrogate what has been learnt by making inferences, and finding evidence to support the generalizations inherent within that knowledge or skill, propose alternatives to what has been learnt, and to judge the validity or quality of the acquired knowledge or skill based on appropriate criteria.

THE INTERNATIONAL MANDATE FOR CRITICAL THINKING IN SCHOOLS

Twenty-first century society is characterized by globalization, the diffusion of information technology, and a growing knowledge economy driven by innovation, competition, and the need for constant renewal. The demands of living and working in this kind of society necessitates that every aspect of education (from pre-school to post-secondary education) be focused on preparing citizens with 21st century skills. A summary of the needed skill sets for 21st century life and work has been developed by Partnership for 21st Century Skills (2008) as a collaborative effort for guiding change in education. Three of the identified 21st century skill sets are directly related to our conceptualization of critical thinking:

1.   The ability to think critically and making judgments;
2.   The ability to solve complex, multi-disciplinary, open ended problems; and
3.   The ability to make innovative use of knowledge, information, and opportunities to create new services, processes, and products.

Let us take a closer look at the 21st century mandate for schools. The first skills set identified is the ability to think critically and making judgments. The mandate is for schools to produce citizens who are able to assess the credibility, accuracy, and value of information received everyday via the Web, media, home, and workplace, and to analyze and evaluate information to make reasoned decisions and take purposeful action. As it relates to the second skill set – the ability to solve complex multidisciplinary and open-ended problems, workers are needed who can think unconventionally; who can face challenges which have no clear-cut answers; who are able to identify problems, think thorough solutions, and alternatives, and explore new options when an implemented approach does not work. And finally, workers are needed who can make innovative use of existing knowledge, information, and opportunities to create new services, processes, and products. Partnership for 21st Century Skills (2008) in advocating for these changes in education sees students' having these skills as an indispensable currency for their successful participation, achievement, and competitiveness in the global economy.

Given the essential nature of critical thinking skills to life and work in today's society, many believe that the minds of the young must be carefully guided towards refining their critical thinking skills. They must be taught strategies they can regularly utilize to think more critically (Choy and Cheah, 2009). One of the most important objectives of schooling today, therefore, must be enhancing students' abilities as it relates to thinking critically and making rational decisions (Slavin, 2006; 2018; Finn, 2018). In this 21st century, an age marked by rapidly changing information and technology, the ability of educated people to engage in critical thought and reflection has become fundamental to their ability to cope successfully as workers, and as citizens (Cotton, 1991; ten Dam & Volman, 2004). In fact, some education psychologists argue that the most crucial and valuable skills that students should learn in school is not necessarily the specific knowledge taught in content areas, but rather the ability to learn, and use the information and skills learnt to solve problems (Slavin, 2006; 2018; Gough, 1991).

Given this mandate for critical thinking, schools and teachers who teach in them have therefore been under heavy scrutiny and criticism as researchers have examined the development of thinking skills in the educational experiences of students over the years (Beyers, 1987; Pithers & Soden, 2000; Abrami et al, 2008; Ku, 2009; Marin & Halpern, 2011). Although a significant number of these studies on critical thinking in students tend to be focused on tertiary level students (Abrami, et al, 2008; Butler, Dwyer, Hogan, Franco, Rivas, Siaz, & Almeida, 2012; Elliot, Oty, McArthur, & Clark 2001; Shim & Walczak, 2012; Dunn, Halonen, & Smith, 2008), research studies on developing critical thinking skills in young children also have much support (Hudgins & Edelman, 1986; Freseman, 1990; Cuypers & Haji, 2006; Salmon, 2008; Marin & Halpern, 2011).

Teachers are an indispensable part of the debate surrounding the development of critical thinking skills in schools. As such, examining teachers' thinking skills, as well as empowering them for more effective delivery of these skills for instruction is necessary (Cotton, 1991; Choy & Cheah, 2009; Duron et al 2006; Abrami et al, 2008). For example, research supports that the most effective teachers who register gains in their students' critical thinking skills are those who receive special training in teaching critical thinking (Cotton, 1991; Abram et al., 2008). Through the use of appropriate questioning, computer assisted instructional technology, appropriate classroom climate, and other instructional strategies, teachers are able to promote the development of critical reasoning habits in their students.

EMPOWERING TEACHERS FOR BUILDING STUDENTS' CRITICAL THINKING SKILLS

Asking teachers to reflect on their classroom practice and on student behaviors which may signal challenges in critical thinking, provides insight not only into current aspects of student instruction which need to be improved upon for strengthening students' thinking skills in schools. It also provides valuable insight into teachers' weaknesses, and areas where training will need to be focused in order to better empower teachers for nurturing consistent critical thought in regular classroom instruction (Cochran-Smith & Villegas, 2015).

Consequently, more professional development for teachers is an essential variable if needed changes are to be achieved so that schools produce the kinds of citizens that 21st century society needs (Sedova, Sedlacek, & Svaricek, 2016; Wagner, 2008; Partnership for 21st Century Skills, 2008). Moreover, the provision of specialized training for teachers in critical thinking has been proven to be effective in registering gains in students' critical thinking skills (Cotton, 1991; Choy & Cheah, 2009; Duron et al., 2006; Abrami et al., 2008).

Ritchart (2015) also emphasized the need for empowering teachers to better manage the cultural forces present in the classroom which have the potential to negatively impact their efforts to build cultures of thinking in the classroom space. Given the identified affective deficits which students at times exhibit, empowering teachers so that they are better able to create classroom cultures that are supportive of consistent higher order thinking is critical to addressing, for example, challenges in the classroom regarding students' self-confidence and self-esteem.

CONCLUSION

Educational institutions today have been given an international mandate to better prepare citizens for life and work in a 21st century society characterized by complex business, political, scientific, technological, health, and environmental challenges. The ability to think critically is one of the most essential skills identified for 21st century living. As such, there is greater need for continued research to deepen our understanding of what constitutes critical thinking, and the strategies which can be implemented in developing critical thinking in students. It is also necessary to understand the nature of the challenges facing educators and educational institutions as they seek to improve their capacity to infuse critical thinking into regular instruction. Educational contexts differ, and so will the approach to shaping teacher education and teacher pedagogy in the important area of critical thinking.

REFERENCES

Abrami, P. C., Bernard, R. M., Borokhovski, E., Wade, A., Surkes, M. A., Tamim, R., & Zhang, D. (2008). Instructional interventions affecting critical thinking skills and dispositions: A stage 1 meta-analysis. *Review of Educational Research*, *78*(4), 1102–1134. doi:10.3102/0034654308326084

Anderson, L. W., Krathwohl, D. R., & Bloom, B. S. (2001). *A taxonomy for learning, teaching, and assessing: A revision of Bloom's taxonomy of educational objectives*. Boston, MA: Allyn & Bacon.

Barahal, S. L. (2008). Thinking about thinking: Preservice teachers strengthen their thinking artfully. *Phi Delta Kappan*, *90*(4), 298–302. doi:10.1177/003172170809000412

Beyer, B. K. (1987). *Practical strategies for the teaching of thinking*. Boston, MA: Allyn and Bacon.

Bloom, B. S. (1956). Taxonomy of educational objectives: The classification of educational goals.

Beyer, B. (1995). *Critical thinking*. Bloomington, IN: Phi Delta Kappa Educational Foundation.

Brookfield, S. D. (2011). *Teaching for Critical Thinking: Tools and techniques to help students questions their assumptions*. San Francisco: Jossey Bass.

Browne, M. N., & Freeman, K. (2000). Distinguishing features of critical thinking classrooms. *Teaching in Higher Education*, *5*(3), 301–309. doi:10.1080/713699143

Butler, H. A., Dwyer, C. P., Hogan, M. J., Franco, A., Rivas, S. F., Saiz, C., & Almeida, L. S. (2012). The Halpern critical thinking assessment and real-world outcomes: Cross-national applications. *Thinking Skills and Creativity*, *7*(2), 112–121. doi:10.1016/j.tsc.2012.04.001

Campbell, M. (2015). Collaborating on critical thinking: The team critique. *Journal of Curriculum and Teaching*, *4*(2), 86–95. doi:10.5430/jct.v4n2p86

Chenault, T. G., & Duclos-Orsello, E. D. (2008). An act of translation: The need to understand students' understanding of critical thinking in the undergraduate classroom. *The Journal of Effective Teaching*, *8*(2), 5–20.

Choy, S. C., & Cheah, P. K. (2009). Teacher perceptions of critical thinking among students and its influence on higher education. *International Journal on Teaching and Learning in Higher Education, 20*(2), 198–206.

Cochran-Smith, M., & Villegas, A. M. (2015). Research on teacher preparation: Charting the landscape of a sprawling field. In D. H. Gitomer & C. A. Bell (Eds.), *Handbook of research on teaching* (5th ed., pp. 439–548). Washington, DC: American Educational Research Association.

Cole, D., & Zhou, J. (2014). Diversity and collegiate experiences affecting self-perceived gains in critical thinking: Which works and who benefits? *The Journal of General Education, 63*(1), 15–34. doi:10.1353/jge.2014.0000

Cotton, K. (1991). Close-Up #11: Teaching thinking skills. Northwest Regional Educational. Retrieved from http://educationnorthwest.org/6/cu11.html

Cox, J. (2018). Teaching strategies that enhance higher-order thinking. *Teachhub.* Retrieved from http://www.teachhub.com/teaching-strategies-enhance-higher-order-thinking

Cuypers, S., & Haji, I. (2006). Education for critical thinking: Can it be nonindoctrinative? *Educational Philosophy and Theory, 38*(6), 723–743. doi:10.1111/j.1469-5812.2006.00227.x

Dam, G., & Volman, M. (2004). Critical thinking as a citizenship competence: Teaching strategies. *Learning and Instruction, 14*, 359–379.

Dewey, J. (1933). *How we think.* Boston: Heath and Co.

Dilley, A., Kaufman, J. C., Kennedy, C., & Plucker, J. A. (2015). What we know about critical thinking. Partnership For 21st Century Learning. Retrieved from http://www.p21.org/ourwork/4csresearchseries/criticalthinking

Donovan, L., Green, T. D., & Mason, C. (2014). Examining the 21st century classroom: Developing an innovation configuration map. *Journal of Educational Computing Research, 50*(2), 161–178. doi:10.2190/EC.50.2.a

Duron, R., Limbach, B., & Waugh, W. (2006). Critical thinking framework for any discipline. *International Journal on Teaching and Learning in Higher Education, 17*(2), 160–166.

Dunn, D. S., Halonen, J. S., & Smith, R. A. (Eds.). (2008). *Teaching critical thinking in psychology: A handbook of best practices.* Oxford, UK: Wiley-Blackwell. doi:10.1002/9781444305173

Elder, L., & Paul, R. (2010). Critical thinking development: A stage theory. *Critical Thinking.org.* Retrieved from www.criticalthinking.org

Elliott, B., Oty, K., McArthur, J., & Clark, B. (2001). The effect of an interdisciplinary algebra/science course on students' problem solving skills, critical thinking skills and attitudes towards mathematics. *International Journal of Mathematical Education in Science and Technology, 32*(6), 811–816. doi:10.1080/00207390110053784

Ennis, R. H. (2011). Critical thinking: Reflection and perspective (Part I). *Inquiry: Critical Thinking across the Disciplines, 26*(1), 4-18. doi:10.5840/inquiryctnews20112613

Erickson, L. H. (2007). *Concept based curriculum and instruction for the thinking classroom.* Thousand Oaks, CA: Corwin Press.

Facione, P. A. (1990). *Executive Summary- Critical thinking: A statement of expert consensus for purposes of educational assessment and instruction* (The Delphi Report). Retrieved from http://assessment. aas.duke.edu/documents/Delphi_Report.pdf

Facione, P. A., Facione, N. C., & Giancarlo, C. A. (2000). The disposition toward critical thinking. *Informal Logic, 20*(1), 61–84. doi:10.22329/il.v20i1.2254

Faulkner, J., & Latham, G. (2016). Adventurous lives: Teacher qualities for 21st century learning. *Australian Journal of Teacher Education, 41*(4), 137–150. doi:10.14221/ajte.2016v41n4.9

Finn, P. (2018). Critical thinking for future helping professionals: why, what, and how. *ASHA.* Retrieved from https://www.asha.org/Articles/Critical-Thinking-for-Future-Helping-Professionals-Why-What-and-How/

Freseman, R. D. (1990). *Improving higher order thinking of middle school geography students by teaching skills directly.* Fort Lauderdale, FL: Nova University.

Fullan, M. (1994). *Change forces: probing the depths of educational reform.* London: The Falmer Press.

Fullan, M., & Hargreaves, A. (2016). *Bringing the profession back in: Call to action.* Oxford, OH: Learning Forward.

Gardner, H. (2011). *The unschooled mind: How children think and how schools should teach.* New York: Basic Books.

Guest, K. (2000). Introducing critical thinking to non-standard entry students: The use of a catalyst to spark debate. *Teaching in Higher Education, 5*(3), 289–299. doi:10.1080/713699139

Gokhale, A. A. (1995). Collaborative learning enhances critical thinking. *Journal of Technology Education, 7*(1), 22–30. doi:10.21061/jte.v7i1.a.2

Gough, D. (1991). Thinking about thinking. Alexandria, VA: National Association of Elementary School Principals.

Halpern, D. F. (1998). Teaching critical thinking for transfer across domains: Dispositions, skills, structure training, and metacognitive monitoring. *The American Psychologist, 53*(4), 449–455. doi:10.1037/0003-066X.53.4.449 PMID:9572008

Hudgins, B., & Edelman, S. (1986). Teaching Critical Thinking Skills to Fourth and Fifth Graders Through Teacher-Led Small-Group Discussions. *The Journal of Educational Research, 79*(6), 333–342.

Kahneman, D. (2011). Thinking, fast and slow. New York, NY: Farrar, Straus and Giroux. doi:10.1080/00220671.1986.10885702

Ku, K. Y. L. (2009). Assessing students' critical thinking performance: Urging for measurements using multi-response format. *Thinking Skills and Creativity, 4*(1), 70–76. doi:10.1016/j.tsc.2009.02.001

Lau, J. Y. F. (2011). *An introduction to critical thinking and creativity: Think more, think better*. Indianapolis, IN: Wiley. doi:10.1002/9781118033449

Lauer, T. (2005). Teaching critical-thinking skills using course content material. *Journal of College Science Teaching, 34*(6), 34–44.

Leu, D. J. Jr, & Kinzer, C. K. (2000). The convergence of literacy instruction and networked technologies for information and communication. *Reading Research Quarterly, 35*(1), 108–127. doi:10.1598/RRQ.35.1.8

Leu, D. J. Jr, Kinzer, C. K., Coiro, J., & Cammack, D. (2004). Toward a theory of new literacies emerging from the Internet and other information and communication technologies. In R. B. Ruddell & N. J. Unrau (Eds.), *Theoretical models and processes of reading* (5th ed., pp. 1570–1613). Newark, DE: International Reading Association. doi:10.1598/0872075028.54

Marin, L. M., & Halpern, D. F. (2011). Pedagogy for developing critical thinking in adolescents: Explicit instruction produces greatest gains. *Thinking Skills and Creativity, 6*(1), 1–13. doi:10.1016/j.tsc.2010.08.002

Paul, R. W., & Binkler, J. A. (1990). *Critical Thinking: What Every Person Needs to Survive in a Rapidly Changing World*. Rohnert Park, CA: Center for Critical Thinking and Moral Critique.

Paul, R. W., & Elder, L. (2006). Critical thinking: The nature of critical and creative thought. *Journal of Developmental Education, 30*(2), 34–35.

Piaget, J. (1959). *The language and thought of the child* (Vol. 5). Psychology Press.

Pithers, R. T., & Soden, R. (2000). Critical thinking in education. *Review of Educational Research, 42*, 237–249.

Perkins, D. N. (2014). *Futurewise: Educating our children for a changing world*. San Francisco: Jossey Bass.

Pogrow, S. (1988). Teaching thinking to at-risk elementary students. *Educational Leadership, 5/7*, 79–85.

Riddell, T. (2007). Critical assumptions: Thinking critically about critical thinking. *The Journal of Nursing Education, 46*(3), 121–126. PMID:17396551

Ritchhart, R., & Perkins, D. N. (2008). Making thinking visible. *Educational Leadership*, 57–61.

Ritchhart, R., & Perkins, D. (2005). *Cultures of Thinking Project*. Project Zero, Harvard Graduate School of Education. Retrieved from http://www.ronritchhart.com/COT_Resources_files/6Principles%20of%20COT_V2.pdf

Salmon, A. K. (2008). Promoting a culture of thinking in young children. *Early Childhood Education Journal, 35*(5), 457–461. doi:10.100710643-007-0227-y

Sedova, K., Sedlacek, M., & Svaricek, R. (2016). Teacher professional development as a means of transforming student classroom talk. *Teaching and Teacher Education, 57*, 14–25. doi:10.1016/j.tate.2016.03.005

Shim, W., & Walczak, K. (2012). The impact of faculty teaching practices on the development of students' critical thinking skills. *International Journal on Teaching and Learning in Higher Education*, *24*(1), 16–30.

Slavin, R. (2006). Education psychology: Theory and practice (8th ed.). Boston: Pearson.

Slavin, R. (2018). Education psychology: Theory and practice (12th ed.). Boston: Pearson.

Tang, R. (2009). Developing a critical ethos in higher education: What undergraduate students gain from a reader response task? *Reflections on English Language Teaching*, *8*(1), 1–20.

ten Dam, G., & Volman, M. (2004). Critical thinking as a citizenship competence: Teaching strategies. *Learning and Instruction*, *14*(4), 359–379. doi:10.1016/j.learninstruc.2004.01.005

The Foundation for Critical Thinking. (2015). Our Concept and Definition of Critical Thinking. Retrieved from http://www.criticalthinking.org/pages/our-concept-and-definition-of-critical-thinking/411

Tremblay, K. R. Jr, & Downey, E. P. (2004, Summer). Identifying and evaluating research-based publications: Enhancing undergraduate student critical thinking skills. *Education*, *124*(4), 734–740.

Tsui, L. (2001). Faculty attitudes and the development of students' critical thinking. *The Journal of General Education*, *50*(1), 1–28. doi:10.1353/jge.2001.0008

Brande, S. (n.d.). *Thinking Skills in Bloom's Taxonomy* [illustration]. Retrieved from https://www.google.com/search?q=bloom%27s+taxonomy&source=lnms&tbm=isch&sa=X&ved=0ahUKEwj68Za3pqXdAhXKxVkKHb3YB1IQ_AUICigB&biw=1366&bih=631#imgrc=xnjvagWNqNGFTM

Vesely, P., & Sherlock, J. (2005). Pedagogical Tools to Develop Critical Thinking. *Academic Exchange Quarterly*, *9*(4), 155–161.

Vygotsky, L. S. (1978). *Mind in society: The development of higher psychological processes*. Cambridge, MA: Harvard University Press.

Wagner, T. (2008). *The global achievement Gap: Why even our best schools don't teach the new survival skills our children need—and what we can do about it*. New York: Basic Books.

KEY TERMS AND DEFINITIONS

Classroom Instruction: "The purposeful direction of the learning process"; one of the major teacher class activities (along with planning and management).

Critical Thinkers: Critical thinkers possess cognitive skills such as interpretation, analysis, evaluation, inference, explanation and self-regulation (Facione, Facione, & Giancarlo, 2000; Dilley, Kaufman, Kennedy, and Plucker, 2015; Riddell, 2007).

Critical Thinking Skills: The skills that needed in order to be able to think critically are varied and include observation, analysis, interpretation, reflection, evaluation, inference, explanation, problem solving, and decision making.

Cultural Forces: Influences or energies present in every group learning situation which act as shapers of the group's cultural dynamic. Eight cultural forces are identified as: language, time, environment, opportunities, routines, modeling, interactions, and expectations.

Cultures of Thinking: Places/spaces where an individual (or group's) thinking is valued, visible, and actively promoted as part of the regular, day-to-day experience.

Hierarchical Taxonomy: Classification of behaviors into cognitive reasoning and thinking skills. Differentiates clearly between lower and higher order thinking skills.

Pedagogical Tools: Pedagogical tools are designed to convey important lessons and allow people to improve their understanding of a problem or undertaking. Resources used to enhance, support and facilitate the teaching/learning situation.

Reflective Thinking: Part of the critical thinking process; refers specifically to the processes of analyzing and making judgments about what has happened.

Stages of Critical Thinking: A pretest-posttest design is a kind of experiment in which a group is tested/studied before and after the particular experiment or activity is administered. In this way it is possible to determine what changes if any have taken place and thereby judge the effect or value of the experiment.

Thinking Disposition: Being habitually inquisitive, well-informed, trustful of reason, open-minded, flexible, fair-minded, cognizant of personal biases, prudent in making judgments, willing to reconsider, clear about issues, orderly in complex matters, diligent in seeking relevant information, reasonable in the selection of criteria, focused in inquiry, and persistent in seeking results (APA, 1990; Ennis, 2011). The most common thought patterns, or "thinking dispositions," are based on characteristics like motivation, attitude and emotion.

Chapter 2
Teachers in the "Process of Becoming":
The Role of Pre-Service Teachers' Narratives in Developing Critical Reflective Practice

Jacqueline Manuel
University of Sydney, Australia

Janet Dutton
Macquarie University, Australia

ABSTRACT

This chapter focuses on exploring the role of pre-service teacher (PST) narratives in a research-based model of initial teacher education (ITE) for secondary English teachers across three semesters of a two-year graduate entry, Master of Teaching (Secondary) degree at the University of Sydney, Australia. The model is underpinned by the belief that the development of the teacher's professional identity is an antecedent and generator of their ways of knowing and teacher quality. Initially, the chapter frames the model of ITE through a discussion of the relevant research literature in the field of pre-service teacher development. It then delineates the features of the model at the University of Sydney and provides a close analysis of the sequential narratives of a pre-service English teacher over the course of the first semester of study in the ITE program. Finally, the chapter reflects on the affordances of narratives in shaping PSTs' ways of knowing and professional identity.

INTRODUCTION

Learning to teach is not a mere matter of applying decontextualized skills or of mirroring predetermined images; it is a time when one's past, present, and future are set in dynamic tension. Learning to teach – like teaching itself – is always the process of becoming: a time of formation and transformation, of scrutiny into what one is doing, and who one can become. (Britzman, 1991, p. 8).

DOI: 10.4018/978-1-5225-7829-1.ch002

Copyright © 2019, IGI Global. Copying or distributing in print or electronic forms without written permission of IGI Global is prohibited.

In current educational research and policy there is broad consensus that 'teacher quality' is one of the most salient influences on student learning and achievement (Day, 2017; Hattie, 2009). There is far less unanimity, however, when it comes to defining 'teacher quality' and the optimal means of preparing and retaining 'quality teachers' for diverse and often complex professional roles. In the field of Initial Teacher Education (ITE), research and practice over recent decades have increasingly concentrated on understanding and theorising the concept of teacher professional identity as "the core of the teaching profession" (Sachs, 2005, p. 15).

The concept of teacher professional identity assumes that a teacher's beliefs, values, motivations, personal history, and cultural context, shape their attitudes, aspirations, and ways of knowing, being, and behaving. These facets of a teacher's personal and professional identity converge to drive practical decision-making, functional capacities, resilience and continued investment in teaching as a career. As Day (2017) explains,

Professional identity fashions teachers' expectations of themselves, what they perceive to be the expectations and perceptions of others from inside and outside the school, and their efficacy and agency, the strength of their beliefs that they can, or cannot, succeed in their work with pupils (p. 49).

When teachers are viewed as "active, thinking decision-makers who make instructional choices by drawing on complex, practically-oriented, personalised and context-sensitive networks of knowledge, thought and beliefs" (Borg, 2003, p. 81), the emphases and goals of ITE programs inevitably shift. They shift from a predominant focus on the technical, skills-based components of learning to teach to incorporate a more person-centred, constructivist paradigm that recognises the "symbiotic relationship between professional and personal, cognitive and emotional influences on teachers' identities" (Day, 2017, p. 31). Such a paradigm is typically characterised by attention to fostering the professional identity of pre-service teachers (PSTs) through integrating abundant opportunities for sustained critical reflection.

Critical reflective narratives of the self-as-teacher offer the potential to cultivate in the PST practice-focused and engaged inquiry by balancing the outwardly-focused dimensions of becoming an educator with the equally essential development of the teacher's interiority, or professional identity (Day, 2017). In this way, narratives created over time in an ITE program can encourage "beginning teachers to think about the self contextually and developmentally and can stretch their imaginations to consider alternative conceptions of teaching and self-as-teacher" (Bullough & Stokes, 1994, pp. 220-21).

FOCUS OF THE CHAPTER

This chapter focuses on exploring the role of PST narratives in a research-based model of ITE for pre-service secondary English teachers across three semesters of a two-year graduate entry, Master of Teaching (Secondary) degree at the University of Sydney, Australia. The model is underpinned by the belief that the development of the teacher's professional identity is an antecedent and generator of their ways of knowing and teacher quality. As Bullough (1997) argues,

teacher identity – what beginning teachers believe about teaching and learning and self-as-a-teacher – is of vital concern to teacher education; it is the basis for meaning making and decision making. Teacher education must begin then, by exploring the teaching self (p. 21).

On this basis, the ITE program at the University of Sydney is designed to develop PSTs' critical reflective practice and professional identity through the application of a suite of inquiry, case, and arts-based principles and pedagogies (Bullough & Stokes, 1994; Clandinin, 2007; Connelly & Clandinin, 1998) firmly located within a social constructivist epistemological and ontological paradigm.

In particular, the chapter aims to describe and illustrate the integration of PST narratives intended to open up the spaces to generate critical reflective thinking as they construct, critique and chronicle their evolving story as teachers in the "process of becoming" (Britzman, 1991, p. 8). A narrative approach to identity development and narratives as "stories to live by" (Clandinin, Downey & Huber, 2009, p. 141) are both deeply embedded within and intuitively appropriate to the disciplinary norms and characteristics of English as a subject, given its emphasis on language, story, human experience and meaning-making.

Initially, the chapter frames the model of ITE through a discussion of the relevant research literature on: teacher identity and its significance in pre-service teacher education; the role of beliefs in teacher identity development; and the affordances of critical reflection in the form of narratives in ITE. It then delineates the features of the model at the University of Sydney and provides a close analysis of the sequential narratives of a pre-service English teacher over the course of the first semester of study in the ITE program. Finally, the chapter reflects on the role of narratives in shaping PSTs' ways of knowing and professional identity.

BACKGROUND

Defining Teacher Identity

Teacher identity has been defined in many ways including "what beginning teachers believe about teaching and learning and self-as-a-teacher" (Bullough, 1997, p. 21) and "teachers' sense of self in relation to others in professional environments" (Lee & Schallert, 2016, p. 73). Within the social constructivist paradigm, identity is broadly understood as being influenced by multiple personal and contextual factors that interact in a reciprocal and dynamic way "so identity is continually reshaped over the life of an individual" (Beltman, Glass, Dinham, Chalk & Nguyen, 2015, p. 2).

Bullough's (2005) research highlights the multifaceted nature of teacher identity and argues that the exploration of the teaching self is a priority for ITE (Bullough, 1997). For Bullough, the personal or 'core' identity is viewed as the more stable, continuing dimension of an individual's point of view that persists behind the 'situational' or more public identities that typify the ways teachers perform in different contexts. In the same vein, Markus and Nurius (1986) conceptualise teacher identity as the process of acquiring or resisting certain possible selves. Similarly, Rodgers and Scott (2008) perceive alignment between the notion of 'situational selves' and identity by distinguishing between 'self' and 'identity' whereby "the self [is] the meaning maker and identity [is] the meaning made, with both evolving over time" (Lee & Schallert, 2016, p. 73).

Contemporary conceptualisations of teacher identity thus conceive identity formation not as a "trajectory to an end point but rather an ongoing, discursive process that is dynamic, complex, negotiated and contingent" (Dinham et al., 2016). This discursive process encompasses a host of elements including developing and constructing personal and professional knowledge during the "boundary space" (Beauchamp & Thomas, 2011, p. 7) of transition into initial practice as a teacher (Danielewicz, 2001; Day, Kington, Stobart & Sammons, 2006).

The Role of Prior Beliefs About Teaching in PSTs' Identity Development

Pre-service teachers begin their initial teacher education with powerful embodied perceptions, beliefs, 'ways of knowing' and lay theories about teaching (Calderhead, 1991; Fajet, Bello, Leftwisch, Mesler, & Shaver, 2005; Knowles & Holt-Reynolds, 1991; Sugrue, 1997; Taylor & Sobel, 2000). Salisbury-Glennon and Stevens (1999) call beliefs of this nature "personal history beliefs" (p. 471), emphasising the unique biographical dimension of the understandings about teaching that pre-service teachers carry as they commence ITE programs. Kagan (1992a) defines these beliefs as "tacit, often unconsciously held assumptions about students, classrooms and the academic material to be taught" (p. 65). These personal beliefs about classrooms, students and their conception of themselves as teachers are often influenced by memorable models of teachers and other authority figures along with pre-service teachers' own experiences as learners. Pre-service teachers "often extrapolate from their own experiences as learners, assuming that the pupils they will teach will possess aptitudes, problems, and learning styles similar to their own" (Kagan, 1992b, p. 154).

Much of the research literature in the field notes that these initial beliefs and ways of knowing are relatively inflexible and resistant to change (Holt-Reynolds, 1992; Massengill, Mahlios & Barry, 2005; Tillema, 1997; Wilke & Losh, 2008). They have been accrued over many years in schools and by observing teachers. Lortie (1975) and others note that such observations and experiences may be based on atypical episodes, draw on implicit theories of teaching and are often far removed from the realities of teachers' work (Burn, 2007; Sutherland, Howard, & Markauskaite, 2010; Taylor & Sobel, 2001).

A crucial function of ITE programs then is to facilitate opportunities for this pre-teaching identity to be opened up to scrutiny as PSTs move through their ITE and initial classroom experiences. As Pajares (1992) notes,

few would argue that the beliefs teachers hold influence their perceptions and judgments, which in turn, affect their behaviour in the classroom, or that understanding the belief structures of teachers and teacher candidates is essential to improving their professional preparation and teaching practices (p. 307).

Pajares' (1992) research confirms that these prior beliefs and ways of knowing are only disrupted and eventually affirmed or transformed in response to new information if the justification is compelling: otherwise new information will likely be dismissed (Pajares, 1992). When PSTs engage in composing and critiquing their own unfolding narratives of the self-as-teacher, this pre-teaching identity and embedded belief structures can be opened up to scrutiny through critical reflection, enabling the emerging professional identity to be consciously shaped and articulated in powerful ways.

The Role of Critical Reflective Practice in ITE

The concept of critical reflective practice has assumed an increasingly prominent role in ITE (see Hatton & Smith, 1995; Jay & Johnson, 2002; Larrivee, 2000; Otteson, 2007; Schön, 1987). Embedded in critical reflective practice is "the art of analysing and evaluating thinking with a view to improving it" (Elder & Paul, 2010) which in turn, can shape teacher identity, ways of knowing and pedagogy. Critical thinking involves the internalised capacity to question, critique, and confirm or revise beliefs, thoughts, perspectives and attitudes. For these reasons, ITE programs that have as their goal the development of critical reflective practitioners and activist professionals (Sachs, 2005) draw on theories of teacher identity development that conceptualise identity as malleable and evolving.

ITE programs that assume a deficit view of the pre-service teacher, however, are often driven by "an unashamed attempt to replace [lay theories and beliefs] by privileging what we as teacher educators regard as more scientific and more grounded theory and research based versions" (Furlong, 2013, p. 80). Such programs tend to undervalue or ignore the role of prior beliefs shaped over decades of an "apprenticeship of observation" (Lortie, 1975). Furlong (2013) likens this approach to laying a veneer on top of a wooden surface. Because the veneer is not as established or robust as the original layer underneath, it can be easily "chipped away by the pervasive culture of the school" or be 'washed out' by the survival tactics the pre-service teacher resorts to (Furlong, 2013, p. 80) when confronted with the unprecedented 'newness' of teaching students and the school setting. The educational theories from ITE are therefore displaced and pre-service teachers default to their more familiar and therefore less disruptive lay theories for their theories of practice. For many, not surprisingly, this means teaching the way they were taught (Burke, 1992, p. 116).

Miller and Shifflet (2016) critique this deficit view of PST identity and argue that "teacher education programs have erroneously assumed that coursework can fully shape the beliefs and actions of pre-service teachers, whilst ignoring students' past experiences" (p. 21). Since professional learning is "never a mere technical process of acquiring knowledge and skills, but always implies the personal integration of the new insights with the knowledge and beliefs that a person already holds" (Kelchtermans, 2009, p. 43), PSTs' beliefs and prior experiences of education become central to the "process of becoming" (Britzman, 1991, p. 8). Challenging tacit and entrenched belief schemes therefore has the potential to produce cognitive dissonance that can be perturbing and trigger strong emotional responses (Hargreaves, 1998). Importantly, it can also be argued that this challenging of beliefs, certainties and assumptions is a necessary dimension of the pre-service teacher journey to teaching (Cook, 2009; Kelchtermans, 2009).

In light of these understandings about pre-service teachers' initially entrenched belief schemes about teaching (Conway, 2001; Hallman, 2007; Hatton & Smith, 1995; Lee, 2005; Miller & Shifflet, 2016; Schön, 1983, 1987), a multidimensional concept of identity offers an alternative to a strictly linear framework of teacher identity development and as such may accommodate the reflexive, cyclic and complex nature of pre-service teacher development that has been observed in studies such as, for example, those by Conway and Clark (2003).

Critical Reflective Practice as Pedagogy and Process

Pedagogies that enable critical reflective practice provide opportunities for PSTs to experience cognitive dissonance which, as noted above, is seen by some as essential to making explicit, challenging and subsequently prompting a re-evaluation or affirmation of pre-service teachers' initial beliefs. A critically reflective process involves both the capacity for critical inquiry *and* self-reflection. Critical inquiry involves the "conscious consideration of the moral and ethical implications and consequences of classroom practices on students" (Larrivee, 2000, p. 294).

Self-reflection moves beyond critical inquiry by adding the dimension of a deep examination of the personal values, beliefs and expectations about students and teachers' work. A pedagogy of critical reflection incorporates these two dimensions and involves an exploratory process that exposes often unexamined assumptions, beliefs and expectations making visible the reflexive loops and their status relative to broader socio-political, educational and moral contexts. Importantly, critical reflection is not merely an end-point in a linear progression from less complex to more complex forms of reflection. Rather it is part of a holistic, "intertwined" process (Jay & Johnson, 2002, p. 80) that can result in a rich and complex contemplation of the ideas and experiences which underpin the emerging identity of a pre-service teacher. PST narratives offer a vehicle for activating and sustaining this exploratory process of identity development.

Narratives as Vehicles for Professional Identity Development

Through the telling of stories, humans keep the memory of their experiences, the history of their communities. At the same time, the narrative mode imposes order on the heterogeneity of experience and therefore does not merely reflect it but constructs it (Fina & Georgakopoulou, 2012, p. 17).

Reflective writing in the form of narratives provides powerful prismatic windows into perceptions and beliefs of the self-as-teacher (Massengill, Mahlios & Barry, 2005). It is understood that the narrative mode is not based on truth, but on verisimilitude. Nias (1989) argues that heightened self-understanding emerges from the "persistent self–referentialism" (p. 5) of teachers whereby their questioning of and critical thinking and dialogue about their professional actions inevitably leads them to speak about themselves. Consequently, a teacher's "sense of self is very prominently present in [her/his] accounts about their practice" (Kelchtermans, 2009, p. 38).

Furthermore, Bullough and Stokes (1994) contend that narratives can encourage "beginning teachers to think about the self contextually and developmentally and can stretch their imaginations to consider alternative conceptions of teaching and self-as-teacher" (pp. 220-21). This process of self-examination affords the opportunity to articulate potential links between existing lay theories and the established theoretical bases of teaching. The use of narratives in ITE thereby promises a "powerful way to unravel and understand the complex processes of sense-making that constitute teaching" (Kelchtermans, 2009, p. 31), situating the stories of PSTs both temporally and spatially. As Shulman (1986) states, a "professional is capable of not only practising and understanding his or her craft, but of communicating the reasons for professional decisions and actions to others" (p. 8) in a range of forms, including narrative.

In this sense, the use of narratives in ITE facilitates the development of what Batchelor (2012) labels the ontological voice or the "voice for being and becoming" (p. 598). The concept of voice spans "literal, metaphorical, and political terrains. In its literal sense voice represents the speech and perspectives of the speaker; metaphorically, voice spans inflection, tone, accent, style, and the qualities and feelings conveyed by the speaker's words" (Britzman, 1991, p. 146). Politically, the notion of voice aligns with Sachs's definition of the "activist professional" (2005) and legitimates the rights of the individual to 'speak', to be 'heard' and have her/his unique self-as-teacher represented.

THE MODEL OF ITE FOR SECONDARY PRE-SERVICE ENGLISH TEACHERS AT THE UNIVERSITY OF SYDNEY

The ITE program for secondary pre-service teachers of English at the University of Sydney draws on the theoretical and epistemological paradigms outlined above. It is premised on a cyclical, reflexive model of teacher development (Conway & Clark, 2003) with the goal of engendering quality teaching, agency and "activist professionalism" (Sachs, 2005) defined by: transformative practices; the production of new knowledge; practitioner inquiry – teacher as researcher; and teachers working collaboratively towards ongoing improvement (Sachs, 2005). To achieve this goal, the program integrates a range of pedagogies under the umbrella of critical reflective practice, with narratives figuring prominently within and across the English curriculum methodology units (Bullough & Stokes, 1994; Clandinin, 2007; Connelly & Clandinin, 1998).

An Overview of the Structure and Features of the ITE Program

The graduate-entry Master of Teaching (Secondary) degree is a professional teaching qualification accredited at the state level in NSW and recognised nationally and internationally. The degree consists of four semesters of sequential study over two years. The program attracts a diverse candidature of high-quality graduates who experience a teaching and learning environment that integrates the principles of critical thinking and reflective practice through "self-directed inquiry and case-study learning experiences in small seminars, augmented by lecture, tutorials and technology-based learning experiences" (University of Sydney, n.d.).

Epistemological and Ontological Basis of English Curriculum Methodology Units

PSTs specialising in teaching secondary English undertake three sequential semester-long methodology units: English Curriculum 1 in semester 1 of Year 1; English Curriculum 2 in semester 2 of Year 1; and English Curriculum 3 in semester 1 of Year 2. English curriculum PSTs are encouraged to embed theory-in-practice in all aspects of their learning. They work collaboratively and at the same time, are expected to take increasing responsibility for their professional learning and goals.

The English curriculum units include explicit engagement with the nature of the transition to teaching including consideration of the journey from the perspective of Van Gennep's *rites de passage* (Turner, 1964; Van Gennep, 1997). As a means of offering a meta-language that the pre-service teachers can invoke when conceptualising and critically reflecting on their experiences, the course materials and activities make explicit reference to the inter-structural "period of margin" or "liminality" (Turner, 1964, p. 46) that occurs when an individual is on the threshold (Batchelor, 2012) of a transition from one state to another in a process of "becoming" or "transformation" (Turner, 1964, pp. 46-7). This model from anthropology poses that "all rites of passage are marked by three phases: separation, margin (*limen*), and aggregation.

During English curriculum workshops the Van Gennep/Turner model is explicated and interrogated for applicability to the transition to English teaching in the belief that critical thinking and meaningful learning requires PSTs to commit to a dynamic process that involves grappling with their own assumptions, "weighed against different perspectives, circumstances, and ideas" and that undergoing this "uncomfortable and disorienting metamorphosis" (Nelson & Harper, 2006, p. 10) requires tenacity. Acknowledgement is made that ITE might be experienced as a period of being 'betwixt and between' the original status and the new status (teacher) being sought and that this ambiguous stage can generate feelings of confusion, challenge and perturbation (Batchelor, 2012; Cook- Sather, 2006; Nelson & Harper, 2006; Turner, 1964).

If PSTs are equipped with a discourse and theory with which to articulate the phases of their transition to teaching, it can enable them to navigate and manage the inevitable challenges they will encounter.

Informed by research, the concept of Liminality can function as a 'road map' (Nelson & Harper, 2006) through the learning journey to teaching and as such complement the activities, readings and pedagogy in the English curriculum units. It is concept that also has the potential to help normalise pre-service teachers' uncertainties and encourage tenacity and resilience if their beliefs and assumptions are disrupted by new knowledge.

When PSTs enter the program, they are explicitly positioned as 'beginning teachers' (rather than as education 'students'). The adaptation of this pedagogy, known as the 'mantle of the expert' (Heathcote, 2009; Heathcote & Bolton, 1994) is a vital component of the program. Through adopting the mantle of the expert – itself a metaphor – PSTs consciously envision and begin to embody the qualities, behaviours, perspectives, self-expectations and ethical stance of a teaching professional. The approach is an amalgam of inquiry-based learning, drama as a learning medium, and expert framing. By enacting the mantle of the expert, PSTs engage in 'real world' experiences of being a teacher, collaborating with their peers in a staffroom (simulated in workshops and seminars), raising and addressing questions of theory and practice, taking responsibility for their learning, and being guided by the leadership and expertise of the lecturer (in the role of Head Teacher when appropriate).

Integrating PST Narratives of the Self-As-Teacher for Developing Critical Thinking, Reflective Practice and Ways of Knowing

Narratives of the self-as-teacher constitute a core component of the ITE program for pre-service English teachers and, along with other arts-based and inquiry approaches, are integrated into the three sequential English curriculum units over three semesters. Table 1 below provides an overview of where and when this pedagogical strategy is introduced and foregrounded in relation to other components of the ITE program.

Narratives of the Emerging Self-As-Teacher

Early on in the first semester of the ITE program, PSTs begin to construct narratives (1, 2, 3 and 4, Phase 1) of the self-as-teacher based on their own beliefs, values, motivations, expectations, ideals and life experiences. These initial Phase 1 narratives are created prior to PSTs' immersion in English curriculum seminars, workshops, course readings, and collaborative discussions. To support the process of developing the narratives, PSTs are offered a series of prompts, intended to bring to the surface and stimulate questioning of, critical thinking about and reflection on their existing beliefs and the formative influences on their ways of knowing. Prompts for the Phase 1 narratives are:

Narrative 1: Describe a well-remembered event from your secondary school English experiences and reflect on its significance;

Narrative 2: Describe a well-remembered English teacher and explain why this teacher is significant;

Narrative 3: Articulate your reasons for choosing to teach; and

Narrative 4: "I'd like to be an English teacher who ..." including reference to your chosen metaphor for the self-as-teacher.

Narrative 5 (Phase 2) is developed towards the end of the first semester of English Curriculum 1 and is therefore shaped and informed by PSTs' learning and new knowledge gained since entering the program.

Table 1. Key features of ITE program English Curriculum sequence of units

Stage in Program	Pedagogy and PST Activity
Semester 1, Year 1 (Entry level)	• An initial survey of PSTs' motivations, beliefs, expectations, goals, assumptions about teaching/the teacher/learning, own school experience, mentors. • Individual survey responses followed by group discussion. Identification and critique of responses. PSTs begin to theorise and critique assumptions and beliefs. • Introduced to the 'mantle of the expert (Heathcote & Bolton, 1994): Required to 'act as if' (not treated as a 'student'). • Establishment of professional learning groups. • Introduced to case study method. • Introduced to concept of liminality (Van Gennep, 1997; Turner, 1964). • Development of metaphor for self-as-teacher: o Draw/Paint/Photograph o Create 3D artefact o Select objective correlative (representative object/s) o Reflective statement to accompany metaphor, informed by critical readings. • Development of: • Narratives 1 and 2 (Phase 1) – initial beliefs, memorable experiences of English as a student and formative influences • Narrative 3 (Phase 1) – motivations to choose to teach, beliefs, expectations, and aspirations, guided by the chosen metaphor • Narrative 4 (Phase 1) – the English teacher they'd like to be • Narrative 5 (Phase 2) – building on previous narratives to develop an anticipatory narrative of their sense-of-self as teacher, including a philosophy of teaching and a statement of goals and values. • Case study and inquiry-based tasks relevant to theory, pedagogy and the implementation of junior secondary English syllabus and support documents. • Narratives are revised and annotated prior to commencing the first block of Professional Experience in schools.
Semester 2, Year 1	• Professional Experience – 20 consecutive days (4-week block). • Narrative 6 is developed post-Professional Experience and focuses on key learnings, unexpected experiences and challenges to prior beliefs and ways of knowing. • Case study and inquiry-based tasks relevant to theory, pedagogy and the implementation of senior secondary English syllabus and support documents.
Semester 3, Year 2	• Professional Experience – 20 consecutive days (4-week block). • Narratives are critically annotated to identify shifts, continuities and 'voices' influencing PSTs' beliefs and identity.
Semester 4, Year 2	• In-school Internship (9-week block) • Research Project and post-Internship research conference.

This Phase 2 narrative is constructed immediately prior to commencing the first block of Professional Experience. It is a revision and extension of previous narratives to incorporate a philosophy of teaching and a statement of goals and values. For this narrative, PSTs are asked to reflect on the prompt: "the English teacher I'd like to be".

In the following discussion, excerpts from the Phase 1 and Phase 2 narratives of one PST – Odetta – are analysed to illustrate the application and affordances of a narrative approach to professional identity development. The narratives of Odetta are representative of the process of identity development in other PSTs in the program whose narratives formed part of a broader research inquiry (Dutton, 2017). Limitations of space preclude an analysis of each one of Odetta's narratives in its entirety, or narratives written in the subsequent two semesters of English curriculum. Consequently, the discussion below concentrates on excerpts from Odetta's narratives 3, 4 and 5. The analysis is followed by an overview of the discernible continuities and shifts in Odetta's beliefs, values, motivations, expectations, goals and ways of knowing that occur in the span of a semester of ITE in English Curriculum 1. The comparative analysis draws attention to areas of stability or modification in the PST's developing identity prior to her first in-school experience and demonstrates the iterative process of critical thinking and reflection that occur during this phase of ITE.

NARRATIVES: PHASE 1

The narratives written in Phase 1 are designed to bring to the fore the beliefs, values, motivations, expectations and assumptions about teaching.

Narrative 3

Prompt: Why did you decide to become an English teacher?

I have decided to become an English teacher because I love English and I love working with people, so I can't imagine a better profession. I see many students who hate English and I believe that is because it is taught in a detached, sterile way and bogged down with literary jargon. I think if students could see that English is all about celebrating story-telling, expression and exploring human experience, then more children would grow to love it. This is what I hope to be able to achieve.

Odetta's decision to teach emerges unambiguously from her intrinsic motivation to sustain her passionate engagement with English, to interact with others and make a difference in their lives. The repetition of emotive language – e.g. "love" and "I love English" – constructs Odetta's all-encompassing passion for the subject. She implicitly values the role of collaboration and interpersonal relations. Part of her motivation to teach is a desire to rescue English education from the perceived negative impact of ineffective teaching.

A significant other is anonymously present in her exemplum of perceived bad teaching. What is judged to be an undesirable approach to English teaching is juxtaposed with her assertion that "if students could see that English is all about celebrating story-telling, expression and exploring human experience, then more children would grow to love it". This opposition constructs the rejected approach to English as emotionless, closed, static and technical with the preferred approach being open, celebratory, creative and positive. Of note is the selection of verb endings with the simple past tense "ed" form in "detach*ed* … and bogg*ed* down" suggesting fixed and closed processes whereas the "ing" participle form in "celebrat*ing* story-telling … explor*ing* human experience" connotes an ongoing, future-directed and dynamic process of English teaching and learning.

Odetta's judgements about how best to teach English are based on anecdotal experience and beliefs ("I see … I believe … I think") rather than empirical evidence or theory, but her statements are associated with relatively high modality conveying a sense of certainty. Strongly evident is Odetta's belief in the cycle of influence with her desire for students to love English as she does. The use of the metaphoric "grow" represents Odetta's sense of self-as-teacher who nurtures and nourishes her students. Largely omitted in the early narrative is a consideration of the reasons why this ideal would be beneficial for the students: Odetta believes it as a given that a love of English is inherently valuable. The hyperbolic "celebrating" constructs the strength of her belief and the aspects of English she names all represent ways of constructing meaning that are not fixed or purely functional. They are processes that are open, dynamic and gesture to possibilities as well as being fluid in allowing multiple ways of seeing the world.

Although Odetta conveys a high degree of confidence about her decision to teach English, the likely success of her aim is less certain. Her decision is problematised to an extent in the final statement, slightly tempering her certainty and revealing a reflexive awareness of what she may recognise as naïve idealism: "This is what I hope to be able to achieve". Her final statement is an articulation of her hopes and aspirations for herself as an English teacher and a recognition of the power of teachers to challenge hegemonic pedagogies in order to affect change.

Narrative 4

Prompt: I'd like to be an English teacher who …? Include a metaphor that you think captures your sense of you as an English teacher.

As a teacher, I envisage myself as a gardener and all my students the various plants of the garden. I acknowledge I will encounter a range of vegetation in my garden, from all kinds of flowers and vegetables, to all sorts of shrubs and trees! Every plant will come from its own unique patch of soil and will grow and develop in vastly different ways. I hope to be able to be there to nourish them with knowledge and support, but also allow them to branch out for themselves and explore everything they can within the garden. In terms of practice, I envisage this garden taking the form of a warm, open classroom, in which I plant the seeds for discussion and equip students with the tools to undertake exercises, allowing the students to work both independently and collaboratively at different times, and ideally finish each class with a group chat about what we have learnt. I hope students feel comfortable to push the boundaries of their thinking and are prompted to think in ways which don't stop once they leave my classroom.

Odetta articulates her conception of herself as an English teacher wholly framed by her metaphor of a gardener tending her plants. Inherent in her choice of this metaphor is a pervasive impetus towards altruism and the nurturing of student growth, building on the growth-oriented perspectives evident in the previous narrative. She sees her knowledge and expertise – particularly in understanding individual difference and students' unique contexts – as the necessary factors to encourage the "vegetation" to flourish and extend their knowledge. The terms "range", "kinds", and "sorts" construct the notion of breadth and the reference to "different soils" is used to symbolise Odetta's awareness of the significance of contextual factors to a student's development. The exclamation marks convey a celebratory tone, removing any doubt concerning Odetta's positivity in relation to the array of students she will encounter in her English teaching.

Part of Odetta's focus is a determination to establish conditions that will maximise the potential growth of her students. This perspective is conveyed by language choices such as "nourish", "support", "warm, open classroom", and "comfortable". This ideal of warmth and safety works in concert with an awareness of the need to cater to individual differences and extend the boundaries of students' learning. The metaphorical "garden" (a demarcated space) hints at the extent to which exploration may be stiffled given the institutional constraints and boundaries imposed on classrooms and learning in schools. The garden is not appropriated as a symbol of restriction but rather as a metaphor to capture Odetta's aspirations to nurture and support students in a cultivated, tended and therefore safe context. A patterning of references to outward movement ("grow", "branch out", "comfortable to push the boundaries") suggests an awareness of the as yet uncertain challenges in her role as teacher but also implies that students will actively engage in and sustain their learning. She believes that students' motivation to learn will naturally occur as result of an optimal classroom environment that she will curate.

This anticipation of enacting a transformative pedagogy is evidence of Odetta's intention to contribute to her students' broader social education. She expresses a clear intent to equip students with the "tools" to work effectively in a range of modes and contexts. While she represents herself as holding status and power, positioned as central to the facilitation of the learning process and context – "I plant the seeds for discussion and equip students" – this is not an authoritarian positioning. Her potential power as teacher is portrayed as more nuanced by its association with "nourish" and the notion of 'being there' as an encouraging presence in the learning situation – of working alongside the students rather than dictating through a hierarchical power relationship. Space will be literally and metaphorically provided for student voice and action.

Her perspective on student/teacher roles consequently underpins the approaches to learning that Odetta envisages for her classroom. She sees students working "both independently and collaboratively at different times" thus expressing her awareness of the need for flexible learning configurations depending on the context, activity or intended outcome. Elided is any reference to inspiring students to share her passion for English. In this narrative, English is considered to be the vehicle through which to accomplish student growth. Odetta's conception of herself-as-teacher is represented as being less about her subject matter and more about the way she will interact with the individuals she will be teaching.

The opening sequence in the narrative employs mostly metaphoric verbs ("grow and develop", "nourish them"). The middle section, however, is a blend of metaphoric and more education-specific, specialist terminology. It is almost as if the richness of metaphorical language is preferred as it more powerfully captures the vivid perceptions she seeks to convey. The shift towards the incorporation of more literal, utilitarian terminology can also be read as a *reaching* for a suitable lexis with which to articulate the complex processes of learning and adolescent development.

This inconsistency in style can be read as evidence of the liminal phase of the transition to becoming a teacher. It is possible that the preponderance of metaphorical terms signifies the stance of being 'betwixt and between' with the lexical choices representative of a not-yet-developed education-specific vocabulary which could be used to articulate Odetta's sense of self-as-teacher. As she reflects on her future English classroom, Odetta articulates high certainty associated with the potentially diverse contextual and personal lives of her students. ("I acknowledge I will" encounter; "Every plant will"). This is in contrast to then lower modality evident when anticipating the outcomes of her teaching ("I envisage"; "I hope students feel comfortable"). The latter are expressed as anticipatory feelings of hope, acknowledging the uncertainty of future, untested situations and her current positioning as a PST who is yet to begin her classroom practice.

NARRATIVE: PHASE 2

This narrative marks the culmination of reflective writing undertaken throughout the first semester of ITE in English curriculum.

Narrative 5

Prompt: The English teacher I'd like to be ...

The real problem that the teacher of English has to face is not how to supply his (sic) pupils with 'matter' to write about; it is rather how to develop within a classroom a climate of personal relationships within which it becomes possible for them to write about the concerns which already matter to them intently (Frank Whitehead's Group, as cited in Walshe, 2009, p. 256).

The above quotation resonates with me deeply as I believe it captures the essence of what studies in English so uniquely allow us to do – build relationships with the text, with the world and with ourselves. In expressing my goals and values as a teacher, I would like to extend on the above quote, not to include only writing, but to include every facet of the English subject. What this quote does so beautifully is identify the fact that the people we teach are not empty vessels needing to be filled with knowledge in order merely to jump through hoops and perform on tests to be labelled with a number at the conclusion of their education. Rather the students we encounter as teachers are human beings, just as any of us are, filled with emotions, memories, experiences and passions. From what I have learnt in this unit and from my life experience in general, a good teacher recognises this, and creates a climate where the student can express all of these things, to continue the accumulation of these valuable life experiences.

I understand although this may be a romantic ideal, the reality of enacting such pedagogy involves hard work. It will require rigorous planning based on a real understanding of my students and their needs. From my experience in my first semester as a pre-service teacher, most valuable have been the ideas espoused about the importance of normalising reading, writing, speaking and listening in the classroom. This normalisation takes practice, as I have learnt even over the course of the semester, becoming more confident in many tasks through consistent practice of skills in seminars and outside class. I suppose one of my main concerns is being able to achieve my goal of an open learning environment while still ensuring my students perform strongly on standardised testing, like NAPLAN. However, from my reading, I can see I am not alone in this concern. My strategy at this point is to make the most of my practical experiences and try to establish how the best teachers achieve both.

In completing this body of work I have found myself reflecting on the idea of liminality at length. It is fascinating engaging in reading positioning myself as a teacher, while at points suddenly realising that I am still simply a student to whom many of the teaching strategies apply. The more I think about it the more I believe I will never fully transcend this phase, as there will always be something else to learn. This is both a comforting and daunting sensation, but one I believe will make me a better teacher for it.

A comparative analysis of this narrative (5, Phase 2) with the earlier narratives (3 and 4, Phase 1) provides insights into both the continuities and the shifts in Odetta's developing identity as a teacher. A comparative analysis of sequential narratives also actualises Bruner's (1991) notion of 'narrative accrual'. Individual narratives considered in isolation reference particular happenings ('particularity') but taken together with other narratives the threads of stories can be woven together to produce "coherence by contemporaneity" (Bruner, 1991, p.19). This process of accrual can eventually create a 'culture' or 'history' or 'tradition' or in the case of PSTs, their unfolding storyline of their "process of becoming" (Britzman, 1991, p.8).

CONTINUITIES BETWEEN ODETTA'S PHASE 1 AND PHASE 2 NARRATIVES

Philosophical and Theoretical Beliefs

Odetta's love for the subject is sustained as she envisions herself engaged in a cycle of influence, teaching the subject she believes has the unique capacity to "build relationships with the text, with the world and with ourselves". This humanist perspective is a key dimension of Odetta's sense of self-as-teacher evident in her earlier choice of a gardener as her metaphor and in the articulation of her intrinsic and altruistic motivations to teach. She continues to construct her identity as an English teacher who will manage the learning environment so that it is conducive to the expression of student voice, appropriating Whitehead's authoritative voice to emphasise the belief that personal experience and relationships need to be the starting point in order to "develop within a classroom a climate of personal relationships".

Odetta's narrative (5) highlights her awareness that her emphasis on personal experience and relationships carries with it a need to ensure the wellbeing and safety of her students. In an echo of the "warm, open classroom" she described in a previous narrative, the tactile imagery here of "climate" depicts a classroom where students can reveal their "emotions, memories, experiences and passions" with safety. Her recognition of the role of individual differences is apparent from the outset in her amending of the Whitehead quotation ("his [*sic*] pupils") to remediate its gender exclusivity. The re-categorisation of students to "human beings" foregrounds a belief in inclusivity that is coupled with a commitment to valuing the distinctive qualities that each student brings to the classroom. Odetta concedes there are challenges inherent in her preferred approach to teaching and alludes to the need for differentiation in stating the requirement for "rigorous planning based on a real understanding of my students and their needs".

Odetta aspires to choreograph classroom experiences that are not only relevant to life but also encompass a bi-directional link with the world beyond the classroom. The Whitehead quotation posits that learning should commence with the concerns "which already matter to (students) intently" and then move further. Odetta endorses this Personal Growth model of English (Dixon, 1967, 1984) but notes the reciprocal process that leads to students clarifying their personal understandings about self and the self in the broader world. With the guidance of a "good teacher" Odetta anticipates that her students will be able to "continue the accumulation of … valuable life experiences" and in so doing, flourish.

This statement constructs teaching and learning as a shared encounter through the use of the collective pronoun "us". Odetta positioning herself, her students and other teachers in the same category. She sustains her way of conceptualising teaching and learning as organic, nurturing and connection-focused, intimated by a chain of references associated with feelings and experiences: "the students we encounter as teachers are human beings, just as any of us are". She continues to reject English teaching that is predominantly content and test driven, seeking instead to become one of those teachers who values students' personal accomplishments as much their achievement as is measured by external, standardised tests.

A Desire to Transcend Boundaries

English so uniquely allows us to … build relationships with the text, with the world and with ourselves.

In this central image of her teaching, Odetta conceptualises English as an endless, spiraling process of expansion – from text to world and from world to the complexities of self. This desire to expand and transcend reveals continuity with two earlier narratives, which also explicitly stated the desire for students to "branch out for themselves and explore everything they can within the garden" and to "feel comfortable to push the boundaries of their thinking". She extends the scope of the writing-focused quotation to a "include every facet of the English subject" and critiques reductive approaches where student learning is repetitive, employing the pejorative metaphor "jump through hoops" to censure pedagogy that relies on conformist expectations.

The Teacher's Role

Odetta's initial belief that a source of power resides in students' existing knowledge is consolidated in this Phase 2 narrative which offers a more detailed consideration of how, as a teacher, Odetta will empower students through normalising "reading, writing, speaking and listening" and through a strident advocacy of an "open learning environment". She continues to express the belief that students' life experiences are the foundations for learning but in this narrative, the belief is articulated with greater confidence and authority accrued through her critical thinking, new knowledge and understandings gained from readings, workshops and case studies.

A further marker of continuity is Odetta's reference to a classroom that maintains both a sense of the full class (*"within a classroom"*) and the individuals within in ("climate where the student can express all of these things", "real understanding of my students and their needs"). This counterpoising of the needs of the group with the needs of the individual underpins her anticipated teaching approach and is informed by theoretical knowledge. Student engagement, in Odetta's view, will naturally emerge from the innate power of 'story' when it is harnessed to students' experiences. Her belief is that students will be engaged when they "write about the concerns which already matter to them intently" and "can express all of these things".

The perspective on the teacher's role in this narrative provides another point of continuity with Odetta's earlier narratives. Previously she had stated: "I hope to be able to be there to nourish with knowledge and support". This belief is sustained through her affirmation of the teacher as an active and agentic force in shaping student learning and in nurturing student development. In this narrative, her view is nuanced by explicit reference to being responsive to student needs, signaling an informed awareness of the role of individual difference and student voice in shaping the teacher's pedagogy. Nonetheless, it is evident that she altruistically believes that the teacher is responsible for developing the "climate" for learning, although there is little detail about how such a climate will be created in pedagogical terms.

SHIFTS BETWEEN ODETTA'S PHASE 1 AND PHASE 2 NARRATIVES

The Status of Prior Experience and Beliefs

Although Odetta's sense of self-as-teacher is still strongly underpinned by her positive and negative experiences at school, in this narrative (5) a shift occurs as she articulates the way her recently acquired knowledge from teacher education has, through a process of critical thinking and reflection, been assimilated with prior experience and belief structures to create new understandings of students, learning and herself as English teacher: "From what I have learnt in this unit and from my life experiences in general …". The understandings are expressed in strongly introspective, reflective terms: "I believe … I understand".

These amplified 'ways of knowing' do not equate to a dramatic reversal in philosophy but rather align with and deepen her long-held beliefs. What does shift, however, are the sources of her knowledge, which now include her courses in education and the extent to which she is now able to situate her beliefs and ideology within larger educational, theoretical and philosophical frameworks. Whereas previously Odetta's beliefs about English teaching were supported by anecdotal examples from her past school experience, now her philosophy is located within the academic and professional discourses encountered during professional readings in English Curriculum 1.

By making deliberate, extended references to literacy practices, this narrative marks a significant departure from Odetta's earlier statements about her English teaching. Previously she had made brief references to "the tools to undertake exercises" but did not explicate her philosophy or pedagogical orientation in any depth. In this post English Curriculum 1 narrative, Odetta's philosophy explicitly offers a theoretical justification that coheres with the Personal Growth model (Dixon, 1967, 1984), demonstrating the outcomes of a process of critical thinking and reflection.

Appropriation of Specialist Discourses

As noted previously, the Phase 1 narratives employ generalised lay terms and metaphoric expressions in preference to subject-specific terminology: educational discourse is an emerging rather than a predominant feature in the early narratives. In this Phase 2 narrative, however, the metaphoric treatment of educational concepts continues to be in evidence but, in the main, it is employed as a rhetorical device. This narrative is framed by the use of a rubric that is a quote from an authoritative educator in the field. Points of distinction are made between Odetta's informed view (supported by reference to academic scholars) can be seen as emblematic of her broader shift towards the more confident appropriation of educational discourse in expressing a philosophy of English teaching and professional identity. It can also be interpreted as a 'trying on' of a voice inflected with the prevailing educational discourses and evidence of a growing sense of membership of a community of professionals.

This marked shift towards appropriating educational discourses is equally apparent in the second paragraph where rhetorical devices are employed to bolster confidence in her emerging professional voice and negate possible counter-arguments to her already stated perspective. Further weight of argument is accrued through an increase in the frequency of technical, specialist terms to articulate her burgeoning understanding of educational concepts and processes.

In the final paragraph Odetta deploys a blend of technical, specialist, generalised and metaphorical terms as she strives to represent her perspective on English teaching using both her already well-developed personal idiom and her growing knowledge of educational theory and discourse. In an image drawn from the familiar discourse of literary criticism and textual practice, the rich complexity of English teaching is aptly encapsulated in the paradoxical, metaphoric closing statement: "This is both a comforting and daunting sensation, but one I believe will make me a better teacher …".

Understanding Broader Contextual Forces

While this Phase 2 narrative sustains clear continuity in relation to valuing student voice, it concurrently marks a significant shift in its recognition of the societal expectations, institutional constraints and external testing conventions that Odetta believes work against the valuing of student voice, interests and needs. Indeed, this narrative reveals a series of shifts in voice and language choices when compared with her earlier narratives.

A significant shift occurs in Odetta's awareness of the limiting factors that emerge when her personal beliefs clash with perceived institutional or societal beliefs and expectations. She describes the tension between these potential limitations and the desire to open up possibilities, listing a series of oppositions. It could be argued that these perceived or anticipated conflicts encapsulate the dissonance between notions of the 'real versus the ideal'. She offers, however, a more nuanced treatment of these concerns as a consequence of her self-awareness, critical thinking and a willingness to interrogate the methods required to bring her philosophy to fruition: "I understand although this may be a romantic ideal, the reality of enacting such pedagogy involves hard work".

Understandings of Liminality

Arguably the most pronounced shift is Odetta's candid reflection on and acceptance of the liminal phase in which she sees herself situated. In previous narratives, it was argued that notions of Liminality were evident in the patterning of terminology and modality. In this later narrative, Odetta registers her cognisance of being 'betwixt and between' and her understanding of the role that educational discourses will play in shaping her identity as an English teacher. She embraces Liminality as a productively destabilising experience by expressing the emotive oxymoron of "comforting and daunting". Her belief that her own learning will make her a "better teacher" and is therefore a necessary endeavour, is expressed with certainty as a definitive closing statement to the reflexive narrative.

Her stated intention to embrace the dislocating effects of the transition to teaching and be "a better teacher" can be interpreted as Odetta seeking to challenge the traditional deficit view of her status as a pre-service teacher. This reading is supported by Odetta's representation of herself as a life-long learner with multiple possibilities ahead in her teaching life. Together these insights position Odetta as seeking to transcend the likely boundaries imposed by the liminal phase she is experiencing. The tension and conflicting emotions of this period are apparent in the closing statement that philosophically evokes the acceptance of contradiction inherent in Keats's Romantic notion of Negative Capabilities or being "capable of being in uncertainties, Mysteries, doubts, without any irritable reaching after fact and reason" (n.d.):

The more I think about it the more I believe I will never fully transcend this phase, as there will always be something else to learn. This is both a comforting and daunting sensation, but one I believe will make me a better teacher for it.

SYNTHESIS OF KEY FEATURES OF THE NARRATIVES

A comparative analysis of Odetta's initial narratives with that composed at the end of the first semester of the ITE program underscores the view that "narrative uniquely affords the analyst a glimpse of how people construct a sense of self ... (and) is so closely linked with life and experiences ... it is the prime way of making sense of them in the form of stories about self" (Fina & Georgakopoulou, 2012, p. 160). From the earliest narratives through to the culminating narrative (5), it is evident that the process of critical thinking and reflection has enabled Odetta to:

- Bring to the fore and examine her prior-held beliefs and experiences;
- Reaffirm the epicentre of her motivation for choosing to teach as her intrinsic love of English, the altruistic desire to empower and influence the life-chances of her students, and her personal belief in the transformative power of human stories;
- Test, problematise, clarify, deepen and legitimate her beliefs, values and expectations through an immersion in the scholarly and research literature in the field;
- Develop her professional identity and voice through the meaning-making tool of narrative integrating a metaphor of the self-as-teacher that invokes processes of 'natural' growth, nurturance and transformation;
- Mature in confidence, incrementally consolidating her philosophical and epistemic affiliation with the English teaching profession, partly by acquiring the specialist language to theorise and lend authority to her beliefs, values, motivations and expectations; and
- Acknowledge and embody the concept of liminality as a useful metacognitive frame for explaining and understanding the uncertainties, anxieties, hesitancies and inner conflict experienced during the pre-service teacher's transition teaching.

In the early stages of ITE the narratives conflate Odetta's interests and needs with those of her imagined students (see Kagan, 1992b; Lee & Schallert, 2016) offering a largely unproblematised version of teacher-student relations and student learning. Whilst this representation may seem naïve, the beliefs on which the perspectives are based are deeply-held, as are the instrinsic and altruistic motivations that led her to teaching (Holt- Reynolds, 1992; Massengill, Mahlios & Barry, 2005; Tillema, 1997; Wilke & Losh, 2008). From the outset she recognises that her optimism could be viewed as naïve hope but despite this she remains steadfastly hopeful of success and even more resolute about her agentic aspirations to become "a better teacher".

CONCLUSION

In the end, the narrative study tells the story of individuals unfolding in a chronology of their experiences, set within their personal, social, and historical context, and including the important themes in those lived experiences (Cresswell, 2007, p. 57).

The aim of this chapter has been to describe and illustrate the pedagogy and process of integrating pre-service English teachers' narratives of the self-as-teacher into an inquiry and case-based model of ITE. The narratives highlight the range of experiences that a pre-service teacher brings to their ITE and the significance of the internalised set of "epistemic assumptions" (Reid, 1996, p. 32) concerning "the purpose and significance of the subject in their own lives and its anticipated impact on the selfhood and life chances of the students they will teach" (Manuel & Carter, 2016, p. 91). The development of narratives facilitated a recursive 'toing and froing' between and critical thinking about initial beliefs, values, motivations, expectations and ideals and new knowledge constructed during the transition to teaching.

The narratives point to the resilience of these initial belief structures that constitute what Bullough has termed the 'core' identity (1997). The process of constructing the narratives did not involve the "shattering" confrontation (Furlong, 2013) and "giving up of previously held beliefs" (Kelchtermans, 2009, p. 43) that typically contributes to dissonance and tension during ITE. Contrary to the view that PSTs' initial beliefs must be jettisoned and replaced by research and theory taught in ITE (Beauchamp & Thomas, 2009; Furlong, 2013), Odetta's narratives point to the fundamental role they can play in shaping an increasingly confident, informed and theorised sense of self-as-teacher. In this way, the constellation of intrinsic and altruistic beliefs, values, motivations and expectations brought to ITE can be understood as the necessary wellspring for the elaborative process of teacher identity development.

Although Odetta's narratives were written prior to any Professional Experience, they suggest that tensions and uncertainties during ITE do not need to be conceptualised as negative (Pillen, Beijaard & den Brok, 2013; Zeichner, 2010). Instead, they can be understood as 'productive friction' (Ward, Nolen & Horn, 2011) or 'productive disequilibrium' (Cook, 2009). The narratives indicate that when tension or conflict is contextualised within a framework such as Liminality that advocates embracing rather than avoiding change and discomfort (Cook, 2009), the pre-service teacher can be equipped to recognise and manage dissonance, build resilience through critical thinking and expand their ways of knowing.

Limited research exists with regard to the use of the concept of Liminality with pre-service teachers (Cook-Sather, 2006; Nelson & Harper, 2006) or the coupling of this concept with PST narratives. Odetta's narratives – as an exemplar of the research conducted with PSTs (Dutton, 2017) at the University of Sydney – point to rich possibilities for the use of narratives of the self-as-teacher and Liminality as a conceptual frame for the pre-service teacher journey. As this chapter has argued, the pedagogy and process of integrating narratives in ITE can enable the PST to articulate and deepen their altruistic beliefs in the transformative power of teaching and galvanise their optimism and hopefulness as they forge their professional identity during Initial Teacher Education.

REFERENCES

Batchelor, D. (2012). Borderline space for voice. *International Journal of Inclusive Education, 16*(5-6), 597–608. doi:10.1080/13603116.2012.655501

Beauchamp, C., & Thomas, L. (2011). New teachers' identity shifts at the boundary of teacher education and initial practice. *International Journal of Educational Research, 50*(1), 6–13. doi:10.1016/j.ijer.2011.04.003

Beltman, S., Glass, C., Dinham, J., Chalk, B., & Nguyen, B. H. N. (2015). Drawing identity: Beginning pre-service teachers' professional identities. *Issues in Educational Research, 25*(3), 225–245.

Britzman, D. (1991). *Practice makes practice: A critical study of learning to teach*. Albany, NY: State University of New York.

Bruner, J. (1991). Narrative construction of reality. *Critical Inquiry, 18*(1), 1–21. doi:10.1086/448619

Bullough, R. (1997). Practicing theory and theorizing practice in teacher education. In J. Loughran & T. Russell (Eds.), *Purpose, passion and pedagogy in teacher education* (pp. 13–31). London, England: Falmer Press.

Bullough, R. Jr. (2005). Being and becoming a mentor: School based teacher educators and teacher education identity. *Teaching and Teacher Education, 21*(2), 143–155. doi:10.1016/j.tate.2004.12.002

Bullough, R. Jr, & Stokes, D. (1994). Analyzing personal teaching metaphors in preservice teacher education as a means for encouraging professional development. *American Educational Research Journal, 31*(1), 197–224. doi:10.3102/00028312031001197

Burke, A. (1992). *Teaching - retrospect and prospect.* Dublin: Stationery Office.

Burn, K. (2007). Professional knowledge and identity in a contested discipline: Challenges for student teachers and teacher educators. *Oxford Review of Education, 33*(4), 445–467. doi:10.1080/03054980701450886

Calderhead, J., & Robson, M. (1991). Images of teaching: Student teachers' early conception of classroom practice. *Teaching and Teacher Education, 7*(1), 1–8. doi:10.1016/0742-051X(91)90053-R

Carter, K. (1993). The place of story in the study of teaching and teacher education. *Educational Researcher, 22*(1), 5–12. doi:10.3102/0013189X022001005

Clandinin, D. (2007). *Handbook of narrative inquiry.* Thousand Oaks: SAGE Publications. doi:10.4135/9781452226552

Clandinin, D., Downey, C. A., & Huber, J. (2009). Attending to changing landscapes: Shaping the interwoven identities of teachers and teacher educators. *Asia-Pacific Journal of Teacher Education, 37*(2), 141–154. doi:10.1080/13598660902806316

Connelly, F., & Clandinin, D. (1988). *Teachers as Curriculum Planners: Narratives of Experience.* New York, USA: Teachers College Press.

Conway, P. (2001). Anticipatory reflection while learning to teach: From a temporally truncated to a temporally distributed model of reflection in teacher education. *Teaching and Teacher Education, 17*(1), 89–106. doi:10.1016/S0742-051X(00)00040-8

Conway, P., & Clark, C. (2003). The journey outward: A re-examination of Fuller's concerns-based model of teacher development. *Teaching and Teacher Education, 19*(5), 465–482. doi:10.1016/S0742-051X(03)00046-5

Cook, J. (2009). Coming into my own as a teacher: Identity, disequilibrium, and the first year. *New Educator, 5*(4), 274–292. doi:10.1080/1547688X.2009.10399580

Cook-Sather, A. (2006). Newly betwixt and between: Revising liminality in the context of a teacher preparation Program. Retrieved from http://repository.brynmawr.edu/cgi/viewcontent.cgi?article=1009&context=edu_pubs

Creswell, J. (2007). *Qualitative inquiry* (2nd ed.). Thousand Oaks, CA: SAGE Publications.

Danielewicz, J. (2001). *Teaching selves: Identity, pedagogy, and teacher education.* Albany, NY, USA: State University of New York Press.

Day, C. (2017). *Teachers' worlds and work: Understanding complexity, building quality.* Milton Park, UK: Routledge. doi:10.4324/9781315170091

Day, C., Kington, A., Stobart, B., & Sammons, P. (2006). The personal and professional selves of teachers: Stable and unstable identities. *British Educational Research Journal, 32*(4), 601–616. doi:10.1080/01411920600775316

Dinham, J., Chalk, B., Beltman, S., Glass, C., & Nguyen, B. (2016). Pathways to resilience: How drawings reveal pre-service teachers' core narratives underpinning their future teacher-selves. *Asia-Pacific Journal of Teacher Education,* 1–9.

Dutton, J. L. (2017). *English teachers in the making: Portraits of pre-service teachers' journeys to teaching.* Unpublished PhD thesis, University of Sydney, Sydney, Australia.

Elbaz, F. (1991). Research on teachers' knowledge. *Journal of Curriculum Studies, 23,* 1–19. doi:10.1080/0022027910230101

Elder, L., & Paul, R. (2010). Critical thinking: Competency standards essential for the cultivation of intellectual skills. *Journal of Developmental Education, 34*(2), 39–40.

Fajet, W., Bello, M., Leftwisch, J., Mesler, J., & Shaver, A. (2005). Pre-service teachers' perceptions in beginning education classes. *Teaching and Teacher Education, 21*(6), 717–727. doi:10.1016/j.tate.2005.05.002

Fina, A., & Georgakopoulou, A. (2012). *Analyzing narrative: Discourse and sociolinguistic perspectives.* Cambridge, UK: Cambridge University Press.

Furlong, C. (2013). The teacher I wish to be: Exploring the influence of life histories on student teacher idealised identities. *European Journal of Teacher Education, 36*(1), 68–83. doi:10.1080/02619768.2012.678486

Hallman, H. (2007). Negotiating teacher identity: Exploring the use of electronic teaching portfolios with preservice English teachers. *International Reading Association, 50*(6), 474-485.

Hargreaves, A. (1998). The emotional practice of teaching. *Teaching and Teacher Education, 14*(8), 835–854. doi:10.1016/S0742-051X(98)00025-0

Haritos, C. (2004). Understanding teaching through the minds of teacher candidates: A curious blend of realism and idealism. *Teaching Education, 20,* 637–654.

Hatton, N., & Smith, D. (1995). Reflection in teacher education: Towards definition and implementation. *Teaching and Teacher Education, 11*(1), 3–49. doi:10.1016/0742-051X(94)00012-U

Holt-Reynolds, D. (1992). Personal history-based beliefs as relevant prior knowledge in course work. *American Educational Research Journal, 29*(2), 325–349. doi:10.3102/00028312029002325

Jay, J., & Johnson, K. (2002). Capturing complexity: A typology of reflective practice for teacher education. *Teaching and Teacher Education, 18*(1), 73–85. doi:10.1016/S0742-051X(01)00051-8

Kagan, D. (1992a). Implications of research on teacher belief. *Educational Psychologist, 27*(1), 65–90. doi:10.120715326985ep2701_6

Kagan, D. (1992b). Professional growth among pre-service and beginning teachers. *Review of Educational Research, 62*(2), 129–169. doi:10.3102/00346543062002129

Keats, J. (n.d.). *Letter to his brothers, 1817*. Retrieved from http://englishhistory.net/keats/letters.html

Kelchtermans, G. (2009). Career stories as a gateway to understanding teacher development. In M. Bayer, U. Brinkkjaer, H. Plauborg, & S. Rolls (Eds.), *Teachers' career trajectories and work lives. Professional learning and development in school and higher education, 3* (pp. 29–47). Amsterdam: Springer Netherlands. doi:10.1007/978-90-481-2358-2_3

Knowles, J. G., & Holt-Reynolds, D. (1991). Shaping pedagogies through personal histories in pre-service teacher education. *Teachers College Record, 93*, 87–113.

Larrivee, B. (2000). Transforming teaching practice: Becoming the critically reflective teacher. *Reflective Practice, 1*(3), 297–307. doi:10.1080/713693162

Lee, H.-J. (2005). Understanding and assessing preservice teachers' reflective thinking. *Teaching and Teacher Education, 21*(6), 699–715. doi:10.1016/j.tate.2005.05.007

Lee, S., & Schallert, D. (2016). Becoming a teacher: Coordinating past, present, and future selves with perspectival understandings about teaching. *Teaching and Teacher Education, 56*, 72–83. doi:10.1016/j.tate.2016.02.004

Lortie, D. (1975). *School-teacher: A sociological study*. Chicago: University of Chicago Press.

Manuel, J., & Carter, D. (2016). Sustaining hope and possibility: Early–career English teachers' perspective on their first years of teaching. *Engineers Australia, 51*, 91–103.

Markus, H., & Nurius, P. (1986). Possible selves. *The American Psychologist, 41*(9), 954–969. doi:10.1037/0003-066X.41.9.954

Massengill, D., Mahlios, M., & Barry, A. (2005). Making sense of teaching through metaphors: A review across three studies. *Teachers and Teaching, 16*(1), 49–71.

Miller, K., & Shifflet, R. (2016). How memories of school inform PST's feared and desired selves as teachers. *Teaching and Teacher Education, 53*, 20–29. doi:10.1016/j.tate.2015.10.002

Nelson, C., & Harper, V. (2006). A pedagogy of difficulty: Preparing teachers to understand and integrate complexity in teaching and learning. *Teacher Education Quarterly, 33*(2), 7–21.

Nias, J. (1989). Teaching and the self. In M. L. Holly & C. S. McLoughlin (Eds.), *Perspectives on teacher professional development* (pp. 155–173). London, England: The Falmer Press.

Otteson, E. (2007). Reflection in teacher education. *Reflective Practice*, *8*(1), 31–46. doi:10.1080/14623940601138899

Pajares, M. (1992). Teachers' beliefs and educational research: Cleaning up a messy construct. *Review of Educational Research*, *62*(3), 307–332. doi:10.3102/00346543062003307

Pillen, M., Beijaard, D., & den Brok, P. (2013). Tensions in beginning teachers' professional identity development, accompanying feelings and coping strategies. *European Journal of Teacher Education*, *36*(3), 240–260. doi:10.1080/02619768.2012.696192

Reid, I. (1996). Romantic ideologies, educational practices, and institutional formations of English. *Journal of Educational Administration and History*, *28*(1), 22–41. doi:10.1080/0022062960280102

Rodgers, C. R., & Scott, K. H. (2008). The development of the personal self and professional identity in learning to teach. In M. Cochrane-Smith, S. Freiman-Demers, D. McIntrye & K. Demers (Eds.), Handbook of research on teacher education, New York, NY: Routledge.

Sachs, J. (2005). Teacher education and the development of professional identity: learning to be a teacher. In M. Kompf & P. Denicolo (Eds.), *Connecting Policy and Practice: Challenges for Teaching and Learning in Schools and Universities* (pp. 5–21). London, UK: Routledge.

Salisbury-Glennon, J., & Stevens, R. (1999). Addressing preservice teachers' conceptions of motivation. *Teaching and Teacher Education*, *15*, 74–752. doi:10.1016/S0742-051X(99)00023-2

Schön, D. (1983). *The reflective practitioner: How professionals think in action*. New York: Basic Books.

Schön, D. (1987). *Educating the reflective practitioner: Towards a new design for teaching and learning in the professions*. San Francisco, CA: Jossey-Bass.

Shulman, L. S. (1986). Knowledge and teaching: Foundations of the new reform. *Harvard Educational Review*, *19*(2).

Sugrue, C. (1997). Student teachers' lay theories and teaching identities: Their implications for professional development. *European Journal of Teacher Education*, *20*(3), 213–225. doi:10.1080/0261976970200302

Sutherland, L., Howard, S., & Markauskaite, L. (2010). Professional identity creation: Examining the development of beginning preservice teachers' understanding of their work as teachers. *Teaching and Teacher Education*, *26*(3), 455–465. doi:10.1016/j.tate.2009.06.006

Taylor, S., & Sobel, D. (2000). Addressing the discontinuity of students' and teachers' diversity: A preliminary study of preservice teachers' beliefs and perceived skills. *Teaching and Teacher Education*, *17*(4), 487–503. doi:10.1016/S0742-051X(01)00008-7

Tillema, H. H. (1997). Stability and change in student teachers' beliefs. *European Journal of Teacher Education*, *20*(3), 209–212. doi:10.1080/0261976970200301

Turner, V. (1964). Betwixt and Between: The liminal period in *Rites de Passage*. *International Journal of the American Ethnological Society*, 4-20.

University of Sydney. (n.d.). Master of teaching. Retrieved from https://sydney.edu.au/education_social_work/future_students/graduate_entry/r esources/MTeach_web.pdf

Van Gennep, A. (1977). *Rites of Passage*. London, UK: Routledge and Kegan Paul.

Ward, J., Nolen, S., & Horn, I. (2011). Productive fiction: How conflict in student teaching creates opportunities for learning at the boundary. *International Journal of Educational Research*, *50*(1), 14–20. doi:10.1016/j.ijer.2011.04.004

Wilke, R., & Losh, S. (2008). Beyond beliefs: Preservice teachers' planned instructional strategies. *Action in Teacher Education*, *30*(3), 213–238. doi:10.1080/01626620.2008.10463503

Zeichner, K. (2010). Rethinking the connections between campus courses and field experiences in college and university-based teacher education. *Journal of Teacher Education*, *61*(1-2), 89–99. doi:10.1177/0022487109347671

Chapter 3

Moving Away From the "Chalk and Board":
Lessons From a Critical Pedagogical Standpoint

Talia Randa Esnard
The University of the West Indies – St. Augustine Campus, Trinidad and Tobago

Linda Lila Mohammed
University of Trinidad and Tobago, Trinidad and Tobago

ABSTRACT

Freire contended that teachers' knowledge sets are incomplete without the critical engagement and dialogic exchange with students. Such non-hierarchical and collaborative arrangements are perceived to be at the crux of transformative praxis. As a way of testing the possibilities around this pedagogical alternative, this project encouraged teachers to creatively explore critical pedagogical approaches (CPA) in the classroom and the extent to which this enhanced the engagement of students, and, ultimately, their ability to critically apply their understanding of existing knowledge frames to the formation and presentation of new forms of knowledge. Written observations and self-reflections point to the salience of systemic constraints that were rooted in the structural and cultural facets of the school system, and the effect of these both on teachers' adoption of a bimodal model of instruction, and, on their partial success in this endeavor. Implications for theory and practices are herein discussed.

INTRODUCTION

We live in a world today that is fast paced and ever-changing and where success is largely dependent on our ability to creatively apply our knowledge, skills and abilities to further our economic development. However, teachers in the classroom face an everyday conundrum. That is, they are challenged to prepare students for standardized assessments, "while still adding creativity to the curriculum" (Longo, 2010, p. 54). This is on account of the growing movement towards an instrumental approach to education where

DOI: 10.4018/978-1-5225-7829-1.ch003

Copyright © 2019, IGI Global. Copying or distributing in print or electronic forms without written permission of IGI Global is prohibited.

the emphasis has been on increasing pass rates, standardizing formal testing systems, and enhancing existing levels of efficiency and effectiveness within schools. With increasing calls for accountability, schools are further pressed to provide high quality instruction with increasing structures of surveillance (UNESCO, 2007). The inherent emphasis in this case is on ensuring that students are given the necessary skills and knowledge sets that are deemed necessary to function within the labor market, and, by extension, the broader society. In fact, citing the early works of Apple (1979), Cho (2013, p.19) contended that such a system "treats educational issues-curriculum, teaching, learning, evaluation, discipline and classroom management-as both technical and non-political, and thus has focused on coming up with procedural models."

Such technical rationality presents a challenge for education systems to equip students with the ability to think critically, act constructively, and aptly adapt to move their societies forward. The persistence of such instrumental logic challenges the potential for criticality and creativity in the classroom (Craft, Jeffrey, & Leibling, 2001; Burnard & White, 2008; Hove, 2011). This is particularly the case for teachers who struggle with creative strategies in their teaching (Fleith, 2000; Robinson, 2006), the critical engagement of students (Sternberg, Grigorenko & Singer, 2004), and the possibilities for self-directed learning (Robinson, 2006; Hove, 2011; Beghetto & Kaufman, 2014). Given the importance of creative teaching to critical thinking (Meyer, 1986; Mayfield, 1997; Eckhoff & Urbach, 2008; Rinkevich, 2011), student engagement (Beghetto & Kaufman, 2014) and academic success (Schachter, Thum & Zifkin, 2006; Vasudevan, 2013), the question then becomes that of whether teachers are trained to promote critical thinking in the classroom. We also argue for deeper interrogations of the underlining philosophy of teacher training programs, the processes through which teachers are prepared to creatively and critically engage students, the actual realities of the classroom, and, the collective effects on teachers ability to move beyond or to transform the chalk and board of the classroom.

TEACHER TRAINING AND PREPAREDNESS

We contend that the issue of teachers' pedagogical approaches within the classroom requires an examination of the teacher training programs. The authors start therefore, with a recognition of the many reforms of teacher training programs in Trinidad and Tobago. To a large extent, the authors note these reforms have been locked within attempts to regularize teacher education in Trinidad and Tobago, to standardization of the criteria for employment or promotion of teachers in the service, to increase access to teacher training institutions. The latter has resulted in the particular expansion of many teacher training institutions, programs, and specializations in Trinidad and Tobago.

Despite such enlargement, teacher training programs remain somewhat fragmented with conflicting epistemological assumptions that drive teaching practices (George, Worrell, & Rampersad, 2002; Steward & Thomas, 1997). A key issue that remains therefore, is the lack of consensus on the "essential knowledge, skills, and competencies that new primary teachers should acquire during pre-service training (Lewin & Stuart, 2003, p. 699). A related matter is also a lack of more pointed discussions of the ontological role and purpose of teacher education and that of how do teachers contribute to the betterment of the wider society that schools serve. These raise many related questions on the type and level of preparedness of teachers to engage in the everyday classroom, and, with the specific concern of whether they are prepared to creatively and critically engage students in the classroom.

These questions also make a strong case for revisiting the assumptions, inherent objectives, and embedded meanings and practices of teacher education and training programs in Trinidad and Tobago. In this regard, the authors start with an acknowledgement of the attempt by a few teacher training institutions in Trinidad and Tobago to constructively prepare teachers to critically engage students and their wider society through their pedagogical approaches. One such program trains teachers to use more of a developmental, constructivist or inquiry-based approach to teacher education (George & Quamina-Aiyejina, 2003; Baldeo, 2011). Under this model, teachers are afforded the opportunity to enter into the field/in schools, and, to function either as observers, apprentices, or interns, with varying time periods and levels of involvement over a four-year period of the program. While the program is at an embryonic stage, with under fifteen years of experimentation around this model, the time is ripe to assess teachers' ability to consciously and actively become agents of social change in the school system. In this case, the authors explore teachers' ability (both pre-service and in-service) to move beyond the culture of talk and chalk to more creative and critical approaches within the classroom.

THE CHALLENGE OF CRITICAL THINKING

For Ticusan & Elena (2015, p. 309), critical thinking "is a way of approaching and solving problems based on convincing, logical and rational arguments, which involve verifying, evaluating and choosing the right response for a given task and reasoned rejection of the other alternative solutions." While this is often considered as a fundamental goal of classroom instruction, it is one that presents major challenges for teachers within existing school systems (Abrami et al., 2008; Baildon & Sim, 2009; Hove, 2011). Several factors emerge as central to this challenge.

A major source of contention in the literature is the extent to which teachers actively promote critical thinking in the classroom (Choy & Cheah, 2009; Moore & Stanley, 2010; Zachary, 2011). Thus, on one hand, there is evidence to suggest that some teachers see critical thinking as an innate ability (Choy & Cheah, 2009; Moore & Stanley, 2010, Sternberg & Williams, 2002). On the other, is a body of literature that speaks to the need to train teachers on how to think and teach critically (Skaggs, 2004; Duron, Limbach & Waugh, 2006; Synder & Synder, 2008; Choy & Cheah, 2009). Two related sources of controversy within such a debate are: (i) the lack of clearly defined notions of what constitutes critical thinking (Paul, Binker, Jensen, & Kreklau, 1990), and; (ii) a dearth of knowledge among teachers as to methods that are necessary to foster critical thinking in the classroom (Hawker, 2000; Fisher, 2007; Stapleton, 2011; Zachary, 2011).

A major argument in the literature is that creative teaching (as an imaginative way of making learning more interesting) can promote critical thinking (Cremin, 2009; Forrester, 2008). Here, researchers stress on the use of problem-based teaching and probing questions as key strategies to be employed in the delivery of the curriculum (Wiggins & McTighe, 2005; Mc Collister &, Sayler, 2010; Rinkervich, 2011). A general call within that literature is for more innovative lesson plans (Sarsani, 2008; Kaufman & Beghetto, 2009; Bolden, Harries & Newton, 2010), as well as, collaborative and nonhierarchical models of teaching that encourage self-regulated learning (Portelli, 1994; Freire, 2005; Simonton, 2012). However, for this to be realized, scholars also underscore the need to examine the psychological factors that affect engagement in the classroom (Hennessey & Amabile, 2010; Turner, 2013). While the idea of how to use creative teaching can evoke critical thought remains substantively under-investigated, there are many approaches that offer some insight. Such is the case of critical pedagogy; which has as its hallmark the potential to critical consciousness and transformative praxis. This is discussed in the following paragraph.

CRITICAL PEDAGOGY

Critical pedagogy has been represented in the literature as a conscious way of thinking about, negotiating and transforming relationships between knowledge, authority, and power in teaching and learning contexts (Ayers, Michie, & Rome, 2004; Giroux, 2004a). As a theory and praxis that is rooted in critical theory, its fundamental goals exist around the need to link the pedagogical approaches in the classroom to the critical negotiation and transformation of the social, material, and ideological contexts that frame the classroom experience (Mc Laren, 1998, 2009; Giroux, 2004b; Freire, 2000; Brookfield, 2005). As a practice of hope and freedom, an underlying expectation for teachers who subscribe to critical pedagogical approaches (CPA) is that of encouraging students to "deal critically and creatively with reality, and, discover how to participate in the transformation of their world" (Freire, 1996, p. 16). Here, these critical pedagogical approaches underscore the relevance of questioning the structural processes that are necessary for creating democratic educational environments. The emphasis therefore is on using critical questions, drawing on context specific applications, as well as, on the strengths of learners to creatively transmit both knowledge and skills sets. Through this approach, the expectation is for students and teachers to move beyond the confines of technicist concerns that inform teaching and learning practices, to more constructivist engagements that open the possibilities for critical thought and action (Freire, 2005). The inherent contention within this line of thinking is that the process of using imaginative or creative approaches to teaching in the classroom remains at the center of that democratization process (Gillian, 1999; Creamin, 2009). Despite the theorized connection between creativity and criticality and the pedagogical strategies for so doing, the experiences of teachers around this expectation for critical pedagogy remains less understood. The objectives of this paper are therefore four-fold.

1. To explore the possibilities for using CPA within the classroom
2. To examine the extent to which such CPA fosters the creativity and criticality of teachers and students
3. To address the factors that hinder or foster the design and implementation of CPA within the classroom
4. To assess the implications of these for moving beyond the *chalk and talk* of the classroom

METHODOLOGY

Methodologically, the authors use CPA to encourage, according to Harman & McClure (2011, p. 382) "critical discussions that focuses on issues related to social equity." As a problem posing approach to education, the methodologically emphasis of CPA is on that of praxis; that being, the method through which teachers and students are able to critically connect, reflect on, and transform their knowledge of and engagement in their social world (Freire, 2005). Given this foci around CPA and the use of teachers as our unit of analysis, the study centered on the examinations of the design of their lesson plans, the delivery of these lessons, and their reflections of the same.

Participants

Five female teachers specializing in the teaching of Social Studies (secondary school program) volunteered to participate in this study after being debriefed on the rationale and processes surrounding the current study. These teachers were all registered in a Bachelor of Education training program in Trinidad and Tobago. At the time of the study, all teachers were all in the final year of their training program with varied years of experience in the classroom. Two of the five teachers were in-service teachers with prior years of teaching within the secondary school system before their entry into the training program. The other three teachers were all pre-service teachers with no teaching experience.

Data Collection

Over an eight-week period, the researchers collected data around teachers lesson plans, reflections of their lessons and actual teaching. In the first two weeks, researchers provided teachers/participants in the study with two articles[1] related to creative teaching and critical thinking in the classroom. These teachers were each instructed to read the selected articles on their own, and, invited to (i) incorporate strategies around creativity and critical thinking in the development of three lesson plans, and (ii) to write a reflection on that process. During those two weeks, teachers were supported by the current researchers in the preparation of these lessons plans and evaluated on various occasions to assess their attempts in that regard. In the six weeks that followed, researchers observed the delivery of fifteen lessons; with three lessons per teacher. Researchers also used the post lesson sessions to debrief teachers on some of the assessments that were made during the observations. Teachers were given the opportunity to respond to these assessments. Written comments were made on all observed lessons and shared with teachers.

Data Sources and Analysis

For this study, teachers lesson plans, personal reflections on the preparation of the lesson plans, and researchers' observations around the delivery of these lessons served as the three main sources of data for this study. Collectively, these sources of data provided thick sets of written data from which researchers were able to draw on in the analysis of whether teachers were able to engage and transform their classrooms. In analyzing these data sets, they were segmented to draw on: analytical categories or specific characteristics related to how teachers incorporated CPA into the classroom, the challenges therein, and the effects of these on their own relations with students. These initial categories were subsequently merged into two major themes; those being, the prospects of using creativity as a vehicle for critical praxis and the challenges of moving beyond the structural and cultural constraints inherent within observed classrooms.

FINDINGS

Creativity as a Vehicle for Critical Praxis

Examinations of the findings indicated that all five teachers attempted to creatively apply novel ways to promote critical thinking in the classrooms. In this case, the creative use of songs, application of students' cultural references, use of games, and roleplaying emerged as effective strategies that encouraged critical thinking among students. These are discussed below.

The Use of Songs

The use of songs unfolded as one of the creative ways to encourage critical thinking among students. In fact, teacher J for instance introduced her lesson with a song that spoke to the problems that persons face in their communities. The originality of that set induction came through her modification of the lyrics of a popular local calypso to capture contemporary manifestations of the social issues that were addressed in the original composition. Here, observed noted that the set induction to the lesson both stimulated students interests and prompted a critique of the social problems that were left out in the calypso. While students' slightly deviated from the teachers' presentation, it was clear that the teaching strategy provoked a critical analysis of the composition.

Using Cultural References

From a critical pedagogical standpoint, critical thinking can be encouraged through the recognition of students' existing knowledge sets and ability to explore new forms of knowledge (McManus, 2001; Reid, Burn, & Parker, 2002; Powers, 2011). What was also clear in the findings was that the creative alignment of students' cultural experience also stimulated critical thought. In addressing the importance of students' cultural reference, *teacher T* suggested that:

One such way to maintain student's interest is to provide examples that relate to real life situations, so that students can connect to the content. Creativity can also be expressed in the strategies the teacher uses to encourage students to generate new ideas and to get them actively involved in generating their own knowledge.

This reflection brings into the discussion the extent to which such creative teaching can affect the perceived applicability and relevance to the lived experiences of students. In fact, *teacher T* commented that, "it made me realize that knowledge acquisition should be more of a student's responsibility and less of the teacher's responsibility". An important aspect of her reflection therefore is that of the functional role of students' involvement in promoting critical thinking in the classroom. Further endorsement comes from Woods (2002), who contends that the more relevant teaching is to student's needs, their lives, cultures and interests, the greater the propensity for them to regulate their personal learning processes.

As a way of addressing how teachers use students' cultural reference to add to the critical application of knowledge, observers noted that teachers attempted to explore the use of students' individual contributions. In a particular instance, observer B remarked that teacher J "related [her treatment of social problem] to the experiences of the students directly, by asking them to describe their own experiences to their peers. This was quite effective". Such questioning also emerged as a way of encouraging students to problematize their existing knowledge around social issues and of soliciting a cognitive and affective response. Observer B therefore remarked that teacher J also "asked students to say how they felt about what they described in their skit". Observer B also commented that "her questioning skills …touched on several levels of Bloom's taxonomy…this was indicative of her understanding of what is required for students to think critically." In fact, researchers contended that such questioning should remain an integral aspect of getting students to move along the continuum of knowledge acquisition to critical applications of skills that knowledge (Fisher, 2004; Beghetto & Kaufman, 2007). When creativity is embodied in such a way then it holds promise for the ability of students to engage in critical and imaginative thoughts about a given entity (Fisher, 2004). To some extent, this was evident in the observations of the five teachers.

Use of Roleplay

Role playing emerged as a creative strategy for encouraging critical thinking in the classroom. In one such case, teacher J flipped the classroom to allow students to explore role playing as medium through which they can represent the specific problems that surface in their respective communities. As such, Observer A mentioned:

Another creative element of the lesson [for teacher J] was the use of role-play to demonstrate the way they understand the notion of problems in the community. Teacher also walks around the classroom while students were planning their presentation to assist in their role-playing.

Here, teachers modelled the use of role playing as an innovative way of encourage students to critically evaluate the problems within their communities. In all cases, teachers not only embodied the issues and personalities that they portrayed. This emerged as a particular strategy for teacher H, who also used role play to introduce a lesson on the structure and workings of the parliamentary system. In addressing this initiative, Observer A remarked that "the lesson started in a creative way with the teacher wearing a gown over her attire and declaring that the Bill has become law and that students should take note. She then related her actions to the topic of the lesson". Similar statements were expressed by Observer B, who remarked "the set induction to the lesson was good, with the teacher entering the classroom dressed in parliamentary regalia". This was also the case of teacher N who used the sounds of drums and appropriate attire to reenact some aspects of the Butler riots in Trinidad and Tobago. A laudable addition to this strategy was the use of role play by the teacher to depict the involvement of trade unionist Uriah Butler and the inclusion of the students, who actively played the roles as supporters in the reenactment. According to teacher N "…I was able to include the students to give them an active role in the teaching-learning process". By giving students a role in the reenactment of the Butler riots, this strategy helped students to critically synthesize the issues surrounding the Butler riots. In that regard, Observer B remarked that:

The set induction to this lesson should be commended. Given the [historical] nature of the topic, it was quite innovative for the teacher to re-enact a riot scene similar to what took place in the Butler Riots of the 1930s in this country. The musical accompaniment enhanced the teacher's performance. The teacher displayed great passion and conviction in her demonstration. This introduction definitely got the student's attention.

Here, researchers observed that students were clothed in working attire, used musical instruments as part of their role play, and moved in sequence with the teacher, who played the role of Uriah Butler. It is through this engagement of students within this reenactment that teacher H offered an effective means to scaffold students' learning and ultimately to foster their own ability to critically engage with the significance and implications of the riots. The value of such an approach is in the extent to which it can encourage the morphing of students into critical beings (Jeffries, 2005; Paul, 2006). However, sustaining this development requires the use of debriefing sessions, or other forms of assessments that allow for the assimilation of that learning (Jeffries, 2005; Goel & Aggarwal, 2012; Earl, 2003). Here, the requirement is for teachers to move into more informal sessions, where they can dialogue through the meanings and effects of the role playing activities on students' learning. However, observers noted that this debriefing was not applied by teachers. Perhaps, this remains an area for further exploration, both by the teachers in this case, and by future researchers who wish to explore this area of research.

The Use of Games

Where both teachers H and N used the game of 'jeopardy' as a summative aspect of the lesson, observers noted that the use of jeopardy provided additional opportunities to engage students, to reinforce learning, and to strengthen their abilities to apply these in different contexts and scenarios. Here, the game formatted lessons served as an important tool for encouraging student centered classrooms (Marzano, Pickering, & Pollock, 2001; Marzano, 2007). The cognitive and affective impact of using games to assist critical thought cannot be underestimated. In fact, researchers stress on the potential for role playing within the classroom to stimulate the cognitive, behavioral, and affective engagement of students (Jeffries, 2005; Possin, 2008). In the moments where such creative engagement of students were employed, teachers were able to nurture their discernibility and criticality; thus, confirming the use of CPA as a practice of hope. In many ways therefore, such creative pedagogical initiatives also represented an important aspect of reconfiguring the power relations between teachers and students in the classroom (McLaren & Da Silva 1993; Freire, 1996; Irwin, 2012).

On Moving Beyond the Structural and Cultural Constraints

The promise of a critical education is the extent to which it can increase the freedoms and possibilities of those who operate within that space. However, analysis of the data sets underlined the challenges of fully implementing CPA in the classrooms. In many cases, the difficulties were associated with the structural and cultural realities of that classroom; which were often in direct contention with the laboratory thrust of CPA.

Dominance and Effect of Didactic Pedagogy

The prevalence of didactic approaches within the school system remained a major issue for teachers in this study. In fact, teachers spoke to the pervasive use and ideological support for what Freire (1996) referred to as didactic pedagogy; an approach that silences that critical consciousness and subjectivities of learners in the classroom. In her reflection, teacher J highlighted the struggles around that process and the role of broader structural constraints within the school system. Teacher J recorded the following:

Too much emphasis is placed on completing syllabi in preparation for standardized tests and prior to the new exposure that I now have I too would have been guilty of directing full energy into standardized tests. What I found was planning a 'chalk and board' type lesson was quite quick and easy, but it compromised the learning process. Often most teachers will overuse this as an excuse and claim that it is too time consuming to sit and plan a creative lesson as they strive to complete content in preparation for standardized examination.

The main issue of contention in this case was the dominant use and application of standardized teaching in schools and the effect of such processes on how teachers' deliver instruction in the classroom. Inadvertently, many authors note that such didactic patterns negatively affect the possibilities of exploring alternative forms of teaching in the classroom (Abrams, Pedulla, & Madaus, 2003; Jeffries, 2005). In fact, we found that dominance of didactic teaching within the schools under observation negatively affected the ability of teachers who intended (at least in the design of their lesson plan) to deliver a lesson using the fundamentals of CPA.

Thus, while teacher C succeeded in involving students within collaborative learning exercises, she stressed on her own inability to negotiate the behavioral outcomes of that process. She wrote that "some of the students were talking a bit too much during the teaching of the lesson. This made me realize that I need to work on my classroom management skills and to be more assertive towards the students". A major limitation in this case was the inability of teacher C to recognize how her own perception of the need for more controlled spaces and for more 'assertive' responses reproduce the power and authority between the teacher and the student, and inadvertently diminishes for the potential for individualized freedoms in the classroom. While the main factor here may be the fear of classrooms becoming too disorderly (Scott, 1999), her response goes against the promise of democratizing the classroom (McLaren, 1995; Giroux, 2004a).

Other researchers have linked such classroom structures and cultures to the bureaucratizing of the education system (Bailey, 2000; Kennedy, 2005). The inherent thinking in this case is that such rationalization directly affects teachers' conceptualization and execution of their lessons. This emerged as a particular issue for teacher H and T. In these cases, both teachers reported on the pressure to complete the curriculum, and on the need to be strategic more than creative. In speaking to this, teacher H remarked that it may be easier to "just give notes;" an expectation she elucidated emerged from her discussions with other teachers within the school. In reflecting on difficulties of this structural reality, teacher T indicated that:

Having the right creative ideas is only a small part of the creative teaching/learning process since execution of these ideas is also important. I believe that my creative ideas as well as the adjustments I've made to my teaching. However, it will only be effective if I have achieved my specified objectives. In this lesson however, I experienced some difficulty executing my ideas in an effective way, the catastrophe was further fueled by time constraints. Therefore, I need to work on executing my ideas, proper time management and classroom management.

In this case, teacher T reinforced the challenges of context and the impact of the evaluation of her lesson. Teacher T alluded in this case, that the difficulties around "poor time and classroom-management", were both on account of "students were reluctant to join groups and I experienced difficulty trying to motivate students to engage in classroom activities" and the collective effect of these on the required procedures for these lessons. In this case, the teacher noted that the students struggled with making the shift to collaborative learning in the classrooms. This can be linked to the dominant and more traditional practices around teaching and learning in the classroom. In speaking to this, she underscored the ways in which the classes are structured (by time allocations and physical layout of schools), how students are expected to behave, how teachers are required to manage the processes around these, and, the extent to which these introduced broader constrains on the execution of the lesson. For this teacher, it became a challenge of responding to how both teachers and students have been imagined within the broader parameters of traditional classrooms. In this case, teachers underscored that the dominance of traditional modes and restrictive practices inherent in these classrooms restricted the possibilities of CPA. Even teachers are faced with such structural barriers, it often presents an added layer for negotiating the social and ideological underpinnings of learning and teaching within traditional classrooms (McLaren, 1998; Giroux 2004b; Brookfield, 2005).

Making a Compromise; the Use of Bimodal Models

The significance of these structural and cultural barriers to the use of CPA was also evident in the use of a bimodal model of teaching and learning, as a compromise between the dominant uses of didactic approaches to that of the intended CPA. In fact, our observations and examinations of teachers' reflections revealed that all five teachers adopted varying forms and degrees of bimodality in the delivery of their third lesson.

In speaking to the case of teacher J, both observers noted that teacher J shifted between asking critical questions to that of simply dictating concepts that were perceived to be pertinent to the lesson. By so doing, teacher J moved from explorations of a CPA to that of the dominant didactic model and from serving as facilitators to disseminators of knowledge. Such switching therefore raises pertinent questions as to teacher J's own perceptions on relative compatibility, functionality and applicability of both models. Observers noted in this case that while teacher J incorporated some of probing strategy into her lesson, she regulated the extent to which such probing shaped the delivery of her lesson. In speaking to this, Observer B commented that "too often, teachers resort to telling students rather than simply asking a question". As a way of extending a more dialogic approach, observer B opined that "it might have been a good idea to question students to elicit from them what they thought the lesson was going to be about, rather than simply telling them at the outset". Where such questioning holds the potential for critical thought (Mills, 1998) and for a dialogic exchange between teachers and students, then it becomes an issue of how these emerge as a central and consistent aspects of their pedagogical practice, if CPAs are to be fully embraced.

Freire (1996) however cautioned that genuine criticality cannot coexist with the strict application of instrumental models of education. Our findings confirmed this. In fact, what we also found however is that even with the adoption of this bimodal approach; teachers were also uniquely positioned in a space of in-betweenity that raise the tensions in the classroom. In this case, observers noted that while teachers creatively explored the integration of CPA in the delivery of their bimodal model, they generally failed to sustain a critical understanding and application of the content and context. In that regard, teacher H noted that she "tried to apply both student and teacher centered approaches to the delivery of the lesson". Like teacher J, she expounded that this approach was driven by the need to "capture [her] students' attention" and to complete the syllabus. However, Observer B indicated that while the use of the diorama enhanced the creativity of the lesson that the teacher stopped short of "peaking students' interest and critical thinking around issues of population distribution". Observer B also recommended that "more could have been done with the resources to further stimulate the students. Maybe she could have simply passed it around from one group to the next. They would have enjoyed the opportunity to manipulate it". Thus, the conclusion in that case from observer B, was that "while there was some attempt at being creative, more could have been done with the lesson" to stimulate critical thinking among students. Likewise, observers noted that while teacher H attempted to design a creative lesson[2] that speaks to the roles and responsibilities of persons within the judiciary, her blending of this lesson with more traditional forms led to low levels of student participation. In fact, observer A noted that "the teaching was poorly designed.... there was poor engagement of the student, the concepts [remained] abstract, [and the students were not able to answer questions related to the lesson]. Observer B also indicated that while teacher H was within her parliamentary regalia, that "this [did not sustain the] interest …throughout the lesson"; particularly in this case because this was neither accompanied, nor followed, by the application of more constructive approaches to learning".

In lieu of this approach, Observer B commented that teacher H "asked and answered her own questions, instead of giving the students the time needed to respond. Questions were all knowledge type which simply required recall and regurgitation without any meaningful thought". In this case, the use of recall did not allow for drawing on higher order thinking and for critically applying that knowledge to more specific contexts or contextual issues. When one considers the tendency for questions to stimulate both creative and critical thinking among students (Kazemi, 1998; Scales, 2013), then it calls for carefully planned integration of specific question types and levels that challenge the thinking and application of students' knowledge sets. This was clearly missing in this case. What resulted on the other hand was that "students appeared disconnected and demotivated" (Observer B).

A disconnection between the objectives of the lesson and the delivery also emerged as an issue for teacher C. In that regard, observers noted that while she seemingly embraced creative teaching to promote critical thinking, her pedagogical approaches remained grounded within the wider frame of a teacher centered lesson. In speaking to this case, Observer A wrote that while she attempted to deliver a lesson on scale measurement to an upper form, she relied on direct instruction without encouraging students to think and to share. By so doing, Observer A noted that she failed to "engage the students during questioning, [with] no encouragement for critical thinking or application of concepts." In fact, observer A noted that even with the reliance on direct instruction that there was "no demonstration of how to work the sum to produce the answers". Observer B also recorded the following:

There were no reinforcement exercises. It was a very poor approach for the teacher to dictate a defini-tion of "statement scale" to the students....[it is also an indication of the poor preparation on the part of the teacher...Additionally, it is also evidence that she failed to consider the visual learners in her class. Telling is a good strategy to use in the classroom but should be utilized when students simply do not know. Rather than elicit information from them, the teacher engaged in telling them the information. The teacher also talked while facing the whiteboard rather than the students.

The issues affecting teacher C therefore remained a pedagogical one. In fact, observers noted that she failed to capture the multiple intelligences and situated realities of students within the classroom. Observer A noted that "a direct result of this was that students made many mistakes in the calculation of the scale while participating in the game". It is under similar evaluations that Observer B also recommended that "students could have been allowed to manipulate this apparatus and this would have not only provided hands-on participation but might have peaked students interest and motivation for the lesson. It is clear in this case that while teacher C attempted to creatively deliver the lesson that she also suffered from her own inability to move beyond the narrowness of traditional approaches to teaching and learning in the classroom. Her tendency to face the board rather than the students is also indicative of the failure to connect with students and perhaps of her own insecurities around her inability to creatively foster critical thinking in the classroom. This situation calls attention to the pressures of teaching to the test (McNeil, 2000; Hatch, 2002; Evans, 2014), and on teachers beliefs in their ability to effectively respond to these (Hennessey & Amabile, 2010; Turner, 2013).

SOLUTIONS AND RECOMMENDATIONS

Where critical pedagogy remains wary of existing educational philosophies, structures and practices, then the call is for teachers to use CPA as an alternative mode of thinking and doing within the classroom. This demands that teachers resist existing ontological and epistemological notions of learning and resituate both the position of students and the relations between themselves and their students. This is a tall but important task. Where teachers attempted to creatively restructure learning modes of inquiry, moments, and spaces, they soon became conscious of, sensitive and responsive to, the dominant ideological, cultural, and structural realities of the school system. In this sense, they recoiled into the crafting of a bimodal model that advances a notion of change as limited and teaching as comprise.

Thus, it was clear that the use of creativity in the delivery of their lessons, allowed teachers to draw on issues of relevance, innovation and participation in the delivery of their lesson (Woods, 2002). This was clear in the extent to which they were able to create critical learning moments or opportunities that allowed students to connect to their own constructions and expressions of their lived realities. However, while this blended model presented an opportunity to respond to both calls for engagement in the classroom (those being, didactic and dialogic), the findings underscored that student engagement were highest, when the latter remained the underlining aspects and approach to the lesson. In this case, the very blending and switching of their approaches in the classroom limited the potential or transformative capacities of CPA.

It is clear therefore that when using this bimodal approach to instruction teachers only partially succeeded in moving beyond the chalk and talk of the classroom. In fact, while teachers made the effort to teach creatively and encourage critical thinking in their students, their overall success was largely hindered by the bureaucratic constraints therein, a lack of repertoire of essential skills necessary for teaching creatively, and promoting critical thinking in their students. It is clear therefore that there are many predicaments that teachers and schools have to resolve if they are to improve creativity and critical thinking in their teaching and learning processes. A few recommendations therefore emerge from such the previously discussed findings around the creative strategies employed by teachers and the structural challenges associated with that process.

1. As a starting point, such findings call for greater scrutiny of the structures and processes that underpin the education system. Central aspects of such interrogation should include:
    a. initial discussion of and consensus on the vision of the education system
    b. the structures and resources that are needed to support such a vision
    c. a clear and well thought out position on the approach or approaches to learning and teaching within the classroom, and;
    d. considerations of the pedagogical ways in which this vision can be enacted within the classroom.

2. Stakeholder consultations- with all stakeholders in the education system should be perceived as necessary aspects of encouraging a participatory approach to educational reform.
3. Revision of existing curriculum and methods of assessing these. An important aspect of this is to enhance the overall quality, relevance, criticality, and openness of developmental models that are used to revise and restructure classroom assessments and curricula.
4. Training of teachers-the emphases here are on the need to provide teachers with the:
   a. Requisite skills, competencies and mindset that can encourage creative and critical thinking.
   b. treatment of the *how* and *why* of CPA that encourages teachers to explore the potential for CPA, perhaps even other viable models, and the possible outcomes of these, particularly for students.
   c. A relevant and effective toolkit for the design and implementation of CPA.
   d. continuous opportunities for professional development

FUTURE RESEARCH DIRECTIONS

The findings suggested that the use of a bimodal approach to classroom engagement emerged as a response to, and was constrained by, the (i) teachers personal beliefs, skills, and strengths, and (ii) the dominant educational structures and processes that exist in the school system. Such findings strengthen existing calls for greater scrutiny of the structural factors that work against innovative and constructive approaches in the classroom. Part of this requires needed historicization of existing educational structures, and the use of such understanding to comparatively address possibilities of change, or continuity, or continuity with change. In so doing, researchers, policy makers, and educators can begin to understand the nature, dynamics, and prospects for reframing or reconfiguring teaching and learning within the school system. This can also allow for some rethinking of the underlining philosophies that guide such practice and the lenses through which educational reform unfolds. Future research therefore should explore questions related to:

1. What are the structures of power that exist within the education system and how do these affect teaching and learning in the classroom?
2. How do such structures of power affect the personal and professional dispositions of teachers?
3. What are the existing methods of classroom instruction and how do these affect the relations of power within the classroom?
4. How, and under what conditions, can CPA address educational inequalities within the school system?
5. How can teachers create and sustain critical support systems that help students to direct their own learning?
6. What are the developmental issues which teachers must address in the process of promoting creativity and criticality in the classroom?
7. How can teachers respond to the structures and cultures that influence their potential to engage in acts of resistance?
8. What kind of support and resources are required for teachers to fully engage in the use and implementation of CPA?
9. What are the implications of CPA for teacher training programs?

If addressed, such problematization can provide useful interrogative starting points for researchers within the field, and deeper insights into the underlying complexities that operate within the school system and the effects of these on how teachers can constructively engage students. Such examinations can also provide empirically driven responses to such systemic constrains.

CONCLUSION

Education as a practice of freedom draws on the need to move beyond the logic of control and conformity to that of participation, democratization and ultimately transformation. Such a dialogical approach, both displaces dominant systems of hierarchy within the classroom, and, encourages active participation and empowerment of all stakeholders involved in the process. Such problematizing of classroom engagement makes visible the ways in which students and teachers are marginalized within the education system, the effects of these on educational outcomes, and the possibilities for addressing these. Irwin (2012, p. 60) insisted that such 'problematization' avoids "fatalism and determinism; aspects of behavior which Freire sees as plaguing the oppressed and their conditions, as well as, their possibilities for overcoming oppression." An essential aspect of this is the need to locate the discursive practices within broader contextual and structural realities of the education system (Freire, 1996; Giroux, 2011).

Where teachers in this study attempted to fuse more traditional approaches to classroom instruction with the critical pedagogical alternative, the findings underscore the salience of their sensitivity to dominant structures and cultures and the multiple challenges that were associated with taking a position of what can be termed here as pedagogical inbetweenity. Thus, while the use of creativity prompted the critical engagement of students at the cognitive and affective levels, the findings point to the general failure of this model to sustain students' interest, to develop self-regulated learning within the classroom, and to transform both the structural and relational aspects of the school system. Such insights also strengthen the need for more pointed questioning of the underlying vision and mission of the education system and the extent to which these frame social and spatial relations within the classroom. At the very least, this requires some rethinking of the educational system, critical consciousness around the social and political contexts of the classroom, a commitment to move towards socially just spaces and places, and the creation of a holistic system to support these. These are critical if teachers are to move away from the chalk and board of the classroom.

ACKNOWLEDGMENT

This research received no specific grant from any funding agency in the public, commercial, or not-for-profit sectors. However, we would like to recognize the valuable contributions of the teachers who participated in this project.

REFERENCES

Abrami, P. C., Bernard, R. M., Borokhowski, E., Wade, A., Surkes, M. A., & Tamim, R. (2008). Instructional interventions affecting critical thinking skills and dispositions: A stage 1 meta-analysis. *Review of Educational Research, 78*(4), 1102–1134. doi:10.3102/0034654308326084

Abrams, L., Pedulla, J., & Madaus, G. F. (2003). Views from the classroom: Teachers' opinions of statewide testing programs. *Theory into Practice, 42*(1), 18–29. doi:10.120715430421tip4201_4

Apple, M. (1979). *Ideology and Curriculum.* NY: Routledge. doi:10.4324/9780203241219

Ayers, W., Michie, G., & Rome, A. (2004). Embers of hope: In search of a meaningful critical pedagogy. *Teacher Education Quarterly, 31,* 123–130.

Baildon, M. C., & Sim, J. B. Y. (2009). Notions of criticality: Singaporean teachers' perspectives of critical thinking in social studies. *Cambridge Journal of Education, 39*(4), 407–422. doi:10.1080/03057640903352481

Bailey, B. (2000). The impact of mandated change on teachers. In N. Bascia & A. Hargreaves (Eds.), *The sharp edge of educational change: Teaching, leading, and the realities of reform* (pp. 112–128). New York: Routledge.

Baldeo, F. N. (2011). *Primary Teacher education in Trinidad and Tobago: A best Practice Framework.* Germany: VDM Verlag Dr. Muller GmbH and Co. KG.

Beghetto, R. A., & Kaufman, J. C. (2007). Towards a broader conception of creativity: A case for "mini-c" creativity. *Psychology of Aesthetics, Creativity, and the Arts, 1*(2), 73–79. doi:10.1037/1931-3896.1.2.73

Beghetto, R. A., & Kaufman, J. C. (2014). Classroom contexts for creativity. *High Ability Studies, 25*(1), 53–69. doi:10.1080/13598139.2014.905247

Bolden, D. S., Harries, T. V., & Newton, D. P. (2010). Pre-service primary teachers' conceptions of creativity in mathematics. *Educational Studies in Mathematics, 73*(2), 143–157. doi:10.100710649-009-9207-z

Brookfield, S. (2005). *The power of critical theory for adult learning and teaching.* San Francisco, CA: Jossey-Bass.

Burnard, P., & White, J. (2008). Creativity and performativity: Counterpoints in British and Australian education. *British Journal of Educational Research, 34*(5), 667–682. doi:10.1080/01411920802224238

Cho, S. (2013). *Critical pedagogy and social change: Critical Analysis on the Language of Possibility.* NY: Routledge.

Choy, S., & Cheah, P. (2009). Teacher perceptions of critical thinking among students and its influence on higher education. *International Journal on Teaching and Learning in Higher Education, 20*(2), 198–206.

Craft, A., Jeffrey, B., & Leibling, M. (Eds.). (2001). *Creativity in education.* London: Continuum.

Cremin, T. (2009). Creative teachers and creative teaching. In A. Wilson (Ed.), *Creativity in Primary Education: Achieving QTS Cross-Curricular Strand* (2nd ed., pp. 36–46). Exeter: Learning Matters.

Duron, R., Limbach, B., & Waugh, W. (2006). Critical thinking framework for any discipline. *International Journal on Teaching and Learning in Higher Education, 17*(2), 160–166.

Earl, L. (2003). *Assessment as Learning: Using classroom assessment to maximize student learning.* Thousand Oaks, CA: Corwin Press, Inc.

Eckhoff, A., & Urbach, J. (2008). Understanding imaginative thinking during early childhood: Sociocultural conceptions of creativity and imaginative thought. *Early Childhood Education Journal, 36*(2), 179–185. doi:10.100710643-008-0261-4

Evans, J. (2014). Problems with Standardized Testing. *Education Today,* 2-6.

Fisher, A. (2007). *Critical thinking: An introduction.* Cambridge, UK: Cambridge University Press.

Fisher, R. (2004). What is creativity? In R. Fisher & M. Williams (Eds.), *Unlocking Creativity: Teaching Across the Curriculum* (pp. 6–20). New York, NY: David Fulton Publishers.

Fleith, D. (2000). Teacher and student perceptions of creativity in the classroom. *Roeper Review, 22*(3), 148–153. doi:10.1080/02783190009554022

Forrester, J. C. (2008). Thinking creatively; Thinking Critically. *Asian Social Science, 4*(5), 100–105.

Freire, P. (1996). *Pedagogy of the oppressed* (2nd ed.). New York: Penguin.

Freire, P. (2000). *Pedagogy of Freedom: Ethics, Democracy, and Civic Courage.* Lanham, MD: Rowman & Littlefield Publishers, Inc.

Freire, P. (2005). *Teachers as cultural workers: Letters to those who dare teach* (D. Macedo, D. Koike, & A. Oliveira, Trans.). Cambridge, MA: Westview Press.

George, J., & Quamina-Aiyejina, L. (2003). *An Analysis of primary education in Trinidad and Tobago. United Kingdom.* Seven Oaks: Department of International Development Publications.

George, J., Worrell, P., & Rampersad, J. (2002). Messages about good teaching: Primary teacher trainees' experiences of the practicum in Trinidad and Tobago. *International Journal of Educational Development, 22*(3-4), 291–304. doi:10.1016/S0738-0593(01)00067-0

Gilligan, A. L. (1999). Education towards a feminist imagination. In B. Connolly & A. B. Ryan (Eds.), *Women and Education in Ireland* (Vol. 1, pp. 201–213). Maynooth: MACE.

Giroux, H. (2004a). *Teachers as intellectuals: Towards a critical pedagogy of learning.* South Hadley, MA: Bergin and Garvey.

Giroux, H. A. (2004b). Critical pedagogy and postmodern/modern divide: Towards pedagogy of democratization. *Teacher Education Quarterly, 31*(1), 31–47.

Giroux, H. A. (2011). *On critical pedagogy.* London: The Continuum International Publishing Group.

Goel, M., & Aggarwal, P. (2012). A comparative study of self-confidence of single child and child with sibling. *The International Journal of Social Sciences (Islamabad), 2*(3), 89–98.

Harman, R., & McClure, G. (2011). All the school's a stage: Critical performative pedagogy in urban teacher education. *Equity & Excellence in Education, 44*(3), 379–402. doi:10.1080/10665684.2011.589278

Hatch, J. (2002). Accountability shovedown: Resisting the standards movement in early childhood education. *Phi Delta Kappan, 83*(6), 457–463. doi:10.1177/003172170208300611

Hawker, L. (2000). From teacher dependence to learner independence: case study from the Dubai Women's College. *Paper presented at The Technological Education and National Development Conference (TEND)*, Abu Dhabi, United Arab Emirates.

Hennessey, B. A., & Amabile, T. M. (2010). Creativity. *Annual Review of Psychology, 61*(1), 569–598. doi:10.1146/annurev.psych.093008.100416 PMID:19575609

Hove, G. (2011). *Developing critical thinking skills in the high school classroom* [Master's Research Paper]. University of Wisconsin, WI.

Irwin, J. (2012). *Paulo Freire's philosophy of education: Origins, developments, impacts and legacies.* London: Bloomsbury Publishing.

Jeffery, B. (2006). Creative teaching and learning: Towards a common discourse and practice. *Cambridge Journal of Education, 36*(3), 394–114.

Jeffries, P. R. (2005). A framework for designing, implementing, and evaluating simulations used as teaching strategies in nursing. *Nursing Education Perspectives, 26*(2), 96–103. PMID:15921126

Kaufman, J. C., & Beghetto, R. A. (2009). Beyond big and little: The four c model of creativity. *Review of General Psychology, 13*(1), 1–12. doi:10.1037/a0013688

Kazemi, E. (1998). Discourse that promotes conceptual understanding. *Teaching Children Mathematics, 4*(7), 410–414.

Kennedy, M. (2005). *Inside teaching: How classroom life undermines reform.* Cambridge, MA: Harvard University Press. doi:10.4159/9780674039513

Lewin, K. M., & Stuart, J. M. (2003). Insights into the policy and practice of teacher education in low-income countries: The Multi-Site Teacher Education Research Project. *British Educational Research Journal, 29*(5), 691–707. doi:10.1080/0141192032000133703

Longo, C. (2010). Fostering creativity or teaching to the Test? Implications of state testing on the delivery of science instruction. *The Clearing House: A Journal of Educational Strategies, Issues and Ideas, 83*(2), 54–57. doi:10.1080/00098650903505399

Marzano, R. (2007). *The art and science of teaching.* Alexandria, VA: Association for Supervision and Curriculum Development.

Marzano, R., Pickering, D., & Pollock, J. (2001). *Classroom instruction that works: Research based strategies for increasing student achievement.* Upper Saddle River, NJ: Pearson.

Mayfield, M. (1997). *Thinking for yourself: Developing critical thinking skills through reading and writing.* Belmont, CA: Wadsworth Publishing Co.

McCollister, K., & Sayler, M. F. (2010). Lift the ceiling: Increase in rigor with critical thinking skills. *Gifted Child Today*, *31*(1), 41–47. doi:10.1177/107621751003300110

McLaren, P. (1998). *Life in schools: An introduction to critical pedagogy in the foundations of education* (3rd ed.). New York: Longman.

McLaren, P. (2009). Critical pedagogy: A look at the major concepts. In A. Darder, M. P. Baltodano, & R. D. Torres (Eds.), *The critical pedagogy reader* (2nd ed., pp. 61–83). New York, NY: Routledge.

McLaren, P., & Da Silva, T. (1993). Decentering pedagogy: Critical literacy, resistance and the resistance and politics of memory. In P. McLaren & P. Leonarded (Eds.), *Paulo Freire: A Critical Encounter* (pp. 47–89). New York: Routledge. doi:10.4324/9780203420263_chapter_4

McManus, D. A. (2001). The two paradigms of education and the peer review of teaching. *Journal of Geoscience Education*, *49*(5), 423–434. doi:10.5408/1089-9995-49.5.423

McNeil, L. (2000). *Contradictions of school reform: Educational costs of standardized testing*. New York: Routledge.

Meyers, C. (1986). *Teaching students to think critically*. San Francisco, CA: Josey-Bass.

Mills, J. (1998). Better teaching through provocation. *College Teaching*, *46*(1), 21–25. doi:10.1080/87567559809596228

Moore, B., & Stanley, T. (2010). *Critical thinking and formative assessments: Increasing rigor in your classroom*. Larchmont, NY: Eye on Education Inc.

Paul, R. (2006). *Critical thinking: How to prepare students for a rapidly changing world*. CA: Foundations for Critical Thinking Press.

Paul, R., Binker, A. J. A., Jensen, K., & Kreklau, H. (1990). *Critical thinking handbook: 4th – 6th grades. A guide for Remodeling Lesson Plans in Language Arts, Social Studies and Science*. CA: Foundation for Critical Thinking.

Portelli, J. P. (1994). The challenge of teaching for critical thinking. *McGill Journal of Education*, *29*(2), 137–152.

Possin, K. (2008). A field guide to critical-thinking assessment. *Teaching Philosophy*, *31*(3), 221–228. doi:10.5840/teachphil200831324

Powers, K. (2011). Going mental: How music education can help develop critical thinking. *Teaching Music*, *18*(6), 40–45.

Reid, M., Burn, A., & Parker, D. (2002). *Evaluation report of the becta digital video pilot project. British Film Industry (bfi)*.

Rinkevich, J. L. (2011). Creative teaching: Why it matters and where to begin. *The Clearing House: A Journal of Educational Strategies, Issues and Ideas*, *89*(5), 219–223.

Robinson, K. (2006). Do school kills creativity? [Video file]. *TED Talk*. Retrieved from http:www.ted. com/talks/ken_robinson_says_schools_kill_creativity.html

Sarsani, M. (2008). Do high and low creative children differ in their cognition and motivation? *Creativity Research Journal, 20*(2), 155–170. doi:10.1080/10400410802059861

Scales, P. (2013). *Teaching in the lifelong learning sector*. Maidenhead: Open University Press.

Schachter, J., Thum, Y. M., & Zifkin, D. (2006). How much does creative teaching enhance elementary school students' achievement? *The Journal of Creative Behavior, 40*(1), 47–72. doi:10.1002/j.2162-6057.2006. tb01266.x

Scott, C. L. (1999). Teachers' bias towards creative children. *Creativity Research Journal, 12*(4), 321–328. doi:10.120715326934crj1204_10

Simonton, D. K. (2012). Taking the US patent office criteria seriously: A quantitative three-criterion creativity definition and its implications. *Creativity Research Journal, 24*(2-3), 97-106.

Skaggs, K. (2004). Childhood and adolescence. In J. L. Kincheloe & D. Weil (Eds.), *Critical thinking and learning: An encyclopedia for parents and teachers* (pp. 149–154). Westport, CT: Greenwood Press.

Snyder, L., & Snyder, M. J. (2008). Teaching critical thinking and problem solving skills. *Delta Pi Epsilon Journal, 50*(2), 90–99.

Stapleton, P. (2011). A survey of attitudes towards critical thinking among Hong Kong secondary school teachers: Implications for policy change. *Thinking Skills and Creativity, 6*(1), 14–23. doi:10.1016/j. tsc.2010.11.002

Sternberg, R. J., Grigorenko, E. L., & Singer, J. L. (Eds.). (2004). *Creativity: From potential to realization*. Washington, DC: American Psychological Association. doi:10.1037/10692-000

Sternberg, R. J., & Williams, W. M. (2002). *Educational psychology*. Boston, MA: Allyn and Bacon.

Steward, L., & Thomas, E. (Eds.). (1997). *Caribbean issues and development. Teacher education in the Commonwealth series*. London: Commonwealth Secretariat.

Ticusan, M., & Elena, H. (2015). Critical thinking in development of creativity. *Paper presented at International Conference of Scientific Paper AFASES*, Brasov, Romania.

Turner, S. (2013). Teachers' and pupils' perceptions of creativity across different key stages. *Research in Education, 89*(1), 23–40. doi:10.7227/RIE.89.1.3

United Nations Educational, Scientific, and Cultural Organization [UNESCO]. (2007). *Accountability in Education: Meeting our Commitments. Global Education Monitoring Report*. Paris: UNESCO.

Vasudevan, H. (2013). The influence of teacher creativity, attitude and commitment and students' proficiency of the English Language. *Journal of Research and Methods in Education, 1*(2), 12–19.

Wiggins, G., & McTighe, J. (2005). *Understanding by design*. Alexandria, VA: Association for Supervision and Curriculum Development.

Woods, P. (2002). Teaching and learning in the new millennium. In C. Day & C. Sugrue (Eds.), Developing Teaching and Teachers: International Research Perspectives (pp. 73-91). London: Falmer.

Zachary, S. (2011). *The challenge: Challenging students to think critically* [Master's Research Paper]. University of Wisconsin, WI.

ADDITIONAL READING

Apple, W. M. (2013). *Can education change society?* NY: Routledge.

Birgili, B. (2015). Creative and critical thinking skills in problem-based learning environments. *Journal of Gifted Education and Creativity*, *2*(2), 71–80. doi:10.18200/JGEDC.2015214253

Fischer, B., & Golden, J. (2018). Modelling and fostering creativity: Two post-secondary EAL teachers' journey. *Canadian Journal of Education*, *41*(1), 99–123.

Koh, A. (2002). Towards a critical pedagogy: Creating 'thinking schools' in Singapore. *Journal of Curriculum Studies*, *34*(3), 255–264. doi:10.1080/00220270110092608

Martin, D. S., Craft, A. R., & Tillema, H. H. (2002). Developing critical and creative thinking strategies in primary school pupils: An intercultural study of teachers' learning. *Journal of In-service Education*, *28*(1), 115–134. doi:10.1080/13674580200200198

Mayo, P. (2013). *Echoes from Freire for a critically engaged pedagogy*. London, UK: Bloomsbury.

Peterson, J. F., Frankham, N., McWhinnie, L., & Forsyth, G. (2015). Leading creative practice pedagogy futures. *Art. Design and Communication in Higher Education*, *14*(1), 71–86. doi:10.1386/adch.14.1.71_1

Rahaela, V. (2011). The importance of enhancing critical thinking skill of pre-service teachers. *Theory into Practice*, *9*(1), 97–106.

Tanggaard, L. (2011). Stories about creative teaching and productive learning. *European Journal of Teacher Education*, *34*(2), 219–232. doi:10.1080/02619768.2011.558078

Turner, S. (2013). Teachers' and pupils' perceptions of creativity across different key stages. *Research in Education*, *89*(1), 23–40. doi:10.7227/RIE.89.1.3

KEY TERMS AND DEFINITIONS

Chalk and Board: This typically refers to the use of a traditional, directed, or didactic teaching and learning method where the teacher who remains at the center of that process delivers a lesson through the use of the chalk and board. These are typically employed to highlight information about pertinent concepts, relevant skills or competencies. In the more contemporary period, this is replaced in some schools with the white board and the marker.

Creativity: In teaching involves the use of innovative, flexible, relevant tools and methods that allow for making connections between existing systems of knowledge, one's own reality, and the possibilities for framing new knowledge frames around these.

Critical Pedagogy: Emerges as both a theory and a praxis. At the core of this is the need for teachers to situate learning and teaching within the social and political contexts of the education system. As such, it therefore presents a method or medium of teaching through which teachers can transform the nature of classroom relations, the capacities of and possibilities for both teachers and students.

Critical Thinking: Is often perceived as an applied skill through which an individual can logically (or through well-reasoned skills), make sense of and analyze information, in the process of solving a given problem or making a decision.

Standardized Curriculum: Speaks to the notion that all schools should be guided by expectations for specific knowledge, skills, and competencies that are deemed suitable to a certain group or developmental level of students. These usually provide standards, methods of instruction and assessment, as well as benchmarks from which the objectives can be measured and evaluated.

Student-Centered Classrooms: Are used to capture learning environment in which there is a co-construction of knowledge (that is, by the teacher and the student). These are driven by philosophical frameworks that place students and teachers within collaborative and non-hierarchical environments.

Teacher-Centered Classroom: Places the teacher at the center of teaching and learning in the classroom. Such classroom environments are often referred to as traditional and didactic.

ENDNOTES

[1]   The two articles included: (i) Jeffery, B. (2006). Creative teaching and learning: towards a common discourse and practice. *Cambridge Journal of Education*, 36 (3) 394-114, and (ii) Longo, C. (2010). Fostering creativity or Teaching to the test? Implications of State Testing on the Delivery of Science Instruction. *The clearing house: A Journal of Educational Strategies, Issues and Ideas*, 83(2), 54-57. An underlying assumption in this case was that the exposure to constructivist learning in their teacher training program provided effective starting points to engage in this project. The articles were used in this case to stimulate and refresh their ideas around the role, methods, and outcomes of creativity within the contemporary classroom.

[2]   Teacher H used both roleplay to open the lesson and the game of jeopardy to close.

Chapter 4
Developing a Critical Stance Through Teacher Candidate Coaching

Kimberly S. Reinhardt
(iD) https://orcid.org/0000-0002-4339-4973
Texas A&M University – Corpus Christi, USA

ABSTRACT

This chapter seeks to illustrate how one field-based professor used her instructional coaching knowledge and applied it in a field-based course to develop reflection and ultimately encourage teacher candidates to challenge themselves and take risks in their clinical placements. It reveals how approaches to teacher candidate coaching differ from traditional instructional coaching, which is focused on student outcomes, and how this coaching encourages teacher candidates to push themselves and think deeply about their emerging practice. Through an analysis of five coaching sessions, the use of effective coaching strategies that foster growth for the candidate were examined. The analysis of coaching as critical pedagogy is important to understand not only how the characteristics of dialogical conversations shape teacher candidates' goal choices, but also to situate the place of skilled feedback in the context of learning to teach.

INTRODUCTION

The journey to become a teacher educator began for me while I was a high school teacher when I was selected by my school district to become an instructional coach. Our school district hired consultants to implement a year-long professional development program to train teacher leaders in the theory behind Instructional Coaching (Fitterer, Harwood, Locklear, & Lapid, 2008) as well as in the use of a specific Teach for Success Classroom Observation Protocol (T4S, 2013) in order to improve rigor and engagement to improve student performance at our school. This professional development afforded me the opportunity to dig deep into pedagogy and practices used in the classroom in order to scaffold the growth of my colleagues through instructional coaching. The scaffolded professional development focused on all aspects of planning, teaching, and assessment through modules focused on student engagement, assessment

DOI: 10.4018/978-1-5225-7829-1.ch004

Copyright © 2019, IGI Global. Copying or distributing in print or electronic forms without written permission of IGI Global is prohibited.

practices, cognitive levels of questioning, instructional approaches, and learning environments (Fitterer, Harwood, Locklear, & Lapid, 2008). As an instructional coach, I was trained to use specific protocols for coaching and observation using an observation instrument to identify instructional attributes within a lesson (T4S, 2013). This experience changed my career. While I was often at odds with taking time from my own students in order to attend professional development and observe and coach my peers, the experience was transformational for me as an educator and inspired me to follow a path into graduate school with the goal of impacting teacher preparation through this type of targeted professional growth.

After graduate school, I was offered a position in a teacher preparation program with a strong regional reputation for preparing high-quality teachers, many of whom remain in the area to support the local school districts. The program offers extensive field-based experiences for the teacher candidates during their preparation, and my position embedded me, with my teacher candidates, in a local area partner school. In the semester prior to clinical teaching, the teacher candidates are placed in a classroom two days a week, and during that time I spanned the boundary from university to school sites to work alongside the teacher candidates to develop their pedagogical practices through seminar, lesson planning, observation, and coaching using an Instructional Coaching Protocol developed specifically to foster growth in this field placement (Tejeda-Delgado & Johnson, 2018). Teacher candidates are expected to use the experiences they have during this time, through both observation and teaching, to connect teaching, assessment and technology to their emerging practice. I served as a facilitator for their seminar, but more importantly, I spent time in their classroom observing their teaching and strengthening their impact with targeted, pedagogical goal setting connected to practice during one to one instructional coaching sessions. With instructional coaching as a passion that drives me as a teacher educator, this chapter explores how instructional coaching with teacher candidates fosters their pedagogical growth and challenges them to think critically about their instructional practices during their initial clinical experience.

BACKGROUND

Instructional coaching, for classroom teachers, is an embedded form of professional development that is focused on individual teaching and learning needs with the goal of improving student outcomes (Fitterer, Harwood, Locklear, & Lapid, 2008; Heineke, 2013; Knight, 2009; Reddy, Dudek, & Lekwa, 2017). Instructional coaching is defined as a partnering to strengthen teaching through personalized, purposeful feedback that incorporates research-based strategies aimed at improving practice (Fitterer, Harwood, Locklear, & Lapid, 2008; Knight, 2009; Sharpin, Garth, & Kehrwald, 2017). Through the integration of evidence-based practices that focus on content planning, formative assessment, specific instructional practices, and building community in the classroom, coaches working with classroom teachers collaborate toward meeting the goals of the classroom teacher (Knight, 2009; Van Nieuwerburgh, 2017). Models of instructional coaching cycles share key components including feedback on instruction, dialectical conversations, and goal setting (Artman-Meeker, 2015; Bean, Draper, Hall, Vandermolen, & Zigmond, 2010; Conner, 2017; Costa & Gramston, 2002; Crawford, Zucker, Van Horne, & Landry, 2017; Desimone & Pak, 2016; Drake, 2016; Gardiner & Weisling, 2016; Sharplin, Kherwald & Garth, 2017; Tejeda-Delgado & Johnson, 2018). Instructional coaching is often focused on classroom teachers, and rooted in school improvement efforts, and instructional coaches draw upon their own classroom experience and leadership to deliver instructional coaching to their peers.

Instructional coaching draws on a set of roles for the coach such as data provider, mentor, curriculum and instructional specialist, classroom supporter, learning facilitator, school leader and catalyst for change and learning (Killion, 2009). These roles overlap with a set of principles, including equality, choice, voice, dialogue, reflection, praxis, and reciprocity, which guide the collaborative partnership that instructional coaching requires (Knight, 2009). A framework developed by Knight (2009) for assessing the impact of instructional coaching addresses "The Big Four" (p. 34). The Big Four framework includes classroom management, content, instruction, and formative assessment. Knight (2009) posits that throughout the instructional coaching conversation, skillful instructional coaches construct conversations about the positive aspects of the observed lesson enacting an authentic voice. The conversation focuses the teacher candidate on metacognitive examination of their practice while examining classroom management, content knowledge, instructional practices, and formative assessment. Further, Ellison and Hayes (2009) claim that instructional coaching "clarifies a way of working with intentionality" (p. 73) by identifying these key aspects of teaching and refining the strategies involved in the development of the cognitive capacity. When teacher candidates have an awareness of impact of their practice, they are better able to take responsibility for instructional choices and outcomes (Van Nieuwerburgh, 2017) and Kretlow and Bartholomew (2010) found that instructional coaching facilitates "accurate and sustained implementation of new teaching practices" (p. 280).

Theoretically, the study draws from the situated conception of mentoring (Tang, 2012; Putnam and Borko, 2000). Teacher education pedagogies are situated within the context of schooling; therefore, the knowledge base from which instructional coaches working with teacher candidates draw is based in the practice of the teacher candidates. Using the teacher candidates' experience from a generative approach allows space for new knowledge to emerge with the opportunity to apply it directly to practice.

Within this framework, this chapter addresses the question:

How does the use of an Instructional Coaching Protocol in a field-based experience transform the praxis to practice gap?

Through an analysis of five instructional coaching sessions related to the initial teaching experiences of a teacher candidate during their first clinical semester, this chapter examines how effective instructional coaching strategies foster growth for the candidate (Reddy, et al., 2017; Soslau, 2015). This analysis is important to understand how the characteristics of dialogical conversations shape teacher candidate's goal choices, but also to situate the place of skilled feedback in the context of learning to teach (Adams, Ross, Burns, & Gibbs, 2015; Burke, 2017; Grossman, Compton, Igra, Ronfeldt, Shahan, & Williamson, 2009; Heineke, 2013; Soslau, 2015).

Instructional Coaching Protocol in Teacher Preparation

Accounts of instructional coaching in teacher preparation are less common, although descriptions of pre- and post-teaching conferences often include feedback on instruction and identification of goals for future lesson planning and delivery. Burke (2017) studied 14 teacher candidates that participated in instructional coaching sessions during their clinical placements and found that instructional coaching sessions are valuable in helping teacher candidates focus on their teaching episodes in ways that they may not realize on their own. There are various accounts of teacher educators using instructional coaching protocols with teacher candidates including the Instructional Coaching Protocol used in this teacher preparation program, which was developed to reflect the key components of instructional coaching (Tejeda-Delgado & Johnson, 2018). The protocol, which is used by the teacher education faculty who teach the field-based experience seminar course, was developed in 2009 to ensure consistent feedback to improve the teacher candidates' practice (Sharplin, Kehrwald, & Garth, 2017; Tejeda-Delgado & Johnson, 2018). Throughout the field-based semester, the teacher candidates develop and teach five lessons. Teaching and learning outcomes are the focus of the embedded seminar course that the teacher candidates attend during this clinical semester. The Instructional Coaching Protocol is used before each lesson to set goals, then revisited after each lesson to discuss the instructional planning process and to assess if the goals were met during the lesson delivery. Within the instructional coaching session, the field-based faculty member and the teacher candidate discuss the instructional choices made during the planning process, the goals met during teaching with evidence of positive student outcomes, and the candidates' developmental observations based on teaching. Using this data, the teacher candidates set goals for their next lesson (Van Nieuwerburgh, 2017). This reflective cycle creates a space for the teacher candidates to critically explore their own assumptions about teaching and direct their own growth in their teaching practice through goal setting and instructional planning (Van Nieuwerburgh, 2017). The use of the Instructional Coaching Protocol provides structure for the field-based faculty member to link teaching strategies and learning outcomes from the field-based seminar course directly to the teacher candidate's practice. However, to promote teacher candidate learning, it is important to allow the candidate to not only reflect on, but also talk about their teaching (Heineke, 2013). The lessons are delivered starting in the fifth week of the semester and the instructional coaching, planning, teaching cycle is designed to allow sufficient time to plan for each lesson and for the teacher candidates to reflect upon their increased knowledge and experience as they gradually move from observation to actively teaching in their clinical placements.

Instructional Coaching Conversations in Clinical Practice

Clinical practice is a key learning experience for teacher candidates (AACTE, 2018). Instructional coaching between a field-based university professor and teacher candidates offers an opportunity to strengthen the theory and practice connection while developing a sense of pedagogical awareness for the teacher candidate (Van Nieuwerburgh, 2017). Instructional coaching serves to develop reflective and metacognitive thinking in candidates to improve their efficacy. Through instructional coaching conversations, instructional coaching help candidates "notice the unnoticed" (Burke, 2017) which in turn allows the teacher candidates to ground their clinical practice in positive aspects of their growth. Instructional coaching conversations can serve to move teacher candidates beyond the practical aspects of learning to teach toward strategies based in their real experience of teaching, thus pushing teacher candidates to think deeply and critically about their emerging practice (Reinhardt, 2017).

In traditional K-12 instructional coaching, there is typically no evaluative element related to the teacher-coach relationship (Costa & Garmston, 2002; Joyce & Showers, 1982). Instructional coaches observe teaching, develop conversations focused on the positive aspects of practice, and offer concrete instructional strategies for the teacher to consider. Through the development of trust and interpersonal relationships, instructional coaches work in partnership with teachers in other content areas to improve teaching, with the goal to improve overall student outcomes (Knight, 2009). The instructional strategies offered by instructional coaches are not part of the teacher's annual evaluation, but rather a collaborative effort to grow the teaching capacity as a team (Costa & Garmston, 2002).

In contrast, as a university professor, my instructional coaching of teacher candidates serves to have an impact on teaching practice by leveraging high impact practices (Grossman, et al., 2009). However, my positionality as the teacher candidates' course instructor required a close examination of my own instructional coaching voice to ensure that I developed a relationship that was not prescriptive, but instead descriptive and collaborative (Adams, et al., 2015; Knight, 2009) and that my questioning strategies and feedback were based in the needs of the teacher candidates (Heineke, 2013), while knowing that their success or failure in this clinical semester was my responsibility.

Instructional coaching with my teacher candidates required understanding who they were and having a keen awareness of their individual context (Heineke, 2013). Each teacher candidates were at a different place in their development, and I recognized the need to meet them "where they are" (Horton, Freire, Bell, & Gaventa, 1990) in order to co-discover where they needed to go. Therefore, my ability to push them required me to be responsive to their emotional needs and also consider the type of classroom in which they were placed.

Based on the existing literature on instructional coaching, there is a gap regarding how instructional coaching is effective in the growth of teacher candidates as they develop their practice, and within this development the importance of effective instructional coaching in bridging the theory and practice gap. This is significant considering the impact of clinical experiences on learning to teach (AACTE, 2018).

METHODS

This exploratory qualitative study examined the one-to-one instructional coaching sessions between a teacher candidate and a field-based teacher educator. The instructional coaching was part of the regular course expectations and was facilitated by the use of the Instructional Coaching Protocol (Tejeda-Delgado & Johnson, 2018). The focus of this study was intended to reveal the ways in which teacher candidate instructional coaching pushed the candidate to critically examine her emerging practice; therefore, a complete analysis of the use of instructional coaching across a semester was appropriate.

Participants and Context of Study

The participant for this study was enrolled in the field-base course titled "Planning, Teaching, Assessment and Technology," and therefore was a convenience sample. The teacher candidates enrolled in this teacher preparation program consent to and regularly participate in research projects with faculty members. During this semester there were 14 students in the course; the course was embedded in a junior high school all day on Tuesday and Thursday, and the teacher candidates were preparing for various content areas. The junior high houses seventh and eighth graders and has just over 850 students. This chapter focuses on five instructional coaching sessions with one teacher candidate that occurred over a 15-week academic semester. This candidate was a female student studying to become certified in 4-8 mathematics.

The course in which the participant was enrolled was considered a field-based experience because it included not only field observation, but also initial teaching episodes. These experiences are designed to prepare the teacher candidates for their clinical teaching semester when they will be teaching five days a week. The course is not content specific, and each section of the course typically includes teacher candidates from across secondary disciplines, including science, math, history, English language arts, special education, physical education, music, and theater.

Data Sources

As the field-based faculty member teaching this course, I was involved in all aspects of learning to teach with the teacher candidates, including lesson planning and delivery, lesson observation, and instruction in the seminar course focused on instructional methods. For this research, I focused specifically on the five instructional coaching sessions related to the candidate's lesson delivery, which included recorded audio and copies of the Instructional Coaching Protocol (Tejeda-Delgado & Johnson, 2018). Each observed lesson was for one class period, which was 50 minutes. The instructional coaching cycle was iterative in that each session served as both a post- and pre-conference. Each instructional coaching session lasted about 30 minutes and was audio recorded. The recordings were provided to the teacher candidate for their own self-reflection and each was transcribed for analysis. To triangulate the findings, the teacher candidate's final reflection on instructional coaching and teaching was analyzed to provide her perspective on the impact of instructional coaching sessions.

Analysis

After transcription of the audio from the instructional coaching sessions, the data was loaded into Dedoose for coding (Dedoose Version 8.0.35., 2018). The initial analysis was focused only on codes that were derived from the Instructional Coaching Protocol (Tejeda-Delgado & Johnson, 2018), which concentrated on four areas a) teacher candidate goals b) specific instructional choices to incorporate the goals c) goals met during teaching episode with evidence of positive student outcomes d) developmental observations based on teaching. Subcodes for the other reflective responses to the protocol framework were also added: praise, questions, techniques. These subcodes were applied to identify areas when I praised the participant's lesson delivery, questions were posed in response to areas the participant sought to improve, and techniques were coded when I offered an instructional strategy for the teacher candidate to consider for their next lesson. In a second pass of coding, the data was analyzed based on the framework set forth by Knight (2009), which identified four areas for effective instructional coaching, which are classroom management, content, instruction, and formative assessment. Data was also chunked by a code for the opening and closing of each instructional coaching session.

FINDINGS

To begin my analysis, I sought to understand how Knight's (2009) "The Big Four" framework overlaid the excerpts coded based on the Instructional Coaching Protocol (Tejeda-Delgado & Johnson, 2018). The framework provided a cross section of the aspects of the instructional coaching sessions based on the actual content in the instructional coaching conversations. In other words, I was able to identify how frequently the instructional coaching addressed "The Big Four" while following the Instructional Coaching Protocol adapted in this teacher preparation program.

Instructional Coaching for The Big Four

Each instructional coaching conversation was both a reflection of the Instructional Coaching Protocol (Tejeda-Delgado & Johnson, 2018) and the themes that occurred in relation to The Big Four framework (Knight, 2009). Figure 1 represents this data across all instructional coaching sessions.

The data show that instructional coaching conversations with the teacher candidate focused on instruction twice as often as it did classroom management, although classroom management is of great concern for all new teachers. When drilling down into the coded excerpts related to these areas, the majority of the excerpts for instruction were sub-coded as goal setting, which occurred at the end of each instructional coaching session and goals reviewed at the beginning of each instructional coaching session. Goal setting with the teacher candidate was a generative process that drew upon her own classroom experience. Using both our seminar content and my own observations of her learning, my instructional coaching sessions were intended to guide the teacher candidate toward personalized goals based on her own needs in their practice. Erica, the teacher candidate in this study, was very interested in ensuring equity in her classroom, and set a goal of grouping her students intentionally to understand how certain combinations of students resulted in different outcomes. I offered her encouragement that included intentionality and accountability:

Grouping with purpose, so thinking about what we already said here, I don't feel like you quite got a chance to do that, so thinking about grouping for diversity ... I want you to plan really intentionally, choose how you want to do it, but try to plan some kind of really intentional grouping. I want you to report back on it, so report back to me.

Figure 1. The topics of the instructional coaching conversation related to Knight's (2009) "Big 4" framework

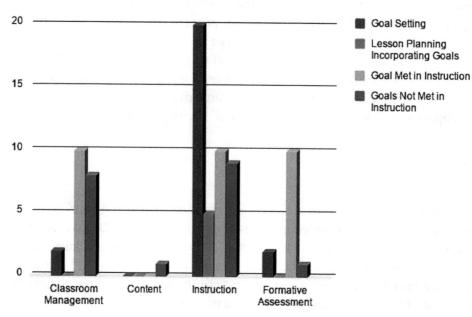

Ultimately throughout the semester, I urged Erica to return to this goal from different angles using questioning strategies and differentiation to understand the diverse learning needs of her students.

The other significant co-occurrence was with classroom management. The instructional coaching conversation in this area focused mainly on the goals that Erica met or did not met during her instruction. Across the sessions, the instructional coaching conversation about positive management outcomes occurred about 20% more often, although this success was reflected after lessons four and five, while unmet goals related to classroom management were persistent for Erica in each lesson. Early on, when Erica was speaking about her management, I gave notice to the situations she described, such as labeling a situation she described during a lesson in which students were slightly off task as "approximating." Additionally, I was able to help Erica understand the punitive nature of some instructional techniques as illustrated in this exchange:

Erica: *I didn't want to call them out and be like, you know like call on them, obviously no one wants to be called on when they don't know what's going on.*
Author: *Yeah, and that's punishment behavior.*
Erica: *Yeah.*
Author: *That's a punishment teacher behavior, to call on students you know that aren't paying attention.*

This "gotcha" method of classroom management is a topic of discussion in seminar, and I was able to draw it into Erica's practice and reinforce in the instructional coaching sessions after each lesson.

While the overall occurrences of instruction and classroom management totaled the greatest number of coded excerpts, formative assessment was equal in the occurrences of goals being met during instruction. From the first lesson, our instructional coaching sessions focused on including the key formative assessment. When Erica told me that she used journals to have her students analyze similarities in mathematical problems, I prompted by asking her, "What did you learn from their journals?". To encourage Erica to think about formative assessment, I would prompt her to explain the evidence she had to prove her students grasped the objective of the lesson. Pushing the teacher candidate in this way opened her understanding of the purpose of assessment. Throughout the semester, Erica implemented exit slips, the use of thumbs up or down, and smartboard quizzes, and was able to articulate how she met her objective for her lessons. Across the interviews, there was no significant attention given to content as an area for instructional coaching with this teacher candidate. The Planning, Teaching, Assessment, and Technology course itself does not lend to this type of content instructional coaching. While all of the teacher candidates enrolled in the course were seeking secondary certification, their content area preparation occurred before they entered their clinical semesters and this field-based course.

When using the Knight's (2009) "The Big Four" framework, instructional coaching of teacher candidates using the Instructional Coaching Protocol (Tejeda-Delgado & Johnson, 2018) along with probing questions allowed me to personalize my instructional coaching to the teacher candidate's specific learning needs and reveal intent and practice issues related to pedagogical practice. While the goals set by the teacher candidate were mostly related to instruction, her successes while teaching reflected her ability to recognize classroom management and formative assessment as integral areas for growth, which opened the opportunity for me to coach her in these areas.

Instructional Coaching Across Planning and Teaching

Each instructional coaching session was connected to one of the five lessons that the teacher candidate taught throughout a 15-week semester. A goal of this study was to see the impact of these instructional coaching sessions as they scaffolded the teacher candidates' thinking during praxis. While goals were set for each lesson, Erica did not always meet the goals that she set, and more often, needed to be coached toward noticing the ways in which her ideas of teaching successes were not always transparent in the delivery of her actual lesson. As a coach, I worked to bring clarity to Erica's experience in the way that offered her space for critical reflection.

To understand the foci of my instructional coaching conversation, Figure 2 displays the percentage within each instructional coaching session that addresses the specific part of the protocol. This included the opening and closing of each instructional coaching session, the goals set by the teacher candidate for teaching, how the teacher candidate planned instruction to meet those goals, and the result of planning in relation to goals met or not met during instruction. Across the five instructional coaching sessions, which were cyclical and generative, there is a positive correlation between articulating and setting goals with Erica and positive outcomes for her instruction. In particular, during her second instructional coaching session, we spent about half of the time discussing goals. Erica had already noticed the impact of collaboration in her classroom and identified differentiation as a goal she sought to incorporate. Erica noted:

You know it takes care of the working together, you know designing groups, scaffolding... walking around and observing who understands. So it's like working in your assessment and using all of those tools to orchestrate what you're gonna do with the rest of your class period.

Based on this conversation, Erica planned with intentionality to design her groups in a way that would "set them up for success" for her next lesson. In setting her goals, I encouraged her to plan her groups,

Figure 2. Goal setting and enactment across instructional coaching sessions

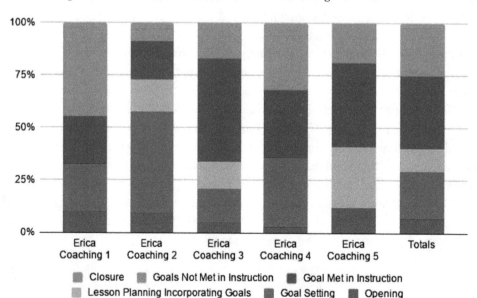

and to "orchestrate" the classroom activities in a way that would allow her to observe her students and assess their mastery of the lesson objective. In our conversation, I started by asking, "Tell me more about it. We already talked about it a little, so setting them up for success and questioning… what you were thinking and what did it look like in your classroom?" Erica described her use of a "Think-Pair-Share" to ensure her students were engaged in her lesson. This allowed her to observe, question, and assess her students while they were working.

Keeping your students engaged and making sure that learning is mandatory for all students, doesn't necessarily mean they have to raise their hand and they have to answer to the whole class. It sounds like you recognized that with your student Amanda and you still knew where she was, you still knew she did share her knowledge with you in a way that helped you assess that without having to put her in a position that was maybe not what, you know, the best way for her to do that. I think you did a good job, it sounds like it.

To push her a little further in her instruction, I used her success in engaging students with one another and her focus on small group questioning to challenge her to engage in multiple modalities and offered rationale for the use of small groups as a way to ensure all students arrived at the mastery of the concept. I shared

If they don't write something, they sometimes talk things out differently than what they thought them out as. That helps it be real intentional and then, of course you know the sharing is picking and you know, then having the students having already compared, pretty much they have the answer. You can pick any student you wanted to.

While this seemingly simple step of writing as well as speaking is a best practice, during this critical time of learning to teach, the nuances of the delivery of teaching can sometimes be blurred by the teacher candidate's anticipation of initial teaching experiences. By situating the growth toward stronger practice within the immediate success of Erica's lesson, she was able to better envision how she might adapt her teaching for subsequent lessons.

Through the use of the Instructional Coaching Protocol, the foci of my conversations about planning and teaching were driven by the personal needs of my teacher candidate and were goal driven. Each goal was evidenced by the successes and failures in the teaching episodes, and if necessary revisited, but always extended to broaden the teacher candidate's capacity for planning and teaching.

The Impact of the Instructional Coaching Conversation

One of the unique aspects of instructional coaching with the protocol used in this teacher preparation program was the focus on goal setting. While findings suggest that instructional coaching sessions in which the conversation was focused on goal setting resulted in lessons with positive outcomes, it was important to also consider how this teacher candidate received this iterative process. At the end of the semester, the teacher candidate composed a final reflection in which she was asked to evaluate her personal growth through her initial teaching episodes. Erica commented that the goal setting, a key component during the instructional coaching sessions, was integral in her growth.

My focus changed as I set goals and incorporated them into my lesson plan because I know had a starting point and advice from my clinical teacher and my professor. I know had a specific focus every lesson about how to improve my teaching…I discussed differentiation in most coaching sessions because it is something I want to incorporate into my future classroom to meet every students' learning needs. When I am able to meet every students' needs, the relationship I have with them will improve.

The next experience for the teacher candidate was to begin her clinical teaching semester. In a culminating reflection, she was asked to set a final goal based on her initial teaching experiences and the goals from this field-based semester. Erica reflected:

What impacted this growth was the field based class and the coaching sessions where I learned more effective ways to ask questions. I started writing personal scripts that included these questions and, my last lesson I printed out the questions and displayed some of the board. My goals for student teaching are to differentiate instruction and know where my students are at in the learning process. My goal as a teacher is to meet my students' needs. I will continue to develop my formative assessment strategies and how to connect mathematics content to the students' known world to increase engagement in learning.

Through instructional coaching, Erica critically recognized her areas for future growth and was able to articulate how and why she intended to follow these goals. Each of the strategies she identified were part of her ongoing growth throughout the semester.

DISCUSSION

The role of instructional coaches is draw upon their own expertise to uncover aspects of the teacher candidates' practice in order to develop an awareness of their actions and to reflect upon how these actions impact the classroom learning and student interaction. In reflecting upon instructional coaching conversations, so often I realized the difficulty with which I resisted what Drake (2016) described as "teacher lust" to share everything I know. The use of the Instructional Coaching Protocol (Tejeda-Delgado & Johnson, 2018; Van Nieuwerburgh, 2017) focused the instructional coaching conversation by rooting the conversation in the teacher candidates' situated experience (Knight, 2009; Tang, 2012; Putnam & Borko, 2000). To be an effective coach, I gave up my teaching authority in order to allow a partnership that drives the instructional coaching cycle to allow teacher candidates the opportunity to become self-directed practitioners (Knight 2009; Van Nieuwerburgh, 2017).

A key to impactful instructional coaching was the development of a partnership through the dialectical conversation within a instructional coaching session (Artman-Meeker, et al., 2015; Bean, et al., 2010; Conner, 2017; Costa, 2002; Crawford, 2016; Desimone & Pak, 2016; Drake, 2016; Gardiner, et al., 2016; Sharplin, Kherwald & Garth, 2017; Tejeda-Delgado & Johnson, 2018). These instructional coaching conversations with the teacher candidate led her to greater outcomes than she might not have had without instructional coaching (Burke, 2017). As she reflected, she recognized the impact that instructional coaching had on her instructional choices, and within that realization, she identified ways in which she intended to continue to capitalize on what she learned about her own practice, thus directing her own growth.

The roles enacted and principles guiding a traditional instructional coach reach beyond that of a coach for a teacher candidate (Killion, 2009; Knight 2009). Teacher candidate instructional coaching maintains that I remain a mentor, instructional expert, and learning facilitator. In the initial teaching experiences described in this chapter, I maintained these roles, although it was necessary for me at all times to be aware of my evaluative role and how this may impact the choices the teacher candidate made during our instructional coaching sessions. In reflection, Erica's decision to sustain the goals she set during her field-based semester indicates her value in, and my ability to, appreciate her learning needs beyond the context of this course (Kretlow & Bartholomew, 2010).

A key factor that provided me with the ability to transform my instructional coaching skills from those suited for experienced teachers to those that are valuable for teacher candidates was the use of the Instructional Coaching Protocol. Its generative and iterative design provided a targeted and scaffolded way to personalize teacher candidate learning (Burke, 2017; Tejeda-Delgado & Johnson, 2018). Further, the instructional coaching conversations were constructivist in nature and provided not only valuable room for growth, but also modeled best practices that can be transferred to classroom teaching (Kretlow & Bartholomew, 2010). The data collected in this study was drawn mainly from the transcription and analysis of the audio sessions that are routinely provided for the teacher candidates. The teacher candidate reported that she found that the audio of the instructional coaching session provided her with further insight into her growth.

IMPLICATIONS AND FUTURE RESEARCH

Teacher preparation programs that involve a clinical practice typically employ some sort of conferencing with teacher candidates about their practice. While intense focus has been paid to the structure of clinical practice in teacher education, far less focus has been aimed at the personalized ways in which teacher educators, including not only site-based faculty, but also cooperating teachers and supervisors, scaffold learning experiences for the teacher candidates. One reason for this may be the varied contexts of the clinical experiences as well as the potential instructional coach's experience with these types of dialectical conversations. The use of an Instructional Coaching Protocol that focuses on developing goals that are specific to the candidate's initial teaching experience contextually offers a scaffold for self-directed learning. It provides consistency in feedback, while allowing the candidate to drive the direction. The refinement from conferencing to instructional coaching provides clarity for growth in clinical placements.

CONCLUSION

Finally, the Instructional Coaching Protocol was focused on goal-oriented actions, which lead to high impact practices for this beginning teacher (Burke, 2017; Grossman, et al., 2009; Soslau, 2015). This provided a situated context in which a teacher candidate was able to cross the boundary from theory to practice. In the high-stakes environment of today's contemporary classroom, newly qualified teachers need to have a solid repertoire of practices that move beyond the practical aspects of learning to teach (Reinhardt, 2017). While the teacher candidate in this study may not have mastered the skills of differentiation or ensuring equitable practices that result in meeting the needs of all learners, she was able to identify the importance of these practices to her effectiveness in the classroom. The instructional coaching conversations developed for working with teacher candidates focused on developing these skills while rooting the understanding in the teacher candidates' lived experiences in learning to teach.

REFERENCES

T4S. (2013). TeachforSuccess — WestEd. Retrieved from https://www.wested.org/teachforsuccess/

AACTE. (2018). A pivot toward clinical practice, its lexicon, and the renewal of educator preparation. *A Report of the AACTE Clinical Practice Commission.* Retrieved from https://aacte.org/professional-development-and-events/clinical-practice-commission-press-conference

Adams, A., Ross, D., Burns, J., & Gibbs, L. (2015). Talking points: Data displays are an effective way to engage teachers. *Journal of Staff Development, 36*(1), 24–29.

Artman-Meeker, K., Fettig, A., Barton, E. E., Penney, A., & Zeng, S. (2015). Applying an evidence-based framework to the early childhood coaching literature. *Topics in Early Childhood Special Education, 35*(3), 183–196. doi:10.1177/0271121415595550

Bean, R. M., Draper, J. A., Hall, V., Vandermolen, J., & Zigmond, N. (2010). Coaches and instructional coaching in reading first schools: A reality check. *The Elementary School Journal, 111*(1), 87–114. doi:10.1086/653471

Burke, A. J. (2017). Coaching teacher candidates- what does it look like? What does it sound like? *Journal of Curriculum, Teaching. Learning and Leadership in Education, 2*(1), 5–10.

Connor, C. M. (2017). Commentary on the special issue on instructional coaching models: Common elements of effective coaching models. *Theory into Practice, 56*(1), 78–83. doi:10.1080/00405841.2016.1274575

Costa, A. L., & Garmston, R. J. (2002). *Cognitive coaching: A foundation for renaissance schools.* Boston, MA: Christopher-Gordon Publishers.

Crawford, A., Zucker, T., Van Horne, B., & Landry, S. (2016). Integrating professional development content and formative assessment with the coaching process: The Texas school ready model. *Theory into Practice, 56*(1), 56–65. doi:10.1080/00405841.2016.1241945

Dedoose Version 8.0.35. (2018). Web application for managing, analyzing, and presenting qualitative and mixed method research data. Los Angeles, CA: SocioCultural Research Consultants, LLC. Retrieved from www.dedoose.com

Desimone, L. M., & Pak, K. (2016). Instructional coaching as high-quality professional development. *Theory into Practice, 56*(1), 3–12. doi:10.1080/00405841.2016.1241947

Drake, M. R. (2016). Learning to coach in practice-based teacher education: A self-study. *Studying Teacher Education, 12*(3), 244–266. doi:10.1080/17425964.2016.1237871

Ellison, J., & Hayes, C. (2009). *Cognitive coaching. Coaching: Approaches and perspectives* (pp. 70–90). Thousand Oaks, CA: Corwin Press.

Fitterer, H., Harwood, S., Locklear, K., & Lapid, J. (2008). *T4S Teach for success*. WestEd.

Gallucci, C., Van Lare, M. D., Yoon, I. H., & Boatright, B. (2010). Instructional coaching: Building theory about the role and organizational support for professional learning. *American Educational Research Journal*, *47*(4), 919–963. doi:10.3102/0002831210371497

Gardiner, W., & Weisling, N. (2016). Mentoring 'inside' the action of teaching: Induction coaches' perspectives and practices. *Professional Development in Education*, *42*(5), 671–686. doi:10.1080/19415257.2015.1084645

Grossman, P., Compton, C., Igra, D., Ronfeldt, M., Shahan, E., & Williamson, P. (2009). Teaching practice a cross-professional perspective. *Teachers College Record*, *111*(9), 2055–2100.

Heineke, S. F. (2013). Coaching discourse: Supporting teachers' professional learning. *The Elementary School Journal*, *113*(3), 409–433. doi:10.1086/668767

Horton, M., Freire, P., Bell, B., & Gaventa, J. (1990). *We make the road by walking: Conversations on education and social change*. Temple University Press.

Joyce, B., & Showers, B. (1982). The coaching of teaching. *Educational Leadership*, *40*(1), 4.

Killion, J. (2009). Coaches' roles, responsibilities, and reach. *Coaching Approaches and Perspectives*, 7-28.

Knight, J. (2009). Coaching. *Journal of Staff Development*, *30*(1), 18–22.

Knight, J. (2009). *Instructional coaching. In Coaching Approaches and Perspectives* (pp. 29–55). Thousand Oaks, CA: Corwin Press.

Kretlow, A. G., & Bartholomew, C. C. (2010). Using coaching to improve the fidelity of evidence-based practices: A review of studies. *Teacher Education and Special Education*, *33*(4), 279–299. doi:10.1177/0888406410371643

Reddy, L. A., Dudek, C. M., & Lekwa, A. (2017). Classroom strategies coaching model: Integration of formative assessment and instructional coaching. *Theory into Practice*, *56*(1), 46–55. doi:10.1080/00405841.2016.1241944

Reinhardt, K. S. (2017) Beyond the practical aspects of learning to teach: Mentoring teacher candidates toward the diverse needs of students. *TxEP: Texas Educator Preparation*. Retrieved from https://www.csotte.com/assets/txep/2017-txep-reinhardt.pdf

Sharplin, E., Kehrwald, B., Garth, S., Sharplin, E., & Kehrwald, B. (2017). *Real-time coaching and pre-service teacher education*. Singapore: Springer.

Soslau, E. (2015). Development of a post-lesson observation conferencing protocol- Situated in theory, research, and practice. *Teaching and Teacher Education*, *49*, 22–35. doi:10.1016/j.tate.2015.02.012

Tang, S. (2012). Knowledge base of mentoring and mentor preparation. In S. Fletcher & C. A. Mullen (Eds.), *The SAGE Handbook of Mentoring and Coaching in Education* (pp. 478–494). London, UK: SAGE; doi:10.4135/9781446247549.n32

Tejeda-Delgado, C. & Johnson, R.D. (2018). A field experience instructional coaching and mentoring model.

Van Nieuwerburgh, C. (2017). *An introduction to coaching skills: A practical guide.* Los Angeles, CA: Sage.

Wang, J., & Odell, S. J. (2002) Mentored learning to teach according to standards-based reform- A critical review. *Review of Educational Research, 72*(3), 481–546. doi:10.3102_00346543072003481

ADDITIONAL READING

AACTE. (2018). A pivot toward clinical practice, its lexicon, and the renewal of educator preparation. *A Report of the AACTE Clinical Practice Commission.* Retrieved from https://aacte.org/professional-development-and-events/clinical-practice-commission-press-conference

Horton, M., Freire, P., Bell, B., & Gaventa, J. (1990). *We make the road by walking: Conversations on education and social change.* Temple University Press.

Knight, J. (2009). *Instructional coaching. Coaching Approaches and Perspectives* (pp. 29–55). Thousand Oaks, CA: Corwin.

Reinhardt, K. S. (2017) Beyond the practical aspects of learning to teach: Mentoring teacher candidates toward the diverse needs of students. *TxEP: Texas Educator Preparation.* Retrieved from https://www.csotte.com/assets/txep/2017-txep-reinhardt.pdf

Reinhardt, K. S. (2017). Mentoring in clinical placements: Conceptualization of role and its impact on practices. *Action in Teacher Education, 39*(4), 381–396. doi:10.1080/01626620.2017.1347533

Reinhardt, K. S. (2018). Discourse and power: Implementation of a funds of knowledge curriculum. *Power and Education.* doi:10.1177/1757743818787530

KEY TERMS AND DEFINITIONS

Clinical Teaching Semester: The academic term that a clinical teacher spends working full-time with a cooperating teacher.

Dialogical Conversation: A dialogue between the teacher candidate and the instructional coach aimed to encourage the teacher candidate's voice and agency through meaning conversation about pedagogy that results in decision making.

Field-Based Experience: An experience for a teacher candidate within a school site that involves immersion in the work of a classroom teacher. this involves observation, collaboration, and teaching.

Field-Based Semester: The academic term that a teacher candidate spends embedded two days a week in a school site.

Praxis: The process of enacting pedagogy that is reflective of research-based practice.

School-University Partnerships: A collaboration between a school district or school site with a teacher preparation program.

Teacher Candidates: Students enrolled in a teacher preparation program that leads to initial teacher certification.

Teacher Preparation Program: Academic program designed to prepare education majors for initial teacher certification.

Teaching Episode: The lessons taught by the teacher candidates throughout the field-based experience.

Chapter 5
The Role of Student Feedback in Building Reflexive Teachers

Kerri Pilling Burchill
Southern Illinois Healthcare, USA

David Anderson
Eastern Michigan University, USA

ABSTRACT

The contemporary demands of the education environment today require that teachers refine their reflective thinking skills and shift towards the deeper critical thinking skills inherent in reflexive thinking. Reflexivity is a deeper level of critical thinking that assumes a degree of metacognition and "knowing-in-action" (Schon, 1983, p. 50). Metacognition is a critical tool in helping individuals become more aware of their deeply seeded biases and tacit assumptions about the way the world works. Through a phenomenological analysis of four individual case studies, this study found that student feedback was a key catalyst for building reflexivity skills. Specifically, the study details the key ways by which feedback prompted novice teachers to metacognitively think through their knowing-in-action and ultimately improve their teaching practice. The research details important implications in three areas: 1) practice, 2) theory, and 3) future research.

INTRODUCTION: STUDENT FEEDBACK AS A CATALYST FOR REFLEXIVITY IN EDUCATION

There is a relationship between the quality of teaching and the quality of student learning (Angelo & Cross, n.d., p.1, Ramsden, 1992; Stark & Lowther, 1980). Teacher training programs emphasize student feedback as one means through which teachers can adjust their lessons to better meet the needs of learners (Hattie and Timperley, 2007). In the classroom, teachers generally receive student feedback in three ways: 1) conversations held directly with students; 2) written feedback from students; and, 3) assessments of the quality of the students' work. These multiple forms of student feedback are "a key practice for lifelong learning in the workplace" (Boud & Molloy, 2013, p. 203).

DOI: 10.4018/978-1-5225-7829-1.ch005

Copyright © 2019, IGI Global. Copying or distributing in print or electronic forms without written permission of IGI Global is prohibited.

While the literature attests to the importance of student feedback in improving the quality of teaching, "the benefits of feedback in the classroom… are often diluted…" (Hattie & Timperley, 2007, p. 101). Too often, teachers see feedback as a statement about the student's performance rather than insights about their own teaching (Timperley & Wiseman, 2002) and miss insights about how feedback informs teaching practice. In short, "faculty and students need better ways to monitor learning throughout the semester" (Angelo & Cross, n.d., p. 1).

Bruno et al. (2011) highlight studies that traditionally explore reflection and learning "have been focused on children" (2011, p. 2), and less on how teachers reflect and learn to become more proficient. However, reflection does not bring us to the critical thinking that emerges from reflexivity. When teachers engage in reflexivity, critically analyzing their students' feedback, they create professional knowledge and can adjust their teaching to better meet students' learning needs.

This chapter contributes to the growing body of research describing how novice professors engage in reflexive thinking to make sense of student feedback and improve their delivery of quality education. More specifically, this chapter examines how teachers translate their tacit knowledge about their students' feedback to explicit understanding, and ultimately make changes in their teaching practice.

LITERATURE REVIEW

Student Feedback

For the purposes of this chapter, student feedback is defined as "information provided by an agent (e.g., teacher, peer, book, parent, self, experience) regarding aspects of one's performance or understanding" (Hattie & Timperley, 2007, p. 82). Extending this definition, Hattie and Timperley observe that "feedback thus is a 'consequence' of performance" (Hattie & Timperley, 2007, p. 81). In the classroom, feedback presents through three broad areas: 1) dialogue between teacher and student regarding the learning taking place; 2) written comments from students regarding the class or assignment; and, 3) students' performance on assignments and exams, through formal student feedback. Teachers use student feedback; Angelo and Cross highlight a three-step process: 1) planning, which involves selecting an assessment tool; 2) implement the tool; and, 3) respond to students by "letting them know what you learned from the assessment and what difference that information will make" (Angelo & Cross, n.d., p. 3).

Feedback plays a critical role in the learning process as it influences one's concept of self-efficacy related to learning, "which in turn leads to further learning" (Hattie and Timperley, 2007, p. 101). In addition to enhancing learning, student feedback is also a valuable tool for teachers in identifying how they can adjust the learning experience to improve learning. In a research project involving over 250 case studies, Black and William (1998) conclude that learning gains and effective feedback go hand-in-hand. Confirming the importance of feedback, Hattie and Timperley (2007) reference Hattie's study of "over 500 meta-analyses which identified that the top three most influential types of feedback are cues, feedback and reinforcement" (p. 83). Less effective strategies broadly include "programmed instruction, praise, punishment, and extrinsic rewards" (p. 84).

Clearly feedback plays an essential role in the learning process. However, Hattie and Timperley (2007) argue, "Feedback by itself may not have the power to initiate further action" (p. 82). Reflecting on student feedback can initiate action, thus a deeper exploration of reflection is in the following section.

Reflection

For the purposes of this chapter, the definition of reflection is borrowed from Mezirow, who defines reflection as "our own orientation to perceiving, knowing, believing, feeling and acting" (p. 13). This process places a focus on "awareness of self in action" (Bruno et al., p. 2). The awareness of self is driven by an individual's "beliefs, values, feelings and implicit assumptions" (Bruno et al, 2011, p. 2) about how the world works. Mezirow (1990) underscores the importance of reflection when he states, ". . . by far, the most significant learning experiences in adulthood involve critical [reflection] - reassessing the way we have posed problems and reassessing our own orientation" (Mezirow, p. 13). Angelo and Cross affirm the importance of reflection, "The type of assessment most likely to improve teaching and learning is conducted by faculty to answer questions they themselves have formulated in response to issues or problems in their own teaching" (Angelo & Cross, 1993, p. 9). As teachers attempt to answer questions that have emerged from their practice, they actively engage in reflection.

Shulman (1998) articulated the essentiality of reflection in professional development, "While an academic knowledge base may be necessary for professional work, it is far from sufficient. Therefore, members of professions have to develop the capacity to learn from the experience and contemplation of their own practice" (p. 519). It is through contemplation and reflection that individuals can engage in reflexivity, thus better understanding their mental models and knowing-in-action. Student feedback can be a catalyst for a teacher's engagement in reflexivity and an essential tool in responding to the contemporary demands of the education environment today.

Schon argues, "Through reflection, (the individual) can surface and criticize the tacit understandings that have grown up around the repetitive experiences of a specialized practice" (Schon, 1983, p. 61). Taggart and Wilson (2005) describe reflective thinking as "the process of making informed and logical decisions on educational matters, then assessing the consequences of those decisions" (p. 1).

Taggart and Wilson (2005) introduce a reflective thinking model and references the work of Dewey (1993), Eby and Kujawa (1994), Pugach and Johnson (1990) and Schon (1983) to depict a cyclical process of reflective thinking involving five steps: 1) identify a problem; 2) framing the problem through observation, reflection, data gathering, moral judgment, schema and context; 3) identify possible interventions; 4) experiment with interventions; 5) evaluate success of the implementations. Furthering the theory of reflective thinking, Argyris introduces "single-loop learning [which] occurs when errors are corrected without altering the underlying governing values" (Taggart & Wilson, p. 206). Schon extends our understanding of reflection suggesting, "Reflection tends to focus interactively on the outcomes of action, the action itself, and the intuitive knowing implicit in the action" (Schon, 1983, 56).

Reflection engages teachers in problem solving and what they can do to address identified issues in their students' learning. Reflexivity, discussed in the next section, is a deeper level of critical thinking to better understand how one's own thoughts, beliefs and reflections influence their actions.

Reflexivity

Reflexivity, different from reflection which places an emphasis on "awareness of self in action" (Bruno et al., 2011, p. 2), can be defined as the relationship between the self and the environment (Schon, 1983). Reflexivity involves an awareness of the environment and the thoughts, beliefs, and reflections of those individuals sharing that the environment (Bruno et al., 2011). Boud and Walker (1998) argue that reflexivity also includes an individual's feeling and wishing about a given situation. Reflexivity becomes a critical process in delivering quality teaching because the changing nature of education requires that teachers refine their reflective thinking skills and shift towards the development of critical thinking skill inherent in reflexive thinking. Further underscoring the importance of reflexivity, Bruno et al., assert, "Reflexivity is a primary requirement for professional work" (Bruno et al., 2010, p. 1).

Reflexivity is a deeper level of critical thinking that assumes a degree of "knowing-in-action" (Schon, 1983, p. 50). Schon suggests that knowing-in-action "does not stem from a prior intellectual operation" (p. 50). Much of one's knowing-in-action is deeply embedded in the biases and views that that are formed as individuals unconsciously make sense of their life experiences. One way individuals become conscious of how their life experiences influence their perception of the world is through metacognition, or "thinking about thinking" (Miller et al, 1970, p. 613). Metacognition involves thinking about what is not typically conscious. Metacognition naturally lends an individual to engage in reflexive thinking.

Reflexivity has a critical role in construction of knowledge and influence on learning processes (Bruno et al., 2011). Kaneklin and Olivetti Manoukian (1990) suggest that learning and teaching processes often promote reflexivity by prompting "the capacity to think one's own and others' thoughts, emotions, assumptions and to think through internal and external conditions of one's own professional life and on them, *through language*, keep up a dialogue" (p. 155). After their study examining how psychologists in training engage in reflexivity, Bruno et al. (2011) suggest that "reflexive practices include cognitive, emotional and volitive dimensions" (p. 14).

Reflexivity plays a critical role in knowing what to do with feedback teachers receive in the classroom. As Boud and Molloy (2013) argue, "It is only the learner who can ultimately act to change what they do" (p. 203). Student feedback serves as a catalyst for reflexivity, discussed in the following section.

Student Feedback as Catalyst for Reflexivity

Student feedback can be a catalyst for reflexivity and is a critical tool in helping teachers become meta-cognitively aware of their tacit knowledge. Nicole et al. that assert that "student feedback is recognised as a core component of the learning process" (Nicole et al., 2014, p. 101). More specifically, Major et al. argue that teachers learn by "looking closely at students and their work" (Major et al, p. 621). When teachers use student feedback to improve their practice, they take on the role of learners, essentially learning how to better meet their students' learning needs. In this role as learners, Boud and Molloy underscore the importance of teachers taking an active role in feedback, "If they are passive recipients of inputs from others, feedback for learning is not occurring" (Boud & Molloy, 2013, p. 203).

This process of looking closely at student work is an impetus to engage in reflexive thinking regarding student learning needs and what the teacher has done to support those needs. In a study of problem-based learning classrooms, Major and Palmer (1006) noted that the experience of teachers reflecting on the feedback they gained from examining their students' performance "changed their understanding of pedagogy" (Major and Palmer, 2006, p. 635). Further, the process of reflecting on student feedback caused teachers to note "a distinct change in the way they think about their teaching" (Ibid., p. 635).

Explicit and Implicit Knowledge

Knowledge can be described as "information that is relevant, actionable, and based at lest partially on experience" (Leonard & Sensiper, 1998, p. 113). More specifically, explicit knowledge refers to one's concrete thinking, or that knowledge which is "expressed in words and numbers and shared in the form of data, scientific formulae, specifications manuals, and the like" (Nonaka & Konno, 1998, p. 42). Adding to this definition, Wyatt (2001) suggests that explicit knowledge is made of "facts, rules, relationships and policies" (p. 6) that can be deconstructed and shared. Nonaka and Konno argue that explicit knowledge is more prevalent in the West. This type of knowledge is more easily shared between individuals than tacit knowledge.

Tacit knowledge is described as "semiconscious and unconscious knowledge held in peoples' heads and bodies" (Leonard & Sensiper, 1998, p. 113). Arguably, tacit knowledge is so deeply unconscious that it cannot be written out or electronically shared (Wyatt, 2001). Because tacit knowledge is not easily visible, it is more challenging to convey to others. Nonaka and Konno (1998) argue, "Subjective insights, intuitions, and hunches" are examples of tacit knowledge (p. 42). Like knowing-in-action, tacit knowledge is deeply formed from one's life experiences, values, ideals and emotions. In short, tacit knowledge shapes one's perception of the world (Nonaka & Konno, 1998). Understanding the interplay between explicit and tacit knowledge is important as this interplay helps individuals become metacognitively aware of how they perceive the world.

Looking more deeply at one's tacit knowledge requires examining mental models. Mental models are formed from one's assumptions about the way the world works and are "often tacit and even contradictory to what people espouse" (Senge, 1990, p. 18). Nonaka and Konno (1998) introduce a SECI model which serves to better understand the interactions between explicit and tacit knowledge.

Conceptual Framework: The SECI Model

In 1998, Nanaka and Konno, researchers in the field of management, published the SECI model, which deconstructs how implicit knowledge is transformed into explicit knowledge. The SECI model extends the concept of "ba", originally introduced by Japanese philosopher Kitaro Nishida (Nanaka and Konno, 1998). Simply defined, ba is the context wherein knowledge is created (Crepelet, 2001). Nanaka and Konno (1998) argue, "Knowledge creation is a spiraling process of interactions between explicit and tacit knowledge" (p. 42). This spiraling process is captured in the SECI model which explores four steps in the knowledge conversion process: socialization, externalization, combination and internalization (Nonaka & Konno, 1998). As individuals engage in these for steps, they create new knowledge. The steps build on each other, explored below.

Socialization is the first step in the SECI model. Socialization involves a physically shared space wherein individuals share tacit knowledge. It is within this shared space that individuals can directly interact with each other. More specifically, the tacit knowledge is shared through social activities, such as working and living together, attending a class together, or playing on a sporting team. Sharing a social space is not enough, however, for knowledge to be created. For knowledge to be created, each person in social space must be open to integrating the other individual's tacit knowledge. In essence, one person's knowledge can strengthen another's understanding. The authors argue that when learners are more empathetic with each other, rather than sympathetic, there is a stronger transference of tacit knowledge. This sharing of tacit knowledge between individuals supports those individuals in becoming "a larger self" (p. 42) as the sharing of tacit knowledge extends one's knowledge base and understanding. The ability to think beyond one's self is essential in sharing tacit knowledge.

In externalization, the second step in the SECI model, an individual is able to commit to the group. This integration with the group comes as an individual expresses tacit knowledge in ways the group understands. By more explicitly expressing tacit knowledge, the individual commits to the group. The commitment to the group comes as the individuals in the group have a shared understanding and in essence "become integrated with the group's mental world" (p. 43-44). This concept of becoming one with the group's mental world occurs through two factors. First, individuals articulate tacit knowledge through metaphors, analogies, stories, and visual aids in relation to how they perceive the world, which supports convey tacit knowledge in more explicit terms. Second, sharing tacit knowledge about their perceptions of the world in ways others can easily understand, making that tacit knowledge more explicit. Sharing tacit knowledge in ways others can understand informs a shared understanding of how the group perceives the world. Gaining a shared understanding of how the group perceives the world relies heavily on listening skills of the members in the group.

The third step in the SECI model is combination. Combination takes the explicit knowledge shared in the second step and develops more complex sets of explicit knowledge. The development of more complex sets of explicit knowledge involves the integration and capture of new explicit knowledge so that others can more easily understand the knowledge. The development of sets of explicit knowledge can be captured in three processes. First, individuals may collect more explicit knowledge from inside or outside the shared context. Second, individuals disseminate the newly collected explicit knowledge with others in the group. By sharing knowledge within the group, there is a higher chance of spreading to other groups associated with the shared environment. The final process involves editing the explicit knowledge so that the group can better use the explicit knowledge. Throughout combination, agreement amongst the group takes place.

Internalization, the final step in the SECI model, relies on individuals' engagement in the aforementioned three steps. With an understanding of the group's mental world gained through the socialization, externalization and internalization steps, individuals are able to convert their explicit knowledge into "explicit knowledge into the organization's tacit knowledge" (p. 45). Converting explicit knowledge into the organization's tacit knowledge is done as individuals apply knowledge that is "relevant for one's self within the organizational knowledge" (45). In other words, individuals are not sharing all of their explicit knowledge with the group. Rather, individuals share explicit knowledge that best aligns with the group's mental world. Broadly, this final stage has the potential to help individuals more deeply understand the organization and themselves.

Each of these steps mentioned above is critical in becoming aware of one's mental model and developing new knowledge. The SECI model described above is explored as it relates to the participants in this study through a qualitative methodological approach, outlined in the following section.

RESEARCH METHODOLOGY

This study employed a phenomenological approach to analyze individual case studies of three teachers, focusing on how student feedback improved their teaching skills. More specifically, the study serves to understand how these novice teachers convert tacit knowledge to explicit knowledge, and what, if any, the impact of that conversion has on their teaching practices. Because this study closely examines the way in which novice teachers engage in reflexivity, using their student feedback as a catalyst to improve the quality of teaching, incorporating phenomenology as a form of research and a qualitative case study design is appropriate.

Researchers who utilize phenomenology as a form of research acknowledge that an individual's experience is "a situated context and it is embedded in time, space, embodiment and relationships" (Munhall,

2007, p. 148). The phenomenological approach allows the researcher to fulfill five key criteria, as outlined by Maxwell: 1) understanding for meaning; 2) understanding the particular context within which the participants act; 3) identifying unanticipated phenomena; 4) understanding the process by which events and actions take place; and, 5) developing causal explanations" (Maxwell, 1996, pp. 17-20). In short, phenomenology allows the researcher to delve into the metacognitive thinking of the participants.

Qualitative case studies allow the researcher to capture participants' voice and story, while simultaneously exploring how context influences participants' experiences (Guba & Lincoln, 1994). Careful analysis of participants' voices and story allow qualitative researchers to provide "rich insight into human behaviour" (Ibid., p. 106). Such insights will be useful in better capturing the story of how student feedback helped strengthen teachers' teaching skills.

In this study, participants' voices were captured through a case study approach that included interviews and classroom teaching observations that took place over two semesters. Once collected, the data was analysed with a systemic coding processes which included initial, axial, and focused coding procedures. Glaser and Strauss (1967) advocate for a systemic coding process that protects researchers against the possibility of "forcing of 'round data' into 'square categories'" (p. 37). Charmaz (2006) suggests that relating and comparing data to existing codes highlights similarities and differences between the data, strengthens an existing code, and highlights a gap in the researcher's understanding of the phenomenon under study.

THE PARTICIPANTS AND THEIR TEACHING CONTEXTS

This study captures how student feedback helped improve three teachers' pedagogical skills. The participants in this qualitative study, Ryan, Darcie and Josephine, were chosen for three criteria. First, the participants all demonstrated willingness to engage in their development, which was determined through their voluntary involvement in the university's professional development courses. Secondly, they all teach in the same Canadian university, serving approximately 15,000 students. The final selection criterion was that all participants have taught for less than three years. Research suggests that within the first three years, teachers experience an intense socialization period (Boice, 1991). Understanding teachers' reflexivity during this intense socialization period serves to better understand the ways in which reflexivity can support novice teachers in their development of the teaching skills necessary to deliver quality education.

Ryan and Josephine taught in the same science department, whereas Darcie taught in the social sciences. At the beginning of the study, Ryan was completing his first year of teaching. Although Ryan had the least amount of teaching experience of the three participants, he was not new to Northern University. He had completed a Master's degree from Northern University before pursuing international doctoral and postdoctoral degrees. Ryan's enthusiasm for his subject and passion for teaching were infectious. Ryan's speech quickened, whether he was talking about his subject matter, his shortfalls as a new teacher or proudly describing how he improved his teaching skills.

Darcie had taught a year and a half at the time of the study. She is the only participant to have earned her doctorate at Northern University. When discussing her career path, she giggles about how much she loves teaching even though she did not plan on teaching. Darcie originally saw her career in community research or developing social policy. When she talked about her work as an educator, she radiated happiness and a deep sense of purpose found through the connection she generates with her students. Depicting her deep connection with her students, Darcie quipped that she viewed herself as a "Care Bear," the stuffed animal known for its compassion and love. While compassionate and caring, Darcie recognized that she has to self-manage her own emotional health as being emotionally available for her students was personally demanding. She described her alone time as being rejuvenating. Josephine taught the largest groups of the three participants, with class sizes of approximately 250 students. She taught in a newly constructed large classroom with eight rising platform that accommodated 20 round tables with four to six chairs arranged around a table. Despite the intimidating space, Josephine radiated a grace and calm as she spoke into the microphone and addressed her class.

DISCUSSION: CAPTURING THE KNOWLEDGE CONVERSION PROCESS

As these novice teachers began teaching, they each identified relying on student feedback as a means to better understand what they needed to do to improve the quality of teaching they delivered. While each participant was acutely aware that they lacked teaching expertise, student feedback helped them identify where they needed to make changes to improve their teaching skills. The student feedback they described as being instrumental in their growth as teachers came in three forms: 1) conversations held directly with students; 2) written feedback from students; and, 3) assessments of the quality of the students' work.

Perhaps Darcie's words best captured how the participants in this study relied on student feedback when she said:

I would stay that I am very – student feedback is very important to me. I take it really seriously. Especially like if there are things that didn't work for them. That really matters to me. Why it didn't work. What were the consequences of that for them? And then thinking through – you know, okay. They are saying that this experience didn't work. They aren't necessarily articulating to me why it didn't work. It's my obligation to figure out why it didn't work.

The following section captures how each teacher used student feedback in exploring the interchange between tacit and explicit knowledge.

Step 1: Socialization

As described in the Literature Review, the first step in the SECI model, socialization, involves the sharing of tacit knowledge between individuals, typically "exchanged through joint activities" (Nonaka & Konno, 1998, p. 42). This step emphasizes how individuals engage in social processes to share tacit knowledge.

Each of the teachers in this study described two distinct social exchanges with their students that were influential in changes they made to their practices. Ryan identified office hours as an opportunity for social exchange with his students. He would ask students to come to his office to delve into a particular learning challenge, thus creating face-to-face interactions with his students. Second, Ryan circulated his classroom and in doing so, interacted with each student and inquired about their understanding regarding the questions that were projected on the screen.

Darcie created an "incentivized" social opportunity with students by offering bonus points if they come and "spend 20 minutes just getting to know me." Second, Darcie used her interactions with students as another means of student feedback that drives her teaching practice.

Josephine had informal one-on-one discussions with her students. Josephine described these interactions as part of her routine teaching where she "I have time to walk through the class, let them work on stuff. They ask me questions." Finally, Josephine referenced comments students shared in spontaneous conversations between her and the students.

The next step in the SECI model, externalization, explores how the tacit knowledge gained through these social contexts described above are converted into explicit knowledge.

Step 2: Externalization

The externalization step involves these teachers' articulation of their tacit knowledge. The following section explores how these professors shifted their tacit understanding of their students' feedback into a more explicit awareness of their mental models.

Ryan received feedback that he gave assignments that were too large during the casual discussions held during his office hours. In reflection, Ryan shared that he had intentionally designed the course to have large assignments, thinking that it was important to "have the whole picture built up." He built up the whole picture by giving students "relatively large homework assignments." His students, however, found large assignments more challenging compared to a series of smaller assignments.

As Ryan shared his rationale for how he set up his assignments, Ryan articulates his tacit knowledge, which captures some of his mental model. More specifically, Ryan's decision to create large assignments aligns with his "meritocratic way of looking at the world." For him, "ability is the thing that means something, in the way I look at the world." This mental model created a situation where Ryan challenged his students with large assignments as a way for his students to demonstrate their abilities.

Darcie referenced her initial impression of a group of male students in her class who "were not engaged . . . chirping at each other . . . eating his snack . . . talking to someone else." Darcie articulated her tacit assumptions and admitted thinking that that these students were bound to "piss me off." As Darcie shared her feelings about this group of male students, she reflected on her thinking at the time, sharing that she consciously thought: "I don't feel right about this particular group."

Josephine's mental model presented as she processed student feedback that the noise was too loud. Josephine shared her explicit thinking about this student's comment, "But I also don't like hearing students say oh – I said in class but I couldn't do a thing because everyone was too noisy. So I just can't let that happen"

As Josephine described her determination to not let the noise in the classroom interfere with her students' learning, she articulated part of her mental model, "You know, I didn't want to be policing any of this. You know, everyone – it is up to them if they want to learn." In this instance. Josephine struggles with wanting to reduce the noise and in the same breath, unhappy at having to "police" the students in her classroom. Josephine not wanting to "police" the students unveils an underlying mental model of the teacher holding a more traditional role in the classroom where the teacher is the expert and the students' responsibility it to absorb the content.

Each of the participants' mental models came as a result of their willingness to listen to and reflect on their students' feedback. By being open to listening to their students and reflecting on the feedback, these teachers were able to convert tacit knowledge to explicit knowledge. Their understanding of their explicit knowledge was then foundational to their engagement in the combination step.

Step 3: Combination

The combination step involves converting the explicit understanding of their students' feedback, described above, into more complex sets of explicit knowledge. Individuals engaging in the combination step gather new data, share their explicit understandings of a given experience and create new knowledge. This section will explore how each of the participants in this study drew new knowledge which resulted in changes to their teaching practice.

Ryan recognized that his mental model of his students needing to see "the whole picture" is not what his students needed and consequently made changes his assignments. For example, he added several additional to a lab assignment and offered theoretical considerations that read more like tips to help his students understand the work. He adjusted the size and frequency of his assignments and made changes to his syllabus as well that included "a homework assignment every week." It is interesting to note that Ryan did not dissolve his mental model that students needed the whole picture; rather, he shifted how he presented the whole picture to his students.

Darcie and Josephine are working on a much more complex mental model. For Darcie, change began when she noticed her deficit perspective in her mental model, an awareness that surfaced through her practice of having a 20-minute discussion with each student. In a tone of surprise, Darcie recognized that these discussions helped her gather develop feedback that led to a more accurate judgement about the students. Darcie's explicit understanding of these boys' behavior changed after she met with them. She shared, "Being able to meet them, and get some sense of that helped me parse out my judgment of these are just some annoying kids who are they don't care, they are not invested." In other words, through these conversations, Darcie was able to have a different understanding of these boys' behaviors. However, prior to the conversation, Darcie identified a mental model that was shaped by her deficit perspective of male students in her class.

After the 20-minute discussion, Darcie's observations of these students' behaviors in class in class and her reflections of their performance on assignments further shifted her mental model. She shared an adjusted explicit understanding of these males' behavior, "They are not used to engaging in class. They are shy. So they were talking to each other because like they feel more comfortable with that . . . then I see the writing assignments, and I see that they are the best students in the class!" Here, Darcie used her observations of these male students' behavior in class, as well as their performance on assignments, to develop new explicit knowledge. The shift is captured in contrasting her own words, thinking that originally the students were going to "piss me off," to a new knowledge that these students were the "best students in the class."

Like Darcie, Josephine's development of explicit knowledge stemmed from her students' feedback that the class was too noisy. Demonstrating an acceptance of that feedback, Josephine began to observe various student behaviors that contributed to the noise of her classroom. These observations of her students' behaviors gave her more data which added to her explicit knowledge base and connected how her students' off-task behaviors contribute to the larger issue of the classroom being distractingly noisy. More importantly, however, is Josephine's openness to adjust her mental model. The two examples below capture this process of adjusting her mental model and creating new explicit knowledge.

First, Josephine observed how her students were off-task, "Every so often, was it last week? I saw one table all of a sudden [cry] 'Ahhhhhhh!' They were playing cards. Someone must have gotten yukred or something!" In a similar demonstration of off-task behavior, Josephine noticed a student who was on his tablet, "It looked like some video game on there." Her explicit observations about her students' off-task behaviors helped Josephine understand the nuances contributing to the noise issues in her class.

With these observations, Josephine took on a more "policing" role. In the first example, Josephine addressed the class before they left on a short break, stating, "If you are going to come back and continue to talk, I recommend that you do not come back . . . It makes learning difficult."

In a secondary example of Josephine's response to the noise in the classroom and her openness to policing her students, she identified reflecting on how she asked her students questions:

I find that if I stand at the front and I am lecturing and I say are there any questions? There's no questions. As soon as I walk out, and I haven't said anything and I walk around, I get someone that oh – and asks me a question about what I just talked about. But, they didn't want to ask it in front of everyone. They want that close, you know, type of contact.

As described in this section, each of the teachers' mental models shifted as they reflected more on their students' feedback. In response to their students' feedback, they each took action that lead to further action. For Ryan, it was changes to his assignments and syllabus. Darcie became aware of her deficit perspective and shifted her perception of a group of male students, and Josephine altered her view of the role of a teacher in the classroom and began addressing the noise issues in her class.

Changing one's mental model is significant in and of itself. The greater gain, however, is when such changes are socialized into a larger group. It is through socialization that change can have a much deeper and broader influence on the delivery of quality education, which is explained in the internalization step of the SECI model, explored in the next section.

Step 4: Internalization

The internalization step examines how individuals share their explicit knowledge and socialize others. This socialization step creates an influence of change much larger than an individual's efforts to change mental models. When individuals engage in the internalization step, changes to their mental models are so deep that the changes become tacit. When deep changes become tacit, individuals are freeer to think through other mental models and engage in the SECI steps over again.

In this study, Darcie is the only participant that showed some evidence of engaging in the internalization step. Darcie's demonstration of the internalization step builds off of the first three SECI steps. In summary of the first three steps, Darcie became more explicitly aware of her mental model around the importance of teachers connecting with their students. As she took action to connect with students, she identified some assumptions and biases she had towards male students and realized that her 20-minute discussions helped her become more explicitly aware of her assumptions and biases towards the male students. Darcie recognized that her 20-minute conversations with her students were influential in shifting her mental model of her students and socialized her students to have the similar experience. Paralleling her own experience previously referenced, Darcie wanted to create a situation where her students received "meaningful feedback" from each other, become aware of their deficit perspectives, and shift their mental models.

Darcie admitted that initially the students' discussions were "kind of a disaster" and were not "structured enough." Making modifications, Darcie gave "guidelines for what their meetings would look like" so that her students could know each other more. She concluded that introducing the structure "works so much better" in setting the stage for her students to give meaningful feedback.

Each of the three cases outlined above capture how these novice teachers engaged in steps in the SECI model. From their experiences, several themes emerge, discussed below.

FINDINGS: EMERGENT THEMES

Theme #1: All Participants Changed Shifted their Mental Models

In this study, all three novice teachers shifted their mental models. Ryan maintained his belief that students needed the whole picture, though he introduced the whole picture to his students through smaller and more frequent assignments. Darcie's deficit perspective changed regarding the male students in her class and Josephine adjusted the role she played in her classroom. These teachers' changes to their mental models occurred by engaging in the first three steps of the SECI model, beginning first with their openness to hear students' feedback, reflecting, and implementing changes. Student feedback played a key role in these teachers' changes to their mental models, discussed below.

Theme #2: Student Feedback as Catalyst for Reflection

The teachers in this study relied on the students' indirect and direct student feedback as a catalyst for reflection and these teachers' explicit understanding of their mental model. Each teacher highlighted the value of their students' feedback. For example, Ryan synonymized student feedback he received as "advice."

I never would have thought of that, but of course! That makes perfect sense. I was really pleased that I asked for this feedback from the students because I actually got some really helpful advice . . . Like that was super helpful in terms of the things that I did change for this course.

Darcie's comments underscored her strategies to gather on-going feedback from her students, "The process of getting feedback from them and observing and reflecting on what I think is happening, and then linking the two, refining the process over time."

Josephine succinctly argued, "You need to feedback to make use of the experience."

For each participant, reflection was a cornerstone in their ability to transition tacit knowledge into a more explicit understanding of various aspects of their teaching practice, discussed in the next section.

Theme #3: Explicit Understanding of Mental Models led to Changes in Teaching Practice

As discussed above, student feedback was a catalyst for these teachers' explicit understanding of their mental models. As these teachers engaged in reflexivity, they recognized that their mental models were not delivering the quality education they hoped to provide their students. Consequently, they made changes to their practice.

In summary, Ryan created smaller assignments, reflected in his course syllabus. Darcie implemented structures in her classroom to make connection and used this connection to dissolve some assumptions and biases she had about a group of male students. Josephine shifted her perception of what she thought the role of teachers was in the classroom and verbalized her expectations in the classroom.

Theme #4: Little Evidence of Internalization

While these teachers made changes to their teaching practice, there is limited evidence to suggest that these teachers' awareness of their mental models resulted in their engagement in the internalizations step of the SECI model. Without internalization, the shifts in one's mental models and the delivery of quality education are limited to individual teachers' practice. In other words, socialization is critical to making changes to the delivery of education on a larger scale. In this study, only Darcie's journey captured how she integrated her changes into her classroom, a decision that in turn has the potential to impact her class' deficit perspective and mental models.

CONCLUSION

This research closely examined how the participants in this study developed explicit knowledge about their teaching practice and skills. Specifically, the study addresses ways through which student feedback facilitated a reflexive process wherein teachers identified deeply held biases and tacit assumptions around their instructional practices. This study is unique in as it identifies how the participants transitioned their tacit to explicit knowledge. The study also presents empirical evidence that reflexivity resulted in significant changes in practice.

Naturally, individuals draw conclusions based on the limited world view fostered by their mental models. The development of one's mental model and deficit perspectives are not conscious, but a product of an individual's life experiences. Holding a limited world view is not a choice; rather, an individual's mental model leaves individuals no alternative but to view a situation in the same way. Once individuals engage in reflexivity, they increase the potential of making changes to their mental models, and incon-sequence, to their world views. In this study, these teachers were not explicitly aware of their mental models until they received the student feedback that was the catalyst for their reflection. In these cases, the participants' metacognitive thinking encouraged reflection on their mental models, which helped the teachers become more explicitly aware of their mental models.

More specifically, Ryan described how reflection influenced his ability to understand those teaching strategies that worked in his classroom, "I think hindsight is really the only tool I feel like that I have to to know what worked and what didn't. And I can only sort of change based on what happened in the past." Similarly, Darcie shared, "I think it is just practice and becoming more aware of yourself in those moments." Josephine highlighted how reflection helped her gain clarity about her classroom, "It is nice to be able to reflect and to see exactly what is going on. When you're in the moment, it is distorted."

Through these teachers' engagement in the steps of the SECI model, these teachers connected their explicit understanding of their mental models to the decisions and changes they made in their teaching practice.

Future Research Recommendations

From this study, there are four recommendations for future research. First, it would be interesting to see how veteran teachers engage with the SECI model throughout their careers. Second, a similar methodological study could be conducted in a K-12 setting, a different university or a different country. Third, a qualitative study could explore how the SECI model applies to a larger sample population, with a particular focus on how larger groups engage in the internalization step.

REFERENCES

Angelo, T. A., & Cross, K. P. (2005). Classroom assessment techniques. In Classroom assessment techniques: a handbook for college teachers (2nd ed., pp. 1-3). John Wiley & Sons Incorporated.

Argyris, C. (1982). The executive mind and double-loop learning. *Organizational Dynamics*, 5–24.

Argyris, C. (2002). Double-loop learning, teaching and research. *Academy of Management Learning & Education*, *1*(2), 206–218. doi:10.5465/amle.2002.8509400

Armstrong, L. (2016). *Institute barriers to innovation and change in education*. TIAA-CREF Financial Institution.

Black, P., & William, D. (1998). Assessment and classroom learning. *Assessment in Education: Principles, Policy & Practice*, *5*(1), 7–74. doi:10.1080/0969595980050102

Boice, R. (1991). New teachers colleagues. *International Journal of Qualitative Studies in Education: QSE*, *4*(1), 29–44. doi:10.1080/0951839910040103

Boud, D., & Molloy, E. (2013). Decision-making for feedback. In D. Boud & E. Molloy (Eds.), Feedback in Higher and Professional Education (pp. 202-217). London. UK: Routledge.

Boud, D., & Walker, D. (1998). Promoting reflection in professional discourses. The challenge of context. *Studies in Higher Education*, *23*(2), 191–206. doi:10.1080/03075079812331380384

Bruno, A., Galuppo, L., & Gilardi, S. (2011). Evaluating the reflective practices in a learning experience. *European Journal of Psychology of Education*, 2–17.

Charmaz, K. (2006). *Constructing grounded theory: A practical guide through qualitative analysis*. Thousand Oaks, CA: SAGE Publications Ltd.

Chickering, A. W., & Gamson, Z. F. (n.d.). Seven principles for good practice in undergraduate education.

Dewey, J. (1933). *How we think*. Boston, MA: DC Health.

Eby, J. W., & Kujawa, E. (1994). *Reflective planning, teaching, and evaluation: K-12*. New York, NY: Macmillan.

Glaser, B., & Strauss, A. (1967). *The discovery of grounded theory: Strategies for qualitative research*. Hawthorne, NY: Aldine Publishing Company.

Guba, E. G., & Lincoln, Y. S. (1994). Competing paradigms in qualitative research. In N. K. Denzin & Y. S. Lincoln (Eds.), *Handbook of qualitative research* (pp. 105–117). Thousand Oaks, CA: Sage Publications, Inc.

Hattie, J., & Timperley, H. (2007). The power of feedback. *Review of Educational Research*, *77*(1), 81–112. doi:10.3102/003465430298487

Kaneklin, C., & Olivetti Manoukain, F. (1990). *Conoscere l'organizzazione*. Milan: Carocci.

Major, C. H., & Palmer, B. (2006). Reshaping teaching and learning: The transformation of teachers pedagogical content knowledge. *Education*, *51*, 619–647.

Maxwell, J. (1996). *Qualitative research methods* (Vol. 41). Thousand Oaks, CA: SAGE Publications.

Mezirow, J. (1990). *Fostering critical reflection in adulthood: A guide to transformative and emancipatory learning*. San Francisco, CA: Jossey-Bass.

Miller, P. H., Kessel, F. S., & Flavell, J. H. (1971). Thinking about people thinking about people thinking about…: A study of social cognitive development. *Child Development*, *41*(3), 613–623.

Morgan, G. (2006). *Images of Organization*. Beverly Hills, CA: Sage Publications.

Nicol, D., Thomson, A., & Breslin, C. (2014). Rethinking feedback practices in education: A peer review perspective. *Assessment & Evaluation in Education*, *39*(1), 102–122. doi:10.1080/02602938.2013.795518

Nonaka, I., & Konno, N. (1998). The concept of "ba": Building a foundation for knowledge creation. *California Management Review*, *40*(3), 40–54. doi:10.2307/41165942

Pugach, M. C., & Johnson, L. (1990). Meeting diverse needs through professional peer collaboration. In W. Stainback & S. Stainback (Eds.), *Support networks for inclusive schooling: Interdependent integrated evaluation* (pp. 123-137). PH Brookes Pub. Co.

Schon, D. (1983). *The reflective practitioner: How professionals think in action*. New York, NY: Basic Books, Inc., Publishers.

Taggart, G. L., & Wilson, A. P. (2005). Promoting reflective thinking in teachers: 50 action strategies. Thousand Oaks, CA: A Sage Publications Company.

Tandberg, D. A., & Griffith, C. (2013). State support of education: Data, measures, findings and directions for future research. Springer. doi:10.1007/978-94-007-5836-0_13

Timperley, H. S., & Wiseman, J. (2002). *The sustainability of professional development in literacy*. Wellington: New Zealand Ministry of Education.

Yun, J. H., Baldi, B., & Sorcinelli, M. D. (2016, January). Mutual mentoring for early-career and underrepresented teachers: Model, research and practice. *Innovación Educativa (México, D.F.)*.

Chapter 6
The Power of Praxis:
Critical Thinking and Reflection in Teacher Development

Sandra L. Guzman Foster
University of the Incarnate Word, USA

Stephen J. Fleenor
Seidlitz Education, USA

ABSTRACT

This chapter introduces the concept of infusing critical thinking and reflection as part of professional development for teachers, as well as provides recommendations for schools to promote critical thinking and reflection as part of teachers' daily practice. Constructs, such as problem posing and dialogue, are introduced to provide examples of promising practices to consider implementing as a means to enhance critical thinking and reflection amongst teachers when participating in professional development. Additionally, professional learning communities and self-directed professional development are introduced as spaces for teachers to practice these constructs to transform their praxis. Providing opportunities for critical thinking and reflection is one of many steps schools and districts must take, to bring about the positive change required for future success of the education system.

INTRODUCTION

In today's classrooms, teachers are inundated with extensive curricula along with the pressure of increased accountability and high-stakes testing. To be effective in the modern educational environment, teachers are required to think about their lesson plans; interactions with students, peers, and parents; grading; alignment of curricula to standards; promoting student engagement and learning; and development and analysis of formative and summative assessments.

In practice, efforts to promote critical thinking about all of the facets of modern teaching practice are limited to lesson plan templates and data meetings centered around Tier II intervention decisions. Largely absent is ongoing support to promote critical thinking as a tool to improve practice and better

DOI: 10.4018/978-1-5225-7829-1.ch006

Copyright © 2019, IGI Global. Copying or distributing in print or electronic forms without written permission of IGI Global is prohibited.

manage the plethora of daily demands placed on teachers. Essential to this support is the role of teacher reflection. Critical reflective thinking helps teachers understand the specific contexts of their classroom environments and develops their professional artistry of their practice.

Teaching is not a neutral act (Freire, 2000). In fact, what occurs outside the classroom affects what happens inside the classroom with teaching and learning. Students' lives, teachers' lives, the social, cultural, and political happenings that occur outside the classroom do not stop at the schoolhouse door. This can be seen today in the current politically charged climate were are currently experiencing in the United States and seeing over and over on television, social media, and on radio. Teachers and students do not forget about these happenings when they enter schools. Therefore, teachers need opportunities to critically think and reflect on how these outside social and political forces impact what happens in their classrooms. For example, if one teaches at a school, located in an impoverished area where students of color are constantly moving from one foster home to another and never really feeling like they have a place to call home, the teacher should understand that what is happening outside of the school to these students impacts what happens inside the classroom. Students may have experienced trauma, violence, death of a parent, abandonment, etc. They may not have the support they need in their foster home to help them learn coping skills; so many of these children's needs go unheard and untreated. As a result, the student goes to school traumatized, scared, hungry, sick, etc. Some of these children may act out while others disengage but yet teachers expect them to learn without even knowing what is really going on in their lives. Critically reflecting how governmental institutions like the foster care system work and what it fails to do for some of these children will help teachers find ways to navigate the school system in a way to reach their students so they find some kind of success in their schooling.

Another example would be if teachers teach students who live in a neighborhood where their community is constantly under surveillance by the police. When these students come to school they may see school resource officers as a threat rather than a resource. Teachers would need to critically reflect on their discipline policies and determine if school resource officers are being used as resources or as a punitive measure when the behavior could have been addressed in the classroom where the teacher has a sound discipline policy. How can they de-escalate a situation in the classroom and work with the student to bring about dialogue and understanding? Critically thinking and reflecting on the social and political forces that exist outside of the classroom can help teachers learn to be deliberate and intentional in their classroom (Bognar & Krumes, 2017).

The goal of this chapter is to examine how instructional practices in critical thinking and reflection are best applied to/in classroom practice and professional development for teachers, and to provide recommendations for schools to promote critical thinking and reflection as part of teachers' daily practice. The relationship between critical thinking, reflection, and praxis, or the iterative marriage between theory and practice, is detailed. This chapter also describes how dialogue and problem-posing support these constructs. Lastly, the role of instructional coaching and professional learning communities (PLCs) in promoting critical thinking and reflection by facilitating dialogue and problem posing is addressed. Teachers are in a position of power. What they say, do not say, and what they do and do not do will impact their students' lives every day they step into the classroom, leaving their mark on their students. Providing opportunities for critical thinking and reflection is one of many steps schools and districts must take, if we want to see the change that is needed in our education system.

BACKGROUND

Some teacher preparation programs infuse critical thinking and reflection in some of their courses. However, it is unclear the extent to which critical thinking and reflection by pre-service teachers about their pedagogy (teachers' values, beliefs and assumptions about education generally) occur. What we do know is that critical thinking and being a reflective practitioner are skills that one must develop and practice; it is much more than "recall and repeat" what one reads in the textbook. Teacher preparation programs should be opportunities when pre-service teachers develop and practice critical thinking and reflection while preparing to be a teacher (Anderson & Freebody, 2012). Furthermore, critical thinking and reflection should be infused in every required teacher preparation course so it becomes second nature to their practices in the classroom. To encourage pre-service teachers to think on their own and critically think and reflect, teacher educators should embrace critical thinking and reflection by modeling what it means to be a critical thinking and reflective practitioner (Bognar & Krumes, 2017).

In many teacher preparation programs, pre-service teachers are basically learning distinct skills or "how to" methods which they can apply in the classroom. As a result, pre-service teachers are not being prepared to critically examine the political and social contexts of teaching that exist outside the classroom. Following pre-service education and certification courses, teacher professional development exists in many forms, including workshops, instructional coaching, mentor relationships, and PLCs. In workshops, new skills, strategies, or ideas are explicitly taught typically in a single setting removed from the classroom. While goal-oriented and participant-centered instruction has been shown to improve effectiveness of workshops in long-term pedagogical change (Lauer, Christopher, Firpo-Triplett, & Buchting, 2014), the effectiveness of workshops most critically depends on continuous, sustained reflection over the course of the school year (Darling-Hammond, Hyler, & Gardner, 2017; Lauer et. al., 2014).

Such reflection is achieved through instructional coaching, mentor relationships, and PLCs. Instructional coaching involves a professional, the coach (usually a central office specialist, member of campus leadership, or hired consultant), regularly observing and conferencing with the teacher in a cyclical manner. Interest in investing in instructional coaches among school districts has risen significantly over the past decade (Galey, 2016; Mangin & Dunsmore, 2015) because instructional coaches are in a unique position to provide targeted, comprehensive, and thorough support. Unlike administrators who are tasked with attendance, discipline, and other duties in addition to instructional leadership, instructional coaches are able to commit deeply to individual teachers' development full-time.

Instructional coaches promote critical thinking and reflection by recording goal-oriented, objective observations of lessons, and asking reflective questions about the observations in follow-up conferences. This model is particularly effective in promoting critical thinking and reflection because it provides a lens for the teacher that is unclouded by the many considerations teachers face during a lesson, such as student behavior, diverse learning needs, and responses to checks for understanding. With focused observation data and reflective questions, teachers can think critically and reflect about their practice and make adjustments. Instructional coaching as a practice depends on critical thinking and reflection itself, as instructional coaches learn to make more meaningful, focused observations and ask more targeted reflective questions. In one study, for example, student mathematics performance rose concomitantly with increasing experience of mathematics elementary coaches (Campbell & Malkus, 2011). Instructional coaching, therefore, is a powerful conduit for promoting teachers' critical thinking and reflection.

In partnership with or in the absence of instructional coaching, mentor relationships and PLCs are strong avenues for continuous professional development. Both of these models require the engagement of senior teacher-leaders. In a mentor relationship, the teacher-leader focuses specifically on the development of a struggling (often new) teacher. However, this relationship is one-sided and does not provide any obvious instructional support for the teacher-leader. PLCs, by contrast, function much more horizontally as teams of teachers in shared content, grade-level, student population or interest work together towards common goals in instructional growth. Such goals might include (but are not limited to) instructional strategies, achievement gains of specific student subpopulations, or improved interactions to address students' socio-emotional needs. An effective PLC is unambiguous in its purpose and is centered around norms of participation (Tam, 2015; Mangin & Dunsmore, 2015). As one example, strategies were modelled to PLCs of high school biology teachers, who were then encouraged to participate in structured conversations about their experience as learners and necessary pedagogical adaptations before and during implementations (Greenleaf, Litman, Hanson, Rosen, Boscardin, Herman, Schneider, Madden, & Jones, 2011). Combined with peer observation and follow-up conversations, PLCs have the power to provide insight for improved practice and ensure accountability of implementation for teachers (Schuck, Aubusson, & Buchanan, 2008).

In all of these models of teacher professional development, critical thinking and reflection about specific and generalized practice can play key roles in shaping beliefs and improving student outcomes.

CONCEPTUAL FRAMEWORK

In addition to our experiences as teachers and as professional development facilitators, our passion for educating all students drives our desire to share this work. As educators, learning should never stop; hence, professional development for teachers is critical. Helping teachers to recognize their own social location is so important because it impacts everything they do and do not do in their classrooms.

Figure 1 provides a visual of the relationships between the different constructs (critical thinking, reflection, problem posing, praxis, and dialogue) that we address in this chapter. Praxis is ultimately developed through critical thinking and reflection, which is promoted by instructional coaching, mentor relationships, and PLCs. Importantly, dialogue is stimulated through this professional development infrastructure, which leads to deeper critical thinking. Praxis is additionally influenced by theories proposed in published literature, one's worldview, and one's cultural frame of reference. These structures, however, are outside of the scope of influence of a school or district. Importantly, our focus in this chapter are the roles in which schools and districts (via instructional coaches, mentor relationships, and PLCs) can influence praxis by promoting critical thinking and reflection.

MAIN FOCUS OF THE CHAPTER

Critical Thinking

Critical thinking is a process of uncovering the root causes of events by making connections between multiple factors which may be directly or indirectly related to the events. In teaching, critical thinking is essential to understand how outcomes, such as student learning or behavior outcomes, can be tied to a teacher's actions or factors extrinsic to the classroom. Critical thinking should not be confused with criticism, however, as a teacher's involvement in negative outcomes is only as relevant as the teacher's

Figure 1. A cyclical model of the drivers of praxis. Professional development infrastructure, including PLCs, mentoring, and instructional coaching, promote teachers' critical thinking. Critical thinking informs reflection, which informs problem posing, which informs praxis. Reflection, problem posing, and praxis guide dialogue, and dialogue leads to deeper critical thinking. The theoretical nature of problems affecting the educational space in which a teacher operates, as well as the theoretical component of a teacher's pedagogy, can be additionally informed by published literature, one's worldview, and the cultural frame of reference from which one operates.

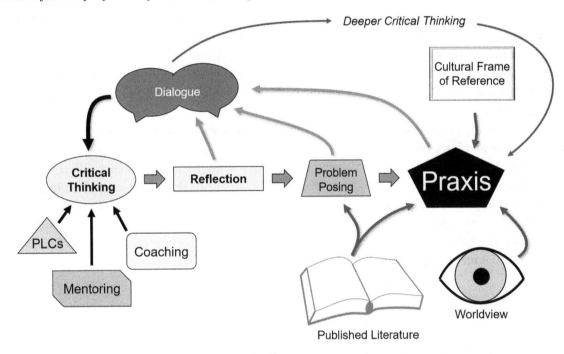

future capacity to prevent such outcomes (Liu, 2015). For example, a multitude of events could have occurred to lead up to a student's misbehavior, several of which might have been within the teacher's control. Critical thinking to understand how one event led to another, leading to the student's eventual misbehavior would paint a clear picture for the teacher about possible future action to mitigate misbehavior. Continuous critical thinking can increase the likelihood and magnitude of positive outcomes and commensurately decrease negative outcomes.

A key component of critical thinking in teaching is the ability to interpret events during a lesson through multiple perspectives. This includes the perspective of a potential colleague observing the lesson as well as student perspectives. Importantly, increasingly diverse student bodies means that multiple points of view affect the relationship between teaching and learning (Tripp, Love, Thomas, & Russell, 2018).

For example, a teacher might observe that, after calling on a specific student with a question in a whole-group setting, the student put his head down and answered "I don't know." The teacher might perceive the student's affective filter impeding his ability to answer confidently. An outside observer might perceive emotional impediments, or might perceive that the student was academically unprepared because of his off-task behavior in the preceding moments before the question. The student might have perceived being punished for off-task behavior by being called upon, or might have felt tested by the question. Another student, by contrast, might wonder why a student of one race/ethnicity/social group was chosen for that question and not herself or a representative student of her group, and question how the teacher might differentially believe in the capacities of certain students in that classroom.

In this example, visualizing distinct perspectives is essential for understanding the socio-emotional nature of the student answering the question, the requisite learning and metacognition necessary for the student to answer the question, and the teacher's own intentionality in asking that question to that student. The ability to view multiple perspectives is not intuitive, however, as the imagination of other people's points of views is often shrouded in one's own assumptions about those people. Critical thinking about points of view is therefore very much a practiced skill greatly enhanced by active coaching, mentoring, and/or peer-to-peer discussion. Importantly, understanding the students' perspectives is developed only through critical analysis of avenues by which students express themselves. Student surveys are often underemployed in schools, but when they have been used they have been found to not only be highly insightful but also highly predictive of academic performance (Downer, Stuhlman, Schweig, Martinez, & Ruzek, 2015).

Teacher training programs, therefore, have significant potential to influence not just preparedness for the first day of school, but also a teacher's ability to self-develop over the course of a teaching career by developing "a habit of mind to think critically in order to ensure effective teaching" (Low & Cai, 2017). Teacher-leaders and mentors who reinforce and model critical thinking contribute to a culture of continuous improvement in schools. The practice of critical thinking is the start of creating a culture of continuous improvement in schools. In order for teachers to understand what this means for them as teachers and what this looks like in practice, they must be comfortable questioning and examining everything about themselves, their practices and what they do in the classroom.

Reflection

To be reflective teachers means to question the goals and values that guide their teaching, the institutional and cultural contexts in which they teach and examining his or her assumptions he or she brings to the classroom relative to their students' cultures and lived experiences (Zeichner & Liston, 1996). Reflection requires one to be self-critical in order to be better prepared to teach children who bring a variety of experiences and backgrounds to the classroom. According to Schon (1983), there are two ways in which teachers can participate in reflective practice. First, teachers can reflect before and after an action; this is known as reflection *on* action. This occurs before and after an action in the classroom. Schon asserts that teachers reflect before a lesson, when they think about the lesson and after execution of the lesson when they reflect on what occurred during the lesson. Next, Schon asserts that there are times when teachers reflect when they encounter an unexpected student reaction or perception and attempt to make immediate adjustments to instruction as a result of these reactions. Schon identifies this as reflection *in* action. For example, a teacher is discussing the preamble to the United States Constitution. During the discussion of the different parts of the preamble, the teacher notices two students talking with each other. In this case, the teacher may respond intuitively and negatively to this scenario. However, knowing these students and realizing that the behavior being displayed is incompatible to how these students typically behave, i.e. attentively. The teacher takes this into consideration and attempts to reframe the situation. Maybe they are confused about what is being said about the preamble, rather than choosing to be rude and talking while the teacher is talking. The teacher continues to discuss the preamble while observing the students' nonverbal behavior via the looks on their faces, which indicates that they are confused. The teacher realizes that there may be other students who are also confused and decides to approach teaching about the different parts of the preamble in a different way. The teacher has just reflected in action.

Reflective teachers reflect both "in" and "on" action. For many teachers, the ability to be more consciously aware of how to bring tacit knowledge and understandings to the surface is reflective teaching. By doing this, teachers can criticize, examine, and improve their practices based on this tacit knowledge. Reflection in and on action are tools reflective teachers use that help them to develop and learn from their experiences.

These tacit understandings can sometimes manifest as assumptions teachers harbor about how others share and respond to their experiences. Understanding one's own assumptions about the personal experiences students bring to school is essential for "assessing the accuracy and validity of these assumptions against lived experience," which establishes a real platform from which positive changes can be implemented (Liu, 2015).

Turning assumptions into perceptions which mirror the lived experiences of one's students is critical not only for teacher growth, but also for social justice. Because the non-White student population continues to increase far faster than that of the predominantly White teacher population, culturally relevant pedagogy is essential for student achievement and, in turn, more socially just economic and social outcomes for non-White members of the general population (Howard, 2003). Reflecting on the extent to which one's pedagogy serves equitably a heterogeneous student body results in improved interactions and delivery of content, an essential for closing achievement gaps.

We assert reflecting in and on action helps teachers discover the "why" behind their actions and the decisions they make in their classroom. By reflecting, teachers are able to change their practices; an analysis of the self in teaching. This results in the ability to identify areas for future professional growth and development so they can improve their practice. Reflective practice is necessary in education. It is a lifelong activity that establishes a foundation for teachers to embark on a learning journey that leads to constructive change, change that will benefit not only the teachers, but also the students in their classrooms.

Problem Posing

Problem-posing is an approach developed by Freire (2000), a Brazilian educator well known for disparaging "banking education," a common approach to education where "deposits" of information are made by teachers into students. In other words, students are seen as receptors rather than autonomous individuals. Developed as a method to use in the classroom with students, we contend that problem- posing can also be applied in professional development with teachers. For example, problem-posing would provide teachers with the opportunity to become critical thinkers. With problem posing, teachers engage in acts of dialogic enrichment to effectively gain knowledge from each other via an inductive questioning process that structures dialogue in a professional development environment. Problem-posing is a method for developing and strengthening critical thinking skills. According to Freire (2000), problem-posing is a method that transforms learners (in this case, the teachers) into "critical co-investigators in dialogue with the teacher" (in this case the facilitator of professional development workshop, a coach, or mentor) (p. 68). Problem-posing requires teachers to name the problem; understand how it applies to them, their classroom, and their students; determine the causes of the problem; generalize to others; and finally suggest alternatives to the problem via dialogue. "Problem posing ignites praxis and leads to action" (Wink, 2011, p. 75); teachers become reflective agents of change who are able to engage in collaborative and mutually transformative practices.

What does problem-posing look like in teacher professional development? Facilitators and learners (in this case teachers) pose questions as a catalyst for learning. In this kind of environment, learners (in this case teachers) quickly see themselves as knowledgeable persons. Questions that arise from problem-posing draw from the learners' awareness and experiences. For example, teachers can videotape themselves teaching and reflect on their practice with their PLC that consists only of teachers (the presence of administrators would change the dynamics and the culture of the PLC). Teachers would name the problem they identified through reflection, understand how it applies to all of them, their classroom and their students, determine the cause of the problem, generalize to others and together suggest alternatives to the problem via dialogue. A shift towards problem posing in professional development is analogous to a pedagogical shift towards student-centered instruction. The most impactful solutions to the problems of classrooms come from within teachers themselves. A critically reflective teacher who regularly exercises problem posing is able to find those solutions and grow professionally.

Praxis

Praxis is an iterative, reflective approach to taking action. It is an ongoing process of moving between practice and theory. Praxis is a synthesis of theory and practice in which each informs the other (Freire, 1985). You cannot have one without the other. Some teachers leave teacher preparation programs without a lot of knowledge about theory. Instead they may learn to improvise and utilize cookie cutter techniques they learned in their teacher preparation programs. To grow in practice, teachers must learn more theory. By theorizing, teachers respond differently when faced with certain situations in their classroom (Schon, 1983). Our practices are about how we do methods in the classroom, our theory is about why we do things one way or the other.

Therefore, it is imperative that teachers are knowledgeable and have the skills necessary to be effective educators. However, teaching is more than knowledge and skills; it is a form of praxis. Praxis emphasizes the moral, ethical and caring dimensions of teaching. One who is praxis-oriented, is clearly aware that she/he continually makes pedagogical decisions that are morally informed and value-laden. Additionally, a praxis-oriented teacher deeply understands that all learning occurs in relationship with others (Kemmis & Smith, 2008; Grotenboer, 2013). Praxis enables educators to reflect on our roles and actions as members of a classroom, school, district, school community, etc. Teachers make decisions and act in the moment of activities that occur in the classroom. A teacher immersed in praxis brings theoretical thoughts to every decision is made. Additionally, what makes one engaged in praxis is the fact that teachers think about the moral implication of their actions and how they will impact the students in their classroom. Praxis is a form of critical thinking and comprises both reflection and action. Freire (2000) describes praxis as reflection and action directed at structures, such as the classroom, to be transformed. Praxis is learning through action, reflection and change. Praxis is powerful because it challenges structures in place and leads to transformative action. Teachers engaged in praxis means being active in the world, to be agents of change.

Community of praxis, which is a combination of the tenants of community of practice and the understanding of praxis is an approach one should consider when providing professional development learning opportunities for teachers. The goal of a community of praxis is to assist teachers in bridging the gap between theory and practice, enabling them to make connections between the approaches they use in the classroom and the education theory behind those approaches in a safe and supportive environment

(Anderson & Freebody, 2012). Teachers benefit from participating in communities of praxis because teachers work together to reflect on their development while at the same time, creating a reflective understanding of teaching.

With community of praxis there is an emphasis on reflection and teachers conceptualizing the theory of learning in their classrooms with the goal of putting what they learned about the learning theory into practice (Anderson & Freebody, 2012). To be more specific, communities of praxis choose to participate beyond spaces of dialogue and critical reflection. For example, teachers observe each other and teachers team teach. Following these experiences, teachers reflect, building on Schon's (1983) "reflection-on action." Reflecting on actions and events that occurred during the observation and team teaching provide teachers with an opportunity to understand how multiple perspectives that are influenced by multiple historical and socio-political contexts impact teaching and learning. As a result of observing their peers or team teaching with their peers, teachers start to be more proactive in making changes in their approaches to teaching so their students are more engaged in learning (Anderson & Freebody, 2012). A community of praxis offers teachers a model that can be achieved within the current constraints that schools are facing, such as budget cuts, time, access to professional development, etc., if teachers are willing to engage in such a community. "Educational praxis as a dialectics of theory and practice, reflection and action, leads us to focus on the dynamics of movement and changes in our thinking and acting in specific and concrete educational situations" (Torres & Mercado, 2004, pp. 60-61).

Dialogue

Along with self reflection, active dialogue among teachers in a professional development space is vital if we want teachers to reflect on their thoughts and feelings about their pedagogical practices. Reflection must occur before transformative dialogue takes place. According to Freire (1995), dialogue is a cooperative activity that involves respect. Dialogue contributes to a more transformative learning environment and removes the traditional "banking" model (a deposit of concepts taught in the professional development space by the instructional coach or the professional development facilitator). For Freire, dialogue is not just about deepening students' (in this case teachers') understanding of new concepts but is also about helping students (in this case teachers) to see that by learning these concepts via dialogue they have a chance to make a difference in the world. Teachers are asked to reflect both inwardly at their own practice and outwardly at the social conditions in which their practice is situated and to participate in dialogue to address what this means for them as teachers.

The goal is for teachers to dialogue and come to an understanding about the sociopolitical and sociocultural contexts of everything that encompasses education and how these forces impact everything they do in the classroom. As professional development proponents, we must provide an environment of comfort, safety, and trust where teachers are open to questioning their long held beliefs about people who are culturally, linguistically, and socioeconomically different from them and are willing to examine the consequences of their actions. Dialogue encourages the voices of the learners (in this case teachers). Further, it creates a sense of belonging among teachers within the school community, which can drive a teacher's commitment towards professional growth (Tam, 2015). If there are no opportunities for participation in critical and reflective dialogue, the risk is loss of engagement among teachers. Without engagement in critical reflection and dialogue, teachers are not able to grow in their practice. Further, a loss of engagement can lead to a sense of hopelessness in teachers to be able to positively impact the communities they serve. This, in turn, can lead to decreased affective support in the classroom, which has a clear and potent effect on student educational outcomes (Sakis, Pape & Hoy, 2012; Klem & Connell, 2009).

By contrast, teachers who are engaged in dialogue with fellow teachers and school leaders can be a significant source of educational progress not just to the classrooms they serve, but also to the broader school community in which they operate. This is because critically reflective teachers are able to realize within themselves solutions to fundamental problems: problems of pedagogy in the classroom, yes, but also more systemic problems within the school and/or community. By providing a learning environment that provides opportunity to dialogue about pedagogical practices, teachers are apt to learn to see things in a different light from what they are currently practicing.

In order to practice dialogue as we describe in this chapter, it is important to first understand that in order for it to be considered dialogue, it requires a shared commitment from the community members (in this case teachers). In other words, they must be willing to work with others despite any differences. In fact, there should be differences because these differences provide the impetus for reflection and inquiry that occur in dialogue. However, for dialogue to work, community members, must be cognizant of not only their responses, but also how they respond when their own views are challenged by other members of the learning community. It is also important for those who speak to be cognizant of dominating the dialogue. In fact, other members have a right to intervene when necessary to allow other community members to participate in the dialogue. It is not uncommon to find that not all members of the learning community will voice their views immediately. This is okay since silence can mean teachers are participating in quiet critical reflection before deciding to share their views. Finally, key to dialogue is one's ability to listen to their fellow community members. This is how teachers learn and gain new knowledge. It is crucial to accept that part of lifelong learning is that learning never stops and this should be what teachers practice, because each new year brings in new students who may be different from the group that preceded them (Roberts, 2008).

SOLUTIONS AND RECOMMENDATIONS

Recommendations to Promote Critical Reflection in Schools

Widespread practice of critical reflection depends on structures in place in the school that facilitate collaboration, dialogue, and introspection. Providing a space that encourages open dialogue and interaction within PLCs and with instructional coaches, gives teachers the opportunity to strengthen their critical reflective practices.

An example of a structure which promotes critical reflection is the establishment of coaching relationships between teachers and instructional leaders. To best facilitate these relationships, philosophical changes must take place about the role of instructional leadership in teacher development. Departing from a common model in which campus instructional leadership serves primarily as evaluators or officers of accountability, educational leaders must instead partner with teachers to promote their professional development. In such a model, the coach adopts a mindset not of "expert with all of the answers," but rather a mindset of learner in how to promote success in the particular setting of the particular teacher. This mindset drives the coach towards asking reflective questions in the context of the teacher's unique professional development path, allowing the teacher to focus specifically on the factors influencing his/

her educational space. To this end, instructional coaches must critically reflect on their own practice to better engage with teachers at their own levels of understanding.

Another promising example is establishing time and norms for PLCs. During these regular meetings, teachers can have structured conversations about their practice to develop critical thinking. This is an example of reflection on action. Reflection in action can be developed through the coaching cycle, in which instructional coaches provide observations which teachers can use to help draw connections between outcomes and causes. Such practice can help teachers make focused observations and take corrective measures in action. Absent the availability of instructional coaches, effective PLCs can employ focused peer observations with regular follow-up conversations to similarly develop in-action critical reflection. Additionally, helping teachers find reflective strategies to help them reflect both on and in action would be beneficial. Strategies such as note taking, requesting feedback, setting up checkpoints, and adjusting to improve practice are some ideas to help teachers start these practices (Giaimo-Ballard & Hyatt, 2012). There is also a possibility of finding strategies with technology. However, this will depend on the capacity a school has to use technological tools.

Utilizing a socially collaborative process as described above provides teachers the opportunity to practice critical reflection that is more likely to result in action which then leads to change in practices in the classroom. According to Freire (1978), "Authentic help means that all who are involved help each other mutually, growing together in the common effort to understand the reality in which they seek to transform." (p. 8). Listening to and learning from each other, not just through what is being said, but the reason it is being said helps move the learning community forward toward progress and change. Therefore, developing trust amongst all participants is critical in order to create an effective PLC. Professional development should provide opportunities for problem posing that is entrenched in praxis and should consist of the realities teachers face in their classrooms (Bragelman, 2015).

Implementing structures which promote critical reflection as it relates to developing the broader school environment is imperative. An essential component of critical reflection is an examination of factors extrinsic to a teacher's control (such as school policies or community issues) as they relate to social justice (Nagle, 2008). If fostered well, a base of critically reflective teachers can play a fundamental role in driving and innovating schools. Furthermore, teachers' professional pedagogical identities must be strong; they must see themselves as capable of impacting change (Grootenboer, 2013). A model for self-directed professional development was previously developed to address the needs of resource-deprived schools; notably, the researchers who proposed this model highlight that such a model depends on a collaborative and interconnected community of professional learners (Mushayikwa & Lubben, 2009). Policy committees composed majorly of teachers, for example, can stimulate reflection about school-wide practices that affect learning and instruction in all classrooms. Taken together, a shift of school cultures towards critically reflective practice can have profound and lasting impacts on the student learning experience.

How Can Districts Implement These Constructs

Every district is different. However, most districts want to see improvement in student performance and outcomes. We recommend two specific actions districts can take as they work towards these goals. First, districts should install instructional coaches and/or expand instructional coaching roles within current personnel's job assignments, and provide ongoing professional development to these coaches to improve their practice. Importantly, this ongoing professional development should provide structured opportunities for coaches to reflect on their practice. For example, coaches can practice scenarios (based on real or invented events) in triads, with alternating roles of mock coach, mock teacher, and observer.

Secondly, districts can support the campus' implementation of norm-based PLCs which are focused specifically on the instructional targets of the campus. The establishment of common meeting times and the generalized purpose of improving student success is often not sufficient structure, because it might devolve into planning meetings. Instead, instructional leaders (including teacher leaders) can provide structure to PLCs by setting agendas, finding resources to inform discussion (such as books or articles), and providing protocols for analyzing student performance data and artifacts. When supported by campus and district leadership, these structures can drive critical thinking and reflection towards becoming a habit, resulting in long-term, sustained development of praxis and improvement of student outcomes.

FUTURE RESEARCH DIRECTIONS

Schools should consider implementing a plan of support for ongoing professional development facilitated by leaders in their schools. These plans can be designed to include many of the recommendations suggested throughout this chapter. Most importantly, a professional development plan must include fostering a culture of dialogue and professional learning. Without a long-term plan for implementation of professional development, any new learning that occurs in the traditional one-stop workshop will by and large prove fruitless. Many of the examples provided can be a starting point for schools and districts to design their own way of implementing reflection, problem posing, praxis, dialogue, PLCs, and other skills to enhance professional development and growth for teachers. If schools took the initiative to lead in providing spaces where teachers can practice these skills, more change would occur in our schools in relation to practices in the classroom, which then would translate to outside of the school, where students would utilize what they learned in their personal lives. As a result, we strongly believe more research must be conducted to examine innovative teacher professional development models that will help teachers integrate theory and practice.

CONCLUSION

What is key to this chapter, is that we are placing teachers in the role of learners who are invested in learning beyond the traditional one day professional development workshops and who want to transform the lives of their students with new ways to engage them in learning. In order for them to be this kind of learners, they need opportunities to learn what it means to critically think, reflect, problem pose, and dialogue that will lead to praxis that is transformative for not only the themselves, but their students. These are only some ideas of what districts and schools can do to help teachers grow and develop so they continue to inspire, empower, and lead in their classrooms. Our hope is that this chapter not only provides "food for thought" for teacher preparation programs to collaborate with local districts and school leaders, but also that these districts and school leaders who are trying to figure out how they can provide ongoing professional development for their faculty will see the value of partnering with teacher preparation programs to be proactive so that pre-service teachers are already practicing these constructs prior to getting their own classroom. A dialogue must be started about how to enhance professional learning opportunities so that teachers are shifting their practices. As we have asserted, there needs to be opportunities for both pre-service and practicing teachers to explore, collaborate, reflect, and dialogue with each other. Furthermore, once they participate in problem-posing, they can go back to their classrooms and apply new knowledge. It is this new knowledge that leads to innovative ideas and practice. Teachers who experience these kinds of opportunities will see that being a part of some kind of ongoing professional development is beneficial.

Critical thinking and reflective practice are seen as central to the theory of transformative learning. Opportunities for personal growth and development through critical thinking and reflection will provide teachers with the tools they need that leads to action and transformation of society, even if it means challenging teachers to move beyond their comfort zone. Something we cannot ignore is the reality that social forces outside of our classrooms impact what happens inside our classrooms. The goal is to help our teachers learn about themselves and their students and how best to engage them in learning that is so powerful that students leave their classrooms as agents of change with the ability to transfer their learning beyond the classroom, whether it be to the individual level, the family level, the community level, or at the level of the society. As educators, we should want to help our students learn and become the best versions of themselves. We assert that the same applies to teachers. Shouldn't they be allowed to grow and develop to be the best versions of themselves? Imagine the possibilities of innovative professional development that transforms the lives of both teachers and students.

REFERENCES

Anderson, M. J., & Freebody, K. (2012). Developing communities of praxis: Bridging the theory practice divide in teacher education. *McGill Journal of Education, 47*(3), 359–378. doi:10.7202/1014864ar

Bognar, B., & Krumes, I. (2017). Encouraging reflection and critical friendship in preservice teacher education. *CEPS Journal, 7*(3), 87–112.

Bragelman, J. (2015). Praxis as dialogue: Teacher and administrator. *Journal of Urban Mathematics Education, 8*(2), 27–43.

Campbell, P. F., & Malkus, N. N. (2011). The impact of elementary mathematics coaches on student achievement. *The Elementary School Journal, 111*(3), 430–454. doi:10.1086/657654

Darling-Hammond, L., Hyler, M., & Gardner, M. (2017). *Effective Teacher Professional Development.* Palo Alto, CA: Learning Policy Institute.

Downer, J. T., Stuhlman, M., Schweig, J., Martinez, J. F., & Ruzek, E. (2018). Measuring effective teacher-student interactions from a student perspective: A multi-level analysis. *The Journal of Early Adolescence, 35*(5-6), 722–758. doi:10.1177/0272431614564059

Freire, P. (1978). *Pedagogy in process: The letters to Guinea Bissau.* New York, NY: The Seabury.

Freire, P. (1985). *The politics of education: Culture, power and liberation.* South Hadley, MA: Bergin & Garvey Publishers. doi:10.1007/978-1-349-17771-4

Freire, P. (1995). *Pedagogy of hope. Reliving pedagogy of the oppressed.* New York, NY: Continuum.

Freire, P. (2000). *Pedagogy of the oppressed. 30th Anniversary edition.* New York, NY: Continuum.

Galey, S. (2016). The evolving role of instructional coaches in U.S. policy contexts. *The William & Mary Educational Review*, *4*(2), 54–71.

Giaimo-Ballard, C., & Hyatt, L. (2012, Fall). Reflection-in-action teaching strategies used by faculty to enhance teaching and learning. *Networks: An Online Teaching Journal for Teacher Research*, *14*(2), 1–11.

Greenleaf, C. L., Litman, C., Hanson, T. L., Rosen, R., Boscardin, C. K., Herman, J., ... Jones, B. (2011). Integrating literacy and science in biology: Teaching and learning impacts of reading apprenticeship professional development. *American Educational Research Journal*, *48*(3), 647–717. doi:10.3102/0002831210384839

Grootenboer, P. (2013). The praxis of mathematics teaching: Developing mathematics identities. *Pedagogy, Culture & Society*, *21*(3), 321–342. doi:10.1080/14681366.2012.759131

Howard, T. C. (2003). Culturally relevant pedagogy: Ingredients for critical teacher reflection. *Theory into Practice*, *42*(3), 195–202. doi:10.120715430421tip4203_5

Kemmis, S., & Smith, T. J. (2008). *Enabling praxis: Challenges for education*. Rotterdam, NL: Sense Publishers.

Klem, A. M., & Connell, J. P. (2004). Relationships matter: Linking teacher support to student engagement and achievement. *The Journal of School Health*, *74*(7), 262–273. doi:10.1111/j.1746-1561.2004.tb08283.x PMID:15493703

Lauer, P. A., Christopher, D. E., Firpo-Triplett, R., & Buchting, F. (2014). The impact of short-term professional development on participant outcomes: A review of the literature. *Professional Development in Education*, *40*(2), 207–227. doi:10.1080/19415257.2013.776619

Liu, K. (2015). Critical reflection as a framework for transformative learning in teacher education. *Educational Review*, *67*(2), 135–157. doi:10.1080/00131911.2013.839546

Low, E. L., & Cai, C. H. (2017). Developing student teachers' critical thinking and professional values: A case study of a teacher educator in Singapore. *Asia Pacific Journal of Education*, *37*(4), 535–551. doi:10.1080/02188791.2017.1386093

Mangin, M., & Dunsmore, K. (2015). How the framing of instructional coaching as a lever for systemic or individual reform influences the enactment of coaching. *Educational Administration Quarterly*, *51*(2), 179–213. doi:10.1177/0013161X14522814

Mushayikwa, E., & Lubben, F. (2009). Self-directed professional development – Hope for teachers working in deprived environments? *Teaching and Teacher Education*, *25*(3), 375–382. doi:10.1016/j.tate.2008.12.003

Nagle, J. (2008). Becoming a reflective practitioner in the age of accountability. *The Educational Forum*, *73*(1), 76–86. doi:10.1080/00131720802539697

Roberts, P. (2008). Teaching as an ethical and political process: A Freirean process. In V. Carpenter, J. Jesson, P. Roberts et al. (Eds.), Ngā Kaupapa here: Connections and contradictions in education (pp. 99-108). Melbourne, AU: Cengage.

Sakiz, G., Pape, S. J., & Hoy, A. W. (2012). Does perceived teacher affective support matter for middle school students in mathematics classrooms? *Journal of School Psychology, 50*(2), 235–255. doi:10.1016/j.jsp.2011.10.005 PMID:22386122

Schon, D. (1983). *The reflective practitioner*. New York, NY: Basic Books.

Schuck, S., Aubusson, P., & Buchanan, J. (2008). Enhancing teacher education practice through professional learning conversations. *European Journal of Teacher Education, 31*(2), 215–227. doi:10.1080/02619760802000297

Stoll, L., Bolam, R., McMahon, A., Wallace, M., & Thomas, S. (2006). Professional learning communities: A review of the literature. *Journal of Educational Change, 7*(4), 221–258. doi:10.100710833-006-0001-8

Tam, A. (2015). The role of a professional learning community in teacher change: A perspective from beliefs and practices. *Teachers and Teaching, 21*(1), 22–43. doi:10.1080/13540602.2014.928122

Torres, M. N. & Mercado, M. (2004). Living the praxis of teacher education through teacher research. *A Journal for the Scholar-Practitioner Leader, 2*(2), 59-73.

Tripp, L. O., Love, A., Thomas, C. M., & Russell, J. (2018). Teacher education advocacy for multiple perspectives and culturally sensitive teaching. In U. Thomas (Ed.), Advocacy and academia and the role of teacher preparation programs (161-181). Hershey, PA: IGI Global. doi:10.4018/978-1-5225-2906-4.ch009

Wink, J. (2011). *Critical pedagogy: Notes from the real world* (4th ed.). Upper Saddle River, NJ: Pearson Education.

Zeichner, K. M., & Liston, D. P. (2013). *Reflective teaching: An introduction* (2nd ed.). New York, NY: Routledge. doi:10.4324/9780203822289

ADDITIONAL READINGS

Aktekin, N. C. (2014). Teacher professional development: The critical friends group (CFG) model. Latvia, European Union: SIA OmniScriptum Publishing.

Brookfield, S. D. (2017). *Becoming a critically reflective teacher* (2nd ed.). San Francisco, CA: Jossey Bass.

Freire, P. (2018). *Pedagogy of the oppressed: 50th anniversary edition* (4th ed.). New York, NY: Bloomsbury Publishing.

Hinchey, P. H. (2006). *Becoming a critical educator: Defining a classroom identity, designing a critical pedagogy* (3rd ed.). New York, NY: Peter Lang.

Knight, J. (2007). *Instructional coaching: A partnership approach*. Thousand Oaks, CA: Corwin Press.

Milner, H. R. IV. (2015). *Start where you are, but don't stay there: Understanding diversity, opportunity gaps, and teaching in today's classroom*. Cambridge, MA: Harvard Education Press.

Sensoy, P., & DiAngelo, R. (2017). *Is everyone really equal? An introduction to key concepts in social justice education* (2nd ed.). New York, NY: Teachers College Press.

Sirrakos, G. Jr, & Emdin, C. (2017). *Between the world and the urban classroom*. Boston, MA: Sense Publishers. doi:10.1007/978-94-6351-032-5

Souto-Manning, M. (2010). *Freire, teaching, and learning: Cultural circles across contexts*. New York, NY: Peter Lang.

KEY TERMS AND DEFINITIONS

Critical Thinking: The process of mapping out relationships between observations to understand the causality and interconnectedness between events.

Dialogue: According to Freire (1995), dialogue is a co-operative activity that involves respect. Dialogue contributes to a more transformative learning environment and removes the traditional "banking" model (a deposit of concepts taught in the professional development space by the instructional coach or the professional development facilitator).

Praxis: Praxis is an iterative, reflective approach to taking action. It is an ongoing process of moving between practice and theory. Praxis is a synthesis of theory and practice in which each informs the other (Freire, 1985).

Problem Posing: According to Freire (1970), problem posing is a method that transforms learners (in this case, the teachers) into "critical co-investigators in dialogue with the teacher" (in this case the facilitator of professional development workshop, a coach, or mentor) (p. 68).

Professional Learning Communities: While "there is no universal definition of a professional learning community," a professional learning community can generally be defined as a group of individuals which regularly collaborate to critically reflect on their practice for the purpose of individual professional growth as well as advancement of the group (Stoll, Bolam, McMahon, Wallace, & Thomas, 2006).

Reflection: To be a reflective teacher means to question the goals and values that guide one's teaching, the institutional and cultural contexts in which he or she teaches and examining the assumptions one brings to the classroom relative to one's students' cultures and lived experiences (Zeichner & Liston, 1996).

Reflection in Action: This occurs during instruction. Teachers reflect an unexpected student reaction or perception and attempt to make immediate adjustments to instruction as a result of these reactions (Schon, 1983).

Reflection on Action: This occurs before and after an action in the classroom. Schon (1983) asserts that teachers reflect before a lesson, when they think about their lesson and after execution of the lesson when they reflect on what occurred during the lesson.

Self-Directed Professional Development: Professional learning that is driven by oneself. While it should depend on a collaborative peer network, it occurs in the absence of administrative oversight, unsolicited coaching, or policy structures which require regular meeting, documentation, or other actions.

Chapter 7
Planning Curriculum for Teaching Thinking Skills Needed for 21st Century Education

Harpreet Kaur Dhir
Hacienda La Puente Unified School District, USA

ABSTRACT

This chapter provides a method for meeting the educational demands of the 21st century. The Content through Action method (CTA) provides a process to plan integrated instructional units for connecting various subject matter areas. Based on the researcher's experience in designing interdisciplinary units, the chapter includes the CTA process of building a unit and the research-based rationale behind each step of the process. The literature review includes discussion of the Four Cs, the 21st-century classroom, the motivation of learners, and the teacher's role. The theoretical framework is built on the foundation provided by constructivism, heutagogy, design thinking, the theory of change, and the growth mindset. After teaching other methods such as problem-based and design-based learning, the author asserts that the CTA method of instructional planning promotes the development of thinking skills compatible with the needs of the 21st-century learner.

INTRODUCTION: 21ST CENTURY EDUCATION

As the world of education completes two decades of the 21st century, it continues to transform the practices, multiple theories, and methods implemented to develop instructional plans compatible with the demands of the modern era. Donovan, Green, and Mason (2014) mention the recent focus on educational reform to develop 21st century skills. The authors point out some commonalities in various frameworks concerned with these necessary skills as they examine the Partnership for 21st Century Skills (P21), enGauge 21st century skills, the American Association of Colleges and Universities, and the Organization

DOI: 10.4018/978-1-5225-7829-1.ch007

Copyright © 2019, IGI Global. Copying or distributing in print or electronic forms without written permission of IGI Global is prohibited.

for Economic Cooperation and Development. This chapter focuses on the P21 framework that includes critical thinking, creativity, collaboration, and communication, or the Four Cs. In schools, the Four Cs are positioned as the foundations of instructional planning.

Being a successful learner in the 21st century consists of a two-pronged process. Developing the needed skills that the Four Cs represent forms one branch; the other branch requires students to develop metacognition to reflect on personal capabilities. Hargreaves (2016) describes reflective competency as essential to maximizing deep learning. Metacognitive skill facilitates the learner's construction of the meaning as a form of mental processing. I argue that planning instruction using the Four Cs framework is incomplete without developing the reflective practice as learners engage in the meaning-making process.

The meaning-making process could be rooted in cultural practices despite the standardized view presented by Bruner (1986). Young children make meaning from the egocentric perspective being unaware of the other perspectives. Through unmediated experiences, having direct encounters with the world leads to developing knowledge about the world. Ultimately, cognition develops as cognition, affect, and action. In the 21st century education, a learner needs to shift from solely having an egocentric perspective to that of cognition and action in collaboration with peers as enabled by the Four C's.

As a practicing educator, I find that theoretical frameworks need methods to materialize research into practice. The goal of this chapter is to facilitate instructional planning and to provide classroom teachers with examples of 21st century-compatible teaching, including the Four Cs and reflective learning. My public-school teaching experience of 25 years enriches the chapter with insights developed throughout those years.

The experience of teaching general education K–6, special education, university teaching to train teachers, and being in the role of a Teacher on a Special Assignment, along with various other leadership roles in 25 years of teaching, has provided the researcher with a vantage point for viewing experience-based learning as the most beneficial to students. During those years of teaching, I have implemented design-based and project-based learning methods, and these methods provide a launching pad to innovate other methods using experience-based professional insights.

BACKGROUND: LITERATURE REVIEW

Defining Thinking Skills

Postman (1985) laments the direction America has been taking towards technology serving as a distraction to thinking where all subject matter is presented in a multi-media format to present it in an entertaining manner. He predicts that the country's attraction towards entertainment will lead to a Hollywood actor becoming the president of the United States. Ronald Reagan and Donald Trump as presidents have materialized the author's concerns with serious public issues turning into entertainment.

This begs the definition of thinking skills if the trend must be shifted from technological entertainment to the necessities of the 21st century education. According to Donovan, Green, and Mason (2014), teaching thinking skills is compatible with the 21st century skills (termed the Four Cs) in the framework of the Partnership for 21st Century Skills (P21). The P21 framework defines thinking skills as a range of ideas and the techniques necessary to create those ideas. The study includes subskills of the umbrella term "thinking skills": creative thinking and critical thinking, in addition to communication and collaboration.

Creativity and Innovation

The authors describe creativity and innovation to include creative thinking, creative collaboration, and implementation of innovations. Creative thinking consists of revising, creating, evaluating, and developing new ideas. Creative collaboration incorporates various perspectives on traditional methods of face-to-face collaboration or working with a team in a virtual setting (e.g., creating products on Google Docs). The team members in a virtual environment could collaborate in real time from distant locations. Another element of creativity and innovation is the possibility of a failed design. But the innovative environment encourages experiencing failure as a learning opportunity in the context of participating in projects and integrating cross-curricular concepts.

Critical Thinking

Critical thinking and problem-solving are associated with thinking skills. One of the components of critical thinking is effective reasoning, including inductive and deductive thinking. Experiencing concepts through a systems-thinking process, where the learners design products using objects combined with technological resources, facilitates the development of reasoning skills. Decision-making is another component in which the learners practice supporting claims with evidence, drawing conclusions, making connections between pieces of information, and reflecting on learning experiences. Problem-solving is concerned with tackling unfamiliar problems in innovative ways.

Communication and Collaboration

Articulation of thoughts and listening to others to create meaning are part of developing communication skills. Using multimedia to present ideas is also encouraged, with the added benefit of collaborative communication must be experienced by the learners to develop 21st century-compatible thinking skills. Along with taking pride in presenting individually created solutions, participating in group assignments by assuming responsibility for the elements of the task promotes collaboration.

Teaching thinking skills using the Four Cs provides a framework for teachers to plan instruction in the form of unit planning. Implementing the Four Cs empowers the learner's individual and social identity. Friere, as cited in Hahn Tapper (2013), asserts that every student possesses a unique personal identity and has the freedom to construct a social identity simultaneously, a part of social identity theory. Therefore, the inclusion of the Four Cs is also compatible with empowering the student's overall identity formation, including individual and social personalities.

21st Century Classroom

The Four Cs provide a framework for developing the thinking skills the modern learner needs, so the classroom environment and instructional planning are factors requiring examination. The importance of implementing evidence-based practices in the classroom and in the school must be understood in the current context. The learning environment of the 21st century classroom must demonstrate the alignment of instructional practices related to educational research if reform of the classroom environment is expected. The 21st century classroom environment must emphasize the progression of improvement over time, stressing the process of learning (Biesta, 2007).

Classroom Environment and Instruction

The traditional instructional models assess successful learning through a learner's ability to replicate existing knowledge and provide perfect answers in the early stages of the learning process—a model considered obsolete in the 21st century. Teaching thinking skills requires learning over time, emphasizing a process-based learning through the experiential journey. Dewey's philosophy of education, as he wrote in 1938, was of, by, and for experience containing longitudinal (historical) and lateral (social) dimensions (School of Educators, 2011). I agree with Dewey's view of experience-oriented learning as the "true learning," emphasizing process over time rather than a product of the moment.

The classroom environment must reflect the process of learning, and assignments must be designed in a way that provides experience to students. John Dewey, as cited in Boyte (2017), did not separate thoughts (intellect) and actions (work), believing that all education reflects the experience that consists of experimenting, observing, and reflecting. Donovan et al. (2014) describe the experience-based learning environment as group or individual projects where students might be at various stages of learning and process completion. One might see students using a range of materials, from textbooks to the digital devices to experience the stages of the learning process in a collaborative setting.

The instructional strategies might also include student journals or online blogs to record the information and reflections related to the topics explored. The final products or the solutions could be presented in creative ways, such as in multimedia presentations and artistic representations. Experience-based teaching methods are associated with pragmatism, and John Dewey's pedagogy of teaching is based on pragmatic values (Ilica, 2016). Experiential learning is a method of instruction that guides students in constructing the meaning of the concept.

Motivating the Learners

I have listened to many teachers express frustration over lack of motivation on the part of the learners, which requires spending some instructional time on motivating individuals to learn. This concern might result from the fact that different motivating forces drive 21st century learners from those that drove the generations of the predigital age. Millennials born between 1981 and 2000 view education differently from the way previous generations did. Sedden and Clark (2016) report that millennials consider college a path to a high-paying career and perceive education as acquiring the means to an end.

Sedden and Clark (2016) provide instructional strategies to increase motivation of modern learners by connecting and engaging with the learners where they build trust with peers and the instructor. The focus on individual student success is more powerful than focusing on class achievement to motivate the learner. The authors recommend creating a classroom where learners are active in discussions, simulations, and hands-on tasks. Problem-based assignments where students work in groups improve motivation, as they incorporate a sense of self-direction and independent thinking.

The 21st century learners possess qualities that differ from the learners of the predigital age. Faulkner and Latham (2016) remind us that the world has shifted from an industrial economy to a knowledge economy. With that shift, instruction had to shift from emphasizing the teaching of routine skills to developing skills of problem-solving and using knowledge to innovate and create. In addition to using existing knowledge, the creation of new knowledge through collaboration with others must become part of educational programs.

The Teacher's Role

The teacher's role of facilitator in the 21st century learning environment is mainly to interact with learners to monitor and guide progress. I believe that the teacher might not always provide corrections for errors right away but might do so in following lessons as the teacher's observations provide the points of instruction. According to Donovan et al. (2014), instead of stating an objective, lessons would begin with expressing the status of the project and setting its direction. John Dewey promoted the individual growth of a student and development of the intellect as the necessary ingredients for citizens of a democratic society (Pouwels & Biesta, 2017). Assigning the task of student intellectual growth, Dewey places teachers in the important role of forming the citizenry of a democratic society.

The National Education Association (NEA, n.d.) describes the role of a teacher in the teacher's ethical code of conduct. Requiring a commitment to guide the students in realizing their potential and learning through inquiry is considered a professional principle. The professional code of conduct enforces Dewey's philosophy of teaching students through experience.

Theoretical Framework

The push to impose educational practices that originated in the field of medicine was an inaccurate practice. Not being ill, the learners learned through interactions with people and their surroundings. Factors such as the teaching style of the teacher, the size of the class, and the school building's design influenced learning experiences (Biesta, 2007). The author examines theories that base education on building student values instead of on the connection to medical theories that promoted the effectiveness of treatment. As Biesta (2007) reports, John Dewey reflected on "knowing"—learning based not on acquiring knowledge through intervention-like treatments, but instead on learning experiences. Dewey's theory of "knowing" promotes the interactions between actions and the impact of those actions, interactions between living beings, and interactions between problem and solutions.

Constructivism

The theory of constructivism views learning as a product of an experience. All human beings construct understanding of the world through their experience (McWilliams, 2016). Viewing knowledge as a practical act reinforces the need for experience-based education. The author argues that fixed and permanent ideas were associated with objectivism, an obstacle to progress through action.

John Dewey's pedagogy was consistent with the theory of constructivism. He believed that schools must create the relevance of education by relating educational programs to the world in which the learners live (Kilfoye, 2013). Constructivism promotes the learner as an active participant in the educational process. The focus on the learner includes the context of life outside of school. Piaget, as cited in Dongo-Montoya (2018), promoted the idea of a learner being a part of the social context. Although Piaget was criticized for following Marx's socialist ideas, his work supported the need to make education concrete and close to the learner's reality. Technology being a major feature of the modern society, the context of the 21st century world consists of the need to develop digital literacy, since technology is embedded in many aspects of the learner's life.

The efforts to update schools to meet the technological needs of the 21st century appear to focus on purchasing more computers and new furniture. I found constructivists such as Dewey describing inquiry as technological thinking (Waddington & Weeth, 2016). Perceiving the time in front of a screen as a 21st century learning method based on this research was inaccurate. Experiential learning develops the innovator's skills, using technology as a tool in the learning process compatible with the 21st century learning. Bruner (1986) found the mind to be the most essential tool of construction along with the hands. Vygotsky, as cited in Bruner (1986), agreed that hands and the mind must collaborate and if left alone without the cooperation of the two, neither the hands nor the mind would achieve much in the learning process. Creating experiences where mind (thinking) and hands (action) coexist is the original technology which must be employed along with the modern tools such as computers and other devices.

Dewey (1990), originally published in 1956, promotes experiential learning as "work" in the classroom. Considering the importance of work, the author emphasizes that experience engages the students by keeping them active and prepares them for the practicalities of the later years. But Dewey cautioned against viewing education as a preparation for the future. Instead the experience was perceived as an instrument to learn about living life itself.

Life Span Theory of Development

Having emerged from the field of developmental psychology, the life span theory is grounded in ideas related to the individual's personality and intellectual functioning. Lapp and Spaniol (2016) describe the life span theory as promoting the idea that individual goals change as time passes and humans acquire the ability to adapt to diminishing resources. The changing phases, along with the changes of age, create the need to adapt.

According to Lapp and Spaniol (2016), at younger phases of life people are likely to pursue acquisition. Focusing on growth and acquiring necessities relate to meeting life's goals, and the need to meet the demands of the 21st century impacts current learners such as the Millennials. At an older age, the focus shifts to maintaining resources and preventing any losses. In the later years of life, declining physical functioning leads to having less control over multiple aspects of living as one adapts to aging (Fiske & O'Riley, 2016). Whether one is younger or older, the common needs involve a sense of continuity and interpersonal relations as time passes.

Heutagogy

The life span theory assists in understanding younger generations such as the Millennials. Mishra, Fahnoe, and Henriksen (2013) describe 21st century demands such as having the skills to employ online sources, integrating knowledge from across disciplines and applying them in a practical sense, problem-solving, and engaging with innovation and creativity. Online learning has gained prominence as learners in the modern era demonstrate the ability to practice self-directed learning using digital skills. Technology enables the inclusion of real-world context in the learning environment, where the learner develops internal characteristics of self-determination through a sense of independence and control over the world in a virtual setting. As defined by Blaschke (2012), heutagogy was a net-centric theory reinforcing the life span theory's idea of younger generations as growth-oriented.

Blaschke (2012) described heutagogy as promoting self-determination. A learner in the context of the 21st century must play an active role in the learning process, and along with learning the content, test personal values. As a practitioner of heutagogy, the teacher's role shifts to becoming a resource for the self-determined learner. The life span theory illuminated the needs of the younger generation, representing most of these learners as attracted to growth and goal achievement, in addition to internalizing the characteristics of a self-determined learner.

Design Thinking

Whitty and Koeplin (2011) express the need for teachers and learners to reinvent themselves on an ongoing basis. Associated with experiential learning, design thinking facilitates the practice of teaching through design by integrating curriculum using unifying ideas. As cited in School of Educators (2011), John Dewey asserted in 1938 that educational philosophy was a philosophy of experience. Education had to afford an experience to the learner in which, by engaging personal capacities, the learner constructs the meaning of the knowledge the adult world imposes.

Dewey considers means and ends a collaborative process, rather than one leading to the other (Biesta, 2007). Design thinking accomplishes this model of instruction, in which a problem is solved by designing a solution, and the solution itself is a problem to be solved. Remodeling of a home where replacing the old tiles with the new ones creates the need to paint the walls to match the color of the tiles illustrates how the solution becomes a new problem to solve. Dewey (Biesta, 2007) considers ends as new hypotheses open to experimentation, calling this intelligent problem-solving. Organizing the various experiences in a connected chain in instructional planning would create the learning process as a collaboration between means and ends.

A learner engaging in designing a solution activates human intuition and imagination. According to Whitty and Koeplin (2011), the human faculties such as the intuition employed during meditation and spiritual and musical experiences are the same faculties responsible for deep learning. Design thinking connects the inner factors of intuition and external factors associated with the building process to create an experience-based process leading to deep learning.

Transformational Learning: The Theory of Change

During the industrial age in the United States in the early years of the 20th century, the education system was confronted with the need to transform to accommodate the industrial and economic shifts. Philosophers such as John Dewey were involved in the process of change. Dewey (1990) warns in the beginning of the 20th century that the industrial shifts caused by scientific discoveries and inventions have controlled and overshadowed all other changes in the society. The economic system's need to produce citizens who no longer needed to think but to act according to the industry's criteria raised concerns for John Dewey. His goal was to transform the schools to such places where students were free to learn without the stresses caused by the economy. But schools became places of repetition of lessons lacking expressions of individual personalities while oppressing the use of language in a social setting.

John Dewey's concern appears to be alive today as well when the scholars and the educators are aware of the need for transforming education, but the system is struggling to shift the instructional practices. As the postindustrial digital world demands educational programs to evaluate existing practices, a sense of transformation is difficult to ignore. Dewey believed that education must reflect the needs of the changing world because education concerns learning that extends beyond the school walls (Kilfoye, 2013). The dissonance in being aware of the need for change and accepting change by transforming instructional practices, as described by Gopaul (2011), seems to be in the air in educational institutions. The theory of change lists the four stages of socialization in the changing world of instruction as educators take steps to transform the learning experience to meet 21st century demands.

As novices of 21st century teaching and learning, individuals progress through the stages of change: anticipatory, formal, informal, and personal. Gopaul (2011) describes the anticipatory stage as being aware of the needed transformation. I believe that teachers and learners have moved beyond the awareness stage. The formal stage includes some level of experience with the shifting dynamics, leading to the informal stage where, in addition to the experience, some expectations are internalized by the learner. The final stage of change is at the personal level, where new knowledge is integrated with existing knowledge, forming a new identity.

According to Van De Ven and Sun (2011), both the experience and the reflection are a part of constructing understanding. The instructional planning for the 21st century learner must include the stages in which the learner journeys through the process of anticipation of the learning, experiencing the learning, and reflecting on the newly created self-identity. This provides a structure for building an instructional method in which experience leads to reflection. I believe that reflection includes the point of connection linking the experience to the required content from across the curricular areas.

Growth Mindset

Dewey (1990) conceives mind as a process of growth as opposed to a fixed system. Dewey's work from the early 1900s still resonates with the modern thinking of the 21st century. The tragedy noticed in the field of education is that the conclusions drawn in the early 1900s have yet to be transformed into a practical approach. My focus has been to teach using the methods which cultivate the growth mindset.

My teaching experience has included the authorities from outside the classroom regulating the classroom environment. Focus walls displaying the components of the programs adopted from a publishing company, data walls with test scores, seating charts with symbols to represent the categories of the students (such as English Language Learners) all waste learning space too sacred to be occupied for compliance purposes. The little room that was left required me, as a practitioner of constructivism, to find creative solutions for arranging the classroom environment in a way that would encourage the development of a growth mindset.

According to Donovan et al. (2014), classroom management involves organizing the resources for learners, including access to the teacher as a resource. The organization of the physical environment must be user-friendly, so learners can access materials easily. Instructional strategies associated with developing the growth mindset include the implementation of the Four Cs: critical thinking, creativity, collaboration, and communication. The interactive lessons relevant to the learner create the conditions for a classroom environment conducive to the development of a growth mindset.

Incorporating active play embedding problem-solving raised curiosity and childlike perspective encouraging the growth mindset. Faulkner and Latham (2016) report that NASA asked astronauts for their childhood hobbies, to tap into the childlike perspective that brings curiosity and innovation. Teachers must enjoy the same freedom to innovate instructional planning by introducing play into the learning experiences. The authenticity of a teacher would enable the creation of the kind of teaching practice conducive to the learner's playfulness. According to Faulkner and Latham (2016), playfulness creates environment, leading to innovation as the positive state of mind that encourages risk-taking, adventurous activities.

In addition to the learners, teachers also must move from a fixed mindset to a growth mindset. Faulkner and Latham (2016) define a fixed mindset as the belief that the ability to practice creativity is predetermined. This type of biased thinking, where the teacher views the learner as lacking creative ability, would be an obstacle to the learner participating in creative tasks. The growth mindset would focus on change by assuming the risks and progressing through the challenges purposefully, with expectations of growth. Educational institutions must include teachers in creating such shifts, so they can become active participants in the changing environment.

MAIN FOCUS: COMPATIBLE METHODS

Problem-Based Learning Method

Problem-based learning advocates create the learning environment compatible with 21st century learning. Donovan et al. (2014) illustrate the problem-based classroom to include individual and group projects. The learners might progress at different stages, supported by such resources as access to the Internet, textbooks, and peer and teacher support. Collaborative work, recorded in journals or online blogs, is presented using multimedia programs or through other media. The energetic classroom environment includes the teacher as a facilitator who instructs learners in a formal lesson-delivery setting and through informal interactions.

The problem-based classroom in the 21st century setting does not include technology as a catalyst for teaching. The problem-based culture of the classroom is the main ingredient in building the capacity to become a 21st century learner. Creativity, collaboration, critical thinking, and communication are the main components of that culture. Technology is a tool to support learning.

Human-Centered Design Method

The industrial environment of the past focused on manufacturing products, and the schools designed educational programs to focus on product creation as well. In the postindustrial world, the emphasis of educational programs had to shift from focus on product to human-centeredness (Bowie & Cassim, 2016). Human-centered methods of instruction include the components of community building, collaboration, and social responsibility. Dewey (1990) mentions the humanity involved in teaching and learning practices demonstrating the consistency of thought with the human-centered design method. Capturing the nature of a child or an adult was the key to learning according to Dewey (1990), and it is a key to the human-centered design method as well. The human-centered design method is centered around the idea of seizing the humanity in the teaching methods impacting the students. The four Rs of human-centered method—respect, reciprocity, relevance, and reflection—are the components of all experiential learning, which has four stages: experience, reflection, conceptualization, and action. According to Bowie and Cassim (2016), human-centered teaching methods employ the use of design to solve problems and plan instruction by integrating the disciplines. The authors of the study assert that including the process of design is essential for making the world a culturally sensitive place embedded in higher consciousness.

Design Thinking Method

Although design thinking is applicable at any age level, I found that work with primary students specifically benefitted from methods involving design. The design thinking methods incorporated problem-based learning and human-centered learning, where students built and tested prototypes (Noel & Liub, 2017). The authors claim the design thinking methods are instrumental in bringing a paradigm shift to teaching and learning, to reform the instructional practices for 21st century education. Vande Zande developed six steps to plan for a design process that included defining the problem, investigating and researching, generating ideas, making the prototype, presenting solutions, and evaluating and researching. Dorst listed a five-step process of formulating a problem, using multiple representations of solutions, moving or creating generators, evaluating by reflecting on action, and managing. Meredith Davis argued that the design process should begin by identifying the problem, researching, testing multiple solutions through building prototypes, and evaluating the prototypes using the performance criteria created through social mediation. The various methods follow the underlying principles of the design thinking theory. My field knowledge of 20 years resulted in the development of a method called Content Through Action (CTA) as connected to the design thinking.

SOLUTIONS FROM MY CLASSROOM

Content Through Action (CTA) Part One: The Experience First

Having been impacted positively by design thinking, my professional practice developed over the years to include the components of problem-based learning and design methods. As illustrated in Figure 1, the process uses the model of the matryoshka dolls to demonstrate its connectivity, beginning with the largest doll to represent the broad theme and progressing toward the conclusion of the experience. The narrative-style organization was essential as Bruner (1986) promotes the human experience to be organized in the format of a narrative, story, or drama. The narrative-style connectivity of the learning process relates to the interaction of the self with the social world.

The process is initiated by sifting through various subjects to form a unifying theme. One can imagine a teacher sitting with all the teacher manuals, looking ahead to plan for the next six to eight weeks. The challenge is to connect the important concepts under one experience. This part is important for the instructor as it allows examination of the curricular areas prior to launching the instructional unit. In relation to the needed unification of the subject matters, Gardner (2000) adds that when arts and sciences integrate, and the processes of inventions and transformations occur, only then the learning will be enhanced, and educational technology will see changes. Bruner (1986) considered the avoidance of a humanistic stance in learning mathematics or sciences as impossible, given the fact of the human mind using language to understand and express opinions and facts. The CTA method promotes the integration across the subjects to achieve the enhanced learning experience in which ideas either merge or show a parallel system of thoughts from one subject's content to another.

The integration of multiple subjects appears to be a difficult point for many teachers as I have witnessed the struggle in various settings such as school-based planning meetings or the district level committee meetings. The teachers following a template of a lesson plan to teach the skills react with confusion and

116

frustration if suggestions to rearrange the sequence of the steps or to begin the study with a universal concept are made.

In planning to teach the plant's parts, most traditional lessons tend to begin with observing the plants, whereas the CTA method would begin with a problem of structure, which is a broad unifying idea. Analyzing the parts of a desk, a pencil box, or a pair of scissors would build the prior knowledge of objects having structures. Observing the plant's parts would follow as a study of the plant's structure. Dewey (1990) lamented the state of education as an effort to create intellectuals full of information rather than being a vehicle for the development of natural human impulses. Instead of the traditional lesson planning template where a lesson begins with the topic of study, Dewey (1990) promoted the introduction of learning a new topic through the learner's context.

The unifying experience of viewing the learning through the lens of structures or other unifying themes provides a path to creating system thinking. Integrating the subject matter with another unifying theme such as preservation creates a system like the solar system where, like the planets, the content areas orbit around the unifying theme. Teachers planning instruction in an integrative manner are called interactionists, creating an atmosphere of active learning in a cooperative setting. This is the opposite of the teacher's role as an interventionist, separating subjects and viewing students as passive learners (Bray & Thomas, 1995).

The next part of the process is to launch a problem that could be possible in a real-world context. An example of such a problem with the theme of preservation could be how one preserves nature, artifacts, and ideas. Dewey promoted problem-solving as part of the learning process, considering that solutions could be designed once the problem was made explicit (Biesta, 2007). This step also involves a mini-research opportunity to prepare for the following step of creating a prototype representing a system which can preserve nature, artifacts, and ideas. Nelson Goodman, the founder of Project Zero, as cited in Gardner (2000), asserts that to help someone become more creative, a teacher must present obstacles which are productive. This further establishes the need to include problem-solving in the teaching method compatible with the 21st century education.

Designing the first prototype of a system that could preserve nature, artifacts, and ideas belongs to the action container. Finding a solution to respond to a problem, according to Dewey, occurs through experimentation by choosing various actions (Biesta, 2007). According to Noel and Liub (2017), prototype creation is a component of design thinking, employing the skills of creativity and resourcefulness identified as early predictors of success. Yet, as Noel and Liub (2017) explain, problem-solving is a skill in the list of skills missing from educational programs and labelled as a 21st century gap. Building a solution to a problem led to improvement in the learner's problem-solving skills.

The design-based learning that I had practiced earlier did not allow research until after the prototype was built. The CTA method differs due to the increased access to information through technology. Self-directed learners are expected to acquire knowledge independently, in addition to the instruction provided in a teacher-directed setting. According to Hill (2012), knowledge exists everywhere in the digital world, and it became essential to develop the skills to process, synthesize, and connect the knowledge holistically without the overemphasis on details. One of the dimensions of education is described as accessibility for all groups and for all ages as a human right (Crosco, 2013). The reality of the modern world includes technology making the abundance of information accessible and avoiding the use of technology throughout the learning path despite the expectations of the world might be considered an element of poor education.

To tackle the fear of lacking originality with access to information through technology, the process did not provide any performance standards to guide the building of the prototype. Instead, the process liberates the learner to build using the personal interpretation of an ideal solution. Teachers might expect to give instructions or performance standards to the learners before designing the prototype but introducing the performance standards would formalize the process too early, at the point where the creativity and insights would be in danger of becoming programming (Mintzberg, 2003). The performance standards are placed later in the process after the prototype is built, which might be a difficult step for the teachers who might display concern in the changed classroom environment.

The learner-centered classroom would look and sound different from the traditionally structured classroom. Dewey (1990) compared the classroom to a laboratory where a learner does not learn as an individual but as a representative of the humanity. Traditionally, sitting in straight rows facing the front, the learners participated in the classroom setting as individuals rarely working in collaboration with the others. The 21st century shifts would impact the classroom environment where peer collaboration would be emphasized.

The next step includes the performance standards that could guide the revision of the prototype and be used as a quantitative rubric if point value were attached to the required standards. According to Bresciani (2010), the measurement instrument (i.e., the performance standards) must state the indicators of success in an age-appropriate, comprehensible manner, by including information to refine the prototypes. The tools of evaluation could be in the form of a rubric, a set of criteria, or a survey. According to Bruner (1986), performance standards assess the appropriate levels of performance in a given context, and the cause for concern arises if the child does not demonstrate the expectations leading to negotiations and talks. The performance standards guide the revision process through renegotiating or discussing the improvement plan.

Along with the evaluation and revisions using performance standards, this is a step in the process for revisiting the research. After the initial experience of designing, a learner would benefit from reexamining the informational sources from a new perspective. The best practices leading to student achievement promote methods whereby learners attain their goals through experience and research (Wise & Hammack, 2011). Combining experience and research accomplishes the teaching of both conceptual and procedural learning included in the theory of instruction (Lynch, Chin, & Blazar, 2017). By this step, the learner has developed a unique view of the original problem through the exposure to the multiple representations of the problem and the solutions by watching the peers in the classroom. As Dewey (1990) mentions, a thought can only be a thought if the learner formed it in a way that is unique to the individual experience. The unique way of viewing the experience leads to the culmination of the process in which the learner is to design the revised prototype of the solution to the problem. This stage involves the learner returning to the design action. At this point, the learner is invested in the prototype, having gone through the process of creating it. At the beginning of the process, the externally provided problem presents a gateway into shaping an action and refining it through the process, using socially and culturally influenced capital (Gopaul, 2011).

Comparative Study

Learning the content across the disciplines or textbook learning is important. Using the theme of preservation of nature, artifacts, and ideas combines topics from the fields of science, social science, math, and literature. Building the conceptual understanding during the experiential stage and transferring the understanding to the content areas requires the learner to realize the similarities and differences between the two phases. Bray and Thomas (1995) reveal this to be the thinking behind the practice of comparative education, where two or more phenomena are compared as part of the study.

According to Bray and Thomas (1995), comparative education consists of three dimensions of the learning process. The first dimension concerns locational aspects of learning, just as the setting is crucial to the story's events. Learning must be situated in a real-world setting. Crossley (2010) found context to be an influential factor in learning, considering it a best practice not to be missed. The second dimension of the comparative education process is related to demographics, such as the characters in a story. Who performed the actions and why? The third and final dimension focuses on the expectations of the society driving the story, such as curriculum and instruction. The connection to action facilitates deep learning as the learner develops the conceptual understanding of the content. Resnick's research from 1995 continues to be of significance in terms of content teaching. As cited in Wise and Hammack (2011), Resnick warned against a decade-old practice of separating learners based on the teacher's ability-based perception of intelligence. All students have the ability to learn the content, based on the efforts of the learners and instructional methods of the teacher.

The comparative study, used for illustrating the CTA overview, provides a structured framework (Noah & Agbaire, 2013). Out of five major comparative methods (i.e., historical analysis, area studies, national character approach, problem-solving method, and social science method), I used the problem-solving approach to organize the CTA overview. Although mostly used for multilevel analysis, the comparative method is employed to organize the multistep process of CTA. Figure 1 illustrates the experience-based process of the CTA method, and Figure 2 provides an overview of the entire process including the content-based teaching.

Grade 2: Examples of the Assignments and Pacing

Having taught all elementary grades, I provide examples of Grade Two assignments, since the content embedded in the theme of preservation belonged to the California Grade Two standards. The examples could be adapted to fit the demands of various grade levels. The assignments below demonstrate the connection to the action of digging the physical model of a volcano to find fossils. Storing the fossils in the preservation prototype built by the students in Part One would be the next step, providing more opportunities to teach art, math, collaborative presentations, and writing. Another intentional feature of each of the assignments is the possible lead into creating writing tasks to teach descriptive, informational, opinion, and narrative styles of writing. The writing could be an informal entry in a journal or used to conduct a formal genre study. Donovan et al. (2014) add that process-oriented learning experiences develop the ability to reflect. Armed with experiential learning, learners are motivated to express their reflections orally and through written and multimedia presentations.

Included in the Figure 7 series, the year-long pacing illustrates the expected grade-level content across subject areas. Having the content organized in this manner reduces the need to flip through the pages of large teacher manuals from each subject. As the district adoptions change over time, the pacing plans would require revisions, but the reason for providing the plans in this chapter was to offer an example of the pacing conducive to the CTA method and to promote content integration. Planning for the CTA units with efficiency provided by the year-long content map makes it convenient to align the content across the subject areas compatible with the district-recommended pacing.

Figure 1. CTA part one: The Experience first

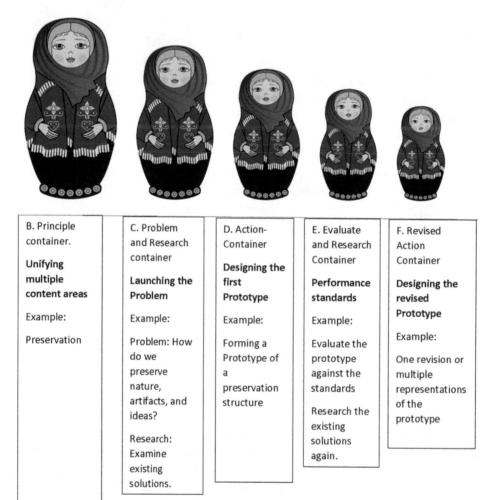

Content through Action (CTA) Method

Part One: The Experience First

A. Content Connections: Teacher examines the content across disciplines to generate the unifying instructional themes

B. Principle container.	C. Problem and Research container	D. Action-Container	E. Evaluate and Research Container	F. Revised Action Container
Unifying multiple content areas	**Launching the Problem**	**Designing the first Prototype**	**Performance standards**	**Designing the revised Prototype**
Example:	Example:	Example:	Example:	Example:
Preservation	Problem: How do we preserve nature, artifacts, and ideas?	Forming a Prototype of a preservation structure	Evaluate the prototype against the standards	One revision or multiple representations of the prototype
	Research: Examine existing solutions.		Research the existing solutions again.	

Donovan et al. (2014) explain that in a content-based learning plan, academic standards and periodic benchmarks drive the instructional plans. Despite considering the standards and benchmark testing as the forces behind the instruction in a traditional method of teaching, I found it necessary to include these factors of unit planning in the CTA method. The CTA method is compatible with the 21st century problem-based learning environment, but the reality of the current learning environment demands that standards and assessment requirements be embedded in the instructional planning. It is important to attend to pacing demands since the district benchmark assessments are connected to the pacing of the

Figure 2. Overview of the CTA: The experience leading to content learning

Content through Action (CTA)	
Overview: Experience Leading to Content Learning	
The examples were provided from an integrated curriculum unit using the theme of preservation. The overview included the experience phase in the first and second dimensions and focused on the content in the third dimension.	
Dimensions of Study	**Experience and Content Instruction**
1st Dimension: The Context Component of the Part I: The Experience First	The preservation of artifacts found under a "volcano" on a table with student made fossils hiding under the butcher paper. The problem was to build a system of preservation for the fossils discovered by digging the volcano.
2nd Dimension: The Learner's Role and Actions Component of the Part I: The Experience First	The learner assumed the role of a geologist at the volcano dig site responsible for discovering and preserving the artifacts, nature, and ideas.
3rd Dimension: Experience Leading to Content Learning Component of the Part II: The Content Next Incorporate instructional structures to include the 4C's: • Communication • Collaboration • Critical thinking • Creativity	Curriculum Integration Examples: The readers can add other subject areas to the list such as art. • **Math reasoning and writing:** Measuring the linear dimensions of the fossils and the preservation system for the fossils • **Reading comprehension and writing:** -Writing a descriptive paragraph describing the preservation system. -Reading the **science** text book and articles on the topics of fossils, earth, volcanoes, and the rock cycle. -Read the **social science** textbook on the topics of primary and secondary sources and create a timeline of the process from the beginning to the end of the volcano discovery process. • **Using technology:** -publish and present the products using a platform such as the Google Classroom slides. -Watch videos and use other resources posted by the instructor for the learners to respond to.

content from each subject area. Figures 3–7 provide examples of CTA student assignments and a year-long content map facilitating the integration of the multiple subject areas.

FUTURE RESEARCH DIRECTIONS

Teacher as Transformational Leader in a CTA Classroom

At one professional development training, I was disappointed to hear the lead administrator begin the training by announcing to the teachers that their role was to be that of implementors, and not designers of the curriculum. Lacking awareness of the fact that teachers design instructional plans according to class composition, schedules, and the theme to connect subject areas, the administrator's perception

Figure 3. Unit cover sign

Universal Theme: Preservation

It is important to preserve nature, animals, laws, artifacts, ideas, events and memories.

Problems To Solve

How do we preserve important things?

Why do we preserve important things?

Figure 4. Assignment one

Scientist's Name: _____   Date: _____

Volcanic Fossils

Time Period: 1,000 years ago

Location: The Volcano Dig Site

Content Study: Where were the fossils found? Describe the Fossils.

| Region it was found in: _____ |
| Illustrate the fossil at the volcano dig site where you found it. |

Dimensions	Inches/Feet 12 inches=1 foot	Centimeters/Meters 100 centimeters/1 meter
Length		
Width		
Height		
Properties to Observe		
Shape		
Color		
Texture		
Luster		
Physical Characteristics		

Figure 5. Assignment two

Scientist's Name: _____   Date: _____

Volcano Fossils

Time Period: Artifacts from 1,000 years ago

Location: The volcano dig site

Content Study: How does my fossil compare to the fossil discovered by another scientist?

1. My partner's fossil is _____ inches long. My fossil is

    _____ inches long. Whose fossil is longer and by how many more inches.

Draw this problem:

Solution: _____ 's fossil was longer by_____ more inches.

Number Sentence_____

Explain how you solved this problem:

of the teacher's role was that of a consumer of the change, and not an active participant. Faulkner and Latham (2016) assert that teachers must become change agents instead of passive victims of change. Future research could conduct studies on changing this perception, viewing the teacher's role as a transformational leader in the classroom.

Teaching using the CTA method would lead the teacher to become a transformational leader who guides learners to deep learning. A teacher who plans a curriculum for teaching thinking skills also must

Figure 6. Assignment two

_____ Inches =1 Foot

_____ Feet=1 Yard

_____ Centimeters=I Meter

_____ Meters=1 Kilometer

Draw an object in the classroom that is:	
measured in inches	
measured in feet	
measured in cm	
measured in meters	

be an activist and advocate for learners. Teaching thinking skills in Dewey's style of constructivism challenges the old school model, and a teacher would need the courage to continue that work by practicing inclusive education, promoting diversity, and focusing on one's own liberating teaching practice. At the same time, strategically finding a way to accomplish all of the above in the ecology of existing school models requires the teacher to plan the curriculum in a creative manner.

A teacher assuming the role of a transformational leader and a change agent in the classroom characterizes the teacher as someone who establishes an environment of high standards and supports the learners' achievement of expectations by recognizing strengths and concerns (Kareem, 2016). According

Figure 7. Prewriting organizer

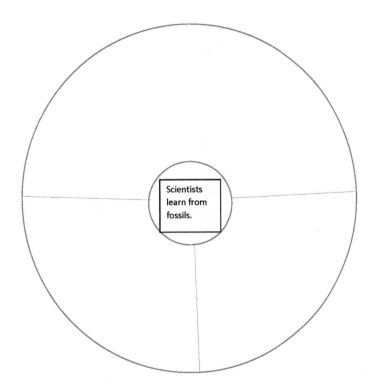

Scientist's Name: _____   Date: _____

Volcano Fossils

Time Period: From 1,000 years ago

Location: Volcano Dig Site

Content Study: What do scientists learn by studying the fossils?

to the author, leadership is a process of leading others to goal attainment by influencing them through building positive relations. A teacher leader has the power to transform the learner by strengthening abilities through a positive and supportive relationship. Kareem (2016) reports that educational organizations such as schools must progress from a transactional to a transformational style of leadership, which leads to the necessary shift in the role of the teacher to that of a transformational leader in the context of a classroom.

Some of the obstacles in the way of creating a 21st century classroom continue to exist in the current school environment, such as staff and leader attitudes based on personal beliefs impacting professional actions. Quek (2013) reports that personal attitudes do influence teaching practice. Chan and Wong (2014) also add that one's beliefs represent what one perceives as one's truths, and individual beliefs

Figure 8. Year-long content map

Year Long Content Map

Teacher: Harpreet K. Dhir   Grade: 2

Resources Used: District Pacing Calendars, Grade Level Expectations Per Trimester, Teacher Editions

	Sept.	Oct.	Nov.	Dec.	Jan.	Feb.	March	April	May	June
Social St. Standards	U.1 H.SS3.1: Describe the physical/human geography, use maps, graphs, photos to organize info about people, places and environment in a spatial context	U.2 H-ss 3.2: Describe the native Indian nations in the local region long ago and in the recent past		U.3 H-SS 3.3: Draw from historic and community resources to organize the sequence of local historic events and describe how each period of settlement left its mark on the land		U.4 H-SS 3.4: Students understand the role of rules and laws in our daily lives and the basic structure of the U.S. govt.			U.5 H-SS 3.5: Demonstrate basic economic reasoning skills and an understanding of the economy of the local region	
Social Studies Pacing Overview	U.1. Land and water in your area L.1 L/water in your area L.2 How people use land in your region	U.2 Calif. Indians Past/Present L.1 Indians in your region alike/different L2 How they used their environment	U.2 cont. L.3 How do Indian groups function L4 How Europeans changed life for Indians	U.3 Your community over time L.1 Who came to your region	U.3 cont. L.2 How did early settlers affect region economy L.3 How did people help place to grow	U.4 Rules/Laws L.1how laws help you stay together L.2 why is good citizenship important	u.4 cont. L.3 What brings community and country together L.4 How govt. works	u.4 conti L.5 how state, Indians, Country govt. works together L.6 how people worked for freedom	U.5 Economy of your region L.1 kinds of resources we use L.2 where are goods made	U.5 cont. L.3 How do we decide what we want L.4 How does your work in school help you.
Science Inquiries related to big concepts	Dir. Inquiry: How can you describe a position Guid. Inquiry: Can a magnet move an object without touching the object	Dir. Inquiry: How can sound made by vibrating obj. change? Guid. Inquiry: How can you change sound?	Full Inqu. How can you make a marble move faster: high/low ramp	Dir. Inquiry: How do baby animals look like their parents? Guided Inquiry: What are some ways shells vary?	Dir.Inqu.: What are the stages of a butterfly's life cycle? Guided Inqu: What is the life cycle of a grain beetle?	Dir.Inqu.: How can light affect how a plant grows? Guided Inqu: How can gravity affect the growth of roots?	U.B. Full Inquiry: How can soil affect the growth of plants?	Dir.Inqu.: How can you compare properties of earth materials? Guid. Inqu.: compare/sort minerals,rock	Dir.Inqu.: How can you study fossils? How can you make model of a fossil?	U.C. full inquiry: How much water do different soils hold?
Science Pacing Overview of concepts through vocabulary	U.A Physical Ch.1: Forces and Motions Position Motion Force Push/pull Friction Gravity Attract Repel Machine/tool Magnet	U.A cont. Ch.2 Sound Vibrate: quick/ slow Volume: loud/ soft Pitch: high/low	Assessment	U.B Life S. Ch.3 plant/Animal in envirn. Offspring Inherit: alike/different Environment: Color sunlight	U.B cont. Ch4: Animal Life Cycles Life cycle: stages Mammal Insect Amphibians Tadpole Larva pupa	U.B. Cont. Ch.5: All about plants Stem Pollen Seed coat Germinate Seedling Need to grow: air water root stem, flowers, fruits(function of each part)	Assess	U.C Earth Science Ch.6: Rocks/Soil Rock Minerals Luster:shiny/dull Weathering Soil Natural reso fuel	U.C. cont. Ch. 7: Fossils/Dinos Fossil Skeleton Dinosaur Life long ago Classify dino	Assess

lead people to the actions they perform. According to the author, fostering an environment to develop the learner's academic, social, and emotional skills involves a non-interventionist model where the teacher avoids imposing personal values on the learner. The teacher's role in the non-interventionist model involves developing a learner's thinking skills to empower the growth of the individual's values or mindset.

The interventionist model, a teacher-centered model, continues to be the more common method in school systems, in which the growth of the individual learner's mindset is based on the external regulations imposed on the learner (Quek, 2013). The author explains that most beginning teachers find it necessary to manage students through a strict classroom tone. A teacher's role while practicing the CTA method must balance the two extremes of a student-centered non-interventionist model and the teacher-centered interventionist model, based on the needs of the learners.

According to Sohmen (2015), creative leaders motivated to transform society are aware of the vision. They possess the ability to innovate and use diverse methods to practice new ideas. The teaching of thinking skills and planning the curriculum to meet the instructional goals demand creativity from the teacher. Sohmen (2015) agrees that planning for teaching thinking skills for 21st century education could be achieved through the methods associated with design thinking. The thinking skills of the human

Figure 9. Year-long content writing map

	Sept.	Oct.	Nov.	Dec.	Jan.	Feb.	Mar.	Apr.	May	June
Lang. Arts:										
Word Analysis	**Spelling:** T1, T2 **High Freq assess.,** writing samples **Syllabication:** T1, T2 **Reading:** benchmark assessment, reading folders Weekly Fluency folder-70 words/minute			**Spelling:** T3, T4 **High Freq assess.,** writing samples **Syllabication:** T3, T4 **Reading:** benchmark assessment, reading folders , Fluency folder-70 words/minute *Abbreviations:* Jan, Mr., St., T3, T4, Class assess. **Plural:** s, es, ies, leaves t3, t4				**Spelling:** T5, T6 **High Freq assess.,** writing samples **Syllabication:** T5, T6 **Reading:** benchmark assessment, reading folders , Fluency folder-70 words/minute *Abbreviations:* Jan, Mr., St., T6, Class assess. **Plural:** s, es, ies, leaves , spelling tests		
Vocabulary	Ant/syn. T1, T2 **Mult.meaning words:** academic(social/science) Houghton vocab., ELL handbook, **Compound word parts:** Vocabulary sheets, T2			Ant/syn. T_, T_ **Mult.meaning words:** academic(social/science) Houghton vocab., ELL handbook, **Compound word parts:** Vocabulary sheets, T3 *Prefixes, suffixes:* T3				Ant/syn. T_, T_ **Mult.meaning words:** T5, T6 academic(social/science) Houghton vocab., ELL handbook, **Compound word parts:** Vocabulary sheets, *Prefixes, suffixes:* T5, T6		
Cmprhen.	**Struc.devices:** **Title, t.able of .cont, headings:** T2 Resp. to Lit. folders **Questions:** what, what if, how, T1, T2 **Restate facts/detals** T1, T2, (not taught till T3 in book) **Alternative ending to plot** T1, Resp. to Lit. Folders			**Struc.devices:** **Title, t.able of .cont, headings:** T3 Resp. to Lit. folders **Questions:** what, what if, how, T3, T4 **Restate facts/detals** T3, T4, **Alternative ending to plot** T3, Resp. to Lit. Folders **Author's Purpose:** T3, Resp. To lit. **Cause/Effect (give reasons):** T3, T4, Resp. to Lit. **Interpret info from charts, graphs, diagrams:** T3, T4, **Follow 2 step written directions:** T3, T4 **Compre/contrast versions of the same story from different cultures:** Class Assess				**Struc.devices:** **Title, t.able of .cont, headings:** T5, T6, Reseach Report, Resp. to Lit. folders **Questions:** what, what if, how, T5, T6, Report **Restate facts/detals** T5, T6, Report **Alternative ending to plot** T5, Resp. to Lit. Folders **Author's Purpose:** T5, Resp. To lit. **Cause/Effect (give reasons):** T5, Resp. to Lit. **Interpret info from charts, graphs, diagrams:** T5, T6, **Follow 2 step written directions:** T5, T6, Report **Compre/contrast versions of the same story from different cultures:** Class Assess **Compare Plots, setting, character in different stories:** Class assessment, T5 **Use of rhythm, rhyme, alliteration in poetry,** T5, Class Assess.		
Writing Applications	**Narrative: setting/ characters** T1, T2 Writing Sample, District Writing Test			**Narrative: setting/ characters** T3, Writing Sample, **Friendly Letter:** District Writing test, T3, T4, Letter Sample				**Narrative: setting/ characters** T5, T6, Writing Sample, Dist. TEst **Friendly Letter:** Letter SAmple		
Writing Strategies	**Group related ideas:** T1, T2 Nrrative Writng Sample, District Writng Test **Revise:** T1 T2, Narrative Writing sample, District Test			**Group related ideas:** T3, T4 Letter Writng Sample, District Writng Test **Revise:** T3, T4, Letter Writing sample, District Test **Legible Handwriting:** T3, T4, Lettr sample, DWT **Reference materials:** dict, thesaurus, T3, T4, Vocab. Sheet				**Group related ideas:** T5, T6 Letter, Report, DWT **Revise:** T5, T6, Letter Writing sample, District Test, Report **Legible Handwriting:** Lettr sample, DWT, Narrative, Report **Reference materials:** dict, thesaurus, T5, T6, Vocab. Sheet		
Lang. Conven.	**Comp/income senten.** T1, T2 Narrative Writing Sampes, District Wrtng Test **Nouns/verbs:** T1, T2 Vocabulary sheets **Capital:** prop noun, letr parts, month,day, initials: T1, T2, Letter writing, Narrative Sample, District Writing Test **Frequently used words, Sho/lon.vowels, r-con. Blends:** T1, T2, spelling test of High Freq. words,			**Comp/income senten.** T3, Writing Sampes, District Wrtng Test **Nouns/verbs:** T3, T4 Vocabulary sheets **Capital:** prop noun, letr parts, month,day, initials: T3, T4, Letter writing, District Writing Test **Frequently used words, Sho/lon.vowels, r-con.** T3, T4, High Frequency Test **Correct Word Order in Sentences:** Letter Samples, DWT **Commas in letters, dates, between city/state:** T3, Writing Sample,				**Comp/income senten.** T6, Writing Sampes, District Writing Test, Report **Nouns/verbs:** T5, T6 Vocabulary sheets **Capital:** prop noun, letr parts, month,day, initials: T5, T6, Letter writing, District Writing Test, Report **Frequently used words, Sho/lon.vowels, r-con.** T5, T6, High Frequency Test		

psyche develop intellectual, moral, spiritual, and emotional components as the individual travels from being consciously unskilled to being unconsciously skilled. Teaching thinking skills asks the teacher to dive into the unique capabilities of creative thinking, so that learners can experience the dive into their own capabilities.

CONCLUSION

The topic of how a teacher teaches thinking skills, by strategically examining the curriculum, integrating the multiple subjects, aligning various components of the study by providing a real-world context, and forming a meaningful and relevant experience for the learners, was complex but necessary. The 21st century skills, including creativity, critical thinking, collaboration, and communication abilities, require educators and the school as an organization to emphasize the inclusion of these skills in interdisciplinary units of study. The CTA accomplishes this task by incorporating the Four Cs and integrating curriculum while connecting the experience of an action to the instructional unit.

Figure 10. Year-long content map

	Sept.	Oct.	Nov.	Dec.	Jan.	Feb.	Mar.	Apr.	May	June
Lang. Arts:										
Word Analysis	**Spelling:** T1, T2 **High Freq assess.,** *writing samples* **Syllabication:** T1, T2 **Reading:** benchmark assessment, *reading folders* *Weekly Fluency folder-70 words/minute*			**Spelling:** T3, T4 **High Freq assess.,** *writing samples* **Syllabication:** T3, T4 **Reading:** benchmark assessment, *reading folders*, Fluency folder-70 *words/minute* ***Abbreviations:*** Jan, Mr., St., T3, T4, Class assess. **Plural:** s, es, ies, leaves t3, t4				**Spelling:** T5, T6 **High Freq assess.,** *writing samples* **Syllabication:** T5, T6 **Reading:** benchmark assessment, *reading folders*, Fluency folder/minute ***Abbreviations:*** Jan, Mr., St., T6, Class assess. **Plural:** s, es, ies, leaves , spelling tests		
Vocabulary	**Ant/syn.** T1, T2 **Mult.meaning words:** academic(social/science) Houghton vocab., ELL handbook, **Compound word parts:** *Vocabulary sheets,* T2			**Ant/syn.** T_, T_ **Mult.meaning words:** academic(social/science) Houghton vocab., ELL handbook, **Compound word parts:** *Vocabulary sheets,* T3 ***Prefixes, suffixes:*** T3				**Ant/syn.** T_, T_, **Mult.meaning words:** T5, T6 academic(social/science) Houghton vocab., ELL handbook, **Compound word parts:** *Vocabulary sheets,* ***Prefixes, suffixes:*** T5, T6		
Cmprhen.	**Struc.devices:** **Title, t.able of .cont, headings:** T2 *Resp. to Lit. folders* **Questions: what, what if, how,** T1, T2 **Restate facts/details** T1, T2, (not taught till T3 in book) **Alternative ending to plot** T1, *Resp. to Lit. Folders*			**Struc.devices:** **Title, t.able of .cont, headings:** T3 *Resp. to Lit. folders* **Questions: what, what if, how,** T3, T4 **Restate facts/details** T3, T4, **Alternative ending to plot** T3, *Resp. to Lit. Folders* **Author's Purpose:** T3, *Resp. To lit.* **Cause/Effect (give reasons):** T3, T4, *Resp. to Lit.* **Interpret info from charts, graphs, diagrams:** T3, T4, **Follow 2 step written directions:** T3, T4 **Compre/contrast versions of the same story from different cultures:** Class Assess				**Struc.devices:** **Title, t.able of .cont, headings:** T5, T6, *Reseach Report, Resp. to Lit. folders* **Questions: what, what if, how,** T5, T6, *Report* **Restate facts/details** T5, T6, *Report* **Alternative ending to plot** T5, *Resp. to Lit. Folders* **Author's Purpose:** T5, *Resp. To lit.* **Cause/Effect (give reasons):** T5, *Resp. to Lit.* **Interpret info from charts, graphs, diagrams:** T5, T6, **Follow 2 step written directions:** T5, T6, *Report* **Compre/contrast versions of the same story from different cultures:** Class Assess **Compare Plots, setting, character in different stories:** Class assessment, T5 **Use of rhythm, rhyme, alliteration in poetry,** T5, Class Assess.		
Writing Applications	**Narrative: setting/ characters** T1, T2 *Writing Sample, District Writing Test*			**Narrative: setting/ characters** T3, *Writing Sample,* **Friendly Letter:** *District Writing test,* T3, T4, *Letter Sample*				**Narrative: setting/ characters** T5, T6, *Writing Sample, Dist. TEst* **Friendly Letter:** *Letter SAmple*		
Writing Strategies	**Group related ideas:** T1, T2 *Nrrative Writng Sample, District Writing Test* **Revise:** T1 T2, *Narrative Writing sample, District Test*			**Group related ideas:** T3, T4 *Letter Writng Sample, District Writng Test* **Revise:** T3, T4, *Letter Writing sample, District Test* **Legible Handwriting:** T3, T4, *Lettr sample, DWT* **Reference materials:** dict, thesaurus, T3, T4, *Vocab. Sheet*				**Group related ideas:** T5, T6 *Letter, Report, DWT* **Revise:** T5, T6, *Letter Writing sample, District Test, Report* **Legible Handwriting:** *Lettr sample, DWT, Narrative, Report* **Reference materials:** dict, thesaurus, T5, T6, *Vocab. Sheet*		
Lang. Conven.	**Comp/income senten.** T1, T2 *Narrative Writing Sampes, District Wrtng Test* **Nouns/verbs:** T1, T2 *Vocabulary sheets* **Capital:** prop noun, letr parts, month,day, initials: T1, T2, *Letter writing, Narrative Sample, District Writing Test* **Frequently used words, Sho/lon.vowels, r-con. Blends:** T1, T2, *spelling test of High Freq. words,*			**Comp/income senten.** T3, *Writing Sampes, District Wrtng Test* **Nouns/verbs:** T3, T4 *Vocabulary sheets* **Capital:** prop noun, letr parts, month,day, initials: T3, T4, *Letter writing, District Writing Test* **Frequently used words, Sho/lon.vowels, r-con.** T3, T4, *High Frequency Test* **Correct Word Order in Sentences:** *Letter Samples, DWT* **Commas in letters, dates, between city/state:** T3, *Writing Sample,*				**Comp/income senten.** T6, *Writing Sampes, District Wrtng Test, Report* **Nouns/verbs:** T5, T6 *Vocabulary sheets* **Capital:** prop noun, letr parts, month,day, initials: T5, T6, *Letter writing, District Writing Test, Report* **Frequently used words, Sho/lon.vowels, r-con.** T5, T6, *High Frequency Test*		

I have practiced teaching using design thinking since the turn of the century but did not see the school as a system transitioning to 21st century teaching practice. As Hill (2012) explains, most educational systems still reflect the methods of learning from the 12th century. The rigidity of the instruction and the emphasis on rote learning do not represent the needs of modern learners. It might be appropriate to stop the practice of giving spelling tests and holding award assemblies to reward the number of high frequency words the learners can read, or the number of multiplication tables learners can recite in a certain time period.

The teacher evaluation systems and the benchmark assessments administered to learners also fail to reflect the current shifts in educational demands. For that reason, a teacher making a commitment to teach the thinking skills compatible with 21st century competencies could be a lone practitioner on campus and might have to develop the courageous spirit to keep moving forward for the success of each student. Educating even one learner was, is, and will be an act of service to humanity.

REFERENCES

Biesta, G. (2007). Why "what works" won't work: Evidence-based practice and the democratic deficit in educational research. *Educational Theory*, *87*(1), 1–22. doi:10.1111/j.1741-5446.2006.00241.x

Blaschke, L. M. (2012). Heutagogy and lifelong learning: A review of heutagogical practice and self-determined learning. *International Review of Research in Open and Distance Learning*, *13*(1), 56–71. doi:10.19173/irrodl.v13i1.1076

Bowie, A. A., & Cassim, F. (2016). Linking classroom and community: A theoretical alignment of service learning and a human-centered design methodology in contemporary communication design education. *Education as Change*, *20*(1), 126–148. doi:10.17159/1947-9417/2016/556

Boyte, H. C. (2017). John Dewey and citizen politics: How democracy can survive artificial intelligence and the credo of efficiency. *Education and Culture*, *33*(2), 13–47. doi:10.5703/educationculture.33.2.0013

Bray, M., & Thomas, R. M. (1995). Levels of comparison in educational studies: Different insights from different literatures and the value of multilevel analyses. *Harvard Educational Review*, *65*(3), 472–490. doi:10.17763/haer.65.3.g3228437224v4877

Bresciani, M. J. (2010). Data-driven planning: Using assessment in strategic planning. *New Directions for Student Services*, *2010*(132), 39–50. doi:10.1002s.374

Bruner, J. (1986). *Actual minds, possible worlds*. Cambridge, MA: Harvard University Press.

Chan, Y., & Wong, N. (2014). Worldviews, religions, and beliefs about teaching and learning: Perception of mathematics teachers with different religious backgrounds. *Educational Studies in Mathematics*, *87*(3), 251–277. doi:10.100710649-014-9555-1

Croso, C. (2013). Human rights are the key to the world we want. *Adult Education and Development*, *80*, 78–85.

Crossley, M. (2010). Context matters in educational research and international development: Learning from the small states experience. *Prospects*, *40*(4), 421–429. doi:10.100711125-010-9172-4

Dewey, J. (1990). *The school and society and the child and the curriculum*. Chicago, IL: The University of Chicago Press. (Originally published 1956) doi:10.7208/chicago/9780226112114.001.0001

Dongo-Montoya, A. O. (2018). Marx and Piaget: Theoretical and epistemological approaches. *Educação e Realidade*, *43*(1), 7–22. doi:10.1590/2175-623660803

Donovan, L., Green, T. D., & Mason, C. (2014). Examining the 21st century classroom: Developing an innovation configuration map. *Journal of Educational Computing Research*, *50*(2), 161–178. doi:10.2190/EC.50.2.a

Faulkner, J., & Latham, G. (2016). Adventurous lives: Teacher qualities for 21st century learning. *Australian Journal of Teacher Education*, *41*(4), 137–150. doi:10.14221/ajte.2016v41n4.9

Fiske, A., & O'Riley, A. A. (2016). Toward an understanding of late life suicidal behavior: The role of lifespan developmental theory. *Aging & Mental Health, 20*(2), 123–130. doi:10.1080/13607863.2015. 1078282 PMID:26305860

Gardner, H. (2000). Project zero: Nelson Goodman's legacy in arts education. *The Journal of Aesthetics and Art Criticism, 245*(3), 245. doi:10.2307/432107

Gopaul, B. (2011). Distinction in doctoral education: Using Bourdieu's tools to assess the socialization of doctoral students. *Equity & Excellence in Education, 44*(1), 10–21. doi:10.1080/10665684.2011.539468

Hahn Tapper, A. J. (2013). A pedagogy of social justice education: Social identity theory, intersectionality, and empowerment. *Conflict Resolution Quarterly, 30*(4), 411–445. doi:10.1002/crq.21072

Hargreaves, K. (2016). Reflection in medical education. *Journal of University Teaching & Learning Practice, 13*(2), 1–19.

Hill, I. (2012). An international model of world-class education: The international baccalaureate. *Prospects: Quarterly Review of Comparative Education, 42*(3), 341–359. doi:10.100711125-012-9243-9

Ilica, A. (2016). On John Dewey's philosophy of education and its impact on contemporary education. *Journal Plus Education / Educatia Plus, 14*(1), 7-13.

Kareem, J. (2016). The influence of leadership in building a learning organization. *IUP Journal of Organizational Behavior, 15*(1), 7–18.

Kilfoye, C. (2013). A voice from the past calls for classroom technology: John Dewey's writings on educational reform tell us we should embrace technology in the classroom so that we can prepare students with 21st century skills. *Phi Delta Kappan, 94*(7), 53–56. doi:10.1177/003172171309400717

Lang Froggatt, D. (2015). The informationally underserved: Not always diverse, but always a social justice advocacy model. *School Libraries Worldwide, 21*(1), 54–72. doi:10.14265.21.1.004

Lapp, L. K., & Spaniol, J. (2016). Aging and self-discrepancy: Evidence for adaptive change across the life span. *Experimental Aging Research, 42*(2), 212–219. doi:10.1080/0361073X.2016.1132900 PMID:26890636

Lynch, K., Chin, M., & Blazar, D. (2017). Relationships between observations of elementary mathematics instruction and student achievement: Exploring variability across districts. *American Journal of Education, 123*(4), 615–646. doi:10.1086/692662

McWilliams, S. A. (2016). Cultivating constructivism: Inspiring intuition and promoting process and pragmatism. *Journal of Constructivist Psychology, 29*(1), 1–29. doi:10.1080/10720537.2014.980871

Mintzberg, H. (2003). Unconventional wisdom: A conversation with Henry Mintzberg. *Leadership in Action, 23*(4), 8–10. doi:10.1002/lia.1028

Mishra, P., Fahnoe, C., & Henriksen, D. (2013). Creativity, self-directed learning and the architecture of technology rich environments. *TechTrends, 57*(1), 10–13. doi:10.100711528-012-0623-z

National Education Association (NEA). (n.d.) *Code of ethics.* Retrieved from http://www.nea.org/home/30442.htm

Noah, M., & Agbaire, J. J. (2013). Methodological issues in comparative education studies: An exploration of the approaches of Kandel and Holmes. *Journal of Educational Review, 6*(3), 349–356.

Noel, L., & Liub, T. L. (2017). Using Design Thinking to Create a New Education Paradigm for Elementary Level Children for Higher Student Engagement and Success. *Journal of Design and Technology Education, 22*(1), 1.

Postman, N. (1985). Amusing Ourselves to Death. *Etc.; a Review of General Semantics, 42*(1), 13–18. Retrieved from http://search.ebscohost.com/login.aspx?direct=true&AuthType=sso&db=eue&AN=15901018&site=eds-live&scope=site&authtype=sso&custid=ns083389

Pouwels, J., & Biesta, G. (2017). With Socrates on your heels and Descartes in your hand: On the notion of conflict in John Dewey's democracy and education. *Education in Science, 7*(1), 1–14. doi:10.3390/educsci7010007

Quek, C. L. (2013). Exploring beginning teachers' attitudes and beliefs on classroom management. *New Horizons in Education, 61*(2), 13–33.

School of Educators. (2011, December). Experience & education-John Dewey (1938 publication). Retrieved from http://schoolofeducators.com/2011/12/experience-education-john-dewey/

Sedden, M. L., & Clark, K. R. (2016). Motivating students in the 21st century. *Radiologic Technology, 87*(6), 609–616. PMID:27390228

Sohmen, V. S. (2015). Reflections on creative leadership. *International Journal of Global Business, 8*(1), 1–14.

Van de Ven, A. H., & Sun, K. (2011). Breakdowns in implementing models of organization change. *The Academy of Management Perspectives, 25*(3), 58–74.

Waddington, D. I., & Weeth Feinstein, N. (2016). Beyond the search for truth: Dewey's humble and humanistic vision of science education. *Educational Theory, 66*(1/2), 111–126. doi:10.1111/edth.12157

Whitty, M., & Koeplin, J. (2011). Putting more soul into our work: Teaching the whole person. *Business Renaissance Quarterly, 6*(1), 21–28.

Wise, D., & Hammack, M. (2012). Leadership coaching: Coaching competencies and best practices. *Journal of School Leadership, 21*(3), 449–477. doi:10.1177/105268461102100306

ADDITIONAL READING

Czerniawski, G. (2011). Emerging teachers-emerging identities: Trust and accountability in the construction of newly qualified teachers in Norway, Germany, and England. *European Journal of Teacher Education, 34*(4), 431–447. doi:10.1080/02619768.2011.587114

Herrington, D., Kelsey, C., Barker, K., & Kearney, W. S. (2010). The role of trust in establishing an educational leadership program in a recently created urban university (2009-2010). *The John Ben Shepperd Journal of Practical Leadership*, (5), 72–80.

Kopelman, R. E., Gardberg, N. A., & Brandwein, A. C. (2011). Using a recognition and reward initiative to improve service quality: A quasi-experimental field study in a public higher education institution. *Public Personnel Management*, *40*(2), 133–149. doi:10.1177/009102601104000204

Kreber, C. (2013). Empowering the scholarship of teaching: An Arendtian and critical perspective. *Studies in Higher Education*, *38*(6), 857–869. doi:10.1080/03075079.2011.602396

Niu, W., & Sternberg, R. J. (2001). Cultural influences on artistic creativity and its evaluation. *International Journal of Psychology*, *36*(4), 225–241. doi:10.1080/00207590143000036

Ohler, J. (2011, February). Character education for the digital age. *Educational Leadership*, *68*(5). Retrieved from http://www.ascd.org/publications/educational-leadership/feb11/vol68/num05/Character-Education-for-the-Digital-Age.aspx

Oxley, C. (2011). Digital citizenship: Developing an ethical and responsible online culture. *Access*, *25*(3), 5–9.

Stanton, K., Stasik-O'Brien, S., Ellickson-Larew, S., & Watson, D. (2016). Positive affectivity: Specificity of its facet level relations with psychopathology. *Cognitive Therapy and Research*, *40*(5), 593–605. doi:10.100710608-016-9773-1

KEY TERMS AND DEFINITIONS

Constructivism: A theory leading to the teaching methods in which learners construct meaning through process-oriented experience.

Content Through Action (CTA): A teaching method designed by the author, based on the theory of constructivism and associated with methods such as human-centered design, design-based learning, and problem-based learning. The CTA method focuses on teaching content by integrating the curriculum through process-oriented experience.

Curriculum Integration: Connecting various subject matters such as science, social science, math, and language arts under a unifying theme such as preservation.

Design Thinking: A theory associated with the theory of constructivism, leading to teaching methods in which learners design prototypes of solutions to problems in a real-world context.

Four Cs: Based on the P21 framework, a guide for the learner to develop creativity and innovation, critical thinking and problem-solving, collaboration, and communication skills. The 21st century skills embedded in the Four Cs are necessary in life and career environments beyond the school walls.

Multimedia: Description of providing various media to communicate ideas requiring technology, maintenance of the technology, and training to develop digital literacy. Multimedia presentations or collaborations employ visual, symbolic, audio, and linguistic forms of communication styles.

Partnership for 21st Century Skills (P21): An organization providing a framework for the skills needed to be successful in the 21st century environment, including the framework of the Four Cs implemented in schools in the United States.

Teacher as a Transformational Leader: Concept of the teacher influencing learners by demonstrating value-based behavior to build trust, establishing a vision with expectations, encouraging problem-solving and risk-taking, and intentionally focused on the growth and achievement through process-oriented instruction

Section 2

Interrogating Teachers' Critical Thinking Pedagogy Across Multidisciplinary Contexts

Chapter 8
Using Argumentation to Develop Critical Thinking About Social Issues in the Classroom:
A Dialogic Model of Critical Thinking Education

N. Leigh Boyd
Columbia University, USA

ABSTRACT

Thanks to the polarized nature of politics in the world today, students need to learn how to think critically about social issues. Argumentation can be both a type of critical thinking and a tool with which to teach students to think critically about social issues. This chapter lays out a framework for teaching students how to develop critical thinking about real world issues through the use of dialogic argumentation. The impact of dialogic argumentative activities in the classroom are discussed, particularly as they relate to the development of metacognition and theory of mind, as well as how they help students develop an "inner-locutor" that allows them to evaluate both their position and opposing positions. Finally, a model for how these elements contribute to students' value-loaded critical thinking about social issues is outlined.

INTRODUCTION

In an increasingly polarized world with multiple streams of false or biased information, critical thinking and argumentation in the arena of social justice and social issues are important. Adolescents are tuned in and plugged in around the clock, resulting in near-constant exposure to sources of information that can be misleading. And unlike their parents and grandparents, today's teens have the ability to (and in some ways are required to) receive information that aligns with their interests and confirms their positions. Adolescents self-tailor their news by getting it online and picking what stories they want to see, a phe-

DOI: 10.4018/978-1-5225-7829-1.ch008

Copyright © 2019, IGI Global. Copying or distributing in print or electronic forms without written permission of IGI Global is prohibited.

nomenon aided by the algorithms that shape web use. They are also more likely to get news from social media and satiric news shows like the *Daily Show* rather than traditional news outlets (Marchi, 2012).

At the same time, the internet offers a platform for extreme voices. When social issues are raised online, it is often the most extreme ends of the spectrum whose ideas are "heard" by adolescents and others. So, how can students make sense of the information and issues they are exposed to everyday?

One way of helping students make sense of information and social issues is via critical thinking. Critical thinking is not a new concept, nor is it only applicable to dealing with current social issues. Frijters, ten Dam, & Rijlaarsdam (2008) point out that when analytic thought is combined with the development of values, the resulting "value-loaded critical thinking" builds a stronger citizenry. In addition, studies show that having critical thinking skills helps people differentiate between fake news and real news stories (Beavers, 2011; Hobbs, 2010; Pennycook & Rand, 2017). Thus, aside from the importance of critical thinking in general, it is imperative for students to learn this skill if they are to make sense of the world around them and generate solutions to some of the world's problems.

If it is important for students to learn this type of critical thinking, it is important for teachers to provide training that helps them do so. There are many ways of approaching critical thinking skills in the classroom. In this chapter, the ways that dialogic argumentation can be a tool to help students develop critical thinking about social issues will be examined. First, the multiple ways to define critical thinking and the ways argumentation can serve as a key critical thinking skill will be discussed. Then the literature on how dialogue and argumentation work in the classroom will be presented, followed by the ways in which dialogic argumentation leads students to flexible thinking, including understanding of multiple viewpoints and development of values, which is a cornerstone of critical thinking about social justice issues outside the classroom. Finally, suggestions for future research directions will be presented.

BACKGROUND

Defining Critical Thinking

Following the industrial revolution, education of the late 19th century and most of the 20th century was focused on teaching students the acquisition of skills and facts. This made sense for that era, as this type of learning prepared students for the types of jobs available to them. However, at the end of the 20th century and into the 21st century, it has become more important for students to learn how to sort through information to find what is important and to make value judgments about issues than to simply memorize facts. That is, critical thinking skills have become crucial and educators increasingly understand that it is better to teach the skills associated with acquiring knowledge and understanding than to teach knowledge itself (Kuhn, 2007).

As part of the process of acquiring knowledge and understanding, students need to be taught how to evaluate the information in front of them. They need to learn how to figure out what's true and what's not; what is important and what is not; what is just and what is not. This is part of the task of critical thinking: to help students evaluate sources, information, and ideas.

There are many different definitions of critical thinking, though most include higher-order thinking as part of that skill. A surprisingly good definition comes from the Wikipedia page for critical thinking. There, critical thinking is defined as "the objective analysis of facts to form a judgment," with a note that it is "self-directed, self-disciplined, self-monitored, and self-corrective thinking" (Wikipedia.org, n.d.). Thus, a student who engages in critical thinking is not only evaluating and judging information and positions, that student is also utilizing regulatory and metacognitive skills to control engagement with the material or issue being critically thought about.

A 1990 report commissioned by the American Philosophical Association commonly referred to as the Delphi Report tried its own hand at defining critical thinking by bringing together 46 experts in the field and finding consensus in what critical thinking is. The Delphi Report conceptualizes critical thinking from the view of two domains, cognitive skills and dispositions. Cognitive skills involve things like analysis, evaluation, and self-regulation. Dispositions, on the other hand, are the emotional elements required for critical thinking, such as inquisitiveness, open-mindedness, and perseverance (Facione, 1990). These traits help students engage in the taxing work required of them when they engage their cognitive skills. For example, a student who is open-minded and inquisitive is more likely to seek out and analyze information presented from different viewpoints. Likewise, a student who is high in perseverance can engage in the self-regulation required to continue working through a difficult concept.

Perhaps one of the most influential 21st century scholars in the world of critical thinking is Halpern, whose definition of critical thinking is worth quoting in full. According to Halpern (2014),

Critical thinking is the use of those cognitive skills or strategies that increase the probability of a desirable outcome. It is used to describe thinking that is purposeful, reasoned, and goal directed—the kind of thinking involved in solving problems, formulating inferences, calculating likelihoods, and making decisions, when the thinker is using skills that are thoughtful and effective for the particular context and type of thinking task. (p. 8)

Halpern's definition is a thorough one and can be divided into several key areas. Based on her framework, the product of critical thinking is a better chance at a "desirable outcome." The elements of critical thinking are that it is "purposeful, reasoned, and goal directed." The cognitive skills involved in critical thinking include "solving problems, formulating inferences, calculating likelihoods, and making decisions." Finally, the utilization of critical thinking requires "using skills that are thoughtful and effective for the…context and…task" (Halpern, 2014, p. 8).

The product of critical thinking requires that students are working towards success. Whether that success involves making judgments about a source or a social issue, critical thinking is about increasing the chance that a student will come to a "good" or "right" answer. For example, a student evaluating the arguments on different sides of a social issue might come to a "good" answer by pointing out the relative strengths and weaknesses of both sides. This result can lead to better, stronger thinking, as discussed later in this chapter, and thus increases the chances of student success not only on this task but also others.

The elements of Halpern's definition give guidance as to what is required of this type of thinking. Students who think in ways that are systematic, logical, and focused on the purpose and goal of a task are engaging with information critically. A student who analyzes an argument's logic is activating Halpern's elements, specifically reasoning, to get to the heart of an argument.

Cognitive skills are the heart of critical thinking, and they involve the intellectual work required when using Halpern's elements. Problem-solving, decision-making, drawing inferences, and probability analysis are all about using purposeful and reasoned thinking to approach an issue or problem. For example, as mentioned above, a student's analysis of an argument's logic involves the elements of critical thinking. But the actual work, the thinking, involved in that analysis, requires cognitive skills such as drawing inferences or making decisions.

Finally, the utilization of critical thinking, according to Halpern, is contextual. That is, the application of critical thinking must fit the specific problem or context. Analyzing the logic of an argument works for many contexts, from academic reading to scrolling through a Twitter feed, but the specific approach of analysis must work within the context of the problem. Student, then, are not going to analyze the argument in an academic text in the same way that they will analyze the argument in a tweet, nor should they. Thus, Halpern's definition ends with the point that critical thinking happens in context and must be applied differently in different contexts.

Thus far, the definitions of critical thinking presented have focused on critical thinking as a higher-order process requiring the use of cognitive, emotional, and contextual practices to evaluate and/or analyze issues. Insofar as argumentation involves identifying, evaluating, and countering reasons for or against an issue, it falls within these definitions of critical thinking. Thus, argumentation is a critical thinking skill.

However, it is more than that. Bowell & Kemp (2005) use argument as both a part of and reason for critical thinking. As they point out, "every day, we are bombarded with messages apparently telling us what to do or not to do, what to believe or not to believe" (p. 1). People need to think critically about those messages, the authors argue, and doing so requires mastering argumentation. Thus, the barrage of daily persuasive (i.e., argumentative) messages people encounter is the reason they need critical thinking, and the way to think critically about those messages is to become fluent in their language, the language of argumentation. To understand Bowell & Kemp's point, it is important to turn attention to argumentation and its purpose and outcomes in education.

Argumentation as a Type of and Tool for Critical Thinking

Many educators and psychologists identify argumentation as a key critical thinking skill (Bowell & Kemp, 2005; Halpern, 2014; Kuhn, 2007). In this way, argumentation is a type of critical thinking. However, it is also a tool *for* critical thinking. Through argumentation, students can learn how to reason, how to evaluate arguments and evidence, how to think flexibly, and how to acknowledge others' viewpoints. Thus, argumentation is not only a type of critical thinking; it is a way of developing critical thinking skills.

All the way back with Piaget and Vygotsky, psychologists have known that argumentation plays a key role in the development of children's thinking. Vygotsky understood that "the higher functions of child thought first appear…in the form of argumentation" (Vygotsky, 1981, p. 157). In other words, argumentation is the natural state of young minds. As such, it is a good starting point for learning other skills, since children do it and like to do it, even if they do not do it well at first.

Indeed, using argumentation within subject areas can broaden and deepen student understanding. For example, Walker & Zeidler (2007) found that socioscientific inquiry and debate led to better understanding of the social side of science. Further, argumentation forces students to think about other perspectives, as discussed further later in this chapter. Cozolino (2013) writes of how this can lead to wisdom through students' "shift[ing] focus" to "broader perspectives" (p. 213).

Thus, argumentation can help students think critically about the world around them, the issues facing them, and the sources of evidence and opinions. But how does it work? To answer that, let us turn to what the research says works in teaching critical thinking via argumentation.

TEACHING CRITICAL THINKING: WHAT WORKS?

As already discussed, critical thinking is a complex topic. Nevertheless, it is a crucial skill to learn and therefore should be a central part of education. And as the previous section hints, argumentation within the classroom is a tool that can help build critical thinking skills. The following sections will highlight the specific ways argumentation, and particularly dialogic argumentation, can help students become better thinkers about social issues. The first of these sections will examine research on argumentation and social issues, in particular how argumentative classroom activities can help students develop values and evaluate ideas and reasons. Following that, the ways in which metacognition develops and plays a role in argumentation is explored. Two final sections look at the power of conflict and disagreement in dialogic activities when developing an inner voice that allows students to understand, evaluate, and respond to the other side of a social issue.

Argumentation and Social Issues

Though the research discussed earlier in this chapter demonstrates that argumentation can be successful in teaching subject matter and general thinking (Cozolino, 2013; Kuhn, 2007; Walker & Zeidler, 2007), the question remains: how does argumentation teach students to think? More specifically, how can argumentation engage students in critical thinking, especially in terms of real-world issues? Perhaps more than other skills or activities, argumentation allows for students to grapple with real world social issues. The nature of argumentative activity means that students are able to analyze and evaluate both their own and others' positions on a topic. This has been shown to promote flexible thinking, engage students in metacognitive thought and talk, and increase the quality of student persuasive writing (Fallahi, 2012; Kuhn, Hemberger, & Khait, 2017; Zillmer, 2016).

In large part, results like these are due to the more or less structured classroom environment. Adolescents argue all the time, but arguing about an issue in a social setting often leads to simple my-side reasons and opinions not supported by evidence and/or not analyzed critically (Halpern, 2014; Kuhn & Crowell, 2011; Wolfe, 2012). In contrast, argumentation in the classroom opens space for students to question, argue, and explore social issues in an environment that prizes logic, reason, and critical thinking. As a result, students begin to engage with issues in deeper, more critical ways. A curriculum developed by Kuhn and extensively researched has found just that (Kuhn & Crowell, 2011; Kuhn et al., 2017; Kuhn, Zillmer, Crowell, & Zavala, 2013; Zillmer, 2016). In the curriculum, students engage deeply with social issues for 15 class sessions. During that time, students pick a side, work with others from both their same side and the opposing side to create, evaluate, and counter arguments with reason and evidence, participate in a whole-class debate, and write an argumentative persuasive essay. Each session of the curriculum is student-centered and dialogic in nature, meaning that students engage in deep conversation about both the topic and the task (Kuhn et al., 2017). Students are also asked to work together to evaluate and reflect upon different arguments and counterarguments in each class session. After grappling with a social issue for 15 sessions and writing a position paper, students then repeat the curriculum sequence with a new social issue. The circular nature of the curriculum allows students to work within several social issues over the course of a single school year. Examples of issues addressed in the curriculum include the ethics of animal testing, government policies meant to control the population (such as China's one-birth policy), whether organ sales should be legal, and abortion. Among the more popular topics in the curriculum is the issue of juvenile justice. Specifically, the prompt for that issue asks students to think about whether teens who commit serious crimes should be tried and sentenced as adults (Kuhn et al., 2017).

The way students engage in argumentation through the lens of the juvenile justice topic demonstrates how argumentation in a classroom allows students to utilize critical thinking skills about a social issue. During a mid-topic activity, students who collaborate to write an essay with an opposing-side partner often engage in their own debates about the topic (Boyd, 2018). These writing partner discussions can lead to the type of critical thinking that exemplifies the power of argumentation. For example, in one such exchange between seventh graders on the topic, the two students weigh the severity of punishment against its efficacy. The exchange begins with one student offering reasons to back up her position that serious crimes should be severely punished:

Student 1: *I feel that adult court is better because, you know, it's a place of high, serious crime. They gonna continue doing the same thing. You know, if they have a history and they, um*

Student 2: *Well, I disagree because teenagers who commit a crime shouldn't be sent to adult court. They should go to juvenile court because at adult court they have electric chairs and many things that could kill a person. They should be sent to therapy.*

Student 1: *That won't do anything. For example, the teenagers in our neighborhood, they have constant behavior like having disrespect and stuff like that and they may have committed a serious crime and they gonna go to*

Student 2: *But think about this: they're still kids!* (Boyd, 2018)

The exchange above illustrates the way in which even young adolescents are able to engage in deep discussion requiring critical thinking when faced with a social issue they care about. Notice how the students both build on and critique each other's reasons. When student 2 suggests that the solution is to provide juvenile offenders with therapy, his partner points out that therapy might not be effective for serious offenders. This response is just one of several in this short exchange that demonstrates critical thinking about arguments.

Imbedded within the discussion is more than simple evaluative thinking, though. Student 1's skepticism about therapy is not untethered; it is grounded in her own experience of the world, as demonstrated in her next sentence ("…the teenagers in our neighborhood…"). Thus, the power of argumentation is not simply that it allows and encourages critical thinking in general, but that it engages students in the real world in which they live. This grounded engagement makes real the issues, encouraging students to think about social problems in both concrete and abstract ways.

The critical evaluation that develops as a result of these kinds of exchange is focused on evaluating ideas and reasons. This leads to understanding that some ideas are better than others (Felton & Kuhn, 2001). A student who suggests that juvenile offenders who commit serious crimes should not be tried at all (in either juvenile or adult court systems) will quickly be called out by peers as they point out the flaws in such an argument. Thus, students learn to critically evaluate arguments.

This critical thinking about ideas also leads to an understanding that not every argument they themselves make is a good one. As students are exposed to argumentation curricula, they become better able to understand the weaknesses of their own position and the strengths of the opposing side (Boyd, 2018;

Gélat, 2003; Kuhn et al., 2013; Newell, Beach, Smith, & Vanderheide, 2011). This is an important understanding, as Cozolino (2013) writes, for "wise individuals…transcend the notion of a single correct perspective…and recognize the inescapable distortions inherent in one's own perspective" (p. 211). As students become more and more able to "recognize the inescapable distortions inherent in one's own perspective," they also begin to be able to recognize the distortions in sources. Questions of the validity of sources, as well as their angles and biases, naturally begin to arise when students are engaging in critical, evaluative thinking. Thus, the evaluation of ideas and reasons leads down a path towards the evaluations of resources.

It is more than just the evaluation of ideas, though. While argumentation teaches students to think critically about ideas and sources, it also promotes the value of others. Notice in the exchange above that the students are critical of each other's ideas, but not of each other. Despite being middle schoolers, a notoriously vicious age, they do not call each other names or attack each other. They simply question and counter the arguments presented.

Partly, this comes from the nature of this particular argumentation curriculum. Specifically, it comes from the collaborative and dialogic nature of the activities in which the students participate. Put simply, working with others helps students understand others. Collaborative reasoning methods help students co-construct understanding while also allowing them to question and evaluate (Boyd, 2018; Chinn, Anderson, & Waggoner, 2001; Kuhn et al., 2017). Through this co-construction, students begin to understand both how they think and how others think, a topic explored in the next section.

Argumentation and Metacognition

As discussed in the previous section, argumentation in the classroom can teach students how to evaluate ideas and sources. Both as part of this evaluation and as an extension of it, argumentation teaches students how people think and how to evaluate thought processes (Boyd, 2018; Chinn et al., 2001; Larkin, 2009; Zillmer, 2016). This leads to the development of two important mental competencies: metacognition and theory of mind.

Metacognition broadly encompasses a set of skills that involve thinking about thinking (Livingston, 2003). More specifically, metacognition requires students to understand the ways that they and others conceptualize problems and to regulate their own learning (Larkin, 2009; Livingston, 2003). The evaluation of ideas that springs from collaborative argumentation leads into metacognition as students become aware that not everyone thinks the same way or approaches problems in the same manner. Indeed, research has shown that the longer students are exposed to argumentation as a practice, the more they tend to engage in metacognitive discourse (Boyd, 2018). That is, as students argue with others in a classroom setting, the more their discussion focuses on the ways to approach the issue and what value specific ideas and strategies have. A student's first time collaborating on a persuasive essay, for example, might be filled with simple listing of arguments. The more a student collaborates on the argumentative essay, though, the more that student is likely to discuss with partners whose arguments and approaches are most persuasive. As they engage with others more, they become aware that thinking (and talking) about metacognition is an important part of crafting an argument (Boyd, 2018). In other words, they are learning how to direct their argumentative efforts.

This shift towards metacognitive dialogue (or what Zillmer (2016) calls "metatalk") occurs because of the power of argumentation to focus students on evaluating ideas and not people. The more comfortable people are with their collaborative partners, the more they engage in metatalk (Zillmer, 2016). This suggests that there needs to be trust and safety for successful collaboration, and while those things never happen automatically, keeping the argumentative focus on evaluation of ideas can help to build both. There is also evidence that students will engage in metatalk even in the absence of teacher direction (Larkin, 2009) and that students will often engage in metatalk better when the teacher is not present (Boyd, 2018). Thus, though metacognition is often thought of as a skill that must be explicitly taught, to an extent it can also emerge organically through the process of argumentation. Whether organic or explicit, though, the fact remains that argumentation boosts student metacognition.

As part of metacognition, students become aware not only of how they themselves think but also how others think. Working collaboratively on argumentative tasks is particularly good for this, as it promotes the understanding that others think and know different things than you do. Psychologists call this theory of mind. Theory of mind leads students to understand that others view things differently from the way they do, which leads them to evaluate their reasons and positions (as well as those of others). A student who is faced with arguments from an opposing side partner is actively confronted with the fact others think differently. Evaluating a partner's reasoning, is likely to lead to an evaluation of one's own reasoning. This can then lead to a deeper understanding of what Cozolino (2013) refers to as "the inescapable distortions inherent in one's own perspective" (p. 211). Thus, argumentation builds theory of mind which builds both theory of mind and metacognition.

Theory of mind plays a role in both the way students manage their own learning and the way they understand and relate to others. As Mercer (2013) defines it, theory of mind involves "both assessments of what others think and know and metacognitive reflections on our own thought processes" (p. 151). Thus, theory of mind allows students to understand what they know and what others know and what understandings, skills, and knowledge they share with others (Mercer, 2013). In this way, theory of mind strengthens understanding and empathy. As one student works with another, they both become aware that they understand and know different things. Not only can this cause them to reflect and evaluate their own thinking, it can also help them understand the unique perspective of each other. This is particularly true in a collaborative argumentative setting, where students are asked to explicitly discuss, evaluate, and justify their position. Insofar as this explicit discourse plays a major role in supplying the benefits of argumentative curricula, it is worth exploring on its own, as will be done in the following section.

Dialogue, Conflict, & Growth

What makes dialogue so powerful in the classroom? And, must it remain conflict-free in order to aid student growth? To answer that, it is important to discuss first what dialogue is and how it works in the classroom, particularly as it pertains to argumentation. Dialogic processes involve students engaging with each other in discourse. As a social process, dialogue employs students in discussion with others, particularly with peers. In argumentation, this often takes the form of debate as students push each other to justify and to think critically about arguments. This dialogic argumentation is exactly the type of classroom work that leads to student growth in critical thinking and metacognitive skills (Boyd, 2018; Kuhn et al., 2017).

It has long been known that dialogue leads to deeper understanding and engagement in the developing mind (Piaget, 1929; Tudge & Rogoff, 1989; Vygotsky, 1981; Vygotsky, 1978). Both Piaget and Vygotsky acknowledged the role of discourse in cognitive development, including the power of dialogue to increase metacognitive awareness. Piaget (1929) wrote that "it is through contact with others and the practice of discussion that the mind is forced to realise its subjective nature and thus to become aware of the process of thought itself" (p. 87). In other words, talking with others increases the ability of students to evaluate their own thoughts and engage in meta-level reflection on how they have arrived at their conclusions.

Vygotsky likewise saw dialogue as critical for cognitive development, arguing that thought begins as discussion. In Vygotskian terms, dialogue allows students to move understanding from inter-psychological discourse to intra-psychological understanding (Vygotsky, 1981). In other words, dialogue between students leads to co-constructed knowledge. This co-constructed knowledge becomes internalized by each student and develops into an internal part of their individual cognitive landscape. For example, debate with others often becomes part of a student's internal dialogue, shaping the way that student thinks about the issue at hand (Garcia-Mila & Andersen, 2007).

In addition, dialogue requires active engagement of students, as opposed to passive learning activities like lecture. As Chinn et al. (2001) write, "discussion is the everyday implementation of the principle that learners must be active agents in their own learning" (p. 378). In other words, students in a dialogic classroom engage with the content in an active way, grappling with issues and understanding in conjunction with others. The very nature of dialogue means that students are active: a conversation cannot happen if one of the conversers is not participating. Inter-psychological co-construction is impossible with only one person working; thus students engaged in dialogic work often become active participants out of necessity.

Indeed, socioconstruction is at the heart of collaboration. Any type of collaboration requires some form of co-construction, either socioconstruction of a product and/or of ideas and understanding. Dialogic argumentation is particularly good at encouraging the latter (Felton & Kuhn, 2001; Tudge & Hogan, 1997), and it is this co-construction of ideas and understanding that is most important in the development of critical thinking. As students argue with each other, they sort through ways of conceptualizing an issue. Through this dialogic argumentation, as already discussed, students then evaluate each other's ideas and their own, working together to construct an understanding of what arguments, evidence, and sources are best.

Despite the proven effectiveness of dialogic argumentation, many educators still think of collaboration and socioconstruction as requiring a primarily agreement-based and conflict-free process. Often, educators worry about problems inherent in disagreement and conflict. Though disagreement-based dialogue can be difficult to manage (Järvelä, Volet, & Järvenoja, 2010), it is through disagreement that students can learn to better understand others' perspectives and think more critically about their own positions (Boyd, 2018; Howe, 2010; Rojas-Drummond, Albarrán, & Littleton, 2008). In fact, some research has found that even when students do not come to a successful consensus during dialogic collaboration, growth can still be seen in subsequent individual measures (Howe, 2010; Kapur, 2008; Skoumios, 2009).

This growth partly springs from the very act of discussion with someone who disagrees with you (Howe, 2010; Skoumios, 2009). As students work with others who disagree, their thoughts about topics often change. According to Cozolino (2013), maturation of thought occurs as adolescents move from believing that there are simple solutions to complex issues to understanding that "solutions to human problems are hardly ever simple or straightforward" (p. 214). This is the very type of cognitive development that can occur as students work in disagreement-based collaborative environments. Indeed, the very nature of dialogue is that it requires more than simple agreement. As Adey and Shayer (2010) ask of discourse with minimum disagreement, "What would generate the dialogue?" (p. 19). Thus, true growth in metacognition and theory of mind requires not only collaboration, or dialogic collaboration, but disagreement-based dialogue. It is the sociocognitive conflict created through dialogue with someone from an opposing side that allows students the most space to grow and understand both themselves and others.

Developing an "Inner-Locutor"

The focus of the previous sections has been on the ways that disagreement-based dialogic argumentation in the classroom can build critical thinking skills as students engage with each other and grapple with social issues. Often, argumentation in the classroom leads up to and is measured by argumentative writing (Boyd, 2018; Howe, 2010; Kuhn et al., 2017). When it comes to social issues, this written argumentation most often takes the form of persuasive position papers. However, a common issue in argumentative writing is what Graff (2008) calls the "missing interlocutor;" that is, students are writing without recognizing or taking into account the opposing position.

This type of "my-side bias" is common in many students and here, too, dialogic argumentation can help students mitigate this tendency. As discussed previously, engagement in discursive argumentation can lead students to understanding and evaluating first the other side's positions and, subsequently, their own positions. This process of evaluation, closely linked to the development of theory of mind, can help students better construct argumentative essays that address the opposing side (Boyd, 2018; Kuhn et al., 2013).

Dialogic argumentation, then, can help students fill in Graff's missing interlocutor with an internalized one. This "inner-locutor" develops as the inter-psychological discourse becomes intra-psychological and students begin to understand how others understand and conceptualize social issues. In other words, students begin to develop an inner voice that evaluates various positions, pointing out the flaws in their position and any strengths in the opposing position. As they write, this inner-locutor guides them and allows them to evaluate their argument and to think flexibly and critically about all sides of an issue. Thus, this type of classroom activity builds critical thinking skills that become more and more internalized as students are exposed to them (Boyd, 2018; Kuhn et al., 2017).

A DIALOGIC MODEL FOR CRITICAL THINKING AND SOCIAL ISSUES

The previous sections outlined some of the research demonstrating the strengths of dialogic collaboration for developing critical thinking skills in students, particularly as they relate to student engagement with social issues. But how does the development of critical thinking skills and the inner-locutor help students engage with social issues in a way that promotes value-loaded critical thinking?

Argumentation, metacognition, theory of mind, and the development of an inner-locutor work together to contribute to critical thinking about the real world in additive ways. Dialogic argumentation leads to critical thinking through the development of metacognition and theory of mind. These then lead to the development of an inner-locutor, which further supports critical thinking.

The route through which each of these feeds into each other can be summarized in three steps which have implementation implications for educators. First, disagreement-based dialogic collaboration focused on social issues leads to the development of theory of mind, the act of socioconstruction, and the evaluation of ideas and sources. As has already been outlined, students from opposite sides of an issue working together in a dialogic setting learn to evaluate ideas and sources while valuing people through dialogic argumentation. The development of theory of mind, which is closely tied to socioconstruction, further undergirds understanding of differences in viewpoints and approaches to issues.

Secondly, building these skills (theory of mind, socioconstruction, and evaluation) via dialogic activities leads to flexible, value-loaded cognition (Frijters et al., 2008). Value-loaded cognition involves reflecting on and applying values to analysis and other cognitive processes. Thus, as dialogue helps students build theory of mind, socioconstruction skills, and learn to evaluate ideas, they begin to be able to think about values and how they relate to the social issues they are confronted with. Alongside value-loaded cognition, cognitive flexibility emerges. This occurs as students' metacognitive skills develop and they begin to understand how different problems require different approaches. The development of both flexible and value-loaded cognition means that students are able to understand multiple viewpoints and develop values around what is important.

Finally, flexible, value-loaded cognition leads to critical thinking about social issues and the media that presents them. Armed with the ability to think flexibly and to apply values to issues, students are able to evaluate both positions and sources of information. Their full understanding both of how others think and how they themselves think (i.e., metacognition) can lead them to understand that not all solutions and not all positions are equal. Thus, in order to create critical thinkers (and good citizens), teachers need to incorporate disagreement-based dialogic activities into their classroom, especially those rooted in real world social issues.

FUTURE RESEARCH DIRECTIONS

Future research directions might include examining the impact of teacher intervention on student outcome. Emerging research in this area is promising (Biesta, Priestley, & Robinson, 2017; Sedova, Sedlacek, & Svaricek, 2016). Still more research is needed to understand the ways in which both large- and small-scale teacher education regarding dialogic teaching can impact student learning outcomes, including critical thinking skills.

In addition, this chapter has not touched upon the existing research on the impact of the demographic make-up of dialogic partners on the actual dialogue. Specifically, issues of gender, race, power, and privilege intersecting with discourse in the classroom can lead to both self-imposed and other-imposed restrictions on some students (see, for example, Keogh, Barnes, Joiner, & Littleton, 2000). More research on the ways structural and societal power plays out in dialogue both within and outside the classroom could illuminate the ways in which critical thinking develops in different types of students in the same classroom.

CONCLUSION

This chapter has attempted to bring together the literature on what critical thinking is, how dialogic argumentation builds critical thinking, and how both of these can be applied to addressing social issues in the classroom. One of the central issues of our time is how to engage students in ways that allow them to develop value-loaded critical thinking around social issues. The theoretical model outlined in this chapter is a first step in conceptualizing how teachers can teach students those skills. Specifically, the research suggests that disagreement-based dialogic argumentation activities rooted in real world social issues allow students to interact in ways that bring them to a mindset of value-loaded critical thinking.

In the end, students, teachers, and society at large all benefit from teaching students to think critically about social issues. Through dialogic argumentation, students have the opportunity to develop values-based critical thinking about the real-world scenarios they encounter and the sources they use to justify their positions. In a world as polarized as ours, students with flexible, evaluative thinking skills and the empathy that can come with a robust theory of mind about others can offer hope for the future in the form of today's students.

REFERENCES

Adey, P., & Shayer, M. (2010). The effects of cognitive acceleration – and speculation about causes of these effects. In *AERA Research Conference, Socializing intelligence through academic talk and dialogue* (pp. 1–20). Learning, Research and Development Centre. Retrieved from http://www.kcl.ac.uk/sspp/departments/education/research/crestem/CogAcc/Cognaccel.aspx

Beavers, S. L. (2011). Getting political science in on the joke: Using The Daily Show and their comedy to teach politics. *PS, Political Science & Politics*, *44*(02), 415–419. doi:10.1017/S1049096511000266

Biesta, G., Priestley, M., & Robinson, S. (2017). Talking about education: Exploring the significance of teachers' talk for teacher agency. *Journal of Curriculum Studies*, *49*(1), 38–54. doi:10.1080/00220272.2016.1205143

Bowell, T., & Kemp, G. (2005). *Critical thinking: A concise guide* (2nd ed.). New York: Routledge. doi:10.4324/9780203482889

Boyd, N. (2018). *The effects of collaboration on student writing development*. Columbia University.

Chinn, C. A., Anderson, R. C., & Waggoner, M. A. (2001). Patterns of discourse in two kinds of literature discussion. *Reading Research Quarterly*, *36*(4), 378–411. doi:10.1598/RRQ.36.4.3

Cozolino, L. (2013). *The social neuroscience of education*. New York: W.W. Norton.

Facione, P. A. (1990). Critical thinking: A statement of expert consensus for purposes of educational assessment and instruction. Research findings and recommendations. *American Philosophical Association*. Doi": doi:10.1016/j.tsc.2009.07.002

Fallahi, M. (2012). Text-based Dyadic Conversation: The influence of partners' attitude and level of critical thinking. California State University, Chicago, IL.

Felton, M., & Kuhn, D. (2001). The development of argumentive discourse skill. *Discourse Processes*, *32*(2), 135–153. doi:10.1207/S15326950DP3202&3_03

Frijters, S., ten Dam, G., & Rijlaarsdam, G. (2008). Effects of dialogic learning on value-loaded critical thinking. *Learning and Instruction*, *18*(1), 66–82. doi:10.1016/j.learninstruc.2006.11.001

Garcia-Mila, M., & Andersen, C. (2007). The cognitive foundations of learning argumentation. In S. Erduran & M. P. Jimenez-Aleixandre (Eds.), *Argumentation in science education* (pp. 29–45). Berlin, Germany: Springer. doi:10.1007/978-1-4020-6670-2_2

Gélat, M. (2003). Taking others' perspectives in a peer interactional setting while preparing for a written argument. *Language and Education, 17*(5), 332–354. doi:10.1080/09500780308666855

Graff, G. (2008). *Clueless in academe: How schooling obscures the life of the mind.* New Haven: CT Yale University Press.

Halpern, D. F. (2014). *Thought and knowledge: An introduction to critical thinking* (5th ed.). New York: Psychology Press.

Hobbs, R. (2010). *News literacy: what works and what doesn't.* Association for Education in Journalism and Mass Communication.

Howe, C. (2010). Peer Dialogue and Cognitive Development: A two-way relationship? In K. Littleton & C. Howe (Eds.), *Educational dialogues: Understanding and promoting productive interaction* (pp. 32–47). New York: Routledge. Retrieved from https://books.google.com/books?hl=en&lr=&id=_buLAgAAQBAJ&pgis=1

Järvelä, S., Volet, S., & Järvenoja, H. (2010). Research on motivation in collaborative learning: Moving beyond the cognitive-situative divide and combining individual and social processes. *Educational Psychologist, 45*(1), 15–27. doi:10.1080/00461520903433539

Kapur, M. (2008). Productive failure. *Cognition and Instruction, 26*(3), 379–424. doi:10.1080/07370000802212669

Keogh, T., Barnes, P., Joiner, R., & Littleton, K. (2000). Gender, pair composition and computer versus paper presentations of an English language task. *Educational Psychology, 20*(1), 33–43. doi:10.1080/014434100110362

Kuhn, D. (2007). Is direct instruction an answer to the right question? *Educational Psychologist, 42*(2), 109–113. doi:10.1080/00461520701263376

Kuhn, D., & Crowell, A. (2011). Dialogic argumentation as a vehicle for developing young adolescents' thinking. *Psychological Science, 22*(4), 545–552. doi:10.1177/0956797611402512

Kuhn, D., Hemberger, L., & Khait, V. (2017). *Argue with me: Argument as a path to developing students' thinking and writing* (2nd ed.). New York: Routledge. doi:10.4324/9781315692722

Kuhn, D., Zillmer, N., Crowell, A., & Zavala, J. (2013). Developing norms of argumentation: Metacognitive, epistemological, and social dimensions of developing argumentive competence. *Cognition and Instruction, 31*(4), 456–496. doi:10.1080/07370008.2013.830618

Larkin, S. (2009). Socially mediated metacognition and learning to write. *Thinking Skills and Creativity, 4*(3), 149–159. doi:10.1016/j.tsc.2009.09.003

Livingston, J. A. (2003). *Metacognition: An overview.* Retrieved from http://eric.ed.gov/?id=ED474273

Marchi, R. (2012). With Facebook, blogs, and fake news, teens reject journalistic "objectivity.". *The Journal of Communication Inquiry, 36*(3), 246–262. doi:10.1177/0196859912458700

Mercer, N. (2013). The social brain, language, and goal-directed collective thinking: A social conception of cognition and its implications for understanding how we think, teach, and learn. *Educational Psychologist, 48*(3), 148–168. doi:10.1080/00461520.2013.804394

Newell, G. E., Beach, R., Smith, J., & Vanderheide, J. (2011). Teaching and learning argumentative reading and writing : A review of research. *Reading Research Quarterly, 46*(3), 273–304.

Pennycook, G., & Rand, D. G. (2018). Who falls for fake news? The roles of bullshit receptivity, overclaiming, familiarity, and analytic thinking.

Piaget, J. (1929). *The child's conception of the world.* London: Routledge & Kegan Paul, Ltd.

Rojas-Drummond, S. M., Albarrán, C. D., & Littleton, K. S. (2008). Collaboration, creativity and the co-construction of oral and written texts. *Thinking Skills and Creativity, 3*(3), 177–191. doi:10.1016/j.tsc.2008.09.008

Sedova, K., Sedlacek, M., & Svaricek, R. (2016). Teacher professional development as a means of transforming student classroom talk. *Teaching and Teacher Education, 57,* 14–25. doi:10.1016/j.tate.2016.03.005

Skoumios, M. (2009). The effect of sociocognitive conflict on students' dialogic argumentation about floating and sinking. *International Journal of Environmental and Science Education, 4*(4), 381–399.

Tudge, J., & Hogan, D. (1997). Collaboration from a Vygotskian Perspective, 12.

Tudge, J., & Rogoff, B. (1989). *Peer influences on cognitive development: Piagetian and Vygotskian perspectives.* Lawrence Erlbaum Associates, Inc.

Vygotsky, L. (1981). The Genesis of Higher Mental Functions. In J. V. Wertsch (Ed.), *The concept of activity in Soviet psychology* (pp. 144–188). Armonk, NY: M.E. Sharpe.

Vygotsky, L. S. (1978). *Mind in society: The development of higher psychological processes.* doi:10.1007/978-3-540-92784-6

Walker, K., & Zeidler, D. L. (2007). Promoting discourse about socioscientific issues through scaffolded inquiry. *International Journal of Science Education, 29*(11), 1387–1410. doi:10.1080/09500690601068095

Wikipedia. (n.d.). Critical Thinking. Retrieved November 7, 2018, from https://en.wikipedia.org/wiki/Critical_thinking

Wolfe, C. R. (2012). Individual differences in the "Myside Bias" in reasoning and written argumentation. *Written Communication, 29*(4), 477–501. doi:10.1177/0741088312457909

Zillmer, N. (2016). *Metacognitive dimensions of adolescents' intellectual collaboration* [Dissertation]. Columbia University. doi:10.1017/CBO9781107415324.004

KEY TERMS AND DEFINITIONS

Argumentation: The process of taking positions and backing them up with logic and evidence. The social act of argumentation is sometimes referred to as debate, while argumentative writing is often referred to as persuasive writing.

Critical Thinking: A higher-order thinking skill encompassing cognitive, emotional, and contextual practices to evaluate, analyze, and make judgments.

Dialogic: Programs or processes that engage two or more people in discussion with each other.

Inner-Locutor: An internal interlocutor, or dialogue partner, that allows students to "hear" other perspectives as they work, particularly on argumentative writing.

Metacognition: The process of thinking about and regulating your thinking and others' thinking.

Socioconstruction: When two or more people creating products or ideas together through collaboration. Socioconstruction (as opposed to co-construction) usually focuses on the social aspect of creation.

Theory of Mind: The understanding that others think, believe, and know differently than you do.

Chapter 9
Using Socioscientific Issues to Enhance Evidence-Based Reasoning Among Middle School Students

Wardell Anthony Powell
Framingham State University, USA

Danielle Fuchs
Wellesley High School, USA

ABSTRACT

This study investigated the implementation of a socioscientific issue curricular unit that was designed to enhance evidence-based reasoning among middle school students. Forty-three middle school students (11-12 years old; 20 males, 23 females) from a summer enrichment program operated by a non-profit organization in the northeastern United States participated in this study. The duration of this curricular unit took place over five consecutive 1-hour period blocks. The researchers utilized qualitative procedures to analyze students' abilities to engage in evidence-based reasoning and the impact it might have on students' argumentation quality on whether the air we breathe makes us sick. Comparison of the findings from pre-test and post-test indicate that students were able to use evidence-based reasoning to enhance their argumentation quality. The results from this investigation suggest that perhaps the use of socioscientific issues as a critical pedagogical tool does enhance students' abilities to engage in evidence-based reasoning.

INTRODUCTION

It is no secret that air pollution in the United States and around the world may have adverse effects on human health as well as the health of the environment. Several studies have shown that exposure to air pollution has been associated with a wide range of health-related effects including respiratory diseases, cancers, and even death. Equally troubling is the fact that children from marginalized groups within the

DOI: 10.4018/978-1-5225-7829-1.ch009

Copyright © 2019, IGI Global. Copying or distributing in print or electronic forms without written permission of IGI Global is prohibited.

general population are exposed to more pollutants and are at higher risks of developing health complications, such as asthma, due to air pollution. While the prospect of finding solutions to the pollution crisis in impoverished communities occur very slowly, one thing seems evident is that school-based science has the potential to equip students with the knowledge and skills necessary for them to think and act on pollution issues as well-informed citizens would. The use of socioscientific issues (SSI) to teach scientific concepts has the potential to enhance students' abilities to use evidence to substantiate their claims during argumentation practices in the classroom settings. This, in turn, will increase critical thinking skills, and thus students' abilities to act. In this chapter, we will demonstrate to the science education community, policymakers, and practitioners how to use SSI to engage middle school students in evidence-based reasoning and the results that are achieved when this practice is implemented. Described below is the SSI unit we created, the teaching strategies we adapted, and the results we obtained from a group of middle school students in the northeastern United States who engaged in evidence-based reasoning on the effects of asthma on the health of marginalized populations. This chapter will:

1. Define what are socioscientific issues.
2. Describe the Understanding by Design tenets embedded within the SSI Unit of study to provide long-term achievement gains by students.
3. Discuss how the SSI Unit increased access to and mastery of science content, concepts, and inquiry skills critical for evidence-based reasoning.
4. Describe the population of learners and their unique characteristics.
5. Discuss students' findings and arguments on the disproportionate asthma cases in communities throughout the northeastern United States.

We hope this unit will show that through contemporary teaching methods paired with SSI, we can increase critical thinking skills of students as well as their abilities to make evidence-based decisions as well-informed citizens.

BACKGROUND

What Are Socioscientific Issues?

Socioscientific issues are those issues that are typically contentious in nature, can be considered from a variety of perspectives, do not possess simple conclusions, and frequently involve morality and ethics (Zeidler & Kahn, 2014). Examples of SSI include a range of dilemmas such as biotechnology, hydraulic fracking, environmental issues, health effects of diets, as well as genetic engineering (Sadler & Murakami, 2014; Zeidler, et al., 2009; Zeidler & Kahn, 2014). The SSI framework seeks to involve students in decision making regarding everyday social issues with moral or ethical implications embedded within scientific contexts (Powell, 2014; Yap, 2014; Zeidler, 2007). The disproportionate cases of asthma in underserved communities throughout the United States is a socioscientific issue. Teaching students about what asthma is, the causes, symptoms, and triggers of asthma, the prevalence of asthma in their communities, the relationships between socioeconomic status and the incidence of asthma, and potential ways to reduce asthma cases is best done through the use of socioscientific issues as a critical pedagogical strategy. This will enhance students' ability to analyze, synthesize and evaluate information, develop their moral reasoning and ethical decision-making, in addition to developing students' content knowledge and argumentation skills (Dawson & Venville, 2010; Klosterman & Sadler, 2010; Sadler, Klosterman, & Topcu, 2011; Zeidler & Nichols, 2009; Zeidler, 2014).

Evidence-Based Reasoning

Evidence is described as an observable sign, indicator, or datum that is relevant in deciding whether a hypothesis of interest is true or false (Tecuci, et al., 2016). The scientific enterprise is based on the collection and analysis of evidence. Thus, arguments based on evidence forms the foundation to scientific thinking (Kuhn, 1993; Kuhn & Pearsall, 2000). While some in the United States government are fascinated with the desire to chip away at the bedrock that forms the scientific enterprise by banning phrase such as, evidence-based, the fact still remains that in order to empower citizens to think about scientific situations as scientific-literate citizens would, argumentation exercises in the classroom setting that provide opportunities for students to engage in evidence-based reasoning is of paramount importance. In fact, science education reform efforts advocate for opportunities in the classroom that will allow students to participate in scientific argumentation exercises to enhance their abilities to reason from evidence (National Research Council [NRC], 2012; Next Generation Science Standards [NGSS], 2013). This many believe is paramount to developing critical thinking, problem-solving, and reasoning skills that will allow students to generate and evaluate scientific claims, explanations, models, and experimental designs (Evagorou, Sadler, Tal, 2011). To develop and use arguments that are convincing to others, students need to understand that the presentation of ample evidence in an argument plays a critical role to determine the validity of a conclusion.

What Is Argumentation?

Argumentation is a process of thinking and social interaction in which individuals construct and critique arguments (Golanics & Nussbaum, 2008). Two distinctions that have been made between the word argument. The first (argument 1-visual), is that argument can be seen as a product and the second (argument 2-persuasive), an argument can be seen as a process (Blair, 2015). Discussion in the classroom that allows students to make and evaluate each other's arguments, would be a form of argument-2 (Blair, 2015; Nussbaum, 2011). This is the type of argument that is currently being advocated by standard initiatives such as the Next Generation Science Standards (NGSS) and Common Core State Standards (CCSS) for English Language Arts and Literacy in History/Social Studies, Science, and Technical Subjects (Common Core State Standards Initiative, 2010; Next Generation Science Standards, 2013). For example, the NGSS requires K-12 students to engage in argument from evidence to support or refute the explanation or a model for a phenomenon or a solution to a problem. The above standards advocate for the inclusion of the social and cognitive practices of doing science, which involves higher order thinking (Etkina et al, 2005; Mestre et al, 2009) and evidential reasoning (Cetina, 1999, Osborn, 2010). The standards also advocate for discourse in science that provides opportunities for students to observe, describe, theorize, ask questions, argue, design experiments, follow procedures, judge, evaluate, formulate conclusion, generalize, and report on phenomena (Halliday, 2004). In requiring students to develop argument from evidence, the standards (NGSS, 2013 and CCSS, 2010) require teachers to provide students with opportunities to engage in activities to develop skills in formulating empirically based scientific argument (Driver et al, 2000; Osborne, 2005; Abi-El-Mona & Abd-El-Khalick, 2006; Jimenez-Aleixandre & Eurduran, 2008; Newell et al, 2011). In general, the main purpose of these standards is not mainly to nurture a new generation of scientists, but to create an informed citizenry capable of making well-informed decisions on everyday phenomena. The SSI unit plan we developed for middle school students will provide opportunities for the students to engage in argument from evidence to enhance the skills needed to become well-informed citizens.

METHODS

Education reform efforts over the last two-and-a-half decades have advocated for opportunities in the classroom that will allow students to participate in scientific argumentation exercises to enhance their abilities to reason from evidence (American Association for the Advancement of Science (National Research Council [NRC], 2012; Common Core State Standards Initiative 2010; Next Generation Science Standards [NGSS], 2013). In light of these reform efforts, the following questions and corresponding rationales were used in this investigation to determine:

Research Question 1: What relationships, if any, exist between the use of socioscientific issues and middle school students' abilities to engage in evidence-based reasoning?

Rationale 1: Supporters of the SSI framework have long argued that such pedagogy has the potential to develop students' competencies in making informed decisions on sustainable environmental practices (Bencze, Sperling, & Carter, 2012; Muller, Zeidler, & Jenkins, 2011). Issues such as climate change, water pollution, and air pollution in marginalized communities pose a serious threat to the health and survival of society at large. Finding solutions to these issues will require a generation who can critically think about the potential cause and effect ramification that will result from our actions and inactions in dealing with issues such as energy consumption. Sound pedagogy is a requirement for teaching students to determine potential relationships between the consumption of fossil fuels and environmental issues. Socioscientific issues as a pedagogical strategy are poised to enhance students' ability to think critically as they determine cause and effect relationships and engage in evidence-based reasoning on science issues such as energy consumption that relates to their everyday lives.

Research Question 2: How might middle school students' abilities to think critically about energy consumption impact their argumentation quality?

Rationale 2: Researchers have said that the most efficient and effective way to increase students' critical thinking abilities is through extensive deliberate practice that involves the use of argument mapping (Mulnix, 2010). Such beliefs are aligned with the vision for K-12 science education advocated by the National Research Council (2012). The framework has determined that for students to become the critical consumers of science, they must be given opportunities to use critique and evaluation to judge the merits of any scientifically based argument (NRC, 2012). However, achieving this goal is only possible if teachers adapt and use sound pedagogical practices in the classroom settings that will foster the development of students' abilities to use critique and evaluation to judge the merit of an argument. The use of socioscientific issues as a key pedagogical strategy has the potential to enhance students' critical thinking abilities as they engage in argumentation exercises on scientific issues that are personally relevant and meaningful to their daily lives. The ability to identify connections between energy consumption and its unintended consequences on the environment is paramount for us to engage in sustainability activities.

Study Participants

The participants in this study were 43 middle school students (11–12 years old; 20 males, 23 females) who participated in a summer enrichment program operated by a non-profit organization in the northeastern United States. The program remediates achievement gaps and prepares students for acceptance to and success at top independent, Catholic, and public exam schools in the northeastern United States. The students are generally referred to the program by their teachers from the public school system, and they are admitted in the spring before their fifth or sixth grade year. The racial breakdown of the students is as follows: 19% Asian, 37% Black, 21% Hispanic, 10% Multiracial, 4% White, and 9% other. These students were from 40 distinct feeder schools in a major metropolitan region of the northeastern United States. Seventy-seven percent (77%) of the students attended public schools, nineteen percent (19%) attended charter schools, and four percent (4%) attended parochial schools. The average family income was $41,735, and fifty-one percent (51%) of the students qualify for free and reduced meals. The students came from 16 distinct neighborhoods.

Study Design

This study employed a quasi-experimental pretest-post-test design by using students who were enrolled in three science classes in an enrichment summer program with a non-profit organization in the northeastern United States. Qualitative data were gathered to get a better understanding of the effects of a socioscientific issues curricular unit in promoting students' abilities to engage in evidence-based reasoning on the relationships between wealth and the incidence of asthma. The senior director of teaching and learning for the non-profit organization randomly assigned three classes to be exposed to the socioscientific issues curriculum. The first author taught all three classes. The students in these classes were given the pre-test questionnaire, exposed to the socioscientific issues curriculum unit and activities, and then given the post-test questionnaire to complete. In order to enhance students' engagement and support long- term achievement, the 5E Model of Instruction (Bybee, 2014) and the Understanding by Design Framework (Wiggins & McTighe, 2011) were central in the development of this curricular unit.

5E Model of Instruction

The 5E Model of Instruction is a constructivist design for learning framework that provides students with the required experiences to challenge their conceptions and/or misconceptions. It provides students with activities that facilitate the reconstruction of their ideas and abilities (Bybee, 2014). This model has five phases that include: engaging the learner, providing chances for exploration of material, opportunities for the learners to explain their discovery of new content during the exploration phases, to elaborate upon unfamiliar concepts under investigation, and provide opportunities to evaluate the new knowledge gained by the learner (Bybee, 2014). While the evaluation phase appears at the end of the list, it is important to point out that this process is cyclic in nature and that those formative assessments are frequent evaluative checks done throughout each phase of the cycle. All of the lessons in the unit are developed on the 5E model in conjunction with the Understanding by Design Framework (UbD) elements.

UNDERSTANDING BY DESIGN FRAMEWORK

The Understanding by Design Framework (UbD) supports the notion that long-term achievement gains by students are more likely when teachers teach for the understanding of transferrable concepts and processes while giving learners multiple opportunities to apply their learning in authentic contexts (Wiggins & McTighe, 2011). Two key features of the framework are: 1) teaching and assessing for understanding and knowledge transfer, and 2) the curriculum is designed "backward" from those ends. McTighe and Wiggins (2011) have further identified seven critical tenets of the UbD Framework:

1. Learning is enhanced when teachers think purposefully about curricular planning. The UbD framework helps this process without offering a rigid method or prescriptive recipe.
2. The UbD framework helps focus curriculum and teaching on the development and deepening of student understanding and transfer of learning (i.e., the ability to effectively use content knowledge and skill).
3. Understanding is revealed when students autonomously make sense of and transfer their learning through authentic performance. Six facets of understanding—the capacity to explain, interpret, apply, shift perspective, empathize, and self-assess—can serve as indicators of understanding.
4. An effective curriculum is planned backward from long-term, desired results through a three-stage design process (Desired Results, Evidence, and Learning Plan). This process helps avoid the common problems of treating the textbook as the curriculum rather than a resource, and activity-oriented teaching in which no clear priorities and purposes are apparent.
5. Teachers are coaches of understanding, not mere purveyors of content knowledge, skill, or activity. They focus on ensuring that learning happens, not just teaching (and assuming that what was taught was learned); they always aim and check for successful meaning making and transfer by the learner.
6. Regularly reviewing units and curriculum against design standards enhances curricular quality and effectiveness and provides engaging and professional discussions.
7. The UbD framework reflects a continual improvement approach to student achievement and teacher craft. The results of our designs—student performance—inform needed adjustments to the curriculum as well as the instruction so that student learning is maximized.

The tenets outlined above are an indication that appropriate planning should precede all teaching if we as educators are serious about educating for students' future success. Proper planning should not be an add-on to effective teaching and learning if we want to become well-informed citizens. We cannot start with just giving the content; we must begin with what students are expected to be able to know and do with the content by building off their prior knowledge and skill set. Using the UbD framework is planning with the end goal in mind at the forefront. In this form of planning, we must also include methods to gauge that the students have garnered the skills to transfer information from the content in their decision making through various means of assessment. The stages below outline the methods of planning we undertake to provide the students the opportunity to think critically as they weigh evidence to make informed decisions on socioscientific issues.

STAGE 1: DESIRED RESULTS OF ASTHMA AND ITS EFFECTS IN MASSACHUSETTS

Big Idea: Disproportionate Asthma Cases in Communities Throughout Massachusetts

In this stage of the UbD process, we wanted to identify the long-term transfer goals that were targeted, the meaning that students should make to arrive at important understanding and the essential questions that the students would consider throughout the unit. Additionally, we also wanted to identify the knowledge and skills the students would acquire as a result of their experience. Finally, we wanted to identify the standards that were targeted in this unit. According to Wiggins and McTighe (2011), these tenets will provide us the ability to determine real evidence from the activities the students will be exposed to in the unit. To start off the UbD framework, we came up with an overall theme or 'Big Idea' that we wanted the students to use as a take home message for the SSI unit. It is important while planning units, especially around socioscientific issues, to include a Big Idea message that warrants a question to the students so that the information can be passed on to their peers. Big ideas should be something that is ambiguous and takes some efforts in critical thinking to digest. We chose this big idea for the asthma unit based on the patterns in data and the realizations we hoped the students would observe as they went through the unit and started thinking critically about the data that was presented to them.

Science Standards: From the 2016 Massachusetts Science and Technology/Engineering Curriculum Framework

1. Scientific knowledge can describe the consequences of actions but does not necessarily prescribe the decisions that society takes. (MS-ESS3-4)
2. Construct an argument supported by empirical evidence that changes to physical or biological components of an ecosystem affect populations (MS-LS2-4)

We included the state science curriculum standards as a guide for our planning. This was a useful tool while using the UbD framework that requires the planning of instruction backward. This process allows teachers and curriculum developers to plan instruction and curriculum with the end in mind. Additionally, we used the backward design frameworks to ensure that the learning that was occurring was addressing important standards mandated by the state/institution. This also shows that any curriculum can be designed to adhere to a set of standards even if is different from the norm. Below is a description of the elements used to garner the desired results in this investigation.

- **Disciplinary Core Ideas:** The National Research Council for K-12 science education (2012) identifies the disciplinary core ideas as the fundamental ideas that are necessary for understanding a given science discipline. According to the framework, these ideas extend in a more coherent way across grades K-12 to avoid the coverage of multiple disconnected scientific topics, and instead provide for deep exploration of important concepts to develop a meaningful understanding to actually practice science and engineering. We wanted this unit to provide students with opportunities to formulate a hypothesis about real world scientific issues, engage in research to gather data on such issue, analyze the data, and to think critically about what they have learned from the data before determining a course of action based on evidence. As a result, we purposefully developed this unit around the disciplinary core idea of Human Impacts on Earth Systems (MS-ESS3-3, NGSS, 2013). This we believed would provide students with the pportunity to investigate and take actions on a socioscientific issue topic that plagues many marginalized communities throughout the United States.

- **Crosscutting Concepts:** According to the National Research Council for K-12 science education (2012), these concepts help to provide students with an organizational framework for connecting knowledge from the various disciplines into a coherent and scientifically-based view of the world. For students to critically evaluate scientific data and make evidence-based scientific decisions, it is imperative that they are given opportunities to develop their skill set in identifying patterns and deducing cause and effects relationships based on their observations. The unit under investigation addresses the following crosscutting concepts:
   - **Patterns:** Patterns can be used to identify cause and effect relationships. (MS-LS2-2)
   - **Cause and Effect:** Cause and effect relationships may be used to predict phenomena in or designed systems. (MS-LS2-1)

- **21st Century Skills:** Supporters of the 21st century skills movement have been advocating reforms in schools to meet the social and economic needs of students and society in the 21st century. The main argument driving these reform efforts is based on the notion that there is a specific list of skills that are required for success in the 21st century society. For example, collaboration, communication, creativity, and critical thinking are skills necessary to innovate and develop new technologies to deal with various problems. These skills are required for developing students into global citizens. Therefore, stakeholders such as teachers, educational researchers, policy makers, politicians, and employers have vigorously advocated that competency in dealing with problems of the current century will demand that students be competent in these skills in order for them to function effectively at work, as citizens, and in their leisure time (Dede, 2007; Kalantzis and Cope, 2008). Dealing with issues such as disproportionate asthma cases in any communities throughout the world will require competency in the use of 21st century skills.

- **Habits of Mind:** This is described as having a disposition toward behaving intelligently when confronted with problems, the answers to which are not immediately known (Costa & Kallick, 2008). Dealing with socioscientific issues which are ill-structured problems without clear-cut solutions requires one to be skilled in problem-solving, life-related skills that are necessary to effectively operate in a society to promote strategic reasoning, insightfulness, perseverance, creativity, and craftsmanship (Costa & Kallick, 2008). In this unit, we sought to provide the opportunity for the students to grow in persisting, listening with understanding and empathy, thinking flexibly, questioning and posing problems, thinking and communicating with clarity and precision, and thinking interdependently. These listed habits of mind will provide the opportunity for the students in this investigation to be more thoughtful as they investigate what relationship, if any, exists between the place where one lives and the incidence of asthma.

- **Objectives:** We wanted the students to use what they learned from their research on asthma to determine what, if any, relationships exist between the place one lives, the air one they breathes, and the potential of becoming ill with asthma. We wanted the students to use what they learned from their research to communicate to stakeholders the disproportionate incidence of asthma in underserved communities. We wanted the students to make connections between sources of pollution and the potential incidence of asthma cases. Additionally, we wanted the students to determine a possible course of action that would be needed to reduce the incidence of asthma among minority populations. As a result, we used the following objectives to guide the unit. At the end of this unit, students will be able to:
  - Define what asthma is.
  - Identify the causes, symptoms, and potential triggers of asthma.
  - Determine the prevalence of asthma in their communities through a questionnaire.
  - Recognize that asthma disproportionately impacts certain populations.
  - Conduct air quality testing to identify asthma triggers in an environment.
  - Examine the relationships between socioeconomic status and the incidence of asthma in certain populations.
  - Make recommendations on how to reduce the effects of asthma on certain populations.
- **Essential Questions:** As the students worked through the various activities in the unit, we wanted them to keep their focus on specific questions. This we believe would act as stimulus to sustain their engagement and allow them to think critically about the information presented to them throughout the unit. As a result, we used the following as our essential questions:
  - Does the air we breathe make us sick?
  - Which communities in Massachusetts has the highest incidence of asthma? Why?
  - What are some of the various factors that may be contributing the high asthma rates in these communities?
  - Who is impacted the most by asthma in these communities? Why?
- **Acquisition:** We wanted the students to learn how to ask appropriate scientific questions based on evidence, how to collect and analyze data for patterns, and how to use the data collected and the trends observed to engage in arguments from evidence. Additionally, to communicate persuasively to policymakers and key stakeholders from their communities, we wanted the students to establish cause and effect relationships and patterns from pollution sources, economic status, gender, race, and the incidence of asthma in underserved communities.

STAGE 2: EVIDENCE ABOUT WHO ARE AFFECTED THE MOST BY ASTHMA IN MASSACHUSETTS AND WHY

We are aware that to make changes to the status quo, those who are advocating for such changes must be able to articulate their thoughts and position in an effective manner. As a result, we wanted to create a learning environment that would foster the students' abilities to intelligently use higher order thinking to communicate what they knew about the cause and effect relationships of asthma in marginalized communities. The assessment criteria employed to determine the evidence needed to achieve the desired results indicated in Stage 1 are shown below:

- **Assessment Criteria:** In order for the students to effectively engage in evidence-based reasoning on the cause and effect relationships regarding the disproportionate incidence of asthma in marginalized communities throughout Massachusetts, we believe it was imperative for the students to become competent in:
  - Formulating a claim
  - Providing clear explanations of a claim
  - Use of data to support a claim
  - Formulate conclusion based on evidence

These tenets are critical to the development and enhancement of students' argumentation skills. As described earlier, supporters of reform of K-12 science education believe argumentation plays a critical role in developing scientific literacy (NGSS, 2013 and CCSS, 2010)

- **Performance Tasks:** The students were asked to demonstrate what they learned about the cause and effect relationships, patterns from pollution sources, economic status, gender, race, and the incidence of asthma in underserved communities. The students were given the option to communicate such through a poster, persuasive essay, persuasive letter, and public service announcements. Students did so based on the outlining describe below:
  - What is asthma?
  - What are the triggers of asthma?
  - Is there a disproportionate incidence of asthma in the various communities under investigation?
  - Compare and contrast which demographic is mostly affected by asthma in the different communities Massachusetts?
  - Determine what relationships, if any, exist between socioeconomic status and the incidence of asthma in the various communities under investigation.
  - What actions should be taken to reduce the asthma rates in the city that has the most cases?

STAGE 3: THE LEARNING PLAN

The Unit: Asthma and Its Effects in Poor Communities in the Northeastern United States

Below is an outline of the UbD framework elements and the 5E Model of Instructional practices used to guide this unit. The duration of this unit was 5 hours. This time was distributed over a five-day period (1 hour each day).

Day 1

We chose the local region so that students have a closer connection to the topic. If the topic is close to home, it will be more meaningful to the students. Therefore, we started this unit with the open-ended question: Does the air we breathe make us sick? Why or why not? We used this question to gain a better understanding of what the students know about what is in the air they breathe and if possible, whether there is anything in the air they breathe that has the potential to make them sick.

To further engage the students on the topic of air quality and health, we then showed a 2-minute video aired by WWLP-22News titled I-Team: "Air Pollution in W. Mass". We adapted and used this video to expose the students to something that may be new or familiar to them in order to gather their perspectives. To assess the students' perspectives, we assigned a *see-think-wonder* technique to engage students in inquiry-based thinking through close observation. This allowed us to determine how the students felt about the topic presented to them in the video, in addition to deciding what questions they had about the topic. This then allowed us to relate their feelings and thoughts on the issue of whether the air we breathe makes us sick. Additionally, this activity allowed us to gauge their background knowledge on any issues as well as observe if there were any inherent science-related misconceptions.

To expose the students to the idea of using evidence to substantiate claims, we provided the students with a one-page asthma fact sheet from the National Medical Association. We then asked them to answer questions about what asthma is, some of the triggers of asthma, and what population is affected by asthma the most and why. We presented the students with the fact sheet to guide them in analyzing the facts about asthma as they used their comprehension skills to complete the questions.

To create more relevance, we asked the students who in Massachusetts was most affected by asthma and why? Here we wanted the students to relate to something in their communities to build upon their thoughts on the question.

We then assigned an Asthma Questionnaire for the students to complete as homework. This exercise was used for students to gather information about asthma from people who are close to them. This information would be valuable for the students to use deductive reasoning to make claims later in the unit, and it also would draw on the personal aspect which is what makes SSI units so important (tying together scientific data with real-world social issues).

Day 2

Table 1 was used for the students to organize themselves with their groups based on the teachers' assignment. These will be the groups for their research project. Three students were assigned to each group, and each group was also assigned six cities to investigate. Table 1 shows the assigned cities the students were asked to investigate.

The websites and directions below were used to engage the students in the data gathering process in order to facilitate the efficiency of the data gathering activity and keep the students on task. Table 2 represents a completed table of the toxic sites by town for group 1. The directions for completing table 2 are shown below:

Use the links below to complete the data in table 2.

- Do the following to identify the per capita income of your assigned cities or towns [wealthiest first etc., scroll up and down the pages to determine the ranking]
- Click on the website https://www.census.gov/quickfacts/fact/map/MA/INC910216#viewtop
- Click on Massachusetts
- Click on County Subdivisions
- Type in the names of your assigned cities and towns to get the per capita income between 2012-2016
- Your city/town will appear in a red circle; put your cursor over the name of the city/town to get the per capita income.

Table 1. Assigned cities by groups

Group	Assigned Cities
Group 1	Weston
	Dover
	Carlisle
	Boston
	Lowell
	Springfield
Group 2	Shelbourne
	Sudbury
	Wellesley
	Boston
	Lynn
	Lawrence
Group 3	Winchester
	Manchester
	Lexington
	Boston
	Fitchburg
	Methuen
Group 4	Boxford
	Wayland
	Concord
	Boston
	Quincy
	Brockton
Group 5	Brookline
	Norwell
	Newton
	Boston
	Worcester
	New Bedford

- Identify the number of sites in your assigned cities/towns from the Toxic Towns data on pages 31 to 38 [scroll up and down the pages to determine the number of sites]
- https://www.scribd.com/document/56106447/Toxics-in-Massachusetts-A-town-by-town-profile of https://toxicsaction.org/wp-content/uploads/TAC-toxics-in-massachusetts.pdf
- Use the Diversity map of Massachusetts Town by town diversity link below to determine the population by race and diversity scores for your assigned cities/towns [Hover over the cities of towns to determine population and diversity scores] https://www.bostonglobe.com/2014/12/04/diversity-map-massachusetts/Q3OqhKZEJoLj84vzTClhAN/story.html

Table 2 shows the completed table from group 1. This table shows the assigned cities' per capita income, toxic sources, diversity percentages of the cities, and the diversity score for each city.

Table 2. Toxics sites and diversity by cities/towns for group 1

Per-capita Income	Town	NPL Sites	Tier 1A Sites	Tier 1B, 1C and 1D Sites	Solid Waste Inc.	Large Quantity Hazardous Waste Generators	Partially Capped or Uncapped Landfills	Capped Landfills	White Pop.	Black Pop.	Asian Pop.	One or more race	Div. Score 0-10
$101,393	Dover	0	0	2	0	0	1	0	90.67%	0.57%	6.67%	2.08%	1.84
$94,419	Weston	0	0	0	0	0	0	1	84.52%	2.32%	10.14%	3.01%	2.92
$83,920	Carlisle	0	0	1	0	0	1	0	87.78%	0.60%	8.85%	2.78%	2.35
$37,288	Boston	0	2	43	0	80	6	0	53.83%	25.4%	9.06%	11.71%	6.72
$22,890	Lowell	1	1	10	0	25	0	1	59.28%	6.98%	20.14%	13.62%	6.30
$19,027	Springfield	0	2	12	0	32	1	1	51.51%	21.61%	2.29%	24.57%	6.86

After completing the above table, the students were assigned the *see-think-wonder* technique to engage them in inquiry-based thinking through close observation. Also, the students were assigned the following questions. These are research questions that allow the students to explore the meanings of the data more deeply so that they can better interpret the numbers they have gathered:

1.   What are National Priorities List (NPL) sites?
2.   What, if any, dangers do NPL pose?
3.   What are Tier 1A, 1B, 1C and 1D Sites?
4.   What, if any, dangers do these sites pose?
5.   What are Solid Waste Incinerators?
6.   What, if any, dangers do Solid Waste Incinerators pose?
7.   What are Large Quantity Hazardous Waste Generators?
8.   What, if any, dangers do Large Quantity Hazardous Waste Generators pose?
9.   What are Partially Capped or Uncapped Landfills?
10. What, if any, dangers do Capped and Uncapped landfills pose?

The data gathered in the table above and the responses to the questions were used by the students as evidence as they engaged in the unit to determine if the air we breathe makes us sick. The students also used these data to determine who are affected the most by asthma as well as the possible relationship between asthma and wealth.

Day 3

The students were asked to use the data gathered on day 2 to answer the following questions. A brief overview of the reasons behind each is provided below.

1.   What trend, if any, do you notice?
2.   How would you describe the pattern(s) observed?

These questions tie in the mathematics portion of the unit where students are asked to observe trends (if any) based on the data they have gathered. Here, the students were able to use their knowledge of graphing to interpret the data in the table to tell whether there were any changes in the data.

3.   What are your thoughts on the trend(s) observed?

The above question required the students to form opinions based on the data they had observed. This question was used as a tool to get a basis as to whether the students' initial thoughts on the topic had changed or not. This was important in determining what impact the lesson was having on the students' opinions on whether the air they breathe makes them sick or not.

4.   What relationships, if any, do you believe exist between the trend(s) observed and the cause of asthma in your city (Boston)?

This question required the students to determine if there were any connections between the personal survey data they had gathered and the cities they had studied. This allows them to make the real-life connection to what the data is telling them. Additionally, this is critical in enhancing the students' abilities to engage in evidence-based reasoning on scientific concepts. -

5.   Which city has the most toxic sites?
6.   Which city has the least toxic sites?
7.   What relationships, if any, exist between the population demographics and the location of toxic sites?
8.   What relationships, if any, exist between the per capita income of a community and the number of toxic sites observed?
9.   What relationships, if any, exits between socioeconomic status and exposure to toxins in one's community?

Questions 5-9 were data analysis type questions (mathematics). These questions allowed the students to use their interdisciplinary science and mathematics skills. The students were able to report that in general, the more diverse cities with less wealth had the most toxic sites.

10.   Does the air we breathe make us sick?

We used question 10 to intentionally provide the opportunity for the students to now formulate a claim not based on a perception but based on evidence shown in the data they've collected. This question is now a tool to see if the students can relate real-life data to their perception on the topic of environmental quality and pollution; forming a new kind of thinking pattern. This is paramount in helping the students to get accustomed to using evidence-based reasoning to support their claim.

Day 4

The Massachusetts Department of Public Health established the Community Health Network Area initiative in 1992. This initiative establishes six regions that provide targeted skills development to individuals and teams working to build healthy communities in Massachusetts. To provide the opportunity for the students to determine how widespread the problems of asthma is, we asked the students to identify the regions of their assigned cities. Table 3 shows the regions the students identified.

In addition to determining the regions of their assigned cities, the students were required to use the website below to detail the following:

1.   Asthma mortality for your assigned cities or towns
2.   Asthma Inpatient Hospitalizations for your assigned cities or towns
3.   Asthma Emergency Room Visits for your assigned cities or towns
4.   Asthma Hospital Observation Stays for your assigned cities or towns

The website below provides information on the incidence of asthma in Massachusetts from 2005-2013. http://www.mass.gov/eohhs/researcher/community-health/masschip/asthma-mortality-and-hospital-data.html

Table 3. Community health network regions

Group	Assigned Cities	Region
Group 1	Weston	4
	Dover	4
	Carlisle	4
	Boston	6
	Lowell	2
	Springfield	2
Group 2	Shelbourne	1
	Sudbury	4
	Wellesley	4
	Boston	6
	Lynn	3
	Lawrence	2
Group 3	Winchester	4
	Manchester	3
	Lexington	4
	Boston	6
	Fitchburg	2
	Methuen	3
Group 4	Boxford	3
	Wayland	4
	Concord	4
	Boston	6
	Quincy	4
	Brockton	4
Group 5	Brookline	4
	Norwell	4
	Newton	4
	Boston	6
	Worcester	2
	New Bedford	5

The students gathered the above information in four separate tables. Table 4 shows the data the students in group 5 gathered on Asthma Emergency Room visits. The other three tables show data on asthma mortality, hospitalization. Hospital observation stays are not shown due to space limitations.

The students used the web link we provided to them to gather data for each table. The data gathered provided the students with more concrete examples of the disproportionate cases of asthma in the various communities they investigated. Also, the data the students collected in these tables provided them with the opportunity to formulate appropriate claims on what relationship, if any, exists between asthma rates and the socioeconomics of the cities they were assigned. In addition to the question of whether the air we breathe makes us sick, to engage the students in the type of thinking that would allow them to answer these essential questions, we assigned the following questions based on the data collected.

1. In what region(s) are your wealthiest cities and towns in Massachusetts located?
2. What trend(s) do you notice regarding the asthma mortality rates among your assigned cities/towns?
3. What trend(s) do you notice regarding the asthma Inpatient Hospitalizations among your assigned cities/towns?
4. What trend(s) do you notice regarding the asthma Emergency Room Visits among your assigned cities/towns?
5. What trend(s) do you noticed regarding the asthma Hospital Observation among your assigned cities/towns?

The questions above allowed the students to use their Mathematics and Science skills to do an overall analysis of the cities they were assigned based on the data they had gathered.

Table 4. Asthma emergency room visits for Group 5

Identify your assigned city of town above each area 3-year count	Boston Area 3 Year Count	Brookline Area 3 Year Count	Norwell Area 3 Year Count	Newton Area 3 Year Count	Worcester Area 3 Year Count	New Bedford Area 3 Year Count
Population	685,094	59,157	11,067	88,994	185,677	95,120
Per Capita Income	$33,964	$65,340	$64,205	$63,872	$24,330	$21,056
% of Population	.8556%	.1893%	N	.2191%	.8283%	.7412%
Gender			O			
Male	.4106%	.0964%		.1112%	.4120%	.3259%
Female	.4450%	.0930%	D	.1079%	.4163%	.4153%
Race			A			
White Non-Hispanic	.1711%	.1183%	T	.1517%	.3431%	.4226%
Black Non-Hispanic	.4075%	.0152%	A	.0247%	.1072%	.0736%
Hispanic	.2204%	.0287%		.0180%	.2370%	.1998%
Asian/Pacific Islander Non-Hispanic	.0158%	.0118%		.0135%	.0145%	NA
Age						
0 to 4 yrs.	.1254%	.0507%		.0292%	.1820%	.0452%
5 to 14 yrs.	.1407%	.0287%		.0393%	.1659%	.0746%
15 to 34 yrs.	.2673%	.0592%		.0742%	.2644%	.3417%
35 to 64 yrs.	.2978%	.0440%		.0697%	.2030%	.2775%
65 and older	.0245%	NA		.0090%	.0129%	.0231%

6.   Based on the trends observed, what relationship, if any, exists between wealth and asthma?

We used question 6 to allow the students to draw from all of the data they had collected whether or not there is a connection between wealth (socioeconomic status) and asthma. This is a similar exercise to the first data gathering, except that this is strictly based on health.

7.   Who in Massachusetts seems to be impacted by asthma the most? What might be some of the reasons?

The word 'Impact' is revisited. Students can decide what implications this word has. We specifically do not tell the students whether something is positively or negatively impacted, we want them to deduce this on their own based on the knowledge they have gained.

8.   What relationships, if any, exist between the asthma rates and the number of waste disposal sites in your assigned cities/towns?

Here we ask the students to combine their observations from the pollution data and the health data. This helps students start to see the overall big picture.

9.   Does the air we breathe makes us sick? Why or why not?

Students can formulate a concrete answer to this question based on the data they have gathered now from two kinds of data sets. This is the big connector!

10.   What should be done to reduce the asthma rates in the city that has the most cases?

This question is an action piece. Students can channel their feelings and energy that they may have gained over the process of research to come up with an action plan based on the relationships they have researched between asthma and pollution.

Day 5

Based on the findings from the research conducted by the students, they were asked to use the data collected to make the case that the place a person lives may contribute to that person being diagnosed with asthma. The students were given the opportunity to communicate this either via a poster board presentation, persuasive essay, persuasive letter, or a public service announcement.

ANALYSIS AND FINDINGS

In our analyses of students' initial responses to the question: 'Does the air we breathe make us sick?', we first sought to create categories through qualitatively analyzing students' responses inductively. Such inductive analyses produced three common categories consisting of: (1) Yes; (2) No; and (3) Maybe. Figure 1 below outlines the percentages for each category of response.

Figure 1. Students' initial responses to the question does the air we breathe make us sick? why or why not?

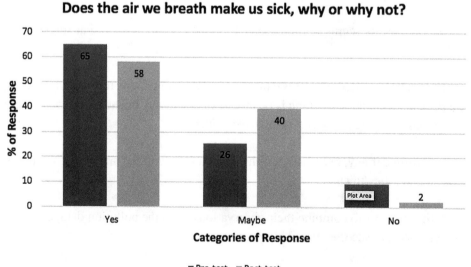

Research Question 1: What relationship, if any, exists between the use of socioscientific issues and middle school students' ability to engage in evidence-based reasoning?

The table above shows that the majority of the students from both the pre-test and post-test (pre-test 65%; post-test 58%) believed that the air we breathe makes us sick. However, the percentage of students who stated that the air we breathe has the potential to make us sick showed a 14% increase post-test. This change is as a result of the exposure to the SSI readings and activities in this unit. Additionally, the percentage of students who stated that the air we breathe does not make us sick showed a slight decrease from pre-test to post-test. These results showed that the unit impacted the students' thinking on whether the air we breathe makes us sick. Our analyses of the students' justification for their claim also revealed several interesting themes and trends. Description of the common reasons the students gave for saying, "yes", "Maybe, or "No" are shown in Table 5.

The initial description above was common among the three classes of students in this investigation. However, due to space limitations, we have provided only three examples. Based on the above descriptions, the students seem to have a basic understanding of air pollution and the potential dangers it poses to human health. However, the students were unable to articulate how the air becomes polluted and if the air is polluted to the same degree everywhere in the world. Additionally, in all three cases above, the

Table 5. Initial justification for saying yes, no, or maybe the air we breathe makes us sick

Categories	Student Responses	Researchers' Interpretations
Yes	"The air we breathe makes us sick because of the air pollution. The air is filled with toxic gases and it can be dangerous for our bodies. (PLL#16)	The student response indicates a superficial understanding of air pollution. The notion that that the air we breathe is filled with dangerous gas is a simplistic view of the various gases that make up the air. Also, they provided no evidence to strengthen their claim that the air we breathe makes us sick.
Maybe	"I think it depends on what type of air it is. If it is clear and healthy, you will not get sick. But when the air is polluted or is filled with unhealthy things, you will most likely get sick." (ACS#9)	The student response clearly shows understanding that if air is void of contaminants, it is generally healthy for living things healthy to breathe. However, the response is superficial and does not provide any evidence that may convince others who may hold the opposite view.
No	"No, because the air we breathe comes from plants which produce oxygen." (PLL#22)	Air is a mixture of mainly nitrogen and oxygen. The student is correct that plants produce oxygen, however, the student neglected to consider that the air in certain locations can be very toxic to the extent that it might be unsafe to one's health.

students did not provide any evidence to support the claim they made. Table 6 provides the description of the justifications the students made after being exposed to the activities, research, and readings of days 1 to 4 above. The justifications are in reference to the question of whether the air we breathe makes us sick. Below are some typical responses observed from the students' statements.

The responses described above show that the students were able to use the data they gathered from the research of their assigned cities to substantiate their claim. In all three examples above, the students associate air pollution with toxins from various sources they researched. Their responses provided examples of how and why the air we breathe makes us sick. This is in stark contrast to the responses they gave prior to their exposure with the SSI unit on asthma. These findings do indicate that the use of SSI can impact students' abilities to engage in evidence-based reasoning.

Research Question 2: How might middle school students' ability to engage in evidence-based reasoning impact their argumentation quality on pollution issues such as the incidence of asthma?

For students to effectively advocate for practices aimed at sustaining the environment and or other scientific issues that are of interest, it is imperative that they are given opportunities to engage in col-

Table 6. Post intervention justification for saying yes, no, or maybe the air we breathe makes us sick

Categories	Student Responses	Researchers' Interpretations
Yes	"There are a number of toxic sites in the city of Boston and those toxic sites in the city makes the air toxic and then get us all kinds of sickness. More people in Boston have asthma than the other cities in Massachusetts." (ACS#12)	The student associated the number of toxic sites in Boston to the incidence of asthma in that city. The student used the findings from the activities on days 1-4 of the unit to make the case that cities like Boston that have more toxic sites pollute the air more and as a result there are more cases of asthma in Boston than any other cities in Massachusetts.
Maybe	"The air we breathe can only make us sick if it is contaminated. In neighborhoods like Worcester, Boston, and New Bedford, they have more toxic sites so people living in these cities get more sick than people living in cleaner places." (PLL#25)	The student used the results from the activities on days 1-4 of the unit to make the case that cities like Worcester, Boston, and New Bedford have more air pollution sources. As a result, more people in these cities are exposed to more toxins in the air which results in more people from these communities having respiratory illness.
No	"The air we breathe does not make us sick, but when the air gets by the National Priority List sites, Large Quantity Hazardous Waste Generators, Solid Waste Generators, the Tiered Waste Sites, and Uncapped Landfills, then we can Get sick." (SEL#29)	The student used the results from the activities on days 1-4 of the unit to make the case that waste sites can pollute the air. If this happens, then people who are exposed to the pollutants from these toxic sites can become sick.

laborative discourse and argumentation exercises in order to enhance their conceptual understanding, skills, and capabilities with scientific reasoning. Our analyses of the initial responses from the students in this investigation showed that they struggled to articulate any meaningful support of their claims regarding whether or not the air we breathe make us sick. However, after exposure to the various activities and readings from our SSI unit on asthma, the students showed improvement in their ability to identify patterns in data, make inferences, and construct evidence-based explanation in order to create persuasive arguments. Below are some common arguments that the students generated as they made their case that the place where one lives may contribute one being diagnosed with asthma.

Below is a common exemplar of the students who said yes, the place one live may cause asthma:

Yes Do you think that where you live affects if you get asthma or not? Well, I believe that where you live does affect if you get asthma or not. It matters if you live in wealthier cities, poorer cities, and close to toxic sites. That's why I believe that where you live does affect if you have asthma or not.

First is the effect of living in a rich city. From my research, if you live in a wealthier city, you're better off. Wealthier cities have less people with asthma. They can afford medication, which lowers mortality rates. They have way fewer toxic sites, which I am going to talk about later. They are just better off.

Second is the effect of living in a poor city. Poor cities, or lower-waged cities have it worse. Let's take Boston as an example. Bostonians make $30,000 annually, which is pretty poor. Boston had more than 10 deaths because of asthma. They had over 5800 emergency room visits. That's very bad. So, living in a poor city kind of sucks.

Now a lot of people say that my opinion is wrong. It could be the case, but I think this one piece of evidence makes a very strong argument against it. My argument is my third reason, toxic sites. Nontoxic sites are the main reason why where you live affects if you'll get asthma or not. Wealthier cities have way fewer toxic sites. Since this is a statistical fact, it very much means they have less people affected by asthma. Guess what? It's true! Some things with poorer cities. Let's talk about Boston. As I've said before, it has a lot of people affected by asthma. Do you hear what else it has a lot of? That's right, it has a lot of toxic sites. In fact, it has more than 130 of these hazardous sites.

I've explained my position. I've explained that where you live does affect the chances of you getting asthma. It matters if you live in a wealthy or poor city. It matters how many toxic sites are around. That's why you should carefully choose where you live. SEL#38

Researchers' Interpretations

The student made a convincing argument that the place one lives may contribute to one being diagnosed with asthma. The student was able to identify patterns in the data (see similar types patterns in Tables 2 and 4) that show that the incidence of asthma is higher among residents who live in less wealthy cities. The student cited data as evidence to support the argument made. For example, the student stated that the per capita income in Boston is in the thirty thousand range and that this city has over 130 toxic sites, which is significantly more than cities with a higher per capita income. The student also cites evidence from the research conducted that more residents of Boston (5800) visited the emergency room due to asthma-related illness. This number is significantly higher than any of the other cities the student researched. This student was also aware that others with an opposing view may disagree with the stance taken and as a result provided supporting data to substantiate the position taken.

Below is another example from a student who said yes, the place one lives may cause asthma:

Yes Have you thought about how people are affected by asthma? Well, there are three main reasons. First, the more money the city has, the less people are affected. While those cities with less money have more citizens affected by asthma. Another reason is the number of waste sites affects citizens. And lastly, some races are affected by asthma more than others. Overall, asthma affects people a lot depending on many things.

First, based on the per capita income of the six cities (Boxford, Wayland, Concord, Boston, Quincy, and Brockton), Boston had the least money. Boston also had the most people with asthma. And what might cause asthma? Air pollution. Because of the number of waste sites in Boston, there is more air pollution that causes asthma. Waste sites release a lot of chemicals into the environment, so the air isn't clean as we thought. And out of all of the races affected by asthma, African Americans are affected the most. Out of the 25 million citizens in America affected by asthma, 4 million are African Americans.

Overall, there are millions of people affected by as asthma. The reasons are the per-capita income and the amount of waste sites. And out of all the people affected, African Americans are affected the most. In summary, asthma can affect you easily and you should be careful. (ACL#9)

Researchers' Interpretations

This student used the patterns identified in the research data to effectively defend the claim that the place one lives may contribute to them being diagnosed with asthma. Of the six cities this student researched, Boston was among the group with the lowest per capita income ($37,288) when compared to Boxford ($62,718), Concord ($68,032), and Wayland ($75,588). However, it was the city with the most hazardous waste sites and the more people affected by asthma. The student was able to use this evidence to make inferences that having more toxic sites in an area may contribute to more air pollution and thus more health effects. The student was also able to use the data collected as evidence to make the case that lower income cities do in fact have more cases of asthma, which means that those who live in more impoverished communities have more of a chance of been diagnosed with asthma. The student also used data from the National Medical Association facts sheet to make the case that African Americans are affected by asthma more than any other race. Based on the United States Census, the African American population is greater in large cities than in smaller cities and towns. The Census also shows that larger cities like Boston have a lower per capita income than smaller less diverse cities and towns. Overall, these students were able to engage in evidence-based reasoning to enhance the effectiveness of their argument after exposure to the SSI unit on asthma.

Below is an example that reflects a common feeling among the students who said maybe the place one live may cause one to get asthma:

Maybe Did you know that the place where people live may contribute to whether someone is diagnosed with asthma or not? Asthma is mostly caused by pollution due to toxic waste sites and other harmful hazards such as smoke, gas, and chemicals. Chemicals and gas from toxic waste sites are the main reasons people have asthma. The more toxic waste sites and polluted air, the higher the rates of asthma and asthma mortality.

I found that the poorest cities and towns have the most cases of asthma and the most toxic waste sites. I've also found that the wealthier cities and towns have the least toxic waste sites and the least cases of asthma. The toxic waste sites are the biggest contributor to the cases of asthma. The polluted air makes us sick from all the diseases and sickness it can cause. For example, Boston has the most toxic waste sites and the most cases of asthma. If we do not do anything now it will be a greater problem.

We need to think of healthy environmentally safe alternatives. To reduce the number of toxic waste sites, we could use environmental energy instead of fossil fuel, such as solar energy and wind turbines. We need to reduce the toxic waste sites to stop pollution and to help bring down the asthma rates. There are more than forty waste sites and more than seventy hazardous waste generators on Boston. We need to stop asthma mortality from happening. We need productive work to make this happen.

In conclusion, the places where people live do increase the risk of them being diagnosed with asthma. Waste sites and generators can make residents sick if they pollute the air. We need to stop the asthma rates from becoming greater. The main reason why people have asthma is due to the level of pollution in the environment and or the town that they live in. (SEL#34)

Researchers' Interpretations

Again, this student was able to use the data to make the case that the place one lives may contribute to one being diagnosed with asthma. The student used the research data to substantiate this claim. The student correctly used the data to argue that more impoverished cities have a higher incidence of asthma in comparison to more wealthy cities. Additionally, the student suggested that environmentally friendly alternatives have the potential to make the air safer for those who live in poorer communities. The student was able to make a claim and used the data collected to effectively infer that safe alternative may produce less waste and thus be friendlier to the environment.

DISCUSSION

Socioscientific issues pedagogy has the potential to enhance students' conceptual understanding of scientific phenomena that affect our daily lives. Our investigation exposed middle school students to the incidence of asthma in marginalized communities throughout a major metropolitan region in the northeastern United States. The findings from our study showed that through productive socioscientific issues pedagogy, the students were able to use the evidence collected from their investigation to validly conclude that the place one lives does contribute to one becoming sick. The students were able to identify that areas in the northeastern United States with lower per capita income have more waste disposal sites, are more racially diverse, and have a higher incidence of asthma. Based on the research the students conducted, they were able to compare and contrast the asthma mortality rates, hospitalization, emergency room visits between affluent communities and those that are less wealthy. The students were able to weigh the evidence collected and make convincing arguments that the incidence of asthma is higher in marginalized communities throughout the northeastern United States. A recent study that investigated middle and high school students' conceptions of climate change mitigation (socioscientific issues) and adaptation strategies reported that high school students provided a higher frequency of valid justifications on the reasons behind climate change (Boffering & Kloser, 2015). The authors further stated that once middle school students experienced the instructional unit, it appears that they became more confident in providing answers to the questions about mitigation and adaptation even though they did not necessarily provide correct responses. The findings from this research show further evidence of the potential impact that socioscientific issues on students conceptual understanding of scientific phenomena.

Another study that focuses on how youth navigate the complex socioscientific issue of a proposed new power plant, Burton and Levine (2012) reported improvements in participants' skepticism towards claims put forth by a corporation. For example, the study indicated that the participants' understanding of the distinction between particulate pollution and carbon dioxide emissions and the implications of each led the participants to question what the Electric Company meant when it referred to the new plant as being ''cleaner.'' The results from this study support the argument that socioscientific issues pedagogy can have on students' conceptual understanding of everyday scientific issues.

Chung, Yoo, Kim, Lee, and Zeidler (2014) conducted a recent study that investigated socioscientific issues as a pedagogical tool for promoting students' communication skills. This investigation involved 132 ninth grade students (80 males, 52 females) attending a 3-year public middle school (grades 7–9) located in the capital city of Seoul, Korea. The students were exposed to a socioscientific issues curriculum that engaged them in a dialogical process in diverse discourse contexts and personal, societal, and global perspectives on the issue of genetic engineering. The results from this investigation demonstrated that SSI instruction brought about a moderately large impact on students' ability to understand the key ideas of others and to value others' perspectives, as well as a marginally positive effect on developing active assertion. The results from these studies as well as the current investigation clearly show that carefully crafted SSI instruction has the potential to effectively engage in active inquiry activities that allow the student to develop their skills in argumentation, evidence-based debates or discussions, and decision-making in school science.

FUTURE RESEARCH DIRECTIONS

Although this study revealed some significant findings, it was not without limitations.

Most notably, the sample size used for this research is too small to generalize the findings since this study was conducted with only 43 students who were enrolled in a summer enrichment program in the northeastern United States. To be able to generalize, this study needs to be conducted with more students from varied locations. Others who are interested may be able to replicate the interventions described earlier in a cross-cultural setting. The results from such investigation might create the scope to generalize.

CONCLUSION

The results obtained from this investigation are every invigorating considering that the study was conducted with middle school students who are 11-12 years old. This suggested that SSI, when implemented effectively in the curriculum, has the potential to enhance students' ability to formulate claims, generate inferences from those claims, engage in research, and analyze the data collected to make evidence-based decisions. The results indicated that students were able to use the data they collected to make the case that wealth, race, and where one lives may contribute to one becoming ill from air pollution. While few of the students in this investigation thought that the place one lives has nothing to do with whether or not they will be diagnosed with asthma, after exposure to the SSI unit they changed their thoughts. Additionally, the students were able to identify patterns that cities that are wealthier have fewer toxic sites and lower incidence of asthma. Consequently, they were able to use these findings to make the case that the places one lives may contribute to one being sick.

A significant strength of this study was the diverse backgrounds of the students who were involved in the investigation. The students came from sixteen (16) distinct neighborhoods in a major metropolitan region of the northeastern United States. Additionally, they were from forty (40) different feeder schools in the area. Seventy-seven percent (77%) of the students attended public schools, nineteen percent (19%) attended charter schools, and four percent (4%) attended parochial schools. The average family income was $41,735, and fifty-one percent (51%) of the students qualify for free and reduced meals. If SSI can have such an impact on such a diverse group of students' ability to engage in evidence-based reasoning, then education policymakers and teachers should perhaps implement such pedagogy in the classroom. This could help in developing the next generation of scientifically literate citizens with the competencies necessary to solve environmental problems of the 21st century and beyond.

ACKNOWLEDGMENT

This work is supported by funding from Center of Excellence in Learning, Teaching, Scholarship, and Service at Framingham State University. Any opinions, findings, and conclusions or recommendations expressed are those of the authors and do not necessarily reflect the views of the Center of Excellence in Learning, Teaching, Scholarship, and Service at Framingham State University.

REFERENCES

Ade-El-Kalick, F. (2006). Socioscientific issues in pre-college science classrooms. In D. L. Zeidler (Ed.), *The role of moral reasoning and discourse on socioscientific issues in science education* (pp. 41–61). Dordrecht, Netherlands: Springer.

Bencze, L., Sperling, E., & Carter, L. (2012). Students' research-informed socio-scientific activism: Re/ visions for a sustainable future. *Research in Science Education, 42*(1), 129–148. doi:10.100711165-011-9260-3

Blair, J. A. (2015). Probative norms for multimodal visual arguments. *Argumentation, 29*(2), 217–233. doi:10.100710503-014-9333-3

Bofferding, L., & Kloser, M. (2015). Middle and high school students' conceptions of climate change mitigation and adaptation strategies. *Environmental Education Research, 21*(2), 275–294. doi:10.1080 /13504622.2014.888401

Bybee, R. W. (2014). The BSCS 5E instructional model: Personal reflections and contemporary implications. *Science and Children*, *51*(8), 10–13. doi:10.2505/4c14_051_08_10

Cetina, K. K. (1999). *Epistemic cultures: how the sciences make knowledge*. Cambridge, MA: Harvard University Press.

Common Core State Standards Initiative. (2010). *Common Core State Standards for English Language Arts and Literacy in History/Social Studies, Science, and Technical Subjects*. National Governors Association Center for Best Practices, Council of Chief State School Officers, Washington DC. Retrieved from http://www.corestandards.org/

Costa, A. L., & Kallick, B. (2008). *Learning and leading with habits of mind: 16 essential characteristics for success*. Alexandria, VA: ASCD.

Dawson, V. M., & Venville, G. (2010). Teaching strategies for developing students' argumentation skills about socio-scientific issues in high school genetics. *Research in Science Education*, *40*(2), 133–148. doi:10.100711165-008-9104-y

Dede, C. (2007). *Transforming education for the 21st century: new pedagogies that help all students attain sophisticated learning outcomes*. Retrieved from http://www.gse.harvard.edu/~dedech/Dede_21stC-skills_semi-final.pdf

Driver, R., Newton, P., & Osborne, J. (2000). Establishing the norms of scientific argumentation in classrooms. *Science Education*, *84*(3), 287–312. doi:10.1002/(SICI)1098-237X(200005)84:3<287::AID-SCE1>3.0.CO;2-A

Etkina, E., Mestre, J. P., & O'Donnell, A. (2005). The Impact of the Cognitive Revolution on Science Learning and Teaching. In J. Royer (Ed.), *The impact of the cognitive revolution on Educational Psychology* (pp. 119–164). Greenwich, CT: Information Age Publishing.

Evagorou, M., Sadler, T. D., & Tal, T. (2011). Metalogue: Assessment, Audience, and Authenticity for Teaching SSI and Argumentation. In T. D. Sadler (Ed.), *Socio-scientific issues in the classroom*. Netherlands: Springer Science Business Media. doi:10.1007/978-94-007-1159-4_9

Golanics, J. D., & Nussbaum, E. M. (2008). Enhancing collaborative online argumentation through question elaboration and goal instructions. *Journal of Computer Assisted Learning*, *24*(3), 167–180. doi:10.1111/j.1365-2729.2007.00251.x

Halliday, M. A. K. (2004). The Language of Science. In J. J. Webster (Ed.), *The Collected Works of M.A.K. Halliday*. London: Continuum.

Jimenez-Aleixandre, M. P., & Eurduran, S. (2008). Argumentation in science education: an overview. In S. Eurduran & M. P. Jimenez-Aleixandre (Eds.), *Argumentation in science education: perspectives from classroom-based research*. Berlin, Germany: Springer.

Kalantzis, M., & Cope, B. (2008). *New learning. elements of a science of education*. Cambridge: Cambridge University Press. doi:10.1017/CBO9780511811951

Klosterman, M.L & Sadler, T.D. (2010). Multi-level Assessment of Scientific Content Knowledge Gains Associated with Socioscientific Issues-based Instruction. *International Journal of Science Education*, *32*(8), 1017-1043. doi:10.1080/09500690902894512

Kuhn, D. (1993). Science as Argument: Implications for teaching and learning scientific thinking. *Science Education*, *77*(3), 257–272. doi:10.1002ce.3730770306

Kuhn, D., & Pearsall, S. (2000). Development origins of scientific thinking. *Journal of Cognition and Development*, *1*(1), 113–127. doi:10.1207/S15327647JCD0101N_11

McTighe, J., & Wiggins, G. (2011). *The understanding by design guide to advanced concepts in creating and reviewing units*. ASCD.

Mestre, J. P., Ross, B. H., Brookes, D. T., Smith, A. D., & Nokes, T. (2009). How Cognitive Science Can Promote Conceptual Understanding in Physics Classrooms. In I. M. Saleh & M. S. Khine (Eds.), *Fostering scientific habits of mind: pedagogical knowledge and best practices in science education* (pp. 145–171). Rotterdam: Sense.

Mueller, M. P., Zeidler, D. L., & Jenkins, L. L. (2011). Earth's role in moral reasoning and functional scientific literacy. In J. L. DeVitis & T. Yu (Eds.), *Character and moral education: a reader* (pp. 382–391). New York: Peter Lang.

Mulnix, J. (2012). Thinking critically about critical thinking. *Educational Philosophy and Theory*, *44*(5), 464–479. doi:10.1111/j.1469-5812.2010.00673.x

National Research Council. (2012). *A framework for K-12 science education: Practices, crosscutting concepts, and core ideas. Committee on Conceptual Framework for the New K-12 Science Education Standards, Board on Science Education, National Research Council*. Washington, DC: National Academies Press.

Newell, G. E., Beach, R., Smith, J., & VanDerHeide, J. (2011). Teaching and learning argumentativer-Reading and writing: A review of research. *Reading Research Quarterly*, *46*, 273–304.

Next Generation Science Standards. (2013). Washington DC: *The National Academies Pres*s. http://nextgenscience.org/next-generation-science-standards

Nussbaum, E. M. (2011). Argumentation, dialogue theory, and probability modeling: Alternative frameworks for argumentation research in education. *Educational Psychologist*, *46*(2), 84–106. doi:10.1080/00461520.2011.558816

Osborne, J. (2005). The Role of Argumentation in Science Education. In K. Boersma (Ed.), *Research and the Quality of Science Education* (pp. 367–380). Amsterdam: Springer. doi:10.1007/1-4020-3673-6_29

Osborne, J. (2010). Arguing to learn in science: The role of collaborative, critical discourse. *Science*, *328*(5977), 463–466. doi:10.1126cience.1183944 PMID:20413492

Powell, W. A. (2014). *The effects of emotive reasoning on secondary school students' decision-making in the context of socioscientific issues*. Unpublished doctoral dissertation, University of South Florida.

Rose, S. L., & Calabrese Barton, A. (2012). Should Great Lakes City build a new power plant? How youth navigate socioscientific issues. *Journal of Research in Science Teaching, 49*(5), 541–567. doi:10.1002/tea.21017

Sadler, T. D., Klosterman, M. L., & Topcu, M. S. (2011). Learning science content and socioscientific reasoning through classroom explorations of global climate change. In T. D. Sadler (Ed.), *Socio-scientific issues in science classrooms: Teaching, learning and research* (pp. 45–77). The Netherlands: Springer. doi:10.1007/978-94-007-1159-4_4

Sadler, T. D., & Murakami, C. D. (2014). Socio-scientific issues-based teaching and learning: Hydro-fracturing as an illustrative context of a framework for implementation and research. *Brazilian Journal of Research in Science Education, 14*(2), 331–342.

Tecuci, G., Boicu, M., Marcu, D., & Schum, D. A. (2016). Evidence-based reasoning: Computational theory and cognitive Assistants. *Romanian Journal of Information Science and Technology, 19*(1-2), 44–64.

Wiggins, G., & McTighe, J. (2011). *The understanding by design guide to creating high-quality units*. Alexandria, VA: ASCD.

Yap, S. F. (2014). Beliefs, values, ethics and moral reasoning in socio-scientific education. *Issues in Educational Research, 24*(3), 299–319.

Yoonsook, C., Yoo, J., Kim, S.-W., Lee, H., & Zeidler, D. L. (2016). Enhancing students' communication skills in the science classroom through socioscientific issues. *International Journal of Science and Mathematics Education, 14*(1), 1–27. doi:10.100710763-014-9557-6

Zeidler, D., Sadler, T., Applebaum, S., & Callahan, B. (2009). Advancing reflective judgment through socioscientific issues. *Journal of Research in Science Teaching, 46*(1), 74–101. doi:10.1002/tea.20281

Zeidler, D. L. (2014a). Socioscientific issues as a curriculum emphasis: Theory, research and practice. In N. G. Lederman & S. K. Abell (Eds.), *Handbook of research in science education* (Vol. 2, pp. 697–726). New York, NY: Routledge.

Zeidler, D. L., & Kahn, S. (2014). *It's debatable! Using socioscientific issues to develop scientific literacy, K-12*. Arlington, VA: NSTA Press.

Zeidler, D. L., & Nichols, B. H. (2009). Socioscientific issues: Theory and practice. *Journal of Elementary Science Education, 21*(2), 49–58. doi:10.1007/BF03173684

Zeidler, D. L., Sadler, T. D., Callahan, B., Burek, K., & Applebaum, S. (2007). Advancing reflective judgment through socioscientific issues. *Paper presented at the 2007 Meeting of the European Science Education Research Association*, Malmö University, Malmö, Sweden.

Chapter 10
Critical Thinking in Science and Technology:
Importance, Rationale, and Strategies

David Florius Samuel
Providence Secondary School, Barbados

ABSTRACT

From as far back as the 1980s, many researchers have cited the importance of critical thinking in the citizens of modern societies. Given this importance, the merits of including critical thinking as a major objective at various levels of the education system and in different subject areas of the school curriculum have been extensively argued. This chapter focuses on science and technology curricula and rationalizes the need for changes both in the development as well as the implementation of the curriculum to facilitate the promotion of critical thinking skills in students. There is also an extensive discussion of particular instructional approaches and strategies needed to facilitate this.

INTRODUCTION

This chapter will trace the development of critical thinking perspectives as occurring in tandem with the development of scientific inquiry from the time of the ancient Greek philosophers. Arguments will be raised that the development of human civilizations required critical thinking even from the earliest human beings. However, with the growth of the scientific enterprise, that thinking was targeted at making sense of natural phenomena as well as altering nature for the benefit of mankind and human civilizations. This way of thinking was formalized in different subject areas in schools and universities. The growth of science and technology, the consequent changes in society, and the impact of that growth on ordinary citizens meant that there was increasing need for higher order thinking skills among human populations. A response was called from the education systems around the world. However, evidence will be highlighted that despite the presence of critical thinking as a goal of many curriculum documents around the world, this has not translated to the kinds of critical thinking required in the general

DOI: 10.4018/978-1-5225-7829-1.ch010

Copyright © 2019, IGI Global. Copying or distributing in print or electronic forms without written permission of IGI Global is prohibited.

population. The chapter will focus on these responses with particular reference to science education. Arguments are raised for the need for curriculum changes as well as instructional changes in science if the goal of a critical thinking human population is to be realized.

BACKGROUND

Critical Thinking: Origins, Definition, and Relevance to The Growth of The Scientific Enterprise

As can probably be expected, there is no consensus in the research literature as to what exactly is critical thinking. Many definitions allude to some generalized thinking skills required for a person to think critically. These include reflective thinking and purposeful, self-regulated judgment (Facione, 2011), and skilful conceptualizing, applying, analysing, synthesizing and/or evaluating information (Paul and Elder, 2004). Facione (2011) also identified the habits of mind of an ideal critical thinker which includes being habitually inquisitive, well informed, open-minded, flexible, prudent in making judgments, and persistent in seeking results which are as precise as the subject of inquiry permit. This seems to be a mouthful, but it may only be the proverbial 'tip of the iceberg' as to all the intricacies of the thinking and habits of mind of a critical thinker. Therefore, for this discussion, a simplified definition by Halpern (2007) is used where critical thinking is referred to as that which requires higher order thinking skills that are relatively complex, and involve judgment, analysis and synthesis of information, and are not applied in a rote or mechanical manner.

Why then is critical thinking regarded by so many philosophers, researchers and educators as important to individuals in modern societies? To understand this, we probably need to go back to what one may consider to be the likely origins of critical thinking. Though authors such as Sternberg (1986) point to the ancient Greek philosophers such as Plato and Aristotle as the initial proponents of critical thinking, it can also be argued that critical thinking is at least as old as human beings. By simply imagining what it took for early man to survive the harshness of earth's environment, it can be reasoned out that a great deal of higher order thinking must have taken place. The inventions of agricultural tools, the wheel, clothing, and the shaping of metals were all done long before the pronouncements of the ancient Greeks. These, and many other inventions, were the result of the thinking of human beings on how to use their physical environment to survive and improve on their way of existence. It can also reasonably be concluded that all the thinking skills and habits of mind identified as constituting critical thinking, did come into play in the process of coming up with these inventions.

Sternberg's (1986) reference to the ancient Greek philosophers as the original proponents of critical thinking is likely due to the historical records that highlight in fair detail the thinking processes involved in their efforts to explain natural phenomena. At that time, it was common for populations in Europe, and indeed around the known world, to ascribe the natural events (both good and bad) affecting them to supernatural forces for example the Greek and Roman gods. According to Wilson (1996), these philosophers relied on careful observation, logic, reasoning, and rational argument to propose natural causes for natural events. A distinction can clearly be seen between this critical thinking of these philosophers and the passive thinking of the 'common people' who simply accepted many important happenings in their lives as the will of the gods, or other supernatural entity. The simple acceptance of these occurrences meant that there was little effort at careful observation, questioning, and objective analysis aimed at considering natural causes. It was simply accepted that, for example, the sun rose in the east and set in the west, the earth was flat, the sky was blue, and all this because of the gods.

It must be noted here that, though we attribute critical thinking to the natural philosophers, and passive thinking to the 'common folk', this is not to say that there could never have been elements of critical thinking in ordinary people dealing with the rigors of everyday living. On the contrary, there must have been. What was different about the natural philosophers was that their thinking, and hence their ideas, were targeted at making sense of the world in a more general way. This was applied in several areas affecting the human condition e.g. natural philosophy, politics, ethics and aesthetics. They also formalized that way of thinking about the world in schools and universities. The philosophy of Aristotle, one of the most famous of these ancient Greek philosophers, was used in university curricula for about 2000 years (Wilson, 1996). This had the unintended effect of stifling the advancement of critical thinking in European scholars until the era of the renaissance.

In the common era (C.E.) up to the 16th century, the growth of Christianity and the increasing powers of papal authorities led to control over university curricula by the church. It was therefore the acceptance of Aristotle's theories by the church, since it supported their teachings, which led to its dominance in university curricula. The authoritative teachings of these theories together with the enforcement of blind adherence to the church's teachings created the environment for stifling the thinking of even the academics of that era until the notable events of the renaissance. The irony of this is that, although there was adherence to the philosophies of the Greek philosophers, it went against one of their most fundamental principles that, as put forward by Socrates, one cannot depend on authoritative sources to have sound knowledge and insight (The foundation for critical thinking, 1997).

In the middle ages, though thinkers such as Thomas Aquinas maintained the adherence to critical thinking as the basis for constructing ideas, it was not until the Renaissance period that this gained prominence among European scholars. It was indeed a significant paradigm shift where there was a new thirst to critically examine previously held ideas about religion, natural processes, and society. This era was also that of what was later referred to as the Scientific Revolution. Several philosophers, key among them Francis Bacon and Rene' Descartes, set the stage for the birth of the scientific enterprise with its fundamental underpinnings of empiricism and critical thinking. If we briefly examine the ideas of these two philosophers, we can clearly justify the argument that critical thinking forms a major aspect of the scientific enterprise.

Though Bacon emphasized the fallibility of human thinking, Wilson (1996) identified the credit given to his book Novam Organum as mainly responsible for the scientific thinking of the era. This, in spite of his major argument that priority should be given to human empiricism in the search for knowledge. On close examination of his writings it can be ascertained that Bacon, rather than decrying the importance of thinking, was accentuating the importance of critical thinking, which, in itself, must stem from careful observation. He alludes to this when he said, "For myself…as having a mind nimble and versatile enough to catch the resemblance of things" (Cited in Critical Thinking on the Web, 2015).

Descartes, unlike Bacon, emphasized the supremacy of the critical thinking mind in the search for knowledge. His philosophy of 'systematic doubt' indicates that nothing that is perceived with the senses is necessarily true. Ultimately, it is through the mind that the world is sensed and made sense of. This he succinctly articulates in his famous quote "I think therefore I am". Descartes, in effect, argued that the search for truth can best be realized through clarity and precision in human thinking. He however also argued that every part of this thinking should be questioned, doubted, and tested (The Foundation for

Critical Thinking, 1997). This marks the essence of a critical thinking mind and forms a fundamental pillar of modern scientific inquiry,

In his 'Structure of Scientific Revolutions', Kuhn (1996) argues that the growth in the scientific enterprise was the result of continuous paradigm shifts. He defined a paradigm as a body of works which for a time serves to "implicitly…define the legitimate problems and methods of a research field for succeeding generations of practitioners" (p.10). New paradigms just do not replace old ones in the minds of scholars. It is more like an evolution of thought where there is gradual declining resistance to new paradigms and increasing opposition to older ones which contradict the new (Samuel, 2013). Both this declining resistance to new paradigms and the increasing opposition to those they succeed, are grounded in the critical thinking of scholars that was espoused by Bacon and Descartes. In the post-Renaissance era and continuing to the modern era, this thinking opened the way for the continued growth of the scientific enterprise, in addition to the political, social, and economic developments that have transformed human societies to what they are today.

Critical Thinking in Modern Societies

It must be re-emphasized here that the average citizen in society will, as part of their daily existence, encounter issues and circumstances that require the use of CT skills such as making reasoned judgments, pondering on the solution to problems, deciding on the best course of action, analysing the arguments put forward by other persons, and so on. The question therefore is not whether CT is important in society, but how effectively is it being used. It may be best to think of CT as occurring at various levels in society. At the lower end of the spectrum are those who do not use CT skills to any meaningful extent in their daily interactions with other persons, materials, and events. These persons may, for example, simply rely on basic instinct or their own (and other persons') experiences in making important decisions. Conversely, at the upper end of the spectrum are those who, as a habit, effectively use CT skills in both their routine as well as major decision making.

It can also be argued that the highest level of CT is that which, as outlined in the last section, resulted in the production and growth of knowledge over the centuries, and hence, the advancement of human civilizations. This begs the question as to what level of CT should be regarded as an important characteristic of the general population in societies. It is a fair argument that the level of CT required by scholars contributing to the advancement of human knowledge is not what is required by the average citizen. It is therefore important to consider, firstly, the reasons why CT is important in the general population to identify the thinking skills and dispositions required. Secondly, it is also important to consider how our current education systems can inculcate the critical thinking skills and dispositions required in the general population as well as those who will go further and contribute to the advancement of knowledge in various subject areas. The first will be dealt with now while the second will be addressed in the next section.

Researchers have identified a number of reasons why critical thinking is an important trait for citizens living in modern societies. This includes its importance in a variety of ways for meaningful personal living (Dem & Volman,2004; Barua & Chakrabarte, 2017), for being an effective and productive citizen in increasingly democratic and plural societies (Viera, Tenreiro-Viera & Martins, 2011; ten Dam & Volman, 2004; National Education Goals Panel' 1992), as well as its importance for successfully dealing with the new demands of the changing global environment (Barua & Chakrabarte, 2017, Barak, Ben-Chim & Zoller, 2007; Gunn, Grigg & Pomahac, 2008). Other researchers refer specifically to the modern demands of an increasingly science and technologically oriented global environment as, more than ever, requiring critically minded citizens (Viera, Tenreiro & Martins, 2011; Santos, 2017). Linked to this is the continued focus in education circles on the need for scientific literacy which has been defined as "...the knowledge and understanding of scientific concepts and processes required for personal decision making, participation in civic and cultural affairs, and economic productivity" (National Research Council, 1996). Implicit in this definition is the presence of critical thinking in scientifically literate populations since it is fundamental to the personal decision making, participation in civic affairs and economic productivity articulated in the definition.

With regards to the importance for meaningful personal living, ten Dam & Volman (2004) rationalizes that critical thinking allows individuals to more effectively manage many private tasks. Barua and Chakrabarte (2017) concurs and adds that it promotes creativity in problem solving, as well as the clarity and rationality of the thinking required. They also identified the importance of language and presentation skills as well as self-reflection in problem solving. These skills are enhanced by the ability to think critically. Many of the personal decisions being made in society are increasingly related to science and technological developments. Hence the need for scientific literacy. Barua & Chakrabarte (2017) identifies critical thinking individuals in society as consistently attempting to think rationally, reasonably, and empathetically. Hence, they are more inclined to be accepting of the increasingly diverse and plural society, and continually strive to improve their physical and social environment.

For being an effective and productive citizen in increasingly democratic and plural societies, it is argued in the literature that a critical thinking population is vital to the proper functioning of such societies (E.g. National Education Goals Panel, 1992). Of critical importance are the decisions related to governance that must be made by the citizens. Researchers such as Viera, Tenreito-Viera & Martins (2011), and Barua & Chakrabarte (2017) all point to the important role of critical thinking to the rational decision making that would result in the selection of suitable political leaders as well as ensure proper discussion and debate of the policies put forward by these leaders. In addition, ten Dam & Volman (2004) and Barua & Chakrabarte (2017) both allude to the increasing need for tolerance and acceptance of differences in culture, beliefs, and lifestyles in these societies. They argue that citizens who can think critically about such issues are more likely to overcome biases, prejudices, and social injustices allowing them to approach the world in a reasonable and fair-minded way.

It can be reasonably argued that there have never been rapid social, economic and technological changes as are presently occurring in societies across the globe. For a number of reasons, meaningful adaptation to these changes require global citizens to more and more make rational decisions based on evaluative critical thinking rather than simply accepting authoritative declarations (Berak, Ben-Chim & Zoller, 2007). The current era has widely been reported as being that of a knowledge economy which is being driven by information and technology. Implicit in this characterization is the recognition that knowledge is increasingly the driver of global productivity and economic growth. Countries who do not embrace these changes face the distinct possibility of economic stagnation and retarded development. Adapting to these changes requires citizens to acquire a range of skills and to constantly adapt these skills based on ever changing challenges. Barua & Chakrabarte (2017) identifies the requirement of what they refer to as flexible intellectual skills allowing individuals to analyse information and integrate diverse sources of knowledge in solving problems. With regards to developments in science and technology, Gunn, Grigg, & Pomahac (2008) correctly predicted that future citizens will need to be informed consumers of the products of science and technology in addition to dealing with a variety of sociological and ethical challenges because of these developments. Therefore, skills such as reasonableness and logical thinking are vital. They concluded that critical thinking skills offer the greatest chance of success with these changes.

With regards to science and technological developments, modern citizens are increasingly being called upon to understand scientific arguments and make decisions on issues that more and more impact on their daily existence. This includes very mundane issues such as grocery shopping, dieting, exercising, and even the manner of communication with other persons. However, it also includes more complex, but just as important, issues such as climate change, genetically modified foods, and energy consumption. According to Viera, Tenreiro & Martins (2011), critical thinking abilities allows individuals to take a stand on these issues by logically rationalizing arguments put forward in the public media.

It is issues such as these that has prompted the emphasis in educational circles on the need for scientifically literate populations. The National Research Council (NRC) of the USA, in putting forward their definition of scientific literacy, articulated that critical thinking abilities is a necessary aspect of scientific literacy. Hence, strategies to promote scientific literacy in students go hand in hand with the promotion of critical thinking. Other researchers (e.g. Gunn, Grigg & Pomahoc, 2007; and Tenreiro-Viera & Viera, 2001) have also suggested that to be scientifically literate involves not only the effective use of scientific knowledge, but also critical thinking. Reference is also made by Viera, Tenreiro & Martins (2011) to the dispositions and attitudes of critical thinking individuals which are also essential to scientific literacy. Related to this are the ideas of Kuhn (1996) who coined the term 'scientific revolutions' as that which resulted in the evolution of the scientific enterprise over the centuries. The continuous cycle of acceptance and rejection of paradigms which facilitated this evolution must, of necessity, have involved the highest levels of critical thinking.

Given the importance of critical thinking to the continued advancement of modern societies, it is a very relevant argument that it should be a main goal of education systems globally. Curriculum documents from many different countries indicate that this is indeed the case. Viera & Tenreiro-Viera (2005) noted at the time that several education systems around the world have included critical thinking as a major goal to be achieved within the context of a variety of subject areas as well as school levels. They also note that this has especially been the case for subject areas in science and technology. The critical question to be answered is how successful these curriculum initiatives have been in increasing the levels of critical thinking in societies. The discussion in the next two sections will focus on the general response of education systems to the need for critical thinking in society, and then specifically on how science and technology curricula could better facilitate the promotion of critical thinking in students.

Infusing Critical Thinking in the Science Curriculum

Many researchers have called for critical thinking to be a principal component of school curricula (e.g. Gunn, Grigg & Pomahac, 2007) and specifically science curricula (e.g. Siegel, 1989). Herbert & Rampersad (2007) refers to the 'higher mental operations' that were evident in the birth and development of the scientific enterprise and, also, forms part of the thinking and methodological nature of scientific inquiry. These mental operations should therefore form a part of the teaching of science. Gunn, Grigg & Pomahac (2007) argue that it is an obligation for educators to equip students with the thinking skills necessary to be an active participant in, rather than a passive recipient of modern day science and technological developments. They add that the skills and dispositions of critical thinking will better ensure that it is society that directs the pace and purpose of science and technological developments rather than the other way around.

As will be discussed later, many science curriculum documents internationally do identify the importance of critical thinking as a component of the development of scientifically literate students. A key question that has arisen over the years is whether critical thinking should be taught in a separate, stand alone, subject, or whether it should be embedded in different subjects. Ennis (1987) makes the distinction between infusion and immersion of critical thinking into school curricula. Infusion takes place when critical thinking principles are made explicit in a subject separate to the normal ones on the school curriculum. Immersion is when these principles are embedded in different subject areas where the focus is the subject matter knowledge, with critical thinking skills forming a part of the goals of instruction. Ennis (1987) argues this point with reference to the relative importance of teaching students to think critically in their everyday lives compared to teaching them to think critically within the boundaries of particular subjects. With regards to embedding critical thinking in different subject areas, he argues that this would be useless to the important goal of helping students to think critically in their everyday lives. This view assumes that the content taught in the various subject offerings is different to what students will encounter in their everyday lives. The frequently cited opposing view is from McPeck (1990) who argues that the content taught in the different school subjects has as its main goal the enlightenment of students about what they need in their everyday life. This argument holds as long as critical thinking is actually embedded in the subject curricula, is actually part of the implementation of that curricula in the classroom and is done in a manner that meaningfully links subject content to everyday experiences. As will be discussed later, there are questions as to the extent to which any of these requirements actually occur.

Notwithstanding these arguments, key curriculum developments in science education throughout the 20th century and into the 21st century have either directly or indirectly identified critical thinking as a key goal of science instruction. The Progressive Education movement that was championed by John Dewey in the early 20th century called for education that developed critically minded and socially engaged individuals as opposed to the authoritative educational environment of the era. The 'Sputnik' initiatives from the late 1950s to the 1960s in the US witnessed the widespread curriculum reform which, for science education, meant a focus on the thinking and methodological processes of scientific inquiry. The benchmarks and standards of the late 20th century and continuing in the 21st century highlighted the importance of inquiry-based instruction, constructivism, and problem solving in the science classroom.

Leading the charge for the development and promotion of standards and benchmarks were the American Association for the Advancement of Science (AAAS) and the National Research Council (NRC). The (AAAS, 1993) produced the Benchmarks for Scientific Literacy which brought the argument that in the increasingly science and technological world, scientifically literate individuals are needed who have the understandings and habits of mind that enable them to think critically and independently when dealing with evidence, logical arguments, and uncertainties in problems encountered in society (AAAS 2003). The National Science Education Standards (NSES) produced by the NRC highlights the importance of complex reasoning which includes critical thinking, non-routine problem solving, and constructing and evaluating evidence-based arguments (NRC, 1996). They refer specifically to the goals of school science which should allow students to intelligently engage in public discourse and debate about science and technological developments as well as being economically productive in their use of the knowledge, understanding, and skills of a scientifically literate person.

A survey of school curricula in countries around the world do indicate that they have heeded the call and included critical thinking in the goals identified for science and technology education, and, in more modern times, STEM education. A brief overview of a few of these curriculum documents will now be done.

In Canada, several high-level meetings and consultations from the end of the 20th century have continually highlighted the importance of critical thinking in school curricula. The 'Common Framework of Science Learning Outcomes, k-12: Pan-Canadian Protocol for collaboration on School Curriculum (Council of Ministers of Education, 1997) identifies a number of goals of science education which includes preparing students to critically address science-related societal, economic, ethical, and environmental issues. For this they identified scientific literacy as vital to all Canadian students. Abrami, Bernard, Borokhovski Wade, Sturkes, Tamin & Zhang (2008) cited a report by the Canadian federal government in 2002 which recommended that schools, colleges, and universities should promote critical thinking at all levels of education. Also in 2015, a revised Canadian and World Studies grade 11 and 12 curriculum identified the need for students to become critically thoughtful and informed citizens (Ontario Ministry of Education, 2015).

In the US, Tsui (2002) cites a national survey of employers, policymakers and educators which concluded that the dispositions and skills of critical thinking should be considered essential outcomes of a college education. The revised benchmarks and standards for education in the US continue to highlight inquiry-based and integrated approaches to science instruction to better enable the critical thinking required in a scientifically literate population. The Framework for k-12 Science Education published by the NRC (2012) built on the important foundational contributions of the Benchmarks for Scientific Literacy (AAAS, 1993) and the National Science Education Standards (NRC, 1996). The overarching goals of the framework alludes to the development of critical thinking students by including the following statements: At the end of the 12th grade all students

- Should possess sufficient knowledge of science and engineering to engage in public discussions on related issues, and
- Are careful consumers of scientific and technological information related to everyday life.

Based on this framework, the publication of The Next Generation Science Standards (NGSS Lead States, 2013) is currently influencing the development of science curricula throughout the US. Osbourne (2014,2) describes these standards as better an understanding of science as a social and cultural practice.

In Singapore, both the primary school and secondary school science curricula contain explicit statements indicating that the development of critical thinking citizens is a major goal of the education system. The primary school curriculum, for example, indicates that 21st century competencies must, of necessity, include critical thinking (Ministry of Education [MOE], 2013). That syllabus also stresses the importance of scientific literacy, indicating that this will allow students to be equipped with the ethics and attitudes to engage in science-related issues as a reflective citizen. The particular skills identified that would allow this includes reasoning and analytical, decision and problem-solving, flexibility to respond to different contexts, and possessing an open and inquiring mind.

In the English-speaking Caribbean, the Caribbean Examining Council (CXC) is the main examining body responsible for regional examinations at the secondary and post-secondary advanced level. The science curricula in the different subject areas also contains explicit statements concerning the importance of the development of critical thinking skills in the implementation of these curricula. The Caribbean Certificate of Secondary Level Competence (CCSLC) is an examination offered to mid-level secondary students (Form 3 or grade 9) as well as adults as a certification of general competence to progress to the final two years of secondary education in the different subject areas. In that curriculum, CXC identifies problem solving and critical thinking as generic competencies, and scientific literacy as a subject-specific competence (CXC.org). CXC also offers the Caribbean Secondary Education Certificate examinations (CSEC) in various subject areas and is targeted at students in the final year of secondary education as well as adults. In all the science curricula, CXC describes the ideal Caribbean person as one who possesses various skills and dispositions including being independent and critical thinkers as well as being able to innovatively apply science and technology to problem solving (CXC.org, n.d.).

These are just examples of the numerous curriculum documents occurring internationally that have critical thinking as a major goal to be achieved in education generally, and specifically in STEM education. The question now is to what extent is this goal being reflected, firstly, in the instructional strategies being implemented in STEM education at the various levels of the education system and, secondly, in the ability of students leaving these educational institutions to use critical thinking processes in their daily living. This will be the subject for the discussion in the next section.

The Status of Current Instructional Strategies in Science and Technological Education and Their Ability to Promote Critical Thinking in Students

The research literature is replete with data indicating that, generally, the science instructional strategies being implemented by teachers in many international jurisdictions do not effectively allow the development of critical thinking skills in students (e.g. Herbert & Rampersad, 2007; Santos, L, 2017). Hence it is no surprise that many studies (e.g. National Education Goals Panel, 1992) also indicate that students who have graduated from secondary and even tertiary institutions have low levels of critical thinking skills.

In a report from the U.S. Department of Education by Perie, Grigg, & Donohue (2005), it was revealed that only 6 percent of high school seniors can actually make informed, critical judgments about written text. Still in the U.S., Shenkman's (2008) book entitled 'Just How Stupid are we? Facing the Truth About the American Voter' reveals very troubling data about the state of critical thinking in American society. It, for example, states that most Americans were willing to accept government policies and decisions even though just a little thought would indicate they were bad for the country. They were also readily swayed by stereotyping, simplistic solutions, irrational fears, and public relations babble. Paul, Elder, & Bartell (1997) cited a study for the California Commission on Teacher Credentialing to determine the extent to which colleges and universities were advancing critical thinking through the general education and teacher preparation curriculum. The study indicated that while 90% of faculty indicated the importance of critical thinking to their instruction, only 19% could meaningfully state what it means. Very few of the faculty could also give any real evidence about how they were fostering critical thinking in their instruction. Other studies even show that many introductory STEM courses are not designed to encourage the development of critical thinking abilities.

Even though the curriculum developments of the late 20th century and the 21st century clearly articulate the importance of critical thinking to effective science and technology education, this has not adequately been reflected in the classroom where even trained teachers seem to constantly resort to these traditional content-focused instructional strategies. Other studies (e.g. Tenreiro-Viera & Viera, 2001) provide evidence that the development of critical thinking abilities is not even taken into consideration in teacher education programmes, school books, and other school resources. With regards to science instruction, it is relevant to this discussion to consider the possible reasons for this. Many researchers have, over the years, voiced their concern that science curricula have generally been implemented at all levels as mainly the traditional teaching of ready-made facts (e.g. Abd-el-Khalick et al, 2004; Jones & Carter, 2007; Santos, 2007). This concern was raised in the early 20th century with John Dewey's progressive movement and has been a constant refrain in the research literature up to the present day. When teachers are primarily focused on getting students to know and understand copious amounts of content, it is likely that the development of critical thinking skills in students would be placed on the backburner despite its presence as a goal in the subject curriculum. Therefore, in order to discuss instructional strategies and curriculum development initiatives that would realistically promote the development of critical thinking students, it maybe worthwhile considering the reason for the current dominance of traditional instructional strategies.

In the traditional mode of science instruction, the teacher is the primary source of knowledge and has the role of presenting that content to students in meaningful and structured ways, mainly using lecture-oriented strategies. It is regarded as traditional since it has arguably remained the primary approach to science instruction even today. It is a teacher-centred approach and the students are generally passive but, hopefully, receptive learners. This mode of instruction actually fits in well with how science itself has traditionally been viewed. Over the centuries, scientific inquiry has resulted in this extensive body of knowledge that is classified as concepts, theories, laws or principles. This body of knowledge has been primarily responsible for advancements in the way of living of human civilizations over the centuries. The perception is that human societies have been transformed by it. It therefore stands to reason that a major goal of education systems across the globe should be the teaching of that body of knowledge to students and, hence, maintaining and improving on it through successive generations. The organization of that body of knowledge into subject areas allowed the organization that simplified this transmission of knowledge. This therefore became the traditional mode of instruction and, as is generally the case, has so entrenched itself at all levels of education that changing it is proving to be very difficult.

It can therefore be argued that this approach has, in effect, sustained itself since teachers would generally be most comfortable using the instructional strategies that they themselves were taught with. In addition, as opined by Bybee (2006), teacher-centred instructional strategies like lecturing are generally easier to plan for and implement since it mainly relies on the knowledge of the content by teachers and the ability to present that knowledge in a meaningful and structured manner. The examination-oriented nature of many educational systems provide a third reason. Duffy & Rayner (2010) highlights the important point that the teachers' focus on preparing students for examinations, particularly those that are high stake, causes them to excessively rely on lecture-dominated strategies. This is especially the case when these examinations are based on extensive areas of content. Plourde (2002) actually cited survey data from Madaus, West, Harmon, Lomas, & Victor (1992) where approximately 20% of science classes heavily emphasized the preparation of students for standardized tests focused on lower level knowledge and skills. Other reasons for a reliance on traditional instructional approaches are provided by Jones & Carter (2007) which includes the belief by some teachers that these are the most effective approaches for instruction as well as teachers who lack either content knowledge or student-centred pedagogical skills and are therefore more comfortable using these approaches.

The skills and dispositions of critical thinking discussed earlier cannot be effectively attained by students through traditional approaches to science instruction. Researchers such as Osbourne (2014, 1) and Barak, Ben Chim, & Zoller (2007) as well as many others attest to a variety of reasons for this. Barak, Ben-Chim and Zoller (2007) argue that traditional instruction emphasizes algorithmic lower order cognitive skills and highlights the modern impetus to educational reform where higher-order thinking skills can be attained through inquiry-based instructional approaches, learning science within students' personal, social, and environmental contexts, and the integration of critical thinking. Osbourne (2014) compares traditional instruction to people being indoctrinated in a faith and cites Driver, Leach, Millar, and Scott (1996) in arguing that students emerging from school science thinks that the ultimate achievement of science is the establishment of a good fact. The current educational reform initiatives do shed light on possible curriculum development initiatives as well as instructional strategies that, when effectively applied, could be a step in the right direction to enhancing critical thinking skills and dispositions in the societies they serve. This will now be discussed.

SOLUTION AND RECOMMENDATIONS

Enhancing Critical Thinking Through Science Education: Curriculum Initiatives and Instructional Strategies

In the curriculum document "A Framework for k-12 Science Education: Practices, Cross-cutting Concepts and Core Ideas" by the NRC (2011), a number of arguments were raised that the current k-12 curriculum in the US fails to achieve some important educational outcomes that more and more are becoming increasingly necessary for citizens to confront current and future challenges in a society increasingly affected by science and technological developments. Included in these arguments were observations that the curriculum was not organized systematically across successive years of k-12 education and there was too much of a focus on 'breadth over depth' where there was shallow coverage of a large number of topics rather than a more in-depth coverage of less. These arguments are relevant to science curricula in many other jurisdictions and are, quite possibly, a large part of the reasons for the low interest, poor attitudes, and poor performance in science that has been reported in the research literature for many years (e.g. Gedrovics, Nozelka & Cedere, 2010). They are also relevant to this discussion since the development of critical thinking skills and habits of mind would less likely occur in an educational environment where the focus is on student learning of a large amount of isolated facts in preparation for high-stakes traditional 'pen-and-paper' examinations. Therefore, the first step to enhancing critical thinking skills in students is probably curriculum reform.

By examining curriculum development theories from as far back as the progressive movement of the early 20th century, it can be realized that the call for school curriculum changes in a manner that better allows the development of higher-order thinking skills in students is not new. Thompson (2011) highlights the views of John Dewey that the role of the teacher should be more than the presentation of subject content to students but should also involve relevant problem-solving and inquiry skills. Based on this and other pronouncements of the progressive movement, several approaches to curriculum development emerged that were argued to better foster critical thinking development. According to Thompson (2011) this included child-centred and activity-centred learning. Later, in the century, the idealism theory of curriculum development, which emerged from Plato's doctrines, re-emphasized the importance of mind over subject matter. Thompson (2011) suggests that this theory promotes holistic learning, which he describes as looking at the big picture as opposed to treating subject knowledge as a collection of disjointed units. This supports the arguments from the NRC (2011) cited earlier for a more systematic organization of curricula to allow a greater focus on depth of content over the current breadth of content that is being implemented in science education.

The increasing popularity of cognitive theories of learning from the 1970s shed new light on the role of critical thinking in human learning and hence, its importance as a primary goal of education. Piaget's stages of cognitive development describe how critical thinking skills develop in children with maturation and their experiences with the physical world: from the pre-operational stage where children critically thinking about objects allowing them to understand what they are and name them, to the concrete operational stage where children are able to logically and critically think about a problem one step at a time, to the formal operational stage where abstract thinking adds to critical thought and hence the ability to solve a variety of more complex problems. Progressing through these stages of cognitive development requires changes in cognitive structures caused by exposure to experiences that are challenging to an individual's current mental development. In education, this equates to instructional activities that develop critical thinking.

Linked to this are the cognitive information processing theories which suggests that information to be learnt by an individual passes, in order, through the following cognitive units in the brain: the sensory register which picks up the information from the environment, the short-term memory which temporarily stores the information, and the long-term memory where effective learning and understanding occurs. As outlined in Thompson (2011), transfer to the long-term memory is not automatic. This transfer is better facilitated by the depth and richness of how the material was encoded in the short-term memory in the first place. In education, this requires student-centred instructional strategies that promote depth to the content being learnt rather than instruction that emphasizes repetition and recall of large amounts of shallow content. Thompson (2011) suitably summarizes what this means for school curricula when he adds that teaching for critical thinking competence necessitates a philosophical shift from drill and practice to problem-based learning, from subject isolation to subject integration, and from output to process. Ten Dam & Volmann (2004) cites Paul (1993) who argues that critical thinking should be the aim of education rather than an aim. For this to be effectively accomplished, there must be a total reform of the current education system with consequences for curriculum goals, textbooks, assessment, staff development, and teacher training.

In the absence of this curriculum reform, critical thinking skills can also be developed in students if appropriate student-centred instructional strategies are used. The assumption that classroom experiences can serve to develop critical thinking skills has been the basis of a number of research studies investigating the effectiveness of particular instructional approaches and strategies in developing such skills (see Herbert & Rampersad, 2007, Cherif & Adams, 2015). The research literature has consistently shown that traditional lecture-oriented classroom experiences facilitate low mental operations while the more student-centred activities facilitate higher order mental operations. Many of these student-centred experiences fall under the inquiry-based instructional approaches that have been recommended by educational researchers for almost a century. These experiences involve a variety of interactions of students with each other, the teacher, and materials in the environment. Herbert & Rampersad (2007) describes examples of these interaction patterns as, for example, working cooperatively in groups to make decisions, collecting data by hands-on manipulation of materials and constructing strategies and generating data to solve problems. They cited research showing that these instructional strategies produce the highest output in terms of complex thinking processes (e.g. Costa, 2001). Viera, Tenreiro-Viera & Martins (2011) adds that encouraging students to express their ideas, explore, take risks, question each other and reflect on their actions effectively promote critical thinking in students. This aptly describes a constructivist learning environment. The following is a brief discussion of some of the instructional strategies that facilitate this.

The development of the process skills of science has been promoted as integral to effective science instruction from the golden era of curriculum reform in the 1960s. This followed the ideas of Jerome Bruner who advocated for the use of inquiry as a process to acquiring scientific knowledge. This led to the promotion of science process skill development in science instruction, the formulation of process objectives, and the focus on students learning how to learn (Ruhf, 2006). Engaging students in the use of both the basic process skills (e.g. observation and communication) and the integrated process skills (e.g. experimenting, inferring, and problem solving) are felt by researchers (e.g. Herbert & Rampersad, 2007; Santos, 2007) to not only enhance conceptual understanding of science, but also to enhance the development of analytical and critical thinking skills. Santos (2007) particularly identifies problem solving as a key way to link science and critical thinking.

With regards to problem-based learning, ten Dam & Volmann (2004) cites Brown (1997) who describes how encouraging students to focus on the solution to real life problems promotes critical thinking and the development of critical thinking skills. She argues that this not only motivates and stimulates the active involvement of students, but that these are the kinds of problems for which critical thinking is needed in real life situations. Slameto (2017) adds that students can develop critical thinking habits by engaging in learning activities in which there is active analysis and solving of a variety of relevant problems.

Questioning and discussion, when effectively implemented as instructional strategies, can also be very effective in promoting the development of critical thinking in students. With regards to questioning, Bloom's taxonomy serves as a framework and guide to the development of questions that require various levels of thinking. Framing questions based on the higher levels of the taxonomy, such as analysis, synthesis and evaluation, are best for eliciting higher thinking responses. However, this is highly dependent on the ability of teachers to engage in proper questioning techniques in the classroom. Santos (2007) identifies the ability to formulate critical questions as one of the most important aspects of science linked to critical thinking. In addition, the ability to vary the levels of questions and using probing techniques with adequate wait time is also critical.

Linked to questioning are the instructional strategies that involve classroom discussions. Santos (2017) identifies the practices of argumentation, discussion, debates and/or defending ideas in the science classroom as effective in developing critical thinking students. A number of studies were cited by ten Dam & Volmann (2004) that focused on instructional strategies in secondary and higher education. For example, in a study by Dennick & Exley (1998) the methods of small-group teaching that were found to enhance critical thinking included focused discussions and student-led seminars. A number of other student-centred instructional strategies can include student dialogue, debate and discussions in a manner that involves critical thinking. These include field trips, demonstrations, drama and role-play activities, and cooperative learning.

Information and Communications Technology (ICT) tools are increasingly being deployed in classrooms to extend students' capacities to interact with the subject matter. These tools can be used to create activities that promote the development of critical thinking skills. According to MacKnight (2000) many of these activities involve students collaborating online with each other, the teacher, and other relevant individuals where critical thinking can be practiced in a more relevant manner than can be achieved in the normal classroom environment. Mansbach (2015) classifies these tools as including:

1. Reflection activities where students are provided opportunities to track their learning and demonstrate their progress through the term or semester (e.g. Using Google Docs).
2. Peer review activities where students give feedback on each other's work and are exposed to alternative perspectives (e.g. as provided by sites like Preze).
3. Discussion forums which allow students to communicate with their peers, discuss issues, and analyse course content (e.g. as provided by sites like Edmodo).

4.   Digital storytelling activities where students tell stories using multimedia to present information. This allows students to evaluate, reflect on, or analyse course content (e.g. by using sites like Smilebox).

CONCLUSION

Given the importance of critical thinking citizens in modern societies, and the multitude of research studies indicating that the levels of critical thinking among global populations is unacceptably low, there must be a response from education systems internationally. This response has first to be at the level of curriculum development and secondly at the level of the educational experiences students are exposed to in the normal classroom environment. Science is one of the key subject areas for infusing critical thinking into school curricula. In order for science education to better facilitate the development of critical thinking, the popular requirement of curriculum documents that large amounts of shallow content be learnt, which encourages the use of traditional lecture-oriented instructional strategies must be replaced by a focus on content-depth, integration of subject areas, and student-centred instructional strategies. It is not simply the use of these strategies that will facilitate the development of critical thinking skills but how they are used by teachers. The development of critical thinking must be regarded as a primary goal of science education and this must be reflected in the kinds of classroom interactions and activities planned by the teacher under each of these instructional strategies.

REFERENCES

Abd-el-Khalick, F., Boujaoude, S., Duschl, R., Lederman, N. G., Mamlok-Naaman, R., Hofstein, A., … Tuan, H. (2004). Inquiry in science education: international perspectives. In E. Krugly-Smolska & P.C. Taylor (Eds.), *Cultural and Comparative Studies* (pp. 397-419). Academic Press. Retrieved from http://www.d.umn.edu/~bmunson/Courses/Educ5560/readings/AbdElKhalick-Inquiry.pdf

Abrami, P., Bernard, R., Borokhovski, E., Wade, A., Surkes, M., Tamim, R., & Zhang, D. (2008). Instructional interventions affecting critical thinking skills and dispositions: A stage 1 meta-analysis. *Review of Educational Research*, 78(4), 1102–1134. doi:10.3102/0034654308326084

Adams, G., Cherif, A. H., Dunning, J., & Movehedzadeh, F. (2015). What if fossils are discovered on planet Mars? Collection of learning activities for promoting active learning. *Pinnacle Journal Publication*. Retrieved from http:/www.pjpub.org

American Association for the Advancement of Science. (2003). *Project 2061*. Retrieved from www.project2061.org

Barak, M., Ben-Chaim, D., & Zoller, U. (2007). Purposively teaching for the development of higher-order thinking skills: A case of critical thinking. *Research in Science Education*, 37(4), 353–369. doi:10.100711165-006-9029-2

Barua, K., & Chakrabarte, P. (2017). A survey on critical thinking in education scenario. *International Journal on Future Revolution in Computer Science & Communication Engineering*, 3(12), 197–203.

Brown, A. (1997). Transforming schools into communities of thinking and learning about serious matters. *The American Psychologist*, *52*(4), 399–413. doi:10.1037/0003-066X.52.4.399 PMID:9109348

Caribbean Examinations Council (CXC). (n.d.). *CCSCC-Caribbean Certificate of Secondary Level Competence*. Retrieved July 01, 2018 from http://www.cxc.org/examinations/ccslc/

Costa, A. L. (2001). Teacher behaviors that enable student thinking. In A. L. Costa (Ed.), *Developing minds: A resource book for teaching thinking* (3rd ed.; pp. 359–369). Alexandria, VA: Association for Supervision and Curriculum Development.

Critical Thinking on the Web. (2015). *What is critical thinking*. Retrieved from www.austhink.com/critical/

Driver, R., Leach, J., Millar, R., & Scott, P. (1996). *Young People's Images of Science*. Buckingham, UK: Open University Press.

Duffy, T. M., & Raymer, P. L. (2010). A practical guide and a constructivist rationale for inquiry-based learning. *Educational Technology*, *46*(3), 3–13.

Elder, L. (2017). IT'S CRITICAL. *USA Today, 145*, 42-43. Retrieved from https://search.proquest.com/docview/1858621016?accountid=45040

Ennis, R. H. (1987). A taxonomy of critical thinking dispositions and abilities. In J. B. Beron & R. J. Sternberg (Eds.), *Teaching Critical Thinking Skills* (pp. 9–26). New York: Freeman.

Facione, P. A. (2007). Critical thinking: What it is and why it counts. Millbrae, LA: Insight Assessment. The California Academic Press.

Gedrovics, J.; Mozelka, D.; Cedere, D. (2010). Alteration of students' interest in science topics in Latvia, 2003-2008. *Problems in Education in the 21st Century, 22*, 45-54.

Gunn, T., Grigg, L., & Pomahac, G. (2006). Critical thinking and bio-ethical decision making in the middle school classroom. *International Journal of Learning*, *13*(5), 129–136.

Gunn, T. M., Grigg, L. M., & Pomahac, G. A. (2008). Critical thinking in education: Can bio-ethical issues and questioning strategies increase science understanding. *The Journal of Educational Thought*, *42*(2), 165–183.

Halpern, D. F. (2007). The nature and nurture of critical thinking. In R. J. Sternberg, H. L. Roediger III, & D. F. Halpern (Eds.), *Critical Thinking in Psychology* (pp. 1–14). Cambridge, NY: Cambridge University Press.

Herbert, S., & Rampersad, J. (2007). The promotion of thinking in selected lower secondary science classrooms in Trinidad and Tobago: Implications for teacher education. In L. Quamina-Aiyejina (Ed.), *Caribbean Curriculum*. St. Augustine: School of Education, University of the West Indies.

Kuhn, T. S. (1996). *The Structure of Scientific Revolutions* (3rd ed.). Chicago: University of Chicago Press. doi:10.7208/chicago/9780226458106.001.0001

MacKnight, C. (2000). Teaching critical thinking through on-line discussions. *Educause Quarterly,* (4). Retrieved from http://eac595b.pbworks.com/f/macknight+2000+questions[1].pdf

Mansbach, J. (2015). *Using technology to develop students' critical thinking skills*. Retrieved July 20, 2018 from https://dl.sps.northwestern.edu/blog/2015/09/using-technology-to-develop-students-critical-thinking-skills/

McPeck, J. E. (1990). Critical thinking and subject-specificity: A reply to Ennis. *Educational Researcher, 19*(4), 10–12. doi:10.3102/0013189X019004010

Ministry of Education. (2013). Singapore: Primary School Curriculum. Retrieved from.

National Education Goals Panel. (1992). *Executive summary: The national education goals report-building a nation of learners*. Washington, DC: Author.

National Research Council. (1996). *National Science Education Standards*. Washington, DC: National Academy Press.

National Research Council. (2011). A Framework for K-12 Science Education: Practices, Crosscutting Concepts, and Core Ideas. Committee on a Conceptual Framework for New K-12 Science Education Standards. Board on Science Education, Division of Behavioral and Social Sciences and Education. Washington, DC: The National Academies Press.

NGSS Lead States. (2013). *Next Generation Science Standards: For States, By States*. Washington, DC: The National Academies Press.

Ontario Ministry of Education. (2015). *The Ontario curriculum: Grades 11 and 12*. Retrieved from http://www.edu.gov.on.ca/eng/curriculum/secondary/2015cws11and12.pdf

Osbourne, J. (2014a). Teaching critical thinking? New directions in science education. *SSR, 95*(352), 53–62.

Osbourne, J. (2014b). Teaching Scientific Practices: Meeting the Challenge of Change. *Journal of Science Teacher Education, 25*, 175–196.

Paul, R., & Elder, L. (2004). *The miniature guide to critical thinking concepts and tools*. Dillon Beach, CA: The Foundation for Critical Thinking.

Paul, R. W. (1993). *Critical thinking — What every person needs to survive in a rapidly changing world* (3rd ed.). Santa Rosa, CA: Foundation for Critical Thinking.

Paul, R. W., Elder, L., Bartell, T., & California Commission on Teacher Credentialing, Sacramento. (1997). *California Teacher Preparation for Instruction in Critical Thinking Research Findings and Policy Recommendations*. Distributed by ERIC Clearinghouse.

Perie, M., Grigg, W. S., & Donahue, P. L. (2005). *The Nation's Report Card: Reading 2005 (NCES 2006–451). U.S. Department of Education, Institute of Education Sciences, National Center for Education Statistics*. Washington, DC: U.S. Government Printing Office.

Plourde, L. A. (2002). Elementary science education: The influence of student teaching-where it all begins. *Education, 123*(2), 253–259.

Ruhf, R. J. (2006). *Analyzing the effects of inquiry-based instruction on the learning atmosphere. Science among pre-service teacher education students* (Doctoral thesis).

Samuel, D. F. (2013). *Teachers' beliefs as predictors of their inquiry-based instructional practices in the implementation of the primary school science and technology curriculum in St. Lucia* (Unpublished doctoral thesis). University of the West Indies, Cave Hill Campus, Bridgetown, Barbados.

Santos, L. F. (2017). The role of critical thinking in science education. *Journal of Education and Practice, 8*(20), 159–173.

Shenkman, R. (2008). *Just how stupid are we? Facing the truth about the American voter*. New York: Basic Books.

Siegel, H. (1989). The rationality of science, critical thinking, and science education. *Synthese, 8*, 9–41.

Slameto. (2017). Critical thinking and its affecting factors. *Jurnal Penelitian Humaniora, 18*(2).

Sternberg, R. J. (1986). *Critical thinking: Its nature, measurement, and improvement*. Washington, DC: National Institute of Education.

ten Dam, G. T. M., & Volman, M. L. L. (2004). Critical thinking as a citizenship competence: Teaching strategies. *Learning and Instruction, 14*(4), 359–379. doi:10.1016/j.learninstruc.2004.01.005

Tenreiro-Vieira, C., & Vieira, R. M. (2001). *Promoting Students Critical Thinking: Concrete proposals for the classroom*. Porto: Porto Editora.

The Foundation for Critical Thinking. (1997). *A brief history of the idea of critical thinking*. Retrieved from http://www.criticalthinking.org/pages/a-brief-history-of-the-idea-of-critical-thinking/408

Thompson, C. (2011). Critical thinking across the curriculum: Process over product. *International Journal of Humanities and Social Science, 1*(9), 1–7.

Tsui, L. (2002). Fostering critical thinking through effective pedagogy. Evidence from four institutional case studies. *The Journal of Higher Education, 73*(6), 740–763.

Vieira, R. M., & Tenreiro-Vieira, C. (2005). *Teaching / Learning strategies: the questions which promote critical thinking*. Lisboa: Instituto Piaget.

Viera, R. M., Tenreiro-Viera, C., & Mertins, I. P. (2011). Critical thinking: Conceptual clarification and its importance in science education. *Science Education International, 22*(1), 43–54.

Wilson, P. K. (1996). Origins of science. *National Forum, 76*(1), 39.

Chapter 11
Pre-Service Teachers Critical Thinking and Developing and Using Models in Science

Lizette A. Burks
University of Kansas, USA

Douglas Huffman
University of Kansas, USA

ABSTRACT

The new science and engineering practice of developing and using models is needed to achieve the vision of three-dimensional teaching and learning and should be an important new component of teacher preparation programs. This chapter examined critical thinking and preservice teachers' preconceptions about critical thinking and the practice of developing and using models. The results of the study indicated that when preservice teachers initially described how this practice might look in the classroom, only two of the six categories outlined in A Science Framework for K-12 Science Education for this practice were described by most participants. Of those two categories described by most participants, the majority were at a novice level. These results emphasize the necessity for elementary teacher education to provide opportunities for preservice teachers to better understand the practice of developing and using models, and how critical thinking can help teachers use models.

INTRODUCTION

The development of critical thinking has been a widely accepted goal in education for many years with varying definitions across fields (Halpern, 2003; Hitchcock, 2018; Horvath & Forte, 2011). Hitchcock (2018) asserts there is a basic concept that anchors differing conceptions of critical thinking: careful thinking directed to a goal. Critical thinking skills encompass the need to retrieve information so that it will be available when needed to test hypotheses, predict or control environments, evaluate evidence, assess claims, monitor comprehension, solve problems, estimate likelihoods, and make decisions (Halpern, 2003). Some of these critical thinking skills are used more often than others in different academic

DOI: 10.4018/978-1-5225-7829-1.ch011

Copyright © 2019, IGI Global. Copying or distributing in print or electronic forms without written permission of IGI Global is prohibited.

disciplines (Halpern, 2003). Conceptions differ depending on the type of goal, criteria or norms for thinking, and the thinking components that are the focus (Hitchcock, 2018).

Critical thinking can be improved in the science classroom by embedding strategies asking students to develop a deep understanding of concepts and competencies required to succeed in science by basing them upon evidence (Halpern, 2003; The Critical Thinking Consortium, 2015). To be competitive in the 21st century, American students are competing with students from across the globe. In 2010 Achieve completed an international benchmarking study of ten countries' science standards, identified through international assessments (Programme for International Student Assessment) and studies (Trends in International Mathematics and Science Study). The study noted a prominent shortcoming from studying leading nations, a call for students to consistently focus on evidence (Achieve, 2010). There is a need to "consistently incorporate science practices that focus on establishing lines of evidence, using evidence to substantiate claims, to develop and refine testable explanations, and to make predictions about natural phenomena" (Achieve, 2010, p. 5). The success of these high performing countries (including Singapore, Finland, Korea, Canada, and Japan) gave guidance to the National Research Council *Framework* (NRC, 2012) and the *Next Generation Science Standards* (NGSS Lead States, 2013) (Achieve, 2010). A primary successful feature noted after studying leading nations in the report was developing students' capacity to understand, design and apply physical, conceptual, and mathematical models as a key ability that should be interwoven in the new U.S. standards. "Scientific model-building is an important tool of science conceptualization and theorizing" (Achieve, 2010. p. 57). Developing and using models can improve critical thinking in science education because models are based on evidence (NRC, 2012). Modeling lies at the core of modern science and engineering providing a way to mediate or negotiate our ideas with empirical data and can help learners better advance their understanding of concepts (Schwarz et al., 2017).

In science, models are used to represent a system (or parts of a system) understudy, to aid in the development of questions and explanations, to generate data that can be used to make predictions, and to communicate ideas to others. Students can be expected to evaluate and refine models through an iterative cycle of comparing their predictions with real world and then adjusting them to gain insights into the phenomenon being modeled. As such, models are based upon evidence. When new evidence is uncovered that models can't explain, models are modified. (NGSS Lead States, 2013, Appendix F p. 6)

This chapter focuses on the critical thinking elicited through the practices of the *Next Generation Science Standards* (*NGSS*) (NGSS Lead States, 2013) and seeks to study first steps in translating this critical thinking strategy through teacher education. Since the release of the NGSS, researchers have noted current classroom practices of using models in science as end products of learning instead of using them for explanatory purposes grounded in evidence when making sense of phenomena in a systematic way (Gouvea & Passmore, 2017). Modeling can aid in supporting learners advance their ideas based on evidence and help teachers teach more effectively when used appropriately (Schwarz et al., 2017). The study included here focused on preservice elementary teachers' preconceptions of the *NGSS* science and engineering practice of developing and using models. The study examined preservice teachers' initial views of models and preservice teachers' preconceptions of the role of student-student and student-teacher discourse in the development of modeling instruction in the classroom.

In a review of research, Davis et al. (2006) described how preservice elementary teachers have little sophisticated understandings of science inquiry in general or related skills due to their limited exposure to environments where true science inquiry is used. Previous to the Next Generation Standards, state adopted standards in the United States were often interpreted and implemented by science teachers as one dimensional, primarily focusing on the disciplinary core idea. It is important for teachers to understand how the disciplinary core ideas, science and engineering practices, and crosscutting concepts of the *NGSS* use elements of each dimension to all for student attainment of the performance expectations. It is critical for teachers to develop a strong knowledge of the practices to help their students engage in phenomena driven three-dimensional learning. Likewise, improving support with educators for the science and engineering practices will be needed. Because models appear in two of the three dimensions (i.e. science and engineering practices, and cross-cutting concepts) and the practice of developing and using models utilizes several of the other practices, it is an area that holds great promise in teacher preparation. In a recent study of 19 preservice teachers, ideas about scientific practices, including modeling instruction, were examined. Ricketts (2014) identified elementary teachers as those that will need the most support due to their lack of a strong science background. Success in implementing modeling instruction will need to be developed from the beginning with preservice teachers and preparatory programs to implement key components of these new national standards. For that reason, elementary preservice teachers were chosen as the focus for this study. The following research question guided the study: What are elementary preservice teachers' preconceptions about developing and using models in the classroom?

BACKGROUND

"Several recent international science education reforms have included scientific literacy, science practices, critical thinking, and socio-scientific issues as learning outcomes" (Vieira & Tenreiro-Vieira, 2016, p. 660). In the United States the *NGSS* (NGSS Lead States, 2013) were released in 2013, and their precursor, *A Framework for K-12 Science Education: Practices, Crosscutting Concepts, and Core Ideas* (the *Framework*) (NRC, 2012) was released in 2012. The *Framework* (NRC, 2012) was the blueprint for the *NGSS* and "expresses a vision in science education that requires students to operate at the nexus of three dimensions of learning: Science and Engineering Practices, Crosscutting Concepts, and Disciplinary Core Ideas" to achieve scientific literacy (NGSS Lead States, 2013, Appendix F p.1). Natural phenomena have been central in science and engineering, but have been traditionally missing from science education, "which too often has focused on teaching general knowledge that students can have difficulty applying to real world contexts" (Achieve, Inc., 2016, p. 1). As students use critical thinking to construct coherent and evidence-based explanations of complex phenomena, the practices are essential to achieving the goal of shifting from "learning about" to "figuring out" in science education (Windschitl et al., 2018).

The science and engineering practices of the *NGSS* provide a means to scientific literacy through critical thinking (NRC, 2012; Vieira & Tenreiro-Vieira, 2016). Vieira & Tenreiro-Vieira (2016) propose a framework for scientific literacy and critical thinking. "The use of critical thinking in such situations should appear closely linked to scientific practices and to the efficient and rational use of scientific knowledge---mainstream scientific literacy for citizenship" (Vieira & Tenreiro-Vieira, 2016, p. 668). The *Framework* (NRC, 2012) describes a helpful way of understanding the practices of scientists and engineers. The science and engineering practices are integrated into both inquiry and design with attention to critical thinking within the spheres of activity for scientists and engineers (NRC, 2012, p. 46). "However, few reforms provide an operational definition of scientific literacy that includes critical thinking, and that is practical and usable by elementary science teachers to guide their planning, classroom teaching, and assessment practices" (Vieira & Tenreiro-Vieira, 2016, p. 660).

McNeill, Katsh-Singer, and Pelletier (2015) describe a shift that educators will need to make towards prioritizing the science practices and this involves needing to move away from "science as a body of memorized facts to science as a way of thinking, talking, and acting that students need to engage in to make sense of the natural world" (p. 22). As educators make those shifts McNeill et al., (2015) have noted in their experiences the challenges educators have in thinking about the eight distinct practices and helping educators make appropriate shifts in using them in classroom instruction. The *Framework* (NRC, 2012) describes the following eight science and engineering practices: 1) asking questions and defining problems, 2) developing and using models, 3) planning and carrying out investigations, 4) analyzing and interpreting data, 5) using mathematics and computational thinking, 6) constructing explanations and designing solutions, 7) engaging in argument from evidence, and 8) obtaining evaluating and communicating information. McNeill et al. (2015) group the practices into three categories (investigating practices, sensemaking practices, and critiquing practices) based on how they were presented in the *Framework* . This categorization can help preservice teacher improve their understanding about how to implement the practices. The practice of developing and using models is one of the few practices that fits into all three categories (investigating, sensemaking, and critiquing). Windschitl et al. (2018) describe the critical importance of modeling, stating that "[r]esearch confirms that, through modeling, students can understand science concepts and learn how ideas evolve, using evidence and new information" (p. 13). However, they continue on to say, "[u]nfortunately modeling is a structured activity that few teachers have ever experienced as learners. It has never been part of common practice in science classrooms" (p. 13-14). The science and engineering practice of developing and using models in *NGSS* is a practice designed to achieve the vision of three-dimensional teaching and learning (NRC, 2012). "Increasingly, more science education researchers and U. S. national standards documents have noted the importance of models in science and engineering and have subsequently called for an increased role for models in K-12 science teaching and learning" (Campbell et al., 2014, p. 159-160). Educators will need support to use the practice of developing and using models as a tool to help students think critically (Gouvea & Passmore, 2017).

Assumptions, Limitations, and Delimitations

The students in this study were in the first weeks of a science methods course at the university. This course was the first science methods course the preservice teachers were about to take, and it was assumed that the *NGSS* (NGSS Lead States, 2013) and the practice of developing and using models was not used for instruction the first two weeks of class. It was also assumed that the participants in this study had little to no knowledge of the *NGSS* and specifically the practice of developing and using models.

This study focused on the science and engineering practice of developing and using models described in the *Framework* (NRC, 2012) and the *NGSS* (NGSS Lead States, 2013). The practices is one of the three dimensions (disciplinary core ideas, science and engineering practices, and crosscutting concepts) students use to make sense of natural phenomena described in the new vision for science education (NGSS Lead States, 2013). This study revealed the preconceptions of the science and engineering practice of developing and using models for a sample of elementary preservice teachers.

First, the preservice teachers were asked about their preconceptions of this practice and a video was analyzed during one phase of the study. The video was not intended to be an intervention, but instead was shown to teachers to get responses to the survey questions. Second, analysis of written responses and interviews was conducted by one person and a more robust study would include more evaluators for inter-rater reliability. Efforts were made to use tools from previous research studies and were pilot tested to improve reliability and validity in the study. Finally, the results are from only two small groups of elementary preservice science teachers at a Midwestern U.S. university and although the implications of the study cannot be generalized to a larger context, they can provide further insight about this practice and the support needed to achieve the critical thinking needed by students in the vision described in the *Framework* (NRC, 2012) .

Method

This descriptive non-experimental study used a mixed methods design. Thirty-six preservice elementary teachers at a large mid-western public university were surveyed to investigate their current state of knowledge about the science practice of developing and using models in the *NGSS*. First, the preservice teachers completed a written survey about their initial views of modeling. Then preservice teachers watched a video of an experienced teacher using modeling in the science classroom. Preservice teachers were then asked to describe the various ways modeling was used in the video, and to describe student-student discourse and the student-teacher discourse around the use of models. Preservice teachers' responses to the survey were coded to develop themes on the use of modeling. Additionally, interviews were conducted with a sample of six preservice teachers. The interview data were qualitatively coded using the themes that emerged from the survey responses. Both types of data in combination with each other provided in-depth examination of preservice teachers views of modeling, an essential component needed to help students think critically about complex natural phenomena.

PRESERVICE TEACHERS' PRECONCEPTIONS

This study analyzed elementary preservice teachers' preconceptions about the science and engineering practice of developing and using models as described in the *Framework* (NRC, 2012) and *NGSS* (NGSS Lead States, 2013). To do this, teachers responded to the survey question below prior to watching a video of modeling being used in a classroom to elicit teachers' preconceptions about the practice. The key question was: What are your perceptions of how the practice of developing and using models should be applied in the classroom?

In a pilot study a discrete scale was adapted from the *Framework* (NRC, 2012) and *NGSS* (NGSS Lead States, 2013) to code responses to the survey questions. The responses to the survey received a score of zero (0) beginner, one (1) novice, two (2) transitional, or three (3) skilled by the authors to interpret their preconceptions for each of the categories that represent the practice in the *Framework* (NRC, 2012) and *NGSS* (NGSS Lead States, 2013). The responses to the survey questions were also coded using an ordinal scale to capture the sophistication of responses so further implications could be made about preservice teacher education (attending and analyzing categories only). This ordinal scale was used in a previous study on preservice science teachers (Barnhart & van Es, 2015) to score the quality of responses regarding sophistication. Responses for sophistication received a score of low sophistication, medium sophistication, or high sophistication in three categories. Tables 1 and 2 include example responses (one category from each scale) that relate to the scores for each of the scales to further clarify how these instruments were used.

Table 1. Discrete scale developing and using models: example survey responses

Example Survey Responses **Discrete Scale: Developing and Using Models**		
Category 1: Types of Models (Represents a Sample of One Category Only)		
Score	**Example Response**	**Coding Rationale**
A Score of 0 (Novice)	"For developing and using models, I would guide students on what to do and set up guidelines. The students will put the model together with the available supplies. I would only have them do models for things where a model would be most beneficial" (Participant #17)	Describes models using no specific descriptions of the different types of models and only describes models generally as a tool used to better visualize or understand the phenomena under investigation
A Score of 1 (Emerging)	"My idea of using models in the classroom would be having the students build or draw out whatever the concept being taught is" (Participants #15)	Describes some specific descriptions of the types of models using general terms to indicate there are different types
A Score of 2 (Transitional)	"I think it is very important to include visual models in the classroom. Whether its posters around the room or demonstrations" (Participant #14)	Describes models to include one or two of the following types of models: diagrams, physical replicas, mathematical representations, analogies, or computer simulations
A Score of 3 (Skilled)	No responses at this level	Describes models to include two or more of the following types of models: diagrams, physical replicas, mathematical representations, analogies, or computer simulations

Table 2. Ordinal scale sophistication of preservice teacher responses: example survey responses

Example Survey Responses **Ordinal Scale: Sophistication of Preservice Teacher Responses**		
Category 1: Attending (Represents a Sample of One Category Only)		
Score	**Example Response**	**Coding Rationale**
Low Sophistication	"Developing and using models might include incorporating different philosophies and ways of teaching a specific content area in a specific study in which some students learn better through different models" (Participant #11)	Highlights classroom events, teacher behavior, student behavior, and or classroom climate. Little to no attention to student or teacher thinking.
Medium Sophistication	"These models should be supplemental to the instruction so that students can further expand their learning. Models should be relevant and not too distracting. Get to know your class beforehand so that you can determine which models should be developed or applied throughout the lesson" (Participants #23)	Highlights student or teacher thinking with more of a procedural focus (teacher use of pedagogy strategies)
High Sophistication	"My interpretation of a model is a physical (usually 3D) representation of something. For example, a model of our solar system using Styrofoam spheres. This can be helpful to students because they have a more tangible way to learn a concept, especially those they cannot see" (Participant #26)	Highlights student or teacher thinking with more of a conceptual focus (teacher analyzing and understanding of appropriate use of pedagogy strategies)

The frequency and percentage statistics when coding preservice teacher survey responses to the first question, regarding the six categories of the discrete scale, are in the Table 3.

Criteria from categories two (models are not exact), three (limitations of models), five (revising models), and six (models in engineering) were not identified by more than 50% of the participants when elementary preservice teachers described how modeling might look in the classroom. No elementary preservice teachers used criteria from category six, models in engineering, in their description of the practice developing and using models. Category one (types of models) and four (using models as a tool

Table 3. Discrete scale developing and using models: frequency and percentage statistics

Category	Statistics	Score				
		0-Novice	1-Emerging	2-Transitional	3-Skilled	No Use
1	Frequency	25	6	1	0	4
	Percentage (n=36)	69.4%	16.7%	2.8%	0%	11.1%
2	Frequency	8	1	0	0	27
	Percentage (n=36)	22.2%	2.8%	0%	0%	75.0%
3	Frequency	14	0	0	0	22
	Percentage (n=36)	38.9%	0%	0%	0%	61.1%
4	Frequency	23	6	0	0	7
	Percentage (n=36)	63.9%	16.7%	0%	0%	19.4%
5	Frequency	1	0	0	0	35
	Percentage (n=36)	2.8%	0%	0%	0%	97.2%
6	Frequency	0	0	0	0	36
	Percentage (n=36)	0%	0%	0%	0%	100%

Frequency and Percentage Statistics
Discrete Scale: Developing and Using Models

for thinking) were used by more than 80% of the elementary preservice teachers when describing the practice of developing and using models. Although category one and category four were identified by more participants, this was done at a novice (score of 0) level by over 60% of participants. This novice level does not meet the expectations of how this practice is used in the classroom defined by the *Framework* (NRC, 2012) and *NGSS* (NGSS Lead States, 2013). The frequency and percentage statistics when coding preservice teacher survey responses to the first question, regarding two categories (attending and analyzing) of the ordinal scale, are in Table 4.

Table 4. Ordinal scale sophistication of preservice teacher responses: frequency and percentage statistics

Statistics	Category	Score		
		Low	Medium	High
Frequency	Attending	20	14	2
Percentage (n=36)		55.6%	38.9%	5.6%
Frequency	Analyzing	20	7	0
Percentage (n=36)		55.6%	19.4%	0%

Frequency and Percentage Statistics
Ordinal Scale: Sophistication of Preservice Teacher Responses

Although the criteria described by the elementary preservice teachers for the practice of developing and using models for this section was low, the capacity to attend to or analyze student thinking (sophistication) was more evenly distributed between the first two scores (low and medium) in the attend category. This even distribution dropped when moving to the analyzing category. Elementary preservice teachers had higher sophistication of responses in the attending category than the analyzing category. The mean of the scores for each of the six categories in the discrete scale used for developing and using models are listed in Table 5. The mean only represents those answers that could be coded for each category, because the responses to the survey for each preservice teacher did not identify criteria in each category.

There were two mean scores for category one and four (lower than 0.5) that show the current knowledge of this practice in relation to achieving the vision (score of 3) in the *Framework* (NRC, 2012) and *NGSS* (NGSS Lead States, 2013).

There were two questions at the end of the survey to help elicit more preconceptions from the elementary preservice teachers about their beginning understanding of the practice developing and using models, and the critical communication patterns needed to use this practice in the classroom. The following mean scores are representative of the data collected to elicit any further preconceptions the preservice teachers could identify from the six categories in the discrete scale identifying criteria from the *Framework* (2012) and *NGSS* (NGSS Lead States, 2013). Although the video was not intended to be an intervention, it has been identified as a limitation to this study. The further identification of criteria from the two categories in Table 6 are after watching the video for the survey.

Table 5. Discrete scale developing and using models: statistical mean of scores

Statistical Mean of Scores Discrete Scale: Developing and Using Models		
Category	Mean Min.=0, Max.=3	Percentage of Participants Who Identified Criteria in This Category
Category 1	0.3	32 of 36 = 88.9%
Category 2	0.1	9 of 36 = 25%
Category 3	0	14 of 36 = 38.9%
Category 4	0.2	29 of 36 = 80.6%
Category 5	1	1 of 36 = 2.8%
Category 6	0	0 of 36 = 0%

Table 6. Discrete scale developing and using models: statistical mean of scores from additional survey questions

Statistical Mean of Scores from Additional Questions Discrete Scale: Developing and Using Models		
Category	Mean Min.=0, Max.=3	Percentage of Participants Who Identified Criteria in this Category
Category 1	1.9	7 of 36 = 19.7%
Category 5	0.5	33 of 36 = 91.7%

More participants in this study could identify category five (revising models), but the mean score was only slightly larger. The video showed students revising models, but the preservice teachers were still not able to identify this category at levels (score of 3) described by the *Framework* and *NGSS*. Not many participants elaborated on the types of models (category 1), but those that did (19.7%) increased the comparison mean score by more than 1.5 points. The video gave them context that helped them identify different types of models, but interviews conducted on a sample of the preservice teachers revealed their ideas tend to fall back in line with those in the data from before the video was watched.

Six participants were interviewed using a protocol that asked preservice teachers to elaborate on their survey responses and to probe for possible influences on their responses. The six participants were asked to describe their current comfort level in teaching science on a scale of zero to ten. The mean current comfort level of teaching science was a score of 6.4. Although their comfort level was above a score of five (middle score), the results indicate that teachers' understanding of the practice of developing and using models was low. Even though participants saw the classroom video, the participants were still at the novice level, and were not able to describe anything different than their original survey responses.

Two emerging themes developed when analyzing the data from the interviews related to this first research question, use of teacher centered models and little previous experience with developing models. Five of the six interview participants originally described the practice of developing and using models as a teacher-centered practice. The models were made and used by the teacher to display some content knowledge to students. One participant described this by saying, "I think I haven't developed that many models in my classes and I feel like I'm learning how to teach way different than I was taught" (Participant #3, October 19, 2016). This does not fit the new vision for this practice and describes developing and using models as a student practice. When asked why they may have responded to the survey question in this manner, participants described their previous experience with the practice of developing and using models. Their collective previous experiences were limited to using models as described above (teacher made, for use by students) or participants describe little experience creating models at all. All six participants described little experience creating or developing models and all participants described doing so after knowledge about the content was already acquired. This also does not fit the new vision for this practice. One participant described creating a representation of what they learned about in their third-grade rain forest unit: "we turned our class into a rain forest displaying the plant and animal life" (Participant #5, October 9, 2016). Another participant described creating a model of a cell, saying, "I was piecing together information from what I had already learned" (Participant #4, October 9, 2016). This experience was mimicked by another student who described making a representation of the solar system with his mother at home in middle school after learning about the planets in class. Their previous experiences with models are very limited compared to the description in the *Framework* (NRC, 2012) and *NGSS* (NGSS Lead States, 2013). The authors attribute the low scores to the lack of experience the elementary preservice teachers have had with models. Their experiences developing models were a rare occurrence in their previous learning as students and they only developed models to display a topic after content learning had occurred. Most of the experiences described with models centered around the teacher creating or showing a model to students to demonstrate a topic. One participant said, "I would say most of the models were given to me to look at" (Participant #5, October 9, 2016) to describe his experiences with this practice.

RECOMMENDATIONS

Hitchcock (2018) asserts there is a basic concept that anchors differing conceptions of critical thinking: careful thinking directed to a goal. The vision set forth by the *Next Generation Science Standards* (NGSS Lead States, 2013) includes critical thinking. Science and engineering practices to help understand complex phenomena is central to the vision and requires critical thinking by students. Research shows it is possible to teach science in better ways than most current practices in the elementary science classroom (Duschl et al., 2007; Donovan & Bransford, 2005; Campbell et al., 2014). "But transforming elementary science teaching from its current status to the more ambitious forms of teaching needed to achieve the goals laid out in the *NGSS* (and other reform documents) will require drastic change" (Roth, 2014, p. 365).

Currently elementary teachers only "take a limited number of science courses and a single science methods course" (NRC, 2012, p. 259). Elementary preservice teachers focus on other content areas in their preservice teacher programs creating a dilemma of time to focus on science teaching and learning. The new vision for science education is complex and will require systematic changes to preservice teacher programs to attend to the higher levels of critical thinking needed by students. The *Framework* "expresses a vision in science education that requires students to operate at the nexus of three dimensions of learning: Science and Engineering Practices, Crosscutting Concepts, and Disciplinary Core Ideas" (NGSS Lead States, 2013, Appendix F p.1).

With the current status of elementary preservice teachers taking one science methods course, the time for teachers to focus on science teaching and learning will need to be carefully designed. Roth (2014) examined research spanning a decade (2000-2012) on elementary science teaching. Roth (2014) acknowledges the new vision for science education and states, "… that the identification of a small set of research-supported, high-leverage science teaching practices could play an important role in closing the gap between what exists and what is needed" (p. 365). Roth (2014) defines high-leverage teaching practices as "teaching practices in which the proficient enactment by a teacher is likely to lead to comparatively large advances in student learning. Ball states "High leverage practices are those that, when done well, give teachers a lot of capability in their work" (as cited in Ball et al., 2009, pp.460-461---p.365). The researcher makes a case for elementary science preservice education to focus on the science and engineering practice of developing and using models when introducing preservice teachers to all eight science and engineering practices as a part of the three-dimensional education teachers will need.

This study used the science and engineering practice of developing and using models as a focus to meet the rigor of critical thinking set forth by the *NGSS* (NGSS Lead States, 2013). Developing and using models is one of the eight identified practices in the science and engineering practices dimension. Similarly, in the dimension of crosscutting concepts, systems and system models is one of seven identified concepts (NGSS Lead States, 2013). The practice of developing and using models has the potential to have a significant impact on teacher preparation because this practice also utilizes several of the other seven practices and modeling has been identified in two of the three dimensions in this new vision for science education (i.e. science and engineering practices, and cross-cutting concepts) (NRC, 2012). Anchoring learning in phenomena is central to the vision and "modeling (together with explanation) is at the heart of knowledge building in the discipline" (Windschitl et al., 2018, p. 13).

Science learning "is an inherently social and cultural process that requires mastery of specialized forms of discourse and comfort with norms of participation in the scientific community of the classroom (NRC, 2007, p. 203). "Each of the eight practices, as it is introduced and elaborated and experienced in the classroom, requires that students externalize their reasoning" (Schwarz et al., 2017, p. 311). Talk and discursive practices are fundamental to all the science practices in the classroom and mimic that of experienced scientists and engineers (Schwarz et al., 2017). The social aspect of the practices make this important idea a necessary inclusion in elementary science preservice education. The practice of developing and using models has also been identified as a practice where discourse is needed in implementation. "There is little debate about the importance of the connection between modeling and other scientific practices, especially discourse" (Campbell et al., 2014, p. 162). The practice of developing and using models also advances instructional shifts to promote science and language learning with English learners (Grapin et al., 2018). Students use language when they develop models and "as students use language to 'do' science, they learn science and language simultaneously" with this language-in-use view in contrast with earlier views of how children learn language with acquisition of vocabulary and grammar (Lee, 2018, p. 1). "Contemporary views emphasize that language learning occurs not as a precursor but as a product of using language in social interaction" (Lee, 2018, p. 1). The combination of the overlapping of other practices within the practice of developing and using models, models identified as a focus in two of the three dimensions for the new science education vision, and the use of discourse in the practice of developing and using models makes this practice a perfect candidate to use as a high-leverage teaching practice. Roth (2014) described using high-leverage teaching practices to close the "gap between what exists and what is needed" (p. 365) and the limitation of time also validates this strategy as one that will be needed as elementary science preservice education is carefully crafted. Roth (2014) describes exploring the idea in the field of "helping teachers be well-started beginners" and that as a field we would benefit "from more studies in thinking about science teaching in terms of a specific framework that is supported by limited number of related teaching strategies that are explored in depth and then implemented in student teaching, internship experiences, and the beginning years of teaching" (p. 387). It is not possible for elementary science preservice teacher to explore in depth all disciplinary core ideas, science and engineering practices, and crosscutting concepts (three dimensions) for their grade band in one science methods course. "This kind of work would represent an important first step in thinking about a continuum of science teacher learning across a career" (Roth, 2014, p. 385).

The purpose of this study was to examine pre-service techers' view of the practice of developing models as a type of critical thinking. All teachers including elementary preservice teachers will need to know the overall vision of this practice as defined in the *Framework* (NRC, 2012) and *NGSS* (NGSS Lead States, 2013) so that they know the end goal of this practice. This study elicited insight into what areas in this high leverage teaching practice will need more support. The vision for this practice in the *NGSS* (NGSS Lead States, 2013) was not understood by the educators in this study; more than 50% were not able to identify four of the six categories that make up the vision for this modeling practice. The two categories identified at a higher frequency were both at a novice level and the use of this practice in meaningful sense-making of phenomena will require educators to know the types of models (category 1) and the affordances each type of model may provide as a way to scaffold sensemaking and critical thinking (category 4) in the science classroom at a minimum (Grapin et al., 2018; Windschitl et al., 2018). There are different affordances in modalities to consider when choosing the type of models to construct during language acquisition for English learners (Grapin et al., 2018). To achieve the vision for this practice educators will need to learn about the types of modeling to be able to apply their use in scaffolding and with equity in mind. Educators in this study were not able to identify the two aforementioned categories at the level needed to make insightful instructional moves in the classroom to help students as they increase in sophistication with the critical thinking needed to make sense of phenomena. In order to implement this practice in the classroom, a framework as described by Roth (2014) will be needed and will require more specificity to the progression grade band and to the purposes and affordances of different types of modeling for this practice for elementary science teachers. Frameworks for middle school science teachers might have some similarities to the frameworks that elementary teachers use, but should increase in sophistication.

Loughran (2014) conducted a literature review on science teacher learning. "It has long been recognized that student teachers' experiences of school science have a major impact on their expectations for and approaches to learning to teach" (Loughran, 2014, p. 812). The interviews in this study mimic the same sentiments and were included in the findings in this chapter. These findings show that elementary science preservice teachers in this study used their previous experiences to describe the practice of developing and using models. Even after watching a video of a successful session of the practice used in a classroom, when asked about their preconceptions about the practice in interviews the participants reverted to using their previous experiences without the new knowledge they may have gained in the video. Richardson states "student teachers find it difficult to move beyond that which they have experienced, are comfortable with, and have been successful at as students" (as cited in Loughran, 2014, p. 812).

"Therefore, a great challenge for teacher education programs is to help student teachers see beyond their own experiences of teaching and find new ways to engage them in conceptualizing practice as something more than how they themselves were taught" (Loughran, 2014, p. 812). The *Framework* (NRC, 2012) says that preservice teachers will need experiences that integrate the three dimensions that will require them to understand in depth what the three dimensions are and how they are used to make sense of phenomena. Preservice teachers will need help with the following: science pedagogical content knowledge for the disciplinary core ideas in the *NGSS*, help understanding how students think critically about phenomena in order to build experiences, experiencing the science and engineering practices for themselves in investigations in order to help students develop those practices, facilitating productive classroom discourse, and how to make the crosscutting concepts a focus when teaching the content through an anchoring phenomena (NRC, 2012). Russell and Martin (2014) are teacher educators reviewing literature about learning to teach science. In their review of literature, they make note that although experience will play a role in developing professional knowledge this experience alone will not be enough (Russell & Martin, 2014). The experiences will need to be integrated with the preservice teachers reflectively thinking about their actions (Russell & Martin, 2014). The authors of this study concluded that a teacher reflection tool will be needed as one of the high-leverage teaching practices needed in achieving the new vision of science education when creating an elementary science preservice education program.

In summary, elementary preservice education programs will need to address and introduce teachers to the critical thinking shifts represented in the *NGSS* (NGSS Lead States, 2013). An understanding of each of the dimensions will be needed and the *Framework* (NRC, 2012) can be used to help teachers in these programs. Ricketts (2014) found that simply reading the *Framework* (NRC, 2012) did not achieve the goal of making significant instructional shifts. Ricketts (2014) concluded that the *Framework* (NRC, 2012) may help preservice teachers begin to develop these understandings. This study exposed the preconceptions of the science and engineering practice of developing and using models for a population of elementary science preservice teachers. This knowledge can be used to strengthen greater areas of deficiencies for this practice to help achieve the increased rigor of critical thinking in the *NGSS* (NGSS Lead States, 2013). Experiences will be needed to help elementary preservice teachers make the needed instructional shifts (Russell & Martin, 2014). The *Framework* (NRC, 2012) states preservice teachers will need experiences that integrate the three dimensions that will require them to understand in depth what the three dimensions are and how they are used in student critical thinking to make sense of natural science phenomena.

Roth (2014) in her review of literature about elementary science teaching regarding the new vision for science education makes some recommendations about the experiences developed for preservice education programs. Roth (2014) states using high-leverage teaching practices will be necessary due to the time constraints with current elementary preservice education programs. These high-leverage teaching practices should give teachers more beginning capability for their work. Roth (2014) also recommends these high-leverage teaching practices should have frameworks with limited teaching strategies. The authors of this study recommend using the practice of developing and using models in preservice teacher education programs. This study has exposed which parts of the practice will need more development with a sample of elementary science preservice teachers.

Loughran (2014) in his review of literature about science teacher learning describes research that reveals how preservice teachers hold tight to the previous experiences they have used and have been successful with as students. The challenge for teacher education programs will be to help these teachers move beyond how and what they were taught and to help students achieve the increased level of rigor in critical thinking for this new vision. Building on the idea that it is difficult for preservice teachers to move beyond how and what they were taught, Russell and Martin (2014) in their review of literature about learning to teach science state that experiences will not be enough to create instructional shifts. Russell & Martin (2014) add that these experiences will need to be integrated with support by the teacher educator to help the preservice teachers reflect thoughtfully about their actions. The authors of this study have concluded that another high-leverage teaching practice will be a reflection tool as Russell and Martin (2014) have described. This tool will need to be chosen carefully so that it aids in achieving the new vision for science education and is appropriate for elementary science preservice teachers. The current state of science teacher preparation will need reform to meet the challenges that come with the *NGSS* (NGSS Lead States, 2013) and the authors of this study have summarized what elementary service teacher preparation programs will need to meet these challenges based on the findings of this study.

FUTURE RESEARCH DIRECTIONS

The future research found in this section center around three areas; modeling instruction in teacher education programs, modeling instruction with in-service teachers, and modeling instruction in relation to student learning. Frameworks that elementary preservice teachers can use in their setting for implementation of the practice of developing and using models will be needed. When asked about what support the teachers would need to implement modeling in the classroom, one teacher noted the need to have a framework to implement the practice with students. This participant described this framework that would be needed and referenced the Biological Sciences Curriculum Study 5E model (engage, explore, explain, elaborate, evaluate) (Bybee et al., 2006) and how this framework provides a flow of steps that helped her implement lessons in the classroom. Roth (2014) describes the need for frameworks as well. A seminal piece of literature used in this study has been the review of literature of modeling instruction conducted by Campbell et al. (2014). "Collectively, in this research, we sought to more generally understand the pedagogical functions that modeling has played in science instruction and research" (Campbell et al.,

2014, p. 173). As noted previously, this study did not investigate implementation of modeling instruction and only sought to investigate the preconceptions teachers hold about the practice of developing and using models as described in the *Framework* (NRC, 2012) and *NGSS* (NGSS Lead States, 2013). "Our aim was also to support the development of our modeling framework in coordination with discursive acts and technology" (Campbell et al., 2014, p. 173). The review of literature conducted by Campbell et al. (2014) will be important when creating frameworks for modeling instruction to achieve this new vision for science education. The framework that Campbell et al. (2014) describe needs to include the need for this practice of developing and using models to increase in sophistication.

More research will be needed regarding a discourse framework that could be used in conjunction with meeting the reformed vision of modeling instruction described in the reform documents (NRC, 2012; NGSS Lead States, 2013). The authors of this study described the need for a high-leverage teaching practice to include a discourse framework that attends to more contemporary views of language acquisition for English learners explored in the recommendations. This type of inclusive framework for discourse is needed because the purpose of a high-leverage teaching practice as Roth (2014) describes it is to help give teachers more capability in their work. If the future work will include all eight science and engineering practices, a discourse framework that helps teachers use the framework to meet each of the practices will be needed.

More research will also need to be done on a reflection tool that could be used in teacher preparation programs that integrate experiences with the preservice teachers reflectively thinking about their actions as Russell & Martin (2014) describe. This is another high-leverage teaching practice that the authors see as critical to elementary science preservice teacher programs. The scale used in this study was developed by Barnhart et al. (2015) to be used in a reflection study. More research would need to be done about the framework that Barnhart et al. (2015) used when thinking about the new vision for science education and research about elementary science preservice educators specifically as they have different challenges as noted in the review of literature in this study.

Finally, future research about teacher education and modeling instruction will be needed to investigate how to change modeling instruction that creates lasting transformation with the elementary science preservice education students will be needed. This can be done by creating a pre- and post-study that investigates changing views of modeling instruction that meets the vision in the *NGSS* (NGSS Lead States, 2013).

The authors of this study investigated elementary science preservice educators' preconceptions of the practice of developing and using models. The following future research studies will be needed to explore more about achieving the new vision for science education and, in particular, modeling instruction with in-service teachers. The current status of how often modeling instruction is used in classrooms will be important in measuring implementation efforts of the new vision for science education that includes the practice of developing and using models in every grade band in differing degrees of sophistication. This current status will need to include the types of modeling instruction that are specific to the vision of the practice of developing and using models described in recent reform documents (NRC, 2012; NGSS Lead States, 2013). The authors of this study included the specificity from these reform documents and this showed findings that will need more development than others. The participants in this study described the practice of developing and using models in relation to their previous experiences as a student. This current status will help as a beginning point for in-service teachers and the professional learning needed to implement the practice of developing and using models in the classroom. In conjunction with this current status of how often modeling instruction is used in science classrooms, a study about practicing teachers and their preconceptions about this practice will be needed to create that beginning point for professional learning is needed.

The same frameworks described for preservice teachers will be needed for in-service teachers, keeping in mind that sophistication of the practice increases when moving across grade bands will need to be included in the frameworks so that we are meeting the vision. Different methods or frameworks to achieve the vision of the science and engineering practice of developing and using models in the *NGSS* (NGSS Lead States, 2013) can also be an area of future research. These different methods that are investigated could allow for more choice by teachers implementing the practice to meet the demands of their teaching environments.

Finally, more research about how to make shifts that are lasting with modeling instruction and in-service teachers will be needed as well. Pre- and post-studies to investigate how to include professional learning that creates lasting change with in-service teachers is needed. In-service teachers have different challenges than those described for preservice teachers in the literature review provided for this study.

This study provides some useful insight into the professional learning development of elementary science preservice teachers to meet the vision of critical thinking for science education described in the recent reform document the *Framework* (NRC, 2012) and *NGSS* (NGSS Lead States, 2013). The results emphasize the components of the overall idea of the science and engineering practice of developing and using models described in the reform documents (NRC, 2012; NGSS Lead States, 2013) that will need more development. The focus of this study on the science and engineering practice of developing and using models is situated in the overall goal of the *NGSS* (NGSS Lead States, 2013) to focus on three dimensions: disciplinary core ideas (science content), science and engineering practices (application of science), and cross cutting concepts (ideas that connect the disciplines in science) that are intended to be integrated for student learning of phenomena. Future research will provide more information so that the education field can continue to learn more about how to provide professional learning development for the practice of developing and using models to increase critical thinking towards the vision in the *NGSS* (NGSS Lead States, 2013).

CONCLUSION

The findings from the survey responses in this study indicated that preservice teachers have a limited understanding of the practice of developing and using models as described in the *Framework* and *NGSS*. Of the six categories evaluated, four were identified by fewer than half of the surveyed teachers. Only the categories of "Types of Models," and "Models as a Tool for Thinking," were identified by a majority of respondents. Further evaluation of the survey responses was made using a discrete scale, scoring responses from zero to three to identify increasing levels of sophistication for each response. Even though the categories of "Types of Models," and "Models as a Tool for Thinking," were identified by many survey takers, the majority of preservice teachers did so at the lowest level of sophistication (69 percent and 64 percent respectively). In the category of "Types of Models," this often meant that participants were not able to give further description of the types of models described in the *NGSS*, but rather only that models were used to better visualize topics (often calling them "hands-on"). Most participants described pre-made teacher models rather than students developing and using models. This was further validated during the interviews when most participants elaborated on their responses to indicate they know this practice to mean pre-made teacher models that students use. Similarly, category four (Models as a Tool for Thinking) was also used with high frequency and most participants scored at the novice (score of 0) level as well. Elementary preservice teachers could describe the idea that models represent a disciplinary core idea that is being taught to students but could not further describe that models represent a system (or parts of a system) that can aid in the development of questions and explanations, are used to generate data that can be used to make predictions, and to communicate ideas to others. The emerging themes described above where the term "model" was used to mean a tool the teacher pre-made for the students to use for thinking was found in this category as well. Although category one and four were identified by many participants, they were still at a novice level (score of 0) because of their limited view on what makes a model and that this practice encompasses more than using a pre-made teacher model as a tool for thinking. The teachers primarily thought of models as simple physical replicas that students might construct, rather than more complex processes or analogies to help students understand and critically think about science.

Preservice teachers will need more preparation to reach all the nuances and level of critical thinking described in the *Framework* (NRC, 2012) and *NGSS* (NGSS Lead States, 2013) to make this practice a sense-making and critiquing practice (McNeill et al., 2015). The results suggest that preservice elementary teachers need to have more opportunities categorizing and thinking about modeling practices as described by McNeill et al. (2015) to help them think about how and when to use models to make sense of phenomena in the classroom, and to help students critically think about science.

REFERENCES

Achieve, Inc. (2010). *International science benchmarking report: Taking the lead in science education forging Next-Generation Science Standards*. Retrieved from https://www.achieve.org/files/ InternationalScienceBenchmarkingReport.pdf

Achieve, Inc. (2016). *Using Phenomena in NGSS-Designed Lessons and Units*. Retrieved from http://www.nextgenscience.org/sites/default/files/Using%20Phenomena%20in%20NGSS.pdf

Ball, D. L., Sleep, L., Boerst, T. A., & Bass, H. (2009). Combining the development of practice and the practice of development in teacher education. *The Elementary School Journal, 109*(5), 458–474. doi:10.1086/596996

Barnhart, T., & van Es, E. (2015). Studying teacher noticing: Examining the relationships among preservice science teachers' ability to attend, analyze, and respond to student thinking. *Teaching and Teacher Education, 45*, 83–93. doi:10.1016/j.tate.2014.09.005

Boston, W. G. B. H. (Producer). Annenberg/CPB Project (Distributed by). (2000). Teaching high school science [Episode 6]. *The physics of optics*. Video file retrieved from https://www.learner.org/resources/series126.html#jump1

Bybee, R. W., Taylor, J. A., Gardner, A., Van Scotter, P., Carlson Powell, J., Westbrook, A., & Landes, N. (2006). *BSCS 5E instructional model: Origins and effectiveness. A report prepared for the Office of Science Education, National Institutes of Health*. Colorado Springs, CO: BSCS.

Campbell, T., Oh, P. S., Maughn, M., Kiriazis, N., & Zuwallack, R. (2014). A review of modeling pedagogies: Pedagogical functions, discursive acts, and technology in modeling instruction. *Eurasia Journal of Mathematics, Science, and Technology Education, 11*, 159–176.

Davis, E. A., Petish, D., & Smithey, J. (2006). Challenges new science teachers face. *Review of Educational Research, 76*(4), 607–651. doi:10.3102/00346543076004607

Donovan, M. S., & Bransford, J. D. (Eds.). (2005). *How students learn: History, mathematics, and science in the classroom.* Washington, DC: National Academy Press.

Duschl, R. A., Schweingruber, H. A., & Shouse, A. W. (Eds.). (2007). *Taking science to school: Learning and teaching science in grades K-8.* Washington, DC: National Academies Press.

Gouvea, J., & Passmore, C. (2017). Models of versus models for: Toward an Agent-based conception of modeling in the science classroom. *Sci & Educ, 26*(49). doi:10.100711191-017-9884-4

Grapin, S., Haas, A., & Lee, O. (2018, July). *Science and language instruction and assessment with all students including English learners.* Workshop presented at National Science Education Leadership Association Summer Leadership Institute, Philadelphia, PA.

Halpern, D. (2003). *Thought and knowledge: An introduction to critical thinking.* Hillsdale, NJ: L. Erlbaum Associates.

Hitchcock, D. (2018). Critical thinking. In *The Stanford Encyclopedia of Philosophy.* Retrieved from https://tc2.ca/uploads/PDFs/TIpsForTeachers/Tips4Teachers_Promotingcriticalthinkinginscience.pdf

Horvath, C., & Forte, J. M. (2011). *Critical thinking* (Education in a competitive and globalizing world series). New York. *Nova Scientia.*

Lee, O. (2018, January). How do children learn science? *At a Glance, News from the Steinhardt School of Culture, Education, and Human Development.* Retrieved from https://steinhardt.nyu.edu/site/ataglance/2018/01/okhee-lee-how-students-learn-science.html

Loughran, J. J. (2014). Developing understandings of practice: Science teacher learning. In N. G. Lederman & S. K. Abell (Eds.), *Handbook of research on science education* (Vol. 2, pp. 811–829). New York, NY: Routledge.

McNeill, K. L., Katsh-Singer, R., & Pelletier, P. (2015). Assessing science practices – Moving your class along a continuum. *Science Scope, 39*(4), 21–28. doi:10.2505/4s15_039_04_21

National Research Council (NRC). (1996). *National science education standards.* Washington, DC: National Academy Press.

National Research Council (NRC). (2012). *A Framework for K-12 science education: Practices, crosscutting concepts, and core ideas.* Washington, DC: The National Academies Press.

NGSS Lead States. (2013). *Next Generation Science Standards: For states, by states.* Washington, DC: The National Academies Press.

Pruitt, S. L. (2014). The Next Generation Science Standards: The features and challenges. *Journal of Science Teacher Education, 25*(2), 145–16. doi:10.100710972-014-9385-0

Ricketts, A. (2014). Preservice elementary teachers' ideas about scientific practices. *Science and Education*, *23*(10), 2119–2135. doi:10.100711191-014-9709-7

Roth, K. J. (2014). Elementary science teaching. In N. G. Lederman & S. K. Abell (Eds.), *Handbook of research on science education* (Vol. 2, pp. 361–394). New York, NY: Routledge.

Russell, T., & Martin, A. K. (2014). Learning to teach science. In N. G. Lederman & S. K. Abell (Eds.), *Handbook of research on science education* (Vol. 2, pp. 871–888). New York, NY: Routledge.

Schwarz, C., Passmore, C., & Reiser, B. J. (2017). *Helping students make sense of the world using next generation science and engineering practices.* Arlington, VA: NSTA Press, National Science Teachers Association.

The Critical Thinking Consortium. (2015). *Tips for Teachers: Promoting critical thinking in science.* Retrieved from https://tc2.ca/uploads/PDFs/TIpsForTeachers/Tips4Teachers_Promotingcriticalthinking inscience.pdf

Vieira, R. M., & Tenreiro-Vieira, C. (2016). Fostering Scientific Literacy and Critical Thinking in Elementary Science Education. *International Journal of Science and Mathematics Education*, *14*(4), 659–680. doi:10.100710763-014-9605-2

Windschitl, M., Thompson, J., & Braaten, M. (2018). *Ambitious Science Teaching.* Cambridge, MA: Harvard Education Press.

ADDITIONAL READING

Campbell, T., Oh, P. S., & Neilson, D. (2013). Reification of five types of modeling pedagogies with model-based inquiry (MBI) modules for high school science classrooms. In M. S. Khine & I. M. Saleh (Eds.), *Approaches and Strategies in Next Generation Science Learning* (pp. 106–126). Hershey, Pennsylvania: IGI Global. doi:10.4018/978-1-4666-2809-0.ch006

Justi, R. S., & Gilbert, J. K. (2002). Modeling, teachers' views on the nature of modeling, and implications for the education of modelers. *International Journal of Science Education*, *24*(4), 369–387. doi:10.1080/09500690110110142

Krajcik, J., & Merritt, J. (2012). Engaging students in scientific practices: What does constructing and revising models look like in the science classroom? Understanding a framework for K-12 science education. *Science Scope*, *35*(7), 6–8.

Lee, O., Goggins, M., Haas, A., Januszyk, R., Llosa, L., & Grapin, S. E. (forthcoming). Making everyday phenomena phenomenal: NGSS-aligned instructional materials using local phenomena with student diversity. In P. Spycher & E. Haynes (Eds.), *Culturally and linguistically diverse learners and STEAM: Teachers and researchers working in partnership to build a better path forward.* Charlotte, NC: Information Age Publishing.

Louca, L. T., Zacharia, Z. C., & Constantinou, C. P. (2011). In quest of productive modeling based learning discourse in elementary school science. *Journal of Research in Science Teaching, 48*(8), 919–951. doi:10.1002/tea.20435

National Research Council (NRC). (2007). *Taking science to school: Learning and teaching science in grades K–8*. Washington, DC: National Academies Press.

Oh, P. S., & Oh, S. J. (2011). What teachers of science need to know about models: An overview. *International Journal of Science Education, 33*(8), 1109–1130. doi:10.1080/09500693.2010.502191

Schwarz, C. (2009). Developing preservice elementary teachers' knowledge and practices through modeling-centered scientific inquiry. *Science Education, 93*(4), 720–744. doi:10.1002ce.20324

Windschitl, M., Schwarz, C., & Passmore, C. (2014). *Supporting the implementation of the Next Generation Science Standards (NGSS) through research: Pre-service teacher education*. Retrieved from https://narst.org/ngsspapers/preservice.cfm

Windschitl, M., Thompson, J., & Braaten, M. (2008). Beyond the scientific method: Model-based inquiry as a new paradigm of preference for school science investigations. *Science Education, 92*(5), 941–967. doi:10.1002ce.20259

Chapter 12

Teaching and Assessing Critical Thinking and Clinical Reasoning Skills in Medical Education

Md. Anwarul Azim Majumder
The University of the West Indies – Cave Hill Campus, Barbados

Bidyadhar Sa
The University of the West Indies – St. Augustine Campus, Trinidad and Tobago

Fahad Abdullah Alateeq
Al Imam Mohammad Ibn Saud Islamic University (IMSIU), Saudi Arabia

Sayeeda Rahman
American University of Integrative Sciences, Barbados

ABSTRACT

In recent years, there has been more emphasis on developing higher order thinking (e.g., critical thinking and clinical reasoning) processes to tackle the recent trends and challenges in medical education. Critical thinking and clinical reasoning are considered to be the cornerstones for teaching and training tomorrow's doctors. Lack of training of critical thinking and clinical reasoning in medical curricula causes medical students and physicians to use cognitive biases in problem solving which ultimately leads to diagnostic errors later in their professional practice. Moreover, there is no consensus on the most effective teaching model to teach the critical thinking and clinical reasoning skills and even the skill is not effectively tested in medical schools. This chapter will focus on concepts, contemporary theories, implications, issues and challenges, characteristics, various steps, teaching models and strategies, measuring and intervention tools, and assessment modalities of critical thinking and clinical reasoning in medical education settings.

DOI: 10.4018/978-1-5225-7829-1.ch012

Copyright © 2019, IGI Global. Copying or distributing in print or electronic forms without written permission of IGI Global is prohibited.

INTRODUCTION AND BACKGROUND OF THE CHAPTER

It has been recognized internationally that undergraduate medical education must adapt to changing needs to equip students with a number of desired transferrable skills including clinical reasoning and critical thinking (Majumder, D'Souza, & Rahman, 2004). According to Facione (1990), critical thinking is "Purposeful, self-regulatory judgment that uses cognitive tools such as interpretation, analysis, evaluation, inference, and explanation of the evidential, conceptual, methodological, criteriological, or contextual considerations on which judgment is based" (p. 3). Though clinical reasoning and critical thinking are interchangeably used in the literature, "Critical thinking involves some skills and attitudes necessary for the development of clinical reasoning, which is based on existing knowledge and context" (da Silva Bastos Cerullo & da Cruz D, 2010, p. 126). Critical thinking includes "analysis, inference, interpretation, explanation, synthesis and self-regulation" (Facione, 2011, p. 21). Clinical reasoning, as Victor-Chmil (2013) mentioned, is the "*application* of critical thinking to the clinical situation" (p. 34). Clinical judgment is also one of frequently used terms in health profession education. Tanner explained the clinical judgment as "an interpretation or conclusion about a patient's needs, concerns, or health problems, and/or decision to take action (or not), use or modify standard approaches, or improvise new ones as deemed appropriate by the patient's response" (Tanner, 2006, p. 206). Other terms which are used in relation to critical thinking and clinical reasoning in the literature include: clinical decision-making, diagnostic reasoning, analytical thinking, critical judgment, creative thinking, problem solving, reflective thinking etc. (da Silva Bastos Cerullo & da Cruz D, 2010).

In recent years, there has been more emphasis on developing higher order thinking (e.g. critical thinking and clinical reasoning) processes to tackle the recent trends and challenges in medical education (Redecker et al., 2011; Scott, 2015). Higher order thinking has become one of the essential features for tomorrow's doctors for maintaining clinical competence and medical professionalism (Trowbridge, Joseph, & Durning, 2015; Victor-Chmil, 2013). These skills traditionally are taught in clinical placements; however, students in many schools receive limited practice and suboptimal supervision. As a result, more than two-thirds of the diagnostic failures are attributed to physicians' lack of critical thinking ability at the given situation (Royce et al., 2018). Medical schools should begin to address these limitations by designing courses with specific learning outcomes that cater to the critical thinking abilities and skills. Critical thinking and clinical reasoning skills could be nurtured by encouraging students to more actively participate in learning activities (Amey, Donald, & Teodorczuk, 2017). Medical educators need to interact with students, more to them often listen, encourage questioning, challenge students, and encourage them to reflect, and explore the answers for themselves (Scott & Chafe, 1997).

This chapter will focus on concepts, contemporary theories, implications, issues and challenges, characteristics, various steps, teaching models and strategies, measuring and intervention tools, and assessment modalities of critical thinking and clinical reasoning in medical education settings. Appropriate recommendations will also be generated for policy makers and medical educators to develop a strategic direction to produce evidence-based critical thinking in undergraduate medical curriculum and training.

CONCEPTS OF CRITICAL THINKING AND CLINICAL REASONING

Critical thinking, the capacity to be deliberate about thinking, is considered as a cornerstone for teaching and training tomorrow's doctors. Critical thinking is an important feature of the Socratic method of teaching which dates back to 470-399 BC during Socrates era (Paul, Elder, & Bartell, 1997). This method of teaching applies thought proving enquiry to enhance students' problem-solving and critical thinking skills. Critical thinking is considered as "accessing, analysing and synthesizing information, and can be taught, practised and mastered" which also includes skills like "communication, information literacy and the ability to examine, analyse, interpret and evaluate evidence" (Scott, 2015, p. 4). Harasym, Tsai, & Hemmati, (2008) mentioned that critical thinking consists of three components which a learner should experience in developing the skill, i.e. (a) *process:* actively and skilfully conceptualizes, applies, analyses, synthesizes, and/or evaluates information/knowledge, (b) *method:* observing, experiencing, reflecting, reasoning, or communicating, and (c) *purpose:* knowledge acquisition and action. Moreover, to be a critical thinker a learner needs to utilize following nine cognitive steps [cited by Harasym, Tsai, & Hemmati, (2008)]:

1. Gather relevant information
2. Formulate clearly defined questions and problems
3. Evaluate relevant information
4. Utilize and interpret abstract ideas effectively
5. Infer well-reasoned conclusions and solutions
6. Pilot outcomes against relevant criteria and standards
7. Use alternative thought processes if needed
8. Consider all assumptions, implications, and practical consequences
9. Communicates effectively with others to solve complex problems

Clinical reasoning is a complex topic and both problem solving and decision-making approaches are fundamental to the understanding of it. Clinical reasoning is a context-dependent way of thinking and decision making in clinical practice to guide practice actions. Trowbridge, Joseph, & Durning (2015) defined clinical reasoning as "the cognitive and non-cognitive process by which a health care professional consciously and unconsciously interacts with the patient and environment to collect and interpret data, weigh the benefits and risks of actions, and understand patients' preferences to determine a working diagnostic and therapeutic management plan whose purpose is to improve a patient's well-being" (p. xvii). Clinical reasoning helps physician to make a diagnosis and arrive at a treatment decision. Thus clinical reasoning is the application of critical thinking to the clinical context (Victor-Chmil, 2013).

It has been emphasized that medical students should have appropriate exposure to critical thinking skills as any physician's ability to provide safe, high-quality care depends upon their ability to reason, think, and judge. The physicians should be able to apply and utilize their critical thinking skills in assessing, diagnosing and treating patients in their daily clinical practice. Critical thinking has been well documented and discussed in nursing literature, but the evidence application in medicine is limited (Batool, 2010; Iranfar et al., 2012; Mahmoodabad, Nadrian, & Nahangi, 2012; Maudsley & Strivens, 2000). Critical thinking, clinical reasoning and clinical judgment should be given due importance in the medical curricula and clinical training to produce competent physicians for the society.

Contemporary Theories and Models of Critical Thinking

While critical thinking was conceptualized by the researchers and educators in a number of ways over the past century, the intellectual root of critical thinking was established 2,500 years ago with the teachings by a Greek philosopher, Socrates who is considered as father of critical thinking (Fahim & Bagheri, 2012). His method of teaching is widely known as 'Socratic Questioning' and is also considered as the best critical thinking teaching strategy. The strategy "established the importance of seeking evidence, closely examining reasoning and assumptions, analysing basic concepts, and tracing out implications not only of what is said but of what is done as well" (The Foundation for Critical Thinking, 2018). Plato, who was most famous disciple of Socrates, recorded his experience with Socrates in the form of a dialogue and carried on the tradition of critical thinking. Aristotle, Plato's outstanding student, and other Greek philosophers refined Socrates' philosophy using systematic thinking and asking questions to discover the deeper and true realities of life (The Foundation for Critical Thinking, 2018).

It is to be noted that African, Arabic, Chinese, and Indian traditions (including Buddhist, Jain, etc.), and philosophy have also contributed to the development of logic and critical thinking (Vaidya, 2017). Charaka, an Ayurveda physician during BC300, emphasize that "Discussion with specialists promotes pursuit and advancement of knowledge, provides dexterity, improves power of speaking, illumines fame, removes doubt in scriptures, if any, by repeating the topics, and creates confidence in case there is any doubt, and brings forth new ideas. The ideas memorized in study from the teacher, will become firm when applied in (competitive) discussion" (Loon, 2002, p. 115-116).

The Scholars of the Middle Ages, the Renaissance, and post Renaissance, and French Enlightenment continued to refine the tradition of systematic critical thinking (Fahim & Bagheri, 2012). All these fundamentals of thought and reasoning have now formed the baseline of critical thinking in various discipline including medical education and medicine.

In the modern era, the theory of critical thinking was highlighted with the works of Bloom and his co-workers (1956) (Khodadady & Karami, 2017). The widely used theoretical model for critical thinking in medical education is Bloom's Taxonomy (Bloom et al., 1956). The taxonomy is a set of three hierarchical models — cognitive, affective, and psychomotor. These models classify the educational learning objectives into levels of complexity and specificity and is based on the belief that one must develop prerequisite basic skills in each area before progressing to more complex, higher order skills. The cognitive domain is most relevant to the teaching of critical thinking, and it included six hierarchical categories: knowledge, comprehension, application, analysis, synthesis and evaluation (Figure 1).

Figure 1. Bloom's taxonomy
Source: (Bloom et al., 1956)

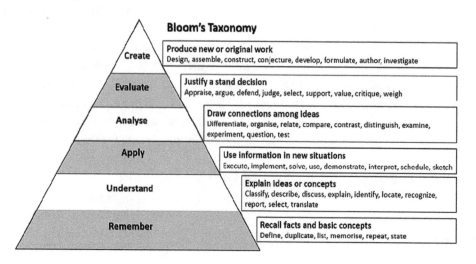

Lorin Anderson, a former student of Bloom, and David Krathwohl revisited the cognitive domain and proposed revised Bloom's taxonomy (Figure 2). The changes occurred in three broad categories: Bloom's six categories were changed from noun to verb forms, and rearrange cognitive domain into two-dimensional table: Knowledge dimension and the Cognitive process dimension (Table 1) (Anderson et al., 2001).

Both the original taxonomy and the revised version provides a valuable framework for teachers to design higher order learning outcomes for their curriculum. By providing a hierarchy of critical thinking, teachers are able to develop performance tasks, creating questions, or constructing cases using these hierarchy of critical thinking.

Importance of Teaching Critical Thinking in Medical Education

In the 21st century, the main goal of medical education is to strengthen students' critical thinking skills as well as acquisition of information, which help them to analyse information critically and then apply

Figure 2. Revised Bloom's taxonomy
Source: (Anderson et al., 2001)

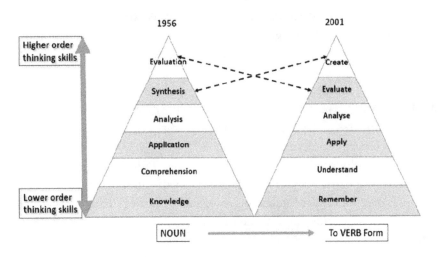

Table 1. Two dimensions of revised Bloom's taxonomy

		Knowledge Dimension			
		1. Factual	2. Conceptual	3. Procedural	4. Metacognitive
Cognitive process dimension	F. Create				
	E. Evaluate				
	D. Analyze				
	C. Apply			C3	
	B. Understand		B2		
	A. Remember	A1			

Source: (Anderson et al., 2001)

those to the existing information. However, lack of training in critical thinking and clinical reasoning in medical curricula causes medical students and physicians to use 'cognitive biases' in problem solving which ultimately leads to 'diagnostic errors' later in their professional practice (Hayes, Chatterjee, & Schwartzstein, 2017). Diagnostic and clinical error is estimated to occur in between 10%-15% of clinical decision making encounters (Graber, 2013; Higgs & Elstein, 1995). A study conducted among 127 hospital-based paediatric consultants and registrars across the Republic of Ireland identified cognitive biases as the most common reasons for diagnostic error (Perrem et al., 2016). Approximately 10% of in-hospital mortality occurs due to medical errors (National Academies of Sciences, Engineering, and Medicine, 2015). The USA data showed that 83% of diagnostic errors in the inpatient setting were preventable (Zwaan et al. 2010) and recoded a consistent 10-20% of missed diagnoses which was confirmed by autopsy studies (Shojana et al. 2003; Winters et al. 2012). In the USA, clinical errors were estimated in 2016 to cause 250,000 deaths per year (Makary and Daniel, 2016) and approximately 5% of US adult patients experience diagnostic errors (Singh, Meyer, & Thomas, 2017). There is a clear evidence of compromise with patient safety and increasing chance of morbidity and mortality rates (Amey et al., 2017; Royce et al., 2018). In developed countries, clinical errors are the main cause of medical malpractice claims which increase the cost of healthcare (Saber Tehrani et al., 2013). An analysis data from over 23,000 malpractice cases, the CRICO Report found that 20% of total cases were attributed to diagnostic errors and 73% of these diagnostic error cases are due to identifiable lapse in clinical reasoning (Table 2) (CRICO Report, 2014). The total estimated incurred cost was $631 million. A 25-Year (1986–2010) analysis of US malpractice claims for diagnostic errors found a cost of US$38.8 billion (mean per-claim pay out US$386 849; median US$213 250) (Saber et al., 2013). The literature with respect to critical thinking in the training of medical students is sparse (Scott & Chafe, 1997). In comparison, the nursing literature on the subject is extensive, and strongly supportive of critical thinking training of nurses (Dobrzykowski, 1994). Various research demonstrated that positive performance of critical thinking and diagnostic reasoning correlates with good clinical decision-making, academic success and professionalism (Ross, Loeffler, Schipper, Vandermeer, & Allan, 2013).

Formalized teaching of clinical decision making to medical students remains a formidable task. Critical cognitive skills form a specific body of knowledge. A novel, innovative course requiring the practice of accepted principles of clinical decision making, as used by Sherlock Holmes in selected short stories, improves students' decision making skills as measured by a series of examinations requiring the use of basic science knowledge to arrive at clinical diagnoses (Ayers, 1997).

Several leading medical education organizations and medical schools emphasized teaching critical thinking in medical schools and include in medical curricula and viewed the skill as a key competency to be cultivated and assessed in medical schools (Core Committee, Institute for International Medical

Table 2. Lapses in clinical judgement

• Overall: 73% lapses in clinical judgement
• Leading issues in clinical judgement:
o 31% failure to or delay in diagnostic test
o 23% misinterpretation of diagnostic test
o 22% failure to establish a differential diagnosis
o 18% failure to or delay in obtaining a consult or referral
o 8% failure to rule out an abnormal finding

Source: (CRICO Report, 2014)

Education, 2002; Simpson et al., 2002; Fuks, Boudreau, & Cassell, 2009; Simpson et al., 2002). Medical educationists also highlighted the importance of critical thinking competency in the medical curriculum to produce better healthcare professionals (Mahdi, Victoria, & Carolina, 2010; Amey et al., 2017; Simpson & Courtney, 2002; Allen, Rubenfeld, Scheffer, 2004; Daly, 2001). It was found that teaching clinical thinking in the early phase of a medical curriculum is necessary to promote 'encapsulation' (Schmidt & Rikers 2007; Amey et al., 2017), an integrated strategy of teaching basic medical knowledge to link to the causal chains of illnesses and diseases taught in courses in pathology and medicine and later observed in the clinic (Mahdi et al., 2010).

Teaching critical thinking and clinical reasoning is found to be challenging, and difficulties associated with assessment are diverse (Willingham, 2007; Norman et al., 2017; Mafinejad et al., 2017). The assessment of critical thinking is a constant challenge and there is considerable debate as to how to identify best assessment methods (Manogue et al., 2002; Staib, 2003). Moreover, medical academics and practitioners have raised concerns about the low levels of critical thinking and clinical reasoning among medical students and physicians. A study conducted to examine the relationship between critical-thinking skills and decision-making ability of medicine students in India identified poor decision-making skills among the students (Irfannuddin, 2009). Students with low critical thinking skills or with inadequate subject knowledge had a higher risk of low clinical reasoning ability (Heidari & Ebrahimi, 2016).

Lack of critical skills and clinical reasoning make up a sizable portion of preventable adverse outcomes in healthcare (Graber, 2005). Moreover, approximately one third of patient problems are mismanaged due to lack diagnostic skills and critical thinking abilities among physicians (Harasym, Tsai, & Hemmati, 2008). A recent study sought feedback on clinical reasoning (wrong, delayed, or missed diagnosis and/or treatment) among Clerkship Directors in Internal Medicine of the US medical schools and found that most institutions (52/91; 57%) surveyed lacked sessions dedicated to these topics and most students enter the clerkship with only poor (25/85; 29%) to fair (47/85; 55%) knowledge of key clinical reasoning concepts (Rencic, Trowbridge, Fagan, Szauter, & Durning, 2017). Lack of curricular time (59/67, 88%) and faculty expertise in teaching these concepts (53/76, 69%) were identified as barriers. Teaching good clinical reasoning should be considered as an important component of medical education. It was emphasised that a structured curriculum in clinical reasoning should be taught in all phases of medical education. Medical teachers and educators also rarely receive adequate training on how to teach and assess this area (Rencic, 2011). Appropriate faculty development programmes need to be organized to develop an understanding of good critical skills and clinical reasoning and how these skills are assessed and evaluated (Iobst, Trowbridge, & Philibert, 2013). Faculty should know explicit ways of teaching these skills so that students can think critically to minimize clinical errors (Iobst et al., 2013). Iobst et al., (2013) proposed framework for defining 'Good Clinical Thinking' (Table 3).

Table 3. Elements of good clinical thinking

• Sensitivity
o Interest in gaining more information
o Seeking alternatives
• Inclination
o Willing to invest energy in thinking the matter through
• Ability
o Possess the cognitive ability

Source: (Iobst et al., 2013)

Various authorities including General Medical Council (GMC) UK, American Association of Medical Council (AAMC) recommended enhancing health care professional education in the area of diagnostic and clinical reasoning and critical thinking. Educating medical students at an early phase of the medical curriculum about the processes of clinical reasoning and critical thinking to develop the skill to avoid diagnostic errors increase patient safety (Amey et al., 2017). Dedicated curriculum developed to teach reasoning, metacognition, cognitive biases, and debiasing strategies will enhance critical thinking and clinical reasoning skills (Hayes, Chatterjee, & Schwartzstein, 2017). Appropriate resources should be in place to develop and implement relevant curricula to improve diagnostic accuracy and reduce diagnostic error among medical students.

Teaching Critical Thinking in Medicine: Evidence-Based Practice

Critical thinking is vital to evidence-based medicine and practice. This section reviews the concepts of the evidence-based practice (EBP) and Evidence-based medicine (EBM) and important strategies to teach, improve and foster critical thinking in medical education. The term EBP was first introduced in 1992 (Evidence-Based Medicine Working Group, 1992) and serves to help develop and practice critical thinking skills. Various research has mentioned that EBP leads to better clinical decisions and improves care, patient outcomes and satisfaction of patients in various healthcare settings (American Association of Colleges of Nursing, 1998; Flodgren, Rojas-Reyes, Cole, & Foxcroft, 2012; Profetto-McGrath, 2005). EBP is defined as "the conscientious, explicit and judicious use of current best evidence in making decisions about the care of the individual patient" (Sackett, Rosenberg, Gray, Haynes, & Richardson, 1996, p. 71). Moore (2007, p. 13) described EBP as "a means of facilitating well-reasoned decisions by encouraging the practitioner to effectively integrate scientific research findings, the preferences, circumstances, and uniqueness of each client, and his or her professional judgment". Critical thinking is considered as one of the important skills (Profetto-McGrath, 2003; Tanner, 1999), which can equip physicians and other healthcare professionals "with the necessary skills and dispositions (habits of mind, attitudes, and traits) to support EBP" (Profetto-McGrath, 2005, p. 364). Critical thinking develops the ability and willingness to assess claims and make objective judgments on the basis of well-supported reasons and evidence rather than emotion or anecdote.

The exponential growth of scientific and clinical knowledge is one of the most pervasive issues in medicine and physicians are unable to cope with the information overload. EBM encourages physicians to use best available clinical evidence and high quality research to make decisions in healthcare settings (Masic, Miokovic, & Muhamedagic, 2008; Ubbink, Guyatt, & Vermeulen, 2013). Physicians are required to adopt lifelong, self-directed, and problem-solving approaches (e.g. literature-search, meta-analysis etc.) to identify and generate evidence and apply those to improve patient care (Masic et al., 2008). The practice of EBM is found to be cost-effective and efficient and bridges the gap between research and practice (Masic et al., 2008; Al-Almaie & Al-Baghli, 2003). Medical students and physicians should be provided with opportunities to learn EBM principles and encourage use of evidence-based research findings (e.g. RCT), systematic reviews/meta-analysis, guidelines and protocols and undertake patient-cantered research to improve patient care and outcomes (Nunan et al., 2017; Farquhar, 2018).

In medical education, most widely used strategies to develop critical thinking and EBP among medical and other health professionals included: problem-based learning (PBL), reflective journals, role modelling, and journal clubs (Profetto-McGrath 2005). First, PBL was pioneered in the health sciences at McMaster University in Canada in 1965 (Barrows & Tamblyn, 1980). Since its inception, many medical schools have adopted PBL method in their curriculum (Hur & Kim, 2007). In PBL, students learn by solving problems and reflecting on their own experiences (Barrows & Tamblyn, 1980). Students deal with a real-life problem or clinical case and engage reflectively to construct their own understanding (Lim, 2011). PBL provides opportunities to the students to relate their new knowledge to their prior understanding (Hmelo-Silver, 2004) which is supported by reflective thinking, critical skills, and problem solving (Si, 2018).

Second, reflection is a strategy to develop critical thinking skills. In medical education, reflection is related to the acquisition of knowledge and skills, personal and professional development to improve critical thinking skills (Mann, Gordon, & MacLeod, 2009). Reflecting "on educational and clinical experiences in medical practice, including one's own behaviour" is essential (Boenink, Oderwald, De, Van & Smal, 2004' p. 369) and acquiring knowledge and practical skills in preclinical years are not enough to become competent medical practitioners (American Association of Medical Colleges, 1984; Metz, Stoelinga, Pels-Rijcken-Van, Taalman Kip, & Van Der Brand-Valkenburg, 1994). Self-report questionnaire, essay writing, portfolio, diaries, logbooks etc. are used to assess students' reflective skills (Mann et al., 2009; Boenink et al., 2004; Niemi, 1997; Sobral, 2000).

Third, reflective writing is one strategy that has been used in undergraduate medical curricula to develop critical thinking among medical students (Sar & Nalbant, 2014, Si 2018). More specifically within reflective writing is reflective journaling, a powerful tool of expressing feelings and to reflect privately upon one's own daily experiences in the clinical setting (Ganesh & Ganesh, 2010). Students usually use diary writings or notes to recode their emotions, experiences and feelings on critical incidents they encounter during patient interactions (Sar & Nalbant, 2014).

Fourth, role modelling is an important and valuable educational method which facilitates student learning and helps to develop professional identity through the observation of their clinical tutors (Brownell & Cote, 2001; Prideaux et al., 2000; Ficklin, Browne, Powell, & Carter, 1988; Paice, Heard, & Moss, 2002). According to Irby (1986, p. 40), role modelling is the "process in which faculty members demonstrate clinical skills, model and articulate thought processes and manifest positive professional characteristics". Research showed the importance of role modelling in medical education as 90% of students identify one or multiple role models during their undergraduate training (Wright, Wong, & Newil, 1997). It is important that medical educators need to be critical thinkers and should create a learning environment that fosters critical thinking, self-directed learning, and problem-solving (Dickerson, 2005). Medical faculty should be 'aware of their responsibilities as teachers and role models, and hold themselves to high standards' (Mileder, Schmidt, & Dimai, 2014). The use of role modelling should take place in formal, informal, and hidden curricula situations (Hafferty & Franks, 1994; Hundert, Hafferty, & Christakis, 1996).

Finally, learning and practicing evidence-based medicine in undergraduate medical education can be achieved through the use of journal clubs (Lucia & Swanberg, 2018; Curtis, Viyasar, Ahluwalia, & Lazarus, 2016). Journal club is a well-established instructional method mainly used in clinical years (Alguire, 1998; Roberts et al., 2015). Journal club critically evaluates current available evidence to improve patient care and provide the opportunity to teach/learn EBM (Mohr et al., 2015; Harris et al., 2011). Despite some challenges, research demonstrated that journal clubs can be successfully implemented in preclinical years to teach critical thinking and real-world application skills which are needed later in their professional life (Lucia & Swanberg, 2018).

Critical thinking is paramount among the competencies required to support EBP. The acquisition of critical thinking and clinical reasoning can equip physicians with the required skills and attitude to practice EBP. Teaching critical thinking in undergraduate medical education is therefore crucial as EBP supports health care and contributes positively to patient outcomes.

Assessment Methods and Tools for Critical Thinking

Despite the widely held belief that physicians should be critical thinkers, there is no consensus on the most effective model to teach and assess the critical thinking and clinical reasoning skills and even the skill is not effectively tested in medical schools (Amey et al., 2017; Scott & Chafe, 1997). Teaching and assessing the skills has faced many difficulties and challenges although critical thinking is now considered as one of the important core competencies in medical education. The main obstacles are lake of operational definition of critical thinking and hence absence of objective assessment tools (Bissell &Lemons, 2006; Sternod & French, 2015; Butler, 2012). Moreover, critical thinking is a complex and multivariate concept and a valid and reliable test is often difficult to design to test its cognitive and dispositional components (Halpern, 1999). In the following sections, the variety of methods and instruments which have been widely used to assess these critical skills and clinical reasoning are discussed.

The common methods which have been employed to develop these skills in medical students include: simulation, problem-based learning, discussion of critical incidences, in-depth clinical experience debriefing, reflective writing and concept mapping, collaborative writing, think-pair-share strategy, brain storming, one minute paper, team based learning, case based instruction, panel discussion, and peer learning have been developed in medical education (Zayapragassarazan et al., 2016; LaMartina & Ward-Smith, 2014).

In medical schools, students are expected to be active learners and take control of their own learning as self-directed learners. Research showed that active learning approach helps students to develop critical thinking and problem solving skills which are essential determinants of quality medical practitioners (Zayapragassarazan et al., 2016). A systematic review of the literature on effective teaching methods used to develop critical thinking in nursing and midwifery undergraduate students identified the most common educational interventions were problem-based learning (PBL), simulation, concept mapping, and a combination of PBL and concept mapping (Carter, Creedy, & Sidebotham, 2016). Other methods used included: narrative pedagogy, critical reading and writing course, videotaped vignettes, information communication technology (ICT) based approach, web-based animated pedagogical agents, reflective writing, grand rounds, interactive videodisc system (IVS), evidence-based nursing education course, and peer active learning strategies approach (PALS).

The tools which are widely used include: California Critical Thinking Skills Test (CCTST), California Critical Thinking Disposition Inventory (CCTDI), Watson-Glaser Critical Thinking Appraisal (WGCTA), Del Bueno's Performance-Based Development System (PBDS) and Health Science Reasoning Test (HSRT) (Zayapragassarazan et al., 2016; LaMartina & Ward-Smith, 2014). These inventories and measures help the faculty and medical educators to examine the critical thinking and clinical reasoning of learners. A systematic review of the literature on teaching critical thinking in nursing and midwifery undergraduate students found that 57% of the studies utilised one of three standardised commercially available tools to measure critical thinking which included CCTDI, CCTST, and HSRT (Carter et al., 2016). Ross et al. (2013) conducted a literature review and meta-analysis to determine whether the three commonly used critical thinking tools (CCTDI, CCTST, and WGCTA) correlate with academic success of health professional trainees and demonstrated that the skill was moderately correlated with academic success. The authors also found that the CCTDI was inferior to the CCTST in correlating with academic success. In a study, Bartlett and Cox (2002) examined the change in critical thinking skills among physical therapy students in preclinical and clinical phases and found that both CCTST and CCTDI detected change over the year, more change was observed by the CCTDI.

The CCTST, a discipline neutral assessment for undergraduate and graduate level students, is a 34-item multiple-choice question quiz, generating six total scores and five subscale scores (Facione, P. A., Facione, N. C., & Blohm, 2007). The test is divided into two groups: three critical-thinking skills, including analysis, evaluation, and inference, are in one group, and deduction and inductions are assessed in another group (Lotfi, Hasankhani, & Mokhtari, 2010). It is trusted worldwide as a valid, objective and reliable measure of core reasoning skills. The CCTST has been increasingly popular to measure critical thinking among undergraduate students (Jacob, 2012; Al-Fadhli & Khalfan, 2009; Miri, David, & Uri, 2007). Studies conducted among medical students in Iran using CCTST found that the critical thinking skills of medical students were lower than the average level and poor (Heidari & Ebrahimi, 2016; Shakurnia & Aslami, 2017). Mafinejad et al. (2017) in their study used the California Critical Thinking Skills Test (CCTST) to assess critical thinking ability of medical students by using multi-response format of assessment (open and closed-ended response questions) and highlighted the importance of such multimodal assessment format to test critical thinking abilities.

The CCTDI assesses the extent to which a person possesses the disposition of the ideal critical thinker and measures affective attitudinal dimensions of critical thinking. Facione (1990) developed the inventory with 46 cross-disciplinary experts as a tool to evaluate critical thinking disposition among college students, adults and professionals (Facione & Facione, 1992). The instrument contains 75 items and consists of the following seven subscales: truth-seeking: 12 items, open-mindedness:12 items, analytical: 11 items, systematic: 11 items, inquisitiveness: 10 items, self-confidence: 9 items), and maturity: 10 items. The instrument has widely been adopted to research the critical thinking disposition of medical and other health personnel (Kabeel & Eisa, 2016; Gurol, Uslu, Polat, Yigit, & Yucel, 2013; Yeh, 2002; Profetto-McGrath, 2003; Kawashima & Petrini, 2004, Gupta et al., 2012; Yuan, Liao, Wang & Chou, 2014).

The WGCTA has 80 items and produces a single score based on the assessment of five critical thinking skills. Scott, Markert, & Dunn, (1998) administered the Watson-Glaser Critical Thinking Assessment (WGCTA) to one class of students at entry to medical school and near the end of year 3 and found that critical thinking skills improve moderately during medical school. Scott & Markert (1994) also used the WGCTA to examine the relationship between critical thinking skills and success during the first two years of medical school and recorded moderately predictive of academic success during the preclinical years of medical education.

However, a number of limitations identified for the use of these instruments in health profession education include lack of specific nature of attributes related to health profession, failure to address the practical reality of health professions, and they do not assess well-established psychometric properties (da Silva Bastos Cerullo & da Cruz D, 2010).

CONCLUSION

In medical education, the important goal is not only acquisition of relevant information, but it is rather to strengthen students' critical thinking skills so that they can able to analyse and then apply the existing information for clinical judgement and apply appropriate treatment. The development of critical thinking is considered as one of the essential skills which medical students should develop to solve problems by assessing and utilizing appropriate evidence. Critical thinking is a cognitive skill that can be taught, learned and assessed through active process and learning. Evidence shows that critical thinkers have better decision-making, problem-solving, and are professionally more competent and confident. Medical teachers should have a clear and cohesive understanding of critical thinking and clinical reasoning skills. There is a need for ongoing faculty development opportunities so that they develop a comprehensive understanding of the concept of these skills.

REFERENCES

Al-Almaie, S. M., & Al-Baghli, N. A. (2003). Evidence-based Medicine: An overview. *Journal of Family & Community Medicine, 10*, 17–24. PMID:23011987

Al-Fadhli, S., & Khalfan, A. (2009). Developing critical thinking in e-learning environment: Kuwait University as a case study. *Assessment & Evaluation in Higher Education, 34*(5), 529–536. doi:10.1080/02602930802117032

Alguire, P. C. (1998). A review of journal clubs in postgraduate medical education. *Journal of General Internal Medicine, 13*(5), 347–353. doi:10.1046/j.1525-1497.1998.00102.x PMID:9613892

Allen, G. D., Rubenfeld, M. G., & Scheffer, B. K. (2004). Reliability of assessment of critical thinking. *Journal of Professional Nursing, 20*(1), 15–22. doi:10.1016/j.profnurs.2003.12.004 PMID:15011189

American Association of Medical Colleges. (1984). Physicians of the 21st century. Report of the Working Group on Personal Qualities, Values and Attitudes. *Journal of Medical Education, 59*, 177–189.

Amey, L., Donald, K. J., & Teodorczuk, A. (2017). Teaching clinical reasoning to medical students. *British Journal of Hospital Medicine, 78*(7), 399–401. doi:10.12968/hmed.2017.78.7.399 PMID:28692355

Anderson, L. W., Krathwohl, D. R., Airasian, P. W., Cruikshank, K. A., Mayer, R. E., Pintrich, P. R., & Wittrock, M. C. (2001). *A Taxonomy for Learning, Teaching, and Assessing: A revision of Bloom's Taxonomy of Educational Objectives*. New York: Pearson, Allyn & Bacon.

Ayers, W. R. (1997). Sherlock Holmes and clinical reasoning: Empiric research on a methodology to teach clinical reasoning. In A. J. J. A. Scherpbier, C. P. M. van der Vleuten, J. J. Rethans, & A. F. W. van der Steeg (Eds.), *Advances in Medical Education* (pp. 600–601). Dordrecht: Springer. doi:10.1007/978-94-011-4886-3_182

Barrows, H. S., & Tamblyn, R. (1980). *Problem-Based Learning: An Approach to Medical Education*. New York: Springer.

Bartlett, D. J., & Cox, P. D. (2002). Measuring change in students' critical thinking ability: Implications for health care education. *Journal of Allied Health, 31*, 64–69. PMID:12040999

Batool, T. (2010). Hyposkillia and critical thinking: Lost skills of doctors. *APS Journal of Case Reports, 1*, 9.

Bissell, A. N., & Lemons, P. P. (2006). A new method for assessing critical thinking in the classroom. *Bioscience, 56*(1), 66–72. doi:10.1641/0006-3568(2006)056[0066:ANMFAC]2.0.CO;2

Bloom, B. S., Engelhart, M. D., Furst, E. J., Hill, W. H., & Krathwohl, D. R. (1956). *Taxonomy of Educational Objectives, Handbook I: The Cognitive Domain.* New York: David McKay Co Inc.

Boenink, A. D., Oderwald, A. K., De, J. P., Van, T. W., & Smal, J. A. (2004). Assessing student reflection in medical practice. The development of an observer-rated instrument: Reliability, validity and initial experiences. *Medical Education, 38*(4), 368–377. doi:10.1046/j.1365-2923.2004.01787.x PMID:15025638

Brownell, A. K., & Cote, L. (2001). Senior residents' views on the meaning of professionalism and how they learn about it. *Academic Medicine, 76*(7), 734–737. doi:10.1097/00001888-200107000-00019 PMID:11448832

Butler, H. A. (2012). Halpern Critical Thinking Assessment Predicts Real-World Outcomes of Critical Thinking. *Applied Cognitive Psychology, 26*(5), 721–729. doi:10.1002/acp.2851

Carter, A. G., Creedy, D. K., & Sidebotham, M. (2016). Efficacy of teaching methods used to develop critical thinking in nursing and midwifery undergraduate students: A systematic review of the literature. *Nurse Education Today, 40*, 209–218. doi:10.1016/j.nedt.2016.03.010 PMID:27125175

Core Committee, Institute for International Medical Education. (2002). Global minimum essential requirements in medical education. *Medical Teacher, 24*(2), 130–135. doi:10.1080/01421590220120731 PMID:12098431

CRICO. (2014). *Malpractice Risks in the Diagnostic Process: 2014 CRICO Strategies National CBS Report.* Retrieved from https://www.rmf.harvard.edu/Malpractice-Data/Annual-Benchmark-Reports/Risks-in-the-Diagnostic-Process

Curtis, A., Viyasar, T., Ahluwalia, V., & Lazarus, K. (2016). Educating medical students: Introducing a journal club. *The Clinical Teacher, 13*(3), 233–234. doi:10.1111/tct.12356 PMID:26013431

da Silva Bastos Cerullo, J. A., & da Cruz, D. (2010). Clinical reasoning and critical thinking. *Revista Latino-Americana de Enfermagem, 18*(1), 124–129. doi:10.1590/S0104-11692010000100019 PMID:20428707

Daly, W. M. (2001). The development of an alternative method in the assessment of critical thinking as an outcome of nursing education. *Journal of Advanced Nursing, 36*(1), 120–130. doi:10.1046/j.1365-2648.2001.01949.x PMID:11555056

Dickerson, P. S. (2005). Nurturing critical thinkers. *Journal of Continuing Education in Nursing, 36*(2), 68–72. doi:10.3928/0022-0124-20050301-06 PMID:15835581

Dobrzykowski, T. M. (1994). Teaching strategies to promote critical thinking skills in nursing staff. *Journal of Continuing Education in Nursing, 25*, 272–276. PMID:7868746

Facione, N. C., & Facione, P. A. J. (1996). Externalizing the critical thinking in clinical judgment. *Nursing Outlook, 44*, 129–136. doi:10.1016/S0029-6554(06)80005-9 PMID:8794454

Facione, P. A. (1990). *Critical thinking: A statement of expert consensus for purposes of educational assessment and instruction—The Delphi report.* Millbrae, CA: California Academic Press.

Facione, P. A. (2011). Critical thinking: What it is and why it counts. *Insight Assessment, 2007,* 1–23.

Facione, P. A., Facione, N. C., & Blohm, S. W. (2007). *The California Critical Thinking Skills Test: CCTST.* Millbrae, CA: California Academic Press.

Fahim, M., & Bagheri, M. B. (2012). Fostering critical thinking through Socrates' questioning in Iranian language institutes. *Journal of Language Teaching and Research, 3*(6), 1122–1127. doi:10.4304/jltr.3.6.1122-1127

Farquhar, C. (2018). Evidence-based medicine - the promise, the reality. *Australian and New Zealand Journal of Obstetrics and Gynaecology, 58*(1), 17–21. doi:10.1111/ajo.12768 PMID:29400399

Ficklin, F. L., Browne, V. L., Powell, R. C., & Carter, J. E. (1988). Faculty and house staff members as role models. *Journal of Medical Education, 63,* 392–396. PMID:3361591

Flodgren, G., Rojas-Reyes, M. X., Cole, N., & Foxcroft, D. R. (2012). Effectiveness of organisational infrastructures to promote evidence-based nursing practice. *The Cochrane Database of Systematic Reviews, 2.* doi:.CD002212.pub2 doi:10.1002/14651858

Fuks, A., Boudreau, J. D., & Cassell, E. J. (2009). Teaching clinical thinking to first-year medical students. *Medical Teacher, 31*(2), 105–111. doi:10.1080/01421590802512979 PMID:19330669

Ganesh, A., & Ganesh, G. (2010). Reflective writing by final year medical students: Lessons for curricular change. *The National Medical Journal of India, 23,* 226–230. PMID:21192519

Graber, M. (2005). Diagnostic errors in medicine: A case of neglect. *Joint Commission Journal on Quality and Patient Safety, 31*(2), 106–113. doi:10.1016/S1553-7250(05)31015-4 PMID:15791770

Graber, M. L. (2013). The incidence of diagnostic error in medicine. *BMJ Quality & Safety, 22*(Suppl 2), ii21–ii27. doi:10.1136/bmjqs-2012-001615 PMID:23771902

Gupta, K., Iranfar, S., Iranfar, K., Mehraban, B., Montazeri, N., & ... . (2012). Validly and Reliability of California Critical Thinking Disposition Inventory (CCTDI) in Kermanshah University of Medical Sciences. *Educational Research in Medical Sciences, 1,* e77064.

Gurol, A., Uslu, S., Polat, O. E., Yigit, N., & Yucel, O. (2013). Critical thinking disposition in students of vocational school of health services. Electronic Journal of Vocational Colleges, 28-36.

Guyatt, G. (1992). Evidence-based medicine. A new approach to teaching the practice of medicine. *Journal of the American Medical Association, 268*(17), 2420–2425. doi:10.1001/jama.1992.03490170092032 PMID:1404801

Hafferty, F. W., & Franks, R. (1994). The hidden curriculum, ethics teaching, and the structure of medical education. *Academic Medicine, 69*(11), 861–871. doi:10.1097/00001888-199411000-00001 PMID:7945681

Halpern, D. F. (1999). Teaching for critical thinking: Helping college students develop the skills and dispositions of a critical thinker. *New Directions for Teaching and Learning, 80*(80), 69–74. doi:10.1002/tl.8005

Harasym, P. H., Tsai, T. C., & Hemmati, P. (2008). Current trends in developing medical students critical thinking abilities. *The Kaohsiung Journal of Medical Sciences*, *24*(7), 341–355. doi:10.1016/S1607-551X(08)70131-1 PMID:18805749

Harris, J., Kearley, K., Heneghan, C., Meats, E., Roberts, N., Perera, R., & Kearley-Shiers, K. (2011). Are journal clubs effective in supporting evidence-based decision making? A systematic review. BEME Guide No. 16. *Medical Teacher*, *33*(1), 9–23. doi:10.3109/0142159X.2011.530321 PMID:21182379

Hayes, M. M., Chatterjee, S., & Schwartzstein, R. M. (2017). Critical Thinking in Critical Care: Five Strategies to Improve Teaching and Learning in the Intensive Care Unit. *Annals of the American Thoracic Society, 14*, 569-575.

Heidari, M., & Ebrahimi, P. (2016). Examining the relationship between critical-thinking skills and decision-making ability of emergency medicine students. *Indian Journal of Critical Care Medicine: Peer-Reviewed, Official Publication of Indian Society of Critical Care Medicine*, *20*(10), 581–586. doi:10.4103/0972-5229.192045 PMID:27829713

Higgs, J., & Elstein, A. (1995). Clinical reasoning in medicine. In J. Higgs (Ed.), *Clinical reasoning in the health professions* (pp. 49–59). Oxford, UK: Butterworth-Heinemann Ltd.

Hmelo-Silver, C. E. (2004). Problem-based learning: What and how do students learn? *Educational Psychology Review*, *16*(3), 235–266. doi:10.1023/B:EDPR.0000034022.16470.f3

Hundert, E. M., Hafferty, F., & Christakis, D. (1996). Characteristics of the informal curriculum and trainees' ethical choices. *Academic Medicine*, *71*(6), 624–633. doi:10.1097/00001888-199606000-00014 PMID:9125919

Hur, Y., & Kim, S. (2007). Different outcomes of active and reflective students in problem-based learning. *Medical Teacher*, *29*(1), e18–e21. doi:10.1080/01421590601045007 PMID:17538825

Iobst, W. F., Trowbridge, R., & Philibert, I. (2013). Teaching and assessing critical reasoning through the use of entrustment. *Journal of Graduate Medical Education*, *5*(3), 517–518. doi:10.4300/JGME-D-13-00211.1 PMID:24404322

Iranfar, S., Sepahi, V., Khoshay, A., Rezaei, M., Matin, B. K., Keshavarzi, F., & Bashiri, H. (2012). Critical thinking disposition among medical students of Kermanshah University of Medical Sciences. *Educational Research in Medical Sciences Journal*, *1*, 63–68.

Irby, D. M. (1986). Clinical teaching and the clinical teacher. *Journal of Medical Education*, *61*, 35–45. PMID:3746867

Irfannuddin, I. (2009). Knowledge and critical thinking skills increase clinical reasoning ability in urogenital disorders: A Universitas Sriwijaya Medical Faculty experience. *Medical Journal of Indonesia*, *18*, 53–59. doi:10.13181/mji.v18i1.341

Jacob, S. M. (2012). Analyzing critical thinking skills using online discussion forums and CCTST. *Procedia: Social and Behavioral Sciences*, *31*, 805–809. doi:10.1016/j.sbspro.2011.12.145

Kabeel, A. R., & Eisa, S. A. E. M. (2016). The Correlation of Critical Thinking Disposition and Approaches to Learning among Baccalaureate Nursing Students. *Journal of Education and Practice*, *7*, 91–103.

Kawashima, A., & Petrini, M. A. (2004). Study of critical thinking skills in nursing students and nurses in Japan. *Nurse Education Today*, *24*(4), 286–292. doi:10.1016/j.nedt.2004.02.001 PMID:15110438

Khodadady, E., & Karami, M. (2017). An Evaluation of Textbooks Designed for Advanced English Learners within a Foreign Context: A Critical Thinking Perspective. *Porta Linguarum*, *28*, 96–109.

LaMartina, K., & Ward-Smith, P. (2014). Developing critical thinking skills in undergraduate nursing students: The potential for strategic management simulations. *Journal of Nursing Education and Practice*, *4*(9), 155–162. doi:10.5430/jnep.v4n9p155

Lim, L. A. (2011). A comparison of students' reflective thinking across different years in a problem-based learning environment. *Instructional Science*, *39*(2), 171–188. doi:10.100711251-009-9123-8

Loon, G. V. (2002). *Charaka Saṃhitā: Handbook on Ayurveda Vol-1. Chaukhambha*. Orientialia Publishers.

Lotfi, H., Hasankhani, H., & Mokhtari, M. (2010). The effectiveness of simulation training and critical-thinking strategies on clinical decision-making of operating room students. *Journal of Nurse-Midwifery*, *5*, 5–11.

Lucia, V. C., & Swanberg, S. M. (2018). Utilizing journal club to facilitate critical thinking in pre-clinical medical students. *International Journal of Medical Education*, *15*, 7–8. doi:10.5116/ijme.5a46.2214 PMID:29334677

Mafinejad, M. K., Arabshahi, S. K. S., Monajemi, A., Jalili, M., Soltani, A., & Rasouli, J. (2017). Use of Multi-Response Format Test in the Assessment of Medical Students' Critical Thinking Ability. *Journal of Clinical and Diagnostic Research: JCDR*, *11*, LC10–LC13. PMID:29207742

Mahdi, T., Victoria, G., & Carolina, P. (2010). Teaching clinical thinking to first-year medical students. *Psihologie*, *4*, 75–85.

Mahmoodabad, S. S. M., Nadrian, H., & Nahangi, H. (2012). Critical thinking ability and its associated factors among preclinical students in Yazd Shaheed Sadoughi University of Medical Sciences (Iran). *Medical Journal of the Islamic Republic of Iran*, *26*, 50–57. PMID:23483755

Majumder, M. A. A., D'Souza, U., & Rahman, S. (2004). Trends in Medical Education: Challenges and Directions for Need-based Reforms of Medical Training in South-East Asia. *Indian Journal of Medical Sciences*, *58*, 369–380. PMID:15470278

Makary, M. A., & Daniel, M. (2016). Medical error-the third leading cause of death in the US. *British Medical Journal*, *353*, i2139. doi:10.1136/bmj.i2139 PMID:27143499

Mann, K., Gordon, J., & MacLeod, A. (2009). Reflection and reflective practice in health professions education: A systematic review. *Advances in Health Sciences Education: Theory and Practice*, *14*(4), 595–621. doi:10.100710459-007-9090-2 PMID:18034364

Manogue, M., Kelly, M., Masaryk, S. B., Brown, G., Catalanotto, F., Choo-Soo, T., & ... . (2002). Evolving methods of assessment. *European Journal of Dental Education*, *6*, 53–66. doi:10.1034/j.1600-0579.6.s3.8.x PMID:12390260

Masic, I., Miokovic, M., & Muhamedagic, B. (2008). Evidence Based Medicine – New Approaches and Challenges. *Acta Informatica Medica*, *16*(4), 219–225. doi:10.5455/aim.2008.16.219-225 PMID:24109156

Maudsley, G., & Strivens, J. (2000). 'Science', 'critical thinking' and 'competence' for tomorrow's doctors. A review of terms and concepts. *Medical Education*, *34*(1), 53–60. doi:10.1046/j.1365-2923.2000.00428.x PMID:10607280

Metz, J. C. M., Stoelinga, G. M., Pels-Rijcken-Van, E., Taalman Kip, E. H., & Van Der Brand-Valkenburg, B. W. M. (Eds.). (1994). Blueprint 1994: Training of Doctors in the Netherlands: Objectives of Undergraduate Medical Education. Nijmegen, University Publication Office.

Mileder, L. P., Schmidt, A., & Dimai, H. P. (2014). Clinicians should be aware of their responsibilities as role models: A case report on the impact of poor role modeling. *Medical Education Online*, *19*(1), 23479. doi:10.3402/meo.v19.23479 PMID:24499869

Miri, B., David, B.-C., & Uri, Z. (2007). Purposely teaching for the promotion of higher-order thinking skills: A case of critical thinking. *Research in Science Education*, *37*(4), 353–369. doi:10.100711165-006-9029-2

Mohr, N. M., Stoltze, A. J., Harland, K. K., Van Heukelom, J. N., Hogrefe, C. P., & Ahmed, A. (2007). An evidence-based medicine curriculum implemented in journal club improves resident performance on the Fresno test. *The Journal of Emergency Medicine*, *48*(2), 222–229. doi:10.1016/j.jemermed.2014.09.011 PMID:25440869

Moore, Z. E. (2007). Critical Thinking and the Evidence-Based Practice of Sport Psychology. *Journal of Clinical Sport Psychology*, *1*(1), 9–22. doi:10.1123/jcsp.1.1.9

National Academies of Sciences, Engineering, and Medicine. (2015). *Improving diagnosis in health care*. Washington, DC: The National Academies Press.

Niemi, P. M. (1997). Medical students' professional identity: Self-reflection during the preclinical years. *Medical Education*, *31*(6), 408–415. doi:10.1046/j.1365-2923.1997.00697.x PMID:9463642

Norman, G. R., Monteiro, S. D., Sherbino, J., Ilgen, J. S., Schmidt, H. G., & Mamede, S. (2017). The causes of errors in clinical reasoning: Cognitive biases, knowledge deficits, and dual process thinking. *Academic Medicine*, *92*(1), 23–30. doi:10.1097/ACM.0000000000001421 PMID:27782919

Nunan, D., O'Sullivan, J., Heneghan, C., Pluddemann, A., Aronson, J., & Mahtani, K. (2017). Ten essential papers for the practice of evidence-based medicine. *Evidence-Based Medicine*, *22*(6), 202–204. doi:10.1136/ebmed-2017-110854 PMID:29170157

Paice, E., Heard, S., & Moss, F. (2002). How important are role models in making good doctors? *British Medical Journal*, *325*(7366), 707–710. doi:10.1136/bmj.325.7366.707 PMID:12351368

Paul, R., Elder, L., & Bartell, T. (1997). *California Teacher Preparation for Instruction in Critical Thinking: Research Findings and Policy Recommendations*. California Commission on Teacher Credentialing, Sacramento.

Perrem, L., Fanshawe, T., Sharif, F., Pluddermann, A., & O'Neill, M. B. (2016). A national physician survey of diagnostic error in pediatrics. *European Journal of Pediatrics, 175*(10), 1387–1392. doi:10.100700431-016-2772-0 PMID:27631589

Prideaux, D., Alexander, H., Bower, A., Dacre, J., Haist, S., Jolly, B., ... Tallett, S. (2000). Clinical teaching: Maintaining an educational role for doctors in the new health care environment. *Medical Education, 34*(10), 820–826. doi:10.1046/j.1365-2923.2000.00756.x PMID:11012932

Profetto-McGrath, J. (2003). The relationship of critical thinking skills and critical thinking dispositions of baccalaureate nursing students. *Journal of Advanced Nursing, 43*(6), 569–577. doi:10.1046/j.1365-2648.2003.02755.x PMID:12950562

Profetto-McGrath, J. (2005). Critical Thinking and Evidence-Based Practice. *Journal of Professional Nursing, 21*(6), 364–371. doi:10.1016/j.profnurs.2005.10.002 PMID:16311232

Redecker, C., Ala-Mutka, K., Leis, M., Leendertse, M., Punie, Y., Gijsbers, G., ... Hoogveld, B. (2011). *The Future of Learning: Preparing for Change*. Luxembourg: Publications Office of the European Union.

Rencic, J. (2011). Twelve tips for teaching expertise in clinical reasoning. *Medical Teacher, 33*(11), 887–892. doi:10.3109/0142159X.2011.558142 PMID:21711217

Rencic, J., Trowbridge, R. L. Jr, Fagan, M., Szauter, K., & Durning, S. (2017). Clinical Reasoning Education at US Medical Schools: Results from a National Survey of Internal Medicine Clerkship Directors. *Journal of General Internal Medicine, 32*(11), 1242–1246. doi:10.100711606-017-4159-y PMID:28840454

Roberts, M. J., Perera, M., Lawrentschuk, N., Romanic, D., Papa, N., & Bolton, D. (2015). Globalization of continuing professional development by journal clubs via microblogging: A systematic review. *Journal of Medical Internet Research, 17*(4), 103. doi:10.2196/jmir.4194 PMID:25908092

Ross, D., Loeffler, K., Schipper, S., Vandermeer, B., & Allan, G. M. (2013). Do scores on three commonly used measures of critical thinking correlate with academic success of health professions trainees? A systematic review and meta-analysis. *Academic Medicine, 88*(5), 724–734. doi:10.1097/ACM.0b013e31828b0823 PMID:23524925

Royce, C. S., Hayes, M. M., & Schwartzstein, R. M. (2018). Teaching Critical Thinking: A Case for Instruction in Cognitive Biases to Reduce Diagnostic Errors and Improve Patient Safety. *Academic Medicine*, 1. doi:10.1097/ACM.0000000000002518 PMID:30398993

Saber, T. A. S., Lee, H., Mathews, S. C., Shore, A., Makary, M. A., Pronovost, P. J., & Newman-Toker, D. E. (2013). 25-year summary of US malpractice claims for diagnostic errors 1986-2010: An analysis from the National Practitioner Data Bank. *BMJ Quality & Safety, 22*(8), 672–680. doi:10.1136/bmjqs-2012-001550 PMID:23610443

Sackett, D. L., Rosenberg, W. M., Gray, J. A., Haynes, R. B., & Richardson, W. S. (1996). Evidence based medicine: What it is and what it isn't. *British Medical Journal, 312*(7023), 71–72. doi:10.1136/bmj.312.7023.71 PMID:8555924

Sar, Ö., & Nalbant, H. (2014). Medical Practice and Review Medical students ' reflections on first clinical experience. *Medical Practice and Review, 5,* 31–35.

Schmidt, H. G., & Rikers, R. M. J. P. (2007). How expertise develops in medicine: Knowledge encapsulation and illness script formation. *Medical Education, 41,* 1133–1139. PMID:18004989

Scott, C. L. (2015). *The futures of learning 2: what kind of learning for the 21st century? ERF Working Papers Series, No. 14.* Paris: UNESCO.

Scott, J. N., & Markert, R. J. (1994). Relationship between critical thinking skills and success in preclinical courses. *Academic Medicine, 69*(11), 920–924. doi:10.1097/00001888-199411000-00015 PMID:7945695

Scott, J. N., Markert, R. J., & Dunn, M. M. (1998). Critical thinking: Change during medical school and relationship to performance in clinical clerkship. *Medical Education, 32*(1), 14–18. doi:10.1046/j.1365-2923.1998.00701.x PMID:9624394

Scott, T. M., & Chafe, L. L. (1997). Critical Thinking in Medical School Exams. In A. J. J. A. Scherpbier, C. P. M. van der Vleuten, J. J. Rethans, & A. F. W. van der Steeg (Eds.), *Advances in Medical Education* (pp. 387–389). Dordrecht: Springer. doi:10.1007/978-94-011-4886-3_117

Shakurnia, A., & Aslami, M. (2017). Critical Thinking Skills of Medical Students at Ahvaz Jundishapur University of Medical Sciences. *Indian Journal of Medical Education, 17,* 420–427.

Shojana, K. G., Burton, E. C., Mcdonald, K. M., Goldman, L., & Page, P. (2013). Changes in rates of autopsy-detected diagonstic errors over time: A systematic review. *Journal of the American Medical Association, 289,* 2849–2856. doi:10.1001/jama.289.21.2849

Si, J. (2018). An analysis of medical students' reflective essays in problem-based learning. *Korean Journal of Medical Education, 30*(1), 57–64. doi:10.3946/kjme.2018.82 PMID:29510609

Simpson, E., & Courtney, M. D. (2002). Critical thinking in nursing education: Literature review. *International Journal of Nursing Practice, 8*(2), 89–98. doi:10.1046/j.1440-172x.2002.00340.x PMID:11993582

Simpson, J., Furnace, J., Crosby, J., Cumming, A., Evans, P., David, M. F. B., ... MacPherson, S. G. (2002). The Scottish doctor--learning outcomes for the medical undergraduate in Scotland: A foundation for competent and reflective practitioners. *Medical Teacher, 24*(2), 136–143. doi:10.1080/01421590220120713 PMID:12098432

Simpson, J., Furnace, J., Crosby, J., Cumming, A., Evans, P., David, M. F. B., ... MacPherson, S. G. (2002). The Scottish doctor—learning outcomes for the medical undergraduate in Scotland: A foundation for competent and reflective practitioners. *Medical Teacher, 24*(2), 136–143. doi:10.1080/01421590220120713 PMID:12098432

Singh, H., Meyer, A. N., & Thomas, E. J. (2014). The frequency of diagnostic errors in outpatient care: Estimations from three large observational studies involving US adult populations. *BMJ Quality & Safety, 23*(9), 727–731. doi:10.1136/bmjqs-2013-002627 PMID:24742777

Sobral, D. T. (2000). An appraisal of medical students' reflection-in-learning. *Medical Education, 34*(3), 182–187. doi:10.1046/j.1365-2923.2000.00473.x PMID:10733703

Staib, S. (2003). Teaching and measuring critical thinking. *The Journal of Nursing Education, 42*(11), 498–508. doi:10.3928/0148-4834-20031101-08 PMID:14626388

Sternod, L., & French, B. (2015). Test Review: Watson-Glaser™ II Critical Thinking Appraisal. *Journal of Psychoeducational Assessment.*

Tanner, C. A. (1999). Evidence-based practice: Research and critical thinking. *The Journal of Nursing Education, 38*(3), 99. doi:10.3928/0148-4834-19990301-03 PMID:10102506

Tanner, C. A. (2006). Thinking like a nurse: A research-based model of clinical judgment in nursing. *The Journal of Nursing Education, 45*, 204–211. PMID:16780008

The American Philosophical Association. (1990). *Critical Thinking: A Statement of Expert Consensus for Purposes of Educational Assessment and Instruction. ERIC Doc. No. ED 315-423.* Millbrae, CA: California Academic Press.

The Foundation for Critical Thinking. (n.d.). Retrieved from http://www.criticalthinking.org/pages/a-brief-history-of-the-idea-of-critical-thinking/408

Trowbridge, R. L., Joseph, J. R., & Durning, S. J. (2015). *Teaching Clinical Reasoning. ACP's Teaching Medicine Series.* Philadelphia: American College of Physicians.

Ubbink, D. T., Guyatt, G. H., & Vermeulen, H. (2013). Framework of policy recommendations for implementation of evidence-based practice: A systematic scoping review. *BMJ Open, 3*(1), e001881. doi:10.1136/bmjopen-2012-001881 PMID:23355664

Vaidya, A. J. (2017). Does Critical Thinking and Logic Education Have a Western Bias? The Case of the Nyaya School of Classical Indian Philosophy. *Journal of Philosophy of Education, 51*(1), 132–160. doi:10.1111/1467-9752.12189

Victor-Chmil, J. (2013). Critical thinking versus clinical reasoning versus clinical judgment: Differential diagnosis. *Nurse Educator, 38*(1), 34–36. doi:10.1097/NNE.0b013e318276dfbe PMID:23222632

Willingham, D. T. (2007). Critical thinking, why is it so hard to teach? *American Educator, 31*, 8–19.

Winters, B., Custer, J., Galvagno, S. M. Jr, Colantuoni, E., Kapoor, S. G., Lee, H. W., ... Newman-Toker, D. (2012). Diagnostic errors in the intensive care unit: A systematic review of autopsy studies. *BMJ Quality & Safety, 21*(11), 894–902. doi:10.1136/bmjqs-2012-000803 PMID:22822241

Wright, S., Wong, A., & Newill, C. (1997). The impact of role models on medical students. *Journal of General Internal Medicine, 12*(1), 53–56. doi:10.100711606-006-0007-1 PMID:9034946

Yeh, M. L. (2002). Assessing the reliability and validity of the Chinese version of the California critical thinking disposition inventory. *International Journal of Nursing Studies, 39*(2), 123–132. doi:10.1016/S0020-7489(01)00019-0 PMID:11755443

Yuan, S., Liao, H., Wang, Y., & Chou, M. (2014). Development of a scale to measure the critical thinking disposition of medical care professionals. *Social Behavior and Personality*, *42*(2), 303–312. doi:10.2224bp.2014.42.2.303

Zayapragassarazan, Z., Menon, V., Kar, S. S., & Batmanabane, G. (2016). Understanding Critical Thinking to Create Better Doctors. *Journal of Advances in Medical Education and Research*, *1*, 9–13.

Zwaan, L., de Bruijne, M., Wagner, C., Thijs, A., Smits, M., van der Wal, G., & Timmermans, D. R. (2010). Patient record review of the incidence, consequences, and causes of diagnostic adverse events. *Archives of Internal Medicine*, *170*(12), 1015–1021. doi:10.1001/archinternmed.2010.146 PMID:20585065

Chapter 13
Critical Thinking and Mathematics Teaching and Learning

Kelli Thomas
University of Kansas, USA

Douglas Huffman
University of Kansas, USA

Mari Caballero
Emporia State University, USA

ABSTRACT

The purpose of this chapter was to investigate pre-service teachers' noticing of children's critical thinking and views towards eliciting and using students' critical thinking in mathematics teaching. A mixed method study was used to provide a range of perspectives on pre-service teachers' views towards mathematics. The results indicated that the pre-service teachers initially held beliefs that mathematics teaching and learning consist of transferring information and students absorbing and memorizing information. The pre-service teachers based their instructional responses on experiences they had as students in elementary mathematics classrooms. The pre-service teachers described what they had observed about teaching mathematics as the ideal without regard for how the teaching behaviors they observed might influence children's critical thinking about mathematics. After completing a mathematics methods course, the pre-service teachers held beliefs more consistent with a reform-oriented classroom and demonstrated growth in their ability to notice children's mathematics thinking.

INTRODUCTION

Globally, education reforms over the past few decades have called for a shift away from classrooms where students passively receive knowledge and practice procedures modeled and demonstrated by teachers to classrooms where students actively construct understanding through authentic learning tasks. There is a need for classrooms that emphasize the development of critical thinking to meet an economic demand

DOI: 10.4018/978-1-5225-7829-1.ch013

Copyright © 2019, IGI Global. Copying or distributing in print or electronic forms without written permission of IGI Global is prohibited.

for a workforce that uses knowledge and information to construct new understandings and to solve problems. In mathematics classrooms around the world, thinking critically about mathematics concepts and ideas is a central goal of teaching and learning. Meeting this goal requires teachers who elicit and help develop students' critical thinking while also thinking critically themselves about pedagogy, subject matter and student learning. The ability to notice and think critically about a child's mathematical thinking is needed to effectively teach children mathematics using reform-based methods. Research has shown that professional noticing of mathematical thinking is developed over time (Jacobs, Lamb, & Philipp, 2010; Stockero, Rupnow, & Pascoe, 2017). As a result, it is important to consider how pre-service teachers are forming the knowledge and skills to effectively teach children mathematics using reform-based practices (Feiman-Nemser, 2001; Schussler, Stooksberry, & Bercaw, 2010).

The intent of this study was to determine how pre-service teachers' views of mathematics teaching and learning, as well as their attention to children's mathematical thinking develop during a university level mathematics methods course with an integrated field experience in an elementary classroom. A mixed-method study approach was employed to examine pre-service teachers' noticing of children's critical thinking and pre-service teachers' views towards eliciting and using students' critical thinking in mathematics teaching. Data sources included both qualitative and quantitative data to provide a range of perspectives on pre-service teachers' views towards mathematics. This chapter presents a study framed by the following guiding questions:

Research Question 1: What are pre-service elementary teachers' views of mathematics teaching and learning?

Research Question 2: How do pre-service teachers notice and propose to elicit and use students' critical thinking in mathematics teaching?

The mathematics methods course that was the context for this study was intentionally designed to engage pre-service teachers to think critically and analytically about both their own experiences as learners and also how instruction can support the development of children's mathematics understanding. The course syllabus included the following course purpose statement:

The purpose of this course is to explore how to help children learn mathematical concepts and skills with understanding. The emphasis will be on teaching children mathematics using an active learning and problem solving approach. We will examine theories and methodologies related to topics in elementary mathematics programs. We will analyze children's mathematical thinking through the lens of various learning theories. We will observe teaching and learning of mathematics and reflect on how teachers can help children make sense of mathematics. You will become familiar with materials and models used in teaching mathematical concepts to children. The field experience component of this course is designed to acquaint you will children and the classroom environment as related to mathematics education. This course will also explore the use of available technology in your learning and teaching.

The mathematics methods course was structured to include 18 days of fieldwork in an elementary classroom. The pre-service teachers started the semester with four to five weeks of study in the university classroom reading about, analyzing, and discussing topics such as Learning with Understanding, Teaching Through Problem-Solving, Problem-Based Instruction, Standards for Teaching and Learning, Building

Assessment into Instruction, Teaching Mathematics to All Students, and Technology in the Mathematics Classroom. This initial work on campus was followed by a three-cycle sequence of two weeks of fieldwork in elementary classrooms and one week of class sessions on campus with one additional week on campus at the end of the semester. While in elementary classrooms, pre-service teachers assisted the classroom teacher with individual students and small groups of students; taught a mini-lesson or center activity to small groups; and co-taught one to two complete lessons to the whole class. Pre-service teachers were expected to think critically about what they were observing and experiencing in the elementary classroom in relationship to what they were reading and learning about in the university-based portion of the course. Through reflective journals written each week during the fieldwork, class discussions to debrief fieldwork, and reflective discussions and written responses to the videos of children solving mathematics problems, the pre-service teachers were actively engaged in critical reflection.

BACKGROUND

The National Council of Teachers of Mathematics (NCTM) and the standards movement which began in the United States in the 1980s, encouraged changes in the way in which mathematics is taught and learned. Reforming mathematics education was based on the premise of teaching children how to understand mathematics conceptually and procedurally by utilizing problem solving and reasoning in instruction (Battista, 1994). Later, the NCTM (2000) Principles and Standards consolidated the initial three separate NCTM standards publications that focused on curriculum, teaching, and assessment into one guiding document. The Principles and Standards (2000) document presented five primary content areas of mathematics including numbers and operations, algebra, geometry, data analysis and probability, and measurement and developed five process standards that NCTM believes should be integrated into mathematics teaching and learning. The five process standards NCTM espoused are problem solving, reasoning and proof, communication, connections, and representation. More recently, the Common Core State Standards (Council of Chief State School Officers & National Governors Association Center for Best Practices, 2010) reflect recommendations and findings from seminal mathematics education documents and literature such as the research synthesis contained in *Adding It Up* (National Research Council, 2001) and numerous NCTM publications about what and how mathematics should be learned.

Because of the robust nature of the mathematics that children need to learn, it is critical that pre-service teachers are prepared to help children learn with deep understanding. Not only do teachers need to develop sophisticated Mathematical Knowledge for Teaching (Ball, Thames, & Phelps, 2008; Hill, Rowan, & Ball, 2005) they also need to have a thorough understanding of how to recognize children's mathematical knowledge and thinking. Pre-service teachers that are preparing to enter the education field need to deepen their understanding of concepts from both a mathematical and pedagogical perspective, which includes their ability to understand and recognize their students' mathematical thinking and reasoning (Chapman, 2007). During initial preparation programs, pre-service teachers need repeated opportunities to thoughtfully practice the interactive work of teaching and gain a better understanding of how children think critically and reason about mathematics (Ball & Forzani, 2009). In order for pre-service teachers to better understand children's mathematical knowledge and thinking, they need to have experiences analyzing children's thinking (Jacobs, Lamb, & Philipp, 2010; Stockero, et al., 2017). Without these experiences, pre-service teachers will have a difficult time helping their future students understand and learn mathematics (Ball & Forzani, 2010). That is why it is so important for teachers to be able to notice their students' mathematical thinking and reasoning skills and then make instructional decisions based on those skills, which in turn will enable children to effectively learn mathematics.

MAIN FOCUS OF THE CHAPTER

Critical Thinking in Classrooms

Critical thinking has numerous conceptions across a variety of fields but is generally espoused as an educational goal (Hitchcock, 2018). While there is contention around a precise definition of critical thinking, Hitchcock asserted that the same basic concept anchors the differing conceptions of critical thinking. The basic concept of critical thinking can be described as careful thinking directed toward a goal (Hitchcock, 2018). Critical thinking has been incorporated into classrooms using either embedded methods where students are asked to engage in higher levels of cognition about content or with explicit instruction in critical thinking skills such as metacognition (Marin & Halpern, 2011). Explicit instruction has been found to produce greater student gains; however, both methods are effective for the development of critical thinking and can lead to positive student learning outcomes (Marin & Halpern, 2011). To support reforms like those called for in mathematics education, Gini-Newman and Case (2018) make a case for a reorientation to "thinking classrooms" where students are asked to think critically throughout the teaching and learning process. They argue for a shift away from classrooms where subject matter information is transferred directly from teachers to students before students are asked to think and reason (Gini-Newman & Case, 2018). One key factor in accomplishing this shift is that teachers' foundational beliefs about teaching and learning place thinking at the heart of classroom practices and activities (Gini-Newman & Case, 2018). A focus on critical thinking in mathematics teaching and learning can help students better understand what they are learning and make reasoned decisions about aspects of mathematics (Thomas, 2006). The Critical Thinking Consortium (CTC) (2013) emphasizes that selecting strategies for building number sense and mastery of basic facts can help students think critically. The CTC also emphasizes strategies such as deciding how to approach a problem for which students have no ready-made solution or procedure, choosing the most appropriate way to represent a mathematical situation, monitoring problem solving progress and adjusting as necessary, and having students analyze their own responses and analyzing if it makes sense (CTC, 2013).

Critical Thinking in Mathematics Education

Reform-based mathematics education encourages student learning through active engagement in constructing understanding of concepts, knowledge and skills. Students develop mathematical understanding through reasoning, reflecting, and refining their ideas (Battista, 1999). If one applies the basic concept of critical thinking as careful thinking toward a goal, this approach to mathematics education relies on critical thinking as teachers pose complex and interesting problems for which students work toward solutions, forming mathematical and logical arguments to support those solutions (Van De Walle, 2007). Further, when students engage in mathematical problem solving, mathematical ideas and mathematical thinking develop interactively with critical thinking (Lesh & Zawojewski, 2007). In this way, critical thinking does not stand alone but rather is inherently intertwined with students' thinking as they reason, reflect, justify, and refine their ideas and solutions through mathematical thinking. More than two decades ago, recommendations were made that in order to "develop powerful mathematical thinking in students, instruction must focus on, guide, and support their personal construction of ideas. Such instruction encourages students to invent, test, and refine their own ideas rather than to blindly follow procedures given to them by others" (Battista, 1999, p. 429). More recently, in *Principles to Actions: Ensuring Mathematical Success for All*, the NCTM proposed key principles derived from research for establishing and maintaining effective mathematics programs (NCTM, 2014). The first guiding principle, Teaching and Learning, includes eight Mathematics Teaching Practices supported by research as essential components for the implementation of effective teaching. One of the eight essential practices supported by research is for teachers to "elicit and use evidence of student thinking" as part of regular classroom instruction and assessment (NCTM, 2014, p. 10). Previous research indicates that teachers' mathematical knowledge for teaching is a key aspect of instructional decision making and that it relates to "habits of the mind" for teaching and learning mathematics (Ball & Hill, 2009, p. 70). One aspect of mathematical knowledge for teaching is a teacher's ability to notice a child's critical thinking about mathematics and adapt instruction accordingly. NCTM called for action from teachers to use evidence of student thinking to "advance student reasoning and sense making about important mathematical ideas and relationships," (NCTM, 2014, p. 57). These skills require critical thinking from the teacher about students' development of mathematics knowledge and skills. When pre-service elementary teachers learn to notice children's mathematical thinking, the beliefs pre-service teachers develop about mathematics as a subject as well as beliefs about mathematics understanding and learning are more sophisticated than if they do not learn those skills (Philipp, Ambrose, Lamb, Sowder, & Schappelle, 2007). Effective mathematics teaching and facilitation of students' growth relies on the knowledge, skills, and beliefs to notice, elicit, and use a child's mathematical thinking and reasoning and necessitates the utilization of critical thinking to respond with appropriate pedagogical patterns (Carpenter, Fennema, Peterson, Chiang, & Loef, 1989; Jacobs, et al., 2010; NCTM, 2014).

Critical Thinking in Educator Preparation

Educator preparation clearly must aim to improve pre-service teachers' knowledge and understanding of the content disciplines they will help students learn. Equally important is the aim to develop pre-service teachers' pedagogical knowledge and understanding relative to content. Teachers not only need to understand how to do mathematics themselves, but they also need to understand how to teach students to understand how to do mathematics (Ball & Forzani, 2010). Mathematical Knowledge for Teaching (MKT) has been conceptualized as the mathematical knowledge necessary for effective mathematics teaching and consists of two main domains– subject matter knowledge and pedagogical-content knowledge– with multiple subdomains (Ball, et al., 2008; Ball & Thames, 2010). MKT includes pedagogical content knowledge, which comprises the ability to understand the students in the classroom, as well as the content, and instruction (Ball & Thames, 2010). Effective teachers know how their students develop understanding of a content area and can use that knowledge to anticipate and respond to students' thinking and reasoning (Darling-Hammond & Bradsford, 2005). Pedagogical preparation in educator preparation programs should encompass a wide range of areas including the study of how students learn, analysis of student thinking, understanding of instructional methods to meet student learning needs, consideration of how to assess learning, and the social and emotional development of students (Wilson, Floden, Ferrini-Mundy, 2001). Opportunities to watch children think and reason about mathematics, whether in person or through video analysis, helps teachers refine their pedagogical practices and improves their MKT (Jacobs, et al., 2010; Roth McDuffie, et al., 2014; Teuscher, Switzer, & Morwood, 2016). Pre-service teachers must have the opportunity to strengthen their MKT, which includes their ability to notice children's mathematical thinking and reasoning.

RESEARCH METHODS

Research Context and Participants

This study examined pre-service teachers' views of elementary mathematics teaching and learning, and their ability to notice and use children's critical thinking about mathematics. The study was conducted by researchers who are teacher educators in a 4-year undergraduate elementary educator preparation program at an institution that identifies critical thinking as one of six core learning goals for earning a degree. The elementary education program curriculum was developed to acknowledge the importance of critical thinking to the practice of teaching. A purposeful, convenience sample of 157 pre-service teachers participated in the study. All of the teachers were from a large public university in the central part of the United States. The pre-service teachers in this project were in their third year of university study to become elementary teachers for children ages 6 years to 11 years old. The study spanned four semesters and included eight sections of the methods course. Two of the researchers also served as instructors of the methods course in addition to a third instructor. The instructors shared a common syllabus and collaborated on course content and delivery. All 157 pre-service teachers completed a video reflection both at the beginning and at the end of the semester in response to a child solving several mathematics problems. In addition, a total of nine case study pre-service teachers volunteered to participate in a semi-structured interview at the start and the close of the university course.

Data Sources and Analysis

The study included both qualitative and quantitative data on pre-service teachers' views of teaching and learning mathematics and on their critical thinking about children's mathematical thinking. Two data sources were analyzed to address the research questions. First, responses to a video reaction activity in which pre-service teachers were asked to watch a young student attempt to solve mathematics problems were analyzed for pre-service teachers' ability to notice and respond instructionally to a child's mathematical thinking. As a team, the researchers reviewed video responses from a pilot sample to refine theoretical categories derived from prior research (Aguirre, et al., 2013; Flake 2014; & Jacob, et al., 2010). This also allowed the researchers to establish a shared understanding of what would constitute a response to the reflection questions within each category. Each researcher categorized and scored the responses of the pre-service teachers independently from each other then compared the independent analysis for consistency. If all three researchers identified a response as the same category, the label was used as the final classification for that response. In cases where there was not initial unanimous agreement about a category label, the researchers discussed the response and usually retained a classification if two of the three researchers were in agreement. Tables 1, 2, and 3 include descriptions of how the responses were analyzed and classified within a category (Thomas, Huffman, & Flake, 2016). The categories were as-

Table 1. Question 1: What did the student do to solve the problem?

Category	Description
Novice	• Incorrect mathematical strategies stated • Incorrect use of mathematical strategies and knowledge • Lack of mathematical knowledge • List without description of strategies
Emerging	• Identified one or two strategies • Emerging description of the strategies used • Lack of attention to details of the strategies used to solve the problem • Lack of connection to mathematical concepts
Transitional	• Multiple strategies identified • Developing description of the strategies used • Strategies described with some connection to mathematics concepts
Skilled	• Multiple strategies identified • Specific and detailed description of the strategies used • Connections are made to the mathematical concepts • Descriptions include mathematically significant details • Evidence of a more sophisticated Mathematical Knowledge of Teaching

Table 2. Question 2: What did you learn about the student's mathematical understanding?

Category	Description
Novice	• No mathematical connection to the strategies used • No description of what the child mathematically understands
Emerging	• Incorrect or immature inferences about the mathematical understandings of the child • Lack of focus on the particular child • No evidence of interpretation of the child's understandings • Commentary on the child but not on the understandings
Transitional	• Descriptions show the ability to infer some basic mathematical understandings • Limited depth on the child's understandings • Some broad or undefined descriptions
Skilled	• Inferences have a richer description of mathematical understandings • Descriptions connect specific examples • Used details of the strategy to explain what the child understood

Table 3. Question 3: What would you do if you were the student's teacher to encourage growth?

Category	Description
Novice	• No evidence based on child understandings • Incorrect interpretation of the future mathematical experiences appropriate for the child • Incorrect mathematical statement • Teacher-centric (what the teacher would do or how *they* think the child should learn)
Emerging	• Very general descriptions for future mathematical teaching • Descriptions could be said without seeing the actual video of the child • Little or no reference to building on the child's understandings
Transitional	• Descriptions consider the child's strategy but does not consider the strategy in relationship to future concept development • Used the child's understandings in more of a general way
Skilled	• Robust description of how the child's strategies will be used for future concept development • Individualized for the students based on their understandings for concept development • Explicitly considers the child's existing strategies when thinking about the next steps • Knowledge about the next steps for children's mathematical development

signed a numeric code to enable quantitative analysis of the data. The pre/post video response scores were analyzed for significant differences through paired-sample t-tests conducted using SPSS.

Second, individual semi-structured interviews with nine pre-service teachers were conducted by two of the researchers during the first week and the last week of the university course. The purpose of the interviews was to gather insights into pre-service teachers' views of teaching and learning mathematics. The interviewers asked pre-service teachers to share their views and beliefs related to mathematics in the elementary classroom, their role as teachers, students' roles as learners, and what they envision as an ideal elementary mathematics lesson and classroom environment. Each interview lasted 15-30 minutes and was recorded, transcribed, and then analyzed to glean teachers' views and beliefs about elementary mathematics and teaching. The interview transcripts were first coded using an inductive process to identify and label distinct words, phrases, and passages. There were 45 initial codes established through the data analysis. Next, a constant comparative method was used to analyze the codes for patterns leading to the consolidation of codes and to inform the development of concepts. The concepts were then analyzed and compared to identify their interconnectedness and relationships to one another. Through this process the concepts were grouped into themes by commonality.

Video Reflection and Response

During a semester-long mathematics methods course pre-service teachers watched three distinct videos throughout the semester that each captured a child solving mathematics problems. The videos were used intentionally as instructional tools to facilitate the development of the teachers' ability to notice and propose how to elicit and use students' critical thinking in mathematics teaching. Each video featured a different child and focused on different stages of number and operation understanding and growth. The problems presented in each video were mathematics situations presented in a context. The contextual situations were written to represent the way in which children develop increasingly sophisticated understanding of numbers and operations (Fennema, Franke, Carpenter, & Carey, 1993; Jacobs, et al., 2010; Mulligan & Mitchelmore, 1997). After the pre-service teachers watched each video, they were given a response sheet, which asked three open-ended questions that prompted them to think critically about the child's mathematical thinking and implications for instruction. After responding to the questions individually, the teachers engaged in small group and whole class discussions facilitated by the instructor with the purpose of making the child's thinking and subsequent instructional implications more explicit. The mid-semester videos provided an opportunity for the teachers to think critically about student mathematical understanding and development.

The three question prompts following each video were:

1. What do you think the student is doing to figure out the answers to the problems?
2. What did you learn about the student's mathematical understandings?
3. What would you do as a teacher to encourage the student's mathematical understanding and growth?

These questions were adapted from a research project conducted by Jacobs, et al., (2010) in which they analyzed the teachers' levels of noticing of students' mathematical thinking. The videos used during the mathematics methods course were recorded to capture the processes and thinking a child used to solve mathematics problems. The problems were presented to the child using an interview protocol including probing questions about children's mathematical thinking. The video protocol was modeled after videos recorded and used by Jacobs, et al., (2010). The protocol included presenting increasingly challenging mathematics problems to the child, allowing the child to solve the problems, and then asking probing questions about how the child solved the problems to elicit the child's mathematical thinking about the problems. The video reflections from these videos were not analyzed for this study. This study analyzed responses to an additional video viewed by pre-service teachers at the beginning and end of the semester. After viewing the pre/post video, the teachers responded to the prompts above without additional discussion.

The pre/post video showed a first-grade girl solving contextual problems involving addition and subtraction. The girl was asked six questions related to numbers and operations. She was provided with concrete objects and paper and pencil to assist her in solving the problems posed in the questions. The first and second questions involved addition, with the second question involving numbers greater than ten. The girl used a pencil and made tally marks to answer the first question and figured out the second question in her head by using base-ten knowledge. The third and fourth questions presented subtraction situations. The girl demonstrated an understanding of the inverse relationship between addition and subtraction by thinking about the problem as an addition problem with a missing addend. The fifth and sixth questions were addition questions with larger two-digit numbers. Question five, the first of the more challenging questions, required her to determine the total number of paint cans on a shelf if originally there were 24 cans and 36 more were added. The girl made tally marks in groups of five and also used the counters. The sixth question involved larger numbers and asked how many paint cans there were if a shelf initially contained 58 paint cans and then 60 more were added. The girl, once again, made many tally marks on her paper and then counted the tally marks. She then used the cotton balls and continued to count up from where she had left off with the tally marks.

RESEARCH FINDINGS

Video Reflection and Response Results

The video reflection responses were analyzed based on theoretical categories derived from prior work of Aguirre, et al., (2013), Flake (2014), and Jacob, et al., (2010). Responses were categorized and scored as either: *novice (0), emerging (1), transitional (2), or skilled (3)*. The reflection questions that pre-service teachers answered reveal insights into their critical thinking about teaching and learning elementary mathematics. Overall, the response questions elicited the pre-service teachers' critical thinking related to mathematics content and pedagogy. Separately, the questions focused on the teachers' ability to notice a child's strategies and thinking to solve a mathematics problem, their awareness of how mathematical ideas develop, what the elementary mathematics instructional context requires for desired learning outcomes to be reached, as well as their inclination to use their knowledge and awareness to propose classroom practice (Schussler, et al., 2010). The video reaction results indicate that more than three quarters of the pre-service teachers embark on a mathematics methods course at the *novice* or *emerging* category of overall skill in noticing children's mathematical thinking (see Table 4). A pre-service teacher identified in these categories responds to the reflection questions in ways that demonstrate a surface level of understand-ing mathematics, a procedural view of learning mathematics, and often a general approach to teaching children mathematics. This is not uncommon for pre-service teachers in the United States (Jacobs, et al., 2010). At the conclusion of the semester, which included more than 45 hours of classroom fieldwork with elementary students, over one quarter of pre-service teachers had moved to either the *transitional* or *skilled* category in noticing children's strategies for solving problems. One third progressed to the *transitional* or *skilled* category for interpreting what the student's thinking revealed about mathematical understanding. One fifth progressed to the *transitional* category in their ability to describe subsequent instructional moves based on children's mathematical development and very few pre-service teachers' responses were categorized as *skilled* in this area at the end of the semester. The results of the paired samples t-test on the three video questions indicated that the pre-service teachers significantly increased their score from pre to post on all three video questions. There was a significant increase on question #1 (M=.45, SD=.82, t(156)=6.91, p=0.00) question #2 (M=.60, SD= .66, t(156)=11.39, p=0.00) and question #3 (M=.59, SD .84, t(156)=8.74, p=0.00. See Table 4. These findings provide evidence that during the semester the pre-service teachers' grew in their ability to recognize the child's strategies, to interpret the child's mathematical thinking and understanding, and in their ability to propose a response to the student based on the child's mathematical understandings.

Interview Results

Analysis of the interview transcripts indicates that after a semester-long mathematics methods course, pre-service teachers developed more sophisticated thinking and moved from *novice/emerging* understanding to *emerging/transitional* understanding of a classroom environment that supports students' critical thinking in mathematics. When pushed to propose specifically how they will enact a classroom environment in which they can elicit and use student critical thinking in mathematics, most of the pre-service teachers can identify general practices that reflect the features of a reform oriented, thinking classroom. However, many struggle to move beyond *novice* and *emerging* levels in their ability to explain specifically how to encourage and support students' growth and understanding of particular mathematics concepts and competencies.

Beginning Views and Beliefs

At the beginning of the mathematics methods course eight of the nine pre-service teachers interviewed described an elementary mathematics classroom from a historical teacher-centered, "review-teach-practice" perspective. Initially, most of the pre-service teachers described elementary mathematics as students memorizing formulas and facts, doing drills, and practicing problems on worksheets. One pre-service

Table 4. Video response scores

Score	Q1 – Pre		Q1 – Post		Q2 – Pre		Q2 – Post		Q3 – Pre		Q3 – Post	
	N	%	N	%	N	%	N	%	N	%	N	%
0	25	15.9	9	5.7	43	27.4	8	5.1	94	59.9	38	24.2
1	92	58.6	66	42.0	96	61.1	79	50.3	56	35.7	77	49.0
2	39	24.8	68	43.3	17	10.8	62	39.5	6	3.8	40	25.5
3	1	0.6	14	8.9	1	0.6	8	5.1	1	0.6	2	1.3
Mean	1.10		1.55		0.85		1.45		0.45		1.04	
SD	(.65)		(.74)		(.62)		(.67)		(.60)		(.74)	

teacher explained, "I would start the day by asking if anyone has questions over the homework and spend a lot of time going over questions. So, spend a lot of time going over the homework and then cover a new concept, do some sort of activity, and yes, there will be worksheets," (A.S. pre 8:30). Another stated, "I think it is important to have a period of time where I am explaining how to do the problem…and I do think it's important that they are able to practice," (E.S. pre 6:52). At the same time, over half of the pre-service teachers expressed the belief that students should be able to connect mathematics to "real world" experiences, that mathematics should be "fun" and that students should do "hands-on" activities. In the section of the interview above where E.S. described that she would explain how to do the problem, she also expressed a desire to "have a lot of hands-on, visual stuff and after I explain the process, give [elementary students] manipulatives and they try the process," (E.S. pre 7:07). T.M.'s explanation followed the same pattern when she said she would "initially introduce the topic of the day and go over homework from the last class and clarify any issues…then definitely include some real life examples of the topic of the day," (T.M. pre 6:57). She thought "there should be a balance between lecture and asking students questions" as well as "working with hands-on but then also stuff on the board" that would be followed by assigning homework and some sort of assessment, (T.M. pre 8:01).

One challenge that pre-service teachers faced at the beginning of the semester was how to use manipulatives or activities to prompt critical thinking about mathematics. Seven of the nine teachers interviewed described how they as the teacher would model using the manipulatives or give step-by-step instructions for how to complete the activities rather than pose investigations or problems that would encourage students to think critically about the mathematics. As one teacher stated, "I'll have an overhead projector and I'll tell the students how I am going to solve the problem, give them a sample easy question that they will follow along with me and I'll show them what I'll do with my base 10 blocks on the overhead. After that, students will get into groups and I will put different problems on the overhead and we will all figure them out together," (N.S. pre 5:57). Another pre-service teacher explained that she would "definitely show students--this is how you can do it," (L.H. pre 4:16), adding that if there was a mathematical problem or scenario she would demonstrate for students "this is what we're going to do, we are going to do it with manipulatives like this, then I would have students do it with pencil and paper, showing them how it all connects together," (L.H. pre 4:21). These case interview results are consistent with the responses to the video reflection question when the teachers were asked how they would encourage student mathematical understanding and growth. At the beginning of the semester, 60% of the pre-service teachers gave responses that were scored at the *novice* level, indicating a teacher-centric approach that relied on rote memorization of procedural knowledge and demonstrated a lack of attention to the child's mathematical thinking or understanding.

Reoriented Views and Beliefs

Interviews conducted at the end of the semester captured the reorientation of pre-service teachers' views about elementary mathematics teaching and learning to a more dynamic view of mathematics as a discipline and of mathematics teaching and learning. They expressed beliefs that mathematics is best learned in a problem-based classroom that focuses on developing an understanding of the relationships among mathematics ideas, concepts, and procedures. The change from viewing mathematics in elementary classrooms as static rules to be memorized to a dynamic discipline that can be used to represent situations and solve problems was shared by several pre-service teachers in their end of semester interview. When asked what comes to mind when she thinks about elementary school mathematics, P.G. said, "it's not plugging numbers into formulas but truly understanding mathematics concepts, relationships and how to use it [mathematics] in real world situations, (P.G. post 0:31). In contrast, when asked the same question during the interview at the beginning of the semester, the first and only thing P.G. described was memorizing rules and procedures such as the long division algorithm and how she struggled in mathematics and was often confused. At the beginning of the semester, L.H. described mathematics in elementary school as "addition, subtraction, early multiplication, and times tables because those were drilled into my head," (L.H. pre 0:09). Following the mathematics methods course her views of mathematics represented the change shared by other pre-service teachers when she said, "I think about a lot of modeling. Math is a way of thinking so having students explain their thinking. Students should use math to solve problems and view it as a tool," (L.H. post 1:02). This statement also captured the way in which pre-service teachers shifted their prospective for thinking about mathematics in elementary classrooms. All nine of the pre-service teachers moved from thinking of themselves as students to thinking of themselves as teachers helping students learn, providing further evidence of their development beyond the *novice* or beginning stages.

At the end of the methods coursework and fieldwork in elementary classrooms, eight of the nine pre-service teachers expressed a desire to utilize student-centered classroom practices that encourage communication about mathematics and that foster student critical thinking. The ninth pre-service teacher shared that she appreciated that there are multiple ways to approach mathematics problems but she did not translate that idea into a description about how she would promote critical thinking in a classroom. A classroom environment where students "learn how to approach problems through problem solving with an overall focus on critical thinking...learn to think things out" is how E.S. explained her views of elementary mathematics, (E.S. post 0:46). A.S. emphasized her belief that "students should learn different ways of solving mathematics problems but first they should have time to figure it [solutions to problems] out themselves. Students need to be able to problem solve on their own and understand basic concepts," (A.S. post 3:25). She elaborated and said, "students need to be interacting and thinking. So instead of just sitting and listening to the teacher they need to be interacting and thinking and problem solving...there should be discussions about the mathematics and the thinking," (A.S. post 4:51). To highlight their views of the importance of developing students' critical thinking, a few of the pre-service teachers described a misalignment between what they believed about elementary mathematics classrooms and what they experienced during the fieldwork. As one explained, "What I have seen is it's not very, well they [students] don't think a lot, it's a lot of processes...instead of being asked to think and figure things out. The teachers I have observed read from a script and told the students, this is exactly how you are supposed to do it and they did not really give students any opportunity to think critically about the mathematics. It went by too fast, they weren't given time to think. Students should be thinking critically about the mathematics ideas and concepts," (R.U. post 0:14). N.S. said that as a teacher he wants to "teach the concepts of math and to get them [students] to think and discover the math ideas conceptually" (N.S. post 2:28), which is different from what he experienced as a learner and what he observed in fieldwork. He shared, "The experience we had in the classroom, they [students] didn't really have much of a foundation or background for the concepts. For me, growing up I was always taught the procedures and didn't necessarily know why I should know the procedures," (N.S. post 0:52). He continued to describe the importance of a classroom environment that supports children's thinking through "hands-on and group activities, giving them [students] choice...and allowing them to have objects in front of them to work things out is huge," (N.S. post 4:15).

When asked to describe an ideal mathematics lesson, eight of the pre-service teachers described beginning the lesson by engaging students in thinking about a problem or an inquiry activity through which students can explore mathematics content and relationships to make conjectures. In contrast to her views at the beginning of the semester, T.M. explained that ideal lessons were those in which students are encouraged to "discover the procedure themselves and are able to articulate" their thinking. She elaborated, "You need to probe for their thinking processes and let them discover things themselves through an inquiry-based lesson," (T.M. post 8:02). She believed "any formal presentation during a lesson should come after students have spent time working individually or with others on an activity," (T.M. post 8:40). At the beginning of the semester, N.S. said he would show students how he would solve problems and demonstrate how to do the mathematics. By the end of the semester, his views were reoriented as evidenced by his explanation of an ideal elementary mathematics lesson as one in which students are given a problem or task and the teacher allows students "to try to figure it out on their own," (N.S. post 5:10). He continued to describe his role during this portion of the lesson as listening to students as they share their thinking and strategies. He would then use what he discovered about their understanding to guide a whole class discussion about the mathematics of the problem or task so that students could "really get that light bulb moment for themselves rather than giving it to them at the beginning of the lesson," (N.S. post 6:03).

All of the nine pre-service teachers interviewed referenced what they observed in elementary classrooms during the fieldwork of the course and how those observations helped reshape their views and beliefs about mathematics teaching and learning. Interestingly, those who described placements in classrooms that reflected a teacher-centric "review-teach-practice" model shared how they believed the classroom environment should be different from what they observed. Their views aligned with the vision of a "thinking classroom" conceptualized by Gini-Newman and Case (2018). These views were represented by A.S. when she said, "it's important for a teacher to discuss with students and not just speak to them. I observed classes that were not like that and the teacher did all the talking without engaging students. But I think there should be discussions about the mathematics and the thinking. Students should be talking with each other and sharing their thinking, utilizing multiple representations of mathematics concepts and ideas and utilizing a variety of tools," (A.S. post 5:55).

SOLUTIONS AND RECOMMENDATIONS

Teacher education programs are a vehicle for pre-service teachers to begin to study the professional work of teaching and to start their professional journey of developing and refining competencies of an effective teacher. While mathematics methods courses only provide a beginning to a teacher's journey, the courses and experiences can be carefully constructed to advance a pre-service teacher's views, beliefs, and abilities to become an effective elementary mathematics teacher. To cultivate improvement in pre-service teachers' abilities, mathematics methods courses need to provide opportunities for them to attend to a child's mathematics thinking through thoughtful reflection (Flake, 2014; Jacobs, et al., 2010). Pre-service teachers should spend time watching children do mathematics, then discussing with their peers, their course instructor, and practicing teachers what they notice. Providing pre-service teachers with opportunities to observe children whether it is in an elementary classroom or through video can help them continue to improve in their ability to attend to children's mathematics growth and development. Pre-service teachers should be prompted to think critically about how the child's strategies and approach to problems reveals the child's knowledge and understanding. Purposeful dialogue between the instructor and the pre-service teachers about what they are seeing and comprehending about the child's understandings is equally important.

Video reflection results of this study showed pre-service teachers improved their ability to notice and interpret student thinking at the conclusion of a mathematics methods course. Interview results with a case sample of the pre-service teachers provided insights into their views of children's mathematics learning and how to teach mathematics to elementary school aged children. The researchers propose that features of the mathematics methods course contributed to the positive results of the study and recommend that mathematics teacher educators include similar elements into mathematics methods courses. In particular, the instructors of the mathematics methods course from this study used the three question prompts as an analytic framework for reflective discussions and written responses to the videos of children solving mathematics problems. Assisting pre-service teachers' in developing the ability to notice and respond to children's mathematical thinking becomes more explicit and effective when an analytic framework is used (Stockero, et al., 2017). The researchers therefore recommend the intentional use of an analytic framework in mathematics methods courses.

FUTURE RESEARCH DIRECTIONS

This study investigated pre-service teachers' views of children's critical thinking and their views towards eliciting and using students' critical thinking in mathematics teaching. While the findings of this study provide evidence of pre-services teachers' re-orientations toward mathematics teaching and learning, and their increased ability to notice children's mathematical thinking, future research that explores how those re-oriented views and beliefs influence actual teaching practices in classrooms is needed. The field needs studies that follow pre-service teachers into their future classrooms and investigate how they attend to and interpret children's mathematics thinking, then make instructional decisions to promote mathematics learning and growth. In their chapter synthesizing research on teacher preparation, Cochran-Smith and Villegas (2015) identified three trends that have influenced major programs of research in teacher education and that align with the shift to a global knowledge-based economy. They credited new understandings about how people learn and what they need to know in a knowledge-based economy as one trend shaping teacher education and teacher education research. These changes also contributed to the widely accepted conception of teaching as engaging students in authentic tasks involving higher levels of thinking and problem-solving with responsiveness to students' developing understanding (Cochran-Smith & Villegas, 2015). In contemporary research literature, Cochran-Smith and Villegas found that, "the practice of teaching is conceptualized broadly to include reflection, collaboration, inquiry, and decision making," (p. 480, 2015). Because this conception of teaching relies on teachers who think critically about their beliefs and how their actions influence learning, teacher education programs need to attend to pre-service teachers' views and beliefs, provide opportunities for pre-service teachers to think critically about their developing roles as teachers, and to reflect on the influence their instructional decisions will have on supporting students' deep learning. The field would benefit from more in-depth studies on teachers' thinking about mathematics instruction.

CONCLUSION

The pre-service teachers in this study began the semester with underlying beliefs that mathematics teaching and learning consist of teachers transferring information and students absorbing and memorizing information. These views served as a filter for what they initially noticed about a child's mathematical thinking and how they proposed to respond instructionally to the child. At the beginning of the semester, a majority of the 157 pre-service teachers responded that they would tell or show the child what to do to correctly add the numbers, most often describing showing the child how to "line up" the digits in the numbers and add each column separately, and then they would give the child more practice problems. These findings are consistent with the seminal work of Dan Lortie (1975) and his notion that years of observation as students in classrooms frame the beliefs that teachers hold about teaching and learning through the "apprenticeship of observation." When the pre-service teachers were students in an elementary mathematics classroom they did not have access to their teacher's reasoning and thinking about teaching and learning. The pre-service teachers in this study initially anchored their responses to experiences they had as students in elementary mathematics classrooms. They intuitively and imitatively described what they had observed about teaching mathematics as the ideal, without regard for how the teaching behaviors they observed might influence what is learned about mathematics.

The beliefs that pre-service teachers bring with them into their preparation program through an apprenticeship of observation can make it difficult for them to change or reorient their views because they tend not to think of themselves as *novice* or having much more to learn (Feiman-Nemser, 2012). Holt-Reynolds (1992) found that pre-service teachers relied on their beliefs about good mathematics teaching developed as learners to justify why they still believed that teacher centered practices like lecturing were superior to student centered practices that encourage student reasoning and thinking about mathematics. Holt-Reynolds (1992) found that pre-service teachers rationalized that "lecturing had helped them learn math; therefore, they saw lecturing as an inherent, necessary feature of good instruction in math," (pp. 334-335). Despite impediments to changing beliefs such as those found by Holt-Reynolds (1992) and Feiman-Nemser (2012), the pre-service teachers in this study ended the semester with views and beliefs more closely aligned with reform-oriented practices for mathematics teaching and learning than they held at the beginning of the semester. Rather than using Lortie's apprenticeship of observation as the explanation for why pre-service teachers go on to replicate the teacher centered practices they observed as learners, those experiences can and should be used in productive ways in mathematics methods courses (Feiman-Nemser, 2001; Mewborn & Tyminski, 2006). An early assignment in the mathematics methods course the pre-service teachers in this study completed was to write and illustrate a Mathematics Life Story. This mathematics autobiography asked pre-service teachers to reflect on their educational backgrounds and throughout the semester served as a baseline for them to reconcile their beliefs with what they were learning from course readings, discussions, and observations.

Schneider and Plasman (2011) advised that in the progression of learning pedagogical content knowledge pre-service teachers first need to think critically about the student doing the learning, then to focus on the instruction, and finally to reflect on both the learning and teaching. Facilitating this learning progression in a mathematics methods course includes pre-service teachers thinking critically about the views and beliefs they bring with them to their preparation program (Boyd, Gorham, Justice, & Anderson, 2013; Feiman-Nemser, 2001; Feiman-Nemser, 2012; Mewborn & Tyminski, 2006), engaging in mathematically rich experiences within their own learning experiences (Turner, et al, 2012), and thinking critically about children's mathematics thinking (Jacobs, et. al., 2010; Stockero, et al., 2017).

A recurring in-class activity during the mathematics methods course was the child video reflection and response that engaged pre-service teachers in analysis of and discussion about a child's thinking while solving problems. The video reflection and response activity served as a catalyst for the teachers to hone their competencies for noticing and responding to children's mathematics thinking. This activity was implemented using an analytic framework reflected in the video question prompts. The class discussions and video question prompts also provided them with metacognitive scaffolding as recommended by Sleep and Boerst (2012) for preparing pre-service teachers to interpret student' mathematical thinking.

The findings of this study demonstrate that pre-service teachers reoriented their views about mathematics teaching and learning. The quantitative findings from the video response showed a statistically significant change toward more sophisticated abilities to notice a child's mathematics thinking and in turn to propose how to encourage the child's mathematical understandings and growth through teaching practices that build on the child's current knowledge of mathematical concepts and relationships. During the interviews at the end of the course nearly all of the pre-service teachers had reoriented their views of mathematics teaching and learning and described an ideal elementary mathematics lesson as centered around students' mathematical thinking and problem solving. The video response results and the interview results demonstrated that the pre-service teachers advanced on the continuum toward reform-based notions and responses that reflect what Gini-Newman and Case (2018) described as "thinking classrooms" as opposed to knowledge transfer classrooms. Because of the positive findings from this study, the researchers suggest that mathematics teacher educators consider incorporating opportunities for pre-service teachers to think critically about how their own experiences as learners of mathematics influence their views and beliefs about children's mathematical thinking as children do mathematics. The researchers also suggest that pre-service teachers think critically about how instructional decisions they make will influence the mathematics classroom environment to promote learning.

REFERENCES

Aguirre, J. M., Turner, E. E., Bartell, T. G., Kalinec-Craig, C., Foote, M. Q., McDuffie, A. R., & Drake, C. (2013). Making connections in practice: How prospective elementary teachers connect to children's mathematical thinking and community funds of knowledge in mathematics instruction. *Journal of Teacher Education, 64*(2), 178–192. doi:10.1177/0022487112466900

Ball, D. L., & Forzani, F. M. (2009). The work of teaching and the challenge for teacher education. *Journal of Teacher Education, 60*(5), 14.

Ball, D. L., & Forzani, F. M. (2010). What does it take to make a teacher? *Phi Delta Kappan, 92*(2), 5. doi:10.1177/003172171009200203

Ball, D. L., & Hill, H. (2009). The curious-and-crucial case of mathematical knowledge for teaching. *Phi Delta Kappan, 91*(2), 3.

Ball, D. L., Thames, M. H., & Phelps, G. (2008). Content knowledge for teaching: What makes it special? *Journal of Teacher Education, 59*(5), 389–407. doi:10.1177/0022487108324554

Battista, M. (1994). Teacher beliefs and the reform movement in mathematics education. *Phi Delta Kappan, 75*, 5.

Battista, M. T. (1999). The mathematical miseducation of America's youth: Ignoring research and scientific study in education. *Phi Delta Kappan, 80*(6), 9.

Boyd, A., Gorham, J., Justice, J., & Anderson, J. (2013). Examining the apprenticeship of observation with preservice teachers: The practice of blogging to facilitate autobiographical reflection and critique. *Teacher Education Quarterly*.

Carpenter, T. P., Fennema, E., Peterson, P. L., Chiang, C., & Loef, M. (1989). Using knowledge of children's mathematics thinking in classroom teaching: An experimental study. *American Educational Research Journal, 26*(4), 32. doi:10.3102/00028312026004499

Chapman, O. (2007). Facilitating preservice teachers' development of mathematics knowledge for teaching arithmetic operations. *Journal of Mathematics Teacher Education, 10*(2), 8.

Cochran-Smith, M., & Villegas, A. M. (2015). Research on teacher preparation: Charting the landscape of a sprawling field. In D. H. Gitomer & C. A. Bell (Eds.), *Handbook of research on teaching* (5th ed.; pp. 439–548). Washington, DC: American Educational Research Association.

Council of Chief State School Officers & National Governors Association Center for Best Practices. (2010). *Common core state standards for mathematics.* Author.

Critical Thinking Consortium. (2013). *Critical thinking in elementary mathematics: What? Why? When? and How?* Retrieved from https://tc2.ca/uploads/PDFs/TIpsForTeachers/CT_elementary_math.pdf

Darling-Hammond, L., & Bransford, J. (2005). *Preparing teachers for a changing world.* San Francisco, CA: John Wiley & Sons, Inc.

Feiman-Nemser, S. (2001). From preparation to practice: Designing a continuum to strengthen and sustain teaching. *Teachers College Record, 103*(6), 42. doi:10.1111/0161-4681.00141

Feiman-Nemser, S. (2012). *Teachers as learners.* Cambridge, MA: Harvard Education Press.

Fennema, E., Franke, M. L., Carpenter, T. P., & Carey, D. (1993). Using children's mathematical knowledge in instruction. *American Educational Research Journal, 30*(3), 28. doi:10.3102/00028312030003555

Flake, M. (2014). *An investigation of how pre-service teachers' ability to professionally notice children's mathematical thinking relates to their own mathematical knowledge for teaching* (Unpublished doctoral dissertation). University of Kansas, Lawrence, KS.

Gini-Newman, G., & Case, R. (2018). *Creating thinking classrooms: Leading educational change for this century.* Thousand Oaks, CA: Sage.

Hill, H. C., Rowan, B., & Ball, D. L. (2005). Effects of teachers' mathematical knowledge for teaching on student achievement. *American Educational Research Journal, 42*(2), 371–406. doi:10.3102/00028312042002371

Hitchcock, D. (2018). Critical thinking. In E. N. Zalta (Ed.), *The Stanford Encyclopedia of Philosophy.* Academic Press. Retrieved from https://plato.stanford.edu/cgibin/encyclopedia/archinfo.cgi?entry=critical-thinking

Holt-Reynolds, D. (1992). Personal history-based beliefs as relevant prior knowledge in coursework. *American Educational Research Journal, 29*(2), 325–349. doi:10.3102/00028312029002325

Jacobs, V. R., Lamb, L. L. C., & Philipp, R. A. (2010). Professional noticing of children's mathematical thinking. *Journal for Research in Mathematics Education, 41*(2), 33.

Lesh, R. A., & Zawojewski, J. (2007). Problem solving and modeling. In F. Lester (Ed.), *Second Handbook of Research on Mathematics Teaching and Learning* (pp. 763–804). Charlotte, NC: Information Age Publishing, Inc.

Lortie, D. (1975). *Schoolteacher: A sociological study*. London: University of Chicago Press.

Marin, L. M., & Halpern, D. F. (2011). Pedagogy for developing critical thinking in adolescents: Explicit instruction produces greatest gains. *Thinking Skills and Creativity, 6*(1), 1–13. doi:10.1016/j.tsc.2010.08.002

Mewborn, D., & Tyminski, A. (2006). Lortie's apprenticeship of observation revisited. *For the Learning of Mathematics, 26*(3), 30–32.

Mulligan, J. T., & Mitchelmore, M. C. (1997). Young children's intuitive models of multiplication and division. *Journal for Research in Mathematics Education, 28*(3), 309–330. doi:10.2307/749783

National Council of Teacher of Mathematics. (2014). *Principles to actions: Ensuring mathematical success for all*. Reston, VA: National Council of Teachers of Mathematics.

National Research Council. (2001). *Adding it up: Helping Children Learn Mathematics*. Washington, DC: The National Academies Press.

Philipp, R. A., Ambrose, R., Lamb, L. L., Sowder, J. T., Schappelle, B. P., Sowder, L., ... Chauvot, J. (2007). Effect of early field experiences on the mathematical content knowledge and beliefs of prospective elementary school teachers: An experimental study. *Journal for Research in Mathematics Education, 38*(5), 38.

Roth McDuffie, A., Foote, M. Q., Bolson, C., Turner, E. E., Aguirre, J. M., Bartell, T. G., ... Land, T. (2014). Using video analysis to support prospecitve K-8 teachers' noticing of students' multiple mathematical knowledge bases. *Journal of Mathematics Teacher Education, 17*(3), 245–258. doi:10.100710857-013-9257-0

Schneider, R. M., & Plasman, K. (2011). Science teacher learning progressions: A review of science teachers' pedagogical content knowledge development. *Review of Educational Research, 81*(4), 35. doi:10.3102/0034654311423382

Schussler, D., Stooksberry, L., & Bercaw, L. (2010). Understanding teacher candidate dispositions: Reflecting to build self-awareness. *Journal of Teacher Education, 61*(4), 350–363. doi:10.1177/0022487110371377

Sleep, L., & Boerst, T. (2012). Preparing beginning teachers to elicit and interpret students' mathematical thinking. *Teaching and Teacher Education, 28*(7), 1038–1048. doi:10.1016/j.tate.2012.04.005

Stockero, S. L., Rupnow, R. L., & Pascoe, A. E. (2017). Learning to notice important student mathematical thinking in complex classroom interactions. *Teaching and Teacher Education*, *63*, 384–395. doi:10.1016/j.tate.2017.01.006

Teuscher, D., Switzer, J. M., & Morwood, T. (2016). Unpacking the practice of probing student thinking. *Mathematics Teacher Educator*, *5*(1), 47–64. doi:10.5951/mathteaceduc.5.1.0047

Thomas, K., Huffman, D., & Flake, M. (2016). Pre-service elementary teacher dispositions and responsive pedagogical patterns in mathematics. In A. G. Welsh & S. Areepattamannil (Eds.), *Dispositions in Teacher Education: A Global Perspective*. Boston, MA: Sense Publishers. doi:10.1007/978-94-6300-552-4_2

Thomas, K. R. (2006). Students THINK: A framework for improving problem solving. *Teaching Children Mathematics*, *13*(2), 86–95.

Turner, E. E., Drake, C., McDuffie, A. R., Aguirre, J., Bartell, T. G., & Foote, M. Q. (2012). Promoting equity in mathematics teacher preparation: A framework for advancing teacher learning of children's multiple mathematics knowledge bases. *Journal of Mathematics Teacher Education*, *15*(1), 15. doi:10.100710857-011-9196-6

Van De Walle, J. A. (2007). *Elementary and middle school mathematics* (6th ed.). Boston, MA: Pearson Education.

Wilson, S. M., Floden, R. E., & Ferrini-Mundy, J. (2001). Teacher preparation research. An insider's view from the outside. *Journal of Teacher Education*, *53*(3), 12.

ADDITIONAL READING

Callejo, M. L., & Zapatera, A. (2017). Prospective primary teachers' noticing of students' understanding of pattern generalization. *Journal of Mathematics Teacher Education*, *20*(4), 309–333. doi:10.100710857-016-9343-1

Doerr, H. M., & Lesh, R. (2003). A modeling perspective on teacher development. In R. Lesh & H. M. Doerr (Eds.), *Beyond constructivism. Models and modeling perspectives on mathematics problem solving, learning, and teaching* (pp. 125–139). Mahwah, NJ: Erlbaum.

Even, R., & Tirosh, D. (2008). Teacher knowledge and understanding of students' mathematical learning and thinking. In L. D. English (Ed.), *Handbook of international research in mathematics education* (2nd ed.; pp. 202–222). New York, NY: Routledge.

Franke, M. L., & Kazemi, E. (2001). Learning to teach mathematics: Focus on student thinking. *Theory into Practice*, *40*(2), 102–109. doi:10.120715430421tip4002_4

Lesh, R., & Doerr, H. M. (2003). Foundations of a models and modeling perspective on mathematics teaching, learning, and problem solving. In R. Lesh & H. M. Doerr (Eds.), *Beyond constructivism. Models and modeling perspectives on mathematics problem solving, learning, and teaching* (pp. 3–34). Mahwah, NJ: Erlbaum. doi:10.4324/9781410607713

Simpson, A., & Haltiwanger, L. (2017). "This is the first time I've done this": Exploring secondary prospective mathematics teachers' noticing of student's mathematics thinking. *Journal of Mathematics Teacher Education*, 20(4), 335–355. doi:10.100710857-016-9352-0

Thomas, K. (2013). Changing mathematics teaching practices and improving student outcomes through collaborative evaluation. *Teacher Education and Practice*, 26(4).

Thomas, K., & Hart, J. (2010). Pre-Service teachers' perceptions of model eliciting activities. In R. Lesh, et al. (Eds.), Modeling Students' Mathematical Modeling Competencies. New York: Springer Science+Business Media, LLC.

KEY TERMS AND DEFINITIONS

Children's Mathematics Thinking: The ways in which children reason about process of doing mathematics and analyze the relationships among the central ideas of mathematics.

Mathematics Education: The systems that encompass aspects of teaching, learning, and assessing mathematics.

Mixed-Methods: The integration of qualitative and quantitative methods of research.

Pre-Service Teachers: Students enrolled in an initial educator preparation program, studying to become practicing teachers.

Problem-Based: The use of problems or tasks as a vehicle for student learning.

Problem-Solving: The process of analyzing a situation or problem to reach a solution.

Teacher Development: The progression of teacher learning during a professional career.

Video Reaction: The act of reflecting on and responding to video recorded events.

Section 3

Situating Critical Thinking in Instructional and Informational Contexts

Chapter 14
Critical Thinking:
Centering Teachers' Knowledge and Understanding

Karen S. C. Thomas
St. Vincent and the Grenadines Community College, Saint Vincent and the Grenadines

ABSTRACT

Teaching critical thinking skills to students has become a central focus the language arts classroom. It is therefore important to examine what critical thinking may look like for the language arts teacher: How do language arts teachers come to know and understand? How do language arts teachers engage in critical thinking in order to enhance their pedagogical practices? This chapter examines the ways in which teachers' involvement in developing their critical thinking skills can aid them in establishing their knowledge and understandings. The chapter explores findings from a study that involved teachers in Grades 2 and 4 in the development of a framework for reading instruction in the primary grades. These findings make a case for encouraging teachers to engage in critical thinking in professional learning communities that foster professional development and collaboration in an active and reflective process.

INTRODUCTION

Interwoven in the evolving quilt that shapes effective pedagogy at all levels of learning is the construct of critical thinking. Critical thinking is one of the skills that employers require of their novice and experienced employees. In the classroom, the ability to think critically is one of the major indicators of successful learning and application. The ability to think critically is an essential life skill (Frijters, ten Dam & Rijlaarsdam, 2008). Often, emphasis is placed primarily on determining exactly how teachers develop critical thinking skills among students. In some professional development sessions, teachers receive resources that provide numerous strategies, activities, routines and protocols that can be used to develop critical thinking skills among their students (Guskey & Suk Yoon, 2009). These approaches have had some success in the classroom. In conjunction with the general consensus that students must be explicitly taught how to think critically across disciplines, is the acknowledgement that the quality of critical thinking in which teachers themselves engage must also be targeted.

DOI: 10.4018/978-1-5225-7829-1.ch014

Copyright © 2019, IGI Global. Copying or distributing in print or electronic forms without written permission of IGI Global is prohibited.

There is an interdependent relationship between teaching and learning and so, the expectation is that language arts teachers who teach critical thinking skills to students, must also be critical thinkers themselves. An essential question that this chapter seeks to address is how language arts teachers can centre their sense of knowing and understanding through critical thinking. There is no one simple response to this question; nonetheless, there are some understandings that teachers can embrace in an effort to harness their critical thinking skills. In an attempt to centre teachers' knowledge and understandings, transactions that result in a collective conceptualization of critical thinking are paramount. Similarly, the processes that facilitate the ways in which language arts teachers come to know and understand must be explored. The anticipated result is that these understandings will highlight some ways in which teachers come to know and come to understand language arts content and pedagogy, in an effort to improve teaching and learning in the language arts classroom. Since the goal of teachers' understandings through critical thinking is improved instructional practice, the contexts that best facilitate teachers' coming to knowledge and deeper understandings must also be examined.

Critical Thinking: An Emerging Definition

Research indicates that there is no consensus regarding a single definition of critical thinking; however, an exploration of different perspectives of critical thinking would help to centre the understandings that undergird this chapter. For instance, in the 1980s, The Delphi Report's contribution to the discourse on critical thinking was one that explained "critical thinking to be purposeful, self-regulatory judgment which results in interpretation, analysis, evaluation, and inference, as well as explanation of the evidential, conceptual, methodological, criteriological, or contextual considerations upon which that judgment is based" (p. 2). Facione, in the Delphi Report (1989) emphasized that critical thinking is essential as a tool of inquiry and as such, critical thinking is a liberating force in education and a powerful resource in one's personal and civic life (p. 3).

Another definition of critical thinking is one in which Paul, Fisher and Nosich (1993) propose that:

Critical thinking is that mode of thinking – about any subject, content or problem – in which the thinker improves the quality of his or her thinking by skilfully taking charge of the structures inherent in thinking and imposing intellectual standards upon them (p. 4).

More recently, Halpern (2011) has defined critical thinking as:

the use of those cognitive skills or strategies that increase the probability of a desirable outcome. It is purposeful, reasoned, and goal directed. It is the kind of thinking involved in solving problems, formulating inferences, calculating likelihoods, and making decisions (p.2).

She further indicates that "critical thinkers use these skills appropriately, without prompting, and usually with conscious intent, in a variety of settings. That is, they are predisposed to think critically" (p. 2). While there are several commonalities among these definitions, the differences are equally nuanced. As a consequence, whatever definition of critical thinking is preferred, is often dependent on the understanding of the roles it should play in a specific context.

What might critical thinking look like for the language arts teacher?

In order to formulate an emerging definition of critical thinking for the language arts teacher, there must be an examination and an application of how teachers teach language arts content by emphasizing the teaching and use of higher order thinking skills. There must also be a concentration on the use of practical strategies such as essential questions and Socratic questions that hone in on the higher order thinking that is anticipated in the language arts classroom. Both the thinking and the instructional strategies must be completed in a context that is driven by corresponding critical reflection. Along with these three components, there is always the underlying understanding that the development of critical thinking skills should serve both academic purposes and personal, civic life. These components are by no means the exclusive way in which language arts teachers can participate in the transactions involved in critical thinking but they are one way to start.

For the purposes of the arguments being offered in this chapter, critical thinking is not defined as one prescribed approach. Instead critical thinking for the language arts teacher, is a series of multifaceted, complex approaches that language arts teachers apply to their pedagogical practice in order to enrich the teaching and learning experience. Considering the anticipated instructional practices for language arts classrooms, critical thinking by characterization, is the art of thinking about thinking with a view to improving it (Paul, 2004). These metacognitive processes require language arts teachers to become immersed in in-depth, systematic reflection on instructional practices so that questions about:

- What teachers do,
- Why they do what they do,
- What evidence supports or contradicts their instructional decisions
- And what practical evidence-based changes can be made in their thinking and practice

are addressed. Language arts teachers who share this philosophy of what critical thinking may entail, participate in developing the very skills that they seek to shape in their students. Halpern (2011) indicates that:

when we think critically, we are evaluating the outcomes of our thought processes--how good a decision is or how well a problem is solved. Critical thinking also involves evaluating the thinking process--the reasoning that went into the conclusion we've arrived at or the kinds of factors considered in making a decision (p. 2).

Through the critical reflective process, language arts teachers consider different aspects of their planning, instruction and assessment. They do so in order to make connections, draw inferences, ask questions and make evidence-based, logical decisions based on continuous assessment and analysis of how they deliver instruction. These are some of the ways in which language arts teachers come to know, understand and validate their pedagogical choices.

CRITICAL THINKING AND THE LANGUAGE ARTS TEACHER

In the language arts classroom, the elementary teacher plays several roles. She focuses on developing all of the language arts skills regardless of the age of her students; and, in that very context, she must also provide numerous opportunities for her students to think critically as they learn. These expectations mean that the language arts teacher herself must conceptualize notions of critical thinking in sufficiently encompassing ways that facilitate both learning and thinking. In considering what critical thinking might look like to the language arts teacher in the primary grades, a few characteristics must be considered. These characteristics will be described further in the chapter.

A CONTEXT FOR KNOWING AND UNDERSTANDING

How do language arts teachers come to know and understand?

The concept of teacher knowledge is as complex as it is varied. Teacher knowledge encompasses a number of variables which may become more relevant or less relevant depending on the quality of the experiences that the teacher encounters (Darling-Hammond & Bransford, 2005). In general, the variables that shape the effective language arts teacher's knowledge and understanding can be broadly categorized into two components: content knowledge and pedagogical content knowledge. The National Council for Teachers of English (NCTE) offers that embedded within the framework of content knowledge in language arts are the teacher's in-depth understanding of language development, language history and analysis, reading, composition and literature among others. Within each component are specific areas of focus with which the teacher must be intimately familiar. Content knowledge in language arts also requires that the knowledge of these elements must be centred on the inter-related relationships of all the language arts: reading, writing, listening, speaking, viewing, visually representing and thinking (NCTE, 2006; Tompkins, 2014).

When students enter the language arts classroom, teachers are responsible for engaging them in the learning process. In order to be successful in teaching so that higher order learning occurs, there are several expectations that must guide the teaching and learning process. Firstly, teachers must remain cognizant that students come to class with their own knowledge base. Secondly, within the learning process, the anticipated actions of the teacher should lead students to learn to synthesize their knowledge with new information. They should also be able to make connections, interpret and analyse information so that new meanings are created. Thirdly, the language arts teacher must be able to match her content knowledge with the appropriate pedagogical approaches in order to guide students in transforming their learning. When all of these elements seamlessly come together the teacher demonstrates strong pedagogical content knowledge. In essence, pedagogical content knowledge refers to more than just discipline - specific knowledge and/or general knowledge about pedagogy. Pedagogical content knowledge encompasses all the skills, approaches, methodologies and activities that specifically relate to the teaching and learning of language arts (NCTE, 2006). The attendant implication is that all language arts teachers must have a knowledge base that will guide how they come to know and to understand and how this understanding is transformed into effective instruction. Shoffner (2005) argues that the merger or intersection of content and pedagogy is at the heart of pedagogical content knowledge. Sound pedagogical content knowledge is characterized by teachers who know and understand how to utilize multiple ways to unpack the language arts content and teach it in such a way that all learners within that given classroom can learn how to think critically about the content being taught, and understand that very content simultaneously. Thinking about how they best manipulate their pedagogical content knowledge is one way in which teachers come to know and understand in a critical way.

Conceptualizing Critical Thinking

This segment of the chapter examines three of the principal characteristics of critical thinking that aid language arts teachers in centering their knowledge and understanding. These characteristics are:

- Thinking (about) and learning English language arts content
- Questioning for critical thinking and
- Critical reflection

Characteristic 1: Thinking (About) and Learning English Language Arts Content

Conceptualizing critical thinking for the language arts teacher is just as complex as the planning that is required for its implementation in the classroom. Critical thinking involves individual reasoning competencies, constructing socially situated thinking and a sustained balance between social practice and inquiry (Kuhn, 2018). Determining how teachers can be guided into developing critical thinking skills is undergirded by a consideration of what constitutes critical thinking. Ennis (2018) presents critical thinking as the kind of reasoning that is reflective in nature and that is focused on deciding what to believe or do. Ennis further explains that critical thinking encompasses a set of dispositions, abilities and competencies that influence the "believing" and "doing". Critical thinkers must be able to engage in continuous reflection on their own thinking. They must also maintain an awareness of what they are learning and how they are learning. For example, language arts teachers must continuously reflect on what they believe about critical thinking in the language arts classroom. In other words, do they believe that critical thinking should be taught explicitly in the language arts class? If so, how should critical thinking skills be developed? Should they be taught parallel to the language arts content or can the teacher actually use critical thinking to teach higher order skills and language arts content simultaneously? Reflections of this nature guide teachers in how they conceptualize critical thinking (Minott, 2011). The kinds of responses that these types of questions provoke from teachers, signpost the kinds of teaching and learning that occur in the language arts classroom.

Effective critical thinking results from the interplay among one's abilities, competencies and dispositions in ways that reshape knowledge and lead to decision-making. Critical thinking encompasses a merger of abilities to question, interpret, infer, synthesize, analyze and apply, both independently and interdependently, in an effort to make balanced decisions (Abrami, Bernard, Borokhovski, Waddington, Wade & Perrson, 2015). As language arts teachers learn to become critical thinkers, their experiences with different dispositions and abilities transform their thinking. When this happens, teachers continually adjust the criteria that they use to assess, analyze and evaluate what and how they think. Often, these frequent interactions and adjustments result in a change in the kinds of instructional decisions that they make (Guskey, 2002; Paul & Elder, 2001). Teachers' frequent participation in these processes provide more positive opportunities for knowledge acquisition and pedagogical growth (Paul & Elder, 2001; Soo Von Esch, 2018). The argument is this: teachers must understand how their own dispositions, competencies and critical thinking skills are developed and adjusted by experience. This understanding can influence how they plan and how they teach language arts within the context of critical thinking.

Some of the most common critical thinking skills which students are taught in the language arts classroom include questioning, inference-making, offering alternative interpretations and perspectives, synthesizing and analyzing information. An argument may be offered that these are general critical thinking principles; however, it is imperative that there be an understanding that the expectations of each of these skills differ according to the discipline in which they are taught. For instance, asking students to provide alternative interpretations may not look the same in a language arts class as it would in another discipline. In other words, teachers must have a clear conceptualization of what each of these higher order skills requires, in relation to teaching and learning in the language arts classroom. When the conceptualization of critical thinking is determined and established among teachers, the planning and execution of language arts lessons can more effectively teach students how to become critical thinkers themselves.

A concentration on higher order thinking is necessary for the development of critical thinking skills. When engaging in instructional planning for language arts, effective teachers consider the content to be taught as well as the critical thinking that is required to fully understand that content. Conceptualizing critical thinking as a mode through which content can be taught facilitates the development of higher order skills (Smith, Rama & Helms, 2018). Often, language arts is taught with a strong emphasis on the content and some focus on higher order skills (Brookhart, 2010). In fact, Tankersley (2005) argues that the goal of the teacher should be to aid learners in developing skills that depend less on recall-based knowledge and rely more on the ability to skillfully synthesize, analyze, interpret and evaluate what they are learning at more complex levels. The challenge is that teachers are unsure of how to incorporate critical thinking skills in their respective lessons (Collins, 2014). In other scenarios, emphasis is placed more so on memorizing the content being taught while limited attention is given to the development of critical thinking skills. An alternative perspective to these traditional approaches is to consider a seamless fusion between critical thinking and the learning of content (Brookhart, 2010; Collins, 2014). There are numerous possibilities for exceptional teaching in the language arts classroom when teachers possess a sound understanding of what critical thinking means; when their instructional decision making is undergirded by that understanding of critical thinking and when their teaching routines reflect a relationship between both (Beach, Thein & Webb, 2016). Teaching routines of this nature help teachers to harness students' creativity, problem-solving, decision-making, communication and language arts skills within the ambit of teaching and learning (Elder & Paul, 2004; Beach, Thein & Webb, 2016). If language arts teachers intend to move students beyond recalling information, and aim to develop higher order thinking skills, the responsibility of conceptualizing critical thinking, and planning with critical thinking in mind, lies in the care of the teacher. In order to decide how to help learners in the language arts classroom to draw conclusions, make inferences and offer logical and accurate responses in their reading, writing and speaking, the language arts teachers should have comprehensive understanding and competence in how they prepare themselves for the classroom.

Effective language arts instruction that fosters critical thinking is based on the understanding that both the content to be taught and the kinds of thinking that would promote learning must work in concert with each other. Teachers who subscribe to this characteristic of critical thinking ensure that as language arts content is being taught, students are encouraged to think about their understandings of these concepts in ways that help them to assess, problem-solve, communicate and make decisions. In this way, students are able to reflect on the subject matter being taught and think about what they are learning so that they can analyze and synthesize information in new ways.

Characteristic 2: Questioning for Critical Thinking

Conceptualizing the processes and procedures involved in the development of critical thinking skills in the language arts classroom is dependent on the teacher's ability to contextualize the ways in which critical thinking can effectively develop listening, speaking, reading, writing, viewing, visually representing and thinking skills. Each of these language arts requires creative ways of matching critical thinking routines to the skill being developed. Equally important is the pedagogical understanding that the language arts and critical thinking routines do not have to be taught in isolation. In fact, they are more effectively taught when teachers understand the connections among all of the language arts and the kinds of thinking that each one requires. To determine how best to conceptualize the different contexts that would aid in centralizing critical thinking skills and the language arts, language arts teachers seek to answer specific questions that are aligned to their teaching and learning goals such as:

1. What kind of thinking is required in the language arts classroom?
2. What are the goals of the kind of thinking that is required in the language arts classroom?
3. What kinds of considerations should the language arts teacher give to the planning and execution of a lesson that seeks to merge the content being taught and the critical thinking skills that help students to move from memorizing and recall to higher order skills?

McTighe and Wiggins (2013) provide what they call "essential questions" that can help teachers to focus on learning about content through thinking. They suggest that centering instruction around essential questions, opens students' understanding through processes that challenge them to engage in higher order thinking. Consequently, the use of conceptual questions helps students to interact with the content being learnt while they receive exposure to the required skills for that particular content or subject area. Open-ended, thought-provoking essential questions help teachers to guide students into deeper understanding of content as students learn to revise their higher order thinking (McTighe & Wiggins, 2013).

Whatever questions language arts teachers choose for their class must be directly related to the content being taught in that discipline. Along with this, essential questions must also be related to the real world so that students transfer these skills to their everyday experiences (McConnell, 2011). Teachers who effectively use essential questions must constantly ask themselves:

- What is the learning that students must acquire at the end of the lesson?
- In what ways can I use critical thinking to teach the particular content to my class?
- What is most important for today's learning?
- What should my students understand?
- How can I plan my instruction to ensure that these essential questions are addressed?
- Are my essential questions detailed enough to facilitate critical thinking about the content being taught?

In the language arts classroom, some of the following essential questions may be explored in order to expose students to critical thinking and teach the necessary content at the same time (McConnell, 2011).

Reading Comprehension Strategies

- Why are reading strategies important?
- How do readers prepare for reading?
- How do readers monitor their reading?
- What can a reader do when he or she does not understand?
- How can I use the writer's techniques to help me understand what I read?
- How does understanding the structure of a text help the reader to understand the meaning of the text?

Responding to Literature

- How do readers make connections?
- How do readers draw conclusions/make inferences?
- How does a reader understand the meaning of a poem?
- How does word choice influence meaning?

Language Appreciation

- What are the benefits of reading?
- What are the benefits of writing?

Writing

- How is language used to influence perspectives/beliefs and actions?
- How does a writer paint a picture with words?
- How does a writer make characters seem real/believable?
- How does using correct grammar and punctuation improve writing?
- How can the use of different types of sentences improve my writing?

Teachers commonly use questioning to formatively assess students' knowledge, to ascertain learning gaps and to monitor students' learning. Research suggests that in order to engage learners in critical thinking, the kinds of questions teachers ask should be more purposeful, probing, systematic and deep, rather than centered on basic recall and memorization (Guan Eng Ho, 2005; Paul & Elder, 2007). Along with essential questions, teachers strengthen their students' critical thinking skills when they use Socratic questioning to guide students' thinking and to model to students the kinds of questions that they should also ask when thinking on their own. Through Socratic questioning, teachers can determine whether they want students to think analytically about general information in the text, the writer's purpose, points of view, interpretation and inference and so forth (Paul & Elder, 2007).

Questioning for thinking is critical for determining how teachers come to know and understand. Teachers who themselves practice the use of the Socratic method and or essential questions in their reflections and preparations of teaching language arts develop clearer understandings and justifications for their instructional choices (Acim, 2018). A natural consequence is that teachers' pedagogical practice can improve when through questioning for thinking, they gain clarity regarding their understanding of content, students' needs and best practices in the teaching of the language arts (McTighe & Wiggins, 2013; Acim, 2018). If the goal of instruction in the language arts classroom is to teach content through critical thinking, teachers must ask and facilitate the asking of questions that provide students with numerous opportunities to adjust their thinking, clarify misconceptions, question inconsistencies and create new understandings. Likewise, teachers themselves must also consistently engage in Socratic questioning and the use of essential questions regarding their pedagogical practice. This is one of the ways in which they can centre their knowledge and understanding of best practices in language arts instruction.

Characteristic 3: Revisiting Critical Reflection

The language arts teacher cannot fully articulate an understanding of critical thinking if the instructional focus is solely on students' performance and abilities to memorize content. The language arts teacher must also consider the relevance of personal critical reflection in order to ensure pedagogical growth. Correspondingly, an understanding of the term critical reflection is necessary. Shandomo (2010) explains critical reflection as "the process by which adults identify the assumptions governing their actions, locate the historical and cultural origins of the assumptions, and develop alternative ways of acting" (p. 101). The language arts teacher must understand the correlation between the acts of thinking and learning discipline specific content. The effective language arts teacher is also expected to utilize appropriate instructional practices that would facilitate the development of critical thinking. Teachers who participate in consistent critical reflection constantly evaluate their pedagogical beliefs, their content knowledge, their pedagogical knowledge and their effectiveness in meeting the goals of instruction in the language arts classroom. As such, during the reflective process, the language arts teacher must consider the following questions:

- What did I do well?
- What was the learning that took place in today's lesson?
- In what ways must I improve in my instructional practice so that my students achieve the given learning goals?

In the context of the specific content that is being taught, the language arts teacher will adjust the questions for critical reflection, based on the specific focus of the students' learning. Ryan and Cooper (2006) offer some practical questions that teachers should ask prior to and after instruction. The researchers stress that teachers should always reflect on what they are doing and why they are making the decisions that they make in their daily teaching. Consideration should also be given to justifications for the post reflection choices that teachers make. One of the goals of critical reflection is to avoid the pitfalls of routinized teaching that focuses on the completion of tasks and activities by both the teacher and the students, without the occurrence of any actual teaching and learning. In essence, successful teachers who are critical thinkers must also embrace the ideals of critical reflection.

Setting a Context for Centering Teachers' Understandings

Language arts teachers generally understand the theoretical principles that guide their teaching. However, in the daily routines of the school day, language arts teachers need specific contexts that facilitate their critical reflections on their instructional practices for the enhancement of teaching and learning. The rest of this chapter examines some contexts in which teachers' involvement in developing their critical thinking skills, can aid them in establishing their knowledge and understandings, as these understandings relate to the teaching of language arts in the primary grades.

Continual Professional Development

One such context that has been found useful among teachers is professional development. Language arts teachers in the primary grades need a professional development agenda that seeks to address their respective professional needs. Kedzior and Fifield (2004) characterize effective professional development as "integrated, logical and on-going [events that incorporate] experiences that are consistent with teachers' goals; [they are] aligned with standards, assessments, other reform initiatives, and [are] beset by the best research evidence (p. 77). Professional development for teachers is essential in order to bring about change in areas of instructional practice, teachers' attitudes, teacher beliefs and students' learning outcomes (Guskey, 2002). As opposed to instructing teachers and then expecting them to change their instructional approaches, Guskey offers an alternative to traditional professional development. He asserts that teachers' involvement in deciding the areas of focus for their professional development is critical to any anticipated change in classroom practice (Guskey, 2002).

In fact, early research on professional development in schools indicates that there are certain characteristics that must be present if professional development is to be effective. Professional development must be supportive of teachers' individual and collective/staff needs and in so doing, encourage intrinsic motivation and commitment to the learning process (Flores, 2005). When professional development addresses the needs of teachers as individuals, in relation to specific grades and schools, teachers are more willing to engage in the professional development processes, since their personal and professional needs are accommodated (Flores, 2005). In this way, professional development for teachers becomes authentic and relevant (Flores, 2005; Tate, 2009).

Authentic professional development addresses teachers' pedagogical needs in ways that do not overly interfere with their other classroom responsibilities. In other words, whatever change is to be implemented and or sustained, must be in concordance with the daily activities of the classroom and by extension the school. Quick, Holtzman and Chaney (2009), explain that effective professional development for teachers must be embedded in school routines. This is evident when professional development is structured, planned for, consistent and continuous. Likewise, they indicate that professional development should encourage and support active learning among teachers and allow time for them to learn, plan, attempt strategies and reflect on their learning (Quick, Holtzman & Chaney, 2009). In effective professional development sessions the incorporation of active learning is demonstrated in activities that are interactive, that encourage the use of authentic artefacts and that provide opportunities for teachers to engage in the same style of learning that they design for their students (Darling-Hammond, Hyler & Gardner, 2017). Professional development activities that teachers consider to be effective generally focus on teachers' active involvement in the learning process, address areas of pedagogical content knowledge and are clearly connected to other teaching and learning activities that occur in the classroom. Guskey (2002) states that professional development activities that have significant, positive effects on teachers' self-reported increases in knowledge and skills as well as changes in classroom practice, have focused on teachers' content and pedagogical knowledge. It therefore means that professional development for language arts teachers should be differentiated so as to meet the content and instructional needs of teachers in adequate ways. This differentiation can be organized according to qualification, grades taught, individual teacher needs and so forth. Professional development that does not cater to these underlying teacher needs are deemed as less effective (Darling-Hammond & Bransford, 2005; Guskey, 2002; King & Newmann, 2004; Lieberman & Pointer Mace, 2008).

Vignette One: Lessons From Teachers' Voices – Professional Development

The author conducted a study aimed at developing a framework for reading instruction in St. Vincent and the Grenadines (SVG) in 2016. The study was conducted in two phases. In the first phase, data were collected on primary school teachers' perceptions of classroom-based reading assessment and reading instruction. Phase two of the study focused on developing a framework for reading instruction, based on findings from the first phase. In the second phase of the study, the researcher collaborated with three (3) teachers, one Grade 2 teacher and two Grade 4 teachers to develop the framework for reading instruction. Prior to working with the teachers in these two specific grades, a series of professional development sessions were conducted with the entire staff of the primary school in the study. Further professional development sessions were also conducted through a professional learning community that included the Grade 2 teacher, the two Grade 4 teachers and the researcher. Initially, the professional development sessions were conducted twice per week.

For one school term (15 weeks), the staff and the researcher examined the requisite research-based knowledge and skills associated with the use of classroom-based reading assessments as well as the pedagogical content knowledge critical to the effective teaching of reading. Prior to the development of the framework for reading instruction, the teachers at the institution discussed what they knew and what they needed to understand about classroom-based reading assessment and reading instruction. Emphasis was placed on both what needed to be taught and how it should be best taught according to the learning goals for the respective classes.

During the 15 week training period, the staff were invited to share their areas of growth and challenge within the professional learning community. They also offered general feedback on the professional development sessions. The staff underscored the importance of consistent professional development when they clearly articulated that for them, professional development must never be offered as a singular event. Here are a few of their comments:

We should have professional development regularly and those who conduct the sessions with us must consider what we as teachers really need. Because we worked on how to teach comprehension strategies and I wanted to know about that, I didn't feel like it was a waste of time.

I prefer [PD] this way than when we do it just before the school year begins. In those 'back to school' PD sessions, everything is pushed together and halfway in the term we forget about everything. This way, when we are meeting different times throughout the term, we are always talking about how we are doing in teaching language arts in our grades.

The teachers' feedback regarding the implementation of continuous professional development indicated their willingness to engage in professional development once it catered to their instructional needs in consistent authentic ways.

Within the context of continuous professional development, teachers receive numerous opportunities to harness their content knowledge and develop their pedagogical content knowledge. During the open discussion sessions in this professional learning community, it became evident that the teachers' knowledge was constructed uniquely, individually and collectively. This was done through the use of multiple, authentic experiences, resources and contexts (Hord, 2009). The staff credited the success of the professional development sessions to the immediate opportunities they received to practice and reinforce both content and pedagogy in settings that were authentic.

The teachers followed three steps. In order to ensure that they shared a common understanding of each classroom-based reading assessment tool, teachers firstly learned about the formative assessment tool. In the second step, they were encouraged to discuss how and why they would use the assessment tool, considering the quality and kind of data it would provide. Finally, the staff practiced using the assessment tool with one or a small group of students in their charge. Upon return to the next professional development session, the teachers discussed and shared their thinking behind their choices as well as how they would use the data collected to address specific learning needs in the classroom. Some of the teachers explained that this routine facilitated their critical reflection of their pedagogical content knowledge. They were also able to critique the effectiveness of the instructional decisions they made based on their reflections. This approach was used in keeping with Guskey's model of professional development which suggests that teachers' behaviours and attitudes change after they have experienced the use of strategies and found them beneficial (Guskey, 2002). Feedback from the teachers supported the recognition that teachers come to know and understand through consistent, interactive practice. As two teachers explained:

What really stayed with me is that it was okay that everybody didn't have the same experience or difficulty using the assessments in class. I liked how my colleagues explained why they had to adjust how they did some things. You know, that really made me think because we always had to share how we came to the teaching decisions we made and why we made those decisions...

I won't forget that you would always ask us 'why did you do it that way? How was that approach going to help your students to meet the learning outcomes?' You know, I don't usually think about why I am doing what I do so that was good for me. I realised that I knew quite a lot. And I realised that some of the decisions I made were sound and some were really not helping me to teach better.

I didn't feel like the PD sessions were too much to cover because we had two days to try the 3P (power point, practice, presentation) technique. I like that you showed us how to use the assessment tools, then we practiced in our class and then we presented how it worked for our different classes. It felt like I was learning without judgement...

Knowing that I had to explain why I chose an assessment tool and how I would teach a concept based on the data really forced me to think more seriously about how I was teaching in the classroom and why. To me, I feel that that process really helped me to understand why what I was doing made sense when it did. I think that having to say why something wasn't working really help me to understand the importance of thinking through my activities and decisions. I proved this when I was teaching the TPRC [Think – Read- Predict-Connect] comprehension strategy. I had to make sure that it was the right strategy to help my students to read to see if what they read supported what they were thinking.

Based on the teachers' responses, it would be fair to assume that appropriate and continual professional development is a critical factor that can impact the implementation of a framework for reading instruction in SVG. The suitability of the professional development must be dependent on the teachers' pedagogical needs as well as the provision of opportunities for the teachers to administer and dialogue on the elements of instructional change that are to be implemented in their classrooms (Guskey, 2002). The feedback provided by the teachers who participated in the study reiterates what research says about teachers learning within a professional community. The teachers' responses indicated that their ways of knowing, understanding and doing are best sustained through on-going/sustained, systematic professional development.

Collaboration

One of the factors that influenced the implementation of the framework for reading instruction was collaboration. Engaging in the collaborative process is another way in which teachers come to know and understand their pedagogical decisions in the language arts classroom. DuFour (2004) characterizes collaboration as the effort made by groups of educators to "work together to analyse and improve their classroom practice...engaging in an ongoing cycle of questions that promote deep team learning" (p. 9). The success of critical reflection in a collaborative setting must take into consideration that teachers come to the experience with their own sets of knowledge, experiences and beliefs (Hord, 2009). Through respectful dialogue teachers participate in a developmental process of "accommodation, assimilation, or rejection to construct new conceptual structures, meaningful representations or new mental models" (Hord, 2009, p. 41). In other words, as the collaborative process continues, teachers are able to acquire new knowledge as well as adjust and reorganize already existing patterns of knowledge that they gain from each other.

Collaboration validates the knowledge that teachers already have. Further, research indicates that when teachers work together in homogeneous groups, in active and interactive ways, the act of collaboration is most beneficial. Consequently, the collaborative process is fostered in learning communities that share problems, ideas, and viewpoints, and work together toward solutions (Guskey, 2002). Through professional learning communities, teachers can meet regularly and learn from each other so as to improve their craft. Collaboration is best sustained when the professional learning communities in which teachers meet are supported by: the leadership of the school, a sense of accountability among teachers when they meet, a willingness to take professional risks and the maintaining of a 'healthy' social interaction among colleagues (Quick, Holtzman & Chaney, 2009). Through the collaborative process, teachers learn to develop trust in each other and in the learning process itself (Hord & Hirsh, 2008). This trust is developed through peer feedback that is respectful and open (Flores, 2005; Guskey & Suk Yoon, 2009). In essence, any collaborative initiative must provide learning opportunities for teachers of the language arts in ways that address the instructional needs of teachers. The approaches used must be authentic, relevant and flexible. As such, the collaborative process must facilitate meaningful critical reflection of pedagogy with the goal of effecting instructional change.

Collaboration within a professional learning community best serves language arts teachers when teachers are encouraged to think about the ways in which they can effectively use higher order thinking skills to teach the language arts content that their students need to learn. Teachers can do so by questioning their instructional actions using the same critical thinking skills that they expect their students to develop based on their teaching. Through the collaborative process language arts teachers must monitor their learning, draw conclusions, make inferences and make connections between the higher order skills they wish to teach and how they would connect these elements to the language arts content that they are teaching.

Vignette Two: Lessons From Teachers' Voices – Collaboration

The teachers who participated in the study (2016) shared what their experience with the collaborative process was like with the researcher.

When I actually started to make anecdotal records on the children in the group I selected, I had some problems at first but I talked with Mr. John and a few others and I followed the steps. I made sure I knew the process, I practiced with my group of children and then I talked with some of the teachers. I find that when I worked in that order, I was better able to do the assessment and use different ones (other classroom-based reading assessments). I slowly got more confidence when I talked with my colleagues in Grade 4 and realised that I was on the right track. I mean, I still have my moments of uncertainty, but I can always talk with the other teachers if I have difficulty.

I liked that you encouraged us to talk about what we were teaching and assessing before we made any assessment checklists. I remember when we were teaching how to retell in the Grade 2 class, all of the Grade 2 teachers worked together. We really had some deep discussions about why it was important for students to learn to retell and sequence events. We talked about what specific things we wanted the students to understand. Although we had different explanations, they were all workable and we tried to include what we were learning from each other.

I wanted to make sure I asked myself the right questions and think about how best to teach the concept in a way that would also help the children to think critically about retelling. I realised that I also had to think critically about why teaching the skill of retelling was important. I wanted to be clear on how I would get the students to understand that this skill was a life skill and not just for the language arts class. I made sure I talked with other teachers and so they gave me some ideas as what to do. That was a first for me. I really liked discussing why I was teaching the way I did and how well it worked.

For me, the small group planning and discussions with the other teachers built up my confidence as an inexperienced teacher.

In my group, it was the discussion on using the mini-lesson to help students make connections that was my 'aha' moment as a teacher. Sometimes while I am doing the reading a little idea may come to me. I would say, I am doing reading so I am not going to touch any grammar part, but I learned that the mini lessons help the reading and the grammar and I learned how to do them (the mini lessons) during the reading. So I am better at helping children to make connections between the reading and writing with the grammar. And I am making better connections too as a teacher. I do more mini lessons in small groups because we talked about how to do them in our groups when we had P.D. (professional development).

When we were talking about the anecdotal records something struck me. It was the first time I was coming to grips with the thought that I must know what my students can't do but I must also know what they really know or can do. So now when I plan my units I think of each child. And I think about what the child can really do in reading, like what skills she really has. Then I think about what she might need help with. And I talk with Mrs Joseph because she taught my class in Grade 2. So we discuss what might really be the best assessment to use with the child. I find that it really helped me to talk with another teacher because when we talked about why we want the assessment and how we will teach after, I felt sure that I was hitting the nail on the head.

The teachers' responses and actions were indicative of the impact that the practice of collaboration had on the implementation process. The teachers engaged in collaboration on their own and in the researcher's presence. The collaborative process facilitated a greater understanding among the teacher-participants regarding what pedagogical decisions met the teaching and learning needs that existed in the classroom. Through a collaborative effort, the teachers' personal growth and development became evident during the implementation of the framework for reading instruction. The teachers did not simply work together; they also developed a strong sense of collegiality among themselves. Harris and Anthony (2001), summarise collegiality as "any interaction that breaks the isolation of teachers [and that contributes] in some fashion to the knowledge, skill, judgment, or commitment that individuals bring to their work, [to] enhance the collective capacity of groups or institutions" (p. 372). The collaborative effort of the teacher-participants was evident in every stage of the model for reading instruction. All three teacher-participants worked together to dialogue about the most effective instructional practices and formative assessment tools best suited for teaching reading in whole class and small group sessions. Mrs Joseph expressed her thoughts on the practice of collaboration at all stages of the implementation of the framework for reading instruction:

I am not accustomed to talking with other teachers about what I am doing in my classroom. I mean there is a literacy person teaching in the class next door but to be honest we don't have that (collaboration) in our school. But I find that talking with a co-worker, even if we are not in the same grade, really builds your confidence and helps you to see something you might have messed up if you didn't get another opinion.

When asked to clarify, she explained:

I remember when we were doing the student-led grouping and I had to do conferencing with Grade 2. I showed Mrs Joseph my checklist that the children would use. She told me it was too hard for them because they had to use it to talk about their work. I didn't know what to do and I told her I didn't know. So we sat down after school and looked online and she helped me to fix up the 2 stars and a wish checklist to fit my students.

The teachers' responses indicated that collaboration among language arts teachers must consider the kinds of knowledge that teachers are bringing to the discussions. The ways in which that knowledge will be expanded on in practical ways must also be given precedence. Darling-Hammond (2006) strongly advocates that teachers are more effective when they work as a community. She argues that teachers must learn "from teaching as well as learn for teaching" (p. 109). This learning best occurs among teachers and their peers. In other words, collaboration is a critical component of professional development

(Guskey, 2002; National Staff Development Council, 2007). In order for in-service training to enhance the instructional practices of teachers effectively, teachers themselves must be actively involved in the learning process.

The responses from the teachers in the study indicated that teachers come to know and understand through collaborative dialoguing. The success of the collaborative process must not be dependent on how successful individual teachers are in the process; it must also demonstrate that the professional growth of the staff or group has resulted from a collective effort during the training. In order for teachers to grow professionally and as a collective, the continuous professional development that is offered must occur in an environment that fosters collegiality among staff. It also means that staff should be given regular opportunities to implement and reflect on the effectiveness of the new learning that has taken place. In this collaborative context, teachers come to confidently know, understand and justify the instructional decisions that they make.

Collaboration was also evident among the three teacher participants. The teacher-participants' collaboration with creating menu cards also built their confidence and showed their creativity. They shared that they were able to overcome the challenge of finding authentic activities rather than relying on seatwork, by working together and seeking advice from each other. Ms Arindell, the trained Grade 4 graduate indicated:

Well as I said, I am moreso a Math teacher. So I really struggled with the menu cards because sometimes I ran out of activities. But I got a suggestion from Mrs. Joseph in Grade 2. So sometimes, to make sure that I have an extra menu card activity, I used to leave space for one activity that they (the class) would make up for the other groups to do. That helped me to always have other activities and everybody wanted to see whose activity I was using on any day. I took her advice with using the menu cards and some of the tests that I gave at the end of the class were exercises based on the menu cards, so like spelling and vocabulary and some of the writing came from what they did during the week in the menu cards.

Mrs Joseph reiterated Miss Arindell's comments. She explained that the menu cards were a challenge and a strength:

The hardest part was coming up with differentiated activities. But that was where the planning with Mrs Collis and then Miss Arindell really helped me see different ways to do some of the activities. It really was good when we put our heads together. It took less time to plan and somebody else always saw something the other one didn't think about. I like how we used to actually try out the activities ourselves before we let the children do them. I tell you, when you do that, you see all kinds of ways the children could misunderstand the activity, so you fix it before you take it to the children.

Collaboration at each stage of execution was beneficial for the framework since it fostered self-efficacy and professional growth among the teacher-participants. As was earlier indicated by Mrs Joseph and Miss Arindell, the collaborative space offered the teacher-participants healthy opportunities to share their inadequacies and solve problems. It was equally noticeable that of the three teachers Mrs Collis was the only trained graduate, yet all three teachers believed they benefited from collaborating with each other. The fact that these three teachers were able to express that they had experienced professional growth, that their planning practices had improved and they were demonstrating episodes of reflective practice, was evidence that the implementation of a framework for reading instruction in SVG must be served by collaboration through communities of practice. As Darling-Hammond (2011, p. 13) emphasises, through collaboration:

Everyone gets to share their knowledge and expertise. Nobody knows it all when it comes to teaching; teaching is infinitely complex and ever-changing. Kids provide all kinds of challenges and interesting differences, while the curriculum is always evolving... The opportunity to share what they know with each other also allows [teachers] to be individually successful and successful as a team—and teaching is definitely a team sport

When teachers embrace professional communities of learning and foster collaboration among themselves, they create stronger opportunities for the sustainability of any practices in language arts instruction that they may wish to implement as a whole school.

FINAL CONSIDERATIONS

At the end of the implementation of the framework for reading instruction in SVG, the teacher-participants were asked to share their overall thoughts regarding the process of developing a framework for reading instruction with the researcher. These are a few of the responses that they gave:

I have a better way of organizing how I use the teaching time to my advantage and to the children's advantage. I plan better, I teach better and I learned to assess and I think the children and I get along better too

For one teacher, developing the skill of monitoring the students and chronicling their reading performance helped her to grow in her ability to provide feedback to parents. She explained:

I feel that I can speak more specifically to parents when they come to parent's day because I now say 'this is what [Suzanne] and I worked on and she has improved' or 'we still have some work to do with the spelling'. You know, I feel good about being able to do that as a teacher. I am sure about what I know and I can clearly talk to parents with confidence. I think that meeting regularly to think and share how we are learning as teachers is a good practice to have regardless of the subject that we teach. It helps us to be able to speak to exactly how the student is performing and it shows the parents that every child in your class is important and that you know what you are doing. It also lets the parents know that we know what we are about and that they can trust us to teach their children well

Other responses included:

I have really improved in the way I teach the comprehension part of reading. I used to really struggle with how I used comprehension strategies. It's not that I didn't know about them or that we have to use them. I used to mention them in my lesson outline. But now that we learned that the strategy is really for the children and not for us, I learn to do the explicit teaching. So in my mind when I am teaching I remind myself that the children need to see what good readers do when they read. That keeps me on track.

I like that I follow the steps to explain the strategy and I like waiting to see my children actually use the strategy in a paragraph. I really feel more confident now in teaching comprehension skills in Grade 2. I don't feel like I don't do a good job of it anymore.

...I think I have really grown because I am not afraid to plan out and try new things. Not just try part of it but plan for a week and connect everything, like the assessment, the teaching and the activities.

The vast wealth of knowledge and understandings that language arts teachers possess must always be acknowledged and validated. Teachers can function more efficiently when they are able to centre their understandings of evidence-based instructional practices, in contexts that support consistent critical thinking about the teaching of language arts. They must have regular opportunities to think about their thinking and use the very skills that they teach students, to examine what they know and understand. Consequently, there is a need for schools and other academic institutions to accommodate teachers' critical reflective practices. Zeichner and Liu (2010) reiterate this necessary consideration:

Reflection ... signifies a recognition that the generation of new knowledge about teaching is not the exclusive property of colleges, universities, and research and development centres. It is a recognition that teachers have ideas, beliefs, and theories too, that can contribute to the betterment of teaching for all teachers. (p. 4-5)

It is therefore desirable that school leadership personnel work assiduously to provide teachers with the contexts required for testing, reviewing and evaluating their competencies in teaching language arts. Measures should be put in place to provide opportunities for structured, sustained and consistent professional development for staff.

Similarly, schools should encourage a collaborative environment for teachers. This is best achieved when collaboration becomes part of the school's professional culture. It is not sufficient to have a general perspective on the issue of collaboration. Schools must have defined goals and expectations for collaborative processes among teachers. Ideally, all staff should be involved in setting goals, making plans of action and actually taking action (Fullan, 2016). Reflective practice must also play a pivotal during the collaborative process. If the responsibility for collaboration is left to a few teachers, taking ownership of the collective understandings regarding teaching and learning would be futile. The responses of teachers who participated in the study support the argument that pedagogical problems can be resolved in schools, and often, the solutions exist right among the staff. In short, the context for teacher collaboration cannot be overestimated.

There must also be an understanding that collaboration is a process. Effective collaboration is built on relationships (Fullan, 2016). Therefore teachers must be careful to guard their interactions as they work collectively to bring about a change or shift in their traditional beliefs, attitudes, practices and prejudices (Williams, 2001). Often, even if teachers are open to professional development, they struggle with the collaborative process. For instance, one teacher indicated to the researcher: "it's not the training that is the problem, it's the implementation." Structured collaborative sessions can minimize challenges of this nature since teachers who are struggling to implement strategies or initiatives can receive support in a collaborative setting.

In summary, the dialogue on centering teachers' knowledge and understanding must move beyond the accumulation of information through predetermined professional development, to the implementation of evidence-based practices that continually support and empower teachers by validating their competencies in teaching language arts. Assumptions must not be made regarding teachers' understandings of or abilities to implement instructional change in the classroom. Teachers need mentoring through communities of learning so that they can receive beneficial on-going, in-service professional development. And so, schools should be encouraged to foster greater collegiality and professional growth among themselves. Establishing research-based contexts for teachers to examine their teaching and learning through critical thinking is realizable. The teacher-participants in the researcher's study (2016) chose to collaborate, to support each other, to seek guidance where necessary and to take risks that challenged their traditional instructional beliefs. It was in this cycle of teaching and learning among themselves that teachers experienced professional growth. The results were greater self-efficacy, the acquisition of new understandings and confidence to share new knowledge with colleagues. This is the goal of centering teachers understandings – to instruct thinking students by teachers who themselves are critical thinkers.

REFERENCES

Abrami, P. C., Bernard, R. M., Borokhovski, E., Waddington, D. I., Wade, C. A., & Persson, T. (2015). Strategies for teaching students to think critically: A meta-analysis. *Review of Educational Research*, *85*(2), 275–314. doi:10.3102/0034654314551063

Acim, R. (2018). The Socratic method of instruction: An experience with a reading comprehension course. *Journal of Educational Research and Practice*, *8*(1), 41–53.

Beach, R., Thein, A., & Webb, A. (2016). Teaching to exceed the English language arts common core state standards: A critical inquiry approach for 6-12 classrooms. New York, NY: Routledge.

Brookhart, S. (2010). *How to assess higher order thinking skills in your classroom*. Alexandria, VA: ASCD.

Collins, R. (2014). Skills for the 21st century: Teaching higher order thinking. *Curriculum and Leadership*, *12*(14). Retrieved from: http://www.curriculum.edu.au/leader/teaching_higher_order_thinking,37431.html?issueID=12910

Darling-Hammond, L. (2006). Constructing 21st-century teacher education. *Journal of Teacher Education*, *57*(3), 300–314. doi:10.1177/0022487105285962

Darling-Hammond, L., & Bransford, J. (2005). *Preparing teachers for a changing world: What teachers should learn and be able to do*. San Francisco, CA: John Wiley & Sons.

Darling-Hammond, L., Hyler, M. E., & Gardner, M. (2017). *Effective Teacher Professional Development*. Palo Alto, CA: Learning Policy Institute.

DuFour, R. (2004). What is a professional learning community? *Educational Leadership*, *61*(8), 6–11.

Elder, L., & Paul, R. (2004). Critical thinking … and the art of close reading, Part III. *Journal of Developmental Education*, *28*(1), 36–37.

Ennis, R. (2018). Critical Thinking Across the Curriculum: A vision. *Topoi*, *37*(1), 165–184. doi:10.100711245-016-9401-4

Facione, P. (1989). *Critical Thinking: A Statement of Expert Consensus for Purposes of Educational Assessment and Instruction (The Delphi Report). Research Findings and Recommendations.* Newark, DE: American Philosophical Association.

Flores, M. (2005). How do teachers learn in the workplace? Findings from an empirical study carried out in Portugal. *Journal of In-service Education, 31*(3), 485–508. doi:10.1080/13674580500200491

Frijters, S., ten Dam, G., & Rijlaarsdam, G. (2008). Effects of dialogic learning on value-loaded critical thinking. *Learning and Instruction, 18*(1), 66–82. doi:10.1016/j.learninstruc.2006.11.001

Fullan, M. (2016). *The new meaning of educational change* (5th ed.). New York, NY: Teachers College Press.

Guan Eng Ho, D. (2005). Why do teachers ask the questions they ask? *Regional Language Centre Journal, 36*(3), 297–310. doi:10.1177/0033688205060052

Guskey, T. (2002). Professional development and teacher change. *Teachers and Teaching, 8*(3), 381–391. doi:10.1080/135406002100000512

Guskey, T., & Suk Yoon, K. (2009). What works in professional development? *Phi Delta Kappan, 90*(7), 495–500. doi:10.1177/003172170909000709

Halpern, D. (2011). *Critical thinking handout: Critical thinking workshop for helping our students become better thinkers.* Retrieved from: https://louisville.edu/ideastoaction/-/files/featured/halpern/critical-thinking.pdf

Harris, D., & Anthony, H. (2001). Collegiality and its role in teacher development: Perspectives from veteran and novice teachers. *Teacher Development, 5*(3), 127–128. doi:10.1080/13664530100200162

Hord, S. M. (2009). Professional learning communities. Educators work together toward a shared purpose – improved student learning. *National Staff Development Council, 30*(1), 40–43.

Hord, S. M., & Hirsh, S. A. (2008). Making the promise a reality. In A. M. Blankstein, P. D. Houston, & R. W. Cole (Eds.), *Sustaining professional learning communities.* Thousand Oaks, CA: Corwin Press.

Kedzior, M., & Fifield, S. (2004). Teacher professional development. *Education Policy Brief, 15*(21), 76–97.

King, B., & Newmann, F. (2004). Key link: Successful professional development must consider school capacity. *Journal of Staff Development, 25*(1), 26–30.

Kuhn, D. (2018). A role for reasoning in a dialogic approach to critical thinking. *Topoi, 37*(1), 121–128. doi:10.100711245-016-9373-4

Lieberman, A., & Pointer-Mace, D. (2008). Teacher learning: The key to education reform. *Journal of Teacher Education, 59*(3), 226–234. doi:10.1177/0022487108317020

McConnell, C. (2011). The essential questions handbook: Grades 4-8. New York, NY: Scholastic.

McTighe, J., & Wiggins, G. (2013). *Essential Questions: Opening doors to student understanding.* Alexandria, VA: ASCD.

Minott, M. (2011). Reflective teaching, critical literacy and the teacher's tasks in the critical literacy classroom. A confirmatory investigation. *Reflective Practice: International and Multidisciplinary Perspectives, 12*(1), 73–85. doi:10.1080/14623943.2011.541096

Paul, R. (2004). *Critical thinking: What every person needs to survive in a rapidly changing world.* Sonomata State University, Centre for Critical Thinking.

Paul, R., & Elder, L. (2001). *Critical thinking: Tools for taking charge of your learning and your life.* Upper Saddle River, NJ: Prentice Hall.

Paul, R., & Elder, L. (2007). *A guide for educators to critical thinking competency standards.* Dillon Beach, CA: Foundation for Critical Thinking.

Paul, R., Fisher, A., & Nosich, G. (1993). *Workshop on critical thinking strategies.* Sonoma State University: Foundation for Critical Thinking.

Quick, H., Holtzman, D., & Chaney, K. (2009). Professional development and instructional practice: Conceptions and evidence of effectiveness. *Journal of Education for Students Placed at Risk, 14*(1), 45–71. doi:10.1080/10824660802715429

Ryan, K., & Cooper, J. M. (2006). *Those who can, teach.* Boston: Houghton Mifflin.

Shandomo, H. M. (2010). The role of critical reflection in teacher education. *School—. University Partnerships, 4*, 101–113.

Shoffner, M. (2005). Alternative Teacher Preparation Programs: Intersection of Content, Pedagogy and Technology. In C. Crawford, R. Carlsen, I. Gibson, K. McFerrin, J. Price, R. Weber & D. Willis (Eds.), *Proceedings of SITE 2005--Society for Information Technology & Teacher Education International Conference* (pp. 2813-2817). Academic Press.

Smith, T. E., Rama, P. S., & Helms, J. R. (2018). Teaching critical thinking in a GE class: A flipped model. *Thinking Skills and Creativity, 28*, 73–83. doi:10.1016/j.tsc.2018.02.010

Soo Von Esch, K. (2018). Teacher leaders as agents of change: Creating contexts for instructional improvement for English learner students. *The Elementary School Journal, 19*(1), 152–178. doi:10.1086/698753

Stover, L. T. (2006). *Guidelines for the preparation of teachers of English language arts.* Urbana, IL: NCTE.

Tankersley, K. (2005). Literacy strategies for grades 4-12: Reinforcing the threads of reading. Alexandria, VA: ASCD.

Tate, M. L. (2009). Workshops: Extend learning beyond your presentation with these brain- friendly strategies. *Journal of Staff Development, 30*(1), 44–46.

Thomas, K. (2016). *Developing a framework for reading instruction in St. Vincent and the Grenadines* (Unpublished doctoral dissertation). University of the West Indies, Bridgetown, Barbados.

Tompkins, G. E. (2014). *Literacy for the 21st century: A balanced approach* (7th ed.). Upper Saddle River, NJ: Merrill Prentice Hall.

Williams, A., Prestage, S., & Bedward, J. (2001). Individualism to collaboration: The significance of teacher culture to the induction of newly qualified teachers. *Journal of Education for Teaching*, 27(3), 253–267. doi:10.1080/02607470120091588

Zeichner, K., & Liu, K. Y. (2010). A Critical Analysis of Reflection as a Goal for Teacher Education. In N. Lyons (Ed.), *Handbook of Reflection and Reflective Inquiry*. Boston, MA: Springer. doi:10.1007/978-0-387-85744-2_4

KEY TERMS AND DEFINITIONS

Collaboration: Teachers working together with their colleagues, through regular and systematic interactions; dialoguing and participating in supportive teamwork in order to improve teaching and learning.

Content Knowledge: The general details, gist, and elements of a subject or discipline that all teachers should know. In language arts, this refers to the elements of language, its structure, components, and concepts such as composition, grammar, and devices that language arts teachers should know.

Critical Reflection: The ways in which teachers use questions to examine and re-examine their instructional practices, justify their decisions and think of ways in which to improve or change their instructional practice.

Critical Thinking: For the language arts teacher, critical thinking refers to the quality of in-depth, multifaceted and complex examination of how teachers think about their teaching, in order to reconstruct that thinking and reshape it into something better that influences decision making and instructional practice.

Pedagogical Content Knowledge: The skills, methodologies, and approaches that language arts teachers use in order to teach the content, in this case, the language arts content to students. Pedagogical content knowledge is the effective union between *how* teachers teach *what* has to be taught.

Professional Development: On-going, regular sessions conducted in a collaborative setting to provide training for teachers. The goals include improving pedagogical skills, content knowledge, and instructional practice in the classroom.

Questioning for Thinking: The art of asking questions that do not focus on memorization and or recall. Questioning for thinking means that teachers ask themselves (and their students) questions that are sufficiently probing to require higher order thinking that requires reasoning, assessing, analyzing, synthesizing, and reshaping thinking and responses.

Chapter 15

A Completely Structured Training on the Angoff Standard–Setting Method for Developing Critical– Thinking Skills of Teachers

Ifeoma Chika Iyioke
Michigan State University, USA

ABSTRACT

This chapter presents a completely structured training (CST) for the Angoff standard-setting method. The CST was developed to address the challenges teachers face in making the required probability judgments about student performance. It includes a comprehensive curriculum and instruction, practice, and feedback to guide participants on task performance. Overall, the approach is useful for developing critical-thinking skills among teachers in the context of assessing and evaluating educational achievement. This chapter also describes and illustrates how to use the training to facilitate professional development for K–12 teachers through programming. Guidelines, lessons and recommendations for implementation and study of CST are also provided.

PURPOSE AND OBJECTIVES OF CHAPTER

This chapter examines a Completely Structured Training (CST) approach for developing critical thinking (CT) of teachers about assessment and evaluation of students' performance. The CST was developed originally to address the complexity of the Angoff standard setting method judgment tasks for K-12 teachers. Thus, this chapter begins with the review of the literature to ground the CST in the perspectives on developing CT. The remaining sections respectively present the standard setting and Angoff method literature, the CST model, and a previous study of its effectiveness, including recommendations for future implementation.

DOI: 10.4018/978-1-5225-7829-1.ch015

Copyright © 2019, IGI Global. Copying or distributing in print or electronic forms without written permission of IGI Global is prohibited.

THE IMPORTANCE AND CHALLENGES OF CRITICAL THINKING

Critical thinking has become a focus of education, especially in the United States and other OECD countries with a knowledge economy characterized by tremendous amounts of information and ill-defined problems with uncertain solutions (e.g., Educational Resource Information Center [ERIC], 1988; Fung, Michael, Townsend & Judy, 2004; Hager & Kaye, 1992). In the U.S., the works of John Dewey on critique in the 1920s; Edward Glaser on CT in 1940s; and Bloom's Taxonomy of educational objectives in 1950s brought CT to the forefront of education (Saeger, 2014). However, no action was generated, until 1980, when the Rockefeller Commission on the Humanities recommended that CT be included in the U.S. Office of Education's definition of basic skills (ERIC, 1988). The CT movement exploded with the U.S. Secretary of Education's Commission on Excellence 1983 publication, *A Nation at Risk: The Imperative for Educational Reform* (National Commission on Excellence in Education, 1983). This report demonstrates that close to 40% of 17-year-olds did not possess the necessary higher-order thinking skills to draw inferences from written material; 80% were unable to write a persuasive essay; and 66% were unable to solve a multi-step mathematical problem. These startling findings ignited educators' efforts to assess and improve CT across the educational landscape in America (Florence, 2014).

However, there is widespread disagreement on the meaning and on strategy for assessing and developing CT in students. Several definitions have been offered in the fields of philosophy and psychology that influence the perspectives for education. The field of philosophy mostly influences the meaning for curricular purposes, while the field of psychology informs the pedagogical approaches. While the philosophical definitions focus on how people should think under ideal conditions, the cognitive psychology perspectives describe how people think (Abrami, 2015; Fung et al., 2004; Saeger, 2014). Even within the philosophical tradition, there are several definitions, which are driven by the debates about the extent to which CT is generalizable or specific to disciplines and whether it consists of skills or dispositions. For this chapter, a review of the most influential definitions and those that build upon them may suffice to underscore this status quo.

Mulnix (2012) defines CT as exercising the ability to grasp inferential relations holding between statements. He shares the dominant view that CT is an intellectual virtue that transcend subject matter divisions, however he believes that identifying relations between statements is the foundational skill. Therefore, he critiques Willingham (2007) as a notable exception of the contemporary views, which favors the generic traits approach. Willingham's (2007) definition of CT is a type of thinking in reasoning, making judgments and decisions, and problem-solving, characterized by effectiveness, novelty, and self-direction. Willingham argues that CT is not a skill on the basis that it is not generalizable from one domain to another. Meanwhile, an earlier consensual definition by the *American Philosophical Association* involving experts, such as Robert Ennis, Peter Facione and Richard Paul in a Delphi Research project indicates CT is a set of skills and dispositions. This study report Facione (1990), defines CT as a purposeful, self-regulatory judgment that results in interpretation, analysis, evaluation, inference and explanations of the basis for judgment. While adopting this definition for a meta-analysis (Abrami et al., 2015) suggest that it is the most broad-based, but not in widespread use. The most popular conceptions are Robert Ennis's. Specifically, Ennis (1989) defines CT as a reasonable reflective thinking focused on deciding what to believe or do. He replaced his earlier formulation in Ennis (1962), as a "correct evaluation of statements," which encountered much criticism, because it was based on skills alone. The penchant for Ennis (1989) conception is because it includes: dispositions and skills; generic and specific skills; and functional characteristics. But, it falls short of distinguishing CT from other higher order thinking. To establish more precision in the definition, Lipman (1988) defines CT as a mode of thinking in judgment that relies upon criteria; corrects itself; and is context-sensitive. Accordingly, CT requires mental processes which are self-correcting when reasoning is found failing to meet the criteria and sensitive to the context where the judgment is made (Saeger, 2014).

The approaches to developing CT skills are predicated on the assumption that human thinking is fallible (Fung et al., 2004). Herbert Simon's account (Simon, 1957) is the paradigm of the CST. It alerts us that human rationality is bounded, especially under conditions of considerable uncertainty and complexity (refer to the section on the CST). Unfortunately, several years after Robert Glaser's foundational work, the debate in instructional design still focuses on whether to view CT as a generic or a discipline-specific skill and on its transferability from one domain to another (Abrami et al., 2015). To facilitate development of curriculum and assessment tools, many theorists tend to identify sets of generic skills for good reasoning while assuming students who have mastered these skills will be able to put them to use in various domains (Fung et al., 2004). This approach applies to CST relying on the general principles of categorization and recall. ERIC (1988) identifies a process and content model of CT pedagogy. They represent the extreme views. Ennis's (1989) is a more comprehensive typology: general, infusion, immersion, and mixed model. The general approach is akin to the process model. It teaches CT separate from the content of a subject matter. While infusion and immersion are both content-based, CT is an explicit objective in the infusion course but not in the immersion course. A mixed-model involves a combination of these approaches. In accordance with this classification, the CST is an infusion model for developing CT skills.

In the 1990s, the perspectives on CT shifted from the general to the infusion approach based on research, which suggested that students have difficulty transferring skills with the general approach. Citing Prawat (1991), Angeli and Valanides (2009) in evaluating infusion for ill-defined issues indicate that this shift assumed that through infusion, transfer to other domains becomes possible. Subsequent research efforts lend support to the infusion method in the fields of science and mathematics education (e.g., Abrami et al., 2015; Aizikovitsh & Amit, 2010; Aizikovitsh-Udi, 2012a, 2012b; Kuntze, Aizikovitsh-Udi, & Clarke, 2017; Zulkpli, Abdullah, Kohar, & Ibrahim, 2017). For instance, Abrami's et al. (2015) meta-analysis indicated a significant effect size of 0.30 and effective strategies, as including opportunities for dialogue and the exposure of students to authentic or situated problems. Some researchers also suggest the benefit of the infusion model for teachers. Zulkpli et al. (2017) found that teachers gained satisfaction in terms of professional developments when applying the infusion approach. Aizitovitsch-Udi (2012a), referencing Feuerstein's study (2002) reported that teachers were able to develop CT in their students when provided theoretical and pedagogical knowledge. However, the efforts to integrate CT into teacher education focus on pre-service preparation (Aizikovitsh, 2012a; Feuerstein, 2002; Furness, Cowie, & Cooper, 2017; Haberlin, 2018; Hager & Kaye, 1992).

Thus, the CST is to fill this gap in the literature on professional development for in-service teachers. The framework of the curriculum is a hybrid combination of the Ennis (1989) and Lipman (1988) definitions, and the formulation of CT skills is thinking that uses experiential, assessment content and process criteria in generating probability judgment. Thus, the curriculum involves simpler principles than Liberman and Tversky's (2001) "Probability in Daily Life" Unit (Aizikovitsh, 2012). Meanwhile, the pedagogy focuses on skills while assuming positive affective dispositions.

The issue of how CT is measured is as important as understanding how CT can be taught. Some standardized instruments include the Watson-Glaser Critical Thinking Appraisal, Cornell and California Critical Thinking Skill Tests (Saeger, 2014). Hager and Kaye (1992) recommended mixed-methods, including structured analysis of the problem-solving process. The latter methods are in sync with the evaluation approaches of CST, which are useful to empower teachers to "work on the inside." Work on the inside implies conducting research on teaching and learning in their classrooms (Aizikovitsh, 2012a). The remaining segments present how to accomplish this through a criterion-referenced standard setting method.

THE CONCEPT AND HISTORY OF STANDARD SETTING

Standard setting refers to approaches for measuring educational achievement in terms of two or more performance levels or *cut scores*, such as designating below, at, or above grade or proficiency level (Cizek, 2001). There is consensus on the meaning of standard setting, but a disagreement on the methodology. The paradigms are parameter estimation and value judgment. Parameter estimation assumes the existence of a correct value for cut scores while value judgment assumes cut scores are constructed and have no right answer (Zieky, 2001; Skorupski, 2012). The CST perspective is parameter estimation and using Reckase's (2009) model, to formalize the process of standard setting and improve the accuracy of cut scores. The propositions of the model are that standard setting judgments begin by establishing performance standards, followed by the development of Performance Level Descriptors (PLD), test design, and then standard translation. The performance standards are achievement goals (Linn, 2001). Accordingly, PLDs constitute operational definitions of performance standards in terms of specific knowledge and skills of students. A test is a sample of the knowledge and skills. Standard setting methods are more appropriately called standard translation methods, because they constitute measurement operations for converting PLDs into cut scores. However, the label "standard setting method" stands, to be consistent with the literature.

The methods of standard setting are norm-referenced or criterion-referenced. Norm-referenced methods compare a student's performance to those of other students, ensuring (for example) that 10% would fail and not receive a license or credential, while for criterion-referenced methods the frame of reference are performance standards (Cizek, 1993, 2001). The U.S. National Assessment of Educational Progress (NAEP) approach to standard setting was norm-referenced prior to 1990. Given that NAEP was the only national assessment of achievement based on a defensible sample, the governing body interpreted the authorizing legislative responsibility as a mandate to set performance standards, which it named achievement levels as part of the 1990 test administration. The achievement levels were descriptive classifications of performance based on the notion of criterion-referenced measurement as conceptualized by Robert Glaser in 1963. The NAEP engaged content experts in generating descriptions of what students should be able to do at different achievement levels and in making judgments about actual performance (Linn, 2001).

Criterion-referenced methods are test-centered, or examinee centered (Skorupski, 2012). Test-centered methods require judgments about individual test items, while examinee-centered methods require holistic judgments about student work. An example of a test-centered standard method is the Angoff method, the focus of this chapter. The techniques are akin to Delphi survey research methods. The Delphi technique is about harnessing and organizing judgment, particularly in problems that are complex (Hsu & Sanford, 2012). Survey instruments typically try to identify "what is," the Delphi technique attempts to address "what could/should be (Miller, 2006)."

In contemporary times, the U.S. Department of Education continues to mandate minimum competency testing through school accountability laws, such as the No Child Left Behind (NCLB) Act of 2001 and the Every Student Succeed Act (ESSA) of 2015. Both have addressed the need to improve the quality of K–12 education and postschool outcomes of students through increasing the rigor of the standards. However, the evidence from the implementation of the NCLB Proficient standard, suggests that without changing the nature of professional development for teachers to include training on the assessment of student performance, these reforms would do little to achieve the goal of improving the quality of education. In retrospect, the Nation at Risk suggested that teachers' judgments of student performance are often inaccurate. In 2010, America ranked 11th in college-completion rates for young adults, and 40% of secondary school graduates did not have the skills to advance in their jobs (United States [US] Department of Education, 2010). Hence, the ESSA College and Career Readiness standard set the goal of helping all American students transition into and complete postsecondary credential by 2020. The premise of this research is that these school reforms will take root if teachers benefit from professional development on CT skills. A review of the state of knowledge on the Angoff method for accomplishing this purpose follows.

THE IMPORTANCE AND CHALLENGES OF THE ANGOFF METHOD

From a historical standpoint, the Angoff method, named after William Angoff, who first proposed it in 1971 in a book chapter on testing, was one of the first prescribed (Zieky, 2001). A footnote in that chapter described the Angoff method as originally formulated in terms of probability. Angoff (1971) also prescribed a Yes/No method that required participants to simply indicate a "yes" response if the target group of students would respond correctly to an item, and a "no" response if the target group of students would not respond correctly to an item. However, the Angoff method has retained the more popular probability method rather than the Yes/No method. It remains one of the most widely researched methods because it presents a more realistic formulation of correct responses to test questions (Impara & Plake, 1997).

Implementation of the Angoff method adopts a participatory approach, using individuals who represent the stakeholders in a test scenario. For studies in K–12 contexts, stakeholders include teachers who interact and are familiar with the performance of student populations (Impara & Plake, 1997, 1998). The participants in the Angoff method review tests and judge the probability that a minimally competent candidate (MCC) will answer the individual questions on a test correctly. In educational measurement parlance, these probability judgments represent "test items difficulty." The common practice is to sum the probability judgments for each participant and obtain the group average as the estimate of the minimum test score (i.e., cut score) that meets the performance standard.

Although the Angoff method has psychometric appeal, research studies in the K–12 context have consistently concluded that participants struggle to make the required judgments (e.g., Impara & Plake, 1997, 1998; McGinty, 2005; Shepard, Glaser, Linn, & Bohrnstedt, 1993; Skaggs & Hein, 2011; Skorupski, 2012). Impara and Plake (1997) report that although teachers could estimate the relative difficulty of test items very well, they were unable to estimate absolute difficulty accurately. The inability of standard-setting participants to estimate absolute difficulty of test items was reported even when participants were familiar with the students and with the test. Specifically, Impara and Plake (1998) found that teachers were more accurate in estimating the performance of the total group than of the MCC, but in neither case was their accuracy level high. Skorupski (2012) reports that participants have problems understanding MCCs. McGinty (2005) finds that participants have a misunderstanding about the difference between prediction and value judgement. Citing Shepard et al.'s (1993) report on the 1992 NAEP, Skaggs and Hein (2011) note that the method is cognitively complex, meaning that it is characterized by uncertainties of using information in judgments. Shepard et al. (1993) concluded that the method presents an infeasible cognitive task. This conclusion was unfounded (Cizek, 1993). However, it was consequential in discontinuation of its use with the NAEP. Most of the criticisms of the Angoff method and the warrants for the conclusion have to do with the training of the participants (Cizek, 1993). Thus, Skorupski (2012) recommends the study of training paradigms.

Reid (1991) identifies the scant structured training on the Angoff method as a gap in the literature. By structured training, he means instruction and practice activities to assist participants in arriving at a conceptualization of the MCCs and applying this conceptualization at the individual-item level. But, the common training focuses on various types of feedback to participants on their judgments. Reckase (2001) provided a framework to organize the feedback, based on the level of cognitive effect: normative feedback; hybrid feedback; and process feedback. Normative feedback is impact data showing the proportion of students in a reference group that would fail if the recommended cut score were implemented. Hybrid feedback are actual students' item-performance data and discussions of the participants' item-difficulty judgments. Process feedback are construct maps—for instance, the Reckase Chart, based on item-response models, such as the Rasch (1960) model that predicts responses to test questions in terms of item difficulty and the ability of the student.

Hybrid feedback are the most commonly researched type (e.g., Clauser, Mee, Baldwin, Margolis, & Dillon, 2009; Fitzpatrick, 1989). Such feedback has the common, seemingly cognitive effect of yielding the convergence of judgments (e.g., Clauser, et al., 2009; Fitzpatrick, 1989). Contrarily, research by Clauser et al. (2009) in the context of professional licensure and certification suggests that the observed positive impacts of performance-data feedback are due to replacing criterion-referenced with norm-referenced judgments. Mee et al. (2013) examine the impact of instructions for how to use feedback in judgments. They report less normative influence than is reported in past studies. Thus, structured feedback design appears to reduce the normative effect of performance-data feedback. But, appropriate implementation of these structured feedback design requires the introduction of more complex judgment principles and may result in less efficient training (Reckase, 2001).

Raymond and Reid (2001) reiterate the need for adequate emphasis on instruction and practice because of the novelty of the tasks. They analyzed the tasks for participants as first to imagine students who barely meet a performance standard, and then to judge their correct-response probabilities on individual test questions. Efforts to provide structured training instruction and practice have focused on the task of conceptualizing the MCCs (Giraud, Impara, & Plake, 2005; Hein & Skaggs, 2010; Impara & Plake, 1997, 1998; Mills, Melican, & Ahluwalia, 1991). The instruction involves the review of and practice defining the attributes of students on the borderline of a performance category (Skorupski, 2012). Defining Borderline Performance Level Descriptors (BLPDs) is essential for participants to achieve a common understanding of minimum competence (Mills, Melican, & Ahluwalia, 1991). The instructions on how to identify the MCCs have asked teachers to think about a hypothetical group. However, the evidence suggests that teachers are inclined to think about specific students than a hypothetical group (Hein & Skaggs, 2010; Impara & Plake, 1997, 1998).

The instruction on item-difficulty judgment for the MCCs review assessment content, while the practice is taking the test (Giraud, Impara, & Plake, 2005; Reid, 1991). Estimating item difficulties requires an adequate understanding of the substantive difficulty of test items, which according to Haertel and Loriè (2004) refer to the cognitive skills they assess. Thus, the practice of requiring teachers to take the test may be inadequate to assist them in identifying the knowledge and skill constructs that test items assess and in differentiating the abilities of students. Because these structured training approaches do not include meaningful activities to assist participants in conceptualizing items and in generating their difficulties, the author designates them as Partially Structured Training (PST).

Furthermore, PST design relies on a limited understanding of cognitive processes of participants (e.g., McGinty, 2005; Skorupski, 2012). Given the striking analogy between the research in cognitive psychology on probability judgment and the Angoff method tasks, it seems appropriate to draw from the ample cognitive processes uncovered in this area and forge ahead with the task of prescription. Thus, this research relies on the judgment literature to fully understand the cognitive processes in the Angoff method and to design a Completely Structured Training (CST).

THE COMPLETELY STRUCTURED TRAINING MODEL

Table 1 contrasts the CST with PST. The elaboration that follow focuses on the CST to avoid redundancy.

Curriculum

The CST curriculum include concepts and cognitive strategies for identifying MCCs and estimating item difficulties. The concepts are students' assessment and performance constructs. The assessment constructs refer to the content and cognitive processes students' test items assess. The performance constructs are the PLDs and MCCs. They depend on the framework of the standards and curriculum.

The curriculum draws from the field of educational psychology, identifying the importance of a curriculum that covers both concepts and cognitive strategy. A cognitive strategy is a mental routine or procedure for accomplishing a cognitive goal (Dole, Nokes, & Drits, 2009). The cognitive strategies rest on the probability-judgment literature, which identifies the cognitive processes of judgment as heuristics. Heuristics rely on little information and limited thinking in judgment. People use heuristics in making

Table 1. Contrast of completely structured training with partially structured training methodology

Process	Completely Structured Training	Partially Structured Training
Curriculum and instruction	Complete Judgment Strategy: Explicated Process for Integration and Use of Students' Knowledge, Skills, and Performance Concepts exemplified by Item Content, Process & PLD Constrained features for categorization by assessment constructs Unconstrained Recall Recall of real instances Direct Instruction on cognitive processes for identifying students and judging item difficulties	Partial Judgment Strategy: Unexplicated Process for Integration and Use of Students' Knowledge, Skills, and Performance Concepts exemplified by Item Content, Process & PLD Unconstrained features for categorization: consider both construct-relevant and irrelevant factors that affect item difficulty Constrained Recall The imagination of hypothetical instances Direct instruction only on cognitive processes for identifying students
Practice	Structured and closed-ended	Unstructured and open-ended
Feedback	Process and intermediate outcomes	Normative, Hybrid, Process and final outcomes

judgments because of the notion of *bounded rationality*, which indicates constraints in resources, such as time for thinking in the real world. In contrast, unbounded rationality assumes no real-world constraints (Simon, 1957). Unbounded rationality underlies the design of PST to provide an array of information to participants. This design may explain the complexity of Angoff judgments.

The heuristics are representativeness, availability, and adjustment from an anchor (see Tversky & Kahneman, 1974). Tversky and Kahneman provide a summary of the heuristics and biases research. The evidence from the research indicates that heuristics are responsible for the biases in judgments. However, the fast and frugal heuristic perspective of Gigerenzer, Todd, and the ABC Research Group (1999) suggests that heuristics can yield judgments comparable to statistical estimates and highlights the need to build prescriptive models.

Thus, the author applies the representativeness and availability heuristics to design CST because the adjustment from an anchor is a norm-referenced approach employed when a relevant value is available. Skorupski (2012) provides evidence that indicate teachers may use this cognitive process when aware of previous cut scores. Rather than give them values, the CST serves to help teachers rely on their content knowledge and personal experiences.

The representativeness heuristic mediates judgments through categorization, while the availability heuristic mediates judgments by recall. Categorization refers to semantic memory operations, while recall refers to episodic memory operations (The interested reader can refer to Baddeley & Hitch, 1974, and Tulving, 1972, in the Additional Readings for distinctions of working, semantic and episodic long-term memory systems). Furthermore, the System II, as opposed to System I mode of heuristic thinking was adopted for the CST. Kahneman (2011) made the distinction. System 1 thinking is a fast, instinctive, and emotional mode of thinking. Conversely, System 2 is a slow, deliberate, and logical mode of thinking. Figure 1 presents the judgment strategy.

Accordingly, the cognitive processes are categorization and recall of student performance information. The strategy for categorization involves sorting and ordering students based on their KSAs, and test items based on KSAs needed to answer them. Based on similarity judgment research, the strategy suggests the importance of common rather than distinctive features for categorizing objects (Tversky, 1977). Thus, the CST gives full weight to KSAs that predict item difficulty. This strategy assumes achievement of a reduction in cognitive complexity by constraining the features used in judgments to the content and processes that tests assess. Meanwhile, the strategy for recall requires an extensive memory search to retrieve test-performance information and mental counting of successful performance events. It draws on research on human memory, suggesting the superiority of exhaustive or reproductive recall compared to biased recall or imagination (see Tversky & Kahneman, 1973, for the availability heuristic,

Figure 1. Judgment strategy

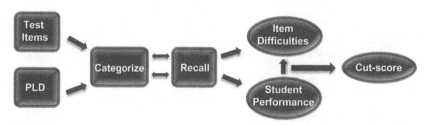

and Schacter & Addis, 2007, for imagination). The process for making the judgment involves two steps. The first requires teachers to identify their students who barely meet a PLD (i.e., Minimally Competent Candidates). The second step requires teachers to recall previously used items in their classrooms that assess the same KSAs as those on the test and to provide judgments by counting the correct responses among the students identified in Step One.

The Methods for Delivering Curriculum

The methods for delivering CST curriculum are a comprehensive approach to addressing the knowledge and skill competencies of the Angoff method through instruction, practice, and feedback to break down its two-component tasks into simpler mental operations.

The methodology for instruction is Direct on both the cognitive processes for identifying students and judging item difficulties. Dole et al. (2009) cite a robust body of research demonstrating the value of direct instruction for teaching cognitive strategies. Direct instruction has roots in cognitivist theories of learning (Kirschner, Sweller, & Clark, 2006).

The CST practice is structured and closed-ended because the procedures break up the Angoff method tasks into categorization and recall strategies. Jonassen (1997) informs the characterization of practice in terms of structure. Problems are structured when they are constrained to engage a limited number of concepts, rules, and principles. The distinction of open-ended vs. closed-ended tasks is made in academic training contexts. While closed-ended tasks are structured, open-ended are ill-structured. The cognitive theories for the design of closed-ended tasks for CST are the depth- and transfer-appropriate processing principles that suggest improvements in memory performance when the instruction and practice activities match with the curriculum (Craik & Lockhart, 1972; Morris, Bransford, & Franks, 1977). The CST uses process feedback, including intermediate outcomes of categorization and recall.

A CASE OF RESEARCH ON THE TRAINING

The purpose of this pilot study (Iyioke, 2013) was to evaluate the effectiveness of the CST and PST with feedback for facilitating the use of assessment constructs in judgment for K-12 teachers. The evaluation design was based on the Kirkpatrick's (1994) training-outcome framework and McGinty's (2005) input, process, output, and outcome model. The inputs are teachers with target characteristics, the process is training, and the outcomes, in accordance with the Kirkpatrick's model includes reaction, satisfaction, knowledge and skills. The methodology was mixed using open-ended and closed-ended questions for assessment, and non-parametric statistical methods, such as the Kruskal's Non-Metric Multidimensional Scaling (NMDS) for structured analysis of the judgment process and independent samples t-tests for hypothesis testing. Kruskal's NMDS computes a lower dimensional space and uses scree plots of stress values to explore the dimensionality of the judgments (Kruskal 1964a, 1964b; Kruskal & Wish 1978; Sturrock & Rocha, 2000). Stress indicates the extent to which judgments can recover the dimensionality of assessment constructs. Scatterplots of the Kruskal's NMDS dimensions investigate skill in categorization and whether the clustering of items recover assumptions about the nature and relationships between the knowledge and skills constructs they assess.

Instruments and Measures

The instruments included a script, participant background questionnaire, skill tests and a training evaluation questionnaire. A script of training was necessary to ensure fidelity in the implementation. The background questionnaire included questions on characteristics, such as demographics, teaching and educational experiences, motivation, emotion, and engagement that could equally influence performance. The skills tested includes classifying, ranking, recalling and recognizing test items based on KSAs needed to answer them. The judgments were in response to "what proportion of barely proficient students would respond correctly to the test items?" The Michigan Educational Assessment Program (MEAP) fourth-grade mathematics assessment and the corresponding Proficient PLD developed in 2005 by the Michigan Department of Education (MDE) were used as references for providing the judgments. Two student tests were used: one for practice and the other for the two rounds of judgment based on feedback. The tests consisted of 15 multiple-choice items each, and the items were samples of the knowledge and skills of the proficient PLD. The items assessed four Michigan Curriculum Framework (MCF) content strands (Number and Operations (N), Geometry (G), Data and Probability (D), and Measurement (M)) and thirteen MCF fourth-Grade Level Content Expectations (GLCE). Additionally, the items assessed Level 1 (Recall) and Level 2 (Skills and Concepts) of the Webb's Depth of Knowledge (DOK) levels. Five items were common on both tests. The unique items on the tests were matched by the MCF content strands and Grade Level Content Expectations (GLCEs), and they differed slightly in DOK levels. Specifically, seven items on the practice test assessed a DOK level of 2, while nine items on the feedback test assessed a DOK level of 2. The evaluation questionnaire included questions on participants process for providing judgments, reactions to and satisfaction with training activities.

Staffing and Participants

A Michigan State University (MSU) policy expert assisted with facilitating the studies, and a graduate student with the feedback data analyses. There were 22 participants in the study—10 and 12 in the CST and PST, respectively—comprising a purposive sample of preservice and inservice teachers in the mid-Michigan area, recruited by listserv and classroom visits. The participants were predominantly Caucasian females. More than half of them were mathematics specialists and had prior teaching experience.

Training and Data-Collection Procedures

The CST was held two weeks before the PST. For the two training sessions, the survey on background characteristics was e-mailed to participants five days before the training, with the instruction to return them on the day of training. Because of scheduling conflicts, 18 of the 22 participants indicated that they would be available to participate on only one of the two training days. The remaining participants were assigned to a training method to balance group sizes. Additionally, participants were assigned to table groups within training to balance their background characteristics. Table 2 presents the CST and PST activities in order of implementation, and a brief elaboration follows.

Summarily, the training activities involved the review of assessment and PLDs, instruction on the Angoff method procedures, practice, and feedback. The instructions were based on scripts and PowerPoint slides the author developed. The CST instruction on assessment involved the review of content strands, GLCEs, and Webb's DOK items. The PST included instruction only on the content strands and GLCEs.

Table 2. Completely structured vs. partially structured training activities

Activity	Completely Structured Training	Partially Structured Training
1	Facilitators reviewed assessment Handouts on mathematics Content Strands and Grade Level Content Expectations (GLCEs) Handout on Webb's DOK	Facilitators reviewed assessment Handouts on mathematics Content Strands and Grade Level Content Expectations (GLCEs)
2	Participants elaborated PLD	Participants took the test
3	Facilitators instructed on the Angoff method Think about the barely proficient students For each item on the test: Think about what it measures (Content strand, GLCE, and DOK level) Think about items that measure these same knowledge and skills Recall the proportion of students who are barely proficient that would respond correctly to items in this category Mark the percentage from 0 to 100	Participants elaborated PLD
4	Participants coded, rank ordered, and judged difficulties of test items Code test items to content strands, GLCEs, and DOK Rank order test items in terms of difficulty Estimate proportion of fourth-grade students who are barely proficient to respond correctly to the items	Facilitator instructed on the Angoff method Think about a classroom made up of 100 barely proficient students For each item on the test: Based on description of barely proficient students, what proportion of the students in the above classroom would answer the item correctly? Mark the percentage from 0 to 100
5	Facilitators provided feedback one Whole group discussion of the bar graph displays of the coding of test items to DOK Whole group discussion of the line chart displays of item difficulty judgments and cut scores A handout containing the content strand, GLCE, DOK, the rank ordering, and the proportions of the students responding correctly to the practice test items	Participants rank ordered and judged difficulties of test items Rank order test items in terms of difficulty Estimate proportion of barely proficient students who would respond correctly to the items
6	Participants rank ordered, recalled, and recognized test items, and judged difficulties Rank order test items in terms of difficulty Recall and recognition of test items Estimate proportion of the fourth-grade students who are barely proficient to respond correctly to the items	Facilitators provided feedback one Whole group discussion of the line chart displays of test item difficulty judgments and cut scores. A handout containing the rank order of items and the proportions of students responding correctly to the practice items.
7	Facilitators provided feedback two Handout on guidelines for discussions Table group discussions of the participants' DOK designations, difficulty ranking of items, estimated item difficulties, and cut scores	Participants rank ordered, recalled, and recognized test items, and judged difficulties Rank order test items in terms of difficulty Recall and recognition of test items based on content. Estimate proportion of the fourth-grade students who are barely proficient to respond correctly to the items
8	Participants rank ordered and judged difficulties of test items Rank order test items in terms of difficulty Estimate proportion of the fourth-grade students who are barely proficient to respond correctly to the items	Facilitators provided feedback two Handout on Reckase Chart Table group discussions of Reckase Chart feedback, participants' items difficulty ranks, and estimates
9	Facilitators administered evaluation survey	Participants rank ordered and judged difficulties of test items
10		Facilitators administered evaluation survey

The CST instruction on the procedure for identifying students asked participants to think about their students, while the PST asked them to think about a hypothetical classroom of 100 students. The practice activities included discussing and elaborating the KSAs of the MCCs, categorizing test items for CST and taking the test for PST, rank ordering, recalling, and recognizing items based on KSAs needed to answer them. The PST training group was also tested on recall and recognition, and on rank ordering of items in terms of difficulty to facilitate the evaluation. There were three rounds of Angoff method judgment. For the CST, the first round of judgment was concurrent with the categorization exercises, while for the PST, it occurred after they took the test. The second and third rounds of judgment followed feedback. Feedback One included whole-group discussions on the charts of participants' item-difficulty and cut-score judgments, and the coding of DOK to items for the CST. Feedback Two for CST was table-group discussions of the participants' coding of DOK to items, item difficulty, and cut-score judgments. For PST, Feedback Two was table group discussions of item-difficulty judgments using the Reckase Chart. Both training methods were concluded with the administration of the evaluation questionnaire.

Data-Analysis Procedures

The judgment data were analyzed using the R version 3.0.1 Development Core (R Development Core Team, 2013) isoMDS function from the MASS package's implementation of Kruskal's NMDS. For the NMDS, the input data consisted of the judgment-data matrices of the 10 participants' 15 items for CST and the 12 participants' 15 items for the PST. The author transposed the judgment datasets for the NMDS analyses. Hence, the data matrices supplied to the NMDS procedure were the 15 items × 10 participants' and the 15 items × 12 participants' item-difficulty judgments for the CST and the PST, respectively. The remainder of the data were analyzed by Excel and SPSS to obtain graphical displays, descriptive statistics and perform t-tests of significance.

Key Findings and Conclusions

This section focuses on the key conclusions of the study, while providing supporting evidence. The interested reader can refer to Iyioke (2013) for the detailed presentation of the results.

The CST participants reacted more positively and were more satisfied with the training. The average evaluation of training by CST participants was 3.70 (vs. 3.25 for PST) while the average evaluation of facilitators by CST participants was 3.80 (vs. 3.09 for PST) on the 4-point Likert scale of assessment: "1" = Poor; "2" = Fair, "3" = Good; and "4" = Very Good. The t-values were significant at $\alpha = .05$.

Participants in both trainings expressed a positive value for the Angoff method and for the discussions on feedback. Based on theme analyses of participants' comments about helpful training procedures, 13 of the 22 comments indicated that discussions were helpful, while the remaining comments suggested that the Angoff method was useful.

The participants of CST and PST provided more meaningful judgments after instruction and practice than feedback. Scree plots of the NMDS stress values indicated the item difficulty judgments can be summarized meaningfully in relatively few dimensions. The scatterplots of the first two NMDS indicated participants' item-difficulty judgments related more to the hypothesized content assessed by the items after instruction and practice compared to feedback, especially for the PST.

The normative effects of feedback were considerably greater for the PST than CST. Table 3 shows the CST participants expressed greater reliance on their educational and classroom experience in their

Table 3. Self-reports of judgment performance

Self- Reports of Performance	CST *M(SD)*	PST *M(SD)*	*t* - Test
Discussion and Feedback Impacted Recommendations	3.30(0.68)	3.75(0.45)	1.87**
Educational or Classroom Experience Impacted Recommendations	3.80(0.42)	3.17(0.84)	2.30**

judgment, while the PST participants reported greater reliance on feedback in making judgments. Table 4 shows the difference between training in the average relationship of participants' judgments with DOK criteria was higher for the CST participants, and it tended toward and eventually became significant with Feedback Two. Table 5 shows the PST participants feedback test cut scores were significantly higher than those estimated based on students' performance data and for the practice test, an easier test.

Hence, the conclusion was that the CST is more effective than the PST for facilitating criterion-referenced judgments with feedback. The findings support Clauser et al.'s (2009) conclusion in a professional licensure and certification context that participants abandon their content-based for norm-referenced judgments with feedback. At the same time, they discredit previous conclusions about the infeasibility of the Angoff method, such as those of Shepard et al. (1993). Rather than suggesting a barrier of cognitive

Table 4. Correlations between item difficulty judgments and validation criteria

Correlations (*r*)	Completely Structured Training *M(SD)*	Partially Structured Training *M(SD)*	*t*-Test
DOK			
Practice	-0.41(0.19)	-0.43(0.16)	0.29
Round One	-0.38(0.15)	-0.31(0.18)	1.08
Round Two	-0.41(0.13)	-0.25(0.10)	3.28**
Group Mean			
Practice	0.67(0.2)	0.77(0.15)	1.26
Round One	0.72(0.1)	0.78(0.08)	1.68
Round Two	0.79(0.05)	0.93(0.03)	6.85**
p-Value			
Practice	0.49(0.24)	0.54(0.20)	0.46
Round One	0.59(0.15)	0.68(0.10)	1.69
Round Two	0.67(0.08)	0.89(0.06)	7.54**

Table 5. Cut score estimates

Cut Score	Completely Structured Training *M(SD)*	Partially Structured Training *M(SD)*	Performance Data Estimate (*M*)	95% LCB	95% UCB
Practice	9.03(1.99)	8.44(0.87)	8.43	7.27	9.45
Round One	10.01(1.19)	10.45(0.87)	8.15	7	9.18
Round Two	10.05(0.83)	10.38(0.82)	8.15	7	9.18

complexity exists in the use of the Angoff method, the evidence here indicated that inappropriate training is the barrier, especially feedback. Even when supplied with the qualitatively better CST instruction and practice, participants were still unable to use normative data feedback, although they were better able to maintain the meaningfulness and stability of their judgments. Therefore, the recommendation is to consider CST instruction and practice with process feedback.

SUMMARY AND RECOMMENDATIONS

This chapter provides a look into a CST approach to developing critical thinking of teachers about assessment and evaluation of students' performance. The study presented in this chapter was small-scale. The limitations pertain to the short test lengths, the small sample size, the less-than-ideal statistical controls, and the simplicity of the design used to test the hypotheses (reader can refer to Iyioke, 2018 for the practical challenges that limited the study design). Because the CST vs. PST did show the prospect of improving the meaningfulness of judgments with feedback and the participants indicated that the group discussions were valuable, the recommendation is to consider the CST with discussions on the process feedback when using the Angoff method for K-12 teachers. The recommendations for future designs of CST, which also draw from the lessons learned from this study address five topical areas: facilitators; participants; materials and discussion; activities; and evaluation.

The appropriate facilitators for CST are individuals with experience in standard setting and from fields in education including policy, curriculum and instruction, and measurement. Managing and implementing the training is the facilitator's responsibility. The effective implementation of any model depends on adequate resources. Thus, it is important to secure adequate funding and minimize cost of implementation through a careful selection of training facility and staff. For instance, this trial run of the CST cost the author (an under-resourced graduate student with no grant funding) $3,960.46 USD. Using a facility in the school rather than booking hotel space was one strategy used for achieving a cost-efficient implementation.

The target population for the CST are inservice teachers at the grade level for standard setting, who have sound working memory and adequate motivation to learn (refer to the Additional Readings for the human memory systems that support CT). Involving teachers in the standard setting is mutually beneficial for the participants and the standard-setting enterprise, facilitating professional development and improving the validity of standard-setting outcomes. In addition, teacher participants transferring acquired skills in educational assessment to self-evaluations of their classroom practices will facilitate the achievement of goals described in accountability laws for school improvement.

One caveat on recruiting teachers in standard settings is that some may participate with the ulterior motive of biasing the judgments in favor of their performance evaluations (see Skorupski, 2012). Hence, the teachers should be oriented appropriately about the benefits of rendering accurate judgments. In addition, incentives such as offering continuing education credits will help to build positive motivation.

Regarding the training materials, including Angoff rating instructions, PLDs, and test items, they should be designed or selected carefully. It is also essential that Angoff rating instructions be printed and handed out to the participants for ease of reference during the rating tasks. Using well-defined PLDs to inform test design and facilitate judgements is important (Giraud et al., 2005; Perie, 2008). Also, piloting test items will control for irrelevant factors (e.g., item format) that could impact their difficulty. Appropriate design and selection of test items with adequate alignment to PLD for Angoff studies would potentially enhance participant performance. Also, appropriate design and selection of test items and documentation of the content-domain constructs they measure would facilitate evaluation of training outcomes. Furthermore, because criterion-referenced standard setting methods are analogous to Delphi methods, the survey research methods should be applied extensively in the design of discussions for collecting and analyzing judgments by participants of CST. Facilitators designing the discussions should account for differences in participant experiences with the target student population by assigning them to table groups to create balance in experience. Administering a survey could obtain information about participant background characteristics before the training. This information could support allocating seat positions by matching participants using experiential variables, and then randomly assigning participants to tables within the matched groups.

The CST is a full-day (eight-hour) training, and there are two recommended options for implementation. The first, based on practical considerations, is to provide instructions and practice activities on categorization and recall, and only one round of practice on item-difficulty judgments, with feedback if the evaluation of skills indicates the participants understand the concepts and strategies involved in the judgment. If an organization is not too constrained by resources, the second recommendation is to provide multiple rounds of feedback. Skorupski (2012) notes the need for more time in training as well as for adequate practical considerations. Thus, the CST serves to achieve efficiency by devoting more time to learning concepts and strategies for making judgments, while de-emphasizing data feedback.

The recommended design of the CST and PST activities in future evaluations are as follows: instruction on assessment constructs; practice categorizing and rank ordering items; practice defining BLPDS; instruction on the judgment procedure; practice judging items' difficulties, including tests of recall and recognition of the similarities and differences between test items based on KSAs they assess; and feedback. Admissible training activities, which were not considered in this implementation of the CST include elaborating the PLDs by theme-analyzing the knowledge and skill attributes of the BLPDs, in addition to their performance, and the instruction to think of a single student. The instruction to think about single students should go with item difficulty judgment instruction to think about the proportion of times the student has been able to respond correctly to similar items as those on the test. Also, an option for instruction on judging item difficulties, if tests align with PLDs is to match items to PLDs, recall and use discussed performance information about the BLPDs as the basis for their judgments.

Iterative feedback is delivered when the judgments do not meet acceptable standards. The recommended feedback on understanding of assessment constructs is group discussion on categorization and rank ordering of items, which includes referencing judgments by content experts. The feedback on the conception of MCCs is a construct map of BLPDs response profiles on test items that assess PLDs. The construct map should delineate the knowledge and skill constructs that items assess, and response probabilities at ability levels that correspond to the Rasch model item-difficulty estimates. The Rasch model is the best option for estimating parameters for evaluating judgments because it is the item-response model closest to the judgment strategy. Participants can be instructed to use the construct map as a reference to adjust recommendations of greater uncertainties that align with a performance level while maintaining substantive-difficulty ordering of items.

The short-term evaluation research question is as follows: What is the effectiveness of the CST vs. PST for facilitating CT skills of pre-disposed teachers for assessment and evaluation of students' performance? The long-term research question is whether the approach to standard setting holds a privileged position with respect to attaining knowledge about students' performance over other thought or model processes.

These future evaluations should be based on continuous assessment of the knowledge and skills of participants before, during, and at the end of training. The framework for evaluation is Kirkpatrick's (1994) training outcome measures. The knowledge and skills to assess prior to and during training should encompass recall, recognition, categorization, and difficulty rank ordering of items. It is essential to measure noncognitive factors that could potentially influence the effects of training, such as participants' motivation and engagement. The assessment at the end of training should include self-report measures on confidence, understanding, satisfaction, factors considered, and strategies that the participants applied in their judgments. The judgments should be evaluated by nonparametric statistics to offer insights about cognitive processes (Refer to Iyioke, 2013, 2015, for the use of these methods. Note that the CST is Heuristic training and PST Normative training in these reports).

REFERENCES

Abrami, P. C., Bernard, R. M., Borokhovski, E., Waddington, D. I., Wade, A., & Persons, T. (2015). Strategies for teaching students to think critically: A meta-analysis. *Review of Educational Research, 85*(2), 275–291. doi:10.3102/0034654314551063

Aizikovitsh, E., & Amit, M. (2010). Evaluating an infusion approach to the teaching of critical thinking skills through mathematics. *Procedia: Social and Behavioral Sciences, 2*(2), 3818–3822. doi:10.1016/j.sbspro.2010.03.596

Aizikovitsh-Udi, E. (2012a). *Developing critical thinking through probability models, intuitive judgments and decision-making under uncertainty* (Doctoral dissertation). Saarbrucken, Germany: LAP Lambert Academic Publishing.

Aizikovitsh-Udi, E. (2012b). Connections between statistical thinking and critical thinking – A case study. *International Congress of Mathematics Education*, Seoul, South Korea.

Angeli, C., & Valanides, N. (2009). Instructional effects on critical thinking: Performance on ill-defined issues. *Learning and Instruction, 19*(4), 322–334. doi:10.1016/j.learninstruc.2008.06.010

Angoff, W. H. (1971). Scales, norms, and equivalent scores. In R. L. Thorndike (Ed.), *Educational measurement* (pp. 508–600). Washington, DC: American Council on Education.

Cizek, G. J. (1993). *Reactions to the National Academy of Education report: Setting performance standards for student achievement*. Washington, DC: National Assessment Governing Board.

Cizek, G. J. (2001). Conjectures on the rise and call of standard setting: An introduction to context and practice. In C. J. Cizek (Ed.), *Setting performance standards: Concepts, methods, and perspectives* (pp. 3–17). Mahwah, NJ: Lawrence Erlbaum.

Clauser, B. E., Mee, J., Baldwin, S. G., Margolis, M. J., & Dillon, G. F. (2009). Judges' use of examinee performance data in an Angoff standard-setting exercise for a medical licensing examination: An experimental study. *Journal of Educational Measurement, 46*(4), 390–407. doi:10.1111/j.1745-3984.2009.00089.x

Craik, F. I. M., & Lockhart, R. S. (1972). Levels of processing: A framework for memory research. *Journal of Verbal Learning and Verbal Behavior, 11*(6), 671–684. doi:10.1016/S0022-5371(72)80001-X

Dole, J. A., Nokes, J. D., & Drits, D. (2009). Cognitive strategy instruction. In G. G. Duffy & S. E. Israel (Eds.), *Handbook of research on reading comprehension* (pp. 347–372). Mahwah, NJ: Erlbaum.

Educational Resources Information Center. (1988). Critical thinking skills and teacher education. Washington, DC: ERIC Clearing house on Teacher Education Digest 3-88.

Ennis, R. H. (1962). A concept of critical thinking. *Harvard Educational Review, 32*(1), 81–111.

Ennis, R. H. (1989). Critical thinking and subject specificity: Clarification and needed research. *Educational Researcher, 18*(3), 4–10. doi:10.3102/0013189X018003004

Facione, P. A. (1990). *Critical thinking: A statement of expert consensus for purposes of educational assessment and instruction—The Delphi report*. Millbrae, CA: California Academic Press.

Feuerstein, M. (2002). *Media literacy in support of critical thinking* (Unpublished doctoral dissertation). University of Liverpool.

Fitzpatrick, A. R. (1989). Social influences in standard-setting: The effects of social interaction on group judgments. *Review of Educational Research, 59*(3), 315–328. doi:10.3102/00346543059003315

Florence, D. C. (2014). A history of critical thinking as an educational goal in graduate theological schools. *Christian Higher Education, 13*(5), 352–361. doi:10.1080/15363759.2014.949164

Fung, I. Y. Y., Townsend, M. A. R., & Parr, J. M. (2004). *Teachers facilitating critical thinking in students: The search for a model and a method*. Paper presented at the European Conference on Educational Research, University of Crete, Rethymno, Greece.

Furness, J., Cowie, B., & Cooper, B. (2017). Scoping the meaning of 'critical' in mathematical thinking for initial teacher education. *Policy Futures in Education, 15*(6), 713–728. doi:10.1177/1478210317719778

Gigerenzer, G., & Todd, P. M. (1999). *Simple heuristics that make us smart*. New York: Oxford University Press.

Giraud, G., Impara, J. C., & Plake, B. S. (2005). Teachers' conceptions of target examinees in Angoff standard setting. *Applied Measurement in Education, 18*(3), 223–232. doi:10.120715324818ame1803_2

Haberlin, S. (2018). Problematizing notions of critical thinking with preservice teachers: A self-study imparting critical thinking strategies to preservice teachers: *A Self-Study. Action in Teacher Education, 40*(3), 305–318. doi:10.1080/01626620.2018.1486751

Haertel, E. H., & Lorie, W. A. (2004). Validating standards-based test score interpretations. *Measurement: Interdisciplinary Research and Perspectives, 2*(2), 61–103. doi:10.120715366359mea0202_1

Hager, P., & Kaye, M. (1992). Critical Thinking in Teacher Education: A Process-Oriented Research Agenda. *Australian Journal of Teacher Education, 17*(2). doi:10.14221/ajte.1992v17n2.4

Hein, S. F., & Skaggs, G. E. (2010). Conceptualizing the classroom of target students: A qualitative investigation of panelists' experiences during standard setting. *Educational Measurement: Issues and Practice, 22*(2), 36–44. doi:10.1111/j.1745-3992.2010.00174.x

Hsu, C., & Sandford, B. A. (2012). The delphi technique: *Making sense of consensus. Practical Assessment, Research & Evaluation, 10*(12), 1531–7714.

Impara, J. C., & Plake, B. S. (1997). Standard setting: An alternative approach. *Journal of Educational Measurement, 34*(4), 353–366. doi:10.1111/j.1745-3984.1997.tb00523.x

Impara, J. C., & Plake, B. S. (1998). Teachers' ability to estimate item difficulty: A test of the assumptions of the Angoff standard setting method. *Journal of Educational Measurement, 35*(1), 69–81. doi:10.1111/j.1745-3984.1998.tb00528.x

Iyioke, I. C. (2013). *Re-conceptualization of modified Angoff standard setting: Unified statistical, measurement, cognitive and social psychological theories* (Unpublished doctoral dissertation). Michigan State University.

Iyioke, I. C. (2015). *A research of heuristic vs. normative training for the Angoff standard setting method.* Paper presented at the Annual Meeting of the American Educational Research Association Conference, Chicago, IL.

Iyioke, I. C. (2018). *Survey Research: Completely structured versus partially structured training on the Angoff method.* London: SAGE Publications, Ltd.; doi:10.4135/9781526436818

Jonassen, D. H. (1997). Instructional design models for well-structured and ill-structured problem-solving learning outcomes. *Educational Technology Research and Development, 45*(1), 65–94. doi:10.1007/BF02299613

Kahneman, D. (2011). *Thinking, fast and slow.* New York, NY: Farrar, Straus and Giroux.

Kirkpatrick, D. (1994). *Evaluating training programs: The four levels.* San Francisco, CA: Berrett-Koehler.

Kirschner, P. A., Sweller, J., & Clark, R. E. (2006). Why minimal guidance during instruction does not work: An analysis of the failure of constructivist, discovery, problem-based, experiential, and inquiry-based teaching. *Educational Psychologist, 41*(2), 75–86. doi:10.120715326985ep4102_1

Kruskal, J. B. (1964a). Multidimensional scaling by optimizing goodness-of-fit to a nonmetric hypothesis. *Psychometrika, 29*(1), 1–27. doi:10.1007/BF02289565

Kruskal, J. B. (1964b). Nonmetric multidimensional scaling: A numerical method. *Psychometrika, 29*(2), 115–129. doi:10.1007/BF02289694

Kruskal, J. B., & Wish, M. (1978). *Multidimensional scaling. Sage University paper series on Quantitative Applications in the Social Sciences # 11.* Beverly Hills, CA: Sage.

Kuntze, S., Aizikovitsh-Udi, E., & Clarke, D. (2017). Hybrid Task Design: Connecting Learning Opportunities Related to Critical Thinking and Statistical Thinking. *ZDM. The International Journal on Mathematics Education, 49*(6), 923–935.

Lieberman, V., & Tversky, A. (2001). *Probability thinking in daily life*. Tel Aviv: Open University. (in Hebrew)

Linn, R. L. (2001). *The Influence of External Evaluations on the National Assessment of Educational Progress* (CSE Technical Report 548). Los Angeles, CA: University of California, Center for Research Evaluation, Standards, and Student Testing.

Lipman, M. (1988). Critical thinking - what can it be? *Educational Leadership, 46*(1), 38–43.

McGinty, D. (2005). Illuminating the "Black Box" of standard setting: An exploratory qualitative study. *Applied Measurement in Education, 18*(3), 269–287. doi:10.120715324818ame1803_5

Mee, J., Clauser, B. E., & Margolis, M. J. (2013). The impact of process instructions on judges' use of examinee performance data in Angoff standard setting exercises. *Educational Measurement: Issues and Practice, 32*(3), 27–35. doi:10.1111/emip.12013

Miller, L. E. (2006, October). *Determining what could/should be: The Delphi technique and its application*. Paper presented at the meeting of the 2006 annual meeting of the Mid-Western.

Mills, C. N., Melican, G. J., & Ahluwalia, N. T. (1991). Defining minimal competence. *Educational Measurement: Issues and Practice, 10*(2), 15–16. doi:10.1111/j.1745-3992.1991.tb00186.x

Morris, C. D., Bransford, J. D., & Franks, J. J. (1977). Levels of processing versus transfer appropriate processing. *Journal of Verbal Learning and Verbal Behavior, 16*(5), 519–533. doi:10.1016/S0022-5371(77)80016-9

Mulnix, J. W. (2012). Thinking critically about critical thinking. *Educational Philosophy and Theory, 44*(5), 464–479. doi:10.1111/j.1469-5812.2010.00673.x

National Commission on Excellence in Education. (1983). *A nation at risk: The imperative for educational reform*. Washington, DC: United States Department of Education.

Perie, M. (2008). A guide to understanding and developing performance-level descriptors. *Educational Measurement: Issues and Practice, 27*(4), 15–29. doi:10.1111/j.1745-3992.2008.00135.x

Prawat, R. S. (1991). The value of ideas: The immersion approach to the development of thinking. *Educational Researcher, 20*(2), 3–10. doi:10.3102/0013189X020002003

R Development Core Team. (2013). *R Version 3.0.1: A language and environment for statistical computing*. Vienna, Austria: The R Foundation for Statistical Computing. Retrieved from http://www.R-project.org

Rasch, G. (1960). *Probabilistic models for some intelligence and attainment tests*. Copenhagen: Danmarks Paedagogiske Institut.

Raymond, M. R., & Reid, J. B. (2001). Who made thee a judge? Selecting and training participants for standard setting. In C. J. Cizek (Ed.), *Setting performance standards: Concepts, methods, and perspectives* (pp. 119–157). Mahwah, NJ: Lawrence Erlbaum.

Reckase, M. D. (2001). Innovative methods for helping standard-setting participants to perform their task: The role of feedback regarding consistency, accuracy, and impact. In C. J. Cizek (Ed.), *Setting performance standards: Concepts, methods, and perspectives* (pp. 159–173). Mahwah, NJ: Lawrence Erlbaum.

Reckase, M. D. (2009). Standard setting theory and practice: Issues and difficulties. In N. Figueras & J. Noijons (Eds.), Linking to the CEFR levels: Research perspectives (pp. 13 - 20). Arnhem, Cito: Institute for Educational Measurement Council of Europe European Association for Language Testing and Assessment (EALTA).

Reid, J. B. (1991). Training judges to generate standard setting data. *Educational Measurement: Issues and Practice, 10*(2), 11–14. doi:10.1111/j.1745-3992.1991.tb00187.x

Saeger, K. J. (2014). The development of critical thinking skills in undergraduate students (2014). *Culminating Projects in Higher Education Administration.* Retrieved from http://repository.stcloudstate.edu/hied_etds/1

Schacter, D. L., & Addis, D. R. (2007). The cognitive neuroscience of constructive memory: Remembering the past and imagining the future. *Philosophical Transactions of the Royal Society of London. Series B, Biological Sciences, 362*(1481), 773–786. doi:10.1098/rstb.2007.2087 PMID:17395575

Shepard, L., Glaser, R., Linn, R., & Bohrnstedt, G. (1993). *Setting standards for student achievement.* Stanford, CA: National Academy of Education.

Simon, H. A. (1957). *Models of man: Social and rational.* New York, NY: Wiley.

Skaggs, G., & Hein, S. F. (2011). Reducing the cognitive complexity associated with standard setting: A comparison of the Single-Passage Bookmark and Yes/No methods. *Educational and Psychological Measurement, 71*(3), 571–592. doi:10.1177/0013164410386948

Skorupski, W. P. (2012). Understanding the cognitive processes of standard setting panelist. In G. J. Cizek (Ed.), *Setting performance standards. Foundations, methods, and innovations* (2nd ed.; pp. 135–147). New York, NY: Routledge.

Sturrock, K., & Rocha, J. (2000). A multidimensional scaling stress evaluation table. *Field Methods, 12*(1), 49–60. doi:10.1177/1525822X0001200104

Tversky, A. (1977). Features of similarity. *Psychological Review, 84*(4), 327–352. doi:10.1037/0033-295X.84.4.327

Tversky, A., & Kahneman, D. (1973). Availability: A heuristic for judging frequency and probability. *Cognitive Psychology, 5*(2), 207–232. doi:10.1016/0010-0285(73)90033-9

Tversky, A., & Kahneman, D. (1974). Judgment under uncertainty: Heuristics and biases. *Science, 185*(4157), 1124–1131. doi:10.1126cience.185.4157.1124 PMID:17835457

United States Department of Education. (2010). *A blueprint for reform: The reauthorization of the Elementary and Secondary Education Act.* Retrieved from www2.ed.gov/policy/elsec/leg/blueprint

Willingham, D. T. (2007). Critical thinking: Why is it so hard to teach? *American Educator, 31*, 8–19.

Zieky, M. J. (2001). So much has changed: How the setting of cut scores has evolved since the 1980s. In C. J. Cizek (Ed.), *Setting performance standards: Concepts, methods, and perspectives* (pp. 19–51). Mahwah, NJ: Lawrence Erlbaum.

Zulkpli, Z., Abdullah, A. H., Kohar, U. H. A., & Ibrahim, N. H. (2017). A review of research on infusion approach in teaching thinking: Advantages and impacts. *Man in India*, *97*(12), 289–298.

ADDITIONAL READING

Baddeley, A. D., & Hitch, G. (1974). Working memory. In G. H. Bower (Ed.), *The psychology of learning and motivation* (Vol. 8). London: Academic Press.

Tulving, E. (1972). Episodic and semantic memory. In E. Tulving & W. Donaldson (Eds.), *Organization of memory* (pp. 381–403). New York: Academic Press.

KEY TERMS AND DEFINITIONS

Assessment Constructs: The hypothetical concepts that educational tests measure.

Completely Structured Training: A type of training that provides full instruction, practice, and feedback on strategies for use of concepts in problem solving.

Curriculum: The content of training, including concepts and strategies for use in solving problems.

Delivery Methods for Curriculum: Pedagogical or teaching methods, including instruction, practice, and feedback.

Heuristics: Resource-efficient strategies for making judgments.

Minimally Competent Candidates: Candidates who barely possess the knowledge, skills, and abilities to be considered as performing at a certain level.

Partially Structured Training: A type of training that provides instruction, practice, and feedback on some, but not all strategies required for using concepts in performing a task.

Performance Level Descriptors: A description of the knowledge, skills, and abilities a student must possess to be determined as performing at a certain level (e.g., at grade level).

APPENDIX

Key Acronyms

BLPDS: Borderline Performance Level Descriptors
CST: Completely Structured Training
CT: Critical Thinking
PLD: Performance Level Descriptors
PST: Partially Structured Training
KSA: Knowledge, Skills, and Abilities
MCC: Minimally Competent Candidates

Chapter 16
Fostering Critical Thinking Using Instructional Strategies in English Classes

Şenol Orakcı
Aksaray University, Turkey

Mehmet Durnali
 https://orcid.org/0000-0002-1318-9362
Hacettepe University, Turkey

Osman Aktan
 https://orcid.org/0000-0001-6583-3765
Düzce RAM Ministry of National Education, Turkey

ABSTRACT

The aim of the chapter is to provide both theoretical and practical ideas about critical thinking development within English language teaching contexts. Encouraging language learners to be critical thinkers is important in teaching English as a foreign language. However, achieving the goal remains a challenge. Using various strategies together seem to be effective when properly implemented. Therefore this chapter outlines these strategies which include communicative language tasks, using authentic meaningful texts, using critical literacy, being aware of whole-brain learning, adopting a reflective teaching, enabling students to become autonomous, using explicit instruction, teacher questioning, using active and cooperative learning strategies, using literature in English classes, using creative drama, and adopting self-assessment. Teachers can enable learners to have critical thinking skills and more efficient English lessons by combining these strategies in a new way or by designing critical thinking activities in the classroom.

DOI: 10.4018/978-1-5225-7829-1.ch016

Copyright © 2019, IGI Global. Copying or distributing in print or electronic forms without written permission of IGI Global is prohibited.

INTRODUCTION

Recent trends in English as a foreign language (EFL) have emphasized the importance and requirement of improving critical thinking as an integral part of English language curriculum (Davidson & Dunham, 1997; Shirkhani & Fahim, 2011; Sun, 2015; Tang, 2016). In English language learning, students need critical thinking skills that are related to quality thinking to analyze, reflect, self-assess, argue, be autonomous, and evaluate during his/her learning. As Kabilan (2000) maintains, only using the target language and knowing the meaning are not enough. Learners must be able to have critical thinking through the language because critical thinking enables students to expand their learning experience and makes language learning deeper and more meaningful in addition to providing learners with a more skillful way of communicating with other people, enabling them to acquire new knowledge, and deal with ideas, beliefs, and attitudes.

A lot of different definitions have been introduced for critical thinking. Norris and Ennis (1989) define critical thinking as "reasonably reflective thinking that is focused on deciding what to believe or do." According to Siegel (1999), Lipman (1991) and Maiorana (1992), critical thinking means achieving, understanding, and evaluating different perspectives, and solving problems. Elder and Paul (1994) state that critical thinking refers to the ability of individuals to take responsibility of their own thinking and improve appropriate criteria and standards for analyzing their own thinking. Zintz and Maggart (1984) inform that critical thinking "involves learning to evaluate, draw inferences and arrive at conclusions based on the evidence". Paul (1991), well known for his works on critical thinking, has described it as reaching conclusions based on observation and knowledge (p. 125). Paul (1991) also defines critical thinking as "thinking about it when it performs the thought action to improve one's own thinking". According to İpşiroğlu (2002), critical thinking is the most developed and advanced form of thinking because critical thinking means objective, reflective and not obsessive thinking. Beyer (1987, p. 32-33) points out that critical thinking is the evaluation of the authenticity and precision of the information and the value of beliefs, arguments and information claims. Smith and Rawley (1997), on the other hand, stated that criticism is a judgement that focuses on accepting or rejecting claims. According to Mayhewv, critical thinking is the process of questioning "how" and "why" (as cited Branch, 2000). Ennis (1985) points out that critical thinking is composed of abilities and tendencies. Norris (1985) also defines critical thinking as "Students put into practice what they have already known and change their pre-learning by valuing their own thinking" (p. 40). Considering these definitions that include temperament, tendency and skill, it can be said that critical thinking is a practical activity.

As a matter of fact, the most basic requirement for being a contemporary society that produces knowledge is educated individuals equipped with critical and creative thinking skills who make new inventions and discoveries and want to initiate social change. In other words, what is expected from educated individuals is that they can make logical inferences, and relate them to everyday life in addition to that they can inquire into what they have learned, accepted and confronted with. Creating these changes in the individual is one of the creative functions of education (Tezcan, 1997, p.188). In education, the existence of critical and creative thinking is also influential in improving the academic achievements of the individuals as it is in daily life (Güven & Kürüm 2006, Koray, Yaman & Altunçekiç, 2004, p. 2).

In general, it is important for a person to learn to criticize in his / her own life for reaching individual enrichment integrality because critical thinking helps an individual to self-govern in his/her life, to clearly see his/her choices, and to help him to liberalize against challenging influences (Chaffee, 2010, p. 519). Watson and Glaser (2010) point out that thanks to critical thinking, learners have the ability to determine assumptions, hidden beliefs, values, and attitudes. Paul (1991), on the other hand, has stated that critical thinking helps learners to form and evaluate their own thinking.

When studies on critical thinking skills are examined, it can be said that the first and most comprehensive study of these belongs to Ennis (1962). Ennis summarized critical thinking skills as 12 items. These are as follow:

1. Understanding the meaning of a statement
2. Judge whether or not there are any ambiguities and assumptions
3. Judge whether or not statements are contradictory to each other
4. Judging whether or not you have reached an absolute result
5. Judge whether or not a statement is sufficiently precise.
6. Judging the application of principles and concepts
7. Judge whether or not an observation-based statement is reliable
8. Judgement of a statement whether or not it ensures an inductive result
9. Judging whether or not a problem is identified
10. Judge whether or not a statement is based on the assumption
11. Judging whether or not a description is sufficient
12. Judge whether or not a statement will be accepted correctly by authorities

This chapter aims to explain critical thinking skills from theory to practice. Therefore, within the literature review, the study is based on both theoretical knowledge and practical activities in EFL classes.

Approaches to Teaching Critical Thinking

There are different approaches to how critical thinking can be achieved. When looked at from the perspective of the literature review, it is observed that there are four basic approaches to the teaching of critical thinking. In subject-based teaching approach, critical thinking instruction is placed deeply and carefully into content-based teaching approach and students are encouraged to use critical thinking when they learn the subject.

In content-based teaching approach, content and principles and rules of critical thinking are combined. Also, students are encouraged to think critically when they learn the content. In this approach, content teaching takes place in the front line and general principles of critical thinking are not explicitly expressed (Ennis, 1989).

In skill-based teaching approach, critical thinking instruction is based on a separate discipline, regardless of context. The content that is structured on the basis of the components and standards of critical thinking skills attempts to give students critical thinking ability and tendency (Ennis, 1997). The main purpose of this approach is to teach students to think critically about contexts outside the school. The mixed teaching approach is composed of a combination of subject-based or content-based approach with the general approach. In this approach, there is a separate course aimed at teaching general principles of critical thinking, but students also participate in a content-based teaching of critical thinking (Ennis, 1989).

Relationship Between Learning Styles and Critical Thinking

The fact that individuals have a lot of different qualities demanded by an information society is one of the most important issues. Among these qualities, abilities for both the critical thinking process and learning styles can be regarded as factors that facilitate an individual's life and his/her learning process. In the studies carried out in recent years, it has been observed that learning style and critical thinking are examined separately in some studies, and these two concepts are brought together in some studies.

In the studies that bring these two concepts together, the theoretical sub-structure of the subject has been tried to be established and this process has been supported with research findings (Toress & Cano, 1995; Colucciello, 1999; Rudd, Baker & Hoover, 2000; Zang & Stenberck, 2000; Myers & Dyer, 2004). Especially in these studies, it has been assumed that individual learning styles influence the development of critical thinking skills. In the light of these explanations, as a result of an extensive literature review that is related to revealing the relationship between learning styles and critical thinking, Torres and Cano (1995) emphasize that different factors play a role in the development of students' complex mental skills such as critical thinking. Among these, learning styles that are in the forefront have an important place in the development of cognitive skills. From this point of view, it can be said that learning styles are utilized in explaining complex mental skills.

Strategies for Promoting Critical Thinking Skills in English Classes

The promotion of critical thinking into the English classes is very significant for several reasons. Firstly, if language learners can undertake their own thinking, they can monitor and evaluate their own ways of learning more successfully. Second, critical thinking enriches the learning experience of the learners and makes the language more meaningful for them. Thirdly, critical thinking increases the learners' achievements. This chapter focuses on instructional strategies which are useful in promoting critical thinking and applicable to English language classrooms. These strategies are as follows:

Using communicative language tasks/activities: Communicative language tasks entail critical thinking. When students engage with using the target language which contains elements such as personalization, investigation and problem solving, then they need to think critically. These kinds of communicative tasks are common as they involve students in authentic communication. These tasks entail the effective use of language together with critical thinking (Hughes, 2014). Teachers also can use a set of practical communicative activities that promote critical thinking. These are as follows:

"Information-Gap Activities"

In this kind of activity that is used a lot in communicative language teaching, a learner knows something that another learner does not know, so they must communicate to "close the gap". Information gap activities can have a number of advantages for learners. First of all, these types of activities support active listening and critical thinking. They also make a contribution to the development of cooperative skills and collective brainstorming. Even though some people consider information gap activities as fill-in-the-blank exercises, the two are not quite the same. In an information gap activity, students find out information needed to understand a larger concept. A sample activity is given below. "Student A is given a map, diagram, chart, timeline, etc. with information on it and Student B has a clear form. Student

A and Student B each have a mostly finished form of a map, diagram, chart, timeline, etc. with various information missing. Student A gives instructions to Student B to enable them to draw or complete a picture or diagram, and the other way around. Students A and B are given similar sets of photographs, picture cards, real objects (toy cars or animals, shapes, etc.) to arrange in an identical way. Student B places objects on a blank picture board or grid to match Student A's board. Pairs understand the differences between two 'spot the difference' pictures" (Great Idea: Barrier Games, 2018).

"Role-Play Activities"

It is a communicative activity in which learners speak each other in different roles from real life, such as "in an airport, in a doctor's office, in a shop, at a railway station, in a mall". For example, two learners have a discussion by answering the questions given in different roles. As a result, they develop critical thinking skills. There are instructions for role play. The procedure for it is given below.

1. **The Choice of the Role Play Situation:** There are various circumstances which lend themselves to the use of role play. These circumstances involve individual dilemmas (e.g., being concerned with a pushy salesperson, observing a crime, or testifying in court) and conflict-resolution situations (e.g., a tenant negotiating with a landlord over the terms of a lease or a police officer confronting a suspected shoplifter). Role-playing can be utilized to overcome a specific issue or problem; for instance, role-playing could be utilized to discuss whether or not adopted persons should be given access to records that demonstrate the name and whereabouts of their natural parents. Finally, role plays are helpful for developing student skills as an interviewer, negotiator, assertive consumer, investigator, or decision maker.

2. **Preparation and Warm-Up:** Students ought to be told the circumstance or issue and taught with regards to the different roles. If role-playing is new to the class, "warm-up" or introductory activities might be useful. For instance, students might be asked to role play greeting a long-lost friend, or to role-play the way someone who had quite recently won a huge whole of money would act.

3. **Choose Participants:** Students can either be assigned roles or the teacher can ask for volunteers. Role plays may be conducted before the whole class or various simultaneous role plays could be conducted by dividing the class into small groups. Students who are not engaged with the role play should act as spectators.

4. **Conduct the Role Play:** Direct students to act out the role the way they think someone faced with the same situation would act in real life. The teacher should not interfere with the role play; however, if the students need some assistance in getting started the teacher should help the students. After performing the role-play it is sometimes useful to have students reverse roles or to perform the same role play using different members. For instance, two students might role play a confrontation between a youth and a police officer. After performing the role play once, the student who acted as the youth could assume the role of the police officer and the other way around.

5. **Debrief:** The role-play activity ought to be questioned and assessed. This is an open door for both the members and the onlookers to analyze the role play and to talk about what happened and why, which supports critical thinking. Typical debriefing questions involve the following:
   a. How did you feel about the role play and each of the different roles?
   b. Was the role play realistic? How was it similar to or different from real life? Was the problem tackled? If so, how? If not, why not?

c. What, if anything, could have been done any other way? What different results were possible?

d. What did you learn from the experience? (Role Play/Simulation, 2018).

"Simulation Activities"

In this kind of activity, the learner performs a role play where he/she plays himself/herself in a given situation from "real world" environments. Simulations promote the use of critical and evaluative thinking. In conclusion, role-playing simulation activities have been found to be an effective solution for improving students' oral performance in English, for not only do they urge students to create a supportive collaborative learning environment, but also give them an opportunity to practice communicating effectively and to think critically to solve problems that may occur in real-life situations (Tipmontree & Tasanameelarp, 2018). A sample activity is given below. The name of the activity is "Will your students steal a car?". This activity is for a group of four students. In this activity, the character cards don't tell the students what decisions they should make, it's completely their choice.

The Story (Don't Tell Your Students): "Four friends are hanging out after school. One of them wants to steal a car but he/she can only steal it if everyone agrees. Will he/she be successful? If yes, there is the second *piece* of the story *which you will let them know* (or show on a slip of paper, so they can read it). Let the students draw their characters, Spring, Summer, Autumn, and Winter. Explain to them they will play 4 friends hanging out and chatting in a simulation about friendship and that they will find some essential information about their characters. However, the rest and they *should* fill themselves as well as any further moves and decisions. Give them the character cards and tell them to think *regarding* their characters a bit and prepare topics to talk about. After they read their cards you shouldn't answer any further questions."

Student Winter: "You are a good kid. You've never stolen anything, you think cheating is nor right and you would never lie to your parents. *Additionally,* it is difficult for you to find new friends and you've recently moved into *another town,* you are the new *child* at school and you want to find new friends and keep them. One day after school, you're hanging out in the shopping *center,* drinking bubble tea and *becoming more acquainted with* your friends. You like student Summer, don't know Student Autumn much and are afraid of Student Spring."

Student Summer: "You are a good kid. You've never stolen anything except a few coins from your mum's purse but that is not stealing anyway. Or the cigarettes you took at the supermarket. You just want to try new things and have some fun. That never hurt anyone. Also, you have a very strict father who you are afraid of. Student Spring is your close friend and you admire him/her. Student Winter is the new kid and you like them and you are *envious of* Student Autumn. One day after school, you're hanging out in the shopping mall, drinking tea and chatting with your friends."

Student Spring: "You are a good kid. You like to have fun and party a bit. You are a bit more mature than your friends. You like stealing fizzy drinks and junk food at the local supermarket. Today you would like to have some fun with your friends. You've seen an old car parked outside. It is easy to break into the car and jump start it and you know how to do that because your cousin taught you. You want to go for a ride around the block with your friends and after that, you just leave the car parked somewhere. You wouldn't be even stealing the car, besides, joyriding isn't even a crime in some countries. You need to persuade your friends to do it with you and you can just do it if everyone agrees. Student Summer is your closest friend, Student Winter is the new kid and you want to impress Student Autumn. One day after school, you're hanging out in the shopping mall, drinking tea and chatting with your friends."

Student Autumn: "You are a good kid. You like to have a great time. Sometimes you do some harmless drugs, sometimes you have a few beverages. You spend time with Summer and Spring because they are younger and sometimes pay you to buy them beer. Sometimes you steal some money from them and they don't even notice, but 'drugs' are *costly* and you like it too much. You were arrested once but it was no big deal, your father paid the bill and made it go away. Right now you would like to earn some quick money, best by stealing something, you have friends who could sell everything. One day after school, you're hanging out in the shopping center, drinking tea and chatting with your friends. You don't know Winter, the new kid."

If all 4 students agree on stealing the car, give them this: "During Your Joy Ride, You Hit Something In A Dark Back Alley. The Car Stops And You Start To Think. It Might Have Been A Human. It Made A Sound Like A Human. What Do You Do?" After the students finish the activity, have a feedback discussion with them. "How did they relate to their characters? Did they imagine any other details *regarding* their characters? Why did they decide the way they did? Did they feel pressured into their decisions? Have they ever been pressured into any decisions in real life?" ("Will your students steal," 2018).

"Jigsaw Activities"

It is a kind of activity that involves re-ordering mixed up information to find its correct order. It helps learners see the connections between parts of information. If you have two news stories that share a theme - for example two separate stories on crime - prepare comprehension questions for each story. Give one half of the class (Group A) one story, and the other half (Group B) the other. The students read their article, answer the questions and check understanding. Students then pair up with someone from the other group and tell them about their story, and listen to the other one. To help students remember their story you may get them to take notes. Alternatively, the students can keep the article with them to refer to. Be careful though, as lazier (or ingenious) students will either read the article aloud, or simply give it to their partner to read! Jigsaw reading is a great way to introduce speaking into a reading lesson. It provides a real opportunity for genuine communication. In real life, we may tell people about a news article we have read, so this is a classroom activity that is fairly authentic (Rees, 2018).

"Surveys"

In this kind of activity, the class is divided into two groups. Learners must work together to write a report about the survey that have been prepared. Topics may be different from each other (*"environmental issues, climate changes, pollution"*, etc.). Learners exchange information in order to finish the task by working together.

"Dialogue Journal"

In this kind of activity, a written diary is exchanged between two learners (learner to learner, learner to teacher). For instance, content is more important than form.

"Picture Strip Story"

In this activity, students are expected to create a story from the pictures by working in pairs. The first learner is given a strip story. He/She shows the first picture of the story to his/her partner and asks him/her to guess what the second picture will be like. At the end of the activity, learners come together and uncover the entire story from the pictures they have had.

"Questionnaire"

Learners ask questions that have been prepared before about some topics given each other.

Describe and Draw

Learners work in pairs. The first learner reads the passage out loud and pauses at the end of every sentence for a few seconds. The other learner listens, and draws the picture. At the end the activity, learners check together what they draw and exchange the roles.

Socratic Questioning

Socratic teaching is the oldest teaching technique that improves critical thinking skills. The teacher here does not provide answers but is instead trained in asking questions: questions that explore, investigate, probe, stimulate and engage. Here are six types of Socratic Questions that both teachers and students can learn to use in classroom activities: a) Questions to clarify (What did you mean by…?, Can you give me an example?, Could you explain a bit more?), b) Questions to challenge assumptions (Why do you assume that…?, Is that always the case?, Why do we include and exclude?) c) Questions to probe evidence/reasons (What do you think causes this to happen?, How do you know this?, Why do you say that?), d) Questions to discover other viewpoints/perspectives (What's another way to look at this?, What are the advantages and disadvantages of…?, Who benefits from this? Who would be affected?, What would be their views?, Why is this the best?) e) Questions that consider implications and consequences (What are some possible consequences of this?, How does ~ affect ~?, How does this tie in with what we already know?), f) Questions about questions (Why did you ask that question?, What did you mean when you said ~?, What are you trying to find out with that question?)

Edward de Bono's Six Thinking Hats

Bono's Six Thinking Hats is a systematic method that enables students to learn to think in six different functions and roles. Here are some ways of using the Six Thinking Hats in your classroom:

- *Teachers could give each student a particular Thinking Hat in order to practice a way of thinking.*
- *Working in groups, each group could be assigned with a particular Thinking Hat in order to encourage and exemplify a way of thinking.*
- *Working in groups, different members of the group could be assigned with a different Thinking Hat in order to promote productive collaboration.*
- *Teachers could get students to change their focus by getting them to put on a different Thinking Hat.*

The Six Thinking Hats are as follows: The White Hat represents 'Facts', The Red Hat – 'Emotions', The Yellow Hat – 'Positivity', The Black Hat – 'The Devil's Advocate', The Green Hat – 'Creativity', and The Blue Hat – 'The Manager' (English Teaching Professional, 2018).

In those mentioned activities above, learners make use of the known and the collected information in order to learn new information, which stimulates critical thinking.

Using Authentic Meaningful Texts

Providing a meaningful context is very important for learners in terms of learning a foreign language. Therefore, it is necessary to use authentic meaningful texts, which enable learners to internalize the language. In the review of literature, a lot of definitions have been made for authentic materials. Nunan (1999) defines authentic material as "any material not specifically produced for language teaching purposes". Peacock (1997) defines "as a material prepared to achieve some social objectives in a target language-speaking society". The most important common point of these definitions is that these materials are not prepared to teach target language. These materials are documents that are intended for use in a society not for any pedagogical purposes. These are used as course materials for foreign language classes, although they are not prepared as a course material. In short, we can define authentic materials used in foreign languages as any document without having any tutorial changes prepared for the target language-speaking individuals, used in the classroom.

In foreign language teaching, authentic materials are used to teach four language skills, such as listening, speaking, reading and writing. In addition, authentic materials can be used effectively for teaching vocabulary and grammar.

With such materials, foreign language teaching becomes more effective as it provides unique examples, increases motivation and interest. They also enable students to be an effective foreign language user with critical thinking ability outside of the classroom environment, one of the main purposes of foreign language teaching in the Common European Language Framework by improving the students' four basic language skills in the target language.

In addition, the most important aim of the use of authentic material is to bring the reality of life to the artificial class environment as much as possible. Herod (2002) also argues that authentic learning materials and activities are designed to imitate real life situations by pointing out that authentic materials are also a kind of documents that enable us to take advantage of a kind of real life situation in an artificial class environment.

Different Types of Authentic Materials

There are many kinds of authentic materials that can be used in teaching foreign languages. They are very important and useful in terms of developing critical thinking skills. Without having any educational purposes, all kinds of songs, magazines, newspapers, television programs, brochures, tickets, literary texts, internet pages, etc. prepared for the target language users, can be used for teaching foreign languages as an authentic material. We can group authentic materials in two main categories: auditory and written. Such documents as television and radio programs, movies, news, weather forecast, airport announcements, electronic books, phone messages, videos, podcasts, job interviews, etc. can be given as examples of auditory authentic materials. Such documents as advertisements, brochures, magazines, newspapers, road signs, calendars, tickets, ATM screens and printouts, poems, manuals, application forms, articles, recipes, restaurant menus, cartoons can also be given as examples of authentic written materials (Laniro, 2007). Genhard (1996) categorizes authentic materials in three main groups: authentic, auditory, written and visual materials. According to this category, radio news, cartoons and songs are auditory; street signs, magazine and newspaper pictures, postcards are visual; sports reports, newspapers, restaurant menus and train tickets can be given as authentic materials. As can be understood from the examples, all materials except auditory materials carry visual items at the same time. Apart from these, Internet is an authentic source of material in itself. All kinds of audio and written authentic materials including visual items that are in target language can be accessed via Internet. It is possible to say that Internet is the most useful, most natural and most accessible authentic material as teachers can use it in the classroom and students can use out-of-class anytime.

When considered in terms of the development of critical thinking skills, different types of authentic materials require understanding the meaning, analyzing the fact from the opinion, and then expressing learners' own views. Especially TV commercials are very effective in developing critical thinking skills.

Features of TV Commercials

The features of TV commercials with the multitude and shortness that help foreign language learners more accessible and usable for language use can be listed as follows:

- **TV Commercials Are Authentic:** TV commercials are prepared for language classes. They target the natural speakers and carry the elements of the real life of society. They can take students far beyond the walls of the language class and introduce themselves to different cultures without the need for travelling. The learning of the cultural and social characteristics of the learned language has great importance in learning foreign languages.
- **TV Commercials Develop Critical Thinking Skills:** The influence of a TV commercial that is the product of intelligence is beyond the pedagogical opportunities and the creative power of a teacher. TV commercials provide an ideal environment for foreign language learners' critical thinking in listening courses. Since advertisements are short, stunner, propaganda and full stories, they can be used as a means in introducing critical thinking skills such as sequencing, predicting, making associations and seeing cause and effect (Smith & Rawley, 1997)

In short, when the authentic materials such as songs, web pages, radio and TV broadcasts, films, leaflets, flyers, posters, news text or a blog post from the real world are presented effectively, learners become more actively involved in English classes by engaging in and responding to authentic materials. Also, they need to understand the meaning, differentiate between the fact and the opinion, and then form their opinions, which foster critical thinking abilities (Anu & Bhaskaran, 2017; Hughes, 2014).

- **Using Active Learning Strategies:** Learner role is very important in the process of active learning applications. In active learning, learners should be educated as an individual who is aware of real situations and who has knowledge about the use of the subject that he/she has learnt in his/her daily life (Seeler, Turnwald, & Bull, 1994). In this way, students are given a more active role in using and practicing knowledge (Dufresne, Gerace, Leonard, Mestre, & Wenk, 1996). While learners gain processes such as organizing, thinking, problem solving and exhibiting democratic behavior as a discipline in active learning, teachers encourage them to take their own learning responsibilities (Dufresne et al, 1996, Baessa, Chesterfield & Ramos, 2002, Mattson, 2005). As a result of students' research-based practices on the subject they will learn using active learning practices, the development of high-level thinking skills is expected (Philips, 2005). Critical thinking that is one of the high-level thinking skills has become one of the major goals of the curricula of different courses with recognition of the importance of it. Thus, the curricula of the different courses should start with primary education, and learning outcomes that are related to students' critical thinking skills and the activities that support these skills should be included (Burbach, Matkin & Fritz, 2004). According to Bevis (1989), active learning is effective in improving high-level thinking skills such as critical thinking and analysis by activating them (Philips, 2005). This motivates students to become self-managing, critical and lifelong learners (Şahinel, 2005).

- **Using Cooperative Learning Strategies:** The century of education in which we live requires citizens who are responsible for their own learning, who can look at events from a wide variety of angles, think critically and creatively, and have problem solving competence. For this reason, creative and critical thinking have become important skills to adapt to the rapidly changing world and to cope with the problems encountered (Dam & Volman, 2004; Penkauskienė, 2010). In order to enable students to have these knowledge and skills, educators use a lot of teaching methods and techniques. Collaborative learning is also one of the most effective teaching methods for students to have critical thinking skills in teaching and learning environments (AbuSeileek, 2012; Kim & Song, 2013). Collaborative learning is a kind of teaching method in which students learn in small groups and help each other in order to achieve a common goal (Johnson & Johnson, 2006, Jenkins, Antil, Wayne & Vadasy, 2003). Within the process, students become critical in the problem-solving process by helping them to work together for group success, helping each other to learn so that higher level learning occurs (Carlan, Rubin & Morgan, 2005). While collaborative learning allows students to take on leadership roles within their own groups, it provides a starting point for students shaping their lives as a democratic citizen (Williamson & Null 2008). Through the interaction between them, students learn to think critically, question, share ideas, clarify differences and construct a new understanding (Gillies & Boyle, 2010). Thanks to the education system to be designed to develop these skills, an important step will be taken towards raising imaginative individuals that have critical thinking. In fact, critical thinking is also the most important food source of creativity.

In sum, active learning strategies and cooperative learning strategies are closely related to each other. Adopting active and cooperative learning strategies promote student participation, cooperation, and interaction, helping students to develop critical thinking. Active group interaction enables students to have chances to exchange ideas, take responsibilities, and become critical thinkers (Slavin, 2011). Some of the proposed strategies involve role play/simulation, a group teaching technique in which students perform a real-life situation (Dennicka & Exley, 1998); group research projects, a method which includes investigation or surveys about a certain topic and the reporting of the findings in different ways, such as presentations, newspapers, plays, skits, debates and peer-critiquing/peer-evaluation (Campbell, 2015; Slavin, 2011; Fung & Howe, 2014). Especially, group discussion, debate, and peer-questioning are suggested as three basic effective strategies that can be used in English classrooms to foster critical thinking skills.

Using literature in English classes: One of the most effective ways that instructors can develop learners' critical thinking is through the materials and especially the texts they use. Nuttall (1982) lists some useful guidelines in selecting a text. These are as follows: "1) Tell the students things they do not know before. 2) Encourage them to think about things they have not thought about before by introducing them to new and relevant ideas. 3) Make it easy for them to understand how other people feel or think. 4) Encourage them to have a desire to read for themselves. 5) Does the text test the students' level of foreign language? 6) If there are unknown lexical items, learning them at this stage is useful and not great in number? 7) Can some of them be inferred from the context? 8) Does the test lend itself to intensive study? 9) Does it encourage you to ask good questions or devise other forms of exploitation?"

Van (2009) lists the advantages of using literature in the English as an EFL classroom as follows: "It offers meaningful contexts; It is composed of a whole range of vocabulary, dialogues and prose; It encourages imagination and increases creativity; It improves cultural awareness; It fosters critical thinking; It is in parallel with CLT (Communicative Language Teaching) principles."

In fact, some studies related to the influence of using literature in the EFL classroom on critical thinking revealed that literary texts used for teaching can play an important role and directly or indirectly help learners in the creation of their thoughts as critical thinkers along with the teaching method (Khatib & Alizadeh, 2012; Külekçi & Kumlu, 2015). Shortly, the constructive role of literature in improving critical thinking is important.

It especially became evident that literary texts such as short stories, poems and novels increase critical thinking skills of the students (Khatip & Nazari, 2012). While analyzing literary texts, students improve a critical attitude towards them, make judgments, hypothesize different point of views, ask questions, and integrate the literary context into the real-life context. As a consequence of these, critical thinking can be promoted among students through teaching and reading literary texts.

- **Using Creative Drama:** Fischer (1989) stated that emotions along with ideas discovered and questioned in the stages of preparation and animation of dramatic activities have led to the realization of thinking processes and strategies. In addition, it has been pointed out that critically-minded individuals are aware of their own thinking process and have observed their own thinking process in order to think in a higher quality way and improve the quality of thinking. Fischer (1989) pointed out that dramas can be an effective tool in the development of critical thinking skills from the point of students' being aware of the process of creating a drama (improvisation, animation, reflection, repetition) as participants were able to get immediate verbal feedback from their friends, to learn spontaneously by seeing and doing it, to have experience of being instantly mingled with thoughts by using or developing the skills they were familiar with.

According to Spence-Campbell (2008), real life situations presented to students in drama environments have great importance. Students who act in the direction of daily purpose investigate some events and problems and solve them in this fictional world. Within this investigation process, they express what they discover physically or verbally. Then, they make sensible decisions through evaluation by activating critical thinking, thus giving meaning to the present situation (Farr Darling & Wright, 2004). Spence-Campbell (2008) stated that dramatic activities are not linear, but rather changeable, and that they intellectually use their imagination to solve difficult or conflicting situations and take joint decisions in this modified structure. Adıgüzel (2010) pointed out that what is created in the creative drama activities is created at that moment and exists for the first time so various viewpoints that are related to the solution of a problem emerge in a natural way. He also stated that different viewpoints and reflections of them should be laid emphasis on without taking account the right or wrong ones of what is created.

Similarly, San (2006) stated that knowledge is learned without memorization as learning is realized through interdisciplinary and interpersonal interactions, taking an active role, improvisation techniques and experiences in drama environments, which enables students to discuss, ask questions and, as a result, to have critical thinking skills.

CONCLUSION

Critical thinking is of a vital importance topic to modern education. The proposed instructional strategies for critical thinking in the study are theoretically sound and research-based. However, no specific method seems to be the best. Teachers are of great importance in terms of developing critical thinking skills in students. They should know how critical thinking relates to language learning in addition to explaining, modelling, and infusing the concept of critical thinking into their lesson designs and classroom activities. They should know how to ask questions beyond memory and factual information and that entail students' greater effort to infer, analyze, and evaluate. For example, open questions and referential questions place the students in an active position by enabling them to have opportunities to think independently and critically (Orlich, Harder, Callahan, Trevisan, Brown, & Miller, 2013). In addition, teachers should use their flexibility and creativity. Effective critical thinking instruction in EFL classrooms depends on teachers' intention and continual efforts. In other words, teachers are likely to achieve the goal of having better critical thinking skills and more efficient English lessons by combining various strategies in a new way or developing alternative methods appropriate to their own classes in designing critical thinking activities in the classroom.

On the other hand, students need to know the value of their own thinking, set their own goals and reflect on their progress if they want to become critical thinkers. According to Xu (2013), learning that is based on learner autonomy both personally and collaboratively promotes critical thinking. Finally, it can be said in the existing literature that students who can read, write, discuss, and interact with lots of learning materials in different ways are more likely to become critical thinkers.

REFERENCES

AbuSeileek, A. F. (2012). The effect of computer-assisted cooperative learning methods and group size on the EFL learners' achievement in communication skills. *Computers & Education*, 58(1), 231–239. doi:10.1016/j.compedu.2011.07.011

Adıgüzel, Ö. (2010). *Eğitimde Yaratıcı Drama*. Ankara: Naturel Yayınevi.

Anu, P., & Bhaskaran, N. (2017). Thinking Outside the Classroom: Developing Critical Thinking Using Authentic Materials in an ELT Classroom. *The Elt Practitioner, 4*(3).

Baessa, Y., Chesterfield, R., & Ramos, T. (2002). Active learning and democratic behavior in Guetamalan Rural Primary Schools. *British Association for International and Comparative Education., 32*(2), 205–218.

Beyer, B. K. (1987). *Practical strategies for the teaching of thinking*. Boston, MA: Allyn and Bacon.

Branch, J. B. (2000). *The relationship among critical thinking, clinical decision-making, and clinical practical: A comparative study (Doktora tezi)*. Idaho: University of Idaho.

Burbach, M. E., Matkin, G. S., & Fritz, S. M. (2004). Teaching critical thinking in an introductory leadership course utilizing active learning strategies: A confirmatory study. *College Student Journal, 38*(3), 482–493.

Campbell, M. (2015). Collaborating on critical thinking: The team critique. *Journal of Curriculum and Teaching, 4*(2), 86–95. doi:10.5430/jct.v4n2p86

Carlan, V., Rubin, R., & Morgan, B. (2005). *Cooperative Learning, Mathematical Problem Solving, and Latinos*. San Diego: American Educational Research Association. Retrieved from http://www.cimt. plymouth.ac.uk/journal/morgan.pdf

Chaffee, J. (2010). *Thinking Critically*. Boston: Houghton Mifflin Company.

Colucciello, M. L. (1999). Relationships between Critical Thinking Dispositions and Learning Styles. *Journal of Professional Nursing, 15*(5), 294–301. doi:10.1016/S8755-7223(99)80055-6 PMID:10554470

Dam, G., & Volman, M. (2004). Critical thinking as a citizenship competence: Teaching strategies. *Learning and Instruction, 14*(4), 359–379. doi:10.1016/j.learninstruc.2004.01.005

Dennicka, R., & Exley, K. (1998). Teaching and learning in groups and teams. *Biochemical Education, 26*(2), 111–115. doi:10.1016/S0307-4412(98)00028-4

Dufresne, J. R., Gerace, W. J., Leonard, W. J., Mestre, J. P., & Wenk, L. (1996). Classtalk: A Classroom Communication System for Active Learning. *Journal of Computing in Higher Education, 7*(2), 3–47. doi:10.1007/BF02948592

Elder, L., & Paul, R. (1994). Critical thinking: Why we must transform our teaching. *Journal of Developmental Education, 18*(1), 34–35.

English Teaching Professional. (2018). *Critical thinking skills in the classroom: Socrates, Bloom and De Bono*. Retrieved from https://www.etprofessional.com/critical-thinking-skills-in-the-classroom-socrates-bloom-and-de-bono

Ennis, R. (1985). Goals for critical thinking curriculum. In A. Costa (Ed.), Developing Minds (pp. 54-57). Alexandria, VA: Association for Supervision and Curriculum Development.

Ennis, R. (1989). Critical thinking and subject specificity: Clarification and needed research. *Educational Researcher, 18*(3), 4–10. doi:10.3102/0013189X018003004

Ennis, R. (1997). Incorporating Critical Thinking in the Curriculum: An Introduction to Some Basic Issues. *Inquiry: Critical Thinking across the Disciplines, 16*(3), 1-9.

Ennis, R. H. (1962). A concept of critical thinking: A proposed basis for research in the teaching and evaluation of critical thinking ability. *Harvard Educational Review, 32*, 81–111.

Ennis, R. H. (1993). Critical Thinking Assessment. *Theory into Practice, 32*(3), 179–186. doi:10.1080/00405849309543594

Farr Darling, L., & Wright, I. (2004). Critical thinking and the social in social studies. In A. Sears & I. Wright (Eds.), *Challenges and Prospects for Canadian Social Studies*. Vancouver, Canada: Pacific Educational Press.

Fischer, C. W. (1989). *Effects of a developmental drama-inquiry process on creative and critical thinking skills in early adolescent students* (Unpublished Doctoral Dissertation). College of Education, Kansas State University.

Fung, D., & Howe, C. (2014). Group work and the learning of critical thinking in the Hong Kong secondary liberal studies curriculum. *Cambridge Journal of Education, 44*(2), 245–270. doi:10.1080/030 5764X.2014.897685

Genhard, J. G. (1996). *Teaching English as a foreign language: A teacher self-development and methodology*. Ann Arbor, MI: The University of Michigan Press.

Gillies, R. M., & Boyle, M. (2010). Teachers' reflections on cooperative learning: Issues of implementation. *Teaching and Teacher Education, 26*(4), 933–940. doi:10.1016/j.tate.2009.10.034

Great Idea. Barrier Games. (2018, December 7). Retrieved from https://ealresources.bell-foundation. org.uk/teachers/great-ideas-barrier-games

Güven, M., & Kürüm, D. (2006). Öğrenme Stilleri ve Eleştirel Düşünme Arasındaki İlişkiye Genel Bir Bakış. *Sosyal Bilimler Dergisi, 6*(1), 75–89.

Herod, L. (2002). *Adult learning from theory to practice*. Heinle and Heinle Publishers. Heinemann.

Hughes, J. (2014). *Critical Thinking in the Language Classroom*. Eli Publishing.

İpşiroğlu, Z. (2002). *Eleştirel Düşünme Öğretilebilir mi?* Retrieved from www.felsefeekibi.com

Jenkins, J. R., Antil, L. R., Wayne, S. K., & Vadasy, P. F. (2003). How cooperative learning Works for special education and remedial students. *Exceptional Children, 69*(3), 279–292. doi:10.1177/001440290306900302

Johnson, D. W., & Johnson, F. P. (2006). *Joining together group theory and group skills*. Boston, MA: Pearson.

Khatib, M., & Alizadeh, M. (2012). Output tasks, noticing, and learning: Teaching English past tense to Iranian EFL learners. *English Language Teaching, 5*(4), 173–186. doi:10.5539/elt.v5n4p173

Khatib, M., & Nazari, O. (2012). The Effect of Literature on Enhancing Critical Thinking. *Journal of Comparative Literature and Culture, 1*(2), 29–33.

Kim, S. H., & Song, K. S. (2013). The Effects of Thinking Style Based Cooperative Learning on Group Creativity. *Creative Education, 3*(8), 20–24. doi:10.4236/ce.2012.38B005

Koray, Ö., Yaman, S., & Altunçekiç, A. (2004). Yaratıcı ve Eleştirel Düşünmeye Dayalı Laboratuar Yönteminin Öğretmen Adaylarının Akademik Başarı, Problem Çözme ve Laboratuar Tutum Düzeylerine Etkisi. Ulusal Eğitim Bilimleri Kurultayı, 6-9 Temmuz 2004, İnönü Üniversitesi, Eğitim Fakültesi, Malatya.

Külekçi, G., & Kumlu, E. (2015). Developiıng Critical Thinking Skills In English Language Teaching Classes Through Novels. *International Journal of Language Academy*, *3*(2), 76–90.

Laniro, S. (2007). Authentic materials. In M. A. Corley & P. Esra (Eds.), Professional Development Fact Sheet. American Institutes for Research.

Lipman, M. (1991). *Thinking in education*. Cambridge, UK: Cambridge University Press.

Maiorana, V. P. (1992). *Critical thinking across the curriculum: Building the analytical classroom.* (ERIC Document Reproduction Service No. ED 347511)

Mattson, K. (2005). Why "Active Learning" Can Be Perilous To The Profession. *Academe*, *91*(1), 23–26. doi:10.2307/40252732

Myers, B. E., & James, E. D. (2004). *The Influence of Student Learning Style on Critical Thinking Skill.* Retrieved May 8, 2018, from http://plaza.ufl.edu/bmyers/Papers/SAERC2004/LearningstyleCT.pdf

Norris, S. P. (1985). Synthesis of research on critical thinking. *Educational Leadership*, *8*, 40–45.

Norris, S. P., & Ennis, R. (1989). *Evaluating critical thinking*. Pacific Grove, CA: Critical Thinking Press and Software.

Nunan, D. (1988). *The Learner-Centred Curriculum*. Cambridge, UK: Cambridge University Press. doi:10.1017/CBO9781139524506

Nunan, D. (1999). *Second language teaching and learning*. Boston: Heinle and Heinle Publishers.

Nuttall, C. (1982). *Teaching reading skills in a foreign language*. London: Heinemann Educational.

Orlich, D. C., Harder, R. J., Callahan, R. C., Trevisan, M. s., Brown, A. H., & Miller, D. E. (2013). *Teaching strategies: A guide to effective instruction* (10th ed.). Belmont, CA: Wadsworth Cengage Learning.

Özdemir, H. (2013). Ortak eylem amaçlı metotla yabancı dil öğretiminde otantik doküman kullanımı. *International Periodical For the Languages. Literature and History of Turkish or Turkic*, *8*(10), 555–560.

Paul, R. W. (1991). Teaching critical thinking in the strong sense. In A. L. Costa (Ed.), Developing minds: A resource book for teaching thinking (Rev. ed.; Vol. 1). Alexandria, VA: ASCD.

Peacock, M. (1997). The effect of authentic materials on the motivation of EFL learners. *ELT Journal*, *51*(2), 144–156. doi:10.1093/elt/51.2.144

Penkauskienė, D. (2010). *Integration of critical thinking principles into the curriculum of secondary schools: Lithuania's case*. Research Report. Retrieved May 8, 2018, from http://www.sdcentras.lt/pr_ctp/Report.pdf

Philips, J. M. (2005). Strategies For Active Learning in Online Continuing Education. *Journal of Continuing Education in Nursing*, *36*(2), 77–83. doi:10.3928/0022-0124-20050301-08 PMID:15835583

Rees, G. (2018). *Jigsaw reading*. Retrieved from https://www.teachingenglish.org.uk/article/jigsaw-reading

Role Play/Simulation. (2018, December 7). Retrieved from https://otis.coe.uky.edu/ccsso/cssapmodules/sbp/sbp/Role%20PlaySimulation.html

Rudd, R., Matt, B., & Tracy, H. (2000). Undergraduate Agriculture Student Learning Styles and Critical Thinking Abilities: Is there a relationship. *Journal of Agricultural Education, 41*(3), 2–12. Retrieved from http://pubs.aged.tamu.edu/jae/pdf/Vol41/41-03-02.pdf

Şahinel, M. (2005). Etkin Öğrenme. In Eğitimde Yeni Yönelimler (pp. 149-165). Ankara: Pegema.

San, İ. (2006). Yaratıcı dramanın eğitsel boyutları, Yaratıcı Drama (1985-1998 Yazılar). İkinci Baskı, Ankara: Naturel Kitap Yayın Dağıtım, 113-122.

Seeler, D. C., Turnwald, K. H., & Bull, K. S. (1994). From Teaching to Learning. *Journal of Veterinary Medical Education, 21*(1). Retrieved from http://ilte.ius.edu/pdf/BarrTagg.pdf

Shirkhani, S., & Fahim, M. (2011). Enhancing critical thinking in foreign language learners. *Procedia: Social and Behavioral Sciences, 29*, 111–115. doi:10.1016/j.sbspro.2011.11.214

Siegel, H. (1999). What are thinking dispositions? *Educational Theory, 49*(2), 207–221. doi:10.1111/j.1741-5446.1999.00207.x

Slavin, R. E. (2011). Instruction based on cooperative learning. In R. E. Mayer & P. A. Alexander (Eds.), *Handbook of research on learning and instruction* (pp. 344–360). New York: Routledge.

Smith, A., & Rawley, L. A. (1997). Using TV Commercials to Teach Listening and Critical Thinking, *The Journal of the Imagination in Language Learning and Teaching, 4*. Retrieved May 8, 2018, from http://www.njcu.edu/CILUvoI4/smith-rawley.html

Spence, S., & Campbell, M. (2008). *Pedagogical Change: Using Drama to Develop the Critical Imagination* (Doctoral Dissertation). University of Alberta, Canada.

Tezcan, M. (1997). Eğitim Sosyolojisi. Yayınevi belirtilmemiş, Ankara.

Tipmontree, S., & Tasanameelarp, A. (2018). The Effects of Role-Playing Simulation Activities on the Improvement of EFL Students' Business English Oral Communication. *The Journal of Asia TEFL, 15*(3), 566–899.

Torres, R. M., & Jamie, C. (1995). Learning Style: A Factor to Critical Thinking? *Journal of Agricultural Education, 36*(4), 55-62. Retrieved May 8, 2018, from http://ssu.missouri.edu/ssu/AGED/naerm/s-g-3.htm.adresinden

Van, T. T. M. (2009). The relevance of literary analysis to teaching literature in the EFL Classroom. *Journal English Teaching Forum, 3*, 2–9.

Watson, G., & Glaser, E. M. (2010). *Technical manual and user guide: Watson–Glaser™ II Critical Thinking Appraisal.* Retrieved from http://us.talentlens.com/request-product-support-materials?leadsource=request-psm

Will your students steal a car? ESL/EFL simulation activity. (2018, December 7). Retrieved from https://eflideas.com/2018/02/26/will-your-students-steal-a-car-esl-efl-simulation-activity

Williamson, A., & Null, J. W. (2008). Ralph Waldo Emerson's Educational Philosophy as a Foundation For Cooperative Learning. *American Educational History Journal, 35*(2), 381–392.

Xu, Q. (2013). Fostering Critical Thinking Competence in EFL Classroom. *Studies in Literature and Language, 7*(1), 6–9.

Zhang, L., & Robert, J. S. (2000). Are Learning Approaches and Thinking Styles Related? A Study in Two Chinese Populations. *The Journal of Psychology, 134*(5), 469–489. doi:10.1080/00223980009598230 PMID:11034129

KEY TERMS AND DEFINITIONS

Active Learning Strategies: A kind of instructional strategy that enables students actively to be involved in in the lessons and the classroom.

Authentic Materials: Materials that enable learners to interiorize the language.

Communicative Language Tasks/Activities: Tasks/activities that require effective use of language together with critical thinking by engaging students in learning activities where authentic communication takes place.

Cooperative Learning Strategies: A kind of instructional strategy in which small groups of students work together on a common task.

Creative Drama: A kind of active learning strategy that helps students to improve academic and social skills communication skills by encouraging students to express themselves.

Critical Thinking: The ability of individuals to undertake responsibility of their own thinking by improving appropriate criteria and standards.

Instructional Strategies: A kind of technique that teachers use to help students become independent and strategic learners by motivating them and helping them focus attention.

Chapter 17
Planning for Critical Thinking in Language Arts Instruction

Shaneise J. Holder
The University of the West Indies – Cave Hill Campus, Barbados

Kahdia L. Jordan
The University of the West Indies – Cave Hill Campus, Barbados

ABSTRACT

This chapter focuses on the importance of planning for critical thinking in language arts instruction based on the Caribbean classroom. It seeks to identify traits of critical thinking, outline suggestions for planning for the inclusion of critical thinking, and highlight methods for incorporating critical thinking into language arts and provide solutions and recommendations. The chapter ends with suggestions for future research directions and summarizes the importance and many benefits associated with critical thinking in language arts.

INTRODUCTION

The overarching goal of most educators is to ensure learning is taking place under his or her watch. The need to foster learning therefore makes planning an essential tool in the educator's toolbox. Unfortunately, planning a lesson can sometimes appear to be a herculean undertaking. On occasion, he or she is tasked with teaching a class that may have many impediments such as overpopulated classrooms with students who have multiple and varying strengths and interests. Regardless of the circumstance, it remains the educator's responsibility to ensure every student under his or her care receives equal access to quality education.

The mandate perpetuated by the concept of facilitating lifelong learners, a key component for the 21st century, posits the need for heavy focus to be placed on fostering critical thinking skills. To this end, it is contingent on teachers who are tasked with the day to day socialization and education of students, to ensure that their charges have a firm grasp of these skills. This mandate is codified in some educational policies. For example, in Barbados, the Ministry of Education recognized the need for students to be able to utilize higher order thinking skills and assigned teachers the job of ensuring that "As lifelong

DOI: 10.4018/978-1-5225-7829-1.ch017

Copyright © 2019, IGI Global. Copying or distributing in print or electronic forms without written permission of IGI Global is prohibited.

learners, persons should be able to engage in critical thinking, generate solutions to complex problems, and gather and synthesize data. In order to facilitate this purpose, Barbadian students must be prepared to read strategically" (Ministry of Education, Youth Affairs and Sports, n.d.). Scott (2015) agreed with this stance when she posited that in order to teach higher order skills, teachers must tailor their lesson to suit "all the characteristics of today's students" (p.2) and should begin as soon as the child commences formal schooling as opposed to further in its educational life. This would allow critical thinking to become second nature to the student, eliminating any awkwardness that may occur from them being unsure of their ability to be rational producers, rather than mindless consumers of knowledge.

This chapter draws upon the experience of teaching and knowledge of the Barbadian education system. To address these concerns, this chapter presents definitions of key concepts: planning and critical thinking, explains the characteristics and identifiable traits of critical thinking, offers suggestions for planning for the inclusion of critical thinking in Language Arts and methods that can be used to incorporate critical thinking into Language Arts. Finally the chapter concludes with solutions and recommendations for these concerns, future research directions and a summary regarding the importance of planning and critical thinking and how they may coincide with Language Arts.

DEFINING KEY CONCEPTS: PLANNING AND CRITICAL THINKING

Thinking is a basic human function in all individuals, manifesting itself in the form of "problem solving, decision making and creative thinking" (Tosuncuoglu, 2018, p. 20). Due to the fact that thinking is natural and automatic to the individual, it occurs without consideration of any intervening factors, and so tends to be selfish, myopic and uninformed. In order to validate one's thoughts, some level of effort must be applied to this automatic thought process to give it some direction (Tosuncuoglu, 2018). One of the most fundamental aspects of critical thinking is its ability to actively encourage educational growth within a technologically changing world. As technology evolves, human thinking should also develop to foster future advancements. Although critical thinking in the classroom may be perceived as a simple task by some, it requires planning to adequately manage and achieve goals within learning environments. Planning and critical thinking coincide as planning requires thorough internal debates about the goal optimistically to be achieved and appropriate methods for achieving it. It "involves deciding on a future desired state and the course of action to get there" (Spoelder, Lockwood, Cowell, Gregersonand, & Henchman, 2015, p. 383). The planning process is a natural occurrence which we often take part in without a conscious awareness. For instance, people often make plans to attend events, for daily and weekly routines or in some cases to achieve academic or business objectives.

Teachers plan before the lesson to give themselves adequate time to instruct, for students to have enough learning experiences and for facilitating assessments within each lesson. Planning before the lesson also allows teachers to choose and prepare teaching aids or materials and strategies which would benefit the students they are working with. During the lesson, there may be interruptions such as meetings, lengthy morning assemblies and other unplanned events. Planning for the lesson, allows things to run smoothly regardless of these interruptions as the teacher already has a clear idea of learning objectives during the class and therefore is better prepared to adapt the strategies and activities to facilitate unexpected interruptions. Similarly, after the lesson, the teacher can gain new insight based on the evaluations. Subsequently, knowledge of what worked and the adjustments which would be needed to effectively maximize learning for students or facilitate reinforcement of any concepts later would be established. In understanding the high importance placed on planning for subcomponents of Language Arts such as Grammar, Composition and Comprehension instruction; equal consideration should be taken with regards to planning for critical thinking.

Pirozzi (2003) defines critical thinking as "a very careful and thoughtful way of dealing with events, issues, problems, decisions or situations" (p. 197). This type of thinking can easily be incorporated to benefit Language Arts topics such as Reading and Comprehension, where students are required to both understand what was read and critique. It can also be used in Composition writing where a student would need to be able to evaluate a topic thoroughly and write from various perspectives or in a manner which engages deep thought for their readers. Therefore, fostering learners who do not accept only but rather question and analyze to develop meaningful, lifelong learning.

Planning for critical thinking in the language arts classroom requires effort and can be divided into three parts. This includes preplanning which refers to what is organized before the teacher meets with the class, planning cooperatively where the teacher uses ideas based on analysis of what has occurred during class and where much of the planning of the teacher stems from the work of the class and daily planning as a result of cooperative planning (Wellington & Wellington, 1960).Most teachers may opt to preplan as it may be convenient, however it is essential that the type of students you are planning for is considered as well as their interests when doing so. Planning cooperatively and daily planning enables students' input to be atthe forefront of the planning process. The teacher has a clear idea of how the students are thinking; their interests and their preferred method of learning.

Planning is essential for effective instruction to take place. Learning comes in many different forms but when it occurs through critical thinking, it allows the learner to link concepts taught to other situations or experiences and establish outcomes for themselves. In other words, learning through critical thinking allows the student to take responsibility for their learning, a trait posited by Donnelly and Linn (2014). Therefore, planning how one is going to get one's students to think critically is important. If one were to reflect on their teaching methods or techniques, many teachers may admit to having used the lecture style, discussion, demonstration and drill and practice methods for teaching. At some point, most would have included questioning as one of their approaches. However, if asked whether they plan for questioning, the general response is often no. Questions are frequently asked based on responses or randomly compiled just for the sake of answering questions. Value is generally not placed on the type of questions asked to generate thought provoking responses, and enough time is not allotted to allow for students to mull over responses or ask questions which could provide valuable knowledge to inform their answers.

Additionally, Benjamin S. Bloom constructed a taxonomy with six major categories in the cognitive domain. The categories were Knowledge, Comprehension, Application, Analysis, Synthesis, and Evaluation. According to Vogler (2005), "the knowledge level is the lowest level. At this level, students are only asked to recall information while at the comprehension level; students are asked only to put information in another form. At application level, students are asked to apply known facts, principles, and/or generalizations to solve a problem. A question at the analysis level asks students to identify and comprehend elements of a process, communication, or series of events. Synthesis requires students to engage in original creative thinking and evaluation is the highest questioning level. Students are asked to determine how closely a concept or idea is consistent with standards or values" (p.99).

The formulation of questions can impact the way students think about content. If students are only permitted to recall information accessible to them, they lack opportunities to use critical thinking strategies that would allow them to correlate and compare new information to what was given or further examine this information. Critical thinking is a lifelong skill that benefits everyone, regardless of age. It is important for educators to ensure that this skill is not only adequately taught in our schools to improve Language Arts learning, but that we plan efficiently to ensure the needs of all of our students are met.

PLANNING FOR CRITICAL THINKING IN LANGUAGE ARTS INSTRUCTION:

Identifying Traits of Critical Thinking in Language Arts

As an educator picks his or her tools or teaching aids and prepares for the type of teaching strategies to be used in advance, it is imperative to deliberately plan for critical thinking to occur in the classroom. Critical thinking should not be a goal left to chance. However, many people are unaware of the identifiable traits which distinguish thinking and thinking critically.

According to Pirozzi (2003), critical thinking requires flexibility, a clear purpose, organization, time and effort, asking questions and finding answers, research and coming to logical conclusions. These attributes or characteristics should be prerequisites of a good teacher, and teachers should become well versed in these strategies before they can be disseminated to students. Ultimately, we as educators are solely responsible for the education of tomorrow's leaders; we must therefore encompass the majority, if not all, of these characteristics. Pirozzi goes on to mention that critical thinking is flexible because it involves a willingness to consider various possibilities before coming to conclusions and it is "deliberate because it involves a clear purpose" (Pirozzi, 2003, p. 198).This is an important facet of any Language Arts class, as it allows the student to think beyond what is obvious and have options before making the best decisions.

Tosuncuoglu (2018), concurred with Pirozzi about the importance and the characteristics of critical thinking. These characteristics or traits as posited by Tosuncuoglu (2018) manifest themselves when the student exhibits "being aware, systematic, flexible and patient, encompassing open-meaning, metacognition, reconstruction, motivation and discussion" (p. 20). This speaks to the difference between the students' thinking because it is an essential part of human beings, and the students' reflecting about why they think the way they do and providing informed responses to questions asked.

Planning for the Inclusion of Critical Thinking in Language Arts

As with planning for any subject or content area, the educator must ensure he/she is well organized in order to maximize the limited time allotted for teaching. If organization is not part of a teacher's daily routine, it can become overwhelming for the teacher to incorporate and plan for critical thinking in the classroom. Due to the enormity of the import of critical thinking skills with their scope which extends beyond the walls of the classroom to touch on the students' everyday lives, it is important to allot time and effort to its incorporation in the classroom, specifically the Language Arts classes. Unfortunately, time for most teachers is a precious commodity. It is scarce but always nice to have. Between grading scripts, school plays and meeting deadlines, time is always fleeting and opportunities for planning scarce. However, in order to adequately impart these skills, as well as ensure that there are opportunities for effective questions to be asked and reflective answers to be given within the Language Arts classes, planning is essential, and time and effort are a must.

If you already know the aspect to be taught and the target audience you are planning for, you are halfway there. Using the curriculum as a guide, teachers can prepare questions, learning activities and materials which would promote critical thinking among students. Teachers are well advised to include these strategies within their lesson plan to ensure they fit within the allotted time slot for the Language Arts class. They must also use language which models critical thinking for students.

Although planning for critical thinking in Language Arts instruction has its strengths, there are also some issues or weaknesses educators may have to be mentally prepared for. It must be noted that with the sharing of multiple points of view or opinions, come strong debates and heated arguments. According to Hawes (1990), "students sometimes associate critical thinking with the words "critic" and "criticism," then conclude that it is synonymous with finding fault" (Geertsen, 2003, p. 5). This predisposition is also dependent on affective aspects like how confident and passionate people become about how they analyze and what they analyze. Teachers must plan how they will ensure that safe and effective learning takes place within the classroom without chaos ensuing. The teacher must maintain effective classroom management, ensuring that the students respect each other's views instead of making their peers feel inadequate.

Teachers must also be prepared to ensure students do not over think and be unable to answer questions or complete tasks adequately. This can occur when students become distracted in their aim to respond to the question being asked or problem to be solved, as they spend time an inordinate amount of time thinking far beyond what is required.

Incorporating Critical Thinking into Language Arts

In Language Arts, emphasis was shifted from teaching particular skills to incorporating critical thinking with all aspects of literacy" (Morgan, 1990, p. 780). Law and Kaufhold (2009) expressed the importance of incorporating critical thinking into Language Arts instructions, noting that a large reason for teachers' inability to do so was their slavish focus on content-centered learning with its heavy focus on rote learning and subsequent neglect of critical thinking application. To this end, educators are encouraged to cultivate students' higher-level cognitive process, and abilities to engage in making inferences, decision making and creative problem-solving through the development of activities (Morgan, 1990). These activities may include plans for students to take part in critical reading, which teaches them to evaluate or question texts. Critical reading is dependent on critical thinking and is therefore described as learning to evaluate, draw inferences and arrive at conclusions based on evidence (Zintz and Maggart, 1984). The reader is then able to distinguish important information from that which is unimportant. The benefits of critical reading to Language Arts learning include an improvement in students' Comprehension and Composition writing along with students' improvement in their oral reading skills, as they may read with more intonation and expression. Improvement in a student's reading can foster better spelling, vocabulary and grammatical skills, hence causing a ripple effect in the Language Arts curricula.

Questioning is also a tool which allows teachers to model critical thinking for their students. Educators should plan the type of questions which they will ask their students to foster critical thinking skills. "A study conducted by McCollister and Sayler (2010) suggested that teachers use questioning techniques that allow students to engage in metacognition and develop activities that require students to evaluate information through collecting and analyzing data; rather than memorizing and recalling facts" (Nappi, 2017, p. 38).These questioning techniques can be incorporated into subcomponents of Language Arts such as Composition writing as well as Comprehension and foster inquiry based learning as well as problem solving skills for the student.

Another strategy for incorporating critical thinking skills in Language Arts was deposed by Elbow (2010) concepts of first order and second-order thinking for writing purposes. "First order thinking is intuitive and creative and does not strive for conscious direction or control" (Elbow, 2010, p. 37). However, "second order thinking is committed to accuracy and strives for logic and control: we examine our premises and assess the validity of each inference" (Elbow, 2010, 37). This is where critical thinking becomes beneficial as the writing process is carefully scrutinized by the student, again separating important from unimportant information. First order thinking allows for the student to respond to questions using existing schema, while second order requires the student not just to use schema to provide random answers, but rather have the students think about their thinking before responding to questions.

Although these strategies are encouraged by teachers, lack of resources for integrating critical thinking instruction into language arts within schools can be an issue limiting the implementation of critical thinking for some teachers (Morgan, 1990). These strategies must be supported by the government or board of directors of schools so that financial aid is put in place to ensure that lack of resources does not become an issue or an excuse. Cassum, Gul, & Profetto-McGrath (2015) noted that the participants of their study identified that "institutional culture, values, program goals, curriculum and assessment policies, support from management as well as availability of the resources affect their ability to create a critical thinking culture in classroom" (p.61).In the case of the Language Arts classroom, if there is no clear understanding of the learning objectives and no support on the curricular level about the import of creating critical thinkers from an early stage, then the Language Arts teacher's hands will be tied. The article cites a very real problem where the curriculum is designed with a focus on content instead of critical thinking, and the allotted time for the lesson is so narrow and stringent that time for actual discussion, deeper thinking and reflection cannot possibly be facilitated (Cassum, Gul, & Profetto-McGrath, 2015). Teachers also seemed to share the complaint that with the roles they were expected to play at the school, the administrative requirements and the frustration resulting from a lack of ready resources, they really could not find the time to "think, reflect, discuss, plan and use creative strategies to engage the students during class" (p.62).

It is not easy for people to master critical thinking (Holmes, Wieman, & Bonn, 2015). According to Holmes, Wieman & Bonn (2015), we can assume that much of the reason students do not take part or frequently exercise critical thinking is because the educational environment provides few chances for this process to occur. Not only should teachers plan the methods in which they will approach their students to effectively construct a critically thinking classroom, but they should pay attention to the environment in which this thinking will be taking place and ensure that there are no barriers that may restrict this process. As previously noted in this chapter, lack of resources can be a barrier for some teachers who aim to construct an appropriate environment. However, critical thinking is extremely important to the way students learn and should therefore become priority to school officials and directors.

Although it is important to demonstrate critical thinking for our Language Arts students to mirror, it is an insufficient method for students to use on their own (Holmes, Wieman, & Bonn, 2015). If a student mirrors a teacher's actions, this does not prove that they understand why these actions are being done or the benefits of doing so. This does not mean that when called upon, the student would be able to live up to expectations. We must teach students how to maneuver on their own through inquiry and experiments.

The complexity of critical thinking expressed by Forte & Horvath (2011) is that critical thinking goes pass the ideology of an internal rationalization to be expressed externally through various means, for example, discourse and writing, to provide a rationale for the fostering of the skill. What separates critical thinking from everyday mundane thinking however is the focus of the train of thoughts as it is commonly used for more stringent conversations, for example, in classrooms or informed discussions about the political landscape. This focus on providing informed input into serious real-world issues seems to be a viable reason as to why critical thinking is an important 21st century skill.

The importance and complexity of critical thinking leads the authors to believe that instead of waiting for adolescence, the skill should be taught early in the child's life. The reason behind this thought process stems from the realization that those who fit into the category of millennials may have a very myopic and selfish way of thinking. They have attained the ability to function with technology but there seems to be a disconnect in the level of contribution they make civically to their respective countries and the global market at large. Connerly (2006), in her research paper admits to a level of frustration where her elementary gifted students were concerned. She seemed to share the authors' opinion of the millennials encountered when she described her students as "naïve and self-absorbed about their thinking" (Connerly, 2006). Connerly's students were in fourth grade when she noted the deficiency in their thought process and sought to correct it.

While reading about Connerly's problem, the authors began to think about the fact that gifted children should really be adept at critical thinking, but this gross misconception was quickly clarified. Critical thinking has nothing to do with the individual's ability to store and replicate information with which they are provided; it has nothing to do with the individual's ability to criticize others and their opinions or their ability to be argumentative and powerful in their convictions. Instead Connerly's problem seems to lie in the students' inability to:

- Understand the logical connections between ideas
- Identify, construct and evaluate arguments
- Detect inconsistencies and common mistakes in reasoning
- Solve problems systematically
- Identify the relevance and importance of ideas
- Reflect on the justification of one's own beliefs and values.

A study conducted in a higher education situation recognized four reasons for the problem of critical thinking in that level, which the writer believes to exist in the primary level. The first identified problem was "teacher's competence" (Cassum, Gul, & Profetto-McGrath, 2015, p. 61). The participants in the study highlighted that "teachers' knowledge, attitude, and skills regarding critical thinking influence their ability to facilitate students to be a critical thinker" (p.61). They also expressed that the lack of knowledge manifested itself in a lack of confidence to step outside of the traditional ways of teaching, to try something new. It appears that traditionally, the focus of teaching was with just getting the students to internalize the new concepts, a read and regurgitate method if you please; the newer way however calls for students to think about the application of knowledge and at times challenge what they are being told. In the Language Arts classroom, one can see this as a problem as students are able to apply a taught principle, but when asked to give a reason for the application, they are unable to.

The "nature of students" (Cassum, Gul, & Profetto-McGrath, 2015, p. 61) was also highlighted. It was revealed that mind set actually was a major player in students' ability to practice critical thinking strategies. If the student does not feel motivated to be an active participant in the lesson, then chances are they will not be able to engage any of the critical thinking strategies taught. In the Language Arts class, a student who is distracted will not be able to focus enough on the tenets being taught during the lesson, far less rationalize why something was done or should be done. Another deterrent that falls under this category is the student who is not as adept at Language Arts as their peers, so they become disruptive in class and their attitude and expressions become off-putting to the teacher who is trying to teach the students.

The study also focused on the impact of the "type of learning environment" (Cassum, Gul, & Profetto-McGrath, 2015, p. 61). One of the participants of the study posited the view that "creating an enabling environment is an art of making the class stimulating, engaging students and motivating shy students as well as controlling the distracting students" (p.61). Warrican (2012), expressed the importance of having a classroom environment that facilitates classroom talk, as it was a means of promoting self-expression (p. 25). It was further stated that the art of listening and speaking were important in the Language Arts classroom and during the time that students are expressing themselves, teachers should not hyper-correct them or seek to discourage them from expressing themselves. If we as educators reflect on our own practices, we may notice that this seems to be quite a problem as we sometimes get caught up in correcting diction and pronunciation which results in invariably frustrating the child to the point that he or she stops sharing views and opinions during class time.

A UNESCO article published on February 26th, 2018, outlined a program undertaken to drive reading and writing for critical thinking in Kazakhstan. The article identified the problem in the country not to be one of a substantial percentage of illiteracy, as the country boasts at the date of the article's publishing an adult literacy rate of 99.3% and youth at 99.83% (UNESCO, 2016, p.1).Though these statistics are exceedingly good, it was realized that the Kazakhstani lacked the ability to think critically. This was due largely to their cultural belief that one should not share their personal beliefs in front of those held in high esteem in the country (elders, professors, teachers), nor challenge the works of respected authors (UNESCO, 2016,p.1). This cultural belief impacted the way schooling took place as the classroom was one where passive learning occurred; as long as the teachers were able to transfer the information to the students, their job was complete. The students were unable to challenge any idea or provide any type of input in the classroom. Though this problem may appear a little archaic to the western world, in classrooms in the Caribbean children are taught at the primary school level in a seemingly similar way, with the end result being success in the exam taken to move from Primary to Secondary level. This becomes the overall and ultimate aim for teachers. Rather than preparing young students for the technologically advancing world, teachers sometime focus on preparing them to be excellent at repetition.

SOLUTIONS AND RECOMMENDATIONS

In order to adequately impart knowledge and foster students' competence of critical thinking, the teacher must be well-versed and skilled in the area (Paul, 2003). If we expect students to mirror us, we must at least know the fundamentals of what we expect them to emulate. However, some teachers are not educated in critical thinking and have neither time nor instructional resources to integrate critical thinking into their daily instruction, (Astleitner, 2002).

As time, effort and consideration is taken to plan for instruction in all subject areas, the same exertion should be used to plan for critical thinking in Language Arts instruction. Kraak (2000) saw critical thinking as "an important, perhaps the most important of all present time educational tasks"(p.51). Both teachers and students reap the benefits of incorporating not only critical thinking in their Language Arts but good planning to ensure that objectives and instructional goals are ultimately met.

Students should be introduced to ways in which experts engage in critical thinking; this in turn exposes them to the nature of knowledge in disciplines, particularly Language Arts. They not only need to be exposed to this way of thinking, but engage in critical thinking process themselves repeatedly with targeted feedback (Holmes, Wieman, & Bonn, 2015).

To effectively plan for any lesson, educators should consider their target audience with regards to their age, gender, race, culture and interests. With these characteristics in mind, it is easier for the teacher to capture the attention of the student body. We can incorporate critical thinking activities into Language Arts instruction which would guide students on how to think critically on their own like 'think, pair share' and other brainstorming activities. These allow students to not only examine but to analyze various topics as well as discuss and hear various opinions from their peers.

There are a number of essential characteristics of a proper attitude toward higher-level thinking (cf. Ennis 1987; Hemming 2000; Siegel 1987; Zechmeister and Johnson 1992:6-7). These include open-mindedness, evidence- mindedness and persistent-mindedness. According to Geertsen (2003), open-minded thinking is associated with having respect for other viewpoints and a willingness to consider those alternative ideas. When your students have an open-minded way of thinking, they can respect views and ideas of others. "It also includes an intellectual curiosity in considering new question and seeking new answers" (Geertsen, 2003, p. 6). As part of planning for critical thinking in Language Arts instruction, planning ways to incorporate open-mindedness during the lesson is essential to having the most effective teaching experiences.

"Evidence-mindedness is the second essential element of proper attitude. With-holding judgment until proper evidence obtained includes a systematic skepticism and objectivity which compels a say" (Geertsen, 2003, p. 6), Persistent-mindedness however, includes a willingness to ask questions as well as a determination to exhaust the possibilities and change directions when necessary" (Geersten, 2003, p. 6). If teachers focus on these three characteristics of proper attitudes, students would be able to gain a lot more from their Language Arts lessons.

Critical thinking should be taught as a component of Language Arts. If this is considered, government officials and board of directors may be keener to ensure that resources are adequately accessible for students wishing to take part in these courses. From the earliest of age, students should encounter critical thinking strategies. They can be adjusted to suit age, gender, ethnic backgrounds and interests. This way, students would become familiar with this method and it would not seem difficult when it is most needed and would eliminate the difficulty of mastering critical thinking at an older age.

A study done by Cassum, Gul, & Profetto-McGrath (2015) revealed that many of the participants in their study were of the belief that critical thinking can be fostered depending on the type of learning environment which the teacher provides for their students. One of the participants in the study stated that "creating an enabling environment is an art of making the class stimulating, engaging students and motivating shy students as well as controlling the distracting students" (Cassum, Gul, & Profetto-McGrath, 2015). English Language has been described by many of its users as a complex discipline with its multiplicity of rules, this being the case, it may not be possible for the student to detect all the nuances or understand the reason behind the application of the taught rules. For this reason, it is important that the teacher create an environment that is conducive to the students' learning while supporting their independent thought process. All students do not learn at the same pace and their perception of events is also different; therefore the students need to have time to process their thoughts and be given an avenue to share their reasoning without fear of recrimination.

Similarly, Wantanabe-Crockett highlighted other strategies which can be useful for the teaching of Language Arts. The first strategy posited was "begin with a question" (p.2). It stands to reason that modern-day pedagogy encourages the teacher to act more in the role of facilitator than main focus; to this end, as facilitator the teacher should foster the child's initial encounter into critically thinking by asking probing questions. The teacher must first think of what it is about the topic that they wish the student to analyze and rationalize, for example, teaching the student about the use of pronouns, question their knowledge of the concept to make sure they understand- can you reword the sentence "Anna, Kim and Pat were waiting on the bus" using a pronoun? Why did you use 'they' and not 'them'? This allows the child to show not just that they are able to apply knowledge learnt, but also defend their use of that knowledge. Wantanabe-Crockett (2018) suggests that the teacher "write down possible answers on a chalkboard or oversized pad as a student reference" (p.3). This was highlighted to be a good way for the student to put the problem into perspective (Wantanabe-Crockett, 2018, p.3).

The second strategy was "create a foundation" (Wantanabe-Crockett, 2018, p.3). In order for the student to think critically, the teacher has to provide some kind of knowledge base from which the student can draw on to make any informed contribution. The impetus behind introducing students to critical thinking is not to have them pull information out of thin air, but rather provide them with information from different mediums which they would then synthesize to understand what they are being exposed to, as well as question formally taught and informally acquired information to be able to know what is going on around them. For example, before students are required to read 'The Three Little Pigs', the teacher would show them a picture of pigs and wolves and have them discuss similarities and differences between them. After the reading, based on the foundation knowledge imparted about the similarities and the differences, the teacher may ask "why do you think the wolf may want to blow downthe pigs' house" to prompt discussion and get the student to interact with the story on a deeper level. This is a very simple method teachers can use to get young children to begin thinking critically rather than reading the story and asking students to recall what was read.

The third strategy suggested was to "consult the classics" (Wantanabe-Crockett, 2018, p.3). Wantanabe-Crockett (2018) stated that "great literary works are a perfect launch pad for critical thinking, with challenging narratives and deep characterization" (p.4). It was understood that this strategy can be used to get students to immerse themselves in the lesson; forcing them to place themselves in the characters' shoes, thinking about the motive behind certain occurrences, thinking about where the plot is going, as well as the theme the writer is trying to demonstrate. In the Language Arts Classroom, as part of the lesson, the teacher can stop between pages and ask the students about what they think would occur on the other page. This allows children to begin thinking beyond what was said to them or make connections based on what was said or taught. This is a popular method used for predicting outcomes.

Also, the teacher can utilize the fourth strategy and have the student create a project based on what was read and how they believe the story would progress. The students can be given some art material and asked to paint or create a scene that represents their thoughts/vision. This is especially appealing to creative and artistic students. It also comes over to them not as work but play. However, the outcome is the same for the teacher- the students are critically thinking and learning is taking place.

The fifth strategy suggested was to have the student practice information fluency. This entails the students collecting information in various ways, thinking about what is relevant to the lesson and what they could discard. The student will also be given the opportunity to think of the reasons that fueled their decision on what is relevant and what was not. This method not only allows students to make decisions but it may also teach them how to solve problems.

The sixth strategy, which is to utilize peer groups, can be employed at this juncture. Wantanabe-Crockett (2018) stated that "Digital kids thrive on environments where critical thinking skills develop through teamwork and collaboration" (p.4). When the students are peered off in the class, the teacher can introduce a topic and have each group share with each other what they know about the particular topic from background knowledge and what they would have researched while practicing information fluency. An example of this is 'think, pair, share' activity mentioned earlier in this chapter.

The other strategies which Wantanabe-Crockett suggests are "try one sentence"- a game the students can play while in groups where a topic is introduced and a sheet of paper is passed around in the group where each student can share what they know about the particular topic and the paper is then passed around with each student reading the previous student's understanding of the topic and folding it before inserting their understanding and passing it down the line; "problem-solving"- the teacher assigns a question or focus and has the students solve the problems using information researched as well as background knowledge; "roleplaying"- where the students are encouraged to play the role of the characters in the books to act out the scenes, allowing them to discuss among themselves their reasons for choosing a particular character and think about similarities and differences in the characters; "speaking with sketch"- the students can create visuals to answer questions asked by the teacher, depicting predictions they make about the stories; "prioritize it"- the teacher should always make sure that they put teaching critical thinking in mind while planning their lessons, making sure that they do not get sidetracked by the need for the students to just be able to read and regurgitate information; and finally, the teacher should be prepared to not only accept the views posited by the students, but have them be open to accept when the teacher or other students put forward informed critiques of information they believe to be true.

FUTURE RESEARCH DIRECTIONS

An interesting area for research would be to analyze whether there are more dangers associated with teaching critical thinking at a young age than benefits in Barbados. Although the authors agree that critical thinking is important, they cannot help but wonder about the dangers associated with teaching it at a very young age. Would the students be mature enough to know when and where they should use critical thinking? An example of critical thinking going wrong is a child being so caught up with their ability to critically analyze information that they over think the simplest questions. Have you ever asked someone a very straight forward question and they gave you an entire story you did not ask for leaving you puzzled? To this regard, how then does a teacher reverse a child's knowledge or try to change how deep students think about certain things?

Another area worthy of research is the extent to which educators engage in critical thinking themselves when planning for Language Arts instruction. How deep do teachers think about their classroom instruction, their students or content to be taught? Do teachers even know how to critically think or analyze to mirror this skill for their students? Are teachers being trained to understand the importance of critical thinking at training colleges? Many questions regarding the teacher's accountability surface under this topic.

Thirdly, research should be based on the difference in overall academic performance for students who are taught critical thinking from a young age and those who are taught in secondary/high school. Guiding questions may include but are not limited to: Are students performing higher when they learn critical thinking skills at an early age? If yes, which subject areas have the highest scores? Do the methods used for teaching critical thinking at an early age vary drastically to the ones used for older students now beginning to learn the skill?

It is important to note that every child's learning capacity and ability will differ. As a result, teachers must be able to plan their lessons according to the students' learning abilities and interests to reap the best results.

CONCLUSION

As educators, it is important to ensure that preparations are made for teaching any subject area. A good teacher knows that planning is essential to their day to day delivery and as critical thinking may not come naturally for many students, a plan should be cultivated to ensure that students are guided and can efficiently perform critical thinking during Language Arts instruction.

This chapter focuses on the importance of critical thinking overall and in Language Arts instruction. Critical thinking allows students to not only accept information given but to analyze, question and solve problems on their own. It is an essential part of learning which is often neglected by teachers when teaching the Language Arts curricula, however it is beneficial to not only Language Arts learning but it prepares students for life's challenges.

Emphasis is also placed on the characteristics of critical thinking in order for it to be easily identified as well as how teachers can efficiently plan for this type of thinking during Language Arts Instruction. Its benefits to Language Arts learning include engaging with material in a decisive way, writing analytically and understanding problems after careful evaluation.

Ultimately, planning for critical thinking may have its problems or issues, however, the benefits of this method to Language Arts instruction surpass any inconveniences educators may have. Therefore, we must all strive to plan for critical thinking in our various Language Arts components to provide students with quality learning experiences that could last them a lifetime.

ACKNOWLEDGMENT

The authors would like to acknowledge the contribution of everyone who took part in the development of this chapter, specifically the editors Dr. Sandra Robinson, and Dr. Verna Knight, The University of the West Indies – Cave Hill Campus, Barbados. Their support and expertise have allowed us to produce a valuable contribution to the book in coherence with fellow authors and for that we thank you.

Our sincere gratitude also goes to our family and friends for their support, patience and inspiration. It would be an impossible task without the smallest contribution.

REFERENCES

Allen, E. G., Wright, J. P., & Laminack, L. L. (1988). The Reading Teacher. *Using Language Experience to ALERT Pupils' Critical Thinking Skills.*

Astleitner, H. (2002). Teaching Critical Thinking Online. *Journal of Instructional Psychology.*

Bean, J. C. (2011). *Engaging Ideas: The Professor's Guide to Integrating Writing, Critical Thinking, and Active Learning in the Classroom.* Jossey-Bass.

Browne, N. M., & Keeley, S. M. (2006). *Asking the Right Questions: A Guide to Critical Thinking.* Longman.

Elbow, P. (2010). *Teaching Thinking by Teaching Writing.* Academic Press.

Geertsen, R. H. (2003). Rethinking Thinking about Higher-Level Thinking. *Teaching Sociology, 31*(1), 1. doi:10.2307/3211421

Goffe, L. C., & Deane, N. H. (1974). *Questioning Our Questions.* Academic Press.

Holmes, N. G., Wieman, C. E., & Bonn, D. A. (2015). Teaching critical thinking. *Proceedings of the National Academy of Sciences of the United States of America.*

Love, S. L., & Stobaugh, R. (2018). *Critical Thinking in the Classroom: A Practitioner's Guide.* Academic Press.

Morgan, M. (1990). *Eric: Encouraging Critical Thinking in the Language Arts.* Academic Press.

Nappi, J. S. (2017). *The Importance of Questioning in Developing Critical Thinking Skills.* International Journal for Professional Educators.

Paul, R. W. (2003). Bloom's Taxonomy and Critical Thinking Instruction. *Educational Leadership.*

Peterson, P. L., Marx, R. W., & Clark, C. M. (1978). Teacher Planning, Teacher Behavior, and Student Achievement. *American Educational Research Journal, 15*(3), 417–432. doi:10.3102/00028312015003417

Pirozzi, R. (2003). *Critical Reading, Critical Thinking: A Contemporary Issues Approach.* Academic Press.

Shaw, R. D. (2014). *How Critical is Critical Thinking.* National Association for Music Education. doi:10.1177/0027432114544376

Spoelder, P., Lockwood, M., Cowell, S., Gregersonand, P., & Henchman, A. (2015). *Protected Area Governance and Management.* ANU Press.

Vogler, K. E. (2005). Improve Your Verbal Questioning. *The Clearing House: A Journal of Educational Strategies, Issues and Ideas, 79*(2), 98–103. doi:10.3200/TCHS.79.2.98-104

Wellington, B. C., & Wellington, J. (1960). *Teaching for Critical Thinking with Emphasis on Secondary Education.* Academic Press.

KEY TERMS AND DEFINITIONS

Barbados: Barbados is an island country in the Lesser Antilles of the West Indies, in the Caribbean region of North America. It is 34 kilometres (21 miles) in length and up to 23 km (14 mi) in width, covering an area of 432 km2 (167 sq mi). It is situated in the western area of the North Atlantic and 100 km (62 mi) east of the Windward Islands and the Caribbean Sea; therein, Barbados is east of the Windwards, part of the Lesser Antilles, roughly at 13°N of the equator. It is about 168 km (104 mi) east of both the countries of Saint Lucia and Saint Vincent and the Grenadines and 400 km (250 mi) northeast of Trinidad and Tobago. Barbados is outside the principal Atlantic hurricane belt. Its capital and largest city is Bridgetown.

Critical Reading: Learning to evaluate, draw inferences and arrive at conclusions based on evidence (Zintz and Maggart, 1984); a skill which is dependent on critical thinking. It teaches students to evaluate or question texts.

Critical Thinking: A skill based on an individual's ability to provide informed opinions on the basis of synthesizing new and existing knowledge.

First Order Thinking: Allows for the student to respond to questions using existing schema, intuitive and creative and does not strive for conscious direction or control (Elbow, 2010, p. 37).

Foundation Knowledge: Information provided to students which they utilize to make informed decisions.

Information Fluency: The ability to not only accumulate but to organize information to determine relevance.

Institutional Culture: A particular set of rules and norms that govern an organization.

Language Arts: A curriculum area which includes the process of studying and constructing meaning, inquiring and presenting ideas through reading, writing, listening, speaking, viewing/visual media.

Language Arts Instruction: A particularly important area in teacher education, that focuses on the teaching of listening, speaking, reading, and writing; instruction in Language Arts is essential to learning and to the demonstration of learning in every content area. Teachers are charged with guiding students toward proficiency in these four language modes, which can be compared and contrasted in several ways.

Planning Cooperatively: A practice where the teacher uses ideas based on analysis of what has occurred during class and where much of the planning of the teacher stems from the work of the class.

Second-Order Thinking: Requires the student not just to use schema to provide random answers, but rather has the students think about their thinking before responding to questions.

Chapter 18
The Instructional Context of Critical Thinking Development in Early Childhood Education:
Theoretical and Curriculum Perspectives

Hannah Mills Mechler
Grays Harbor College, USA

ABSTRACT

This chapter will outline the roles of teachers within early childhood learning environments and how they may promote children's critical thinking skills. Further discussions about how children's cognitive development may be fostered is also addressed. Theoretical frameworks are integrated as well to further decipher and understand how children's critical thinking skills may be promoted within early childhood learning environments. In addition, several curriculum models in early childhood education that are focused on the Montessori, Reggio Emilia, Tools of the Mind, High Scope, and Waldorf approaches are presented and applied to how they may enhance children's critical thinking skills as well as their overall development.

INTRODUCTION

This chapter will focus on the essence of critical thinking and how its application within early childhood environments may foster children's cognitive, social and emotional development. In addressing the practices that promote children's critical thinking skills, theoretical constructs will be outlined. Furthermore, developmentally appropriate practices and concepts associated with these principles will be described and applied to how critical thinking skills may be promoted within early childhood education environments. Curriculum models will also be highlighted in terms of their characteristics and how they may influence children's development of critical thinking skills.

DOI: 10.4018/978-1-5225-7829-1.ch018

Copyright © 2019, IGI Global. Copying or distributing in print or electronic forms without written permission of IGI Global is prohibited.

BACKGROUND

Children's social, emotional, cognitive, and physical development may greatly be influenced by their environments and experiences they gain within these settings. To begin the discussion of how factors within children's environments may affect their critical thinking skills within early childhood contexts, it is important to consider how nature and nurture both interact to influence this potential. Children's ability to engage in critical thinking skills may depend upon a combination of both nature and nurture.

Nature and Nurture

Nature refers to genetics, while nurture is associated with children's environments. Genetics is thought to greatly influence children's temperament, or outward traits and expressions. Nurture has also been found to impact children's behaviors and developmental characteristics. When focusing on both nature and nurture, it is important to consider brain research that has been conducted on young children. According to Feldman (2015), children's early experiences shape their brains. Therefore, the types of experiences that infants have is important for further understanding their brain development, which in turn has been found to be associated with their learning potential. More specifically, developing secure attachments with sensitively attuned caregivers is a key element in ensuring that children's overall development is nourished. Sensitive attunement entails caregivers who consistently respond to their children and are in tune with their needs and routines. By having secure attachments, children's brains have been found to develop in a healthy manner (Dozier, Peloso, Lewis, Laurenceau, & Levine, 2008). A key to establishing healthy attachments between caregivers and children relate to the development of trust. When children have developed a sense of trust with their caregiver and they know their needs will always be met, their stress levels may be lower, as compared to children who do not have this sense of security. Higher stress levels have been found to be related to elevated cortisol levels in the brain. Cortisol is synonymous to a toxin in the brain, as may inhibit normal brain development that occur within synapses and neurons.

In addition to the discussion of nature, the role of temperament may be considered. Temperament is thought to originate primarily from children's genetics. Thomas and Chess (1977) created various categories of temperaments that children may identify with. Temperament may be defined as characteristics and personality traits that children exhibit. There are three common types of temperament, which include: easy, slow to warm up, and difficult. An "easy" temperament may be characterized by children who are adaptable and have fairly stable moods and routines. In comparison, a "slow to warm up" temperament type may include children who are slower to adapting and may have greater variability in their expressions of moods. The other temperament type is "difficult." Children whose characteristics align with difficult may have greater fluctuations of moods and may be wary of change or exhibit protest for changes in routines or schedules.

Juncheng (2014) further discussed these concepts and indicated that individuals' abilities to engage in critical thinking skills may be associated with their temperaments. For example, individuals who are open-minded and exhibit a sense of wonder about their environments may do better in critical thinking skills problems, as compared to others whose temperaments are difficult. Hence, every individual is unique and their critical thinking skills may vary based upon nature and nurture.

In relation to children's environments, or the factors related to nurture, it is important to consider how these components may be connected. According to Bronfenbrenner's (1977) ecological systems theory, certain components have the more direct and others less direct influence on children's growth and development, as well as overall mannerisms associated with socialization. The first of the ecological systems model is the *microsystem*. The *microsystem* involves children's immediate environments, which may influence them the most. Examples of the *microsystem* include home and school environments. For instance, values and beliefs taught at home may influence children's perceptions or their personal beliefs. The next system is termed the *mesosystem* which focuses on connections between microsystems. Children's home environment may intermingle with their school environments. For example, children's beliefs and values may influence their social behaviors at school.

Aside from the microsystem and mesosystem is the *exosystem*, which include less direct influences on children's development, such as parent's jobs and time allotted towards spending time with their children or working. Parents' work schedules may directly influence the types of bonds children have with their parents. In addition, relocation due to parents' jobs may influence the whole dynamics of the microsystem and mesosystem.

As the centric circles move outward, the *macrosystem* emerges, which includes history, culture, and society. One example includes where individuals reside as well as cultural adaptations they are associated with may greatly influence children's development and overall socialization abilities. Finally, the *chronosystem* involves time or the era that individuals live in. For instance, typical family structures in 2018 may differ greatly from those of 1950, in terms of standards established for early childhood environments and schools.

Early childhood environments and children's development greatly relate to both the *microsystem* and *mesosystem*. However, the *chronosystem* in which children live may also influence the type of education they receive due to modifications to school standards as well as use and access to various types of technology.

This chapter will continue by placing a greater focus on the role of the early childhood classroom and how it may be a key factor associated with children's development of critical thinking skills. Furthermore, theories related to child development and early childhood education will be used to justify the inclusion of activities that have been found to promote children's critical thinking skills. In addition, curriculum models will be presented and applied to the concept of children's development of critical thinking skills.

Integrating lessons and activities within early childhood classrooms that promote children's critical thinking skills is an essential component for nourishing their social, emotional, and cognitive development. Piaget (1952) believed that children's active explorations within their environments may be essential for promoting their cognitive skills. In relation, Vygotsky (1978) posited that through interactions with others, children's social and cognitive development are supported. This is due to the perception that learning is actively constructed; thus, through play experiences and exploration within environments, children learn key constructs needed to promote their cognitive development skills. In addition, Vygotsky noted that mental tools are established, which enable children and other individuals to plan and think ahead. The mental tools are referred to as "signs." One example of a "sign" is language, as it promotes children's ability to think about concepts and problems in their minds, while interacting with others in their environments (Vygotsky, 1978).

Vygotsky posited that interactions and associations that children have enable *scaffolding* to occur. *Scaffolding* may be defined as pairing two children together; one with advanced knowledge about a skill and the other with developing knowledge about the content. Due to the pairing, the child with developing knowledge will gain specific tools needed to reach the zone of proximal development. Pairing children together on a task that encourages critical thinking skills to be exercised promotes the concept of *scaffolding*.

At the same time, utilizing manipulates commonly used to encourage critical thinking skills within early childhood environments promotes children's fine and gross motor abilities. When considering the application and immersion of critical thinking skills within early childhood classrooms, connections to key theorists as well as the overarching importance of play are important to consider, as these component further highlight the role of critical thinking in terms of how it promotes children's overall development.

FOSTERING CRITICAL THINKING

Creating environments for children that promote their critical thinking skills is important for further building their cognitive development abilities. Specifically, these abilities enable children to use higher level thinking processes, which are responsible for reasoning, planning, negotiating, and problem solving. These skills are important, as they serve as a foundation for assisting children with thinking more critically as they grow older.

Recommended strategies for encouraging children's development of critical thinking skills include presenting open-ended questions. Open-ended questions facilitate children to think critically about the task that they are engaged with, while making neural connections. Questions that are open-ended include those that involve elaboration, rather than "yes" or "no." Beginning questions with "how" or "why," for instance is a great way to promote children's critical thinking skills, as they enable children to think abstractly about the content. Furthermore, open-ended questions facilitate application of material, so that children can make connections with information they already know when they are learning something new.

Play Interactions

Play is another manner in which children may develop critical thinking skills. The benefits of play surpass the cognitive aspect of development, as children's participation in play activities also promotes their social, emotional, and physical development. For instance, children's participation in play activities have been found to promote their problem solving skills, confidence levels, sharing and negotiation abilities, emotion regulation, fine and gross motor skills, communication and language development, creative and critical thinking abilities, imagination, brain development, and abstract thinking skills (Ginsburg, 2007). In addition, participation in play activities have been found to promote children's physical activity levels, which are related with a reduction in the prevalence of obesity levels.

However, due to the increased focus on media, the amount of play activities that children are engaging in appears to be falling, compared to previous decades (Alper, 2011). Direct communication and exposure with, and exposure to, other children that promote language and vocabulary rich experiences, while building play experiences are truly essential for children's development. Play opportunities also assist children with engaging in life experiences, which in turn will enable them to solve challenges that may arise as they mature (Alper, 2011). Thus, exposure to lower amounts of play activities within children's environments may be problematic if children are not interacting with caregivers, parents, teachers, or other peers (Ginsburg, 2007). Interactions are vital for children's development of social, emotional, cognitive, and physical development. In addition, play and recess have been found to be associated with children's higher academic achievements.

There are different categories of play which may typically be seen at various stages throughout children's lives. Parten (1932) assessed young children's play interactions during free play opportunities throughout the span of an hour. Researchers associated with Parten's research observed children's social behaviors during their play interactions. Among the observations, categorizations and stages of play were formed. The first stage of play is solitary, where children tend to remain occupied with their own play activities; they do not interact with other children. Next, children participate in parallel play, where they tend to play near another child, but do not work together on a same goal while completing the play activity. Following this stage, cooperative play generally emerges, where children begin to engage in collaboration with peers. For instance, during this stage, children may interact with peers during their play activities. These characteristics of play then connect with the goal-directed stage, where children interact and collaborate to achieve common goals (Parten, 1932).

When children interact in their play groups, collaboration and other social and emotional skills are exercised (Leong & Bodrova, 2012). An example includes children's abilities to engage in emotion regulation skills. When they participate in play activities, opportunities present themselves to learn these specific concepts needed to interact with others as they mature. Children's critical thinking skills are fostered due to collaborating with others and engaging in problem solving activities. Through these interactions, the concept of *scaffolding* is highlighted. Thus, *scaffolding* enables children to learn from one another, based upon their unique developmental stages and abilities. When a child with developing knowledge is paired with a child with more advanced knowledge, the learning process is further promoted and enriched.

Developmentally Appropriate Practices

When considering developmentally appropriate practices, it should be noted that every learning opportunity and each lesson presented within early childhood classrooms should be appropriate for children's developmental ages and stages. Furthermore, material that is developmentally appropriate should be items that promote children's development at an individual level. Specifically, children achieve milestones at different rates. Therefore, it is important for teachers in early childhood classrooms to observe and assess children's individual growth and unique abilities. By having baselines that track children's strengths and weaknesses, lessons can be created to uniquely promote their learning and acquisition of developmental milestones.

The National Association for the Education of Young Children (NAEYC) outlines specific standards and competencies related to ensuring that early childhood environments create developmentally appropriate activities for children. Early childhood programs that are NAEYC accredited ensure that teachers obtain knowledge about child development and early childhood education, while promoting professional development opportunities as well. Administrators generally hold college degrees and solid knowledge bases about early childhood education. Furthermore, programs that are NAEYC accredited ensure the curriculum promotes a sense of community and that all children should be welcomed. In relation, promoting a sense of diversity is an important component outlined by NAEYC standards. Celebrating every child and family by highlighting their unique characteristics is essential within these programs. Promoting involvement of families is important for creating a sense of community by embracing and involving all cultural backgrounds and families' unique experiences. In relation, NAEYC has written a position statement, signifying the importance of creating anti-bias educational opportunities to ensure that all children and families feel a sense of community within their classrooms and schools. Promoting multicultural opportunities for all children, while involving families further encourages children and families to develop pride in their cultures and heritages. In turn, this may promote children's self-esteem and overall motivations to learn within inclusive environments.

NAEYC also ensures that early childhood physical environments are developmentally appropriate for children's ages and stages of growth. Furthermore, providing children with a variety of materials is essential for promoting developmentally appropriate experiences for everyone. Children's health and well-being are also a focus of NAEYC accredited early childhood environments, where food is prepared in a healthy manner and cleanliness of all areas within the environments are safe for exploration and discovery. These standards and competencies are important, as they ensure that children have the proper environment needed to nourish their physical, social, emotional, and cognitive development.

Theoretical Considerations

Theoretical concepts developed by Howard Gardner, Jean Piaget, and Lev Vygotsky will be presented below for the purposes of shedding light into how concepts related to each theoretical assumption may be associated with early childhood development and education.

Howard Gardner

Howard Gardner's theory of multiple intelligences underscores the role of integrating critical thinking skills within early childhood environments (Gardner, 1993). Specifically, Gardner postulated that various types of intelligences exist; these types cannot be measured by standardized assessments. The types of multiple intelligences Gardner coined include: *interpersonal, intrapersonal, bodily-kinesthetic, linguistic, logical-mathematical, naturalistic, musical, and spatial. Interpersonal* intelligence refers to doing well in interactions with others, in terms of conversing and reading others' body language. *Intrapersonal* intelligence measures individuals' own processing of emotions and awareness of emotional thoughts. Next, a *bodily-kinesthetic* intelligence relates to characteristics of people who are gifted with working with their hands or bodies; athletes would be an example of this intelligence. In comparison, a *linguistic* intelligence is associated with individuals who do well in social interactions as well as individuals who converse well and perform well in public speaking occasions. The next type of intelligence, *logical-mathematical*, is evident in people who do well with mathematical computations and exhibit logical problem solving skills. *Spatial* intelligence is associated with people who do well with geometric calculations and dimensional objects. Finally, *naturalistic* intelligence is associated with individuals who are in tune with nature and zoology, while individuals with *musical* intelligence may perform well with musical interactions and performances.

Gardner believed that by pluralizing, or presenting material in various ways is beneficial for accommodating multiple intelligences as well as an array of learning styles. Through learning, students should be able to apply the material, which relates to deeper level processing of information. Deep level processing differs from shallow level processing, where information is recited or memorized. When children apply and create, using concepts presented in class, deep level processing occurs. Therefore, when providing children with opportunities to think critically, it may be important to consider activities that enable them to design or create projects that are meaningful to them. Also, as teachers perform observations, assessments, and engage in frequent communication with families, they are further understanding children's unique intelligences. This is essential for creating lessons that bolster children's development and critical thinking skills.

Jean Piaget

Piaget's cognitive development theory may also be applied to the concept of critical thinking. When considering the stages of children's cognitive development and general milestones associated with each stage, critical thinking may be applied in various progressions. Through acquisition of certain skills at each stage of development, children are able to engage in more abstract thought. However, the foundation of being able to think critically begins at the sensorimotor stage, where children's early explorations of their environments are key for enabling them to think more in depth as they mature.

The first stage of Piaget's theory is the sensorimotor, which emerge when children are between the ages of birth to two years (Piaget, 1952). During this period of development, children generally learn through their sensory experiences, as well as their reflexes. As they mature within this stage, they are able to learn associations, such as cause and effect by interacting within their environments. Furthermore, as children interact within their environments, they begin to practice certain skills, such as intentionality, as well as awareness of their own bodies and environments.

The next stage is preoperational, which emerges between the ages of two and seven (Piaget, 1952). During this stage, children are able to apply words to objects due to the growth experienced during the vocabulary spurt. In addition, they are able to think symbolically and represent objects within their environments. This stage is also characterized by egocentrism and centration, where children tend to focus on themselves and cannot accept another person's point of view. Another characteristic of this period involves a lack of abstract understanding related to comprehending time, space, and reversibility. For example, if a child is on a journey whose duration is approximately 100 miles, that child may ask within ten minutes of the trip if the family has arrived at the destination.

To promote children's critical thinking skills during this developmental stage, teachers and caregivers may ask open-ended questions. This questioning may allow children to think critically, while producing original responses based upon their perceptions. Furthermore, early childhood environments that are comprised of open-ended materials, such as those in which children can manipulate and create new products, are also recommended. Through changing the shape or size of manipulatives, children's cognitive skills may be promoted, due to their active experimentation within their environments. Piaget postulated that active experimentation is essential for encouraging growth of children's cognitive development skills, such as imagination, creative thinking, and the ability to think more abstractly as they mature.

The third stage of Piaget's theory is marked by concrete operational thinking (Piaget, 1952). During this period of development, Piaget hypothesized that children are able to think in more abstract manners. The law of conservation is thought to be understood during this stage. The law of conservation refers to children's understanding that there is equal quantity between two comparison groups, even though one group may look larger. An example includes showing children one quarter, versus 25 pennies. A child who has mastered the law of conservation will correctly decide that both quantities of coins have an equal value amount. However, children who believe there is a greater quantity in the group of 25 pennies are thought to have not yet comprehended the concepts associated with the law of conservation. Children in this developmental stage are also likely to attain the abilities to think in reverse. To encourage critical thinking during this stage of development, teachers and caregivers may provide children with opportunities to hypothesize and make connections within their environments.

The final stage of Piaget's theory is referred to as the formal operations stage (Piaget, 1952). During this developmental period, which occurs when children are 12 years of age and older, Piaget believed that children's cognitive abilities enable them to think and reason abstractly and more logically, as compared to the previous stages. To further promote a sense of critical thinking, teachers and adults can encourage children to think in more abstract terms. For instance, the introduction of mathematics that challenge children to manipulate shapes and objects in trigonometry further builds upon skills enabled in the formal operations stage.

Lev Vygotsky

Vygotsky's sociocultural theory describes the ways in which children learn by interacting with others within their environments (1978). Through collaboration with other individuals, children learn skills and concepts necessary for learning. A common application of Vygotsky's theory includes the process of *scaffolding*. By pairing together two children or one child with a teacher, learning is fostered. Specifically, scaffolding is exercised if one child with developing knowledge is paired with another child with more advanced knowledge about a subject matter. Through these interactions, the child with developing knowledge will gain more insight or skills about the concepts, thereby reaching his/her zone of proximal development.

Additional concepts associated with Vygotsky's sociocultural theory include the conceptualizations that learning is actively constructed. Hence, cognitive development could be fostered through interaction within children's environments. Play is also another example of how learning can be actively constructed. By engaging in make believe play, children are provided with opportunities to take roles of the characters they act. These intentional behaviors, in turn, promote children's development of self-regulation and imagination.

Mental tools, or signs are also developed when children interact with others within their environments (Vygotsky, 1978). Through these interactions, children's communication and negotiation skills are fostered, which enable children to plan and engage in higher level thinking processes. Examples of mental tools include speech, writing, and number systems. Children also form their cultural tools by surrounding themselves within their environments and then perceiving those experiences through the lenses of their cultures. Through these experiences, children's attitudes, ideas, and perceptions may be greatly influenced.

Curriculum Models

Critical thinking skills may be applied to various early childhood curriculum models. Curriculum models may be characterized as road maps that teachers and administrators use to teach children based on the philosophy of the school's program. The models that will be addressed in this section include: Montessori, Reggio Emilia, Tools of Minds, High Scope, Waldorf and Anti-bias Education considerations.

Montessori

The Montessori curriculum focuses on a child-centered approach, where teachers serve the roles as guides within early childhood environments. The purpose of acting as a guide rather than engaging in teacher-directed instruction is to promote children's cognitive development skills, such as critical thinking and problem solving. Furthermore, Montessori classrooms are enriched in multi-aged grouping, where children from various ages are generally merged together, rather than dividing children into classrooms based on their chronological ages. Through pairing in mixed-age classrooms, the concept of *scaffolding* is exercised. As mentioned above, *scaffolding* is advantageous, as it provides children with opportunities for children to interact with one another on a common goal. The interactions in turn promote cognitive development, as one child with more advanced knowledge may be paired with another child with developing knowledge. As children are paired together, their critical thinking skills may soar, due to the adoption of the other's perception behind a problem or concept.

Reggio Emilia

A Reggio Emilia curriculum model follows a child-directed approach (Rinaldi, 2006). In this context, teachers may be perceived as guides, as children explore their environments. Emergent curriculum, or a curriculum that is created based upon children's interests is showcased in this model. For instance, if children's interests gravitate towards airplanes, teachers may provide tools and crafts for children to experiment and learn more about these creatures. Teachers may also design the classroom to replicate the interior of an airplane by re-arranging tables and chairs. In relation, children may be provided props, such as dramatic play clothing that allows them to pretend they are pilots or crew members. Furthermore, teachers may read books to children about aviation and also provide them with art supplies that enable them to create aircraft using various open-ended materials. Open-ended materials may include those that allow children to use their imaginations to create limitless possibilities for those items. For instance, with adult supervision, craft sticks and glue may be used to build an airplane.

Key tenants of Vygotsky's sociocultural theory may be applied to the Reggio Emilia curriculum, due to the pairing of children together when engaged in emergent curriculum activities. When children are collaborating, their mental processes become more abstract and they may adopt abilities to develop higher level thinking processes. Higher levels of thinking may include abilities related to planning, reasoning, and abstract thinking.

Tools of the Mind

The Tools of the Mind curriculum integrates many themes of Vygotsky's sociocultural theory. For instance, Vygotsky believed that children learn through interactions with others. Play is an activity that children engage in quite frequently within early childhood. Through participation in play activities, children's cognitive, social, emotional, and physical development is promoted. For instance, when immersed within pretend play, children may adopt characters within play skits. When they play the particular character, their emotional development may be fostered due to acting out emotions the character may display. In turn, through collaboration, children may learn the concept of emotion regulation. Furthermore, as they interact, their language development blossoms and in turn, they process cultural experiences within their environments.

In addition, the Tools of the Mind curriculum promotes scaffolding through teachers' act of pairing two students together, or one teacher and a student. Through this pairing, the individual with developing knowledge gains additional skills and tools from the other individual with advanced knowledge or experience. In relation, the amount of assistance given to the person with developing knowledge may lesson as he or she gains the information or tools needed to perform the activity on his or her own. These interactions develop children's cognitive thinking skills, which in turn also promote their critical thinking and problem solving skills.

High Scope

The High Scope curriculum is another model that will be discussed in this chapter. This curriculum adopts many concepts derived from Vygotsky's theory. Specifically, the curriculum highlights the role of play and active collaboration within children's environments to promote cognitive development. Through active experimentation, children learn from one another, while gaining key skills and concepts related to completing specific tasks within their environments. In addition, *scaffolding* is commonly performed, where teachers pair two children, or one child with one teacher. This pairing entails pairing one individual with developing knowledge with another who may have advanced knowledge. Through this pairing, children gain more knowledge and skill, which assist them with achieving particular skills needed to fulfill the learning objective for particular tasks. As the amount of assistance provided by the individual with advanced knowledge, the amount of assistance given to the other learner with developing knowledge tends to lessen.

Waldorf

The Waldorf curriculum was created by Rudolph Steiner, who believed placing a focus on the whole child; specifically the spiritual aspects of development. Teachers tend to assist children with balancing their thinking skills, feelings, and search for truth so they live moral lives (Armon, 1997). To foster critical thinking skills within the Waldorf model, art projects are commonly integrated. Due to the allowance of free expression and open-ended responses that may be provided during opportunities to engage in art activities, children's critical thinking skills are fostered.

The Waldorf curriculum also references the notion of multiple intelligences that children may have ("Waldorf-Inspired Learning," 2018). Thus, lessons may be developed that focus on fostering children's unique intelligences. The subjects that are taught within Waldorf classrooms coincide to the multiple intelligence theory (Gardner, 1993) due to its focus on language arts, math, science, social studies, foreign languages, music, art, drama, handwork, and physical education. The integration and focus on multiple intelligences may greatly promote children's development of critical thinking skills (Zobisch, Platine, & Swanson, 2015). Specifically, Zobisch et al. (2015) found that educators who integrate opportunities for children to utilize multiple intelligences were more likely to participate in critical thinking activities, as compared to children who were not exposed to lessons that emphasize multiple intelligences.

Anti-Bias Education

Another component to curriculum models involves the discussion of anti-bias education. Anti-bias education may be characterized by early childhood learning environments that are centered on embracing children's unique cultures and backgrounds, while encouraging families' involvement as well (NAEYC, 2018). When children's cultures are integrated into curriculum, a sense of multiculturalism is embraced and children may feel as they belong to warm, welcoming classroom environments. Following principles related to an anti-bias education philosophy are key for embracing diversity and encouraging early childhood learning environments to promote respect for all.

SOLUTIONS AND RECOMMENDATIONS

Solutions and recommendations include promoting critical thinking skills further, while creating welcoming early childhood environments that embrace diversity. By doing so, children may feel comfortable within their classrooms and schools, while growing. In conjunction, assisting teachers with practicing social and emotional learning strategies is suggested. The act of carrying out social and emotional learning techniques within early childhood environments, better prepares children with labeling and identifying emotions. For instance, if teachers label how they feel or how a child may feel and pair these words with facial expressions, children may develop associations between the actual emotions and the proper label for them as well.

Another way to promote an environment that focuses on social and emotional learning includes integrating an emotions chart into the classroom. If children do not know how to label their emotions, they can point to the facial expression exhibited on the chart. Sensory bottles are another tool that may assist children with developing emotion regulation. These bottles are generally filled with water, glitter, and glue and may be used when children need a tool that will assist them with knowing their emotions may be calmed over time. If children shake the bottles, the glitter may emerge throughout the bottle; through time, the glitter may settle to the bottom. This experience provides children with a sensory technique for understanding that emotions can be regulated. In addition, reading books to children that label emotions is a great tool as well. Specifically, books that rhyme are recommended, as children may learn about emotions in a fun way. These suggestions may in turn bolster children's critical thinking skills.

Integrating the most novel ways of teaching and presenting material to students in a way that resonates the best for them is also recommended. Thus, every child and person has unique ways of learning. When material is presented in ways attuned towards kinesthetic, auditory, and visual learners, the information may be better understood and applied. In addition, ensuring that all lessons delve into the importance of fostering diversity and multiculturalism within early childhood programs is essential for creating inclusive and critical thinking environments for all children and families.

FUTURE RESEARCH DIRECTIONS

It is suggested that future research delves into ways in which critical thinking skills may be promoted within early childhood environments that focuses on specific pedagogical approaches aimed towards children's unique learning styles and intelligences. When considering Gardner's (1993) multiple intelligences theory, one may posit that every child has unique strengths. As described previously in this chapter, Gardner's theory describes several types of intelligences that exist. These include: *interpersonal, intrapersonal, bodily-kinesthetic, linguistic, logical-mathematical, naturalistic, musical, and spatial.* By understanding how children learn as well as specific strategies that may be the most effective for them to promote their critical thinking skills, teachers may further encourage the integration of higher level thinking skills within their classrooms.

Furthermore, with changing dynamics to the chronosystem and technology advances associated with the eras in which we reside, it may be influential for researchers to investigate how changing dynamics of play and how technology may play a role with fostering children's critical thinking skills. This may be an influential focus of study, due to the modification and importance placed on technology during the current era, as compared to previous decades.

CONCLUSION

In sum, every opportunity that children have within their environments tends to affect their social, emotional, cognitive, or physical development in some way. Thus, providing enriching and stimulating opportunities to children that bolster their imaginations, creativity, and critical thinking skills is essential for furthering children's cognitive skills and abilities. Critical thinking skills may originate in factors related to both nature and nurture. Specifically, genetics, or nature may affect the children's potentials to engage in critical thinking skills. In comparison, nurture, or the environment as well as children's interactions within their environments may greatly impact their abilities to engage in critical thinking skills. If children are provided with various enriched opportunities that expose them to language, culture, and concepts related to their experiences or educational endeavors, they may be more likely to excel in critical thinking skills. Also, obtaining secure attachments with their caregivers during the first years of life is essential for establishing a foundation for optimal cognitive, social, and emotional development (Dozier et al., 2008).

Teachers may integrate opportunities to promote children's critical thinking skills by continually attuning themselves to children's interests and unique intelligences. When activities are presented, Piaget (1952) believed that children's cognitive development skills; specifically abstract thought and reasoning mature as children grow and obtain experiences within their environments. Higher-level thinking skills are also promoted when children are provided with opportunities to think critically about material. Asking children open-ended questions or posing activities to children that enable them to make predictions or question assumptions are also methods to promote critical thinking skills. Various early childhood curriculum models presented in this chapter shed light into the various methods in which teachers and other individuals working with children within these particular settings may use to promote children's critical thinking skills. By providing children with opportunities to explore within their environments so they may learn through inquiry and collaboration, cognitive development skills soar (Vygotsky, 1978). Through interactions with other children, their exposure to other cultures and perceptions are nourished, which enables them to appreciate diversity and multiculturalism. Incorporating anti-bias education principles is also essential for ensuring that classrooms feel welcoming to all children and families. Thus, the creation of a community within early childhood environments is key to ensuring that children feel respected and valued.

In addition, children who share their perceptions while working on projects together tend to engage in *scaffolding*. Through these *scaffolding* interactions, children with developing knowledge gain skills from other children or teachers with advanced knowledge. This pairing is key for developing sophisticated cognitive development skills. In addition, through collaborative activities, their cultural signs are developed, which enable them to connect experiences to their unique cultures and backgrounds.

REFERENCES

Alper, M. (2011). Developmentally appropriate new media literacies: Supporting cultural competencies and social skills in early childhood education. *Journal of Early Childhood Literacy*, *13*(2), 175–196. doi:10.1177/1468798411430101

Armon, J. R. (1997). *The waldorf curriculum as a framework for moral education: One dimension of a fourfold system.* Paper presented at the American Educational Research Association Conference, Chicago, IL.

Bronfenbrenner, U. (1977). Toward an experimental ecology of human development. *The American Psychologist, 32*(7), 513–531. doi:10.1037/0003-066X.32.7.513

Dozier, M., Peloso, E., Lewis, E., Laurenceau, J. P., & Levine, S. (2008). Effects of an attachment-based intervention on the cortisol production of infants and toddlers in foster care. *Developmental Psychopathy, 20*(3), 845–859. doi:10.1017/S0954579408000400 PMID:18606034

Feldman, R. (2015). The adaptive human parental brain: Implications for children's social development. *Trends in Neurosciences, 38*(6), 1–13. doi:10.1016/j.tins.2015.04.004 PMID:25956962

Gardner, H. (1993). *Frames of mind: The theory of multiple intelligences.* New York, NY: Basic Books.

Ginsburg, K. R. (2007). The importance of play in promoting healthy child development and maintaining strong parent-child bonds. *American Academy of Pediatrics, 119*(182), 182–191. doi:10.1542/peds.2006-2697 PMID:17200287

Juncheng, Y. (2014). Characteristics and inspiration about critical thinking teaching in North America. *Studies in Sociology of Science, 5*(4), 42–46. doi:10.3968/5608

Leong, D., & Bodrova, E. (2012). Assessing and scaffolding: Make believe play. *Young Children, 67*(1), 28–34.

National Association for the Education of Young Children. (2018). *Anti-bias education.* Retrieved from https://www.naeyc.org/resources/topics/anti-bias-education

Parten, M. B. (1932). Social participation among pre-school children. *Journal of Abnormal and Social Psychology, 27*(3), 243–269. doi:10.1037/h0074524

Piaget, J. (1952). *The origins of intelligence in children.* New York, NY: International Universities Press. doi:10.1037/11494-000

Rinaldi, C. (2006). *In dialogue with Reggio Emilia.* New York, NY: Routledge.

Thomas, A., & Chess, S. (1977). *Temperament and development.* New York, NY: Brunner/Mazel.

Vygotsky, L. (1978). *Mind in society: The development of higher psychological processes.* Cambridge, MA: Harvard University Press.

Waldorf-inspired learning. (2018, June 20). Retrieved from http://www.waldorfinspiredlearning.com/the-waldorf-curriculum/

Zobisch, P. J., Platine, D. G., & Swanson, A. (2015). The theory of multiple intelligences and critical thinking. *GLOKALde, 1*(6), 157–176.

ADDITIONAL READING

Aizikovitsh-Udi, E., & Cheng, D. (2015). Developing critical thinking skills from dispositions to abilities: Mathematics education from early childhood to high school. *Creative Education*, 6(4), 455–462. doi:10.4236/ce.2015.64045

Bailey, D. B., Bruer, J. T., Symons, F. J., & Litchman, J. W. (Eds.). (2001). *Critical thinking about critical periods*. Baltimore, MD: Paul H Brookes Publishing.

Bodrova, E. (2008). Make-believe play versus academic skills: A Vygotskian approach to today's dilemma of early childhood education. *European Early Childhood Education Research Journal*, 16(3), 357–369. doi:10.1080/13502930802291777

Chappell, K., Craft, A., Burnard, P., & Cremin, T. (2008). Question-posing and question-responding: The heart of "possibility thinking" in the early years. *Early Years*, 28(3), 267–286. doi:10.1080/09575140802224477

Diamond, A., Barnett, W. S., Thomas, J., & Munro, S. (2007). Preschool program improves cognitive control. *Science*, 318(5855), 1387–1388. doi:10.1126cience.1151148 PMID:18048670

Hewett, V. M. (2001). Examining the Reggio Emilia approach to early childhood education. *Early Childhood Education Journal*, 29(2), 95–100. doi:10.1023/A:1012520828095

Samuelsson, I. P., & Carlsson, M. A. (2008). The playing learning child: Towards a pedagogy of early childhood. *Scandinavian Journal of Educational Research*, 52(6), 623–641. doi:10.1080/00313830802497265

Thompson, R. A., & Nelson, C. A. (2001). Developmental science and the media: Early brain development. *The American Psychologist*, 56(1), 5–15. doi:10.1037/0003-066X.56.1.5 PMID:11242988

KEY TERMS AND DEFINITIONS

Critical Thinking: Critical thinking is defined as providing children with opportunities to exercise their higher level thinking processes by asking open-ended and engaging questions. Examples of open-ended questions include those that do not have "yes" or "no" replies. Rather, these questions typically entail several sentence responses.

Developmentally Appropriate Practices: Developmentally appropriate practices are defined as activities and lessons that are created for children within early childhood education environments that promote their social, emotional, cognitive, and social development. These activities are designed to coincide and foster children's growth within their specific developmental ages and stages of maturation.

Early Childhood Environments: Early childhood environments are defined as educational spaces designed for young children, typically between the ages of 2 to 5 years that promote children's social, emotional, cognitive, and physical development.

High Scope: High scope is defined as an early childhood education curriculum model that focuses on Vygotsky's sociocultural theory due to the incorporation of concepts related to scaffolding and children's active participation within their environments to promote their cognitive development skills.

Montessori: Montessori is defined as an early childhood education curriculum model that is child-centered; teachers are typically perceived as guides that assist children when needed. The Montessori model focuses on providing children with practical life experiences. Examples include utilizing ceramic dishes, rather than plastic dishes. In addition, mixed-age groupings of children typically occur. An example includes two-year old children interacting within a class with five-year old children.

Multiple Intelligences: Multiple intelligences is defined as a theory created by Gardner, who posited there are numerous intelligences that individuals may possess. These include: interpersonal, intrapersonal, bodily-kinesthetic, linguistic, logical-mathematical, naturalistic, spatial, and musical.

National Association for the Education of Young Children: The National Association for the Education of Young Children (NAEYC) is defined as a professional organization that aims to provide early childhood education environments with guidelines and competencies for individuals working with children and families. NAEYC also offers accreditation to early childhood programs who apply and meet the established criterion. These programs ensure that teachers engage in professional development opportunities, while creating nurturing environments for children that promote their cognitive, social, emotional, and physical development using developmentally appropriate practices. In addition, early childhood environments that are NAEYC accredited create warm and welcoming environments for all families, while encouraging their involvement. The embrace of diversity is also highlighted within these programs and environments. Furthermore, children's health and safety are a high priority for professionals working with children and their families.

Reggio Emilia: Reggio Emilia is defined as an early childhood curriculum that focuses on emergent curriculum, where children's interests are followed and pursued. For instance, if children are interested in dinosaurs, teachers may provide props that further enhance their curiosity and knowledge of this topic. In addition, teachers may read books and integrate creative arts activities that further promote children's interest of this material.

Scaffolding: Scaffolding is defined as the process where two individuals are paired together; one with advanced knowledge and another with developing knowledge. As they are paired together, the individual with advanced knowledge will teach the other with developing knowledge certain skills he or she will need to successfully complete the activity by themselves.

Tools of the Mind: The Tools of the Mind curriculum is defined as using many principles from Vygotsky's sociocultural theory. Specifically, scaffolding and the concepts of promoting active exploration within children's environments to promote children's cognitive development is fostered.

Waldorf: Waldorf is defined as an early childhood curriculum that focuses on the whole child. This model emphasizes the importance of promoting children's spirituality and emotional awareness of others within their environments. In addition, the Waldorf model highlights the significance of imitation and creative play for assisting children's overall developmental domains.

Zone of Proximal Development: The zone of proximal development is defined as changing the amount of assistance provided by the individual with advanced knowledge to the other individual with developing knowledge through scaffolding. This commonly occurs as time progresses and the amount of assistance needed by the individual with developing knowledge typically decreases.

Chapter 19
Strategies for Fostering Critical Thinking in Early Childhood Education

Katrina Woolsey Jordan
Northwestern State University, USA

Michelle Fazio-Brunson
Northwestern State University, USA

Shawn Marise Butler
St. Vincent and the Grenadines Community College, Saint Vincent and the Grenadines

ABSTRACT

Critical thinking is not a new concept in the world of education. However, teaching it to university students in teacher education programs can be difficult. Teaching these skills to students in grade school, especially in the early childhood classroom, comes with its own set of challenges. This chapter outlines strategies for teaching critical thinking skills in interesting and innovative ways, both at the university and early childhood level. Of particular interest is the project approach. During the three phases of this approach, children act as young investigators and apply critical thinking skills in their daily work. Future trends in both teacher education and the education of young children are also identified.

INTRODUCTION

This chapter will cover many different approaches to teaching and integrating critical thinking into both teacher education programs and the Early Childhood Education environment. It aims to identify key components of teaching critical thinking to teacher candidates. It will also define and give examples of critical thinking. A major focus will be to identify strategies for teaching critical thinking to teacher candidates as well as key components of teaching critical thinking to students in the early childhood classroom. The chapter will also identify and distinguish among strategies for teaching critical thinking to students in the early childhood classroom. The chapter will culminate with a reflection on ways to teach critical thinking through the Project Approach.

DOI: 10.4018/978-1-5225-7829-1.ch019

Copyright © 2019, IGI Global. Copying or distributing in print or electronic forms without written permission of IGI Global is prohibited.

DEFINING CRITICAL THINKING

Critical Thinking is by no means a recent concept. In fact, Socrates used this concept over 2,500 years ago. Other scholars such as Thomas Aquinas, Colet and Erasmus, Francis Bacon, Descartes, Locke, and Voltaire added to the discipline through the ages (Paul, Elder, & Bartell, 1997). The notion of critical thinking came to the forefront in the 20th century with the publishing of *An Experiment in the Development of Critical thinking* (1941) by Edward Glasser . In his work, Glasser indicated that critical thinking involved three things: (1) an attitude of being disposed to consider in a thoughtful way the problems and subjects that come within the range of one's experiences, (2) knowledge of the methods of logical inquiry and reasoning, and (3) some skill in applying those methods (pp. 5-6).

Contemporary authors continue to explore the relevance of critical thinking. Paul and Elder (2008) define critical thinking as, "… that mode of thinking - about any subject, content, or problem - in which the thinker improves the quality of his or her thinking by skillfully taking charge of the structures inherent in thinking and imposing intellectual standards upon them" (p. 4). Ennis (2011) subdivides critical thinking into dispositions and abilities. His work, which began in the 1950s, focuses on the dispositions and abilities or skills of critical thinking. He stated that these apply whether critical thinking is explicitly taught as a separate skill or embedded in student activities. Ennis also indicated that "...the ideal critical thinker has the ability to clarify, to seek and to judge well the basis for a view, to infer wisely from the basis, to imaginatively suppose and integrate, and to do these things with dispatch, sensitivity, and rhetorical skill" (p. 5).

A further contributor to the discussion of critical thinking is Michael Austin (2012) who discusses elements which he believes compose the critical thinking process: clarity, precision, accuracy, relevance, and consistency. He states, "Clarity of thought is important…; this means that we clearly understand what we believe, and why we believe it" (p. 1). Austin (2012) also indicated that precision can be achieved by asking ourselves specific questions: "What is the problem at issue? What are the possible answers? What are the strengths and weaknesses of each answer?" (p. 1). He also asserts that accuracy is undeniably necessary in this process. Thinkers need information that is both accurate and adequate.

Moving into the 21st century, teaching students how to apply these aspects of critical thinking is a challenge but is also a greater imperative than ever before.

Key Point: Critical thinking involves thought and reasoning, discovering alternative approaches to solve problems and the ability to analyze and reflect on one's thoughts and actions.

BEGINNING THE PROCESS: CRITICAL THINKING SKILLS AND TEACHER EDUCATION CANDIDATES

Given the importance of cultivating critical thinking skills in children, it stands to reason that such skills must first be fostered and developed in teachers. This means that teacher educator programs should promote the development of critical thinking. Currently teacher education programs, as well as grade school programs around the world, consider critical thinking a skill that their graduates need to master (Australian Curriculum, Assessment and Reporting Authority (ACARA), 2018; European Union Education Ministers, 2015; Ijaiya, Alabi, & Fasasi, 2011; International Society for Technology in Education (ISTE), 2016; Lagendijk, 2013; Ren & Tao, 2014).

According to Ren and Tao (2014), "Critical thinking is an important basis for college students' creative ability. In order to develop college students' creative ability and expand creative education, we must pay attention to the cultivation of college students' critical thinking" (p. 206). Likewise, international standards, such as the *Standards for Students* published by the International Society for Technology in Education (ISTE), call for critical thinking to be included as part of students' curriculum (ISTE, 2016). According to Lau (2011), critical thinkers must

- *Understand the logical connections between ideas.*
- *Identify, construct, and evaluate arguments.*
- *Detect inconsistencies and common mistakes in reasoning.*
- *Solve problems systematically.*
- *Identify the relevance and importance of ideas.*
- *Reflect on the justification of one's own beliefs and values. (p. 2).*

For trainee teachers to possess such skills, they must be exposed to them at the level of teacher education.

Fostering Critical Thinking Skills in Teacher Education Candidates

At the heart of critical thinking is analysis and the development of higher order thinking skills. These aspects cannot be promoted through the use of a few strategies but must be imbedded into the teacher education curriculum. This will provide novice teachers with systematic exposure to the critical thinking skills which are an important part of their teacher education. Critical thinking skills can be imparted to teacher education candidates through several methods:

1. Critical thinking must be embedded into the curriculum for Teacher Education Programs. Critical thinking skills should not be viewed as the purview of one course or one teacher educator. Instead they must be invasive throughout the entire teacher education programme.
2. The inclusion of critical thinking skills as a natural aspect of teacher education programs means that teacher educators themselves must incorporate them in their own delivery. Teacher educators need professional development in order to learn the techniques themselves. Then, they will be able to include them seamlessly in their courses. The traditional "Chalk and Talk" method of lecture-heavy instruction does not lend itself to effectively teaching critical thinking skills. Further, teacher educators need to be creative in their course delivery to engage teacher education candidates and to make opportunities for critical thinking in each class. Teacher educators themselves should have knowledge of such skills and through their own pedagogy be able to model how critical skills should be delivered. What should teacher educators do to ensure that their delivery enhances critical thinking skills in their students?
   a. Challenge students to think above the obvious, and provide opportunities for self-critique, reflection and analysis.
   b. Ensure that trainee teachers are involved participants in their own learning and consistently requiring that student response move from knowledge based expressions to analysis, application and evaluation.

c.   The use of questioning strategies which require Higher Order Thinking Skills (HOTS), in order to move students from the Remembering level (lowest level) to the Creating level (highest level).

d.   Another interesting way to teach creative thinking is through the use of Wikis. Wake and Modla (2012) describe a study in which teacher education majors used wikis to collaborate and scrutinize both their work processes and products. Results show that using wikis with the teacher education candidates promoted critical thinking as well as collaboration and the understanding of child development and pedagogical strategies.

e.   The modeling of critical thinking strategies. Strategies and activities leading to the development of critical thinking skills should not simply be recommended and taught but their use should be intentionally modeled. Questioning, how to make inferences, using graphic organizers, mind movies, question and answer relationships (QAR) and other problem solving strategies which facilitate critical thinking skills must be modeled and demonstrated.

f.   Teacher educators should also use assessment forms as a means of enhancing the critical thinking skills of their students. Novice teachers must be educated in the answering of questions through the differentiation of terms such as describe, list, explain and discuss. Papers, presentations, projects, group work, lesson plans, lesson presentations, and formal and informal observations should be created in ways which require analysis and are not solely dependent on knowledge-based responses.

Critical thinking skills are vital for future teachers and must be a part of the pedagogy of teacher educators, be embedded in the curriculum, and be reflected in classroom activities and assessment. The critical skills of teacher education students will be enhanced while they are being equipped with the skills they would be expected to model in their own classrooms.

Key Point: Teacher Educators should model the use of questioning, discussion, using higher order skills and other related strategies to foster critical thinking skills in novice teachers.

TEACHING CRITICAL THINKING TO CHILDREN IN EARLY CHILDHOOD CLASSROOMS

When teachers themselves are critical thinkers who understand the value of deep thought and analysis, then they will create classrooms where critical thinking and refection are a natural component. Processes for facilitating critical thinking skills in teacher education candidates are not much different from processes used with young children. All the techniques previously mentioned as approaches to use with teacher candidates can be modified to teach in early childhood environments. According to Bredekamp (2014), educators can use additional teaching strategies for facilitating critical thinking which are developmentally appropriate for young children, asserting that these strategies should be used in tandem rather than in an isolated fashion. These strategies include:

- Acknowledging and encouraging;
- Giving quality feedback;

- Modeling;
- Demonstrating;
- Giving cues, hints, and offering assistance;
- Creating and adding challenges;
- Questioning;
- Co-constructing;
- Giving direct or explicit instruction; and
- Scaffolding-using strategies in combination.

Each of these strategies is effective and could be discussed in depth, but those which lend themselves most to critical thinking are creating and adding challenges, questioning, and co-constructing. During instruction that includes *creating and adding challenges*, educators incorporate activities that both challenge and interest students. This motivates students to learn without pushing them beyond their zone of proximal development; it also allows children to problem solve and think critically about the challenges presented. *Questioning* involves asking questions that are open-ended rather than closed-ended. Teachers are able to encourage students to think critically while they analyze information, engage in higher order thinking. *Co-constructing* involves educators and children thinking and discussing concepts collaboratively. This strategy is a defining element of the Project Approach, which is discussed in depth later in the chapter.

Early Childhood Approaches Which Foster Critical Thinking

Early Childhood educators can choose from a plethora of developmentally appropriate approaches for helping young children develop critical thinking skills. Some of these approaches are the Reggio Emilia Approach, Montessori Approach, Bank Street Approach, Waldorf Approach, High Scope Approach, and the *Creative Curriculum* (Gestwicki, 2017). The Project Approach is an additional teaching approach which will be explored in depth later in the chapter.

The Reggio Emilia Approach

The Reggio Emilia Approach naturally lends itself to critical thinking exercises (Santin, 2017). This method emerged in post-World War II Italy when concerned parents opened a preschool in a small town, Reggio Emilia, located in northern Italy (Edwards, Gandini, & Forman, 2012). Since then, the philosophy that includes "*The Hundred Languages of Children*" (Gestwicki, 2017, p. 118) has spread across the globe. This approach encourages the view of the child as competent, acknowledges the importance of the environment and values relationships, collaboration, documentation and the importance of provoking the child to thought and action. In sum, children exposed to the Reggio Emilia Approach can be taught critical thinking skills through the following activities:

- Ensuring that learning takes place through research and group sharing, leading ultimately to creativity and curiosity.
- Creating literacy rich classrooms which stimulate children and encourage them to communicate their ideas with each other.

- Provide open ended projects which stimulate thought
- Ensure psychologically safe environments that allow children to explore, experiment and make mistakes

The Montessori Approach

Like the Reggio Emilia Approach, the Montessori Approach emerged in Italy. This approach (Montessori, 1949) was established by Maria Montessori after her observations of children in the early childhood environment led her to recognize that each child is unique, and educators should let children take the lead in their learning (1948). Key components of the Montessori Approach, according to Gestwicki (2017), include: specific training in the approach, partnerships between the schools and children's families, mixed ages and abilities, resources and experiences chosen to meet students' needs and a classroom environment which fosters problem solving and social interaction. Ways through which children's critical thinking skills are fostered through this approach include:

- Allowing students the freedom to pursue their own interest in learning
- Providing open ended questions
- Allowing students to predict an ending to a story and discuss other choices a story book character could make.
- Providing open-ended materials and activities which allow the children the opportunity to make informed choices and to learn from those choices.

The Bank Street Approach / Developmental-Interaction Approach

The Bank Street Approach began when Lucy Sprague Mitchell (1950) established a Play School along with Caroline Pratt (1948) and Harriet Johnson in New York City. This school is recognized as one of the first nursery schools in America. This method of teaching, later renamed the Developmental-Interaction Approach, focuses on building young children's competence, individuality, and socialization (Shapiro & Biber, 1972), and play is a primary vehicle for learning. Those who embrace this approach confirm Mitchell's stated (1934/2001) need for teaching the whole child and treating a classroom like a learning laboratory. Teaching the whole child allows educators in Bank Street schools to foster critical thinking in ways that traditional programs often lack. Teachers who wish to develop critical thinking skills in children in a Bank Street Approach classroom should encourage children to:

- Develop thoughtful engagements with peers and teachers
- Think independently
- Reflect on their own learning
- Be engaged in projects which stimulate thought such as block building, cooking, and field trips

The Waldorf Approach

The Waldorf Approach is rooted in the Rudolf Steiner's work including a book called *The Education of the Child* (1907). The first Waldorf School was opened at the behest of the owner of the Waldorf-Astoria

Cigarette Company. The first schools opened in Stuttgart, Germany, but have spread across the globe, reaching into 60 countries. This method focuses on learning across disciplines and emphasizes the combination of practical, aesthetic, and cognitive elements. Children are encouraged to learn through play, use their imagination, and explore the world through natural rhythms of life (Edwards, 2002). The goal of the Waldorf Approach is "to educate the whole human being, so that thinking, feeling, and doing are integrated" (Gestwicki, 2017, p. 113). Critical thinking is easily incorporated into a curriculum which values imagination, play, and thinking. Teachers who encourage children's critical thinking embrace:

- Questioning
- Providing real life authentic problems and situations
- Delivering lessons which are related to students' immediate experiences
- Encouraging freedom of imagination
- Fostering active and energetic classrooms

HighScope Approach

The HighScope Approach was developed by David Weikart and colleagues. Children in HighScope programs are viewed as active learners who construct their own knowledge as they learn by doing (HighScope Educational Research Foundation, n.d.). As such, much of their day is spent participating in purposefully designed learning centers. Integrating critical thinking into a HighScope environment is seamless. Active learners who construct their own knowledge through learning centers naturally engage in critical thinking activities as they go about their daily routines. Children's critical thinking skills can be fostered through the HighScope approach through the use of:

- Interest areas e.g. a block area, a reading area, an art area, etc.
- Manipulation of materials which encourage freedom of thought, creativity and imagination
- Options— children should be allowed to select what they will explore, how and with whom
- Freedom of thought and expression
- Adult scaffolding when tasks become too challenging for the children.

Creative Curriculum

The Creative Curriculum was created by Diane Trister Dodge, who worked in Head Start and focused on children from poverty (Teaching Strategies, n.d.). The first edition of *The Creative Curriculum* was published in 1978, and the seventh edition was released in 2016 (Dodge, et al, 2016). Currently, the developmentally appropriate curriculum, which is rooted in child development research, is available for children in infant, toddler, preschool, and family child care programs. The five guiding principles of The Creative Curriculum for Preschool are: positive interactions and relations with adults, social-emotional competence, constructive purposive play, physical environment which affects the type and quality of learning interactions and teacher and parent relationships (Teaching Strategies, 2010, p. 2).

Following these principles, educators who use this curriculum organize learning communities to help young children play, explore, and solve problems, which is exactly what students need in order to develop critical thinking skills. Critical thinking skills in children can be further enhanced through the use of:

- Hands on activities which foster creativity and imagination (building blocks, planting a garden etc.)
- Project based investigations which stimulate thought and questioning skills
- Read alouds
- Large and small group activities which encourage collaboration and freedom of thought.

The Project Approach

The Project Approach (Helm & Katz, 2016) is a teaching approach comprising three phases in which children participate in an in-depth investigation, or project. Here, a ***project*** is defined as an in-depth study of a topic (Chard, 1998A; Helm & Katz, 2016). Using this approach, children follow their research interests by identifying questions they want to answer and then conduct research to answer those questions (Helm, 2015).

The children may engage in creative thinking as they "paint, draw, write about, dramatize, or role-play the experiences and understandings they bring to the study" (Chard, 1998B, p. 34). Children examine the data they have gathered along with documentation such as photos, videos, and student-made artifacts and brainstorm how they want to share knowledge gained from project work in a culminating event.

USING THE PROJECT APPROACH TO TEACH CRITICAL THINKING

Project work is characterized by five structural features: *discussions*, *fieldwork, representation, investigation*, and *display* (Chard, 1998B). As children engage in these structural features, teachers take advantage of multiple opportunities to teach children critical thinking skills in meaningful, relevant ways and document children's thoughts and work processes in context. Examples of how children use critical thinking in each feature are presented below.

- **Discussions:** Children engage in initial *discussions* as they communicate prior knowledge and share and compare personal experiences in Phase I (Helm, 2015). Webbing what they know, brainstorming research questions they want to answer, and posing possible resources they can use to answer those questions lead to rich conversations which require critical thinking (Helm & Katz, 2016). Children also strengthen critical thinking skills through dialogue in Phase II as they prepare for field site visits and expert visitors, pondering what they might see and learn, and generating new questions to ask the experts (Helm & Beneke, 2003). Each time they learn something new, they use critical thinking to assimilate and accommodate new information, building or altering their existing background knowledge, or *schema*.
- **Fieldwork:** Second, children participate in *fieldwork* by visiting off-site places to conduct observations, gather data, and interview experts, using critical thinking skills they have learned in the classroom (Chard, Kogan, & Castillo, 2017). Fieldwork is an opportune time for children to practice critical thinking skills in context. They use critical thinking by building theoretical constructs based on what they see, hear, touch, smell, and taste during fieldwork as they build background knowledge and record their findings (Helm & Beneke, 2003).
- **Representation:** Third, children demonstrate creative and critical thinking skills by *representing* new knowledge and current understandings. Projects may be teacher initiated, but they are always

child-driven (Helm & Beneke, 2003). Given many choices, children take ownership of their work as they decide how to document their knowledge. They may write books or other informational texts, chart data, or form diagrams to depict how things relate to one another. They may draw, paint pictures or murals, or use clay to sculpt models depicting what they have seen and learned (Chard, Kogan, & Castillo, 2017). They may make field sketches, design maps, or make manuals. They may use *Loose Parts* (Daly & Beloglovsky, 2015) or *Beautiful Stuff* (Topal & Gandini, 1999) to construct three-dimensional representations, or they may role-play, acting out something they observed in the field or learned from an expert visitor. This kind of choice provides a most important benefit: It encourages students to take ownership of what they do in school.

- **Investigation:** Further, children use creative and critical thinking during *investigation* in Phase II via fieldwork and library research experiences as they answer initial questions and pose new ones (Helm & Beneke, 2003). They use critical thinking skills by making observations and recording findings and by exploring primary and secondary sources, as they analyze and synthesize a variety of information. Further activities which require high order thinking are predicting, experimenting, and confirming (Helm & Katz, 2016). They may conduct surveys, collect data, organize it, and then represent it in a bar graph (Chard, 1998A, p. 40). They may investigate maps, timelines, and charts, and then recreate their own versions. Through investigation, children are intrinsically motivated to make discoveries and be accountable for their learning.

- **Display:** Finally, children use creative and critical thinking to create *displays* which tell their project stories through bulletin boards, documentation panels, murals, wall displays, or gallery walks in Phase III (Chard 1998B, pp. 7-10). On the day of the culminating activity, children share the most important things they learned from the project through individual and shared activities (Chard, Kogan, & Castillo, 2017). They may write a song, paint a mural, or create a clay gallery of models. They may share class books or perform a play to share their knowledge with the audience (Jacobs & Crowley, 2007).

- **Key Point:** Activities such as questioning, open ended projects, and experiments can be used to stimulate critical thinking skills in children regardless of the instructional approach used.

FUTURE RESEARCH DIRECTIONS

Teaching critical thinking, both at grade school and university levels, may seem difficult in this age of accountability. However, some current educational trends lend themselves to critical thinking. According to Jodi Pozo-Olano (2018), STEM (Science, Technology, Engineering, and Math) learning is gaining momentum and will continue to be a focus in education in the years to come. A component of STEM, coding, will also expand to reach learners as early as preschool and kindergarten. Technology, an already important component in education, will continue to dominate the educational landscape, with blended and online learning becoming more prominent in the PK-12 setting. Project-based learning has also enjoyed a boost into the limelight, since recent studies show its effectiveness with students all the way through middle school (Terada, 2018). Additionally, Bates (2018) notes that residency-based teacher preparation programs will be a trend to follow in teacher education practices. Likewise, mentorship for new teachers, which also provides many opportunities for critical thinking, will likely become a trend that sees a resurgence. These trends, along with a call to update research in early childhood education (Lesaux & Jones, 2018), will make for interesting changes in the field of early childhood education in the near future. While all of the approaches described in this chapter facilitate critical thinking, the Project Approach is increasingly relevant because it naturally lends itself to STEM exploration. Throughout each phase, children use higher order thinking skills to investigate their chosen topics of interest. In the words of Albert Einstein, "It is the supreme art of the teacher to awaken joy in creative expression and knowledge" (Edminston, 2008, p. 57). Educators who engage young children in project work marvel at the joy children experience as they co-construct knowledge and use a variety of media to creatively express what they know and can do.

CONCLUSION

Since the birth of the Socratic Method, critical thinking has continued to be a vital part of teaching students to use their minds to make sense of the world around them. Historical and modern philosophers, researchers, and educators agree that critical thinking plays a vital role in our schools and universities. In order to produce educators who can think for themselves, teacher education programs must embed critical thinking into the curriculum. Teacher educators need professional development in order to learn the techniques themselves. Then, they will be able to include them seamlessly in their courses. Processes for facilitating teacher education candidates' critical thinking are not much different from processes used with young children.

In fact, many approaches for teaching young children have guiding elements which foster critical thinking. The Project Approach, Reggio Emilia Approach, Montessori Approach, Bank Street Approach, Waldorf Approach, High Scope Approach, and the *Creative Curriculum* can all be used to teach young children how to think and problem solve. The Project Approach is particularly effective in fostering such an environment in the era of STEM teaching today. Teaching critical thinking, both in the early years and at the university level, can be difficult in this age of accountability. However, current and future educational trends are cause for hope that critical thinking is alive and well and will be fostered by the educational community well into the future.

REFERENCES

Assessment and Reporting Authority (ACARA). (2018). *Australian curriculum: Critical and creative thinking*. Retrieved from https://www.australiancurriculum.edu.au

Bates, A. J. (2018). *10 Important trends in education to expect in 2018*. Retrieved from https://education.cu-portland.edu/

Bredekamp, S. (2014). *Effective practices in early childhood education: Building a foundation* (2nd ed.). Upper Saddle River, NJ: Pearson.

Cadwell, L. B. (1997). *Bringing Reggio Emilia home*. New York, NY: Teachers College Press.

Cadwell, L. B. (2003). *The Reggio approach to early childhood education: Bringing learning to life*. New York, NY: Teachers College Press.

Ceppi, G., & Zini, M. (Eds.). (1998). *Children, spaces, relations*. Modena, Italy: Domas Academy Research Center.

Chard, S. (1998). *The Project Approach: Book one—Making curriculum come alive*. New York, NY: Scholastic.

Chard, S., Kogan, Y., & Castillo, C. (2017). *Picturing the Project Approach: Creative explorations in early learning*. Lewisville, NC: Gryphon House.

Cox, J. (2018). *Teaching strategies that enhance higher-order thinking*. Retrieved from http://www.teachhub.com/teaching-strategies-enhance-higher-order-thinking

Curtis, D., & Carter, M. (2011). *Reflecting children's lives: A handbook for planning child-centered curriculum*. Saint Paul, MN: Redleaf Press.

Curtis, D., & Carter, M. (2013). *The art of awareness: How observation can transform your teaching* (2nd ed.). St. Paul, MN: Redleaf Press.

Daly, L., & Beloglovsky, M. (2015). *Loose parts: Inspiring play in young children*. St. Paul, MN: Redleaf Press.

Dodge, D. T., Heroman, C., Berke, K., Colker, L. J., Bickart, T., Baker, H., ... Tabors, P. O. (2016). *The Creative Curriculum for preschool* (6th ed.). Washington, DC: Teaching Strategies, Inc.

Dunn, R., & Dunn, K. (1999). *The complete guide to the Learning Styles inservice system*. Boston, MA: Allyn & Bacon.

Edwards, C. P. (2002). Three approaches from Europe: Waldorf, Montessori, and Reggio Emilia. *Early Childhood Research & Practice*, *4*(1), 1–24. Retrieved from http://ecrp.uiuc.edu/v4n1/edwards.html

Edwards, C. P., Gandini, L., & Forman, G. (2012). *The hundred languages of children: The Reggio Emilia Experience in Transformation* (3rd ed.). Santa Barbara, CA: Praeger.

European Union Education Ministers. (2015). *Declaration on promoting citizenship and the common values of freedom, tolerance, and non-discrimination through education*. Retrieved from http://ec.europa.eu/dgs/education_culture/repository/education/news/2015/documents/citizenship-education-declaration_en.pdf

Fraser, S., & Gestwicki, C. (2002). *Authentic childhood: Exploring Reggio Emilia in the classroom*. Boston, MA: Delmar.

Gardner, H. (2011). *Frames of mind: The theory of multiple intelligences*. New York, NY: Basic Books.

Gestwicki, C. (2017). *Developmentally appropriate practice: Curriculum and development in early education* (6th ed.). Boston, MA: Cengage Learning.

Glasser, E. M. (1941). *An experiment in the development of critical thinking*. New York, NY: Teachers College, Columbia University.

Helm, J. (2015). *Becoming young thinkers: Deep project work in the classroom*. New York, NY: Teachers College Press.

Helm, J. H., & Beneke, S. (Eds.). (2003). *The power of projects: Meeting contemporary challenges in early childhood classrooms—Strategies and solutions.* New York, NY: Teachers College Press.

Helm, J. H., Beneke, S., & Steinheimer, K. (2007). *Windows on learning: Documenting young children's work* (2nd ed.). New York, NY: Teachers College Press.

Helm, J. H., & Katz, L. (2016). *Young Investigators: The project approach in the early years* (3rd ed.). New York, NY: Teachers College Press.

HighScope. (2018). *Curriculum.* Retrieved from https://highscope.org/curriculum

Ijaiya, N. Y. S., Alabi, A. T., & Fasasi, Y. A. (2011). Teacher education in Africa and critical thinking skills: Needs and strategies. *Research Journal of Business Management, 5*(1), 26–34. doi:10.3923/rjbm.2011.26.34

International Society for Technology in Education (ISTE). (2016). *ISTE Standards for Students (ebook): A practical guide for learning with technology.* ISTE. Available for download at https://www.iste.org/resources/product?ID=4073&ChildProduct=4074

Jacobs, G., & Crowley, K. (2007). *Play, projects, and preschool standards: Nurturing children's sense of wonder and joy in learning.* Thousand Oaks, CA: Corwin Press.

Lagendijk, J. (2013). *The need for critical thinking as new opportunities in higher education arise.* Retrieved from https://www.eaie.org/blog/critical-thinking-for-higher-ed.html

Lau, J. Y. F. (2011). *An introduction to critical thinking and creativity: Think more, think better.* Indianapolis, IN: Wiley. doi:10.1002/9781118033449

Lesaux, N. K., & Jones, S. M. (2018). Early childhood research needs an update. *Education Week, 20*(37), 28.

Mitchell, L. S. (1950). *Our children and our schools.* New York, NY: Simon & Schuster.

Mitchell, L. S. (2001). *Young geographers.* New York, NY: Bank Street College of Education. (Original work published 1934)

Montessori, M. (1948). *The discovery of the child.* Adyar, India: Kalakshetra Press.

Montessori, M. (1949). *The absorbent mind.* Adyar, India: Kalakshetra Press. Retrieved from https://archive.org/details/absorbentmind031961mbp

Paul, R., & Elder, L. (2008). *The miniature guide to critical thinking concepts and tools.* Dillon Beach, CA: Foundation for Critical Thinking.

Paul, R., Elder, L., & Bartell, T. (1997). *California teacher preparation for instruction in critical thinking: Research findings and policy recommendations.* Sacramento, CA: California Commission on Teacher Credentialing.

Pozo-Olano, J. (2018). *A year of disruption? Education trends for 2018.* Retrieved from www.observer.com

Pratt, C. (1948). *I learn from children.* New York, NY: Simon and Schuster.

Ren, Y., & Tao, L. (2014). The critical thinking and Chinese Creative Education. *Canadian Social Science, 10*(6), 206–211.

Santin, F. (2017). Reggio Emilia: An essential tool to develop critical thinking in early childhood. *Journal of New Approaches in Educational Research, 6*(1), 50–56. doi:10.7821/naer.2017.1.207

Shapiro, E. K., & Biber, B. (1972). The education of young children: A developmental-interaction point of view. *Teachers College Record, 74,* 55–79.

Steiner, R. (1907). *The education of the child.* Berlin, Germany: Steiner Books.

Teaching Strategies. (2010). *Research foundation: The Creative Curriculum.* Bethesda, MD: Author.

Teaching Strategies. (n.d.). *Company history.* Retrieved from https://teachingstrategies.com/company/history/

Terada, Y. (2018). *Boosting student engagement through project-based learning.* Retrieved from www.edutopia.org

Topal, C. W., & Gandini, L. (1999). *Beautiful stuff! Learning with found materials.* Worchester, MA: Davis Publishing.

Vecchi, V. (2010). *Art and creativity in Reggio Emilia: Exploring the role and potential of ateliers in early childhood education.* New York, NY: Routledge. doi:10.4324/9780203854679

Weikart, D. P., Deloria, D., Lawser, S., & Wiegerink, R. (1970). *Longitudinal results of the Ypsilanti Perry Preschool Project (Monographs of the High/Scope Educational Research Foundation, 1).* Ypsilanti, MI: High/Scope Press.

Wurm, J. P. (2005). *Working in the Reggio way.* St. Paul, MN: Redleaf Press.

ADDITIONAL READING

Aghayan, C., Schellhaas, A., Wayne, A., Burts, D. C., Buchanan, T. K., & Benedict, J. (2005). Project Katrina. *Early Childhood Research & Practice, 2*(7). Retrieved from http://ecrp.uiuc.edu/v7n2/aghayan.html

Bredekamp, S. (1993). Reflections of Reggio Emilia. *Young Children, 49*(1), 13–17.

Cahill, B., & Theilheimer, R. (2015). *The Developmental-Interaction Approach: Defining and describing New Mexico's curriculum for Early Childhood care & education programs.* Grants, NM: New Mexico Children, Youth and Families Department. Retrieved from https://www.nmaeyc.org/sites/default/files/files/The%20Developmental%20Interaction%20Approach.pdf

Edmiston, A. (2008). A year of personal guidance. *Monitor on Psychology, 39*(10), 57.

Finegan, C. (2001). Alternative early childhood education: Reggio Emilia. *Kappa Delta Pi Record, 37*(2), 82–84. doi:10.1080/00228958.2001.10518468

Gandini, L. (1993). Fundamentals of the Reggio Emilia approach to early childhood education. *Young Children, 49*(1), 4–8.

HighScope Educational Research Foundation. (n.d.). *Overview: The HighScope Preschool Curriculum.* Ypsilanti, MI: Author.

Jennings, D., Hanline, M. F., & Woods, J. (2012). Using routines-based interventions in early childhood special education. *Dimensions of Early Childhood, (40)*2, 14-21. Retrieved from http://www.southernearly-childhood.org/upload/pdf/Using_Routines_Based_Interventions_in_Early_Childhood_Special_Education_Danielle_Jennings_Mary_Frances_Hanline_Juliann_Woods. pdf

Lillard, P. P. (1988). *Montessori: A modern approach: The classic introduction to Montessori for parents and teachers.* New York, NY: Schocken Books.

Morrison, G. (2018). *Early Childhood Education Today* (14th ed.). San Francisco, CA: Pearson.

Nager, N., & Shapiro, E. K. (2007). *A Progressive approach to the education of teachers: Some principles from Bank Street College of Education.* New York, NY: Bank Street College of Education; Retrieved from https://files.eric.ed.gov/fulltext/ED495462.pdf

National Association for the Education of Young Children. (2009). *Developmentally Appropriate Practice in Early Childhood programs serving children from birth through age 8: A position statement of the National Association for the Education of Young Children.* Washington, DC: Author. Retrieved from http://www.naeyc.org/files/naeyc/file/positions/PSDAP.pdf

New, R. S. (2007). Reggio Emilia as cultural activity theory into practice. *Theory into Practice, 46*(1), 5–13. Retrieved from https://reggioalliance.org/downloads/new:theoryintopractice.pdf. doi:10.1080/00405840709336543

Park, S., & Lit, I. (2015). *Learning to play, playing to learn: The Bank Street developmental-interaction approach in Liliana's kindergarten classroom.* Stanford, CA: Stanford Center for Opportunity Policy in Education.

Petrash, J. (2002). *Understanding Waldorf education: Teaching from the inside out.* Lewisville, NC: Gryphon House.

The Project Approach. (2014). *Classroom as a learning environment.* Retrieved from http://projectapproach.org/special-topics/classroom-learning-environment/

KEY TERMS AND DEFINITIONS

Bank Street Approach: Evolved from the original Play School, this teaching approach is based in the works of John Dewey. Bank Street educators see children as active learners who are think, create, explore, and learn in a social setting.

Creative Curriculum: Founded by Diane Trister-Dodge, this curriculum encourages educators to use a wide range of strategies in order to support student learning in all domains. Observation is key in this cross-curricular method which is easily aligned with early learning standards.

Early Childhood: A period of development lasting from birth through around eight or nine years old. Many teacher education programs consider an early childhood degree to cover pre-kindergarten through third grade.

Higher Order Thinking Skills (HOTS): A questioning technique in which instructors encourage their students to move from lower order knowledge-based learning to higher order learning that emphasizes critical thinking skills.

HighScope Approach: An approach to teaching and learning which incorporates learning centers. Benchmarks, anecdotal notes, and student-made plans are all a part of the educational process in a HighScope program.

Montessori Approach: A teaching method often employed in early childhood programs. It is based on sensory experiences and includes specialized training for teachers.

Project Approach: An inquiry-based teaching technique which encourages critical thinking by encouraging students to complete an in-depth study on a topic of interest.

Reggio Emilia Approach: An approach to teaching young children with roots in post-World War II Italy. It is student-centered, and open-ended projects form the core of the method.

Teacher Education Programs: Programs which lead to a license to teach. These often align with a degree program and are usually administered through a university.

Waldorf Approach: In this approach to teaching young children, educators use an interdisciplinary approach which focuses on imagination as a central focus of learning.

APPENDIX

Helpful Websites

- http://www.criticalthinking.org/
- https://highscope.org/
- http://projectapproach.org/
- http://www.reggiochildren.it/identita/reggio-emilia-approach/?lang=en
- https://www.montessori.com/montessori-education/
- https://www.bankstreet.edu/school-children/
- http://www.creativecurriculum.net/
- https://waldorfeducation.org/waldorf_education

Figures

Figure 1. Teacher Webbing with Children to Determine their Schema for Farms

Figure 2. Initial web about farms (recopied)

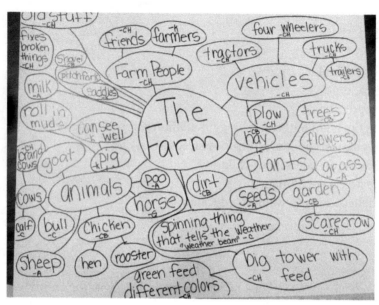

Figure 3. Brainstorm list of research questions about farms

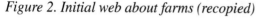

Figure 4. Child petting a baby chick an expert visitor brought to the classroom

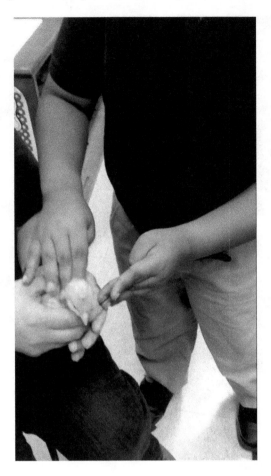

Figure 5. Pig corral constructed with blocks

Figure 6. Silo constructed with blocks

Figure 7. Documentation panel for the farm project

Chapter 20
Information Literacy and Critical Thinking in Higher Education:
Some Considerations

Ann Marie Joanne White
The University of the West Indies – Cave Hill Campus, Barbados

ABSTRACT

This chapter acknowledges the widespread recognition of the importance of instruction in the area of information literacy and shows how information literacy and critical thinking, another vital skill demanded in more and more fields of endeavor, can be integrated as institutions seek to prepare their students to be able to function effectively in today's knowledge-based environment. Some attention is given to Information Literacy frameworks which aim to guide the development of information literacy and enhance delivery and assessment in this field. It recognizes the importance of information specialists and faculty in higher education institutions to be able to work together to establish and develop Information Literacy programs that will equip students with the relevant skills to be considered information literate. It also touches briefly on pedagogical approaches that may be taken in the delivery of Information Literacy instruction and emphasizes the importance of assessment as a means of enhancing the ultimate value of the process to students who participate.

INTRODUCTION

Higher education institutions are expected to produce graduates who can take their place in the world in a variety of productive areas. The challenge, therefore, is to offer programs that will equip the future graduates with the skills and capacity to fulfill the roles that the society requires. Over the centuries and to a very great extent in the last century and in the present, these roles have changed and continue to change rapidly. Preparation of students of the 21st century, the digital age, the age of technology, must of necessity include a focus on elements some of which were not even heard of in the industrial age and subsequently. It is not that progress from the industrial era to the digital age is not a good thing. It is. But somehow it has cheated students in thinking critically or becoming information literate. To understand the present, one should observe the past.

DOI: 10.4018/978-1-5225-7829-1.ch020

Copyright © 2019, IGI Global. Copying or distributing in print or electronic forms without written permission of IGI Global is prohibited.

The industrial era, the 1700s, was a time of great inventions and discoveries in the world, starting the explosion of information. Now has come the digital age, beginning in the 1970s, when there has been an expansion of developments and inventions, when technology creates things to be faster, instantaneous, and obsolete quickly. It has changed the way people learn and want to learn; how they think and do things and how they perceive things. It cannot be that in both eras critical thinking and information literacy were never heard of or known to man. In fact, according to Fisher (2011), critical thinking has been with us for over 2000 years with Socrates beginning this approach to learning. John Dewey is widely considered as the pioneer of the concept of critical thinking in modern times. Information literacy, on the other hand, is a term coined in 1974. According to Andretta (2005), they both reappeared about the time that the educational icon of the 21st century, "life-long learning," also entered the language of formal and informal education.

This chapter draws attention to the relationship between critical thinking and information literacy, and why and how they are important in the context of higher education. The integration of information literacy instruction into the formal curriculum has become an accepted practice. The chapter also gives attention to international standards established in order to guide and enhance the development of information literacy as an integral part of college programs.

BACKGROUND

What Is Information Literacy?

A review of the literature gives a good understanding of the terms "information literacy" and "critical thinking". There is a widely accepted and often repeated definition of critical which runs like this: it is the intellectually disciplined process of actively and skillfully conceptualizing, applying, analyzing, synthesizing and or/evaluating information. Reece (2007) points out that information literacy and critical thinking belong to the cognitive domain and agrees with the same skill sets as outlined above. However, it must be remembered that information literacy is not just critical thinking. For a differentiation of critical thinking and information literacy, Starr and Gaskill (1997) follow Brookfield who explains critical thinking as implying a diligent, open-minded search for understanding, rather than for discovery of a necessary conclusion. Information literacy on the other hand, as Thompson (2000) points out, was spoken of by Henry Brooks Adams some 90 years ago when he expressed the concept by saying "they know enough who know how to learn." That is to say that a person cannot retain all information given but certainly can know how to find, evaluate and use it wisely and effectively. Thompson (2000) goes on to explain that information literacy translates into the ability to derive meaning from information or the ability to access, evaluate and use information from a variety of sources. What information literacy is doing is teaching people how to learn.

The concept of information literacy was re-introduced by Paul Zurkowski, in 1974. Zurkowski makes the point of training in using information resources as a definition of information literacy. Such training would give the person the capacity to use information tools and primary sources to develop solutions to information related problems (Eisenberg, Lowe and Spitzer, 2004). Burchinal suggested that to be information literate one requires a new set of skills (Eisenberg, Lowe and Spitzer, 2004). For Candy (2002), it means that a person can recognize when information is needed and can locate, evaluate and use the required information effectively. According to Blevens (2012), it is the evaluation of the quality and reliability of information paired with the ability to use that information legally and ethically. Information literacy, to take it further, is an important concept because it encompasses conceptual, factual, technical and critical thinking skills. Bearing these definitions in mind, what is important is that the necessary quality instruction should be given to students to meet the objectives of information literacy.

CRITICAL THINKING

To argue is a natural human inclination but the strength of any argument depends on how much critical thought goes into it. According to De Bono (1985), thinking is the ultimate human resource. It is not an easy task because, according to De Bono, the main difficulty associated with thinking is confusion. There is confusion because there are different factors that must come into play when trying to understand a situation so that one can make the correct judgment. Making the right decision challenges people whatever position they may find themselves in. In relation to this, Case and Daniels (n.d.) argue that the term critical thinking draws attention to the quality of thinking required to pose and solve problems competently, reach sound decisions, analyze issues, plan and conduct intellectual inquiries. There is limited value in achieving solutions that are not sensible or reasonable. Simply put by Kreitzberg and Kreitzberg (2010), critical thinking is more than learning techniques; it is a mindset that should be adopted and applied on a consistent basis. It is also a skill that is learned over a period of time and needs to be practiced consistently. Doddington (2008) explains that critical thinking is broadly seen as the kind of logical thinking that helps to analyze and make sense of, or interpret, all forms of situations or information so that the conclusions drawn or interpretations made are sound.

Fisher (2011) emphasizes that the key to better critical thinking is asking the right questions. To be able to ask the right questions at the right time, one needs to master certain skills. These include:

- Identifying reasons and conclusions in everyday language
- Understanding reasoning in the different patterns of reasoning, assumptions, context and thinking map
- Clarifying and interpreting expressions and ideas
- Judging the validity of reasons that are presented

He further posits that mastery of these skills can be developed in many real situations which involve reasoning, argument or dispute.

APPLICATION OF INFORMATION LITERACY

An educational institution that wants to be recognized globally aims to project itself as graduating students who can create innovations that advance development. One aspect of the preparation of such graduates is to teach students to manipulate information and to think critically about information presented. The development of the concept of information literacy indicates a clear movement from strictly tool-based skills to the cognitively complex realm of critical thinking. At the same time, the Information Literacy

Standards 2000 affirm that information literacy competencies provide students with a framework for gaining control over how they interact with information in their environments.

The explosion of information in the digital era provides the libraries of educational institutions the opportunity to assist patrons in sifting through that vast amount of information in electronic and print formats. Librarians have answered the call of anxious students to conduct Information Literacy classes because information literacy is considered to be a core competency of the 21st century (McDonald and McDonald, 2011). Librarians (information specialists) have for some time been conducting information literacy instruction which can be structured to help students think critically so that they produce credible assignments for their lecturers. Librarians show students how to find facts, then, as Hunter (2009) expresses, students must critically think what to believe and what to do with the information gathered.

Andretta (2005) claims further that information literacy also draws on the skills of critical thinking and problem-solving. Kim and Shumaker (2015) concur with ACRL (2000) and Grassian & Kaplowitz (2010) that information literacy and critical thinking are widely seen to be essential for students' success in undergraduate programs and beyond. Information literacy promotes critical thinking and at the same time, the critical thinker is likely to be a more effective in applying the principles of information literacy. "Information literate" and "critical thinkers" are terms being used by universities to categorize the type of students graduating from their institutions. The 2012-2017 strategic plan of The University of the West Indies (UWI) (2012) speaks of a graduate who thinks critically and creatively and is information literate. In our knowledge-based economy, this has become an essential aspect of the focus of universities because of the impact of the rapid expansion of technology and information. Educational institutions must therefore evaluate their information literacy programs regularly if they are to remain true to the mandate to produce information literate graduates. Such an evaluation should include data on the holistic impact of their information literacy programs conducted at the institution. Such a study should, among other things, identify the strengths and weaknesses of the pedagogy used by those who conduct the information literacy sessions.

For centuries libraries have been the significant keepers of information, and they continue to be such repositories, or, perhaps more accurately, they offer additional opportunities of access for students in this information age. Of course, in this era, people have changed the way information is sought, utilizing the ever-advancing technology to obtain the information they desire. Also, the roles of librarians and the library have evolved to respond to different research behaviors. Resources available before the Internet age were in the form of physical print, whether books and journals. However today, resources are available in both physical and electronic formats. The computer has given students the ability to search the Internet and find information, but Roth (1999) laments the fact that often that facility is misused as they "cut and paste" without seeming to appreciate the unethical nature and therefore the seriousness of what they are doing. This does not mean that extracting large amounts of an author's work to insert in an assignment did not happen before the invention of the Internet and the advancement of technology. However, the development of technology has made plagiarism easier to perpetrate and easier to detect. Students in the digital age are comfortable with technology, and the Internet is their primary tool in searching for information. Unfortunately, they often assume that every electronic source is valid without carefully looking at the content, authorship or the credibility of the source; and, importantly, they often do not use the information they gather in appropriate ways.

LIBRARIAN AND FACULTY COLLABORATION

Universities in Europe and the United States since the 1980s have emphasized maintaining and improving the quality of education in order to remain competitive. What may be slowing the process are the rapid changes taking place in the information sphere. Therefore, in this age of competitiveness in the educational industry, it is essential that educators work together to produce the desired information literate graduate. It has been suggested that within higher education institutions individual disciplines have become more inward looking, making it more difficult for disciplines to integrate or blend (Csikszentmihalyi, 2006).

There is a growing number of researchers on the subject of student learning in higher education who indicate that students' knowledge in the area of information literacy can be improved when faculty and librarians work together (Junisbai, Lowe and Tagge, 2016). However, according to Ward (2006), this collaboration requires librarians and faculty to be willing to take risks in reaching out to each other and practice listening without judging. If that works, then the higher educational institution is on its way to producing a critical information literate graduate. However, that is not always the case. Biddiscombe (2000) claims that librarians have had only limited success in convincing their faculty colleagues that their role in the learning process is essential. He states further that there are still librarians who conduct one-shot sessions, trying to cram as much information into the lesson as possible. This does not do justice to the information literacy objective.

It is generally acknowledged that the explosion of information does not make the task of teaching easy, but the frustration often associated with sifting through data can be eased with instruction which is carefully orchestrated by faculty and librarians in collaboration. To achieve the goal of enhancing information skills in higher education, it is essential that academic librarians and administrators be knowledgeable in the theory and practice of information literacy. Iton (2008) has argued that more emphasis should be placed on identifying potential collaborative librarian/faculty relationships to assist in demonstrating by example the benefits of teaching information literacy skills in academic teaching and student research. Some universities have conceded (Getty and Chibnall 2013) that librarians have evolved with technology and have been retooled to collaborate with faculty to help students become information literate. This fact was noted by Franklin (2005) who emphasized that students agreed that involving librarians more directly in the dissertation process was an effective way to help them develop information literacy skills. Collaboration is also a benefit to librarians as Blakeslee (1998), and Harley (2001) acknowledge that their teaching experience enhanced their relationship with teaching faculty.

However, in some instances, this may not be the case, as Armstrong (2010) points out that while "liaison librarians" are frequently invited to give instructions, they have not entirely convinced faculty in the respective disciplines to embed information literacy in their lesson plans. Faculty suggests that librarians should become subject specialist so that they can be more familiar with course objectives and pedagogy in the respective disciplines. The value of this idea is reinforced by Albitz's (2007) claim that teaching faculty is willing to give only a one-shot session in which the librarian is forced to present information too quickly to have any lasting effect. There are still many academics who take a narrow view of information literacy, and there are frustrations and tensions between information professionals and scholars relating to the importance of, need for, and ultimately the construction of information literacy in higher education (Gunasekara, 2008). What can be seen is that the partnership between academic staff and library staff does not seem to be an equal one (Biddiscombe, 2000). Whatever the situation, one thing is sure; without library administration support and strong faculty relationships, it is difficult to develop information literacy instruction, much less sustain and demonstrate its usefulness (Gauder and Jenkins, 2012).

INTERNATIONAL STANDARDS FRAMEWORK FOR INFORMATION LITERACY

It is essential that the information literacy instruction delivered meet international standards for an institution that wants to be globally recognized. There have been challenges in this respect and, as Reece (2007) argues, information literacy has lacked a valid and reliable standard test that can be used to measure outcomes. In some cases, standards are formulated on a national basis in which guidelines for instruction and assessment are set out for use by instructors to integrate information literacy skills into their planned curriculum. The literature indentifies several information literacy standards used by various educational institutions.

For instance, the American Association of School Librarians (AASL) published "Standards for the 21st Century Learner" (2007); and the Association for Educational Communications and Technology (AECT) and AASL published "Information Power: Building Partnerships for Learning" in 1998. These two documents differ slightly in their definition of information literacy and its integration and influence in the student learning experience. The Association of College and Research Libraries (ACRL) developed a standard "Information Literacy Competency Standards for Higher Education" (which was rescinded in 2016). This standard affirms that information literacy initiates, sustains, and extends lifelong learning through abilities which may use technologies, but are ultimately independent of them. In a knowledge-based society, this standard may require reviewing to incorporate technological, visual, textual, and other literacies which would enhance curriculum integration and more collaborative work with faculty involved in learning design (Schroeder and Cahoy, 2010).

HOW THE FRAMEWORK HAS FUNCTIONED

The ACRL higher education framework contains interconnecting core concepts which guide the development of information literacy in higher education. Frames are flexible for easy implementation in any institution.

Frames

- Authority is constructed and contextual
- Information creation as a process
- Information has value
- Research as inquiry
- Scholarship as a conversation
- Searching as strategic exploration

Also, within the framework there exist implementational guidelines.

- Suggestions on how to use the framework for information literacy for higher education
- Introduction to faculty and administrators
- For faculty: how to use the framework
- For administrators: how to support the framework

For example, the component "For faculty: how to use the framework" fosters collaboration between faculty and librarian and faculty and students. The framework emphasizes that information literacy is both a disciplinary and a trans-disciplinary learning agenda which has great potential to transform and enrich the disciplinary curriculum. The following guidelines are suggested:

- Investigate threshold concepts in your discipline and gain an understanding of the approach used in the Framework as it applies to the subject.
  - What are the specialized information skills in the discipline that students should develop, such as using primary sources (history) or accessing and managing large data set (science)?
- Look for workshops at your campus teaching and learning center on the flipped classroom and consider how such practices could be incorporated into your courses.
  - What information and research assignments can students do outside of class to arrive prepared to apply concepts and conduct collaborative projects?
- Partner with your IT department and librarians to develop new kinds of multimedia assignments for courses.
  - What kinds of workshops and other services should be available for students involved in multimedia design and production?
- Help students view themselves as information producers, individually and collaboratively.
  - In your program, how do students interact with, evaluate, produce, and share information in various formats and modes?
- Consider the knowledge practices and dispositions in each information literacy frame for possible integration into your courses and academic program.
  - How might you and a librarian design learning experiences and assignments that will encourage students to assess their attitudes, strengths/weaknesses, and knowledge gaps related to information?

The Framework opens the way for librarians, faculty, and other institutional partners to redesign instruction sessions, assignments, courses, and even curricula; to connect information literacy with student success initiatives; and to create broader conversations about student learning.

FRAMEWORK FOR CRITICAL THINKING

While the framework for information literacy is being scrutinized for collaboration, there are the concepts of critical thinking to be considered. Duron, Limbach, and Waugh (2006) speak of a 5-step analytical thinking framework (Figure 1) that can be implemented in any classroom or training setting to help students develop critical thinking skills.

Figure 1. 5-Step model to move students towards critical thinking
Source: Robert Duron, Barbara Limbach & Wendy Waugh © 2006, (http://www.isetl.org/ijtlhe/cfp.cfm)

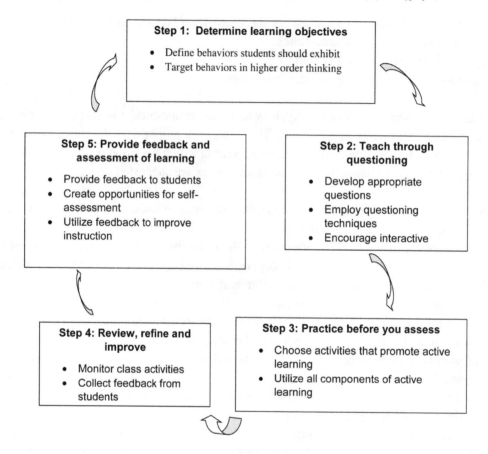

Another critical thinking framework was developed by critical thinking experts Richard Paul and Linda Elder. They simplified the tools and concepts in a mini guide for faculty and students. Users can apply the skills to reading and writing as well as to the way they speak and listen (Paul and Elder, 2006). The framework allows the user to:

- Question information, conclusions, and points of view
- Strive to be clear, accurate, precise, and relevant
- Seek to think beneath the surface, to be logical, and fair
- Apply these skills to their reading and writing as well as speaking and listening
- Apply the framework in all subject disciplines
- Apply the framework in professional and personal life

The framework has the concepts of a universal intellectual standard which is applied to elements of thought such as purpose, questioning, information, interpretation, and point of view. While these elements are being applied, the user develops intellectual virtues or traits such as integrity, humility, confidence in reason, courage and fair mindedness (Paul and Elder, 2006).

PEDAGOGICAL APPROACHES

You can teach a student a lesson for a day; but if you can teach him to learn by creating curiosity, he will continue the learning process as long as he lives. (Clay P. Bedford)

Modern university students approach research differently from earlier generations. Many of them are technology savvy and at some point in their lives perform searches for information of interest. Today, students' first instinct for searching may be to make use of search engines such as Bing, Google and Yahoo on the Internet. In some cases, their search behavior can be characterized as looking for that instant response or the "now" result, which at times may frustrate the research process. This can be attributed, in part, to the fact that they live in a world where fast is excellent and instant is better (Burkhardt and MacDonald, 2010). But research at the university level is not instantaneous and requires specific skills to produce research assignments that are credible.

Students are assisted in acquiring sophisticated research skills through Information Literacy programs implemented by universities and colleges. What has been indicated in the literature is that each university or college and each instructor delivers the instruction in a different way. According to Andretta (2005), the introduction of information literacy marks a fundamental shift in the pedagogy underpinning library instruction, which uses a variety of instructional techniques that address the needs of diverse users.

No matter the instructional approach, the most critical factor for this instruction are the learning outcomes which include the ability of the student to know how to learn. The student should become information literate and be able to use the skills learned for life-long learning. Sharkey (2006) notes that more and more employers are requiring college graduates to have higher levels of critical thinking, research, and technology skills. This qualification is recognized by higher education institutions and incorporated in their strategic plans to introduce information literacy and critical thinking programs so that their graduates will emerge with the requirements that employers demand.

It is widely accepted that the lecture format is inappropriate for these information literacy sessions. According to Duron, Limbach, and Waugh, it frequently does not encourage active learning or critical thinking. That is because topics are discussed sequentially rather than critically, and large amounts of information are memorized rather than thought through and learned. In such sessions students are placed in a passive rather than an active role since the teacher does the talking, the questioning and thus, most of the thinking.

Guidance and practice in the evaluation of resources is a most important element of information literacy instruction. According to Kreitzberg and Kreitzberg (2010), online information can be very unreliable and searchers can easily be misled. Their view is that the Internet is a vast and invaluable but treacherous resource; therefore users must think critically about how information is found, evaluated and applied to searches being carried out. Users have to be helped to bring some critical thinking skills to the web—and some crucial knowledge—to enable them to evaluate what they find there and to separate the wheat from the chaff, so to speak. The acronym CRAAP (currency, relevance, authority, accuracy, and purpose) can be used to evaluate online resources. (Students should, of course, remember that that the same rigorous evaluation should be applied to print resources).

Lesson plans should not be static but flexible. Opportunities for one on one communication between student and instructor to give/receive advice and discuss progress should be emphasized. Students often find this type of interaction helpful in building confidence and in critically thinking about the topic.

Further, Chase and Daniels (n.d.) emphasize that instructors can assist students to improve their critical thinking skills by helping them build a community of thinkers. It must be remembered that critical thinking will not be mastered unless it is reinforced regularly, for example, by posing questions to students to encourage analysis and not just recall.

LEARNING OUTCOMES AND ASSESSMENT

Students cannot respond to an inquiry unless there is first understanding so that the analysis of the questions guides the point to be argued. Evaluation of that understanding further guides the students in deciding what to do with the fact placed before them. Trying to assess or measure critical thinking has its challenges, but if combined with information literacy it can be evaluated meaningfully. Independent learning and critical thinking are important outcomes and require a framework to creatively and sensitively assist students to enhance their independent learning and critical thinking skills (Gunasekara, 2008).

For any educational institution which has implemented a program of information literacy instruction, evaluation by mere observation is not good enough. There should be some empirical evidence to show the impact of instruction on the learning outcomes that students experience. As Brooks (2014) points out, assessment provides essential benchmark data for measuring student information literacy skills and the results inform and guide instructors.

So, there is a need to assess students. One method often used is the pretest- posttest model. In this model, the assessment gauges what students know before taking the session and what they learned in the sessions. The students are required to answer questions that relate to the library and research skills. Once the students have grasped the aim of information literacy, they would be empowered to become lifelong learners. While students are mainly judged on the questions posed in the test, the instructor, by using observation, can make informed decisions on how best to plan or adjust future sessions on a particular topic.

The results of the pretesting element of this model throw up quite contrasting information about entering students. Hodgens, Sendall, and Evans (2012) found that librarians believed that many students exhibited difficulties with basic information literacy skills and suggested that many students entering higher education displayed poor computer and information literacy skills. Singh and Joshi (2013) report that at the University of Agriculture in Abeokuta, Nigeria, 57% of the students showed a need for assistance in the use of electronic information resources and 97% indicated a need for training in computer literacy. Getty and Chibnall (2013) observed that students entering college often do not understand what information literacy is or how it can fit into the college curriculum. Nor do they understand its relevance to their lives after college. On the other hand, Swoger (2011), on assessing students before instruction, found that some had already met some of the goals at the beginning of the college course. Salisbury and Karasmanis (2011), in their assessment, realized that students enter university with strengths in concept identification and basic search formulation but require the most assistance with locating and identifying scholarly literature and how to cite it appropriately in their work.

Active learning techniques may allow students with different learning styles to gain information literacy competencies by seeing, doing, reading and talking and thereby enhance learning outcomes (Houlson, 2007). Furthermore, adapting the classroom from a traditional room with fixed seating to a flexible classroom arrangement can create an environment that encourages teachers to use more interactive methods. An environment where teachers are able to slow down, lecture less, let students explore more, and plan around the students' needs rather than merely following the lesson plan also has its virtues (Julian, 2013).

The learning outcome from the information literacy sessions is vital to the students' progress during the rest of the degree program with the institution. Blakeslee (1998) noted a clear message that students felt the library, information, and computer competencies were the most beneficial parts of the class and that they would like to see even more emphasis on these topics. In a research project the authors, Mery, Newby and Peng (2012) revealed that their pretest results indicated that incoming students enter the university with a need to develop their information literacy skills and the posttest showed that students do not acquire information literacy skills on their own even when they are given a research assignment as part of their regular coursework. All this serves to reinforce the importance of, and indeed the need to have, information literacy programs for incoming college students. After using the Framework Information Literacy Instruction Assessment Cycle (ILIAC), librarians at the North Carolina State University (NCSU) articulated certain learning outcomes. They were able to analyze these more meaningfully, gain important data about student skills, celebrate learning achievements and diagnose problem areas. This Framework facilitated both the documentation and improvement of librarian instructional abilities and student information literacy skills (Oakleaf, 2009). Some universities do not use formal assessments but gauge student outcomes.

CONCLUSION

Access to information and the ability to use that information effectively are vital keys to success in the modern world. Information and more information is always available at the touch of a key on a mobile phone or a computer. The reality is that the virtually limitless amount of information available and the ease with which we have access to it are in themselves no guarantee that that information will be understood or used appropriately or effectively. This is the challenge facing those whose task it is to conceptualize and implement Information Literacy programs as part of the goal of "producing" information literate citizens.

Students need to be guided to an appreciation of the important reality that access to information is not in itself the most important thing. Rather, the capacity to use that information and the practice of using it in a meaningful and profitable way require skills that need to be developed over a period of time. The fact that even experienced researchers can be overwhelmed by this availability of extensive amounts of information reinforces the importance of developing those skills that constitute both information literacy and critical thinking.

REFERENCES

Albitz, R. S. (2007). The What and Who of Information Literacy and Critical Thinking in Higher Education. *portal. Libraries and the Academy*, 7(1), 97–109. doi:10.1353/pla.2007.0000

Andretta, S. (2005). *Information literacy: a practitioner's guide / Susie Andretta*. Oxford, UK: Chandos Pub. doi:10.1533/9781780630755

Armstrong, J. (2010). Designing a writing intensive course with information literacy and critical thinking learning outcomes. *Reference Services Review*, *38*(3), 445–457. doi:10.1108/00907321011070928

Association of College and Research Libraries. (2015). *Framework for information literacy for higher education*. Retrieved from http://www.ala.org/acrl/standards/ilframework

Biddiscombe, R. (2000). The changing role of the information professional in support of learning and research. *Advances in Librarianship*, *23*, 63–92.

Blakeslee, S. (1998). Librarian in a Strange Land: Teaching a Freshman Orientation Course. *Reference Services Review*, *26*(2), 73–78. doi:10.1108/00907329810307678

Blevens, C. (2012). Catching up with information literacy assessment: Resources for program evaluation. *College & Research Libraries News*, *73*(4), 202–206. doi:10.5860/crln.73.4.8742

Brooks, A. (2014). Information literacy and the flipped classroom. *Communications in Information Literacy*, *8*(2), 225–235. doi:10.15760/comminfolit.2014.8.2.168

Brown, S. A. (1997). *500 tips for academic librarians*. London: Library Association.

Burkhardt, J. M. (2010). Teaching information literacy: 50 standards-based exercises for college students (2nd ed.). Chicago: Chicago: American Library Association.

Candy, P. C. (2015). *Lifelong learning and information literacy*. Available from: https://www.researchgate.net/publication/268299706_Lifelong_Learning_and_Information_Literacy

Case, R., & Daniels, L. (n.d.). *Introduction to the TC2 conception of critical thinking: appendix A*. Available from The Critical Thinking Consortium: https://tc2.ca/pdf/About%20Critical%20Thinking/Online%20Articles/Understanding%20Critical%20Thinking/Introduction%20to%20the%20TC2%20Conception%20w_%20new%20copyright.pdf

Csikszentmihalyi, M. (2006). Forward: developing creativity. In N. Jackson, M. Oliver, M. Shaw, & J. Wisdom (Eds.), *Developing creativity in higher education: An imaginative curriculum* (pp. xviii–xx). London: Routledge.

De Bono, E. (1985). *Six thinking hats: The power of focused thinking*. Mamaroneck, NY: The International Center for Creative Thinking.

Doddington, C. (2008). Critical thinking as a source of respect for persons: A critique. In M. Mason (Ed.), *Critical thinking and learning* (pp. 109–119). Oxford: Blackwell Publishing.

Duron, R., Limbach, B., & Waugh, W. (2006). Critical thinking framework for any discipline. *International Journal on Teaching and Learning in Higher Education*, *17*(2), 160–166.

Eisenberg, M. (2004). Information literacy: essential skills for the information age (2nd ed.). Westport, CT: Libraries Unlimited.

Eisenberg, M. B. (2008). Information Literacy: Essential Skills for the Information Age. *DESIDOC Journal of Library and Information Technology*, *28*(2), 39–47. doi:10.14429/djlit.28.2.166

Fisher, A. (2011). *Critical thinking: An introduction* (2nd ed.). Cambridge, NY: Cambridge University Press.

Foundation for Critical Thinking. (2017, July). *Become certified in the Paul-Elder framework for critical thinking*. Available from Foundation for Critical Thinking: http://www.criticalthinking.org/data/pages/62/2241c25a71d4f0d7c7c47a621832551256329c1605487.pdf

Franklin, K. Y. (2005). The importance of information literacy: insights from the next generation of scholars. *ACRL Twelfth National Conference,* 388-396.

Gauder, H., & Jenkins, F. (2012). Engaging undergraduates in discipline-based research. *Reference Services Review, 40*(2), 277–294. doi:10.1108/00907321211228327

Getty, A., & Chibnall, D. (2013). Skillful scaffolding: using information litercy techniques to enhance literature studies. *Currents in Teaching and Learning, 6*(), 53-65.

Grassian, E. S., & Kaplowitz, J. R. (2010). Information literacy instruction: Theory and practice (2nd edition). Journal of Documentation, 66(3), 457-458.

Gunasekara, C.S. (2008). Fostering independent learning and critical thinking in management higher education using an information literacy framework. *Journal of Information Literacy, 2*(2), 74-85.

Hodgens, C., Sendall, M. C., & Evans, L. (2012). Post-graduate health promotion students assess their information literacy. *Reference Services Review, 40*(3), 408–422. doi:10.1108/00907321211254670

Houlson, V. (2007). Getting Results from One-Shot Instruction: A Workshop for First-Year Students. *College & Undergraduate Libraries, 14*(1), 89–108. doi:10.1300/J106v14n01_07

Iton, I. (2008). Breaking into unexplored territory: a case study of the Information Literacy initiative at the Cave Hill Campus of the University of the West Indies. In J. Lau (Ed.), Information Literacy International Perspective. Munchen: IFLA Publications

Julian, S. (2013). Reinventing classroom space to re-energise information literacy instruction. *Journal of Information Literacy, 7*(1), 69–82. doi:10.11645/7.1.1720

Kim, S., & Shumaker, D. (2015). Student, librarian, and instructor perceptions of information literacy instruction and skills in a first year experience program: A case study. *Journal of Academic Librarianship, 41*(4), 449–456.

Kreitzberg, A., & Kreitzberg, C. (2010). *Critical thinking for the twenty-first century: what it is and why it matters to you.* Retrieved from http://www.agilecriticalthinking.com/Portals/0/WhitePapers/Critical%20Thinking%20for%20the%2021st%20Century%20for%20Website.pdf

McDonald, S., & McDonald, J. (2011). *Information literacy for ubiquitous learning.* Available from: https://uts.academia.edu/Sophieherbert/

Mery, Y., Newby, J., & Peng, K. (2012). Why One-Shot Information Literacy Sessions Are Not the Future of Instruction: A Case for Online Credit Courses. *College & Research Libraries, 73*(4), 366–377. doi:10.5860/crl-271

Paul, R., & Elder, L. (2006). *The miniature guide to critical thinking: Concepts and tools.* Retrieved from https://www.criticalthinking.org/files/Concepts_Tools

Reece, G. J. (2005). Critical thinking and cognitive transfer: Implications for the development of online information literacy tutorials. *Research Strategies*, *20*(4), 482–493. doi:10.1016/j.resstr.2006.12.018

Roth, L. (1999). Educating the cut-and- paste generation. *Library Journal*, *124*(18), 42–44.

Salisbury, F., & Karasmanis, S. (2011). Are they ready?: Exploring student information literacy skills in the transition from secondary to tertiary education. *Australian Academic and Research Libraries*, *42*(1), 43–58.

Schroeder, R., & Cahoy, E. S. (2010). Valuing information literacy: Affective learning and the ACRL standards. *Libraries and the Academy*, *10*(2), 127–146. doi:10.1353/pla.0.0096

Sharkey, J. (2006). Towards information fluency: Applying a different model to an information literacy credit course. *Reference Services Review*, *34*(1), 71–85. doi:10.1108/00907320610648770

Singh, D., & Joshi, M. K. (2013). Information literacy competency of post graduate students at Haryana Agricultural University and impact of instruction initiatives; A pilot survey. *RSR. Reference Services Review*, *41*(3), 453–473. doi:10.1108/RSR-11-2012-0074

Starr, G. E., & Gaskill, P. (1997). The community study assignment for leisure studies: Integrating information literacy, leisure theory, and critical thinking. *Research Strategies*, *15*(3), 205–216. doi:10.1016/S0734-3310(97)90041-0

Swoger, B. (2011). Closing the assessment loop using pre- and post-assessment. *RSR. Reference Services Review*, *39*(2), 244–259.

Thompson, H. M., & Henley, S. A. (2000). Fostering information literacy: Connecting national standards, Goals 2000, and the SCANS report. Englewood, CO: Libraries Unlimited and its division Teacher Ideas Press.

KEY TERMS AND DEFINITIONS

Community of Thinkers: A group of learners who come together, supporting each other to address or reflect critically on a particular problem following an agreed procedure. It is sometimes seen as an alternative to the traditional classroom.

CRAAP: A test used as a means of evaluating the process of searching and finding information on websites, in articles and other sources on the basis of the following criteria: *currency, relevance, authority, accuracy, and purpose.*

Frameworks: A framework is a set of rules, guidelines, beliefs that guide how a particular situations or problems are addressed. The standards framework for information literacy would therefore provide guidelines for how information literacy would be defined, understood and applied.

Information Literate: An information literate person is one who is able to recognize the need for information and has the ability to find, assess and use the needed information in a meaningful way, sometimes to create new knowledge.

Pretest-Posttest: A pretest-posttest design is a kind of experiment in which a group is tested/studied before and after the particular experiment or activity is administered. In this way it is possible to determine what changes if any have taken place and thereby judge the effect or value of the experiment.

Compilation of References

AACTE. (2018). A pivot toward clinical practice, its lexicon, and the renewal of educator preparation. *A Report of the AACTE Clinical Practice Commission*. Retrieved from https://aacte.org/professional-development-and-events/clinical-practice-commission-press-conference

Abd-el-Khalick, F., Boujaoude, S., Duschl, R., Lederman, N. G., Mamlok-Naaman, R., Hofstein, A., … Tuan, H. (2004). Inquiry in science education: international perspectives. In E. Krugly-Smolska & P.C. Taylor (Eds.), *Cultural and Comparative Studies* (pp. 397-419). Academic Press. Retrieved from http://www.d.umn.edu/~bmunson/Courses/Educ5560/readings/AbdElKhalick-Inquiry.pdf

Abrami, P. C., Bernard, R. M., Borokhovski, E., Waddington, D. I., Wade, C. A., & Persson, T. (2015). Strategies for teaching students to think critically: A meta-analysis. *Review of Educational Research, 85*(2), 275–314. doi:10.3102/0034654314551063

Abrami, P. C., Bernard, R. M., Borokhovski, E., Wade, A., Surkes, M. A., Tamim, R., & Zhang, D. (2008). Instructional interventions affecting critical thinking skills and dispositions: A stage 1 meta-analysis. *Review of Educational Research, 78*(4), 1102–1134. doi:10.3102/0034654308326084

Abrams, L., Pedulla, J., & Madaus, G. F. (2003). Views from the classroom: Teachers' opinions of statewide testing programs. *Theory into Practice, 42*(1), 18–29. doi:10.120715430421tip4201_4

AbuSeileek, A. F. (2012). The effect of computer-assisted cooperative learning methods and group size on the EFL learners' achievement in communication skills. *Computers & Education, 58*(1), 231–239. doi:10.1016/j.compedu.2011.07.011

Achieve, Inc. (2010). *International science benchmarking report: Taking the lead in science education forging Next-Generation Science Standards*. Retrieved from https://www.achieve.org/files/InternationalScienceBenchmarkingReport.pdf

Achieve, Inc. (2016). *Using Phenomena in NGSS-Designed Lessons and Units*. Retrieved from http://www.nextgenscience.org/sites/default/files/Using%20Phenomena%20in%20NGSS.pdf

Acim, R. (2018). The Socratic method of instruction: An experience with a reading comprehension course. *Journal of Educational Research and Practice, 8*(1), 41–53.

Adams, G., Cherif, A. H., Dunning, J., & Movehedzadeh, F. (2015). What if fossils are discovered on planet Mars? Collection of learning activities for promoting active learning. *Pinnacle Journal Publication*. Retrieved from http:/www.pjpub.org

Adams, A., Ross, D., Burns, J., & Gibbs, L. (2015). Talking points: Data displays are an effective way to engage teachers. *Journal of Staff Development, 36*(1), 24–29.

Ade-El-Kalick, F. (2006). Socioscientific issues in pre-college science classrooms. In D. L. Zeidler (Ed.), *The role of moral reasoning and discourse on socioscientific issues in science education* (pp. 41–61). Dordrecht, Netherlands: Springer.

Adey, P., & Shayer, M. (2010). The effects of cognitive acceleration – and speculation about causes of these effects. In *AERA Research Conference, Socializing intelligence through academic talk and dialogue* (pp. 1–20). Learning, Research and Development Centre. Retrieved from http://www.kcl.ac.uk/sspp/departments/education/research/crestem/CogAcc/Cognaccel.aspx

Adıgüzel, Ö. (2010). *Eğitimde Yaratıcı Drama*. Ankara: Naturel Yayınevi.

Aguirre, J. M., Turner, E. E., Bartell, T. G., Kalinec-Craig, C., Foote, M. Q., McDuffie, A. R., & Drake, C. (2013). Making connections in practice: How prospective elementary teachers connect to children's mathematical thinking and community funds of knowledge in mathematics instruction. *Journal of Teacher Education, 64*(2), 178–192. doi:10.1177/0022487112466900

Aizikovitsh, E., & Amit, M. (2010). Evaluating an infusion approach to the teaching of critical thinking skills through mathematics. *Procedia: Social and Behavioral Sciences, 2*(2), 3818–3822. doi:10.1016/j.sbspro.2010.03.596

Aizikovitsh-Udi, E. (2012a). *Developing critical thinking through probability models, intuitive judgments and decision-making under uncertainty* (Doctoral dissertation). Saarbrucken, Germany: LAP Lambert Academic Publishing.

Aizikovitsh-Udi, E. (2012b). Connections between statistical thinking and critical thinking – A case study. *International Congress of Mathematics Education*, Seoul, South Korea.

Al-Almaie, S. M., & Al-Baghli, N. A. (2003). Evidence-based Medicine: An overview. *Journal of Family & Community Medicine, 10*, 17–24. PMID:23011987

Albitz, R. S. (2007). The What and Who of Information Literacy and Critical Thinking in Higher Education. *portal. Libraries and the Academy, 7*(1), 97–109. doi:10.1353/pla.2007.0000

Al-Fadhli, S., & Khalfan, A. (2009). Developing critical thinking in e-learning environment: Kuwait University as a case study. *Assessment & Evaluation in Higher Education, 34*(5), 529–536. doi:10.1080/02602930802117032

Alguire, P. C. (1998). A review of journal clubs in postgraduate medical education. *Journal of General Internal Medicine, 13*(5), 347–353. doi:10.1046/j.1525-1497.1998.00102.x PMID:9613892

Allen, E. G., Wright, J. P., & Laminack, L. L. (1988). The Reading Teacher. *Using Language Experience to ALERT Pupils' Critical Thinking Skills.*

Allen, G. D., Rubenfeld, M. G., & Scheffer, B. K. (2004). Reliability of assessment of critical thinking. *Journal of Professional Nursing, 20*(1), 15–22. doi:10.1016/j.profnurs.2003.12.004 PMID:15011189

Alper, M. (2011). Developmentally appropriate new media literacies: Supporting cultural competencies and social skills in early childhood education. *Journal of Early Childhood Literacy, 13*(2), 175–196. doi:10.1177/1468798411430101

Alvermann, D. E. (2017). Social media texts and critical inquiry in a post-factual era. *Journal of Adolescent & Adult Literacy, 61*(3), 335–338.

American Association for the Advancement of Science. (2003). *Project 2061*. Retrieved from www.project2061.org

American Association of Medical Colleges. (1984). Physicians of the 21st century. Report of the Working Group on Personal Qualities, Values and Attitudes. *Journal of Medical Education, 59*, 177–189.

Amey, L., Donald, K. J., & Teodorczuk, A. (2017). Teaching clinical reasoning to medical students. *British Journal of Hospital Medicine, 78*(7), 399–401. doi:10.12968/hmed.2017.78.7.399 PMID:28692355

Anderson, L. W., Krathwohl, D. R., Airasian, P. W., Cruikshank, K. A., Mayer, R. E., Pintrich, P. R., & Wittrock, M. C. (2001). *A Taxonomy for Learning, Teaching, and Assessing: A revision of Bloom's Taxonomy of Educational Objectives*. New York: Pearson, Allyn & Bacon.

Anderson, L. W., Krathwohl, D. R., & Bloom, B. S. (2001). *A taxonomy for learning, teaching, and assessing: A revision of Bloom's taxonomy of educational objectives*. Boston, MA: Allyn & Bacon.

Anderson, M. J., & Freebody, K. (2012). Developing communities of praxis: Bridging the theory practice divide in teacher education. *McGill Journal of Education, 47*(3), 359–378. doi:10.7202/1014864ar

Andretta, S. (2005). *Information literacy: a practitioner's guide / Susie Andretta*. Oxford, UK: Chandos Pub. doi:10.1533/9781780630755

Angeli, C., & Valanides, N. (2009). Instructional effects on critical thinking: Performance on ill-defined issues. *Learning and Instruction, 19*(4), 322–334. doi:10.1016/j.learninstruc.2008.06.010

Angelo, T. A., & Cross, K. P. (2005). Classroom assessment techniques. In Classroom assessment techniques: a handbook for college teachers (2nd ed., pp. 1-3). John Wiley & Sons Incorporated.

Angoff, W. H. (1971). Scales, norms, and equivalent scores. In R. L. Thorndike (Ed.), *Educational measurement* (pp. 508–600). Washington, DC: American Council on Education.

Anu, P., & Bhaskaran, N. (2017). Thinking Outside the Classroom: Developing Critical Thinking Using Authentic Materials in an ELT Classroom. *The Elt Practitioner, 4*(3).

Apple, M. (1979). *Ideology and Curriculum*. NY: Routledge. doi:10.4324/9780203241219

Argyris, C. (1982). The executive mind and double-loop learning. *Organizational Dynamics*, 5–24.

Argyris, C. (2002). Double-loop learning, teaching and research. *Academy of Management Learning & Education, 1*(2), 206–218. doi:10.5465/amle.2002.8509400

Armon, J. R. (1997). *The waldorf curriculum as a framework for moral education: One dimension of a fourfold system*. Paper presented at the American Educational Research Association Conference, Chicago, IL.

Armstrong, J. (2010). Designing a writing intensive course with information literacy and critical thinking learning outcomes. *Reference Services Review, 38*(3), 445–457. doi:10.1108/00907321011070928

Armstrong, L. (2016). *Institute barriers to innovation and change in education*. TIAA-CREF Financial Institution.

Artman-Meeker, K., Fettig, A., Barton, E. E., Penney, A., & Zeng, S. (2015). Applying an evidence-based framework to the early childhood coaching literature. *Topics in Early Childhood Special Education, 35*(3), 183–196. doi:10.1177/0271121415595550

Assessment and Reporting Authority (ACARA). (2018). *Australian curriculum: Critical and creative thinking*. Retrieved from https://www.australiancurriculum.edu.au

Association of College and Research Libraries. (2015). *Framework for information literacy for higher education*. Retrieved from http://www.ala.org/acrl/standards/ilframework

Astleitner, H. (2002). Teaching Critical Thinking Online. *Journal of Instructional Psychology*.

Ayers, W. R. (1997). Sherlock Holmes and clinical reasoning: Empiric research on a methodology to teach clinical reasoning. In A. J. J. A. Scherpbier, C. P. M. van der Vleuten, J. J. Rethans, & A. F. W. van der Steeg (Eds.), *Advances in Medical Education* (pp. 600–601). Dordrecht: Springer. doi:10.1007/978-94-011-4886-3_182

Ayers, W., Michie, G., & Rome, A. (2004). Embers of hope: In search of a meaningful critical pedagogy. *Teacher Education Quarterly*, *31*, 123–130.

Baessa, Y., Chesterfield, R., & Ramos, T. (2002). Active learning and democratic behavior in Guetamalan Rural Primary Schools. *British Association for International and Comparative Education.*, *32*(2), 205–218.

Baildon, M. C., & Sim, J. B. Y. (2009). Notions of criticality: Singaporean teachers' perspectives of critical thinking in social studies. *Cambridge Journal of Education*, *39*(4), 407–422. doi:10.1080/03057640903352481

Bailey, B. (2000). The impact of mandated change on teachers. In N. Bascia & A. Hargreaves (Eds.), *The sharp edge of educational change: Teaching, leading, and the realities of reform* (pp. 112–128). New York: Routledge.

Baldeo, F. N. (2011). *Primary Teacher education in Trinidad and Tobago: A best Practice Framework*. Germany: VDM Verlag Dr. Muller GmbH and Co. KG.

Ball, D. L., & Forzani, F. M. (2009). The work of teaching and the challenge for teacher education. *Journal of Teacher Education*, *60*(5), 14.

Ball, D. L., & Forzani, F. M. (2010). What does it take to make a teacher? *Phi Delta Kappan*, *92*(2), 5. doi:10.1177/003172171009200203

Ball, D. L., & Hill, H. (2009). The curious-and-crucial case of mathematical knowledge for teaching. *Phi Delta Kappan*, *91*(2), 3.

Ball, D. L., Sleep, L., Boerst, T. A., & Bass, H. (2009). Combining the development of practice and the practice of development in teacher education. *The Elementary School Journal*, *109*(5), 458–474. doi:10.1086/596996

Ball, D. L., Thames, M. H., & Phelps, G. (2008). Content knowledge for teaching: What makes it special? *Journal of Teacher Education*, *59*(5), 389–407. doi:10.1177/0022487108324554

Barahal, S. L. (2008). Thinking about thinking: Preservice teachers strengthen their thinking artfully. *Phi Delta Kappan*, *90*(4), 298–302. doi:10.1177/003172170809000412

Barak, M., Ben-Chaim, D., & Zoller, U. (2007). Purposively teaching for the development of higher-order thinking skills: A case of critical thinking. *Research in Science Education*, *37*(4), 353–369. doi:10.100711165-006-9029-2

Barnhart, T., & van Es, E. (2015). Studying teacher noticing: Examining the relationships among pre-service science teachers' ability to attend, analyze, and respond to student thinking. *Teaching and Teacher Education*, *45*, 83–93. doi:10.1016/j.tate.2014.09.005

Barrows, H. S., & Tamblyn, R. (1980). *Problem-Based Learning: An Approach to Medical Education*. New York: Springer.

Bartlett, D. J., & Cox, P. D. (2002). Measuring change in students' critical thinking ability: Implications for health care education. *Journal of Allied Health*, *31*, 64–69. PMID:12040999

Barua, K., & Chakrabarte, P. (2017). A survey on critical thinking in education scenario. *International Journal on Future Revolution in Computer Science & Communication Engineering*, *3*(12), 197–203.

Batchelor, D. (2012). Borderline space for voice. *International Journal of Inclusive Education*, *16*(5-6), 597–608. doi:10.1080/13603116.2012.655501

Bates, A. J. (2018). *10 Important trends in education to expect in 2018*. Retrieved from https://education.cu-portland.edu/

Batool, T. (2010). Hyposkillia and critical thinking: Lost skills of doctors. *APS Journal of Case Reports, 1*, 9.

Battista, M. (1994). Teacher beliefs and the reform movement in mathematics education. *Phi Delta Kappan*, *75*, 5.

Battista, M. T. (1999). The mathematical miseducation of America's youth: Ignoring research and scientific study in education. *Phi Delta Kappan, 80*(6), 9.

Beach, R., Thein, A., & Webb, A. (2016). Teaching to exceed the English language arts common core state standards: A critical inquiry approach for 6-12 classrooms. New York, NY: Routledge.

Bean, J. C. (2011). *Engaging Ideas: The Professor's Guide to Integrating Writing, Critical Thinking, and Active Learning in the Classroom.* Jossey-Bass.

Bean, R. M., Draper, J. A., Hall, V., Vandermolen, J., & Zigmond, N. (2010). Coaches and instructional coaching in reading first schools: A reality check. *The Elementary School Journal, 111*(1), 87–114. doi:10.1086/653471

Beauchamp, C., & Thomas, L. (2011). New teachers' identity shifts at the boundary of teacher education and initial practice. *International Journal of Educational Research, 50*(1), 6–13. doi:10.1016/j.ijer.2011.04.003

Beavers, S. L. (2011). Getting political science in on the joke: Using The Daily Show and their comedy to teach politics. *PS, Political Science & Politics, 44*(02), 415–419. doi:10.1017/S1049096511000266

Beghetto, R. A., & Kaufman, J. C. (2007). Towards a broader conception of creativity: A case for "mini-c" creativity. *Psychology of Aesthetics, Creativity, and the Arts, 1*(2), 73–79. doi:10.1037/1931-3896.1.2.73

Beghetto, R. A., & Kaufman, J. C. (2014). Classroom contexts for creativity. *High Ability Studies, 25*(1), 53–69. doi:10.1080/13598139.2014.905247

Beltman, S., Glass, C., Dinham, J., Chalk, B., & Nguyen, B. H. N. (2015). Drawing identity: Beginning pre-service teachers' professional identities. *Issues in Educational Research, 25*(3), 225–245.

Bencze, L., Sperling, E., & Carter, L. (2012). Students' research-informed socio-scientific activism: Re/ visions for a sustainable future. *Research in Science Education, 42*(1), 129–148. doi:10.100711165-011-9260-3

Bensley, D. A. (1998). Critical thinking in psychology: A unified skills approach. Belmont, CA: Academic Press.

Beyer, B. (1995). *Critical thinking.* Bloomington, IN: Phi Delta Kappa Educational Foundation.

Beyer, B. K. (1987). *Practical strategies for the teaching of thinking.* Boston, MA: Allyn and Bacon.

Biddiscombe, R. (2000). The changing role of the information professional in support of learning and research. *Advances in Librarianship, 23*, 63–92.

Biesta, G. (2007). Why "what works" won't work: Evidence-based practice and the democratic deficit in educational research. *Educational Theory, 87*(1), 1–22. doi:10.1111/j.1741-5446.2006.00241.x

Biesta, G., Priestley, M., & Robinson, S. (2017). Talking about education: Exploring the significance of teachers' talk for teacher agency. *Journal of Curriculum Studies, 49*(1), 38–54. doi:10.1080/00220272.2016.1205143

Bissell, A. N., & Lemons, P. P. (2006). A new method for assessing critical thinking in the classroom. *Bioscience, 56*(1), 66–72. doi:10.1641/0006-3568(2006)056[0066:ANMFAC]2.0.CO;2

Black, P., & William, D. (1998). Assessment and classroom learning. *Assessment in Education: Principles, Policy & Practice, 5*(1), 7–74. doi:10.1080/0969595980050102

Blair, J. A. (2015). Probative norms for multimodal visual arguments. *Argumentation, 29*(2), 217–233. doi:10.100710503-014-9333-3

Blakeslee, S. (1998). Librarian in a Strange Land: Teaching a Freshman Orientation Course. *Reference Services Review, 26*(2), 73–78. doi:10.1108/00907329810307678

Blaschke, L. M. (2012). Heutagogy and lifelong learning: A review of heutagogical practice and self-determined learning. *International Review of Research in Open and Distance Learning, 13*(1), 56–71. doi:10.19173/irrodl.v13i1.1076

Blevens, C. (2012). Catching up with information literacy assessment: Resources for program evaluation. *College & Research Libraries News, 73*(4), 202–206. doi:10.5860/crln.73.4.8742

Bloom, B. S. (1956). Taxonomy of educational objectives: The classification of educational goals.

Bloom, B. S., Engelhart, M. D., Furst, E. J., Hill, W. H., & Krathwohl, D. R. (1956). *Taxonomy of Educational Objectives, Handbook I: The Cognitive Domain.* New York: David McKay Co Inc.

Boenink, A. D., Oderwald, A. K., De, J. P., Van, T. W., & Smal, J. A. (2004). Assessing student reflection in medical practice. The development of an observer-rated instrument: Reliability, validity and initial experiences. *Medical Education, 38*(4), 368–377. doi:10.1046/j.1365-2923.2004.01787.x PMID:15025638

Bofferding, L., & Kloser, M. (2015). Middle and high school students' conceptions of climate change mitigation and adaptation strategies. *Environmental Education Research, 21*(2), 275–294. doi:10.1080/13504622.2014.888401

Bognar, B., & Krumes, I. (2017). Encouraging reflection and critical friendship in preservice teacher education. *CEPS Journal, 7*(3), 87–112.

Boice, R. (1991). New teachers colleagues. *International Journal of Qualitative Studies in Education: QSE, 4*(1), 29–44. doi:10.1080/0951839910040103

Bolden, D. S., Harries, T. V., & Newton, D. P. (2010). Pre-service primary teachers' conceptions of creativity in mathematics. *Educational Studies in Mathematics, 73*(2), 143–157. doi:10.100710649-009-9207-z

Boston, W. G. B. H. (Producer). Annenberg/CPB Project (Distributed by). (2000). Teaching high school science [Episode 6]. *The physics of optics.* Video file retrieved from https://www.learner.org/resources/series126.html#jump1

Boud, D., & Molloy, E. (2013). Decision-making for feedback. In D. Boud & E. Molloy (Eds.), Feedback in Higher and Professional Education (pp. 202-217). London. UK: Routledge.

Boud, D., & Walker, D. (1998). Promoting reflection in professional discourses. The challenge of context. *Studies in Higher Education, 23*(2), 191–206. doi:10.1080/03075079812331380384

Bowell, T., & Kemp, G. (2005). *Critical thinking: A concise guide* (2nd ed.). New York: Routledge. doi:10.4324/9780203482889

Bowie, A. A., & Cassim, F. (2016). Linking classroom and community: A theoretical alignment of service learning and a human-centered design methodology in contemporary communication design education. *Education as Change, 20*(1), 126–148. doi:10.17159/1947-9417/2016/556

Boyd, N. (2018). *The effects of collaboration on student writing development.* Columbia University.

Boyd, A., Gorham, J., Justice, J., & Anderson, J. (2013). Examining the apprenticeship of observation with preservice teachers: The practice of blogging to facilitate autobiographical reflection and critique. *Teacher Education Quarterly.*

Boyd, M. P., & Markarian, W. C. (2011). Dialogic teaching: Talk in service of a dialogic stance. *Language and Education, 25*(6), 515–534. doi:10.1080/09500782.2011.597861

Boyte, H. C. (2017). John Dewey and citizen politics: How democracy can survive artificial intelligence and the credo of efficiency. *Education and Culture, 33*(2), 13–47. doi:10.5703/educationculture.33.2.0013

Bragelman, J. (2015). Praxis as dialogue: Teacher and administrator. *Journal of Urban Mathematics Education, 8*(2), 27–43.

Branch, J. B. (2000). *The relationship among critical thinking, clinical decision-making, and clinical practical: A comparative study (Doktora tezi)*. Idaho: University of Idaho.

Brande, S. (n.d.). *Thinking Skills in Bloom's Taxonomy* [illustration]. Retrieved from https://www.google.com/search?q=bloom%27s+taxonomy&source=lnms&tbm=isch&sa=X&ved=0ahUKEwj68Za3pqXdAhXKxVkKHb3YB1IQ_AUICigB&biw=1366&bih=631#imgrc=xnjvagWNqNGFTM

Bray, M., & Thomas, R. M. (1995). Levels of comparison in educational studies: Different insights from different literatures and the value of multilevel analyses. *Harvard Educational Review, 65*(3), 472–490. doi:10.17763/haer.65.3.g3228437224v4877

Bredekamp, S. (2014). *Effective practices in early childhood education: Building a foundation* (2nd ed.). Upper Saddle River, NJ: Pearson.

Bresciani, M. J. (2010). Data-driven planning: Using assessment in strategic planning. *New Directions for Student Services, 2010*(132), 39–50. doi:10.1002s.374

Britzman, D. (1991). *Practice makes practice: A critical study of learning to teach*. Albany, NY: State University of New York.

Bronfenbrenner, U. (1977). Toward an experimental ecology of human development. *The American Psychologist, 32*(7), 513–531. doi:10.1037/0003-066X.32.7.513

Brookfield, S. (2005). *The power of critical theory for adult learning and teaching*. San Francisco, CA: Jossey-Bass.

Brookfield, S. D. (2011). *Teaching for Critical Thinking: Tools and techniques to help students questions their assumptions*. San Francisco: Jossey Bass.

Brookhart, S. (2010). *How to assess higher order thinking skills in your classroom*. Alexandria, VA: ASCD.

Brooks, A. (2014). Information literacy and the flipped classroom. *Communications in Information Literacy, 8*(2), 225–235. doi:10.15760/comminfolit.2014.8.2.168

Brown, A. (1997). Transforming schools into communities of thinking and learning about serious matters. *The American Psychologist, 52*(4), 399–413. doi:10.1037/0003-066X.52.4.399 PMID:9109348

Brownell, A. K., & Cote, L. (2001). Senior residents' views on the meaning of professionalism and how they learn about it. *Academic Medicine, 76*(7), 734–737. doi:10.1097/00001888-200107000-00019 PMID:11448832

Browne, M. N., & Freeman, K. (2000). Distinguishing features of critical thinking classrooms. *Teaching in Higher Education, 5*(3), 301–309. doi:10.1080/713699143

Browne, N. M., & Keeley, S. M. (2006). *Asking the Right Questions: A Guide to Critical Thinking*. Longman.

Brown, S. A. (1997). *500 tips for academic librarians*. London: Library Association.

Bruner, J. (1986). *Actual minds, possible worlds*. Cambridge, MA: Harvard University Press.

Bruner, J. (1991). Narrative construction of reality. *Critical Inquiry, 18*(1), 1–21. doi:10.1086/448619

Bruno, A., Galuppo, L., & Gilardi, S. (2011). Evaluating the reflective practices in a learning experience. *European Journal of Psychology of Education*, 2–17.

Bullough, R. (1997). Practicing theory and theorizing practice in teacher education. In J. Loughran & T. Russell (Eds.), *Purpose, passion and pedagogy in teacher education* (pp. 13–31). London, England: Falmer Press.

Bullough, R. Jr. (2005). Being and becoming a mentor: School based teacher educators and teacher education identity. *Teaching and Teacher Education*, *21*(2), 143–155. doi:10.1016/j.tate.2004.12.002

Bullough, R. Jr, & Stokes, D. (1994). Analyzing personal teaching metaphors in preservice teacher education as a means for encouraging professional development. *American Educational Research Journal*, *31*(1), 197–224. doi:10.3102/00028312031001197

Burbach, M. E., Matkin, G. S., & Fritz, S. M. (2004). Teaching critical thinking in an introductory leadership course utilizing active learning strategies: A confirmatory study. *College Student Journal*, *38*(3), 482–493.

Burke, A. (1992). *Teaching - retrospect and prospect*. Dublin: Stationery Office.

Burke, A. J. (2017). Coaching teacher candidates- what does it look like? What does it sound like? *Journal of Curriculum, Teaching. Learning and Leadership in Education*, *2*(1), 5–10.

Burkhardt, J. M. (2010). Teaching information literacy: 50 standards-based exercises for college students (2nd ed.). Chicago: Chicago: American Library Association.

Burnard, P., & White, J. (2008). Creativity and performativity: Counterpoints in British and Australian education. *British Journal of Educational Research*, *34*(5), 667–682. doi:10.1080/01411920802224238

Burn, K. (2007). Professional knowledge and identity in a contested discipline: Challenges for student teachers and teacher educators. *Oxford Review of Education*, *33*(4), 445–467. doi:10.1080/03054980701450886

Butler, H. A. (2012). Halpern Critical Thinking Assessment Predicts Real-World Outcomes of Critical Thinking. *Applied Cognitive Psychology*, *26*(5), 721–729. doi:10.1002/acp.2851

Butler, H. A., Dwyer, C. P., Hogan, M. J., Franco, A., Rivas, S. F., Saiz, C., & Almeida, L. S. (2012). The Halpern critical thinking assessment and real-world outcomes: Cross-national applications. *Thinking Skills and Creativity*, *7*(2), 112–121. doi:10.1016/j.tsc.2012.04.001

Bybee, R. W. (2014). The BSCS 5E instructional model: Personal reflections and contemporary implications. *Science and Children*, *51*(8), 10–13. doi:10.2505/4c14_051_08_10

Bybee, R. W., Taylor, J. A., Gardner, A., Van Scotter, P., Carlson Powell, J., Westbrook, A., & Landes, N. (2006). *BSCS 5E instructional model: Origins and effectiveness. A report prepared for the Office of Science Education, National Institutes of Health*. Colorado Springs, CO: BSCS.

Cadwell, L. B. (1997). *Bringing Reggio Emilia home*. New York, NY: Teachers College Press.

Cadwell, L. B. (2003). *The Reggio approach to early childhood education: Bringing learning to life*. New York, NY: Teachers College Press.

Calderhead, J., & Robson, M. (1991). Images of teaching: Student teachers' early conception of classroom practice. *Teaching and Teacher Education*, *7*(1), 1–8. doi:10.1016/0742-051X(91)90053-R

Campbell, M. (2015). Collaborating on critical thinking: The team critique. *Journal of Curriculum and Teaching*, *4*(2), 86–95. doi:10.5430/jct.v4n2p86

Campbell, P. F., & Malkus, N. N. (2011). The impact of elementary mathematics coaches on student achievement. *The Elementary School Journal*, *111*(3), 430–454. doi:10.1086/657654

Campbell, T., Oh, P. S., Maughn, M., Kiriazis, N., & Zuwallack, R. (2014). A review of modeling pedagogies: Pedagogical functions, discursive acts, and technology in modeling instruction. *Eurasia Journal of Mathematics, Science, and Technology Education*, *11*, 159–176.

Candy, P. C. (2015). *Lifelong learning and information literacy*. Available from: https://www.researchgate.net/publication/268299706_Lifelong_Learning_and_Information_Literacy

Caribbean Examinations Council (CXC). (n.d.). *CCSCC-Caribbean Certificate of Secondary Level Competence*. Retrieved July 01, 2018 from http://www.cxc.org/examinations/ccslc/

Carlan, V., Rubin, R., & Morgan, B. (2005). *Cooperative Learning, Mathematical Problem Solving, and Latinos*. San Diego: American Educational Research Association. Retrieved from http://www.cimt.plymouth.ac.uk/journal/morgan.pdf

Carpenter, T. P., Fennema, E., Peterson, P. L., Chiang, C., & Loef, M. (1989). Using knowledge of children's mathematics thinking in classroom teaching: An experimental study. *American Educational Research Journal*, *26*(4), 32. doi:10.3102/00028312026004499

Carter, A. G., Creedy, D. K., & Sidebotham, M. (2016). Efficacy of teaching methods used to develop critical thinking in nursing and midwifery undergraduate students: A systematic review of the literature. *Nurse Education Today*, *40*, 209–218. doi:10.1016/j.nedt.2016.03.010 PMID:27125175

Carter, K. (1993). The place of story in the study of teaching and teacher education. *Educational Researcher*, *22*(1), 5–12. doi:10.3102/0013189X022001005

Case, R., & Daniels, L. (n.d.). *Introduction to the TC2 conception of critical thinking: appendix A*. Available from The Critical Thinking Consortium: https://tc2.ca/pdf/About%20Critical%20Thinking/Online%20Articles/Understanding%20Critical%20Thinking/Introduction%20to%20the%20TC2%20Conception%20w_%20new%20copyright.pdf

Ceppi, G., & Zini, M. (Eds.). (1998). *Children, spaces, relations*. Modena, Italy: Domas Academy Research Center.

Cetina, K. K. (1999). *Epistemic cultures: how the sciences make knowledge*. Cambridge, MA: Harvard University Press.

Chaffee, J. (2010). *Thinking Critically*. Boston: Houghton Mifflin Company.

Chan, Y., & Wong, N. (2014). Worldviews, religions, and beliefs about teaching and learning: Perception of mathematics teachers with different religious backgrounds. *Educational Studies in Mathematics*, *87*(3), 251–277. doi:10.100710649-014-9555-1

Chapman, O. (2007). Facilitating preservice teachers' development of mathematics knowledge for teaching arithmetic operations. *Journal of Mathematics Teacher Education*, *10*(2), 8.

Chard, S. (1998). *The Project Approach: Book one—Making curriculum come alive*. New York, NY: Scholastic.

Chard, S., Kogan, Y., & Castillo, C. (2017). *Picturing the Project Approach: Creative explorations in early learning*. Lewisville, NC: Gryphon House.

Charmaz, K. (2006). *Constructing grounded theory: A practical guide through qualitative analysis*. Thousand Oaks, CA: SAGE Publications Ltd.

Chenault, T. G., & Duclos-Orsello, E. D. (2008). An act of translation: The need to understand students' understanding of critical thinking in the undergraduate classroom. *The Journal of Effective Teaching*, *8*(2), 5–20.

Chickering, A. W., & Gamson, Z. F. (n.d.). Seven principles for good practice in undergraduate education.

Chinn, C. A., Anderson, R. C., & Waggoner, M. A. (2001). Patterns of discourse in two kinds of literature discussion. *Reading Research Quarterly*, *36*(4), 378–411. doi:10.1598/RRQ.36.4.3

Cho, S. (2013). *Critical pedagogy and social change: Critical Analysis on the Language of Possibility*. NY: Routledge.

Choy, S. C., & Cheah, P. K. (2009). Teacher perceptions of critical thinking among students and its influence on higher education. *International Journal on Teaching and Learning in Higher Education*, 20(2), 198–206.

Cizek, G. J. (1993). *Reactions to the National Academy of Education report: Setting performance standards for student achievement*. Washington, DC: National Assessment Governing Board.

Cizek, G. J. (2001). Conjectures on the rise and call of standard setting: An introduction to context and practice. In C. J. Cizek (Ed.), *Setting performance standards: Concepts, methods, and perspectives* (pp. 3–17). Mahwah, NJ: Lawrence Erlbaum.

Clandinin, D. (2007). *Handbook of narrative inquiry*. Thousand Oaks: SAGE Publications. doi:10.4135/9781452226552

Clandinin, D., Downey, C. A., & Huber, J. (2009). Attending to changing landscapes: Shaping the interwoven identities of teachers and teacher educators. *Asia-Pacific Journal of Teacher Education*, 37(2), 141–154. doi:10.1080/13598660902806316

Clauser, B. E., Mee, J., Baldwin, S. G., Margolis, M. J., & Dillon, G. F. (2009). Judges' use of examinee performance data in an Angoff standard-setting exercise for a medical licensing examination: An experimental study. *Journal of Educational Measurement*, 46(4), 390–407. doi:10.1111/j.1745-3984.2009.00089.x

Cochran-Smith, M., & Villegas, A. M. (2015). Research on teacher preparation: Charting the landscape of a sprawling field. In D. H. Gitomer & C. A. Bell (Eds.), *Handbook of research on teaching* (5th ed., pp. 439–548). Washington, DC: American Educational Research Association.

Cole, D., & Zhou, J. (2014). Diversity and collegiate experiences affecting self-perceived gains in critical thinking: Which works and who benefits? *The Journal of General Education*, 63(1), 15–34. doi:10.1353/jge.2014.0000

Collins, R. (2014). Skills for the 21st century: Teaching higher order thinking. *Curriculum and Leadership, 12*(14). Retrieved from: http://www.curriculum.edu.au/leader/teaching_higher_order_thinking,37431.html?issueID=12910

Colucciello, M. L. (1999). Relationships between Critical Thinking Dispositions and Learning Styles. *Journal of Professional Nursing*, 15(5), 294–301. doi:10.1016/S8755-7223(99)80055-6 PMID:10554470

Common Core State Standards Initiative. (2010). *Common Core State Standards for English Language Arts and Literacy in History/Social Studies, Science, and Technical Subjects*. National Governors Association Center for Best Practices, Council of Chief State School Officers, Washington DC. Retrieved from http://www.corestandards.org/

Connelly, F., & Clandinin, D. (1988). *Teachers as Curriculum Planners: Narratives of Experience*. New York, USA: Teachers College Press.

Connor, C. M. (2017). Commentary on the special issue on instructional coaching models: Common elements of effective coaching models. *Theory into Practice*, 56(1), 78–83. doi:10.1080/00405841.2016.1274575

Conway, P. (2001). Anticipatory reflection while learning to teach: From a temporally truncated to a temporally distributed model of reflection in teacher education. *Teaching and Teacher Education*, 17(1), 89–106. doi:10.1016/S0742-051X(00)00040-8

Conway, P., & Clark, C. (2003). The journey outward: A re-examination of Fuller's concerns-based model of teacher development. *Teaching and Teacher Education*, 19(5), 465–482. doi:10.1016/S0742-051X(03)00046-5

Cook, J. (2009). Coming into my own as a teacher: Identity, disequilibrium, and the first year. *New Educator*, 5(4), 274–292. doi:10.1080/1547688X.2009.10399580

Cook-Sather, A. (2006). Newly betwixt and between: Revising liminality in the context of a teacher preparation Program. Retrieved from http://repository.brynmawr.edu/cgi/viewcontent.cgi?article=1009&context=edu_pubs

Core Committee, Institute for International Medical Education. (2002). Global minimum essential requirements in medical education. *Medical Teacher*, 24(2), 130–135. doi:10.1080/01421590220120731 PMID:12098431

Costa, A. L. (2001). Teacher behaviors that enable student thinking. In A. L. Costa (Ed.), *Developing minds: A resource book for teaching thinking* (3rd ed.; pp. 359–369). Alexandria, VA: Association for Supervision and Curriculum Development.

Costa, A. L., & Garmston, R. J. (2002). *Cognitive coaching: A foundation for renaissance schools*. Boston, MA: Christopher-Gordon Publishers.

Costa, A. L., & Kallick, B. (2008). *Learning and leading with habits of mind: 16 essential characteristics for success*. Alexandria, VA: ASCD.

Cotton, K. (1991). Close-Up #11: Teaching thinking skills. Northwest Regional Educational. Retrieved from http://educationnorthwest.org/6/cu11.html

Council of Chief State School Officers & National Governors Association Center for Best Practices. (2010). *Common core state standards for mathematics*. Author.

Cox, J. (2018). *Teaching strategies that enhance higher-order thinking*. Retrieved from http://www.teachhub.com/teaching-strategies-enhance-higher-order-thinking

Cox, J. (2018). Teaching strategies that enhance higher-order thinking. *Teachhub*. Retrieved from http://www.teachhub.com/teaching-strategies-enhance-higher-order-thinking

Cozolino, L. (2013). *The social neuroscience of education*. New York: W.W. Norton.

Craft, A., Jeffrey, B., & Leibling, M. (Eds.). (2001). *Creativity in education*. London: Continuum.

Craik, F. I. M., & Lockhart, R. S. (1972). Levels of processing: A framework for memory research. *Journal of Verbal Learning and Verbal Behavior*, 11(6), 671–684. doi:10.1016/S0022-5371(72)80001-X

Crawford, A., Zucker, T., Van Horne, B., & Landry, S. (2016). Integrating professional development content and formative assessment with the coaching process: The Texas school ready model. *Theory into Practice*, 56(1), 56–65. doi:10.1080/00405841.2016.1241945

Cremin, T. (2009). Creative teachers and creative teaching. In A. Wilson (Ed.), *Creativity in Primary Education: Achieving QTS Cross-Curricular Strand* (2nd ed., pp. 36–46). Exeter: Learning Matters.

Creswell, J. (2007). *Qualitative inquiry* (2nd ed.). Thousand Oaks, CA: SAGE Publications.

CRICO. (2014). *Malpractice Risks in the Diagnostic Process: 2014 CRICO Strategies National CBS Report*. Retrieved from https://www.rmf.harvard.edu/Malpractice-Data/Annual-Benchmark-Reports/Risks-in-the-Diagnostic-Process

Critical Thinking Consortium. (2013). *Critical thinking in elementary mathematics: What? Why? When? and How?* Retrieved from https://tc2.ca/uploads/PDFs/TIpsForTeachers/CT_elementary_math.pdf

Critical Thinking on the Web. (2015). *What is critical thinking*. Retrieved from www.austhink.com/critical/

Croso, C. (2013). Human rights are the key to the world we want. *Adult Education and Development*, 80, 78–85.

Crossley, M. (2010). Context matters in educational research and international development: Learning from the small states experience. *Prospects*, 40(4), 421–429. doi:10.100711125-010-9172-4

Csikszentmihalyi, M. (2006). Forward: developing creativity. In N. Jackson, M. Oliver, M. Shaw, & J. Wisdom (Eds.), *Developing creativity in higher education: An imaginative curriculum* (pp. xviii–xx). London: Routledge.

Curtis, A., Viyasar, T., Ahluwalia, V., & Lazarus, K. (2016). Educating medical students: Introducing a journal club. *The Clinical Teacher*, *13*(3), 233–234. doi:10.1111/tct.12356 PMID:26013431

Curtis, D., & Carter, M. (2011). *Reflecting children's lives: A handbook for planning child-centered curriculum.* Saint Paul, MN: Redleaf Press.

Curtis, D., & Carter, M. (2013). *The art of awareness: How observation can transform your teaching* (2nd ed.). St. Paul, MN: Redleaf Press.

Cuypers, S., & Haji, I. (2006). Education for critical thinking: Can it be nonindoctrinative? *Educational Philosophy and Theory*, *38*(6), 723–743. doi:10.1111/j.1469-5812.2006.00227.x

da Silva Bastos Cerullo, J. A., & da Cruz, D. (2010). Clinical reasoning and critical thinking. *Revista Latino-Americana de Enfermagem*, *18*(1), 124–129. doi:10.1590/S0104-11692010000100019 PMID:20428707

Daly, L., & Beloglovsky, M. (2015). *Loose parts: Inspiring play in young children.* St. Paul, MN: Redleaf Press.

Daly, W. M. (2001). The development of an alternative method in the assessment of critical thinking as an outcome of nursing education. *Journal of Advanced Nursing*, *36*(1), 120–130. doi:10.1046/j.1365-2648.2001.01949.x PMID:11555056

Dam, G., & Volman, M. (2004). Critical thinking as a citizenship competence: Teaching strategies. *Learning and Instruction*, *14*, 359–379.

Danielewicz, J. (2001). *Teaching selves: Identity, pedagogy, and teacher education.* Albany, NY, USA: State University of New York Press.

Darling-Hammond, L. (2006). Constructing 21st-century teacher education. *Journal of Teacher Education*, *57*(3), 300–314. doi:10.1177/0022487105285962

Darling-Hammond, L., & Bransford, J. (2005). *Preparing teachers for a changing world.* San Francisco, CA: John Wiley & Sons, Inc.

Darling-Hammond, L., & Bransford, J. (2005). *Preparing teachers for a changing world: What teachers should learn and be able to do.* San Francisco, CA: John Wiley & Sons.

Darling-Hammond, L., Hyler, M., & Gardner, M. (2017). *Effective Teacher Professional Development.* Palo Alto, CA: Learning Policy Institute.

Davis, E. A., Petish, D., & Smithey, J. (2006). Challenges new science teachers face. *Review of Educational Research*, *76*(4), 607–651. doi:10.3102/00346543076004607

Dawson, V. M., & Venville, G. (2010). Teaching strategies for developing students' argumentation skills about socioscientific issues in high school genetics. *Research in Science Education*, *40*(2), 133–148. doi:10.100711165-008-9104-y

Day, C. (2017). *Teachers' worlds and work: Understanding complexity, building quality.* Milton Park, UK: Routledge. doi:10.4324/9781315170091

Day, C., Kington, A., Stobart, B., & Sammons, P. (2006). The personal and professional selves of teachers: Stable and unstable identities. *British Educational Research Journal*, *32*(4), 601–616. doi:10.1080/01411920600775316

De Bono, E. (1985). *Six thinking hats: The power of focused thinking.* Mamaroneck, NY: The International Center for Creative Thinking.

Dede, C. (2007). *Transforming education for the 21st century: new pedagogies that help all students attain sophisticated learning outcomes.* Retrieved from http://www.gse.harvard.edu/~dedech/Dede_21stC-skills_semi-final.pdf

Dedoose Version 8.0.35. (2018). Web application for managing, analyzing, and presenting qualitative and mixed method research data. Los Angeles, CA: SocioCultural Research Consultants, LLC. Retrieved from www.dedoose.com

Deng, S., Sinha, A. P., & Zhao, H. (2016). Adapting sentiment lexicons to domain- specific social media texts. *Decision Support Systems*, *94*, 65–76.

Dennicka, R., & Exley, K. (1998). Teaching and learning in groups and teams. *Biochemical Education*, *26*(2), 111–115. doi:10.1016/S0307-4412(98)00028-4

Desimone, L. M., & Pak, K. (2016). Instructional coaching as high-quality professional development. *Theory into Practice*, *56*(1), 3–12. doi:10.1080/00405841.2016.1241947

Dewey, J. (1933). *How we think*. Boston: Heath and Co.

Dewey, J. (1990). *The school and society and the child and the curriculum*. Chicago, IL: The University of Chicago Press. (Originally published 1956) doi:10.7208/chicago/9780226112114.001.0001

Dickerson, P. S. (2005). Nurturing critical thinkers. *Journal of Continuing Education in Nursing*, *36*(2), 68–72. doi:10.3928/0022-0124-20050301-06 PMID:15835581

Dilley, A., Kaufman, J. C., Kennedy, C., & Plucker, J. A. (2015). What we know about critical thinking. Partnership For 21st Century Learning. Retrieved from http://www.p21.org/ourwork/4csresearchseries/criticalthinking

Dinham, J., Chalk, B., Beltman, S., Glass, C., & Nguyen, B. (2016). Pathways to resilience: How drawings reveal pre-service teachers' core narratives underpinning their future teacher-selves. *Asia-Pacific Journal of Teacher Education*, 1–9.

Dobrzykowski, T. M. (1994). Teaching strategies to promote critical thinking skills in nursing staff. *Journal of Continuing Education in Nursing*, *25*, 272–276. PMID:7868746

Doddington, C. (2008). Critical thinking as a source of respect for persons: A critique. In M. Mason (Ed.), *Critical thinking and learning* (pp. 109–119). Oxford: Blackwell Publishing.

Dodge, D. T., Heroman, C., Berke, K., Colker, L. J., Bickart, T., Baker, H., ... Tabors, P. O. (2016). *The Creative Curriculum for preschool* (6th ed.). Washington, DC: Teaching Strategies, Inc.

Dole, J. A., Nokes, J. D., & Drits, D. (2009). Cognitive strategy instruction. In G. G. Duffy & S. E. Israel (Eds.), *Handbook of research on reading comprehension* (pp. 347–372). Mahwah, NJ: Erlbaum.

Dongo-Montoya, A. O. (2018). Marx and Piaget: Theoretical and epistemological approaches. *Educação e Realidade*, *43*(1), 7–22. doi:10.1590/2175-623660803

Donovan, L., Green, T. D., & Mason, C. (2014). Examining the 21st century classroom: Developing an innovation configuration map. *Journal of Educational Computing Research*, *50*(2), 161–178. doi:10.2190/EC.50.2.a

Donovan, M. S., & Bransford, J. D. (Eds.). (2005). *How students learn: History, mathematics, and science in the classroom*. Washington, DC: National Academy Press.

Downer, J. T., Stuhlman, M., Schweig, J., Martinez, J. F., & Ruzek, E. (2018). Measuring effective teacher-student interactions from a student perspective: A multi-level analysis. *The Journal of Early Adolescence*, *35*(5-6), 722–758. doi:10.1177/0272431614564059

Dozier, M., Peloso, E., Lewis, E., Laurenceau, J. P., & Levine, S. (2008). Effects of an attachment-based intervention on the cortisol production of infants and toddlers in foster care. *Developmental Psychopathy*, *20*(3), 845–859. doi:10.1017/S0954579408000400 PMID:18606034

Drake, M. R. (2016). Learning to coach in practice-based teacher education: A self-study. *Studying Teacher Education*, *12*(3), 244–266. doi:10.1080/17425964.2016.1237871

Driver, R., Leach, J., Millar, R., & Scott, P. (1996). *Young People's Images of Science*. Buckingham, UK: Open University Press.

Driver, R., Newton, P., & Osborne, J. (2000). Establishing the norms of scientific argumentation in classrooms. *Science Education*, *84*(3), 287–312. doi:10.1002/(SICI)1098-237X(200005)84:3<287::AID-SCE1>3.0.CO;2-A

Duffy, T. M., & Raymer, P. L. (2010). A practical guide and a constructivist rationale for inquiry-based learning. *Educational Technology*, *46*(3), 3–13.

DuFour, R. (2004). What is a professional learning community? *Educational Leadership*, *61*(8), 6–11.

Dufresne, J. R., Gerace, W. J., Leonard, W. J., Mestre, J. P., & Wenk, L. (1996). Classtalk: A Classroom Communication System for Active Learning. *Journal of Computing in Higher Education*, *7*(2), 3–47. doi:10.1007/BF02948592

Dunn, D. S., Halonen, J. S., & Smith, R. A. (Eds.). (2008). *Teaching critical thinking in psychology: A handbook of best practices*. Oxford, UK: Wiley-Blackwell. doi:10.1002/9781444305173

Dunn, R., & Dunn, K. (1999). *The complete guide to the Learning Styles inservice system*. Boston, MA: Allyn & Bacon.

Duron, R., Limbach, B., & Waugh, W. (2006). Critical thinking framework for any discipline. *International Journal on Teaching and Learning in Higher Education*, *17*(2), 160–166.

Duschl, R. A., Schweingruber, H. A., & Shouse, A. W. (Eds.). (2007). *Taking science to school: Learning and teaching science in grades K-8*. Washington, DC: National Academies Press.

Dutton, J. L. (2017). *English teachers in the making: Portraits of pre-service teachers' journeys to teaching*. Unpublished PhD thesis, University of Sydney, Sydney, Australia.

Earl, L. (2003). *Assessment as Learning: Using classroom assessment to maximize student learning*. Thousand Oaks, CA: Corwin Press, Inc.

Eby, J. W., & Kujawa, E. (1994). *Reflective planning, teaching, and evaluation: K-12*. New York, NY: Macmillan.

Eckhoff, A., & Urbach, J. (2008). Understanding imaginative thinking during early childhood: Sociocultural conceptions of creativity and imaginative thought. *Early Childhood Education Journal*, *36*(2), 179–185. doi:10.100710643-008-0261-4

Educational Resources Information Center. (1988). Critical thinking skills and teacher education. Washington, DC: ERIC Clearing house on Teacher Education Digest 3-88.

Edwards, C. P. (2002). Three approaches from Europe: Waldorf, Montessori, and Reggio Emilia. *Early Childhood Research & Practice*, *4*(1), 1–24. Retrieved from http://ecrp.uiuc.edu/v4n1/edwards.html

Edwards, C. P., Gandini, L., & Forman, G. (2012). *The hundred languages of children: The Reggio Emilia Experience in Transformation* (3rd ed.). Santa Barbara, CA: Praeger.

Eisenberg, M. (2004). Information literacy: essential skills for the information age (2nd ed.). Westport, CT: Libraries Unlimited.

Eisenberg, M. B. (2008). Information Literacy: Essential Skills for the Information Age. *DESIDOC Journal of Library and Information Technology*, *28*(2), 39–47. doi:10.14429/djlit.28.2.166

Elbaz, F. (1991). Research on teachers' knowledge. *Journal of Curriculum Studies*, *23*, 1–19. doi:10.1080/0022027910230101

Elbow, P. (2010). *Teaching Thinking by Teaching Writing*. Academic Press.

Elder, L. (2017). IT'S CRITICAL. *USA Today, 145*, 42-43. Retrieved from https://search.proquest.com/docview/1858 621016?accountid=45040

Elder, L., & Paul, R. (2010). Critical thinking development: A stage theory. *Critical Thinking.org*. Retrieved from www.criticalthinking.org

Elder, L., & Paul, R. (1994). Critical thinking: Why we must transform our teaching. *Journal of Developmental Education, 18*(1), 34–35.

Elder, L., & Paul, R. (2004). Critical thinking … and the art of close reading, Part III. *Journal of Developmental Education, 28*(1), 36–37.

Elder, L., & Paul, R. (2010). Critical thinking: Competency standards essential for the cultivation of intellectual skills. *Journal of Developmental Education, 34*(2), 39–40.

Elliott, B., Oty, K., McArthur, J., & Clark, B. (2001). The effect of an interdisciplinary algebra/science course on students' problem solving skills, critical thinking skills and attitudes towards mathematics. *International Journal of Mathematical Education in Science and Technology, 32*(6), 811–816. doi:10.1080/00207390110053784

Ellison, J., & Hayes, C. (2009). *Cognitive coaching. Coaching: Approaches and perspectives* (pp. 70–90). Thousand Oaks, CA: Corwin Press.

English Oxford Living Dictionaries. (2016). *Word of the Year 2016*. Retrieved from https://www.oxforddictionaries.com/press/news/2016/12/11/WOTY-16

English Oxford Living Dictionaries. (2018). *Word of the Year 2018*. Retrieved from https://en.oxforddictionaries.com/word-of-the-year/word-of-the-year-2018

English Teaching Professional. (2018). *Critical thinking skills in the classroom: Socrates, Bloom and De Bono*. Retrieved from https://www.etprofessional.com/critical-thinking-skills-in-the-classroom-socrates-bloom-and-de-bono

Ennis, R. (1985). Goals for critical thinking curriculum. In A. Costa (Ed.), Developing Minds (pp. 54-57). Alexandria, VA: Association for Supervision and Curriculum Development.

Ennis, R. (1997). Incorporating Critical Thinking in the Curriculum: An Introduction to Some Basic Issues. *Inquiry: Critical Thinking across the Disciplines, 16*(3), 1-9.

Ennis, R. H. (2011). Critical thinking: Reflection and perspective (Part I). *Inquiry: Critical Thinking across the Disciplines, 26*(1), 4-18. doi:10.5840/inquiryctnews20112613

Ennis, R. (2018). Critical Thinking Across the Curriculum: A vision. *Topoi, 37*(1), 165–184. doi:10.100711245-016-9401-4

Ennis, R. H. (1962). A concept of critical thinking. *Harvard Educational Review, 32*(1), 81–111.

Ennis, R. H. (1962). A concept of critical thinking: A proposed basis for research in the teaching and evaluation of critical thinking ability. *Harvard Educational Review, 32*, 81–111.

Ennis, R. H. (1987). A taxonomy of critical thinking dispositions and abilities. In J. B. Beron & R. J. Sternberg (Eds.), *Teaching Critical Thinking Skills* (pp. 9–26). New York: Freeman.

Ennis, R. H. (1989). Critical thinking and subject specificity: Clarification and needed research. *Educational Researcher, 18*(3), 4–10. doi:10.3102/0013189X018003004

Ennis, R. H. (1993). Critical Thinking Assessment. *Theory into Practice, 32*(3), 179–186. doi:10.1080/00405849309543594

Erickson, L. H. (2007). *Concept based curriculum and instruction for the thinking classroom.* Thousand Oaks, CA: Corwin Press.

Etkina, E., Mestre, J. P., & O'Donnell, A. (2005). The Impact of the Cognitive Revolution on Science Learning and Teaching. In J. Royer (Ed.), *The impact of the cognitive revolution on Educational Psychology* (pp. 119–164). Greenwich, CT: Information Age Publishing.

European Union Education Ministers. (2015). *Declaration on promoting citizenship and the common values of freedom, tolerance, and non-discrimination through education.* Retrieved from http://ec.europa.eu/dgs/education_culture/repository/education/news/2015/documents/citizenship-education-declaration_en.pdf

Evagorou, M., Sadler, T. D., & Tal, T. (2011). Metalogue: Assessment, Audience, and Authenticity for Teaching SSI and Argumentation. In T. D. Sadler (Ed.), *Socio-scientific issues in the classroom.* Netherlands: Springer Science Business Media. doi:10.1007/978-94-007-1159-4_9

Evans, J. (2014). Problems with Standardized Testing. *Education Today*, 2-6.

Facione, P. A. (1990). Critical thinking: A statement of expert consensus for purposes of educational assessment and instruction. Research findings and recommendations. *American Philosophical Association.* Doi": doi:10.1016/j.tsc.2009.07.002

Facione, P. A. (1990). *Executive Summary- Critical thinking: A statement of expert consensus for purposes of educational assessment and instruction* (The Delphi Report). Retrieved from http://assessment.aas.duke.edu/documents/Delphi_Report.pdf

Facione, P. A. (2007). Critical thinking: What it is and why it counts. Millbrae, LA: Insight Assessment. The California Academic Press.

Facione, N. C., & Facione, P. A. J. (1996). Externalizing the critical thinking in clinical judgment. *Nursing Outlook*, *44*, 129–136. doi:10.1016/S0029-6554(06)80005-9 PMID:8794454

Facione, P. (1989). *Critical Thinking: A Statement of Expert Consensus for Purposes of Educational Assessment and Instruction (The Delphi Report). Research Findings and Recommendations.* Newark, DE: American Philosophical Association.

Facione, P. A. (1990). *Critical thinking: A statement of expert consensus for purposes of educational assessment and instruction—The Delphi report.* Millbrae, CA: California Academic Press.

Facione, P. A. (2011). Critical thinking: What it is and why it counts. *Insight Assessment*, *2007*, 1–23.

Facione, P. A., Facione, N. C., & Blohm, S. W. (2007). *The California Critical Thinking Skills Test: CCTST.* Millbrae, CA: California Academic Press.

Facione, P. A., Facione, N. C., & Giancarlo, C. A. (2000). The disposition toward critical thinking. *Informal Logic*, *20*(1), 61–84. doi:10.22329/il.v20i1.2254

Fahim, M., & Bagheri, M. B. (2012). Fostering critical thinking through Socrates' questioning in Iranian language institutes. *Journal of Language Teaching and Research*, *3*(6), 1122–1127. doi:10.4304/jltr.3.6.1122-1127

Fajet, W., Bello, M., Leftwisch, J., Mesler, J., & Shaver, A. (2005). Pre-service teachers' perceptions in beginning education classes. *Teaching and Teacher Education*, *21*(6), 717–727. doi:10.1016/j.tate.2005.05.002

Fallahi, M. (2012). Text-based Dyadic Conversation: The influence of partners' attitude and level of critical thinking. California State University, Chicago, IL.

Farquhar, C. (2018). Evidence-based medicine - the promise, the reality. *Australian and New Zealand Journal of Obstetrics and Gynaecology, 58*(1), 17–21. doi:10.1111/ajo.12768 PMID:29400399

Farr Darling, L., & Wright, I. (2004). Critical thinking and the social in social studies. In A. Sears & I. Wright (Eds.), *Challenges and Prospects for Canadian Social Studies*. Vancouver, Canada: Pacific Educational Press.

Faulkner, J., & Latham, G. (2016). Adventurous lives: Teacher qualities for 21st century learning. *Australian Journal of Teacher Education, 41*(4), 137–150. doi:10.14221/ajte.2016v41n4.9

Feiman-Nemser, S. (2001). From preparation to practice: Designing a continuum to strengthen and sustain teaching. *Teachers College Record, 103*(6), 42. doi:10.1111/0161-4681.00141

Feiman-Nemser, S. (2012). *Teachers as learners*. Cambridge, MA: Harvard Education Press.

Feiman-Nemser, S., & Buchmann, M. (1985). Pitfalls of experience in teacher preparation. *Teachers College Record, 87*(1), 53–65.

Feldman, R. (2015). The adaptive human parental brain: Implications for children's social development. *Trends in Neurosciences, 38*(6), 1–13. doi:10.1016/j.tins.2015.04.004 PMID:25956962

Felton, M., & Kuhn, D. (2001). The development of argumentive discourse skill. *Discourse Processes, 32*(2), 135–153. doi:10.1207/S15326950DP3202&3_03

Fennema, E., Franke, M. L., Carpenter, T. P., & Carey, D. (1993). Using children's mathematical knowledge in instruction. *American Educational Research Journal, 30*(3), 28. doi:10.3102/00028312030003555

Feuerstein, M. (2002). *Media literacy in support of critical thinking* (Unpublished doctoral dissertation). University of Liverpool.

Ficklin, F. L., Browne, V. L., Powell, R. C., & Carter, J. E. (1988). Faculty and house staff members as role models. *Journal of Medical Education, 63*, 392–396. PMID:3361591

Fina, A., & Georgakopoulou, A. (2012). *Analyzing narrative: Discourse and sociolinguistic perspectives*. Cambridge, UK: Cambridge University Press.

Finn, P. (2018). Critical thinking for future helping professionals: why, what, and how. *ASHA*. Retrieved from https://www.asha.org/Articles/Critical-Thinking-for-Future-Helping-Professionals-Why-What-and-How/

Fischer, C. W. (1989). *Effects of a developmental drama-inquiry process on creative and critical thinking skills in early adolescent students* (Unpublished Doctoral Dissertation). College of Education, Kansas State University.

Fisher, A. (2007). *Critical thinking: An introduction*. Cambridge, UK: Cambridge University Press.

Fisher, R. (2004). What is creativity? In R. Fisher & M. Williams (Eds.), *Unlocking Creativity: Teaching Across the Curriculum* (pp. 6–20). New York, NY: David Fulton Publishers.

Fiske, A., & O'Riley, A. A. (2016). Toward an understanding of late life suicidal behavior: The role of lifespan developmental theory. *Aging & Mental Health, 20*(2), 123–130. doi:10.1080/13607863.2015.1078282 PMID:26305860

Fitterer, H., Harwood, S., Locklear, K., & Lapid, J. (2008). *T4S Teach for success*. WestEd.

Fitzpatrick, A. R. (1989). Social influences in standard-setting: The effects of social interaction on group judgments. *Review of Educational Research, 59*(3), 315–328. doi:10.3102/00346543059003315

Flake, M. (2014). *An investigation of how pre-service teachers' ability to professionally notice children's mathematical thinking relates to their own mathematical knowledge for teaching* (Unpublished doctoral dissertation). University of Kansas, Lawrence, KS.

Fleith, D. (2000). Teacher and student perceptions of creativity in the classroom. *Roeper Review, 22*(3), 148–153. doi:10.1080/02783190009554022

Flodgren, G., Rojas-Reyes, M. X., Cole, N., & Foxcroft, D. R. (2012). Effectiveness of organisational infrastructures to promote evidence-based nursing practice. *The Cochrane Database of Systematic Reviews, 2*. doi:.CD002212.pub2 doi:10.1002/14651858

Florence, D. C. (2014). A history of critical thinking as an educational goal in graduate theological schools. *Christian Higher Education, 13*(5), 352–361. doi:10.1080/15363759.2014.949164

Flores, M. (2005). How do teachers learn in the workplace? Findings from an empirical study carried out in Portugal. *Journal of In-service Education, 31*(3), 485–508. doi:10.1080/13674580500200491

Forrester, J. C. (2008). Thinking creatively; Thinking Critically. *Asian Social Science, 4*(5), 100–105.

Foundation for Critical Thinking. (2017, July). *Become certified in the Paul-Elder framework for critical thinking.* Available from Foundation for Critical Thinking: http://www.criticalthinking.org/data/pages/62/2241c25a71d4f0d7c 7c47a621832551256329c1605487.pdf

Franklin, K. Y. (2005). The importance of information literacy: insights from the next generation of scholars. *ACRL Twelfth National Conference,* 388-396.

Fraser, S., & Gestwicki, C. (2002). *Authentic childhood: Exploring Reggio Emilia in the classroom.* Boston, MA: Delmar.

Freire, P. (1978). *Pedagogy in process: The letters to Guinea Bissau.* New York, NY: The Seabury.

Freire, P. (1985). *The politics of education: Culture, power and liberation.* South Hadley, MA: Bergin & Garvey Publishers. doi:10.1007/978-1-349-17771-4

Freire, P. (1995). *Pedagogy of hope. Reliving pedagogy of the oppressed.* New York, NY: Continuum.

Freire, P. (1996). *Pedagogy of the oppressed* (2nd ed.). New York: Penguin.

Freire, P. (2000). *Pedagogy of Freedom: Ethics, Democracy, and Civic Courage.* Lanham, MD: Rowman & Littlefield Publishers, Inc.

Freire, P. (2000). *Pedagogy of the oppressed. 30th Anniversary edition.* New York, NY: Continuum.

Freire, P. (2005). *Teachers as cultural workers: Letters to those who dare teach* (D. Macedo, D. Koike, & A. Oliveira, Trans.). Cambridge, MA: Westview Press.

Freseman, R. D. (1990). *Improving higher order thinking of middle school geography students by teaching skills directly.* Fort Lauderdale, FL: Nova University.

Frijters, S., ten Dam, G., & Rijlaarsdam, G. (2008). Effects of dialogic learning on value-loaded critical thinking. *Learning and Instruction, 18*(1), 66–82. doi:10.1016/j.learninstruc.2006.11.001

Fuks, A., Boudreau, J. D., & Cassell, E. J. (2009). Teaching clinical thinking to first-year medical students. *Medical Teacher, 31*(2), 105–111. doi:10.1080/01421590802512979 PMID:19330669

Fullan, M. (1994). *Change forces: probing the depths of educational reform.* London: The Falmer Press.

Fullan, M. (2016). *The new meaning of educational change* (5th ed.). New York, NY: Teachers College Press.

Fullan, M., & Hargreaves, A. (2016). *Bringing the profession back in: Call to action.* Oxford, OH: Learning Forward.

Fung, I. Y. Y., Townsend, M. A. R., & Parr, J. M. (2004). *Teachers facilitating critical thinking in students: The search for a model and a method.* Paper presented at the European Conference on Educational Research, University of Crete, Rethymno, Greece.

Fung, D., & Howe, C. (2014). Group work and the learning of critical thinking in the Hong Kong secondary liberal studies curriculum. *Cambridge Journal of Education, 44*(2), 245–270. doi:10.1080/0305764X.2014.897685

Furlong, C. (2013). The teacher I wish to be: Exploring the influence of life histories on student teacher idealised identities. *European Journal of Teacher Education, 36*(1), 68–83. doi:10.1080/02619768.2012.678486

Furness, J., Cowie, B., & Cooper, B. (2017). Scoping the meaning of 'critical' in mathematical thinking for initial teacher education. *Policy Futures in Education, 15*(6), 713–728. doi:10.1177/1478210317719778

Galey, S. (2016). The evolving role of instructional coaches in U.S. policy contexts. *The William & Mary Educational Review, 4*(2), 54–71.

Gallucci, C., Van Lare, M. D., Yoon, I. H., & Boatright, B. (2010). Instructional coaching: Building theory about the role and organizational support for professional learning. *American Educational Research Journal, 47*(4), 919–963. doi:10.3102/0002831210371497

Ganesh, A., & Ganesh, G. (2010). Reflective writing by final year medical students: Lessons for curricular change. *The National Medical Journal of India, 23*, 226–230. PMID:21192519

Garcia-Mila, M., & Andersen, C. (2007). The cognitive foundations of learning argumentation. In S. Erduran & M. P. Jimenez-Aleixandre (Eds.), *Argumentation in science education* (pp. 29–45). Berlin, Germany: Springer. doi:10.1007/978-1-4020-6670-2_2

Gardiner, W., & Weisling, N. (2016). Mentoring 'inside' the action of teaching: Induction coaches' perspectives and practices. *Professional Development in Education, 42*(5), 671–686. doi:10.1080/19415257.2015.1084645

Gardner, H. (1993). *Frames of mind: The theory of multiple intelligences.* New York, NY: Basic Books.

Gardner, H. (2000). Project zero: Nelson Goodman's legacy in arts education. *The Journal of Aesthetics and Art Criticism, 245*(3), 245. doi:10.2307/432107

Gardner, H. (2011). *Frames of Mind: The Theory of Multiple Intelligences.* New York: Basic Books.

Gardner, H. (2011). *The unschooled mind: How children think and how schools should teach.* New York: Basic Books.

Gauder, H., & Jenkins, F. (2012). Engaging undergraduates in discipline-based research. *Reference Services Review, 40*(2), 277–294. doi:10.1108/00907321211228327

Gedrovics, J.; Mozelka, D.; Cedere, D. (2010). Alteration of students' interest in science topics in Latvia, 2003-2008. *Problems in Education in the 21st Century, 22*, 45-54.

Geertsen, R. H. (2003). Rethinking Thinking about Higher-Level Thinking. *Teaching Sociology, 31*(1), 1. doi:10.2307/3211421

Gélat, M. (2003). Taking others' perspectives in a peer interactional setting while preparing for a written argument. *Language and Education, 17*(5), 332–354. doi:10.1080/09500780308666855

Genhard, J. G. (1996). *Teaching English as a foreign language: A teacher self-development and methodology*. Ann Arbor, MI: The University of Michigan Press.

George, J., & Quamina-Aiyejina, L. (2003). *An Analysis of primary education in Trinidad and Tobago. United Kingdom*. Seven Oaks: Department of International Development Publications.

George, J., Worrell, P., & Rampersad, J. (2002). Messages about good teaching: Primary teacher trainees' experiences of the practicum in Trinidad and Tobago. *International Journal of Educational Development, 22*(3-4), 291–304. doi:10.1016/S0738-0593(01)00067-0

Gestwicki, C. (2017). *Developmentally appropriate practice: Curriculum and development in early education* (6th ed.). Boston, MA: Cengage Learning.

Getty, A., & Chibnall, D. (2013). Skillful scaffolding: using information litercy techniques to enhance literature studies. *Currents in Teaching and Learning, 6*(), 53-65.

Giaimo-Ballard, C., & Hyatt, L. (2012, Fall). Reflection-in-action teaching strategies used by faculty to enhance teaching and learning. *Networks: An Online Teaching Journal for Teacher Research, 14*(2), 1–11.

Gigerenzer, G., & Todd, P. M. (1999). *Simple heuristics that make us smart*. New York: Oxford University Press.

Gillies, R. M., & Boyle, M. (2010). Teachers' reflections on cooperative learning: Issues of implementation. *Teaching and Teacher Education, 26*(4), 933–940. doi:10.1016/j.tate.2009.10.034

Gilligan, A. L. (1999). Education towards a feminist imagination. In B. Connolly & A. B. Ryan (Eds.), *Women and Education in Ireland* (Vol. 1, pp. 201–213). Maynooth: MACE.

Gini-Newman, G., & Case, R. (2018). *Creating thinking classrooms: Leading educational change for this century*. Thousand Oaks, CA: Sage.

Ginsburg, K. R. (2007). The importance of play in promoting healthy child development and maintaining strong parent-child bonds. *American Academy of Pediatrics, 119*(182), 182–191. doi:10.1542/peds.2006-2697 PMID:17200287

Giraud, G., Impara, J. C., & Plake, B. S. (2005). Teachers' conceptions of target examinees in Angoff standard setting. *Applied Measurement in Education, 18*(3), 223–232. doi:10.120715324818ame1803_2

Giroux, H. (2004a). *Teachers as intellectuals: Towards a critical pedagogy of learning*. South Hadley, MA: Bergin and Garvey.

Giroux, H. A. (2004b). Critical pedagogy and postmodern/modern divide: Towards pedagogy of democratization. *Teacher Education Quarterly, 31*(1), 31–47.

Giroux, H. A. (2011). *On critical pedagogy*. London: The Continuum International Publishing Group.

Glaser, B., & Strauss, A. (1967). *The discovery of grounded theory: Strategies for qualitative research*. Hawthorne, NY: Aldine Publishing Company.

Glasser, E. M. (1941). *An experiment in the development of critical thinking*. New York, NY: Teachers College, Columbia University.

Goel, M., & Aggarwal, P. (2012). A comparative study of self-confidence of single child and child with sibling. *The International Journal of Social Sciences (Islamabad), 2*(3), 89–98.

Goffe, L. C., & Deane, N. H. (1974). *Questioning Our Questions*. Academic Press.

Gokhale, A. A. (1995). Collaborative learning enhances critical thinking. *Journal of Technology Education*, 7(1), 22–30. doi:10.21061/jte.v7i1.a.2

Golanics, J. D., & Nussbaum, E. M. (2008). Enhancing collaborative online argumentation through question elaboration and goal instructions. *Journal of Computer Assisted Learning*, 24(3), 167–180. doi:10.1111/j.1365-2729.2007.00251.x

Gopaul, B. (2011). Distinction in doctoral education: Using Bourdieu's tools to assess the socialization of doctoral students. *Equity & Excellence in Education*, 44(1), 10–21. doi:10.1080/10665684.2011.539468

Gough, D. (1991). Thinking about thinking. Alexandria, VA: National Association of Elementary School Principals.

Gouvea, J., & Passmore, C. (2017). Models of versus models for: Toward an Agent-based conception of modeling in the science classroom. *Sci & Educ*, 26(49). doi:10.100711191-017-9884-4

Graber, M. (2005). Diagnostic errors in medicine: A case of neglect. *Joint Commission Journal on Quality and Patient Safety*, 31(2), 106–113. doi:10.1016/S1553-7250(05)31015-4 PMID:15791770

Graber, M. L. (2013). The incidence of diagnostic error in medicine. *BMJ Quality & Safety*, 22(Suppl 2), ii21–ii27. doi:10.1136/bmjqs-2012-001615 PMID:23771902

Graff, G. (2008). *Clueless in academe: How schooling obscures the life of the mind.* New Haven: CT Yale University Press.

Grapin, S., Haas, A., & Lee, O. (2018, July). *Science and language instruction and assessment with all students including English learners.* Workshop presented at National Science Education Leadership Association Summer Leadership Institute, Philadelphia, PA.

Grassian, E. S., & Kaplowitz, J. R. (2010). Information literacy instruction: Theory and practice (2nd edition). Journal of Documentation, 66(3), 457-458.

Great Idea. Barrier Games. (2018, December 7). Retrieved from https://ealresources.bell-foundation.org.uk/teachers/great-ideas-barrier-games

Greenleaf, C. L., Litman, C., Hanson, T. L., Rosen, R., Boscardin, C. K., Herman, J., ... Jones, B. (2011). Integrating literacy and science in biology: Teaching and learning impacts of reading apprenticeship professional development. *American Educational Research Journal*, 48(3), 647–717. doi:10.3102/0002831210384839

Grootenboer, P. (2013). The praxis of mathematics teaching: Developing mathematics identities. *Pedagogy, Culture & Society*, 21(3), 321–342. doi:10.1080/14681366.2012.759131

Grossman, P., Compton, C., Igra, D., Ronfeldt, M., Shahan, E., & Williamson, P. (2009). Teaching practice a cross-professional perspective. *Teachers College Record*, 111(9), 2055–2100.

Guan Eng Ho, D. (2005). Why do teachers ask the questions they ask? *Regional Language Centre Journal*, 36(3), 297–310. doi:10.1177/0033688205060052

Guba, E. G., & Lincoln, Y. S. (1994). Competing paradigms in qualitative research. In N. K. Denzin & Y. S. Lincoln (Eds.), *Handbook of qualitative research* (pp. 105–117). Thousand Oaks, CA: Sage Publications, Inc.

Guest, K. (2000). Introducing critical thinking to non-standard entry students: The use of a catalyst to spark debate. *Teaching in Higher Education*, 5(3), 289–299. doi:10.1080/713699139

Gunasekara, C.S. (2008). Fostering independent learning and critical thinking in management higher education using an information literacy framework. *Journal of Information Literacy, 2*(2), 74-85.

Gunn, T. M., Grigg, L. M., & Pomahac, G. A. (2008). Critical thinking in education: Can bio-ethical issues and questioning strategies increase science understanding. *The Journal of Educational Thought*, *42*(2), 165–183.

Gunn, T., Grigg, L., & Pomahac, G. (2006). Critical thinking and bio-ethical decision making in the middle school classroom. *International Journal of Learning*, *13*(5), 129–136.

Gupta, K., Iranfar, S., Iranfar, K., Mehraban, B., Montazeri, N., & ... . (2012). Validly and Reliability of California Critical Thinking Disposition Inventory (CCTDI) in Kermanshah University of Medical Sciences. *Educational Research in Medical Sciences*, *1*, e77064.

Gurol, A., Uslu, S., Polat, O. E., Yigit, N., & Yucel, O. (2013). Critical thinking disposition in students of vocational school of health services. Electronic Journal of Vocational Colleges, 28-36.

Guskey, T. (2002). Professional development and teacher change. *Teachers and Teaching*, *8*(3), 381–391. doi:10.1080/135406002100000512

Guskey, T., & Suk Yoon, K. (2009). What works in professional development? *Phi Delta Kappan*, *90*(7), 495–500. doi:10.1177/003172170909000709

Güven, M., & Kürüm, D. (2006). Öğrenme Stilleri ve Eleştirel Düşünme Arasındaki İlişkiye Genel Bir Bakış. *Sosyal Bilimler Dergisi*, *6*(1), 75–89.

Guyatt, G. (1992). Evidence-based medicine. A new approach to teaching the practice of medicine. *Journal of the American Medical Association*, *268*(17), 2420–2425. doi:10.1001/jama.1992.03490170092032 PMID:1404801

Haberlin, S. (2018). Problematizing notions of critical thinking with preservice teachers: A self-study imparting critical thinking strategies to preservice teachers: *A Self-Study. Action in Teacher Education*, *40*(3), 305–318. doi:10.1080/01 626620.2018.1486751

Haertel, E. H., & Lorie, W. A. (2004). Validating standards-based test score interpretations. *Measurement: Interdisciplinary Research and Perspectives*, *2*(2), 61–103. doi:10.120715366359mea0202_1

Hafferty, F. W., & Franks, R. (1994). The hidden curriculum, ethics teaching, and the structure of medical education. *Academic Medicine*, *69*(11), 861–871. doi:10.1097/00001888-199411000-00001 PMID:7945681

Hager, P., & Kaye, M. (1992). Critical Thinking in Teacher Education: A Process-Oriented Research Agenda. *Australian Journal of Teacher Education*, *17*(2). doi:10.14221/ajte.1992v17n2.4

Hahn Tapper, A. J. (2013). A pedagogy of social justice education: Social identity theory, intersectionality, and empowerment. *Conflict Resolution Quarterly*, *30*(4), 411–445. doi:10.1002/crq.21072

Halliday, M. A. K. (2004). The Language of Science. In J. J. Webster (Ed.), *The Collected Works of M.A.K. Halliday*. London: Continuum.

Hallman, H. (2007). Negotiating teacher identity: Exploring the use of electronic teaching portfolios with preservice English teachers. *International Reading Association, 50*(6), 474-485.

Halpern, D. (2011). *Critical thinking handout: Critical thinking workshop for helping our students become better thinkers.* Retrieved from: https://louisville.edu/ideastoaction/-/files/featured/halpern/critical-thinking.pdf

Halpern, D. F. (1998). Teaching critical thinking for transfer across domains: Dispositions, skills, structure training, and metacognitive monitoring. *The American Psychologist*, *53*(4), 449–455. doi:10.1037/0003-066X.53.4.449 PMID:9572008

Halpern, D. F. (1999). Teaching for critical thinking: Helping college students develop the skills and dispositions of a critical thinker. *New Directions for Teaching and Learning*, *80*(80), 69–74. doi:10.1002/tl.8005

Halpern, D. F. (2007). The nature and nurture of critical thinking. In R. J. Sternberg, H. L. Roediger III, & D. F. Halpern (Eds.), *Critical Thinking in Psychology* (pp. 1–14). Cambridge, NY: Cambridge University Press.

Halpern, D. F. (2014). *An Introduction to Critical Thinking* (5th ed.). New York: Psychology Press.

Halpern, D. F. (2014). *Thought and knowledge: An introduction to critical thinking* (5th ed.). New York: Psychology Press.

Harasym, P. H., Tsai, T. C., & Hemmati, P. (2008). Current trends in developing medical students critical thinking abilities. *The Kaohsiung Journal of Medical Sciences*, *24*(7), 341–355. doi:10.1016/S1607-551X(08)70131-1 PMID:18805749

Hargreaves, A. (1998). The emotional practice of teaching. *Teaching and Teacher Education*, *14*(8), 835–854. doi:10.1016/S0742-051X(98)00025-0

Hargreaves, K. (2016). Reflection in medical education. *Journal of University Teaching & Learning Practice*, *13*(2), 1–19.

Haritos, C. (2004). Understanding teaching through the minds of teacher candidates: A curious blend of realism and idealism. *Teaching Education*, *20*, 637–654.

Harman, R., & McClure, G. (2011). All the school's a stage: Critical performative pedagogy in urban teacher education. *Equity & Excellence in Education*, *44*(3), 379–402. doi:10.1080/10665684.2011.589278

Harris, D., & Anthony, H. (2001). Collegiality and its role in teacher development: Perspectives from veteran and novice teachers. *Teacher Development*, *5*(3), 127–128. doi:10.1080/13664530100200162

Harris, J., Kearley, K., Heneghan, C., Meats, E., Roberts, N., Perera, R., & Kearley-Shiers, K. (2011). Are journal clubs effective in supporting evidence-based decision making? A systematic review. BEME Guide No. 16. *Medical Teacher*, *33*(1), 9–23. doi:10.3109/0142159X.2011.530321 PMID:21182379

Hatch, J. (2002). Accountability shovedown: Resisting the standards movement in early childhood education. *Phi Delta Kappan*, *83*(6), 457–463. doi:10.1177/003172170208300611

Hattie, J., & Timperley, H. (2007). The power of feedback. *Review of Educational Research*, *77*(1), 81–112. doi:10.3102/003465430298487

Hatton, N., & Smith, D. (1995). Reflection in teacher education: Towards definition and implementation. *Teaching and Teacher Education*, *11*(1), 3–49. doi:10.1016/0742-051X(94)00012-U

Hawker, L. (2000). From teacher dependence to learner independence: case study from the Dubai Women's College. *Paper presented at The Technological Education and National Development Conference (TEND)*, Abu Dhabi, United Arab Emirates.

Hayes, M. M., Chatterjee, S., & Schwartzstein, R. M. (2017). Critical Thinking in Critical Care: Five Strategies to Improve Teaching and Learning in the Intensive Care Unit. *Annals of the American Thoracic Society, 14*, 569-575.

Heidari, M., & Ebrahimi, P. (2016). Examining the relationship between critical-thinking skills and decision-making ability of emergency medicine students. *Indian Journal of Critical Care Medicine: Peer-Reviewed, Official Publication of Indian Society of Critical Care Medicine*, *20*(10), 581–586. doi:10.4103/0972-5229.192045 PMID:27829713

Heineke, S. F. (2013). Coaching discourse: Supporting teachers' professional learning. *The Elementary School Journal*, *113*(3), 409–433. doi:10.1086/668767

Hein, S. F., & Skaggs, G. E. (2010). Conceptualizing the classroom of target students: A qualitative investigation of panelists' experiences during standard setting. *Educational Measurement: Issues and Practice*, *22*(2), 36–44. doi:10.1111/j.1745-3992.2010.00174.x

Helm, J. (2015). *Becoming young thinkers: Deep project work in the classroom.* New York, NY: Teachers College Press.

Helm, J. H., & Beneke, S. (Eds.). (2003). *The power of projects: Meeting contemporary challenges in early childhood classrooms—Strategies and solutions.* New York, NY: Teachers College Press.

Helm, J. H., Beneke, S., & Steinheimer, K. (2007). *Windows on learning: Documenting young children's work* (2nd ed.). New York, NY: Teachers College Press.

Helm, J. H., & Katz, L. (2016). *Young Investigators: The project approach in the early years* (3rd ed.). New York, NY: Teachers College Press.

Hennessey, B. A., & Amabile, T. M. (2010). Creativity. *Annual Review of Psychology, 61*(1), 569–598. doi:10.1146/annurev.psych.093008.100416 PMID:19575609

Herbert, S., & Rampersad, J. (2007). The promotion of thinking in selected lower secondary science classrooms in Trinidad and Tobago: Implications for teacher education. In L. Quamina-Aiyejina (Ed.), *Caribbean Curriculum.* St. Augustine: School of Education, University of the West Indies.

Herod, L. (2002). *Adult learning from theory to practice.* Heinle and Heinle Publishers. Heinemann.

Higgs, J., & Elstein, A. (1995). Clinical reasoning in medicine. In J. Higgs (Ed.), *Clinical reasoning in the health professions* (pp. 49–59). Oxford, UK: Butterworth-Heinemann Ltd.

HighScope. (2018). *Curriculum.* Retrieved from https://highscope.org/curriculum

Hill, H. C., Rowan, B., & Ball, D. L. (2005). Effects of teachers' mathematical knowledge for teaching on student achievement. *American Educational Research Journal, 42*(2), 371–406. doi:10.3102/00028312042002371

Hill, I. (2012). An international model of world-class education: The international baccalaureate. *Prospects: Quarterly Review of Comparative Education, 42*(3), 341–359. doi:10.100711125-012-9243-9

Hitchcock, D. (2018). Critical thinking. In E. N. Zalta (Ed.), *The Stanford Encyclopedia of Philosophy.* Academic Press. Retrieved from https://plato.stanford.edu/cgibin/encyclopedia/archinfo.cgi?entry=critical-thinking

Hitchcock, D. (2018). Critical thinking. In *The Stanford Encyclopedia of Philosophy.* Retrieved from https://tc2.ca/uploads/PDFs/TIpsForTeachers/Tips4Teachers_Promotingcriticalthinkinginscience.pdf

Hmelo-Silver, C. E. (2004). Problem-based learning: What and how do students learn? *Educational Psychology Review, 16*(3), 235–266. doi:10.1023/B:EDPR.0000034022.16470.f3

Hobbs, R. (2010). *News literacy: what works and what doesn't.* Association for Education in Journalism and Mass Communication.

Hodgens, C., Sendall, M. C., & Evans, L. (2012). Post-graduate health promotion students assess their information literacy. *Reference Services Review, 40*(3), 408–422. doi:10.1108/00907321211254670

Holmes, N. G., Wieman, C. E., & Bonn, D. A. (2015). Teaching critical thinking. *Proceedings of the National Academy of Sciences of the United States of America.*

Holt-Reynolds, D. (1992). Personal history-based beliefs as relevant prior knowledge in course work. *American Educational Research Journal, 29*(2), 325–349. doi:10.3102/00028312029002325

Hord, S. M. (2009). Professional learning communities. Educators work together toward a shared purpose – improved student learning. *National Staff Development Council, 30*(1), 40–43.

Hord, S. M., & Hirsh, S. A. (2008). Making the promise a reality. In A. M. Blankstein, P. D. Houston, & R. W. Cole (Eds.), *Sustaining professional learning communities*. Thousand Oaks, CA: Corwin Press.

Horton, M., Freire, P., Bell, B., & Gaventa, J. (1990). *We make the road by walking: Conversations on education and social change*. Temple University Press.

Horvath, C., & Forte, J. M. (2011). *Critical thinking* (Education in a competitive and globalizing world series). New York. *Nova Scientia*.

Houlson, V. (2007). Getting Results from One-Shot Instruction: A Workshop for First-Year Students. *College & Undergraduate Libraries*, *14*(1), 89–108. doi:10.1300/J106v14n01_07

Hove, G. (2011). *Developing critical thinking skills in the high school classroom* [Master's Research Paper]. University of Wisconsin, WI.

Howard, T. C. (2003). Culturally relevant pedagogy: Ingredients for critical teacher reflection. *Theory into Practice*, *42*(3), 195–202. doi:10.120715430421tip4203_5

Howe, C. (2010). Peer Dialogue and Cognitive Development: A two-way relationship? In K. Littleton & C. Howe (Eds.), *Educational dialogues: Understanding and promoting productive interaction* (pp. 32–47). New York: Routledge. Retrieved from https://books.google.com/books?hl=en&lr=&id=_buLAgAAQBAJ&pgis=1

Hsu, C., & Sandford, B. A. (2012). The delphi technique: *Making sense of consensus. Practical Assessment, Research & Evaluation*, *10*(12), 1531–7714.

Hudgins, B., & Edelman, S. (1986). Teaching Critical Thinking Skills to Fourth and Fifth Graders Through Teacher-Led Small-Group Discussions. *The Journal of Educational Research*, *79*(6), 333–342.

Hughes, J. (2014). *Critical Thinking in the Language Classroom*. Eli Publishing.

Hundert, E. M., Hafferty, F., & Christakis, D. (1996). Characteristics of the informal curriculum and trainees' ethical choices. *Academic Medicine*, *71*(6), 624–633. doi:10.1097/00001888-199606000-00014 PMID:9125919

Hur, Y., & Kim, S. (2007). Different outcomes of active and reflective students in problem-based learning. *Medical Teacher*, *29*(1), e18–e21. doi:10.1080/01421590601045007 PMID:17538825

Ijaiya, N. Y. S., Alabi, A. T., & Fasasi, Y. A. (2011). Teacher education in Africa and critical thinking skills: Needs and strategies. *Research Journal of Business Management*, *5*(1), 26–34. doi:10.3923/rjbm.2011.26.34

Ilica, A. (2016). On John Dewey's philosophy of education and its impact on contemporary education. *Journal Plus Education / Educatia Plus*, *14*(1), 7-13.

Impara, J. C., & Plake, B. S. (1997). Standard setting: An alternative approach. *Journal of Educational Measurement*, *34*(4), 353–366. doi:10.1111/j.1745-3984.1997.tb00523.x

Impara, J. C., & Plake, B. S. (1998). Teachers' ability to estimate item difficulty: A test of the assumptions of the Angoff standard setting method. *Journal of Educational Measurement*, *35*(1), 69–81. doi:10.1111/j.1745-3984.1998.tb00528.x

International Society for Technology in Education (ISTE). (2016). *ISTE Standards for Students (ebook): A practical guide for learning with technology*. ISTE. Available for download at https://www.iste.org/resources/product?ID=4073&ChildProduct=4074

Iobst, W. F., Trowbridge, R., & Philibert, I. (2013). Teaching and assessing critical reasoning through the use of entrustment. *Journal of Graduate Medical Education*, *5*(3), 517–518. doi:10.4300/JGME-D-13-00211.1 PMID:24404322

İpşiroğlu, Z. (2002). *Eleştirel Düşünme Öğretilebilir mi?* Retrieved from www.felsefeekibi.com

Iranfar, S., Sepahi, V., Khoshay, A., Rezaei, M., Matin, B. K., Keshavarzi, F., & Bashiri, H. (2012). Critical thinking disposition among medical students of Kermanshah University of Medical Sciences. *Educational Research in Medical Sciences Journal, 1*, 63–68.

Irby, D. M. (1986). Clinical teaching and the clinical teacher. *Journal of Medical Education, 61*, 35–45. PMID:3746867

Irfannuddin, I. (2009). Knowledge and critical thinking skills increase clinical reasoning ability in urogenital disorders: A Universitas Sriwijaya Medical Faculty experience. *Medical Journal of Indonesia, 18*, 53–59. doi:10.13181/mji.v18i1.341

Irwin, J. (2012). *Paulo Freire's philosophy of education: Origins, developments, impacts and legacies.* London: Bloomsbury Publishing.

Iton, I. (2008). Breaking into unexplored territory: a case study of the Information Literacy initiative at the Cave Hill Campus of the University of the West Indies. In J. Lau (Ed.), Information Literacy International Perspective. Munchen: IFLA Publications

Iyioke, I. C. (2013). *Re-conceptualization of modified Angoff standard setting: Unified statistical, measurement, cognitive and social psychological theories* (Unpublished doctoral dissertation). Michigan State University.

Iyioke, I. C. (2015). *A research of heuristic vs. normative training for the Angoff standard setting method.* Paper presented at the Annual Meeting of the American Educational Research Association Conference, Chicago, IL.

Iyioke, I. C. (2018). *Survey Research: Completely structured versus partially structured training on the Angoff method.* London: SAGE Publications, Ltd.; doi:10.4135/9781526436818

Jacob, S. M. (2012). Analyzing critical thinking skills using online discussion forums and CCTST. *Procedia: Social and Behavioral Sciences, 31*, 805–809. doi:10.1016/j.sbspro.2011.12.145

Jacobs, G., & Crowley, K. (2007). *Play, projects, and preschool standards: Nurturing children's sense of wonder and joy in learning.* Thousand Oaks, CA: Corwin Press.

Jacobs, V. R., Lamb, L. L. C., & Philipp, R. A. (2010). Professional noticing of children's mathematical thinking. *Journal for Research in Mathematics Education, 41*(2), 33.

Järvelä, S., Volet, S., & Järvenoja, H. (2010). Research on motivation in collaborative learning: Moving beyond the cognitive-situative divide and combining individual and social processes. *Educational Psychologist, 45*(1), 15–27. doi:10.1080/00461520903433539

Jay, J., & Johnson, K. (2002). Capturing complexity: A typology of reflective practice for teacher education. *Teaching and Teacher Education, 18*(1), 73–85. doi:10.1016/S0742-051X(01)00051-8

Jeffery, B. (2006). Creative teaching and learning: Towards a common discourse and practice. *Cambridge Journal of Education, 36*(3), 394–114.

Jeffries, P. R. (2005). A framework for designing, implementing, and evaluating simulations used as teaching strategies in nursing. *Nursing Education Perspectives, 26*(2), 96–103. PMID:15921126

Jenkins, J. R., Antil, L. R., Wayne, S. K., & Vadasy, P. F. (2003). How cooperative learning Works for special education and remedial students. *Exceptional Children, 69*(3), 279–292. doi:10.1177/001440290306900302

Jimenez-Aleixandre, M. P., & Eurduran, S. (2008). Argumentation in science education: an overview. In S. Eurduran & M. P. Jimenez-Aleixandre (Eds.), *Argumentation in science education: perspectives from classroom-based research.* Berlin, Germany: Springer.

Johnson, D. W., & Johnson, F. P. (2006). *Joining together group theory and group skills*. Boston, MA: Pearson.

Jonassen, D. H. (1997). Instructional design models for well-structured and ill-structured problem-solving learning outcomes. *Educational Technology Research and Development*, *45*(1), 65–94. doi:10.1007/BF02299613

Joyce, B., & Showers, B. (1982). The coaching of teaching. *Educational Leadership*, *40*(1), 4.

Julian, S. (2013). Reinventing classroom space to re-energise information literacy instruction. *Journal of Information Literacy*, *7*(1), 69–82. doi:10.11645/7.1.1720

Juncheng, Y. (2014). Characteristics and inspiration about critical thinking teaching in North America. *Studies in Sociology of Science*, *5*(4), 42–46. doi:10.3968/5608

Kabeel, A. R., & Eisa, S. A. E. M. (2016). The Correlation of Critical Thinking Disposition and Approaches to Learning among Baccalaureate Nursing Students. *Journal of Education and Practice*, *7*, 91–103.

Kagan, D. (1992a). Implications of research on teacher belief. *Educational Psychologist*, *27*(1), 65–90. doi:10.120715326985ep2701_6

Kagan, D. (1992b). Professional growth among pre-service and beginning teachers. *Review of Educational Research*, *62*(2), 129–169. doi:10.3102/00346543062002129

Kahneman, D. (2011). Thinking, fast and slow. New York, NY: Farrar, Straus and Giroux. doi:10.1080/00220671.1986.10885702

Kahneman, D. (2011). *Thinking, fast and slow*. New York, NY: Farrar, Straus and Giroux.

Kalantzis, M., & Cope, B. (2008). *New learning. elements of a science of education*. Cambridge: Cambridge University Press. doi:10.1017/CBO9780511811951

Kaneklin, C., & Olivetti Manoukain, F. (1990). *Conoscere l'organizzazione*. Milan: Carocci.

Kapur, M. (2008). Productive failure. *Cognition and Instruction*, *26*(3), 379–424. doi:10.1080/07370000802212669

Kareem, J. (2016). The influence of leadership in building a learning organization. *IUP Journal of Organizational Behavior*, *15*(1), 7–18.

Kaufman, J. C., & Beghetto, R. A. (2009). Beyond big and little: The four c model of creativity. *Review of General Psychology*, *13*(1), 1–12. doi:10.1037/a0013688

Kawashima, A., & Petrini, M. A. (2004). Study of critical thinking skills in nursing students and nurses in Japan. *Nurse Education Today*, *24*(4), 286–292. doi:10.1016/j.nedt.2004.02.001 PMID:15110438

Kazemi, E. (1998). Discourse that promotes conceptual understanding. *Teaching Children Mathematics*, *4*(7), 410–414.

Keats, J. (n.d.). *Letter to his brothers, 1817*. Retrieved from http://englishhistory.net/keats/letters.html

Kedzior, M., & Fifield, S. (2004). Teacher professional development. *Education Policy Brief*, *15*(21), 76–97.

Kelchtermans, G. (2009). Career stories as a gateway to understanding teacher development. In M. Bayer, U. Brinkkjaer, H. Plauborg, & S. Rolls (Eds.), *Teachers' career trajectories and work lives. Professional learning and development in school and higher education, 3* (pp. 29–47). Amsterdam: Springer Netherlands. doi:10.1007/978-90-481-2358-2_3

Kemmis, S., & Smith, T. J. (2008). *Enabling praxis: Challenges for education*. Rotterdam, NL: Sense Publishers.

Kennedy, M. (2005). *Inside teaching: How classroom life undermines reform.* Cambridge, MA: Harvard University Press. doi:10.4159/9780674039513

Keogh, T., Barnes, P., Joiner, R., & Littleton, K. (2000). Gender, pair composition and computer versus paper presentations of an English language task. *Educational Psychology, 20*(1), 33–43. doi:10.1080/014434100110362

Khatib, M., & Alizadeh, M. (2012). Output tasks, noticing, and learning: Teaching English past tense to Iranian EFL learners. *English Language Teaching, 5*(4), 173–186. doi:10.5539/elt.v5n4p173

Khatib, M., & Nazari, O. (2012). The Effect of Literature on Enhancing Critical Thinking. *Journal of Comparative Literature and Culture, 1*(2), 29–33.

Khodadady, E., & Karami, M. (2017). An Evaluation of Textbooks Designed for Advanced English Learners within a Foreign Context: A Critical Thinking Perspective. *Porta Linguarum, 28,* 96–109.

Kilfoye, C. (2013). A voice from the past calls for classroom technology: John Dewey's writings on educational reform tell us we should embrace technology in the classroom so that we can prepare students with 21st century skills. *Phi Delta Kappan, 94*(7), 53–56. doi:10.1177/003172171309400717

Killion, J. (2009). Coaches' roles, responsibilities, and reach. *Coaching Approaches and Perspectives,* 7-28.

Kim, S. H., & Song, K. S. (2013). The Effects of Thinking Style Based Cooperative Learning on Group Creativity. *Creative Education, 3*(8), 20–24. doi:10.4236/ce.2012.38B005

Kim, S., & Shumaker, D. (2015). Student, librarian, and instructor perceptions of information literacy instruction and skills in a first year experience program: A case study. *Journal of Academic Librarianship, 41*(4), 449–456.

King, B., & Newmann, F. (2004). Key link: Successful professional development must consider school capacity. *Journal of Staff Development, 25*(1), 26–30.

Kirkpatrick, D. (1994). *Evaluating training programs: The four levels.* San Francisco, CA: Berrett-Koehler.

Kirschner, P. A., Sweller, J., & Clark, R. E. (2006). Why minimal guidance during instruction does not work: An analysis of the failure of constructivist, discovery, problem-based, experiential, and inquiry-based teaching. *Educational Psychologist, 41*(2), 75–86. doi:10.120715326985ep4102_1

Klem, A. M., & Connell, J. P. (2004). Relationships matter: Linking teacher support to student engagement and achievement. *The Journal of School Health, 74*(7), 262–273. doi:10.1111/j.1746-1561.2004.tb08283.x PMID:15493703

Klosterman, M.L & Sadler, T.D. (2010). Multi-level Assessment of Scientific Content Knowledge Gains Associated with Socioscientific Issues-based Instruction. *International Journal of Science Education, 32*(8), 1017-1043. doi:10.1080/09500690902894512

Knight, J. (2009). Coaching. *Journal of Staff Development, 30*(1), 18–22.

Knight, J. (2009). *Instructional coaching. In Coaching Approaches and Perspectives* (pp. 29–55). Thousand Oaks, CA: Corwin Press.

Knowles, J. G., & Holt-Reynolds, D. (1991). Shaping pedagogies through personal histories in pre-service teacher education. *Teachers College Record, 93,* 87–113.

Koray, Ö., Yaman, S., & Altunçekiç, A. (2004). Yaratıcı ve Eleştirel Düşünmeye Dayalı Laboratuar Yönteminin Öğretmen Adaylarının Akademik Başarı, Problem Çözme ve Laboratuar Tutum Düzeylerine Etkisi. Ulusal Eğitim Bilimleri Kurultayı, 6-9 Temmuz 2004, İnönü Üniversitesi, Eğitim Fakültesi, Malatya.

Kreitzberg, A., & Kreitzberg, C. (2010). *Critical thinking for the twenty-first century: what it is and why it matters to you.* Retrieved from http://www.agilecriticalthinking.com/Portals/0/WhitePapers/Critical%20Thinking%20for%20the%20 21st%20Century%20for%20Website.pdf

Kretlow, A. G., & Bartholomew, C. C. (2010). Using coaching to improve the fidelity of evidence-based practices: A review of studies. *Teacher Education and Special Education, 33*(4), 279–299. doi:10.1177/0888406410371643

Kruskal, J. B. (1964a). Multidimensional scaling by optimizing goodness-of-fit to a nonmetric hypothesis. *Psychometrika, 29*(1), 1–27. doi:10.1007/BF02289565

Kruskal, J. B. (1964b). Nonmetric multidimensional scaling: A numerical method. *Psychometrika, 29*(2), 115–129. doi:10.1007/BF02289694

Kruskal, J. B., & Wish, M. (1978). *Multidimensional scaling. Sage University paper series on Quantitative Applications in the Social Sciences # 11.* Beverly Hills, CA: Sage.

Kuhn, D., & Crowell, A. (2011). Dialogic argumentation as a vehicle for developing young adolescents' thinking. *Psychological Science, 22*(4), 545–552. doi:10.1177/0956797611402512

Kuhn, D. (1993). Science as Argument: Implications for teaching and learning scientific thinking. *Science Education, 77*(3), 257–272. doi:10.1002ce.3730770306

Kuhn, D. (1999). A developmental model of critical thinking. *Educational Researcher, 28*(2), 16–46.

Kuhn, D. (2007). Is direct instruction an answer to the right question? *Educational Psychologist, 42*(2), 109–113. doi:10.1080/00461520701263376

Kuhn, D. (2018). A role for reasoning in a dialogic approach to critical thinking. *Topoi, 37*(1), 121–128. doi:10.100711245-016-9373-4

Kuhn, D., Hemberger, L., & Khait, V. (2017). *Argue with me: Argument as a path to developing students' thinking and writing* (2nd ed.). New York: Routledge. doi:10.4324/9781315692722

Kuhn, D., & Pearsall, S. (2000). Development origins of scientific thinking. *Journal of Cognition and Development, 1*(1), 113–127. doi:10.1207/S15327647JCD0101N_11

Kuhn, D., Zillmer, N., Crowell, A., & Zavala, J. (2013). Developing norms of argumentation: Metacognitive, epistemological, and social dimensions of developing argumentive competence. *Cognition and Instruction, 31*(4), 456–496. doi:10.1080/07370008.2013.830618

Kuhn, T. S. (1996). *The Structure of Scientific Revolutions* (3rd ed.). Chicago: University of Chicago Press. doi:10.7208/chicago/9780226458106.001.0001

Ku, K. Y. L. (2009). Assessing students' critical thinking performance: Urging for measurements using multi-response format. *Thinking Skills and Creativity, 4*(1), 70–76. doi:10.1016/j.tsc.2009.02.001

Külekçi, G., & Kumlu, E. (2015). Developing Critical Thinking Skills In English Language Teaching Classes Through Novels. *International Journal of Language Academy, 3*(2), 76–90.

Kuntze, S., Aizikovitsh-Udi, E., & Clarke, D. (2017). Hybrid Task Design: Connecting Learning Opportunities Related to Critical Thinking and Statistical Thinking. *ZDM. The International Journal on Mathematics Education, 49*(6), 923–935.

Lagendijk, J. (2013). *The need for critical thinking as new opportunities in higher education arise.* Retrieved from https://www.eaie.org/blog/critical-thinking-for-higher-ed.html

LaMartina, K., & Ward-Smith, P. (2014). Developing critical thinking skills in undergraduate nursing students: The potential for strategic management simulations. *Journal of Nursing Education and Practice*, *4*(9), 155–162. doi:10.5430/jnep.v4n9p155

Lang Froggatt, D. (2015). The informationally underserved: Not always diverse, but always a social justice advocacy model. *School Libraries Worldwide*, *21*(1), 54–72. doi:10.14265.21.1.004

Laniro, S. (2007). Authentic materials. In M. A. Corley & P. Esra (Eds.), Professional Development Fact Sheet. American Institutes for Research.

Lapp, L. K., & Spaniol, J. (2016). Aging and self-discrepancy: Evidence for adaptive change across the life span. *Experimental Aging Research*, *42*(2), 212–219. doi:10.1080/0361073X.2016.1132900 PMID:26890636

Larkin, S. (2009). Socially mediated metacognition and learning to write. *Thinking Skills and Creativity*, *4*(3), 149–159. doi:10.1016/j.tsc.2009.09.003

Larrivee, B. (2000). Transforming teaching practice: Becoming the critically reflective teacher. *Reflective Practice*, *1*(3), 297–307. doi:10.1080/713693162

Lauer, P. A., Christopher, D. E., Firpo-Triplett, R., & Buchting, F. (2014). The impact of short-term professional development on participant outcomes: A review of the literature. *Professional Development in Education*, *40*(2), 207–227. doi:10.1080/19415257.2013.776619

Lauer, T. (2005). Teaching critical-thinking skills using course content material. *Journal of College Science Teaching*, *34*(6), 34–44.

Lau, J. Y. F. (2011). *An introduction to critical thinking and creativity: Think more, think better*. Indianapolis, IN: Wiley. doi:10.1002/9781118033449

Lee, O. (2018, January). How do children learn science? *At a Glance, News from the Steinhardt School of Culture, Education, and Human Development*. Retrieved from https://steinhardt.nyu.edu/site/ataglance/2018/01/okhee-lee-how-students-learn-science.html

Lee, H.-J. (2005). Understanding and assessing preservice teachers' reflective thinking. *Teaching and Teacher Education*, *21*(6), 699–715. doi:10.1016/j.tate.2005.05.007

Lee, S., & Schallert, D. (2016). Becoming a teacher: Coordinating past, present, and future selves with perspectival understandings about teaching. *Teaching and Teacher Education*, *56*, 72–83. doi:10.1016/j.tate.2016.02.004

Leong, D., & Bodrova, E. (2012). Assessing and scaffolding: Make believe play. *Young Children*, *67*(1), 28–34.

Lesaux, N. K., & Jones, S. M. (2018). Early childhood research needs an update. *Education Week*, *20*(37), 28.

Lesh, R. A., & Zawojewski, J. (2007). Problem solving and modeling. In F. Lester (Ed.), *Second Handbook of Research on Mathematics Teaching and Learning* (pp. 763–804). Charlotte, NC: Information Age Publishing, Inc.

Leu, D. J. Jr, & Kinzer, C. K. (2000). The convergence of literacy instruction and networked technologies for information and communication. *Reading Research Quarterly*, *35*(1), 108–127. doi:10.1598/RRQ.35.1.8

Leu, D. J. Jr, Kinzer, C. K., Coiro, J., & Cammack, D. (2004). Toward a theory of new literacies emerging from the Internet and other information and communication technologies. In R. B. Ruddell & N. J. Unrau (Eds.), *Theoretical models and processes of reading* (5th ed., pp. 1570–1613). Newark, DE: International Reading Association. doi:10.1598/0872075028.54

Lewin, K. M., & Stuart, J. M. (2003). Insights into the policy and practice of teacher education in low-income countries: The Multi-Site Teacher Education Research Project. *British Educational Research Journal, 29*(5), 691–707. doi:10.1080/0141192032000133703

Lieberman, A., & Pointer-Mace, D. (2008). Teacher learning: The key to education reform. *Journal of Teacher Education, 59*(3), 226–234. doi:10.1177/0022487108317020

Lieberman, V., & Tversky, A. (2001). *Probability thinking in daily life*. Tel Aviv: Open University. (in Hebrew)

Lim, L. A. (2011). A comparison of students' reflective thinking across different years in a problem-based learning environment. *Instructional Science, 39*(2), 171–188. doi:10.100711251-009-9123-8

Linn, R. L. (2001). *The Influence of External Evaluations on the National Assessment of Educational Progress* (CSE Technical Report 548). Los Angeles, CA: University of California, Center for Research Evaluation, Standards, and Student Testing.

Lipman, M. (1988). Critical thinking - what can it be? *Educational Leadership, 46*(1), 38–43.

Lipman, M. (1991). *Thinking in education*. Cambridge, UK: Cambridge University Press.

Liu, K. (2015). Critical reflection as a framework for transformative learning in teacher education. *Educational Review, 67*(2), 135–157. doi:10.1080/00131911.2013.839546

Livingston, J. A. (2003). *Metacognition: An overview*. Retrieved from http://eric.ed.gov/?id=ED474273

Longo, C. (2010). Fostering creativity or teaching to the Test? Implications of state testing on the delivery of science instruction. *The Clearing House: A Journal of Educational Strategies, Issues and Ideas, 83*(2), 54–57. doi:10.1080/00098650903505399

Loon, G. V. (2002). *Charaka Saṃhitā: Handbook on Ayurveda Vol-1. Chaukhambha*. Orientialia Publishers.

Lortie, D. (1975). *Schoolteacher: A sociological study*. London: University of Chicago Press.

Lotfi, H., Hasankhani, H., & Mokhtari, M. (2010). The effectiveness of simulation training and critical-thinking strategies on clinical decision-making of operating room students. *Journal of Nurse-Midwifery, 5*, 5–11.

Loughran, J. J. (2014). Developing understandings of practice: Science teacher learning. In N. G. Lederman & S. K. Abell (Eds.), *Handbook of research on science education* (Vol. 2, pp. 811–829). New York, NY: Routledge.

Love, S. L., & Stobaugh, R. (2018). *Critical Thinking in the Classroom: A Practitioner's Guide*. Academic Press.

Low, E. L., & Cai, C. H. (2017). Developing student teachers' critical thinking and professional values: A case study of a teacher educator in Singapore. *Asia Pacific Journal of Education, 37*(4), 535–551. doi:10.1080/02188791.2017.1386093

Lucia, V. C., & Swanberg, S. M. (2018). Utilizing journal club to facilitate critical thinking in pre-clinical medical students. *International Journal of Medical Education, 15*, 7–8. doi:10.5116/ijme.5a46.2214 PMID:29334677

Luke, A. (2000). Critical literacy in Australia: A matter of context and standpoint. *Journal of Adolescent & Adult Literacy, 43*(5), 448–461.

Lynch, K., Chin, M., & Blazar, D. (2017). Relationships between observations of elementary mathematics instruction and student achievement: Exploring variability across districts. *American Journal of Education, 123*(4), 615–646. doi:10.1086/692662

MacKnight, C. (2000). Teaching critical thinking through on-line discussions. *Educause Quarterly,* (4). Retrieved from http://eac595b.pbworks.com/f/macknight+2000+questions[1].pdf

Mafinejad, M. K., Arabshahi, S. K. S., Monajemi, A., Jalili, M., Soltani, A., & Rasouli, J. (2017). Use of Multi-Response Format Test in the Assessment of Medical Students' Critical Thinking Ability. *Journal of Clinical and Diagnostic Research: JCDR*, *11*, LC10–LC13. PMID:29207742

Mahdi, T., Victoria, G., & Carolina, P. (2010). Teaching clinical thinking to first-year medical students. *Psihologie*, *4*, 75–85.

Mahmoodabad, S. S. M., Nadrian, H., & Nahangi, H. (2012). Critical thinking ability and its associated factors among preclinical students in Yazd Shaheed Sadoughi University of Medical Sciences (Iran). *Medical Journal of the Islamic Republic of Iran*, *26*, 50–57. PMID:23483755

Maiorana, V. P. (1992). *Critical thinking across the curriculum: Building the analytical classroom.* (ERIC Document Reproduction Service No. ED 347511)

Major, C. H., & Palmer, B. (2006). Reshaping teaching and learning: The transformation of teachers pedagogical content knowledge. *Education*, *51*, 619–647.

Majumder, M. A. A., D'Souza, U., & Rahman, S. (2004). Trends in Medical Education: Challenges and Directions for Need-based Reforms of Medical Training in South-East Asia. *Indian Journal of Medical Sciences*, *58*, 369–380. PMID:15470278

Makary, M. A., & Daniel, M. (2016). Medical error-the third leading cause of death in the US. *British Medical Journal*, *353*, i2139. doi:10.1136/bmj.i2139 PMID:27143499

Mangin, M., & Dunsmore, K. (2015). How the framing of instructional coaching as a lever for systemic or individual reform influences the enactment of coaching. *Educational Administration Quarterly*, *51*(2), 179–213. doi:10.1177/0013161X14522814

Mann, K., Gordon, J., & MacLeod, A. (2009). Reflection and reflective practice in health professions education: A systematic review. *Advances in Health Sciences Education: Theory and Practice*, *14*(4), 595–621. doi:10.100710459-007-9090-2 PMID:18034364

Manogue, M., Kelly, M., Masaryk, S. B., Brown, G., Catalanotto, F., Choo-Soo, T., & ... . (2002). Evolving methods of assessment. *European Journal of Dental Education*, *6*, 53–66. doi:10.1034/j.1600-0579.6.s3.8.x PMID:12390260

Mansbach, J. (2015). *Using technology to develop students' critical thinking skills*. Retrieved July 20, 2018 from https://dl.sps.northwestern.edu/blog/2015/09/using-technology-to-develop-students-critical-thinking-skills/

Manuel, J., & Carter, D. (2016). Sustaining hope and possibility: Early–career English teachers' perspective on their first years of teaching. *Engineers Australia*, *51*, 91–103.

Marchi, R. (2012). With Facebook, blogs, and fake news, teens reject journalistic "objectivity.". *The Journal of Communication Inquiry*, *36*(3), 246–262. doi:10.1177/0196859912458700

Marin, L. M., & Halpern, D. F. (2011). Pedagogy for developing critical thinking in adolescents: Explicit instruction produces greatest gains. *Thinking Skills and Creativity*, *6*(1), 1–13. doi:10.1016/j.tsc.2010.08.002

Markus, H., & Nurius, P. (1986). Possible selves. *The American Psychologist*, *41*(9), 954–969. doi:10.1037/0003-066X.41.9.954

Marzano, R. (2007). *The art and science of teaching*. Alexandria, VA: Association for Supervision and Curriculum Development.

Marzano, R., Pickering, D., & Pollock, J. (2001). *Classroom instruction that works: Research based strategies for increasing student achievement.* Upper Saddle River, NJ: Pearson.

Masic, I., Miokovic, M., & Muhamedagic, B. (2008). Evidence Based Medicine – New Approaches and Challenges. *Acta Informatica Medica, 16*(4), 219–225. doi:10.5455/aim.2008.16.219-225 PMID:24109156

Massengill, D., Mahlios, M., & Barry, A. (2005). Making sense of teaching through metaphors: A review across three studies. *Teachers and Teaching, 16*(1), 49–71.

Mattson, K. (2005). Why "Active Learning" Can Be Perilous To The Profession. *Academe, 91*(1), 23–26. doi:10.2307/40252732

Maudsley, G., & Strivens, J. (2000). 'Science', 'critical thinking' and 'competence' for tomorrow's doctors. A review of terms and concepts. *Medical Education, 34*(1), 53–60. doi:10.1046/j.1365-2923.2000.00428.x PMID:10607280

Maxwell, J. (1996). *Qualitative research methods* (Vol. 41). Thousand Oaks, CA: SAGE Publications.

Mayfield, M. (1997). *Thinking for yourself: Developing critical thinking skills through reading and writing.* Belmont, CA: Wadsworth Publishing Co.

McBride, R. E. (1991). Critical thinking: An overview with implications for physical education. *Journal of Teaching in Physical Education, 11*(2), 112–125. doi:10.1123/jtpe.11.2.112

McCollister, K., & Sayler, M. F. (2010). Lift the ceiling: Increase in rigor with critical thinking skills. *Gifted Child Today, 31*(1), 41–47. doi:10.1177/107621751003300110

McConnell, C. (2011). The essential questions handbook: Grades 4-8. New York, NY: Scholastic.

McDonald, S., & McDonald, J. (2011). *Information literacy for ubiquitous learning.* Available from: https://uts.academia.edu/Sophieherbert/

McDowell, Z. F. (2017). *Student learning outcomes with Wikipedia-based assignments (Fall 2016 research report).* Amherst, MA: University of Massachusetts.

McGinty, D. (2005). Illuminating the "Black Box" of standard setting: An exploratory qualitative study. *Applied Measurement in Education, 18*(3), 269–287. doi:10.120715324818ame1803_5

McLaren, P. (1998). *Life in schools: An introduction to critical pedagogy in the foundations of education* (3rd ed.). New York: Longman.

McLaren, P. (2009). Critical pedagogy: A look at the major concepts. In A. Darder, M. P. Baltodano, & R. D. Torres (Eds.), *The critical pedagogy reader* (2nd ed., pp. 61–83). New York, NY: Routledge.

McLaren, P., & Da Silva, T. (1993). Decentering pedagogy: Critical literacy, resistance and the resistance and politics of memory. In P. McLaren & P. Leonarded (Eds.), *Paulo Freire: A Critical Encounter* (pp. 47–89). New York: Routledge. doi:10.4324/9780203420263_chapter_4

McManus, D. A. (2001). The two paradigms of education and the peer review of teaching. *Journal of Geoscience Education, 49*(5), 423–434. doi:10.5408/1089-9995-49.5.423

McNeil, L. (2000). *Contradictions of school reform: Educational costs of standardized testing.* New York: Routledge.

McNeill, K. L., Katsh-Singer, R., & Pelletier, P. (2015). Assessing science practices – Moving your class along a continuum. *Science Scope, 39*(4), 21–28. doi:10.2505/4s15_039_04_21

McPeck, J. E. (1990). Critical thinking and subject-specificity: A reply to Ennis. *Educational Researcher, 19*(4), 10–12. doi:10.3102/0013189X019004010

McTighe, J., & Wiggins, G. (2011). *The understanding by design guide to advanced concepts in creating and reviewing units*. ASCD.

McTighe, J., & Wiggins, G. (2013). *Essential Questions: Opening doors to student understanding*. Alexandria, VA: ASCD.

McWilliams, S. A. (2016). Cultivating constructivism: Inspiring intuition and promoting process and pragmatism. *Journal of Constructivist Psychology, 29*(1), 1–29. doi:10.1080/10720537.2014.980871

Mee, J., Clauser, B. E., & Margolis, M. J. (2013). The impact of process instructions on judges' use of examinee performance data in Angoff standard setting exercises. *Educational Measurement: Issues and Practice, 32*(3), 27–35. doi:10.1111/emip.12013

Mercer, N. (2013). The social brain, language, and goal-directed collective thinking: A social conception of cognition and its implications for understanding how we think, teach, and learn. *Educational Psychologist, 48*(3), 148–168. doi:10.1080/00461520.2013.804394

Mery, Y., Newby, J., & Peng, K. (2012). Why One-Shot Information Literacy Sessions Are Not the Future of Instruction: A Case for Online Credit Courses. *College & Research Libraries, 73*(4), 366–377. doi:10.5860/crl-271

Mestre, J. P., Ross, B. H., Brookes, D. T., Smith, A. D., & Nokes, T. (2009). How Cognitive Science Can Promote Conceptual Understanding in Physics Classrooms. In I. M. Saleh & M. S. Khine (Eds.), *Fostering scientific habits of mind: pedagogical knowledge and best practices in science education* (pp. 145–171). Rotterdam: Sense.

Metz, J. C. M., Stoelinga, G. M., Pels-Rijcken-Van, E., Taalman Kip, E. H., & Van Der Brand-Valkenburg, B. W. M. (Eds.). (1994). Blueprint 1994: Training of Doctors in the Netherlands: Objectives of Undergraduate Medical Education. Nijmegen, University Publication Office.

Mewborn, D., & Tyminski, A. (2006). Lortie's apprenticeship of observation revisited. *For the Learning of Mathematics, 26*(3), 30–32.

Meyers, C. (1986). *Teaching students to think critically*. San Francisco, CA: Josey-Bass.

Mezirow, J. (1990). *Fostering critical reflection in adulthood: A guide to transformative and emancipatory learning*. San Francisco, CA: Jossey-Bass.

Mileder, L. P., Schmidt, A., & Dimai, H. P. (2014). Clinicians should be aware of their responsibilities as role models: A case report on the impact of poor role modeling. *Medical Education Online, 19*(1), 23479. doi:10.3402/meo.v19.23479 PMID:24499869

Miller, L. E. (2006, October). *Determining what could/should be: The Delphi technique and its application*. Paper presented at the meeting of the 2006 annual meeting of the Mid-Western.

Miller, K., & Shifflet, R. (2016). How memories of school inform PST's feared and desired selves as teachers. *Teaching and Teacher Education, 53*, 20–29. doi:10.1016/j.tate.2015.10.002

Miller, P. H., Kessel, F. S., & Flavell, J. H. (1971). Thinking about people thinking about people thinking about…: A study of social cognitive development. *Child Development, 41*(3), 613–623.

Mills, C. N., Melican, G. J., & Ahluwalia, N. T. (1991). Defining minimal competence. *Educational Measurement: Issues and Practice, 10*(2), 15–16. doi:10.1111/j.1745-3992.1991.tb00186.x

Mills, J. (1998). Better teaching through provocation. *College Teaching, 46*(1), 21–25. doi:10.1080/87567559809596228

Ministry of Education. (2013). Singapore: Primary School Curriculum. Retrieved from.

Minott, M. (2011). Reflective teaching, critical literacy and the teacher's tasks in the critical literacy classroom. A confirmatory investigation. *Reflective Practice: International and Multidisciplinary Perspectives, 12*(1), 73–85. doi:1 0.1080/14623943.2011.541096

Mintzberg, H. (2003). Unconventional wisdom: A conversation with Henry Mintzberg. *Leadership in Action, 23*(4), 8–10. doi:10.1002/lia.1028

Mishra, P., Fahnoe, C., & Henriksen, D. (2013). Creativity, self-directed learning and the architecture of technology rich environments. *TechTrends, 57*(1), 10–13. doi:10.100711528-012-0623-z

Mitchell, L. S. (1950). *Our children and our schools*. New York, NY: Simon & Schuster.

Mitchell, L. S. (2001). *Young geographers*. New York, NY: Bank Street College of Education. (Original work published 1934)

Mohr, N. M., Stoltze, A. J., Harland, K. K., Van Heukelom, J. N., Hogrefe, C. P., & Ahmed, A. (2007). An evidence-based medicine curriculum implemented in journal club improves resident performance on the Fresno test. *The Journal of Emergency Medicine, 48*(2), 222–229. doi:10.1016/j.jemermed.2014.09.011 PMID:25440869

Montessori, M. (1948). *The discovery of the child*. Adyar, India: Kalakshetra Press.

Montessori, M. (1949). *The absorbent mind*. Adyar, India: Kalakshetra Press. Retrieved from https://archive.org/details/absorbentmind031961mbp

Moore, B., & Stanley, T. (2010). *Critical thinking and formative assessments: Increasing rigor in your classroom*. Larchmont, NY: Eye on Education Inc.

Moore, Z. E. (2007). Critical Thinking and the Evidence-Based Practice of Sport Psychology. *Journal of Clinical Sport Psychology, 1*(1), 9–22. doi:10.1123/jcsp.1.1.9

Morgan, M. (1990). *Eric: Encouraging Critical Thinking in the Language Arts*. Academic Press.

Morgan, G. (2006). *Images of Organization*. Beverly Hills, CA: Sage Publications.

Morris, C. D., Bransford, J. D., & Franks, J. J. (1977). Levels of processing versus transfer appropriate processing. *Journal of Verbal Learning and Verbal Behavior, 16*(5), 519–533. doi:10.1016/S0022-5371(77)80016-9

Mueller, M. P., Zeidler, D. L., & Jenkins, L. L. (2011). Earth's role in moral reasoning and functional scientific literacy. In J. L. DeVitis & T. Yu (Eds.), *Character and moral education: a reader* (pp. 382–391). New York: Peter Lang.

Mulligan, J. T., & Mitchelmore, M. C. (1997). Young children's intuitive models of multiplication and division. *Journal for Research in Mathematics Education, 28*(3), 309–330. doi:10.2307/749783

Mulnix, J. (2012). Thinking critically about critical thinking. *Educational Philosophy and Theory, 44*(5), 464–479. doi:10.1111/j.1469-5812.2010.00673.x

Mushayikwa, E., & Lubben, F. (2009). Self-directed professional development – Hope for teachers working in deprived environments? *Teaching and Teacher Education, 25*(3), 375–382. doi:10.1016/j.tate.2008.12.003

Myers, B. E., & James, E. D. (2004). *The Influence of Student Learning Style on Critical Thinking Skill*. Retrieved May 8, 2018, from http://plaza.ufl.edu/bmyers/Papers/SAERC2004/LearningstyleCT.pdf

Nagle, J. (2008). Becoming a reflective practitioner in the age of accountability. *The Educational Forum, 73*(1), 76–86. doi:10.1080/00131720802539697

Nappi, J. S. (2017). *The Importance of Questioning in Developing Critical Thinking Skills*. International Journal for Professional Educators.

National Academies of Sciences, Engineering, and Medicine. (2015). *Improving diagnosis in health care*. Washington, DC: The National Academies Press.

National Association for the Education of Young Children. (2018). *Anti-bias education*. Retrieved from https://www.naeyc.org/resources/topics/anti-bias-education

National Commission on Excellence in Education. (1983). *A nation at risk: The imperative for educational reform*. Washington, DC: United States Department of Education.

National Council of Teacher of Mathematics. (2014). *Principles to actions: Ensuring mathematical success for all*. Reston, VA: National Council of Teachers of Mathematics.

National Education Association (NEA). (n.d.) *Code of ethics*. Retrieved from http://www.nea.org/home/30442.htm

National Education Goals Panel. (1992). *Executive summary: The national education goals report-building a nation of learners*. Washington, DC: Author.

National Research Council (NRC). (1996). *National science education standards*. Washington, DC: National Academy Press.

National Research Council (NRC). (2012). *A Framework for K-12 science education: Practices, crosscutting concepts, and core ideas*. Washington, DC: The National Academies Press.

National Research Council. (1996). *National Science Education Standards*. Washington, DC: National Academy Press.

National Research Council. (2001). *Adding it up: Helping Children Learn Mathematics*. Washington, DC: The National Academies Press.

National Research Council. (2011). A Framework for K-12 Science Education: Practices, Crosscutting Concepts, and Core Ideas. Committee on a Conceptual Framework for New K-12 Science Education Standards. Board on Science Education, Division of Behavioral and Social Sciences and Education. Washington, DC: The National Academies Press.

National Research Council. (2012). *A framework for K-12 science education: Practices, crosscutting concepts, and core ideas. Committee on Conceptual Framework for the New K-12 Science Education Standards, Board on Science Education, National Research Council*. Washington, DC: National Academies Press.

Nelson, C., & Harper, V. (2006). A pedagogy of difficulty: Preparing teachers to understand and integrate complexity in teaching and learning. *Teacher Education Quarterly*, *33*(2), 7–21.

Newell, G. E., Beach, R., Smith, J., & Vanderheide, J. (2011). Teaching and learning argumentative reading and writing : A review of research. *Reading Research Quarterly*, *46*(3), 273–304.

Newell, G. E., Beach, R., Smith, J., & VanDerHeide, J. (2011). Teaching and learning argumentativerReading and writing: A review of research. *Reading Research Quarterly*, *46*, 273–304.

Next Generation Science Standards. (2013). Washington DC: *The National Academies Press*. http://nextgenscience.org/next-generation-science-standards

NGSS Lead States. (2013). *Next Generation Science Standards: For states, by states*. Washington, DC: The National Academies Press.

NGSS Lead States. (2013). *Next Generation Science Standards: For States, By States*. Washington, DC: The National Academies Press.

Nias, J. (1989). Teaching and the self. In M. L. Holly & C. S. McLoughlin (Eds.), *Perspectives on teacher professional development* (pp. 155–173). London, England: The Falmer Press.

Nicol, D., Thomson, A., & Breslin, C. (2014). Rethinking feedback practices in education: A peer review perspective. *Assessment & Evaluation in Education, 39*(1), 102–122. doi:10.1080/02602938.2013.795518

Niemi, P. M. (1997). Medical students' professional identity: Self-reflection during the preclinical years. *Medical Education, 31*(6), 408–415. doi:10.1046/j.1365-2923.1997.00697.x PMID:9463642

Noah, M., & Agbaire, J. J. (2013). Methodological issues in comparative education studies: An exploration of the approaches of Kandel and Holmes. *Journal of Educational Review, 6*(3), 349–356.

Noel, L., & Liub, T. L. (2017). Using Design Thinking to Create a New Education Paradigm for Elementary Level Children for Higher Student Engagement and Success. *Journal of Design and Technology Education, 22*(1), 1.

Nonaka, I., & Konno, N. (1998). The concept of "ba": Building a foundation for knowledge creation. *California Management Review, 40*(3), 40–54. doi:10.2307/41165942

Norman, G. R., Monteiro, S. D., Sherbino, J., Ilgen, J. S., Schmidt, H. G., & Mamede, S. (2017). The causes of errors in clinical reasoning: Cognitive biases, knowledge deficits, and dual process thinking. *Academic Medicine, 92*(1), 23–30. doi:10.1097/ACM.0000000000001421 PMID:27782919

Norris, S. P. (1985). Synthesis of research on critical thinking. *Educational Leadership, 8*, 40–45.

Norris, S. P., & Ennis, R. (1989). *Evaluating critical thinking*. Pacific Grove, CA: Critical Thinking Press and Software.

Nunan, D. (1988). *The Learner-Centred Curriculum*. Cambridge, UK: Cambridge University Press. doi:10.1017/CBO9781139524506

Nunan, D. (1999). *Second language teaching and learning*. Boston: Heinle and Heinle Publishers.

Nunan, D., O'Sullivan, J., Heneghan, C., Pluddemann, A., Aronson, J., & Mahtani, K. (2017). Ten essential papers for the practice of evidence-based medicine. *Evidence-Based Medicine, 22*(6), 202–204. doi:10.1136/ebmed-2017-110854 PMID:29170157

Nussbaum, E. M. (2011). Argumentation, dialogue theory, and probability modeling: Alternative frameworks for argumentation research in education. *Educational Psychologist, 46*(2), 84–106. doi:10.1080/00461520.2011.558816

Nuttall, C. (1982). *Teaching reading skills in a foreign language*. London: Heinemann Educational.

Ontario Ministry of Education. (2015). *The Ontario curriculum: Grades 11 and 12*. Retrieved from http://www.edu.gov.on.ca/eng/curriculum/secondary/2015cws11and12.pdf

Orlich, D. C., Harder, R. J., Callahan, R. C., Trevisan, M. s., Brown, A. H., & Miller, D. E. (2013). *Teaching strategies: A guide to effective instruction* (10th ed.). Belmont, CA: Wadsworth Cengage Learning.

Osborne, J. (2005). The Role of Argumentation in Science Education. In K. Boersma (Ed.), *Research and the Quality of Science Education* (pp. 367–380). Amsterdam: Springer. doi:10.1007/1-4020-3673-6_29

Osborne, J. (2010). Arguing to learn in science: The role of collaborative, critical discourse. *Science, 328*(5977), 463–466. doi:10.1126cience.1183944 PMID:20413492

Osbourne, J. (2014a). Teaching critical thinking? New directions in science education. *SSR, 95*(352), 53–62.

Osbourne, J. (2014b). Teaching Scientific Practices: Meeting the Challenge of Change. *Journal of Science Teacher Education, 25*, 175–196.

Otteson, E. (2007). Reflection in teacher education. *Reflective Practice, 8*(1), 31–46. doi:10.1080/14623940601138899

Özdemir, H. (2013). Ortak eylem amaçlı metotla yabancı dil öğretiminde otantik doküman kullanımı. *International Periodical For the Languages. Literature and History of Turkish or Turkic, 8*(10), 555–560.

Paice, E., Heard, S., & Moss, F. (2002). How important are role models in making good doctors? *British Medical Journal, 325*(7366), 707–710. doi:10.1136/bmj.325.7366.707 PMID:12351368

Pajares, M. (1992). Teachers' beliefs and educational research: Cleaning up a messy construct. *Review of Educational Research, 62*(3), 307–332. doi:10.3102/00346543062003307

Parten, M. B. (1932). Social participation among pre-school children. *Journal of Abnormal and Social Psychology, 27*(3), 243–269. doi:10.1037/h0074524

Paul, R. W. (1991). Teaching critical thinking in the strong sense. In A. L. Costa (Ed.), Developing minds: A resource book for teaching thinking (Rev. ed.; Vol. 1). Alexandria, VA: ASCD.

Paul, R. W., Elder, L., Bartell, T., & California Commission on Teacher Credentialing, Sacramento. (1997). *California Teacher Preparation for Instruction in Critical Thinking Research Findings and Policy Recommendations.* Distributed by ERIC Clearinghouse.

Paul, R., & Elder, L. (2006). *The miniature guide to critical thinking: Concepts and tools.* Retrieved from https://www.criticalthinking.org/files/Concepts_Tools

Paul, R., Fisher, A., & Nosich, G. (1993). *Workshop on critical thinking strategies.* Sonoma State University: Foundation for Critical Thinking.

Paul, R. (2004). *Critical thinking: What every person needs to survive in a rapidly changing world.* Sonomata State University, Centre for Critical Thinking.

Paul, R. (2006). *Critical thinking: How to prepare students for a rapidly changing world.* CA: Foundations for Critical Thinking Press.

Paul, R. W. (1993). *Critical thinking — What every person needs to survive in a rapidly changing world* (3rd ed.). Santa Rosa, CA: Foundation for Critical Thinking.

Paul, R. W. (2003). Bloom's Taxonomy and Critical Thinking Instruction. *Educational Leadership.*

Paul, R. W., & Binkler, J. A. (1990). *Critical Thinking: What Every Person Needs to Survive in a Rapidly Changing World.* Rohnert Park, CA: Center for Critical Thinking and Moral Critique.

Paul, R. W., & Elder, L. (2006). Critical thinking: The nature of critical and creative thought. *Journal of Developmental Education, 30*(2), 34–35.

Paul, R., Binker, A. J. A., Jensen, K., & Kreklau, H. (1990). *Critical thinking handbook: 4th – 6th grades. A guide for Remodeling Lesson Plans in Language Arts, Social Studies and Science.* CA: Foundation for Critical Thinking.

Paul, R., & Elder, L. (2001). *Critical thinking: Tools for taking charge of your learning and your life.* Upper Saddle River, NJ: Prentice Hall.

Paul, R., & Elder, L. (2004). *The miniature guide to critical thinking concepts and tools.* Dillon Beach, CA: The Foundation for Critical Thinking.

Paul, R., & Elder, L. (2007). *A guide for educators to critical thinking competency standards*. Dillon Beach, CA: Foundation for Critical Thinking.

Paul, R., Elder, L., & Bartell, T. (1997). *California Teacher Preparation for Instruction in Critical Thinking: Research Findings and Policy Recommendations*. California Commission on Teacher Credentialing, Sacramento.

Paul, R., Elder, L., & Bartell, T. (1997). *California teacher preparation for instruction in critical thinking: Research findings and policy recommendations*. Sacramento, CA: California Commission on Teacher Credentialing.

Peacock, M. (1997). The effect of authentic materials on the motivation of EFL learners. *ELT Journal, 51*(2), 144–156. doi:10.1093/elt/51.2.144

Penkauskienė, D. (2010). *Integration of critical thinking principles into the curriculum of secondary schools: Lithuania's case*. Research Report. Retrieved May 8, 2018, from http://www.sdcentras.lt/pr_ctp/Report.pdf

Pennycook, G., & Rand, D. G. (2018). Who falls for fake news? The roles of bullshit receptivity, overclaiming, familiarity, and analytic thinking.

Perie, M. (2008). A guide to understanding and developing performance-level descriptors. *Educational Measurement: Issues and Practice, 27*(4), 15–29. doi:10.1111/j.1745-3992.2008.00135.x

Perie, M., Grigg, W. S., & Donahue, P. L. (2005). *The Nation's Report Card: Reading 2005 (NCES 2006–451)*. U.S. Department of Education, Institute of Education Sciences, National Center for Education Statistics. Washington, DC: U.S. Government Printing Office.

Perkins, D. N. (2014). *Futurewise: Educating our children for a changing world*. San Francisco: Jossey Bass.

Perrem, L., Fanshawe, T., Sharif, F., Pluddermann, A., & O'Neill, M. B. (2016). A national physician survey of diagnostic error in pediatrics. *European Journal of Pediatrics, 175*(10), 1387–1392. doi:10.100700431-016-2772-0 PMID:27631589

Peterson, P. L., Marx, R. W., & Clark, C. M. (1978). Teacher Planning, Teacher Behavior, and Student Achievement. *American Educational Research Journal, 15*(3), 417–432. doi:10.3102/00028312015003417

Philipp, R. A., Ambrose, R., Lamb, L. L., Sowder, J. T., Schappelle, B. P., Sowder, L., ... Chauvot, J. (2007). Effect of early field experiences on the mathematical content knowledge and beliefs of prospective elementary school teachers: An experimental study. *Journal for Research in Mathematics Education, 38*(5), 38.

Philips, J. M. (2005). Strategies For Active Learning in Online Continuing Education. *Journal of Continuing Education in Nursing, 36*(2), 77–83. doi:10.3928/0022-0124-20050301-08 PMID:15835583

Piaget, J. (1929). *The child's conception of the world*. London: Routledge & Kegan Paul, Ltd.

Piaget, J. (1952). *The origins of intelligence in children*. New York, NY: International Universities Press. doi:10.1037/11494-000

Piaget, J. (1959). *The language and thought of the child* (Vol. 5). Psychology Press.

Pillen, M., Beijaard, D., & den Brok, P. (2013). Tensions in beginning teachers' professional identity development, accompanying feelings and coping strategies. *European Journal of Teacher Education, 36*(3), 240–260. doi:10.1080/02619768.2012.696192

Pirozzi, R. (2003). *Critical Reading, Critical Thinking: A Contemporary Issues Approach*. Academic Press.

Pithers, R. T., & Soden, R. (2000). Critical thinking in education. *Review of Educational Research, 42*, 237–249.

Plourde, L. A. (2002). Elementary science education: The influence of student teaching-where it all begins. *Education, 123*(2), 253–259.

Pogrow, S. (1988). Teaching thinking to at-risk elementary students. *Educational Leadership, 5/7,* 79–85.

Portelli, J. P. (1994). The challenge of teaching for critical thinking. *McGill Journal of Education, 29*(2), 137–152.

Possin, K. (2008). A field guide to critical-thinking assessment. *Teaching Philosophy, 31*(3), 221–228. doi:10.5840/teachphil200831324

Postman, N. (1985). Amusing Ourselves to Death. *Etc.; a Review of General Semantics, 42*(1), 13–18. Retrieved from http://search.ebscohost.com/login.aspx?direct=true&AuthType=sso&db=eue&AN=15901018&site=eds-live&scope=site&authtype=sso&custid=ns083389

Pouwels, J., & Biesta, G. (2017). With Socrates on your heels and Descartes in your hand: On the notion of conflict in John Dewey's democracy and education. *Education in Science, 7*(1), 1–14. doi:10.3390/educsci7010007

Powell, W. A. (2014). *The effects of emotive reasoning on secondary school students' decision-making in the context of socioscientific issues.* Unpublished doctoral dissertation, University of South Florida.

Powers, K. (2011). Going mental: How music education can help develop critical thinking. *Teaching Music, 18*(6), 40–45.

Pozo-Olano, J. (2018). *A year of disruption? Education trends for 2018.* Retrieved from www.observer.com

Pratt, C. (1948). *I learn from children.* New York, NY: Simon and Schuster.

Prawat, R. S. (1991). The value of ideas: The immersion approach to the development of thinking. *Educational Researcher, 20*(2), 3–10. doi:10.3102/0013189X020002003

Prideaux, D., Alexander, H., Bower, A., Dacre, J., Haist, S., Jolly, B., ... Tallett, S. (2000). Clinical teaching: Maintaining an educational role for doctors in the new health care environment. *Medical Education, 34*(10), 820–826. doi:10.1046/j.1365-2923.2000.00756.x PMID:11012932

Profetto-McGrath, J. (2003). The relationship of critical thinking skills and critical thinking dispositions of baccalaureate nursing students. *Journal of Advanced Nursing, 43*(6), 569–577. doi:10.1046/j.1365-2648.2003.02755.x PMID:12950562

Profetto-McGrath, J. (2005). Critical Thinking and Evidence-Based Practice. *Journal of Professional Nursing, 21*(6), 364–371. doi:10.1016/j.profnurs.2005.10.002 PMID:16311232

Pruitt, S. L. (2014). The Next Generation Science Standards: The features and challenges. *Journal of Science Teacher Education, 25*(2), 145–16. doi:10.100710972-014-9385-0

Pugach, M. C., & Johnson, L. (1990). Meeting diverse needs through professional peer collaboration. In W. Stainback & S. Stainback (Eds.), *Support networks for inclusive schooling: Interdependent integrated evaluation* (pp. 123-137). PH Brookes Pub. Co.

Quek, C. L. (2013). Exploring beginning teachers' attitudes and beliefs on classroom management. *New Horizons in Education, 61*(2), 13–33.

Quick, H., Holtzman, D., & Chaney, K. (2009). Professional development and instructional practice: Conceptions and evidence of effectiveness. *Journal of Education for Students Placed at Risk, 14*(1), 45–71. doi:10.1080/10824660802715429

R Development Core Team. (2013). *R Version 3.0.1: A language and environment for statistical computing.* Vienna, Austria: The R Foundation for Statistical Computing. Retrieved from http://www.R-project.org

Rasch, G. (1960). *Probabilistic models for some intelligence and attainment tests*. Copenhagen: Danmarks Paedagogiske Institut.

Raymond, M. R., & Reid, J. B. (2001). Who made thee a judge? Selecting and training participants for standard setting. In C. J. Cizek (Ed.), *Setting performance standards: Concepts, methods, and perspectives* (pp. 119–157). Mahwah, NJ: Lawrence Erlbaum.

Reckase, M. D. (2009). Standard setting theory and practice: Issues and difficulties. In N. Figueras & J. Noijons (Eds.), Linking to the CEFR levels: Research perspectives (pp. 13 - 20). Arnhem, Cito: Institute for Educational Measurement Council of Europe European Association for Language Testing and Assessment (EALTA).

Reckase, M. D. (2001). Innovative methods for helping standard-setting participants to perform their task: The role of feedback regarding consistency, accuracy, and impact. In C. J. Cizek (Ed.), *Setting performance standards: Concepts, methods, and perspectives* (pp. 159–173). Mahwah, NJ: Lawrence Erlbaum.

Reddy, L. A., Dudek, C. M., & Lekwa, A. (2017). Classroom strategies coaching model: Integration of formative assessment and instructional coaching. *Theory into Practice*, *56*(1), 46–55. doi:10.1080/00405841.2016.1241944

Redecker, C., Ala-Mutka, K., Leis, M., Leendertse, M., Punie, Y., Gijsbers, G., ... Hoogveld, B. (2011). *The Future of Learning: Preparing for Change*. Luxembourg: Publications Office of the European Union.

Reece, G. J. (2005). Critical thinking and cognitive transfer: Implications for the development of online information literacy tutorials. *Research Strategies*, *20*(4), 482–493. doi:10.1016/j.resstr.2006.12.018

Rees, G. (2018). *Jigsaw reading*. Retrieved from https://www.teachingenglish.org.uk/article/ jigsaw-reading

Reid, M., Burn, A., & Parker, D. (2002). *Evaluation report of the becta digital video pilot project. British Film Industry (bfi)*.

Reid, I. (1996). Romantic ideologies, educational practices, and institutional formations of English. *Journal of Educational Administration and History*, *28*(1), 22–41. doi:10.1080/0022062960280102

Reid, J. B. (1991). Training judges to generate standard setting data. *Educational Measurement: Issues and Practice*, *10*(2), 11–14. doi:10.1111/j.1745-3992.1991.tb00187.x

Reinhardt, K. S. (2017) Beyond the practical aspects of learning to teach: Mentoring teacher candidates toward the diverse needs of students. *TxEP: Texas Educator Preparation*. Retrieved from https://www.csotte.com/assets/txep/2017-txep-reinhardt.pdf

Rencic, J. (2011). Twelve tips for teaching expertise in clinical reasoning. *Medical Teacher*, *33*(11), 887–892. doi:10.3 109/0142159X.2011.558142 PMID:21711217

Rencic, J., Trowbridge, R. L. Jr, Fagan, M., Szauter, K., & Durning, S. (2017). Clinical Reasoning Education at US Medical Schools: Results from a National Survey of Internal Medicine Clerkship Directors. *Journal of General Internal Medicine*, *32*(11), 1242–1246. doi:10.100711606-017-4159-y PMID:28840454

Ren, Y., & Tao, L. (2014). The critical thinking and Chinese Creative Education. *Canadian Social Science*, *10*(6), 206–211.

Ricketts, A. (2014). Preservice elementary teachers' ideas about scientific practices. *Science and Education*, *23*(10), 2119–2135. doi:10.100711191-014-9709-7

Riddell, T. (2007). Critical assumptions: Thinking critically about critical thinking. *The Journal of Nursing Education*, *46*(3), 121–126. PMID:17396551

Rinaldi, C. (2006). *In dialogue with Reggio Emilia*. New York, NY: Routledge.

Rinkevich, J. L. (2011). Creative teaching: Why it matters and where to begin. *The Clearing House: A Journal of Educational Strategies, Issues and Ideas, 89*(5), 219–223.

Ritchhart, R., & Perkins, D. (2005). *Cultures of Thinking Project*. Project Zero, Harvard Graduate School of Education. Retrieved from http://www.ronritchhart.com/COT_Resources_files/6Principles%20of%20COT_V2.pdf

Ritchhart, R., & Perkins, D. N. (2008). Making thinking visible. *Educational Leadership*, 57–61.

Roberts, P. (2008). Teaching as an ethical and political process: A Freirean process. In V. Carpenter, J. Jesson, P. Roberts et al. (Eds.), Ngā Kaupapa here: Connections and contradictions in education (pp. 99-108). Melbourne, AU: Cengage.

Roberts, M. J., Perera, M., Lawrentschuk, N., Romanic, D., Papa, N., & Bolton, D. (2015). Globalization of continuing professional development by journal clubs via microblogging: A systematic review. *Journal of Medical Internet Research, 17*(4), 103. doi:10.2196/jmir.4194 PMID:25908092

Robinson, K. (2006). Do school kills creativity? [Video file]. *TED Talk*. Retrieved from http:www.ted.com/talks/ken_robinson_says_schools_kill_creativity.html

Rodgers, C. R., & Scott, K. H. (2008). The development of the personal self and professional identity in learning to teach. In M. Cochrane-Smith, S. Freiman-Demers, D. McIntrye & K. Demers (Eds.), Handbook of research on teacher education, New York, NY: Routledge.

Rojas-Drummond, S. M., Albarrán, C. D., & Littleton, K. S. (2008). Collaboration, creativity and the co-construction of oral and written texts. *Thinking Skills and Creativity, 3*(3), 177–191. doi:10.1016/j.tsc.2008.09.008

Role Play/Simulation. (2018, December 7). Retrieved from https://otis.coe.uky.edu/ccsso/cssapmodules/sbp/sbp/Role%20PlaySimulation.html

Rose, S. L., & Calabrese Barton, A. (2012). Should Great Lakes City build a new power plant? How youth navigate socioscientific issues. *Journal of Research in Science Teaching, 49*(5), 541–567. doi:10.1002/tea.21017

Ross, D., Loeffler, K., Schipper, S., Vandermeer, B., & Allan, G. M. (2013). Do scores on three commonly used measures of critical thinking correlate with academic success of health professions trainees? A systematic review and meta-analysis. *Academic Medicine, 88*(5), 724–734. doi:10.1097/ACM.0b013e31828b0823 PMID:23524925

Roth McDuffie, A., Foote, M. Q., Bolson, C., Turner, E. E., Aguirre, J. M., Bartell, T. G., ... Land, T. (2014). Using video analysis to support prospecitve K-8 teachers' noticing of students' multiple mathematical knowledge bases. *Journal of Mathematics Teacher Education, 17*(3), 245–258. doi:10.100710857-013-9257-0

Roth, K. J. (2014). Elementary science teaching. In N. G. Lederman & S. K. Abell (Eds.), *Handbook of research on science education* (Vol. 2, pp. 361–394). New York, NY: Routledge.

Roth, L. (1999). Educating the cut-and- paste generation. *Library Journal, 124*(18), 42–44.

Royce, C. S., Hayes, M. M., & Schwartzstein, R. M. (2018). Teaching Critical Thinking: A Case for Instruction in Cognitive Biases to Reduce Diagnostic Errors and Improve Patient Safety. *Academic Medicine*, 1. doi:10.1097/ACM.0000000000002518 PMID:30398993

Rudd, R., Matt, B., & Tracy, H. (2000). Undergraduate Agriculture Student Learning Styles and Critical Thinking Abilities: Is there a relationship. *Journal of Agricultural Education, 41*(3), 2–12. Retrieved from http://pubs.aged.tamu.edu/jae/pdf/Vol41/41-03-02.pdf

Ruhf, R. J. (2006). *Analyzing the effects of inquiry-based instruction on the learning atmosphere. Science among pre-service teacher education students* (Doctoral thesis).

Russell, T., & Martin, A. K. (2014). Learning to teach science. In N. G. Lederman & S. K. Abell (Eds.), *Handbook of research on science education* (Vol. 2, pp. 871–888). New York, NY: Routledge.

Ryan, K., & Cooper, J. M. (2006). *Those who can, teach*. Boston: Houghton Mifflin.

Saber, T. A. S., Lee, H., Mathews, S. C., Shore, A., Makary, M. A., Pronovost, P. J., & Newman-Toker, D. E. (2013). 25-year summary of US malpractice claims for diagnostic errors 1986-2010: An analysis from the National Practitioner Data Bank. *BMJ Quality & Safety*, *22*(8), 672–680. doi:10.1136/bmjqs-2012-001550 PMID:23610443

Sachs, J. (2005). Teacher education and the development of professional identity: learning to be a teacher. In M. Kompf & P. Denicolo (Eds.), *Connecting Policy and Practice: Challenges for Teaching and Learning in Schools and Universities* (pp. 5–21). London, UK: Routledge.

Sackett, D. L., Rosenberg, W. M., Gray, J. A., Haynes, R. B., & Richardson, W. S. (1996). Evidence based medicine: What it is and what it isn't. *British Medical Journal*, *312*(7023), 71–72. doi:10.1136/bmj.312.7023.71 PMID:8555924

Sadler, T. D., Klosterman, M. L., & Topcu, M. S. (2011). Learning science content and socioscientific reasoning through classroom explorations of global climate change. In T. D. Sadler (Ed.), *Socio-scientific issues in science classrooms: Teaching, learning and research* (pp. 45–77). The Netherlands: Springer. doi:10.1007/978-94-007-1159-4_4

Sadler, T. D., & Murakami, C. D. (2014). Socio-scientific issues-based teaching and learning: Hydrofracturing as an illustrative context of a framework for implementation and research. *Brazilian Journal of Research in Science Education*, *14*(2), 331–342.

Saeger, K. J. (2014). The development of critical thinking skills in undergraduate students (2014). *Culminating Projects in Higher Education Administration*. Retrieved from http://repository.stcloudstate.edu/hied_etds/1

Şahinel, M. (2005). Etkin Öğrenme. In Eğitimde Yeni Yönelimler (pp. 149-165). Ankara: Pegema.

Sakiz, G., Pape, S. J., & Hoy, A. W. (2012). Does perceived teacher affective support matter for middle school students in mathematics classrooms? *Journal of School Psychology*, *50*(2), 235–255. doi:10.1016/j.jsp.2011.10.005 PMID:22386122

Salisbury, F., & Karasmanis, S. (2011). Are they ready?: Exploring student information literacy skills in the transition from secondary to tertiary education. *Australian Academic and Research Libraries*, *42*(1), 43–58.

Salisbury-Glennon, J., & Stevens, R. (1999). Addressing preservice teachers' conceptions of motivation. *Teaching and Teacher Education*, *15*, 74–752. doi:10.1016/S0742-051X(99)00023-2

Salmon, A. K. (2008). Promoting a culture of thinking in young children. *Early Childhood Education Journal*, *35*(5), 457–461. doi:10.100710643-007-0227-y

Samuel, D. F. (2013). *Teachers' beliefs as predictors of their inquiry-based instructional practices in the implementation of the primary school science and technology curriculum in St. Lucia* (Unpublished doctoral thesis). University of the West Indies, Cave Hill Campus, Bridgetown, Barbados.

San, İ. (2006). Yaratıcı dramanın eğitsel boyutları, Yaratıcı Drama (1985-1998 Yazılar). İkinci Baskı, Ankara: Naturel Kitap Yayın Dağıtım, 113-122.

Santin, F. (2017). Reggio Emilia: An essential tool to develop critical thinking in early childhood. *Journal of New Approaches in Educational Research*, *6*(1), 50–56. doi:10.7821/naer.2017.1.207

Santos, L. F. (2017). The role of critical thinking in science education. *Journal of Education and Practice*, *8*(20), 159–173.

Sar, Ö., & Nalbant, H. (2014). Medical Practice and Review Medical students ' reflections on first clinical experience. *Medical Practice and Review*, *5*, 31–35.

Sarsani, M. (2008). Do high and low creative children differ in their cognition and motivation? *Creativity Research Journal, 20*(2), 155–170. doi:10.1080/10400410802059861

Scales, P. (2013). *Teaching in the lifelong learning sector*. Maidenhead: Open University Press.

Schachter, J., Thum, Y. M., & Zifkin, D. (2006). How much does creative teaching enhance elementary school students' achievement? *The Journal of Creative Behavior, 40*(1), 47–72. doi:10.1002/j.2162-6057.2006.tb01266.x

Schacter, D. L., & Addis, D. R. (2007). The cognitive neuroscience of constructive memory: Remembering the past and imagining the future. *Philosophical Transactions of the Royal Society of London. Series B, Biological Sciences, 362*(1481), 773–786. doi:10.1098/rstb.2007.2087 PMID:17395575

Schmidt, H. G., & Rikers, R. M. J. P. (2007). How expertise develops in medicine: Knowledge encapsulation and illness script formation. *Medical Education, 41*, 1133–1139. PMID:18004989

Schneider, R. M., & Plasman, K. (2011). Science teacher learning progressions: A review of science teachers' pedagogical content knowledge development. *Review of Educational Research, 81*(4), 35. doi:10.3102/0034654311423382

Schon, D. (1983). *The reflective practitioner*. New York, NY: Basic Books.

Schön, D. (1983). *The reflective practitioner: How professionals think in action*. New York: Basic Books.

Schön, D. (1987). *Educating the reflective practitioner: Towards a new design for teaching and learning in the professions*. San Francisco, CA: Jossey-Bass.

School of Educators. (2011, December). Experience & education-John Dewey (1938 publication). Retrieved from http://schoolofeducators.com/2011/12/experience-education-john-dewey/

Schroeder, R., & Cahoy, E. S. (2010). Valuing information literacy: Affective learning and the ACRL standards. *Libraries and the Academy, 10*(2), 127–146. doi:10.1353/pla.0.0096

Schuck, S., Aubusson, P., & Buchanan, J. (2008). Enhancing teacher education practice through professional learning conversations. *European Journal of Teacher Education, 31*(2), 215–227. doi:10.1080/02619760802000297

Schussler, D., Stooksberry, L., & Bercaw, L. (2010). Understanding teacher candidate dispositions: Reflecting to build self-awareness. *Journal of Teacher Education, 61*(4), 350–363. doi:10.1177/0022487110371377

Schwarz, C., Passmore, C., & Reiser, B. J. (2017). *Helping students make sense of the world using next generation science and engineering practices*. Arlington, VA: NSTA Press, National Science Teachers Association.

Scott, C. L. (2015). *The futures of learning 2: what kind of learning for the 21st century? ERF Working Papers Series, No. 14*. Paris: UNESCO.

Scott, C. L. (1999). Teachers' bias towards creative children. *Creativity Research Journal, 12*(4), 321–328. doi:10.120715326934crj1204_10

Scott, J. N., & Markert, R. J. (1994). Relationship between critical thinking skills and success in preclinical courses. *Academic Medicine, 69*(11), 920–924. doi:10.1097/00001888-199411000-00015 PMID:7945695

Scott, J. N., Markert, R. J., & Dunn, M. M. (1998). Critical thinking: Change during medical school and relationship to performance in clinical clerkship. *Medical Education, 32*(1), 14–18. doi:10.1046/j.1365-2923.1998.00701.x PMID:9624394

Scott, T. M., & Chafe, L. L. (1997). Critical Thinking in Medical School Exams. In A. J. J. A. Scherpbier, C. P. M. van der Vleuten, J. J. Rethans, & A. F. W. van der Steeg (Eds.), *Advances in Medical Education* (pp. 387–389). Dordrecht: Springer. doi:10.1007/978-94-011-4886-3_117

Sedden, M. L., & Clark, K. R. (2016). Motivating students in the 21st century. *Radiologic Technology*, *87*(6), 609–616. PMID:27390228

Sedova, K., Sedlacek, M., & Svaricek, R. (2016). Teacher professional development as a means of transforming student classroom talk. *Teaching and Teacher Education*, *57*, 14–25. doi:10.1016/j.tate.2016.03.005

Seeler, D. C., Turnwald, K. H., & Bull, K. S. (1994). From Teaching to Learning. *Journal of Veterinary Medical Education*, *21*(1). Retrieved from http://ilte.ius.edu/pdf/BarrTagg.pdf

Shakurnia, A., & Aslami, M. (2017). Critical Thinking Skills of Medical Students at Ahvaz Jundishapur University of Medical Sciences. *Indian Journal of Medical Education*, *17*, 420–427.

Shandomo, H. M. (2010). The role of critical reflection in teacher education. *School—. University Partnerships*, *4*, 101–113.

Shapiro, E. K., & Biber, B. (1972). The education of young children: A developmental-interaction point of view. *Teachers College Record*, *74*, 55–79.

Sharkey, J. (2006). Towards information fluency: Applying a different model to an information literacy credit course. *Reference Services Review*, *34*(1), 71–85. doi:10.1108/00907320610648770

Sharplin, E., Kehrwald, B., Garth, S., Sharplin, E., & Kehrwald, B. (2017). *Real-time coaching and pre-service teacher education*. Singapore: Springer.

Shaw, R. D. (2014). *How Critical is Critical Thinking*. National Association for Music Education. doi:10.1177/0027432114544376

Shenkman, R. (2008). *Just how stupid are we? Facing the truth about the American voter*. New York: Basic Books.

Shepard, L., Glaser, R., Linn, R., & Bohrnstedt, G. (1993). *Setting standards for student achievement*. Stanford, CA: National Academy of Education.

Shim, W., & Walczak, K. (2012). The impact of faculty teaching practices on the development of students' critical thinking skills. *International Journal on Teaching and Learning in Higher Education*, *24*(1), 16–30.

Shirkhani, S., & Fahim, M. (2011). Enhancing critical thinking in foreign language learners. *Procedia: Social and Behavioral Sciences*, *29*, 111–115. doi:10.1016/j.sbspro.2011.11.214

Shoffner, M. (2005). Alternative Teacher Preparation Programs: Intersection of Content, Pedagogy and Technology. In C. Crawford, R. Carlsen, I. Gibson, K. McFerrin, J. Price, R. Weber & D. Willis (Eds.), *Proceedings of SITE 2005--Society for Information Technology & Teacher Education International Conference* (pp. 2813-2817). Academic Press.

Shojana, K. G., Burton, E. C., Mcdonald, K. M., Goldman, L., & Page, P. (2013). Changes in rates of autopsy-detected diagonstic errors over time: A systematic review. *Journal of the American Medical Association*, *289*, 2849–2856. doi:10.1001/jama.289.21.2849

Shulman, L. S. (1986). Knowledge and teaching: Foundations of the new reform. *Harvard Educational Review*, *19*(2).

Siegel, H. (1989). The rationality of science, critical thinking, and science education. *Synthese*, *8*, 9–41.

Siegel, H. (1999). What are thinking dispositions? *Educational Theory*, *49*(2), 207–221. doi:10.1111/j.1741-5446.1999.00207.x

Si, J. (2018). An analysis of medical students' reflective essays in problem-based learning. *Korean Journal of Medical Education*, *30*(1), 57–64. doi:10.3946/kjme.2018.82 PMID:29510609

Simon, H. A. (1957). *Models of man: Social and rational*. New York, NY: Wiley.

Simonton, D. K. (2012). Taking the US patent office criteria seriously: A quantitative three-criterion creativity definition and its implications. *Creativity Research Journal, 24*(2-3), 97-106.

Simpson, E., & Courtney, M. D. (2002). Critical thinking in nursing education: Literature review. *International Journal of Nursing Practice, 8*(2), 89–98. doi:10.1046/j.1440-172x.2002.00340.x PMID:11993582

Simpson, J., Furnace, J., Crosby, J., Cumming, A., Evans, P., David, M. F. B., ... MacPherson, S. G. (2002). The Scottish doctor--learning outcomes for the medical undergraduate in Scotland: A foundation for competent and reflective practitioners. *Medical Teacher, 24*(2), 136–143. doi:10.1080/01421590220120713 PMID:12098432

Singh, D., & Joshi, M. K. (2013). Information literacy competency of post graduate students at Haryana Agricultural University and impact of instruction initiatives; A pilot survey. *RSR. Reference Services Review, 41*(3), 453–473. doi:10.1108/RSR-11-2012-0074

Singh, H., Meyer, A. N., & Thomas, E. J. (2014). The frequency of diagnostic errors in outpatient care: Estimations from three large observational studies involving US adult populations. *BMJ Quality & Safety, 23*(9), 727–731. doi:10.1136/bmjqs-2013-002627 PMID:24742777

Skaggs, G., & Hein, S. F. (2011). Reducing the cognitive complexity associated with standard setting: A comparison of the Single-Passage Bookmark and Yes/No methods. *Educational and Psychological Measurement, 71*(3), 571–592. doi:10.1177/0013164410386948

Skaggs, K. (2004). Childhood and adolescence. In J. L. Kincheloe & D. Weil (Eds.), *Critical thinking and learning: An encyclopedia for parents and teachers* (pp. 149–154). Westport, CT: Greenwood Press.

Skorupski, W. P. (2012). Understanding the cognitive processes of standard setting panelist. In G. J. Cizek (Ed.), *Setting performance standards. Foundations, methods, and innovations* (2nd ed.; pp. 135–147). New York, NY: Routledge.

Skoumios, M. (2009). The effect of sociocognitive conflict on students' dialogic argumentation about floating and sinking. *International Journal of Environmental and Science Education, 4*(4), 381–399.

Slameto. (2017). Critical thinking and its affecting factors. *Jurnal Penelitian Humaniora, 18*(2).

Slavin, R. (2006). Education psychology: Theory and practice (8th ed.). Boston: Pearson.

Slavin, R. (2018). Education psychology: Theory and practice (12th ed.). Boston: Pearson.

Slavin, R. E. (2011). Instruction based on cooperative learning. In R. E. Mayer & P. A. Alexander (Eds.), *Handbook of research on learning and instruction* (pp. 344–360). New York: Routledge.

Sleep, L., & Boerst, T. (2012). Preparing beginning teachers to elicit and interpret students' mathematical thinking. *Teaching and Teacher Education, 28*(7), 1038–1048. doi:10.1016/j.tate.2012.04.005

Smith, A., & Rawley, L. A. (1997). Using TV Commercials to Teach Listening and Critical Thinking, *The Journal of the Imagination in Language Learning and Teaching, 4*. Retrieved May 8, 2018, from http://www.njcu.edu/CILUvol4/smith-rawley.html

Smith, T. E., Rama, P. S., & Helms, J. R. (2018). Teaching critical thinking in a GE class: A flipped model. *Thinking Skills and Creativity, 28*, 73–83. doi:10.1016/j.tsc.2018.02.010

Snyder, L., & Snyder, M. J. (2008). Teaching critical thinking and problem solving skills. *Delta Pi Epsilon Journal, 50*(2), 90–99.

Sobral, D. T. (2000). An appraisal of medical students' reflection-in-learning. *Medical Education, 34*(3), 182–187. doi:10.1046/j.1365-2923.2000.00473.x PMID:10733703

Sohmen, V. S. (2015). Reflections on creative leadership. *International Journal of Global Business*, *8*(1), 1–14.

Soo Von Esch, K. (2018). Teacher leaders as agents of change: Creating contexts for instructional improvement for English learner students. *The Elementary School Journal*, *19*(1), 152–178. doi:10.1086/698753

Soslau, E. (2015). Development of a post-lesson observation conferencing protocol- Situated in theory, research, and practice. *Teaching and Teacher Education*, *49*, 22–35. doi:10.1016/j.tate.2015.02.012

Spence, S., & Campbell, M. (2008). *Pedagogical Change: Using Drama to Develop the Critical Imagination* (Doctoral Dissertation). University of Alberta, Canada.

Spoelder, P., Lockwood, M., Cowell, S., Gregersonand, P., & Henchman, A. (2015). *Protected Area Governance and Management*. ANU Press.

Staib, S. (2003). Teaching and measuring critical thinking. *The Journal of Nursing Education*, *42*(11), 498–508. doi:10.3928/0148-4834-20031101-08 PMID:14626388

Stapleton, P. (2011). A survey of attitudes towards critical thinking among Hong Kong secondary school teachers: Implications for policy change. *Thinking Skills and Creativity*, *6*(1), 14–23. doi:10.1016/j.tsc.2010.11.002

Starr, G. E., & Gaskill, P. (1997). The community study assignment for leisure studies: Integrating information literacy, leisure theory, and critical thinking. *Research Strategies*, *15*(3), 205–216. doi:10.1016/S0734-3310(97)90041-0

Steiner, R. (1907). *The education of the child*. Berlin, Germany: Steiner Books.

Sternberg, R. J. (1986). *Critical thinking: Its nature, measurement, and improvement*. Washington, DC: National Institute of Education.

Sternberg, R. J., Grigorenko, E. L., & Singer, J. L. (Eds.). (2004). *Creativity: From potential to realization*. Washington, DC: American Psychological Association. doi:10.1037/10692-000

Sternberg, R. J., & Williams, W. M. (2002). *Educational psychology*. Boston, MA: Allyn and Bacon.

Sternod, L., & French, B. (2015). Test Review: Watson-Glaser™ II Critical Thinking Appraisal. *Journal of Psychoeducational Assessment*.

Steward, L., & Thomas, E. (Eds.). (1997). *Caribbean issues and development. Teacher education in the Commonwealth series*. London: Commonwealth Secretariat.

Stewart, T. (2019). Supporting teacher candidates' development of critical thinking skills through dialogue and reflection. In G. J. Mariano & F. G. Figliano (Eds.), *Handbook of research on critical thinking strategies in pre-service learning environments* (pp. 211–234). Hershey, PA: IGI Global.

Stockero, S. L., Rupnow, R. L., & Pascoe, A. E. (2017). Learning to notice important student mathematical thinking in complex classroom interactions. *Teaching and Teacher Education*, *63*, 384–395. doi:10.1016/j.tate.2017.01.006

Stoll, L., Bolam, R., McMahon, A., Wallace, M., & Thomas, S. (2006). Professional learning communities: A review of the literature. *Journal of Educational Change*, *7*(4), 221–258. doi:10.100710833-006-0001-8

Stover, L. T. (2006). *Guidelines for the preparation of teachers of English language arts*. Urbana, IL: NCTE.

Sturrock, K., & Rocha, J. (2000). A multidimensional scaling stress evaluation table. *Field Methods*, *12*(1), 49–60. doi:10.1177/1525822X0001200104

Sugrue, C. (1997). Student teachers' lay theories and teaching identities: Their implications for professional development. *European Journal of Teacher Education*, *20*(3), 213–225. doi:10.1080/0261976970200302

Sutherland, L., Howard, S., & Markauskaite, L. (2010). Professional identity creation: Examining the development of beginning preservice teachers' understanding of their work as teachers. *Teaching and Teacher Education*, *26*(3), 455–465. doi:10.1016/j.tate.2009.06.006

Swoger, B. (2011). Closing the assessment loop using pre- and post-assessment. *RSR. Reference Services Review*, *39*(2), 244–259.

T4S. (2013). TeachforSuccess — WestEd. Retrieved from https://www.wested.org/teachforsuccess/

Taggart, G. L., & Wilson, A. P. (2005). Promoting reflective thinking in teachers: 50 action strategies. Thousand Oaks, CA: A Sage Publications Company.

Tam, A. (2015). The role of a professional learning community in teacher change: A perspective from beliefs and practices. *Teachers and Teaching*, *21*(1), 22–43. doi:10.1080/13540602.2014.928122

Tandberg, D. A., & Griffith, C. (2013). State support of education: Data, measures, findings and directions for future research. Springer. doi:10.1007/978-94-007-5836-0_13

Tang, R. (2009). Developing a critical ethos in higher education: What undergraduate students gain from a reader response task? *Reflections on English Language Teaching*, *8*(1), 1–20.

Tang, S. (2012). Knowledge base of mentoring and mentor preparation. In S. Fletcher & C. A. Mullen (Eds.), *The SAGE Handbook of Mentoring and Coaching in Education* (pp. 478–494). London, UK: SAGE; doi:10.4135/9781446247549.n32

Tankersley, K. (2005). Literacy strategies for grades 4-12: Reinforcing the threads of reading. Alexandria, VA: ASCD.

Tanner, C. A. (1999). Evidence-based practice: Research and critical thinking. *The Journal of Nursing Education*, *38*(3), 99. doi:10.3928/0148-4834-19990301-03 PMID:10102506

Tanner, C. A. (2006). Thinking like a nurse: A research-based model of clinical judgment in nursing. *The Journal of Nursing Education*, *45*, 204–211. PMID:16780008

Tate, M. L. (2009). Workshops: Extend learning beyond your presentation with these brain- friendly strategies. *Journal of Staff Development*, *30*(1), 44–46.

Taylor, S., & Sobel, D. (2000). Addressing the discontinuity of students' and teachers' diversity: A preliminary study of preservice teachers' beliefs and perceived skills. *Teaching and Teacher Education*, *17*(4), 487–503. doi:10.1016/S0742-051X(01)00008-7

Teaching Strategies. (2010). *Research foundation: The Creative Curriculum*. Bethesda, MD: Author.

Teaching Strategies. (n.d.). *Company history*. Retrieved from https://teachingstrategies.com/company/history/

Tecuci, G., Boicu, M., Marcu, D., & Schum, D. A. (2016). Evidence-based reasoning: Computational theory and cognitive Assistants. *Romanian Journal of Information Science and Technology*, *19*(1-2), 44–64.

Tejeda-Delgado, C. & Johnson, R.D. (2018). A field experience instructional coaching and mentoring model.

Tenreiro-Vieira, C., & Vieira, R. M. (2001). *Promoting Students Critical Thinking: Concrete proposals for the classroom*. Porto: Porto Editora.

Terada, Y. (2018). *Boosting student engagement through project-based learning*. Retrieved from www.edutopia.org

Teuscher, D., Switzer, J. M., & Morwood, T. (2016). Unpacking the practice of probing student thinking. *Mathematics Teacher Educator*, *5*(1), 47–64. doi:10.5951/mathteaceduc.5.1.0047

Tezcan, M. (1997). Eğitim Sosyolojisi. Yayınevi belirtilmemiş, Ankara.

The American Philosophical Association. (1990). *Critical Thinking: A Statement of Expert Consensus for Purposes of Educational Assessment and Instruction. ERIC Doc. No. ED 315-423*. Millbrae, CA: California Academic Press.

The Critical Thinking Consortium. (2015). *Tips for Teachers: Promoting critical thinking in science*. Retrieved from https://tc2.ca/uploads/PDFs/TIpsForTeachers/Tips4Teachers_Promotingcriticalthinking inscience.pdf

The Foundation for Critical Thinking. (1997). *A brief history of the idea of critical thinking*. Retrieved from http://www.criticalthinking.org/pages/a-brief-history-of-the-idea-of-critical-thinking/408

The Foundation for Critical Thinking. (2015). Our Concept and Definition of Critical Thinking. Retrieved from http://www.criticalthinking.org/pages/our-concept-and-definition-of-critical-thinking/411

The Foundation for Critical Thinking. (n.d.). Retrieved from http://www.criticalthinking.org/pages/a-brief-history-of-the-idea-of-critical-thinking/408

Thomas, K. (2016). *Developing a framework for reading instruction in St. Vincent and the Grenadines* (Unpublished doctoral dissertation). University of the West Indies, Bridgetown, Barbados.

Thomas, A., & Chess, S. (1977). *Temperament and development*. New York, NY: Brunner/Mazel.

Thomas, K. R. (2006). Students THINK: A framework for improving problem solving. *Teaching Children Mathematics, 13*(2), 86–95.

Thomas, K., Huffman, D., & Flake, M. (2016). Pre-service elementary teacher dispositions and responsive pedagogical patterns in mathematics. In A. G. Welsh & S. Areepattamannil (Eds.), *Dispositions in Teacher Education: A Global Perspective*. Boston, MA: Sense Publishers. doi:10.1007/978-94-6300-552-4_2

Thompson, H. M., & Henley, S. A. (2000). Fostering information literacy: Connecting national standards, Goals 2000, and the SCANS report. Englewood, CO: Libraries Unlimited and its division Teacher Ideas Press.

Thompson, C. (2011). Critical thinking across the curriculum: Process over product. *International Journal of Humanities and Social Science, 1*(9), 1–7.

Ticusan, M., & Elena, H. (2015). Critical thinking in development of creativity. *Paper presented at International Conference of Scientific Paper AFASES*, Brasov, Romania.

Tillema, H. H. (1997). Stability and change in student teachers' beliefs. *European Journal of Teacher Education, 20*(3), 209–212. doi:10.1080/0261976970200301

Timperley, H. S., & Wiseman, J. (2002). *The sustainability of professional development in literacy*. Wellington: New Zealand Ministry of Education.

Tipmontree, S., & Tasanameelarp, A. (2018). The Effects of Role-Playing Simulation Activities on the Improvement of EFL Students' Business English Oral Communication. *The Journal of Asia TEFL, 15*(3), 566–899.

Tompkins, G. E. (2014). *Literacy for the 21ˢᵗ century: A balanced approach* (7th ed.). Upper Saddle River, NJ: Merrill Prentice Hall.

Topal, C. W., & Gandini, L. (1999). *Beautiful stuff! Learning with found materials*. Worchester, MA: Davis Publishing.

Torres, M. N. & Mercado, M. (2004). Living the praxis of teacher education through teacher research. *A Journal for the Scholar-Practitioner Leader, 2*(2), 59-73.

Torres, R. M., & Jamie, C. (1995). Learning Style: A Factor to Critical Thinking? *Journal of Agricultural Education*, *36*(4), 55-62. Retrieved May 8, 2018, from http://ssu.missouri.edu/ssu/AGED/naerm/s-g-3.htm.adresinden

Tremblay, K. R. Jr, & Downey, E. P. (2004, Summer). Identifying and evaluating research-based publications: Enhancing undergraduate student critical thinking skills. *Education*, *124*(4), 734–740.

Tripp, L. O., Love, A., Thomas, C. M., & Russell, J. (2018). Teacher education advocacy for multiple perspectives and culturally sensitive teaching. In U. Thomas (Ed.), Advocacy and academia and the role of teacher preparation programs (161-181). Hershey, PA: IGI Global. doi:10.4018/978-1-5225-2906-4.ch009

Trowbridge, R. L., Joseph, J. R., & Durning, S. J. (2015). *Teaching Clinical Reasoning. ACP's Teaching Medicine Series*. Philadelphia: American College of Physicians.

Tsui, L. (2001). Faculty attitudes and the development of students' critical thinking. *The Journal of General Education*, *50*(1), 1–28. doi:10.1353/jge.2001.0008

Tsui, L. (2002). Fostering critical thinking through effective pedagogy. Evidence from four institutional case studies. *The Journal of Higher Education*, *73*(6), 740–763.

Tudge, J., & Hogan, D. (1997). Collaboration from a Vygotskian Perspective, 12.

Tudge, J., & Rogoff, B. (1989). *Peer influences on cognitive development: Piagetian and Vygotskian perspectives*. Lawrence Erlbaum Associates, Inc.

Turner, E. E., Drake, C., McDuffie, A. R., Aguirre, J., Bartell, T. G., & Foote, M. Q. (2012). Promoting equity in mathematics teacher preparation: A framework for advancing teacher learning of children's multiple mathematics knowledge bases. *Journal of Mathematics Teacher Education*, *15*(1), 15. doi:10.100710857-011-9196-6

Turner, S. (2013). Teachers' and pupils' perceptions of creativity across different key stages. *Research in Education*, *89*(1), 23–40. doi:10.7227/RIE.89.1.3

Turner, V. (1964). Betwixt and Between: The liminal period in *Rites de Passage. International Journal of the American Ethnological Society*, 4-20.

Tversky, A. (1977). Features of similarity. *Psychological Review*, *84*(4), 327–352. doi:10.1037/0033-295X.84.4.327

Tversky, A., & Kahneman, D. (1973). Availability: A heuristic for judging frequency and probability. *Cognitive Psychology*, *5*(2), 207–232. doi:10.1016/0010-0285(73)90033-9

Tversky, A., & Kahneman, D. (1974). Judgment under uncertainty: Heuristics and biases. *Science*, *185*(4157), 1124–1131. doi:10.1126cience.185.4157.1124 PMID:17835457

Ubbink, D. T., Guyatt, G. H., & Vermeulen, H. (2013). Framework of policy recommendations for implementation of evidence-based practice: A systematic scoping review. *BMJ Open*, *3*(1), e001881. doi:10.1136/bmjopen-2012-001881 PMID:23355664

United Nations Educational, Scientific, and Cultural Organization [UNESCO]. (2007). *Accountability in Education: Meeting our Commitments. Global Education Monitoring Report*. Paris: UNESCO.

United States Department of Education. (2010). *A blueprint for reform: The reauthorization of the Elementary and Secondary Education Act*. Retrieved from www2.ed.gov/policy/elsec/leg/blueprint

University of Sydney. (n.d.). Master of teaching. Retrieved from https://sydney.edu.au/education_social_work/future_students/graduate_entry/r esources/MTeach_web.pdf

Vaidya, A. J. (2017). Does Critical Thinking and Logic Education Have a Western Bias? The Case of the Nyaya School of Classical Indian Philosophy. *Journal of Philosophy of Education*, *51*(1), 132–160. doi:10.1111/1467-9752.12189

Van de Ven, A. H., & Sun, K. (2011). Breakdowns in implementing models of organization change. *The Academy of Management Perspectives*, *25*(3), 58–74.

Van De Walle, J. A. (2007). *Elementary and middle school mathematics* (6th ed.). Boston, MA: Pearson Education.

Van Gennep, A. (1977). *Rites of Passage*. London, UK: Routledge and Kegan Paul.

Van Nieuwerburgh, C. (2017). *An introduction to coaching skills: A practical guide*. Los Angeles, CA: Sage.

Van, T. T. M. (2009). The relevance of literary analysis to teaching literature in the EFL Classroom. *Journal English Teaching Forum*, *3*, 2–9.

Vasudevan, H. (2013). The influence of teacher creativity, attitude and commitment and students' proficiency of the English Language. *Journal of Research and Methods in Education*, *1*(2), 12–19.

Vecchi, V. (2010). *Art and creativity in Reggio Emilia: Exploring the role and potential of ateliers in early childhood education*. New York, NY: Routledge. doi:10.4324/9780203854679

Vesely, P., & Sherlock, J. (2005). Pedagogical Tools to Develop Critical Thinking. *Academic Exchange Quarterly*, *9*(4), 155–161.

Victor-Chmil, J. (2013). Critical thinking versus clinical reasoning versus clinical judgment: Differential diagnosis. *Nurse Educator*, *38*(1), 34–36. doi:10.1097/NNE.0b013e318276dfbe PMID:23222632

Vieira, R. M., & Tenreiro-Vieira, C. (2005). *Teaching / Learning strategies: the questions which promote critical thinking*. Lisboa: Instituto Piaget.

Vieira, R. M., & Tenreiro-Vieira, C. (2016). Fostering Scientific Literacy and Critical Thinking in Elementary Science Education. *International Journal of Science and Mathematics Education*, *14*(4), 659–680. doi:10.100710763-014-9605-2

Viera, R. M., Tenreiro-Viera, C., & Mertins, I. P. (2011). Critical thinking: Conceptual clarification and its importance in science education. *Science Education International*, *22*(1), 43–54.

Vogler, K. E. (2005). Improve Your Verbal Questioning. *The Clearing House: A Journal of Educational Strategies, Issues and Ideas*, *79*(2), 98–103. doi:10.3200/TCHS.79.2.98-104

Vygotsky, L. (1981). The Genesis of Higher Mental Functions. In J. V. Wertsch (Ed.), *The concept of activity in Soviet psychology* (pp. 144–188). Armonk, NY: M.E. Sharpe.

Vygotsky, L. S. (1978). *Mind in society: The development of higher psychological processes*. Cambridge, MA: Harvard University Press.

Waddington, D. I., & Weeth Feinstein, N. (2016). Beyond the search for truth: Dewey's humble and humanistic vision of science education. *Educational Theory*, *66*(1/2), 111–126. doi:10.1111/edth.12157

Wagner, T. (2008). *The global achievement Gap: Why even our best schools don't teach the new survival skills our children need—and what we can do about it*. New York: Basic Books.

Waldorf-inspired learning. (2018, June 20). Retrieved from http://www.waldorfinspiredlearning.com/the-waldorf-curriculum/

Walker, K., & Zeidler, D. L. (2007). Promoting discourse about socioscientific issues through scaffolded inquiry. *International Journal of Science Education*, *29*(11), 1387–1410. doi:10.1080/09500690601068095

Wang, J., & Odell, S. J. (2002) Mentored learning to teach according to standards-based reform- A critical review. *Review of Educational Research, 72*(3), 481–546. doi:10.3102_00346543072003481

Ward, J., Nolen, S., & Horn, I. (2011). Productive fiction: How conflict in student teaching creates opportunities for learning at the boundary. *International Journal of Educational Research, 50*(1), 14–20. doi:10.1016/j.ijer.2011.04.004

Watson, G., & Glaser, E. M. (2010). *Technical manual and user guide: Watson–Glaser™ II Critical Thinking Appraisal.* Retrieved from http://us.talentlens.com/request-product-support-materials?leadsource=request-psm

Weikart, D. P., Deloria, D., Lawser, S., & Wiegerink, R. (1970). *Longitudinal results of the Ypsilanti Perry Preschool Project (Monographs of the High/Scope Educational Research Foundation, 1).* Ypsilanti, MI: High/Scope Press.

Wellington, B. C., & Wellington, J. (1960). *Teaching for Critical Thinking with Emphasis on Secondary Education.* Academic Press.

Whitty, M., & Koeplin, J. (2011). Putting more soul into our work: Teaching the whole person. *Business Renaissance Quarterly, 6*(1), 21–28.

Wiggins, G., & McTighe, J. (2005). *Understanding by design.* Alexandria, VA: Association for Supervision and Curriculum Development.

Wiggins, G., & McTighe, J. (2011). *The understanding by design guide to creating high-quality units.* Alexandria, VA: ASCD.

Wikipedia. (n.d.). Critical Thinking. Retrieved November 7, 2018, from https://en.wikipedia.org/wiki/Critical_thinking

Wilke, R., & Losh, S. (2008). Beyond beliefs: Preservice teachers' planned instructional strategies. *Action in Teacher Education, 30*(3), 213–238. doi:10.1080/01626620.2008.10463503

Will your students steal a car? ESL/EFL simulation activity. (2018, December 7). Retrieved from https://eflideas.com/2018/02/26/will-your-students-steal-a-car-esl-efl-simulation-activity

Williams, A., Prestage, S., & Bedward, J. (2001). Individualism to collaboration: The significance of teacher culture to the induction of newly qualified teachers. *Journal of Education for Teaching, 27*(3), 253–267. doi:10.1080/02607470120091588

Williamson, A., & Null, J. W. (2008). Ralph Waldo Emerson's Educational Philosophy as a Foundation For Cooperative Learning. *American Educational History Journal, 35*(2), 381–392.

Willingham, D. T. (2007). Critical thinking, why is it so hard to teach? *American Educator, 31*, 8–19.

Willingham, D. T. (2007). Critical thinking: Why is it so hard to teach? *American Educator, 31*, 8–19.

Wilson, P. K. (1996). Origins of science. *National Forum, 76*(1), 39.

Wilson, S. M., Floden, R. E., & Ferrini-Mundy, J. (2001). Teacher preparation research. An insider's view from the outside. *Journal of Teacher Education, 53*(3), 12.

Windschitl, M., Thompson, J., & Braaten, M. (2018). *Ambitious Science Teaching.* Cambridge, MA: Harvard Education Press.

Wink, J. (2011). *Critical pedagogy: Notes from the real world* (4th ed.). Upper Saddle River, NJ: Pearson Education.

Winters, B., Custer, J., Galvagno, S. M. Jr, Colantuoni, E., Kapoor, S. G., Lee, H. W., ... Newman-Toker, D. (2012). Diagnostic errors in the intensive care unit: A systematic review of autopsy studies. *BMJ Quality & Safety, 21*(11), 894–902. doi:10.1136/bmjqs-2012-000803 PMID:22822241

Wise, D., & Hammack, M. (2012). Leadership coaching: Coaching competencies and best practices. *Journal of School Leadership*, *21*(3), 449–477. doi:10.1177/105268461102100306

Wolfe, C. R. (2012). Individual differences in the "Myside Bias" in reasoning and written argumentation. *Written Communication*, *29*(4), 477–501. doi:10.1177/0741088312457909

Woods, P. (2002). Teaching and learning in the new millennium. In C. Day & C. Sugrue (Eds.), Developing Teaching and Teachers: International Research Perspectives (pp. 73-91). London: Falmer.

Wright, S., Wong, A., & Newill, C. (1997). The impact of role models on medical students. *Journal of General Internal Medicine*, *12*(1), 53–56. doi:10.100711606-006-0007-1 PMID:9034946

Wurm, J. P. (2005). *Working in the Reggio way*. St. Paul, MN: Redleaf Press.

Xu, Q. (2013). Fostering Critical Thinking Competence in EFL Classroom. *Studies in Literature and Language*, *7*(1), 6–9.

Yap, S. F. (2014). Beliefs, values, ethics and moral reasoning in socio-scientific education. *Issues in Educational Research*, *24*(3), 299–319.

Yeh, M. L. (2002). Assessing the reliability and validity of the Chinese version of the California critical thinking disposition inventory. *International Journal of Nursing Studies*, *39*(2), 123–132. doi:10.1016/S0020-7489(01)00019-0 PMID:11755443

Yoonsook, C., Yoo, J., Kim, S.-W., Lee, H., & Zeidler, D. L. (2016). Enhancing students' communication skills in the science classroom through socioscientific issues. *International Journal of Science and Mathematics Education*, *14*(1), 1–27. doi:10.100710763-014-9557-6

Yuan, S., Liao, H., Wang, Y., & Chou, M. (2014). Development of a scale to measure the critical thinking disposition of medical care professionals. *Social Behavior and Personality*, *42*(2), 303–312. doi:10.2224bp.2014.42.2.303

Yun, J. H., Baldi, B., & Sorcinelli, M. D. (2016, January). Mutual mentoring for early-career and underrepresented teachers: Model, research and practice. *Innovación Educativa (México, D.F.)*.

Zachary, S. (2011). *The challenge: Challenging students to think critically* [Master's Research Paper]. University of Wisconsin, WI.

Zayapragassarazan, Z., Menon, V., Kar, S. S., & Batmanabane, G. (2016). Understanding Critical Thinking to Create Better Doctors. *Journal of Advances in Medical Education and Research*, *1*, 9–13.

Zeichner, K. (2010). Rethinking the connections between campus courses and field experiences in college and university-based teacher education. *Journal of Teacher Education*, *61*(1-2), 89–99. doi:10.1177/0022487109347671

Zeichner, K. M., & Liston, D. P. (2013). *Reflective teaching: An introduction* (2nd ed.). New York, NY: Routledge. doi:10.4324/9780203822289

Zeichner, K., & Liu, K. Y. (2010). A Critical Analysis of Reflection as a Goal for Teacher Education. In N. Lyons (Ed.), *Handbook of Reflection and Reflective Inquiry*. Boston, MA: Springer. doi:10.1007/978-0-387-85744-2_4

Zeidler, D. L., Sadler, T. D., Callahan, B., Burek, K., & Applebaum, S. (2007). Advancing reflective judgment through socioscientific issues. *Paper presented at the 2007 Meeting of the European Science Education Research Association*, Malmö University, Malmö, Sweden.

Zeidler, D. L. (2014a). Socioscientific issues as a curriculum emphasis: Theory, research and practice. In N. G. Lederman & S. K. Abell (Eds.), *Handbook of research in science education* (Vol. 2, pp. 697–726). New York, NY: Routledge.

Zeidler, D. L., & Kahn, S. (2014). *It's debatable! Using socioscientific issues to develop scientific literacy, K-12.* Arlington, VA: NSTA Press.

Zeidler, D. L., & Nichols, B. H. (2009). Socioscientific issues: Theory and practice. *Journal of Elementary Science Education, 21*(2), 49–58. doi:10.1007/BF03173684

Zeidler, D., Sadler, T., Applebaum, S., & Callahan, B. (2009). Advancing reflective judgment through socioscientific issues. *Journal of Research in Science Teaching, 46*(1), 74–101. doi:10.1002/tea.20281

Zhang, L., & Robert, J. S. (2000). Are Learning Approaches and Thinking Styles Related? A Study in Two Chinese Populations. *The Journal of Psychology, 134*(5), 469–489. doi:10.1080/00223980009598230 PMID:11034129

Zieky, M. J. (2001). So much has changed: How the setting of cut scores has evolved since the 1980s. In C. J. Cizek (Ed.), *Setting performance standards: Concepts, methods, and perspectives* (pp. 19–51). Mahwah, NJ: Lawrence Erlbaum.

Zillmer, N. (2016). *Metacognitive dimensions of adolescents' intellectual collaboration* [Dissertation]. Columbia University. doi:10.1017/CBO9781107415324.004

Zobisch, P. J., Platine, D. G., & Swanson, A. (2015). The theory of multiple intelligences and critical thinking. *GLOKALde, 1*(6), 157–176.

Zulkpli, Z., Abdullah, A. H., Kohar, U. H. A., & Ibrahim, N. H. (2017). A review of research on infusion approach in teaching thinking: Advantages and impacts. *Man in India, 97*(12), 289–298.

Zwaan, L., de Bruijne, M., Wagner, C., Thijs, A., Smits, M., van der Wal, G., & Timmermans, D. R. (2010). Patient record review of the incidence, consequences, and causes of diagnostic adverse events. *Archives of Internal Medicine, 170*(12), 1015–1021. doi:10.1001/archinternmed.2010.146 PMID:20585065

Zweirs, J., & Crawford, M. (2011). *Academic Conversations: Classroom Talk that fosters critical Thinking and Content Understandings.* Maine: Stenhouse Publisher.

About the Contributors

Sandra Robinson teaches English Education in the School of Education at the University of the West Indies, Cave Hill Campus, Barbados. She serves also as the English Coordinator for the Eastern Caribbean Joint Board of Teacher Education (ECJBTE) and represents the ECJBTE on the Regional Advisory Board of the Organization of Eastern Caribbean States (OECS) Early Learners Programme for Teachers of Literacy. Sandra's research interests include teacher Education, critical thinking pedagogies in secondary English; Critical Literacy, and the nature, acquisition and development of English teachers' professional knowledge and expertise.

Verna C. Knight is a lecturer in Social Studies Education and the Social Context of Education in the School of Education (SOE), at the University of the West Indies (UWI), Cave Hill Campus Barbados. She earned a Bachelor's degree in Education Administration and a Ph.D. in Education Policy from the University of the West Indies. Currently, she serves as the UWI representative documenting the OECS member states implementation of OECS Education Sector Strategy 2012-2021 and as Coordinator for the SOE's Bachelor of Education programme. Her areas of research include Education Policy development in the Caribbean, Teachers' Professional Development, and Social Studies Education. She is a recipient of the American Educational Research Association (AERA) Outstanding Research Paper Award (2016).

***

Osman Aktan works as a special education teacher in the guidance and recruitment center in the Ministry of Education, Turkey. He has a degree in education programs and his research interests are in special education, cohesion education, values education, thinking skills.

Fahad Abdullah Alateeq, a consultant family medicine and assistant professor, is currently working as the family medicine course organizer in the Faculty of Medicine, Al Imam Mohammad Ibn Saud Islamic University (IMSIU), Riyadh, Saudi Arabia. Previously, he worked as a Chairman of medical education department in Al Imam Mohammad Ibn Saud Islamic University (IMSIU) (2013-2017).

David Anderson has been a teacher, administrator, and associate director of two national reform initiatives, and is currently professor and coordinator of the Eastern Michigan University (EMU) Ph.D. program in Educational Leadership. He has worked in the education field for over 30 years, in a variety of capacities, including significant experience in assessment, program evaluation, and research. Dr. Anderson is currently serving as the lead researcher/evaluator for an NSF ITEST grant supporting career pathways in STEM. Dr. Anderson has published over 60 articles and book chapters, completed over 100 scholarly presentations, and authored over 20 funded grant proposals. He has been awarded the EMU College of Education Innovative Scholarship Award, the EMU College of Education Special Service Award, the Maryland Association of Higher Education Award for Outstanding Research, the EMU Alumni Association Teaching Excellence Award, and the University of Michigan Award for Outstanding Dissertation in School Administration.

N. Leigh Boyd holds a PhD in Cognitive Science in Education from Teachers College, Columbia University. Her research focuses on collaborative cognition and the use of dialogue to develop higher level thinking skills in adolescents and emerging adults.

Kerri Pilling Burchill owns and is President of North Star Coaching, an independent coaching and consultant firm, and also serves in the role of Organizational Development Coordinator at Southern Illinois Healthcare. For over 20 years, she has fulfilled academic and leadership roles in education and healthcare in Canada, the United States and the West Indies. Dr. Burchill completed her Doctorate in Education from Eastern Michigan University, with an academic focus that examines the factors that influence how novice teachers gain their pedagogical knowledge and skill. Dr. Burchill has taught at Johns Hopkins University, the University of Michigan, and Eastern Michigan University. Dr. Burchill was recognized with the Alberta Centennial Medal, a provincial recognition for leadership, volunteerism and community contributions. In 2001, Dr. Burchill was also honored with the Pan Canadian Teacher's Choice Award for having played a significant role in the life of a student.

Lizette Burks is the state science supervisor for the Kansas State Department of Education. Previously, she directed K-12 science programs in a large school district in Kansas. She also served as a science teacher in Texas and Kansas at the high school and middle school levels. Dr. Burks serves on the board of directors for the Kansas Association for Conservation and Environmental Education, the Kansas State Science and Engineering Fair, and the Kansas Association for Teachers of Science. She also serves on committees with the Council of State Science Supervisors and the National Science Education Leadership Association. Dr. Burks was recently selected to serve as co-principal investigator for the Advancing Coherent and Equitable Systems of Science Education 13-state National Science Foundation Grant. Her research interests include studying the pedagogical shifts that emerge alongside science education reform and how pre-service and in-service teachers can more effectively implement instruction that moves towards more equitable science teaching and learning. Dr. Burks earned her B.S. in biology from Texas Tech University, her M.Ed. in Teaching from Emporia State University, and her Ed.D. in Curriculum and Instruction from the University of Kansas.

Shawn Marise Butler is presently a senior lecturer in the areas of language, literacy and literature at the St. Vincent and the Grenadines Community College (SVGS) in the Division of Teacher Education (DTE). She is currently affiliated with the University of the West Indies-St. Augustine. Her PhD thesis focuses on the writing instruction practices of primary teachers in St. Vincent and the Grenadines and the factors which impact and influence those practices.

Mari Caballero is an Assistant Professor at Emporia State University. Her areas of specialization are elementary mathematics and special education. Dr. Caballero has taught in elementary classrooms, in special education, and in teacher education. Her research interests include the development of pre-service and current elementary and special education teachers, specifically their ability to teach mathematics to the wide range of student abilities in their classroom and interpret students' understanding of mathematics.

Harpreet Kaur Dhir received her BA in multiple subjects from University of Redlands, CA and MA in Curriculum and Instruction from California Polytechnic University, Pomona. Teaching elementary grades for the past 25 years at the Ontario-Montclair Unified School District and Hacienda La Puente Unified School District, being an advisory board and a faculty member at the Art Center College of Design and a lecturer at California Polytechnic University, Pomona, and currently a doctoral student at the American College of Education, she has a broad range of field experience. Member of the international honor society, Kappa Delta Pi, Teacher of the Year for the LA Sherriff Youth Organization, Leadership in Education awardee from California Polytechnic University, Pomona, and a nominee for the Disney Teacher of the Year award, her classroom research continues in examining and sharing the suitable methods for 21st century classrooms including experiential learning through curriculum integration.

Mehmet Durnali holds B.Sc. degree in computer and educational technologies, M.A. degree and Ph.D. degree in educational administration awarded by Boğaziçi University -2004-, Hacettepe University -2015- and Hacettepe University -2018- respectively. He has been working in state education sector since 2004 taking different roles. He had worked as ICT teacher and as assistant principal. Then, he has been working for central bodies of Ministry of Turkish National Education as national-based educational project developer and director since 2008. Now he is working at the Department of Open Education under General Directorate of Lifelong Learning as the senior project developer. His main area of expertise is in the field of the use of ICT in education, organizational goals, organizational behaviors, educational supervision, lifelong learning and project management. He has not only contributed to several international book chapters but also to several national and international conference papers and articles. He is also a peer reviewer for Hacettepe University Journal of Education. He was involved in many international courses funded by the European Union, international camps, projects, and conferences.

Janet Dutton is a Lecturer in Secondary English Curriculum in the Department of Educational Studies at Macquarie University, NSW. Australia. Her research interests include secondary English curriculum, the impact of high stakes testing and teacher identity formation, motivation and retention. Janet has a passion for English teaching that promotes creative pedagogy and has worked extensively with primary and secondary teachers in the use of identity texts and drama strategies to develop literacy.

Talia Esnard is a Lecturer in the Department of Behavioral Sciences, Faculty of Social Sciences, The University of the West Indies, St. Augustine. Her research interests center on issues affecting Caribbean women who work within educational and entrepreneurial spheres. Some of her work has been published in the Journal of Asian Academy of Management, NASPA Journal about Women in Higher Education, Journal of the Motherhood Initiative, Mentoring & Tutoring: Partnership in Learning, Journal of Educational Administration and History, as well as, Women, Gender & Families of Color. She was also a recent recipient of Taiwan Research Fellowship (2012) and Caricom-Canada Leadership Program (2015 & 2018). She recently completed a co-authored book on Black Women, Academe, and the Tenure Process in the United States and in the Caribbean.

Michelle Fazio-Brunson directs the graduate programs in Early Childhood Education at Northwestern State University and routinely works with undergraduate and graduate Early Childhood candidates in project-based learning. Additionally, she and her husband, the parish District Defender, collaborate to remap Louisiana's Cradle to Prison Pipeline to a Cradle to College Pipeline through early literacy intervention. Working with families and communities, her undergraduate and graduate students engage in service learning projects to facilitate social justice and literacy learning for all students.

Stephen Fleenor is based in San Antonio, TX as an educational consultant with Seidlitz Education (www.seidlitzeducation.com). Stephen earned his PhD in Developmental Neurobiology from the University of Oxford before teaching and coaching high school science in low-income schools in San Antonio. Stephen's primary focus is the advancement of English learners and other disadvantaged students by promoting growth mindset and academic expression.

Danielle Fuchs is a science educator at Wellesley High School in Wellesley, Massachusetts. Her scholarly interests include engaging, practical, & accessible science curriculum for all students, with a particular focus on creating differentiated learning opportunities for a diverse learning population. Specifically, she is interested in using real-world scientific examples interwoven in the science curriculum through the use of a socioscientific issues-based pedagogical tool to reach students in their path to becoming scientifically literate citizens of the world.

Sandra L. Guzman Foster is the Sister Theophane Power Endowed Chair in Education and an Assistant Professor at the University of the Incarnate Word in San Antonio, Texas. Dr. Guzman Foster currently teaches in the Graduate Studies Program in the Dreeben School of Education at UIW. She has several years of experience in teaching at the K-12 level, the community college level, and at the university level in Texas, Arizona and Colorado. Additionally, Dr. Guzman Foster has experience developing curriculum for both face-to-face and online programs in higher education. She has published works in the areas of technology, pedagogy, curriculum, multicultural education, teacher education/preparation/professional development, and educational policy.

Shaneise J. Holder is currently a graduate student at the University of the West Indies – Cave Hill Campus, specializing in Language and Literacy Education. She is a young educator who enjoys writing scripts, poetry and songs. She recently won a bronze award at NIFCA (National Independence Festival of Creative Arts) in Barbados for her rhythm poetry entitled "Sugar Cane" which was performed by St. Cyprian's Boys' School. The school was also awarded the Barbados Manufacturers Association "Brands of Barbados" Award and Shaneise was awarded the COSCAP writer's award in 2016.

Douglas Huffman, PhD., is a Professor of Science Education at the University of Kansas. Dr. Huffman teaches courses in elementary education and also has expertise in assessment and program evaluation. Dr. Huffman previously served as the associated editor for the Journal of Research in Science Teaching. Additionally, he has publications in numerous journals, such as the American Journal of Evaluation, Journal of Research in Science Teaching School Science & Mathematics and the Journal of Science Teacher Education.

Ifeoma C. Iyioke holds degrees in computer science, applied statistics and educational measurement and quantitative methods, from University of Nigeria, Nsukka, UNN, and Michigan State University, MSU, respectively. She is currently an MSU research faculty under Project Excellence, a long-term program evaluation partnership of the MSU Office of Rehabilitation and Disability Studies (MSU-ORDS) with the State of Michigan Rehabilitation Services. Her responsibilities include designing and implementing research methods (e.g., conducting surveys and interviews), data analyses, and reporting findings of the impact of rehabilitation services provided each year to approximately 40,000 individuals with disabilities in the State of Michigan. Her general research interests include applying statistical and measurement models to educational testing problems with a specialized focus on educational standard setting.

Kahdia L. Jordan is currently a graduate student at the University of the West Indies – Cave Hill Campus, specializing in Language and Literacy Education. She also works as a Library Assistant at the Samuel Jackman Prescod Institute of Technology, in Barbados. Kahdia holds a London Cambridge Certificate in Law, an Associate Degree in Law and Political Science, and a Bachelor's degree in Psychology and Sociology. Her philosophy is that all students deserve an equal opportunity to gain a quality education. She enjoys travelling, research and reading.

Katrina Jordan directs the undergraduate program in Early Childhood Education at Northwestern State University and routinely works with undergraduate and graduate Early Childhood candidates in service learning projects and family literacy. She also serves as the NSU College of Education Assessment Coordinator.

Md Anwarul Azim Majumder, a medical educationist and a public health specialist, is currently working as the Director of Medical Education in the Faculty of Medical Sciences, Cave Hill Campus, The University of the West Indies, Barbados. Previously, he worked as a Lecturer at the Clinical Sciences Department, School of Medical Sciences, University of Bradford, UK (2004-16) and was actively engaged in widening participation of medicine programme and problem-based learning. He also worked in the Centre for Medical Education, Bangladesh (1992-2001), and the Department of Medical Education of the School of Medical Sciences, Universiti Sains Malaysia (2001-04) and was actively involved with innovation and experimentation of medical curricula. Dr Majumder was the Founding Secretary-General of the National Association of Medical Education (NAME), Bangladesh and the President of the Union of Risk Management for Preventive Medicine (URMPM), Bangladesh Society. He is also the Executive Editor of the 'South East Asia Journal of Public Health' (published by the Public Health Foundation Bangladesh) and the Editor-in-Chief of 'Advances in Medical Education and Practice' (published by Dove Medical Press Ltd/Taylor & Francis Group). He has published a number of peer reviewed papers on medical education and health care.

Jacqueline Manuel is Associate Professor in English Education in the Sydney School of Education and Social Work at the University of Sydney. She holds a BA (Hons 1) in English, a Dip Ed and a PhD in English Literature. She is Program Director of the Master of Teaching (Secondary) in the Faculty. Jackie's teaching and research interests include teenagers' reading; creative pedagogies in secondary English; pre-service English teacher motivation; and English curriculum history.

Hannah (Mills) Mechler has been teaching early childhood education, family studies, and child development courses in higher education for the past eight years. Her research interests include: parenting, meta-emotion, and social/emotional learning within early childhood classrooms.

Linda Mohammed holds a PhD in Developmental Psychology from the University of the West Indies. She is currently attached to the Institute for Criminology and Public Safety at the University of Trinidad and Tobago. Her research interests include child and adolescent development, cyber bullying and mental health.

Wardell Powell is an assistant professor of education at Framingham State University. His scholarly interest centers on effective science instruction for students with and without specific learning disabilities and the development of accessible science curriculum for such students. Specifically, he is interested in the use of socioscientific issues as a critical pedagogical strategy to enhance scientific literacy among marginalized students.

Sayeeda Rahman is a Clinical Pharmacologist and an Associate Fellow of the Higher Education Academy, UK. She received her first degree in Pharmacy (BPharm and MPharm) from the University of Dhaka, Bangladesh; MBA from Dundee University, UK; and PhD from Universiti Sains Malaysia. She is also trained in various aspects of public health and medical education. Her research interests include diabetes and cardiovascular diseases. She has contributed to the medical sciences with her research publications. She has work experience at university level (Bangladesh, Malaysia and UK), and different national and multinational pharmaceutical companies (Bangladesh). Dr. Rahman was actively engaged in widening participation of medical education and problem-based learning while working at the University of Bradford, UK. Recently, she has joined in the American University of Integrative Sciences, Bridgetown, Barbados as an Associate Professor of Pharmacology.

Kimberly Reinhardt is an assistant professor at Texas A&M University Corpus Christi. Her research focuses on school-university partnerships, fostering culturally competent mentoring of teacher candidates, and the development of inquiry through reflective practice in teacher preparation. She is a Clinical Fellow with the Association of Teacher Educators and has presented her research at major conferences, including Association of Teacher Educators, American Educational Research Association, and National Association of Professional Development Schools. Dr. Reinhardt teaches field-based courses on planning, teaching, assessment, and technology, and graduate courses in classroom management, secondary teaching methods, and educational foundations.

Bidyadhar Sa graduated from Gangadhar Meher College, Sambalpur, one of the premier colleges in India with Honours in 1994 and attained MA (1998), MPhil (1999) and his Doctorate from Kurukshetra University, India in 2004. He subsequently assumed the role of lecturer at his alma mater until 2003 when he moved as Assistant Professor to the Addis Ababa University, Addis Ababa in Ethiopia. In 2008 he moved to Faculty of Medical Sciences (FMS), the University of the West Indies, St. Augustine Campus and now serves as Director of the Centre for Medical Science Education and Deputy Dean, Quality Assurance and Accreditation, at the FMS. He is a prolific researcher and published more than 41 papers which included book, module, papers in refereed Journals and peer reviewed conferences in the area of medical education, empathy and emotional intelligence among health professional students.

He has supervised over 37 graduate thesis and over 60 undergraduate researches and presently serves on 12 national and international scholarly bodies. Dr. Sa has also found time in his hectic schedule to donate public services to 5 local bodies in Trinidad & Tobago.

David Samuel is a science education professional with 35 years' experience in the education sector in the OECS and beyond. He has effectively functioned at multiple levels in the teaching profession from a graduate science teacher to a principal and then a science education lecturer at the tertiary level. Through this experience, he has become very knowledgeable about the education system in the region as well as the many issues impacting the effectiveness of the teaching-learning process at the various levels of the education system. As an education professional, Dr Samuel is intensely interested in the advancement of science education and education generally in the Eastern Caribbean and beyond. His current interests are in a more integrated approach to science instruction as well the impact of teachers' cognition on their instructional practices.

Karen Thomas is currently a lecturer in English Education at the St Vincent and the Grenadines Community College, Division of Teacher Education, in St. Vincent and the Grenadines. She is an educator with over twenty years teaching experience. She has worked as a literacy expert from 2006 to the present, as a secondary classroom teacher, as curriculum specialist and as a teacher educator. She has designed resources for literacy education and has facilitated numerous professional development training activities for teachers at both the primary and secondary levels. Karen's teaching and research interests include pre-service teacher education; teacher professional development; assessment in literacy; and English education.

Kelli Thomas is Associate Dean for Teacher Education and Undergraduate programs in the School of Education at the University of Kansas and Associate Professor of Mathematics Education in the Department of Curriculum and Teaching. Dr. Thomas joined the KU faculty in the fall of 2002 coming to the university from the University of Central Missouri. Dr. Thomas's professional work has focused on mathematics teaching, learning, and assessment in schools for more than 25 years. She has been involved in educator preparation and professional development of educators in university and K-12 settings. She began her career in education teaching in public school settings including the Department of Defense Dependent Schools (DoDDS) in Germany. Her research agenda focuses on teaching, learning, and assessment of mathematics with a focus on teacher development and classroom practice. Her work is published in journals such as Journal of Educational Research, School Science and Mathematics, Teaching Children Mathematics, Action in Teacher Education, American Journal of Evaluation, New Directions for Evaluation, and Teacher Education & Practice.

Ann Marie White is a librarian by profession. She has a first degree in management with certifications in Records Management and Public Administration. She currently works as a Cataloger in the Special Collection Unit of the Sidney Martin Library, and serves as the liaison librarian for the Institute for Gender and Development Studies: Nita Barrow Unit at the University of the West Indies, Cave Hill Campus. She is also responsible for teaching information literacy, and responding to referencing queries from students and researchers at the university.

Index

Purchase Print, E-Book, or Print + E-Book

IGI Global books are available in three unique pricing formats:
Print Only, E-Book Only, or Print + E-Book. Shipping fees apply.

www.igi-global.com

Recommended Reference Books

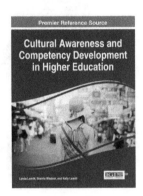

Premier Reference Source

Cultural Awareness and Competency Development in Higher Education

ISBN: 978-1-5225-2145-7
© 2017; 408 pp.
List Price: $210

Premier Reference Source

Cases on STEAM Education in Practice

ISBN: 978-1-5225-2334-5
© 2017 ; 375 pp.
List Price: $195

Handbook of Research on

Writing and Composing in the Age of MOOCs

ISBN: 978-1-5225-1718-4
© 2017; 457 pp.
List Price: $270

Handbook of Research on

Administration, Policy, and Leadership in Higher Education

ISBN: 978-1-5225-0672-0
© 2017; 678 pp.
List Price: $295

Research Insights

Formative Assessment Practices for Pre-Service Teacher Practicum Feedback
Emerging Research and Opportunities

ISBN: 978-1-5225-2630-8
© 2018; 209 pp.
List Price: $145

Research Insights

Technological Pedagogical Content Knowledge (TPACK) Framework for K-12 Teacher Preparation
Emerging Research and Opportunities

ISBN: 978-1-5225-1621-7
© 2017; 173 pp.
List Price: $135

Do you want to stay current on the latest research trends, product announcements, news and special offers?
Join IGI Global's mailing list today and start enjoying exclusive perks sent only to IGI Global members.
Add your name to the list at **www.igi-global.com/newsletters**.

Publisher of Peer-Reviewed, Timely, and Innovative Academic Research

IGI Global
DISSEMINATOR OF KNOWLEDGE

www.igi-global.com   Sign up at www.igi-global.com/newsletters   f facebook.com/igiglobal   t twitter.com/igiglobal   in linkedin.com/igiglobal

Ensure Quality Research is Introduced to the Academic Community

Become an IGI Global Reviewer for Authored Book Projects

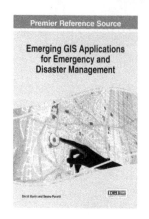
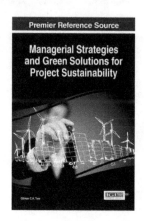

The overall success of an authored book project is dependent on quality and timely reviews.

In this competitive age of scholarly publishing, constructive and timely feedback significantly expedites the turnaround time of manuscripts from submission to acceptance, allowing the publication and discovery of forward-thinking research at a much more expeditious rate. Several IGI Global authored book projects are currently seeking highly qualified experts in the field to fill vacancies on their respective editorial review boards:

Applications may be sent to:
development@igi-global.com

Applicants must have a doctorate (or an equivalent degree) as well as publishing and reviewing experience. Reviewers are asked to write reviews in a timely, collegial, and constructive manner. All reviewers will begin their role on an ad-hoc basis for a period of one year, and upon successful completion of this term can be considered for full editorial review board status, with the potential for a subsequent promotion to Associate Editor.

If you have a colleague that may be interested in this opportunity, we encourage you to share this information with them.

www.igi-global.com

Celebrating 30 Years of Scholarly
Knowledge Creation & Dissemination

InfoSci®-Books

A Collection of 4,000+ Reference Books Containing Over 87,000 Full-Text Chapters Focusing on Emerging Research

This database is a collection of over 4,000+ IGI Global single and multi-volume reference books, handbooks of research, and encyclopedias, encompassing groundbreaking research from prominent experts worldwide. These books are highly cited and currently recognized in prestigious indices such as: Web of Science™ and Scopus®.

Librarian Features:

- No Set-Up or Maintenance Fees
- Guarantee of No More Than A 5% Annual Price Increase
- COUNTER 4 Usage Reports
- Complimentary Archival Access
- Free MARC Records

Researcher Features:

- Unlimited Simultaneous Users
- No Embargo of Content
- Full Book Download
- Full-Text Search Engine
- No DRM

To Find Out More or To Purchase This Database:

www.igi-global.com/infosci-books

eresources@igi-global.com • Toll Free: 1-866-342-6657 ext. 100 • Phone: 717-533-8845 x100

www.igi-global.com

IGI Global Proudly Partners with

Enhance Your Manuscript with
eContent Pro International's Professional
Copy Editing Service

Expert Copy Editing

eContent Pro International copy editors, with over 70 years of combined experience, will provide complete and comprehensive care for your document by resolving all issues with spelling, punctuation, grammar, terminology, jargon, semantics, syntax, consistency, flow, and more. In addition, they will format your document to the style you specify (APA, Chicago, etc.). All edits will be performed using Microsoft Word's Track Changes feature, which allows for fast and simple review and management of edits.

Additional Services

eContent Pro International also offers fast and affordable proofreading to enhance the readability of your document, professional translation in over 100 languages, and market localization services to help businesses and organizations localize their content and grow into new markets around the globe.

IGI Global Authors Save 25% on eContent Pro International's Services!

Scan the QR Code to Receive Your 25% Discount

The 25% discount is applied directly to your eContent Pro International shopping cart when placing an order through IGI Global's referral link. Use the QR code to access this referral link. eContent Pro International has the right to end or modify any promotion at any time.

Email: customerservice@econtentpro.com

econtentpro.com

Are You Ready to Publish Your Research?

IGI Global
DISSEMINATOR OF KNOWLEDGE

IGI Global offers book authorship and editorship opportunities across 11 subject areas, including business, healthcare, computer science, engineering, and more!

Benefits of Publishing with IGI Global:

- Free one-to-one editorial and promotional support.
- Expedited publishing timelines that can take your book from start to finish in less than one (1) year.
- Choose from a variety of formats including: Edited and Authored References, Handbooks of Research, Encyclopedias, and Research Insights.
- Utilize IGI Global's eEditorial Discovery® submission system in support of conducting the submission and blind-review process.

- IGI Global maintains a strict adherence to ethical practices due in part to our full membership to the Committee on Publication Ethics (COPE).
- Indexing potential in prestigious indices such as Scopus®, Web of Science™, PsycINFO®, and ERIC – Education Resources Information Center.
- Ability to connect your ORCID iD to your IGI Global publications.
- Earn royalties on your publication as well as receive complimentary copies and exclusive discounts.

Get Started Today by Contacting the Acquisitions Department at:

acquisition@igi-global.com

Available to Order Now

Order through www.igi-global.com with <u>Free Standard Shipping</u>.

<u>The Premier Reference for Information Science & Information Technology</u>

100% Original Content
Contains 705 new, peer-reviewed articles with color figures covering over 80 categories in 11 subject areas

Diverse Contributions
More than 1,100 experts from 74 unique countries contributed their specialized knowledge

Easy Navigation
Includes two tables of content and a comprehensive index in each volume for the user's convenience

Highly-Cited
Embraces a complete list of references and additional reading sections to allow for further research

Included in:

InfoSci®-Books

Encyclopedia of Information Science and Technology Fourth Edition
A Comprehensive 10-Volume Set

Mehdi Khosrow-Pour, D.B.A. (Information Resources Management Association, USA)
ISBN: 978-1-5225-2255-3; © 2018; Pg: 8,104; Release Date: July 2017

For a limited time, <u>receive the complimentary e-books for the First, Second, and Third editions</u> with the purchase of the *Encyclopedia of Information Science and Technology, Fourth Edition* e-book.*

The **Encyclopedia of Information Science and Technology, Fourth Edition** is a 10-volume set which includes 705 original and previously unpublished research articles covering a full range of perspectives, applications, and techniques contributed by thousands of experts and researchers from around the globe. This authoritative encyclopedia is an all-encompassing, well-established reference source that is ideally designed to disseminate the most forward-thinking and diverse research findings. With critical perspectives on the impact of information science management and new technologies in modern settings, including but not limited to computer science, education, healthcare, government, engineering, business, and natural and physical sciences, it is a pivotal and relevant source of knowledge that will benefit every professional within the field of information science and technology and is an invaluable addition to every academic and corporate library.

Scan for Online Bookstore

Pricing Information

Hardcover: **$5,695**   E-Book: **$5,695**   Hardcover + E-Book: **$6,895**

Both E-Book Prices Include:
- *Encyclopedia of Information Science and Technology, First Edition E-Book*
- *Encyclopedia of Information Science and Technology, Second Edition E-Book*
- *Encyclopedia of Information Science and Technology, Third Edition E-Book*

*Purchase the Encyclopedia of Information Science and Technology, Fourth Edition e-book and receive the first, second, and third e-book editions for free. Offer is only valid with purchase of the fourth edition's e-book through the IGI Global Online Bookstore.

Recommend this Title to Your Institution's Library: www.igi-global.com/books

www.igi-global.com/infosci-ondemand

InfoSci-OnDemand

Continuously updated with new material on a weekly basis, InfoSci®-OnDemand offers the ability to search through thousands of quality full-text research papers. Users can narrow each search by identifying key topic areas of interest, then display a complete listing of relevant papers, and purchase materials specific to their research needs.

Comprehensive Service

- Over 110,800+ journal articles, book chapters, and case studies.
- All content is downloadable in PDF format and can be stored locally for future use.

No Subscription Fees

- One time fee of $37.50 per PDF download.

Instant Access

- Receive a download link immediately after order completion!

"It really provides an excellent entry into the research literature of the field. It presents a manageable number of highly relevant sources on topics of interest to a wide range of researchers. The sources are scholarly, but also accessible to 'practitioners'."

- Lisa Stimatz, MLS, University of North Carolina at Chapel Hill, USA

"It is an excellent and well designed database which will facilitate research, publication and teaching. It is a very very useful tool to have."

- George Ditsa, PhD, University of Wollongong, Australia

"I have accessed the database and find it to be a valuable tool to the IT/IS community. I found valuable articles meeting my search criteria 95% of the time."

- Lynda Louis, Xavier University of Louisiana, USA

Recommended for use by researchers who wish to immediately download PDFs of individual chapters or articles.

www.igi-global.com/e-resources/infosci-ondemand

www.igi-global.com

CPSIA information can be obtained
at www.ICGtesting.com
Printed in the USA
LVHW061252230723
753220LV00008B/711